•UNFINISHED JOURNEY•

THE LEWIS FAMILY

•UNFINISHED JOURNEY•

THE LEWIS FAMILY

Cameron Smith

Summerhill Press

Toronto

© 1989 Cameron Smith

Published by Summerhill Press Ltd.
52 Shaftesbury Avenue
Toronto M4T 1A2

Distributed by University of Toronto Press
5201 Dufferin Street
Downsview, Ontario M3H 5T8

Printed and bound in Canada

Canadian Cataloguing in Publication Data

Smith, Cameron, 1935–   Unfinished journey: the Lewis family

Includes bibliographical references.
ISBN 0-929091-04-3

1. Lewis, David, 1909–1981. 2. Lewis, Stephen, 1937–
3. Lewis family. 4. Canada — Politics and government — 1935-   .* 5. New
Democratic Party — Biography. 6. Politicians — Canada — Biography. 7.
Socialists — Canada — Biography.
I. Title.

FC601.A1S55 1989   971.063 092 2   C89-095155-1
F1034.3.A2S55 1989

•CONTENTS•

A book is not born in its writing but in all that went before. So this book is dedicated to Margaret Cameron Smith, Muriel Smith, and Mary Black for it is in their love and the constancy of their belief that it is rooted.

There is but one key to the present and that is the past.
Max Müller

It is better to go along with the masses in a not totally correct direction than to separate oneself from them and remain a purist.
Vladimir Medem
(as recalled by
Vladimir Kosovsky)

We fought communists all the time.
Doris (Lewis) Andras

THE TAMING OF THE BEAR

T he quotations on the foregoing page tell the story of this book. The first needs no explanation. This is a story about the roots of political action.

The second catches in one sentence the grass-roots focus of the Jewish Labour Bund, an outlawed socialist party that Maishe Lewis — David's father and Stephen's grandfather — belonged to when it was the largest party in Russia at the turn of the twentieth century. Maishe was chairman of the Bund in his home town. The Bund preached revolution, the overthrow of the Tsar, equality for all, and national rights for the Jewish community. As a boy, David was immersed in its philosophy and its programs, and since he left Russia for Canada when he was almost thirteen years old, his most formative years were shaped by that philosophy and those programs.

The quotation emphasizes the approach the Bund took in resolving the tension that inevitably arises in a socialist party between those who insist on ideological correctness and those concerned with the practical steps required in the pursuit of power. Advocates on both sides would acknowledge the need to compromise. The issue always is, by how much?

The quotation from Doris Andras, David's sister, defines in six short words the relationship between the Bund and the Communists (or Bolsheviks). An enormous gulf has always separated democratic socialists from Communists. Lenin didn't see democratic socialists as legitimate in their own right. Either they were in transition to becoming Communists or they were revisionists and enemies. In other words, they were to be remade or they were to be removed. They were not to be allowed to turn what he saw as a way station into a permanent home. With the coming of Lenin's Red Terror, removal as often as not meant execution.

The message was not lost on Canadian socialists. In the end, it was not the Conservatives or Liberals who most effectively confronted the Communists; it was the CCF and the NDP — the socialists. This, then, is also the story of a fierce determination that ran through one political family to combat Communists and any other grouping on the left perceived as trying to undermine or destroy the party.

"Democracy," Lenin declared in one of his better-known essays, "is a form of state whereas we . . . are opposed to *every kind* of state." (Lenin's emphasis.) In another essay he maintained that democracy within a state "is always narrow, hypocritical, spurious and false; it always remains democracy for the rich and a swindle for the poor."[1] Committed socialists, therefore, were seen as a mortal threat to the Communist dream.

In the final analysis, Lenin wanted change from the top down. The Bund, on the other hand, insisted that it should come from the bottom up, and consequently it was prepared to compromise on ideology if it meant retaining mass support.

This same issue of compromise has plagued the CCF/NDP throughout its history. In party mythology, members are divided into two broad groups: the political missionaries and the reformists — those who see ideological conversion as the only route to the New Jerusalem and those who see obtaining political power and hence the ability to precipitate change as the only path. The movement versus the pragmatists.

In the mythology, the missionaries see political power flowing as the consequence of conversion; the reformists see obtaining power as a prerequisite not only to change but also to conversion. The missionaries see reformists as too ready to compromise on principles in order to gain power; the reformists see missionaries as impractical dreamers and sometimes as troublesome ideologues who would doom the party to becoming an inconsequential sect, much like the American Socialist Party.

Like all mythologies, it's simplistic. In this case, it's too simplistic. Too black and white. Almost everyone in the party's history has had a sense of mission and a dedication to socialist philosophy. And almost everyone has been prepared to compromise by adapting ideology to the needs of Canadian voters. Nevertheless, as a philosophic touchstone it has been useful in defining the lineaments of party disputes. And at its best it has supplied a creative tension to the development of policies.

So this, finally, is the story of "The Taming of the Bear." That's the name of a Yiddish tale by a writer who was a favourite of Maishe Lewis. It's a morality tale and, like all such tales when they're well done, its charm captivates while its vision provokes.

It's also a tale that applies to the Lewises. It speaks to the tension between their dreams and how they have pursued them.

The writer of the tale was I.L. Peretz (1851–1915). He wrote at a time when the Jews of Eastern Europe were engaged in a passionate struggle for personal and political liberation. Maishe Lewis was born in 1888 in Russia. He was part of that struggle.

Here is the tale.

ONCE there was a man who could not abide evil. So he turned the little shop he kept over to his wife, shut himself up in a room in his house, and immersed himself in Torah and prayer — studying the revealed scripture and the kabbalah as well.

But even at home, in his very own household, he saw evil. Finally, thinking the matter over, he decided to become a hermit, left his home, and went to study in a corner of the synagogue.

He sits in the synagogue, but the world's evil follows him there. Sometimes a night watchman comes in to warm himself at the stove, or a wanderer comes in to sleep, or a sleepless man blunders into the synagogue — and they sit around the stove talking — but whatever they talk about, the end is always evil upon evil.

Again, the hermit ponders the matter and leaves town to go out into the world to look for a city without evil. And he doesn't find one. It's the same world wherever he goes.

So he gives up on civilization and travels from forest to forest, over hills and valleys until, far from all human habitation, he comes to a stream. What the river is called he does not know, but on its bank there stand the ruins of an ancient palace.

Well, he settles there and busies himself with the kabbalah. But there's no way to escape from evil. . . .

Everywhere the hermit looks, Peretz says, he sees nature at war with itself.

And evil is reasonless. The world thrashes, convulsed without order; and the soul of the world is asleep. Every separate bit of the world looks out for itself, not for the welfare of all.

Do you understand? Right or wrong, this is what the hermit thought.

So he concludes that there is only one thing to do: wake the soul of the world. Once it is awake, then order will reign. The conflicts, the convulsions, the thrashing about of the world's limbs, will stop.

But how does one wake the soul of the world? For *that* there are ideas in the holy books. There are certain things to say and to do. It takes some fervent meditation. One has to dedicate oneself to the task wholeheartedly and with devotion. If not, the words fly off into thin air — into nothing. . . .

So that's what the hermit does — night after night until he senses he's getting somewhere.

But the angry river-spirit becomes aware of what he's doing and says: "No peace for him!". . . so he agitates the river . . . and makes the waves grow huge. Then, snatching a swollen wave, he flings it toward the bank, toward the ruins.

And the wave turns into a bear. A hairy black bear with bloodshot eyes that runs around the ruins, roaring and snarling, interfering with the hermit's meditations once again.

What's to be done? He's not going to kill the bear. That would be evil. Because, in truth, how is the bear guilty of anything? It lives; let it live!

Well, it occurs to the hermit to quiet the bear. To make something decent of him, so that, bear though he is, he will understand what it's all about.

The hermit decides to elevate the bear. He will change him and enlighten his soul.

So, one morning early, the hermit climbs to the top of his ruin and stands there looking down at the bear. No sooner does the bear see him than he falls into a dreadful rage. Digging the ground with his forepaws, he roars and growls and leaps about, his mouth foaming, glaring with bloodshot eyes at the hermit; and the hermit, his eyes filled with loving kindness, looks down at the bear. And there's a war between the two sets of eyes — the hermit's brimming with love and pity, the bear's filled with hatred and rage. But the hermit's eyes are the stronger. Slowly, slowly, they begin to conquer those of the bear.

The conflict between the two pairs of eyes, between the two hearts and the two souls, lasts a long time until, when the sun is in the east, the struggle is over; and when it is high in the heavens, the bear lies humbly before the ruin like a submissive dog; and when the sun sets, the bear rises quietly and sends the hermit a tender pleading look and approaches the gate of the ruins where it knocks quietly, whining like a dog to be let in. . . .

The hermit opens the gate. The bear approaches him and lies down quietly at his feet. And his eyes say: "You are my God. My hopes are in you. I believe in you. Your thoughts are holy. With your meditations you will rebuild the world." And the hermit lovingly caresses the bear, the bear he has himself created, the bear that believes in him.

And he begins to muse, desiring to be immersed in his thoughts once more, to meditate on what is needful to wake the soul of the world.

But there is nothing left for him to think. He himself no longer possesses his former soul, because in the same measure that the bear has ascended to him, he has descended to the bear.

He senses a weariness in all his limbs; his eyelids grow heavy. Falteringly, he goes to his bed, and the bear follows him and lies down beside him.

There is no end to evil. The bear has become partly human, and the human, partly a bear. And a saint who lies down with a bear cannot wake the soul of the world.[2]

So, the savage bear is tamed and the world does become a better place. And evil, although not obliterated, at least is much restrained. But a vision is foreshortened and compromises are made and some evil continues to exist.

Is this a story for rejoicing or for mourning?

Or is it a bittersweet reflection of life?

• NOTES REGARDING DATES AND YIDDISH •

When writing about Russia in periods that span the Revolution, you have to decide whether to refer to the Julian calendar or the Gregorian. Lenin switched Russia from the Julian to the Gregorian in 1918.

The Julian calendar was devised under Julius Caesar and overestimated the length of a year by about eleven minutes. The Gregorian was proclaimed by Pope Gregory XIII in 1582. The eleven-minute difference meant that in the eighteenth century the Julian calendar was about eleven days behind the Gregorian, in the nineteenth century about twelve days behind, and in the twentieth century about thirteen days behind.

For the sake of continuity, I have used the Gregorian calendar throughout. This has some disadvantages. For instance, the October Revolution — a phrase used to describe the seizure of power by the Bolsheviks from the Provisional Government in 1917 — occurred in November under the Gregorian calendar.

On the other hand, it has some advantages. Bloody Sunday at the start of the 1905 Revolution occurred on a Monday (January 9) under the Julian calendar, and on a Sunday (January 22) under the Gregorian. Its greatest advantage, however, is that it allows readers to refer to concurrent dates elsewhere in the world without having to compare calendars.

When I have used English spellings for Yiddish words, I have tried to represent the way in which Yiddish was pronounced in Svisloch.

For instance, I have used "Maishe" instead of "Moishe" because that's how people pronounced his name in that little town. I also have used spellings that do not conform with those that have been accepted as part of an effort to standardize Yiddish spellings — again because I thought it best to retain the spellings that people from Svisloch used. For instance, I have used *kheyder* instead of the now more commonly seen *cheder* as the Yiddish word for "elementary school" — which in towns such as Svisloch was just a room in a teacher's home. In this case, there is an additional incentive to use *kheyder* because an English-speaking person would tend to pronounce *cheder* like the "Cheddar" in Cheddar cheese, which would be totally wrong.

The one exception to this approach is in place names. There I have used the spellings that appear on current maps, the reasoning being that should anyone want to consult a map, similarity in usage would make the task easier.

SVISLOCH IN RELATION TO CURRENT SOVIET-POLISH BORDER

BERNARD BENNELL

Because the border between Poland and Russia (and later the Soviet Union) kept shifting during the period dealt with in this book, the current border is used in the hope that it will be a more recognizable starting point for tracing events.

By 1905 the following cities were important centres of the Bund: Berdichev, Bialystok, Dvinsk, Gomel, Grodno, Kovno, Lodz, Minsk, Mogilev, Odessa, Riga, Vilna, Vitebsk, Warsaw, and Zhitomir.

• C H A P T E R   O N E •

March separately; fight together.
Bund slogan

All day the little town stood motionless in the hot, yellow, summer air, its sawmills quiet, its tanneries empty, its people silent, listening to the faint thumping of artillery as if to their own heartbeats. It came from the east, from beyond the House of Eternity — the Jewish cemetery — from somewhere beyond Poperechny Forest. From far enough away that after each pause, strain as they might, they couldn't tell if it had moved closer.

They waited expressionless. In doorways. By dusty, rutted streets. On rough benches by their homes. Working people for the most part. Dun-shaded. Poor beyond anything Western Europe comprehended. Wondering whose cause they would be harnessed to this time.

So when evening fell and the artillery stopped and weary and beaten Polish soldiers trudged back with their carts of wounded, the only sounds in town were the shuffling, clanking sounds of retreat, the groans of the wounded, and the occasional shouted order. For those who lived there, there was nothing to say and nothing to do and no one stood outdoors to watch.

This was Svisloch — Sislevitz, they called it in Yiddish — and in that last week of July 1920 the Red Army, the Bolsheviks, smashing Polish resistance and even then shouting, "Give us Warsaw," as a battle cry, had stood on the outskirts of the town hot-eyed and triumphant. Warsaw lay but 275 kilometres to the southwest and the Bolsheviks, advancing at the rate of almost twenty kilometres a day, would be there in just two weeks. On July 11 they had overrun Minsk; on July 14, Vilna; during that same final week of July they would capture Bialystok, Pinsk, and Volkovysk; and on August 1, Brest-Litovsk.[1]

Small though Svisloch was, it was crowded with political parties. Each had its factions, its left and right wings, and factions and parties had wrestled one another through fifteen or twenty years. They had survived the Tsar's secret police. They had battled through the 1905 Revolution and endured the savage repression that followed. They had lived through the terrible years of the pogroms. They had risked everything in strikes and speeches and demonstrations. They had weathered the First World War and German occupation and although they were still occupied when the 1917 Revolution occurred, they had shared in the excitement and despaired in the civil war that followed. They had enjoyed a few good years and suffered many more bad when hunger and deprivation disfigured their lives. And now the army of the Bolsheviks stood at their gates and no one knew quite what to expect.

They had heard of the Red Terror. Of the Cheka. Of the shootings, the jailings, the exiling to Siberia. Nevertheless, to most of the workers of Svisloch, critical as they might be of the Bolsheviks, these still were the heroes of the Revolution, fighters for a new dawn of mankind, brave comrades who were the first to smash the chains of capitalism and drive back the bourgeois forces of intervention. And when all was said and done, weren't all socialists brothers?

The civil war had been raging for more than two years, Reds against Whites, with the Western allies supplying arms and matériel to the Whites while at the same time sending in small forces of their own to badger the Bolsheviks.[2] And just when the Bolsheviks thought they finally had won the upper hand, the Poles had attacked.

It came at a bad time. As a report in *Pravda* said on February 26, 1920: "The workers of the towns and of some of the villages choke in the throes of hunger. The railroads barely crawl. The houses are crumbling. The towns are full of refuse. Epidemics spread and death strikes to the right and left. Industry is ruined."[3]

Times had never been worse, said Trotsky.[4]

The Bolsheviks wanted peace with Poland. They needed peace with Poland. After the withdrawal of the German army, Polish forces had taken up positions far to the east of the old, pre-war border, which found them, at the end of 1919, about 175 kilometres west of Kiev. Several times the Bolsheviks proposed negotiations but each time the Poles found a way to avoid them. Then, on April 25, 1920, the Poles attacked, sweeping into Kiev on May 6. Poland proper was jubilant. At last the old boundaries were restored to what they had been 148 years ago before Poland was carved up by land-hungry Russians and Prussians.

It was a short-lived, indeed a foolish, jubilation, for out of the east, thundering across the plains of Ukraine from its position just beyond the Sea of Azov, came Budenny's fearsome Cavalry Army: 16,700 mounted men, forty-eight cannon, five armoured trains, eight armoured cars, and twelve aircraft rushing to join the Bolshevik forces already in place.[5] And in the north, one week after the fall of Kiev, the man whom Stalin would come to call "the demon of the Civil War,"[6] Tukhachevsky, the twenty-seven-year-old aristocrat-turned-revolutionary, commander of the Soviet Western Front, threw his armies at the Polish lines.

Tiny Svisloch, about 300 kilometres on the other side of those lines, lay on Tukhachevsky's direct path to Warsaw. An old market town of about 4,500, of whom 3,500 were Jewish, it lay east of Bialystok and south of Grodno at about the same latitude as Prince Albert in Canada, Nottingham in Britain, and Bremen in West Germany. On today's maps it is in the Soviet Union about seventeen kilometres from the Polish border. In July 1920 the town was still recovering from the German invasion of the First World War: from 1915 to 1918 it had been occupied by German troops. David Lewis would recall in his memoirs that:

> I was barely six [when] our area was occupied by the advancing German army. When fighting came close, we scrambled into a big cellar with many other families. . . . We shared the food and slept in each other's laps, as it were, for several nights. . . . A sound like thunder was heard for hours, but I could not see any rain through the one little window. . . . Then the thunder retreated and we came out into the daylight. The very first sight was unnerving. On the streets and in the market square lay men in pools of blood. Some, I was told, were badly wounded, others were dead. Fearfully I asked my father whether they were Russian or German. "Both," he answered and I was bewildered. I couldn't tell the difference.[7]

Now, barely two years since the Germans had surrendered, another conquering army stood on the doorstep poised and waiting through that long summer night as the Poles, in their westward retreat, trailed past the tanneries clustered at the edge of town, through what looked like a miniature Arc de Triomphe but what actually had been a large toll gate erected in the early eighteenth century by the reigning Polish nobleman, past the Greek Orthodox church, across the broad market square the size of two modern city blocks where junior officers were organizing carts for the wounded and generally trying to bring better order to the passing columns of men, through the heart of the Jewish

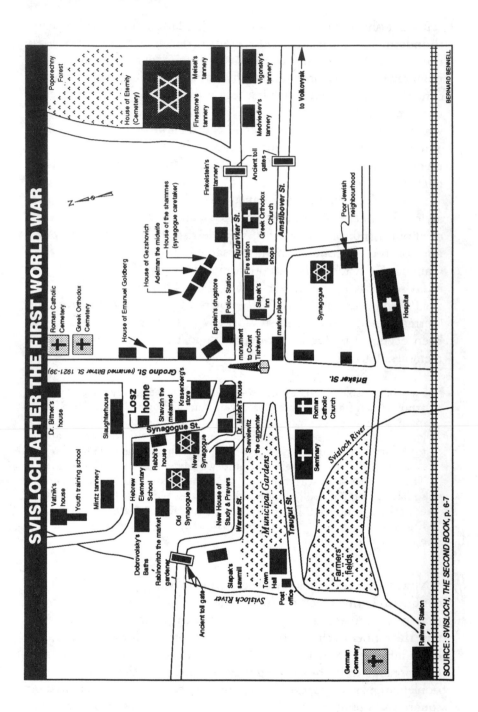

SVISLOCH AFTER THE FIRST WORLD WAR

BERNARD BENNELL

SOURCE: SVISLOCH, THE SECOND BOOK, p. 6-7

community with its houses jostling for space and its synagogues, houses of study, and ritual baths, and then, after passing the city hall and the Municipal Gardens, out Warsaw Street in the direction of the Polish capital, through another former toll-gate arch, across the Svisloch River (which was little more than a good-sized creek) and into the starlit countryside beyond.[8]

In his house up a street running north from market square, Maishe Losz could hear the occasional shouted orders and the clattering of carts and artillery over cobblestones. He was sitting in the back of the house in the main room that served as an eating and sitting room, with its large wood-burning oven that heated the entire building, but instead of listening he was staring pensively at the shadows thrown to the far corners of the room by a kerosene lamp on the table at his elbow. Several times his wife Rose — Raisel, he invariably called her in the affectionate Yiddish diminutive — urged him to come to bed. "Tomorrow will be tomorrow. That you cannot change," was her way of putting it. But still he sat, caught in his concerns, a lean workingman of thirty-two on the verge of becoming stocky, with short dark brown hair, a Charlie Chaplin moustache, a full, sensuous lower lip, and the eyes of a dreamer, dark brown, gentle, and steady. In Canada he would become Maishe Lewis.

In Yiddish there is an old saying: the apple never falls far from the tree. In a family dedicated to socialism for almost 100 years, Maishe was the tree.

That tree had its roots in the Jewish Labour Bund — the Bund, it was called — the socialist party that in the years immediately before and after the 1905 Revolution was the dominant political force among the Jews of Eastern Europe and remained highly influential until the Second World War. It was one of the most remarkable organizations of an eventful age with roots of its own buried deep in the brooding, tormented past of Tsarist Russia.

Maishe was a leading member of the Bund in Svisloch, and in 1920 that meant being a Marxist of one shade or another. For Maishe it meant being a radical Marxist. He gave speeches, he wrote political pamphlets, he organized Jewish workers, he participated in strikes and demonstrations, he had endless discussions with neighbours across his kitchen table, he helped establish Yiddish schools, he did everything he could to promote Yiddish culture, and always the message was the same. For Jews it was pride in being Jewish and power in being organized. For Jewish workers it was straight revolution: smash the capitalists. It was time to establish a society of equality and tolerance where people would contribute according to their ability and receive according to their need. That was the same message that the Communists were delivering, of course. The difference, as Maishe invariably stressed, lay in how you achieved it. The Bolsheviks, he said, were too ruthless, too ready to sacrifice democracy to expediency.

Ever since the Germans had pulled out, the question foremost in the minds of the townspeople had been: "Where will Svisloch end up, in Poland or in Russia?" Maishe had said Poland. Not only that; he had said it vehemently and openly and repeatedly and in the saying he had damned the Bolsheviks. He was not alone in this. Others were doing it, even in St. Petersburg and Moscow, but Bolshevik patience was wearing thin and stories were beginning to circulate that it was not only counter-revolutionaries and "vile plotters" who were being shot.

And now the Bolsheviks were taking his town. So through the night he stared at the shadows in the corner of the room.

The morning, dawning clear and still, brought men into the street where they stood in knots, trading anxious questions or trying to peer into a hovering silence that was exceptional in a town that had to hustle so hard each day just to make ends meet. Rose tried to keep the children indoors, but she succeeded only with Doris, the youngest and the one most resembling her father. At seven years old, she was mature beyond her years. Like a little grandmother already, neighbours used to say.

David, eleven years old, also resembled his father but his features were all edges where Maishe's were rounded, and his eyes burned with an unbridled appetite that throughout his life would be almost unsettling in its intensity. Karpel — Charlie, he would become in Canada — fifteen months younger and fairer, had Rose's square jaw and looks that predicted the movie-star handsomeness he would have at seventeen. People would remember him as "soft," but the word translates poorly from Yiddish where it carries the meaning of big-hearted, generous, considerate, gentle and sensitive. Canadians are more familiar with the French version: *un homme doux*. It was a word also applied to Maishe, but although David would be remembered outside the family for many things, being "soft" was never what sprang to mind.

By mid-morning the silence was unnerving. Even the most vocal of the men were now quiet and women, some still in their aprons, had joined husbands in the square to gaze eastward expectantly. At first it was a murmur so soft they wondered if they had heard it at all. But as quickly as it was gone it was back, rising and falling in waves and odd surges, washing into the square with the breeze and leaving people straining to hear more, slowly growing stronger and clearer until at last they realized what it was. And as recognition started hair tingling, all the dreams, all the nightmares, all the intoxicating excitement of what this could mean crackled around them and 3,000 soldiers marched into town, eight abreast, in full-throated exuberance singing The Internationale:

> Arise, you prisoners of starvation!
> Arise, you wretched of the earth.
> For justice thunders condemnation,
> A better world is now in birth,
> Arise, you slaves no more in thrall.
> The earth shall rise on new foundations,
> We have been naught, we shall be all.

And then the thunderous chorus:

> It is the final fight, and each must stand his place.
> The Internationale shall be the human race![9]

They marched with bedrolls over their shoulders, rifles slung behind, wearing those pointed cloth caps that the Red Army first issued which looked like upturned funnels emblazoned with the red star on the front and with ear flaps that on summer days like this were folded up. The caps, their bedrolls, their loose peasant shirts — rubashka in Russian — that buttoned down the left breast and were gathered in by a belt at the waist, and their baggy khaki pants gave them a softened, almost romantic look. But these were no romantics, no fresh-cheeked recruits. For six years Russia had seen unending fighting and these were the toughened guardians of the revolution. Hardy, battle-experienced soldiers. If anything correctly depicted them as they were, it was their boots: heavy, thick, knee-high, scuffed and scarred and durable, pounding relentlessly across the cobblestones in lockstep.

Seven-year-old Doris remembered those boots more than anything else. Years and worlds later in Ottawa she would flee a performance of the Soviet Army Chorus and Band, terribly upset because the boots of the Cossack dancers reminded her so much of the Bolshevik army marching into Svisloch.

Into the square they swept, filling it with The Internationale and sending it cascading down connecting streets. Townspeople, peasant farmers from the outlying areas, soldiers, children — the square was packed with 6,000 or 7,000 people — plus horses and carts and wagons. Then a "political worker" climbed to the back of a wagon and the speeches began. "Comrades," he shouted, "we bring you a new world. A new life . . . ," and the cheers were deafening.

Kayleh Ain recalled that day in a book of remembrances published many years later in Israel: "I remember the wonderful, beautiful speeches which were delivered in the marketplace. And with what kind of happiness, joy and hope did we listen to those exclamations about equality and freedom."

For hours the speakers went on, long after the soldiers, who paused only briefly, had left, singing their anthem as they marched out Warsaw Street. At times the crowd interrupted speeches with wild cheering; at times it listened attentively to the long descriptions of how reactionary forces had tried to subvert the revolution and how necessary it was to dig out and destroy them root and branch. In the end, said the Bolsheviks, the revolution would prevail; the yoke that had been lifted from their necks had been broken and its pieces would fuel their cooking pots forever. A new industrial society was being created from which all would share, not, as in the past, just owner-thieves. The workers of Svisloch were in the vanguard of an uprising of working classes throughout the world. These were heady words in tough times.

"Oh how naïve we were in believing all that," wrote Kayleh Ain. "Very fast and very bitter was our disappointment. In no time, the liberators showed themselves in their true colours. They were drunk with power and they had a lust for revenge. So they rode undisturbed over the town. It didn't take them too long to shatter all our beliefs and all our hopes. . . .

"For them to sing the words of The Internationale was like a rape. . . . We could hardly wait to be liberated from the liberators. It became a dark period."

Days later, when the Red Army reached Bialystok, the Bolsheviks established a Revolutionary Committee as the supreme authority in Poland, and it immediately issued an appeal to "the Polish working people of city and village" that declared: "We must tear the factories and the coal mines out of the hands of the capitalists and robber-speculators. They shall pass into the possession of the people [along with] estates and forests. . . . Landowners are to be driven away. . . .

"Power in the towns is transferred to workers' deputies; communal Soviets are created in the villages."[10]

The first thing the army had done in Svisloch after the speeches was to establish a local revolutionary committee whose job it was to maintain "firm revolutionary order," and that, among other things, meant locating supplies for the army and, from among Bolshevik sympathizers, arranging for the appointment of deputies and the creation of a communal Soviet to take over the running of the town. It was done within days, but shortly before it was, two soldiers appeared at the tannery where Maishe worked.

"You are Maishe Losz?" they had asked.

"Yes."

"Come with us."

He knew what it meant. Lenin's policy was to look on Bundists as misguided revolutionaries and to try and recruit them to Bolshevism and, failing that, to exile them to Siberia. But there were nagging stories of Bundists from other towns being shot. Somehow Maishe had thought it couldn't happen here. Svisloch was different. He and other Bundists would argue over how the revolution was proceeding, but they would never argue against the revolution itself. But obviously Svisloch was not different enough: recruitment did not begin with sending soldiers to pick you up. With fear tightening about his chest, he realized there wasn't even time to let Rose know.

They took him to the police station and threw him into a cell. Later he learned that he and one or two other townsmen were to be shot.

Barely had the door slammed shut than they began arriving: workers, shopkeepers, rabbis, an elementary school teacher, friends, associates, even political opponents. A steady stream pleading for his life. Yes, he was a Bundist. Yes, he had given speeches attacking the Bolsheviks. Yes, he had favoured incorporation within Poland. But he also was a committed socialist, more so than most in town. And he was a good person. A selfless person. An ornament to the town.

What probably swung the balance was the intervention of two of the deputies. If Maishe and the others were shot so precipitously, they said, it would destroy support for the communal Soviet. These were no bosom friends of Maishe. They were among his toughest political adversaries. But they were shrewd enough to know that, if he could be shot so peremptorily, what that might mean for the rest of the town.

When the cell door swung open two days later, it was not without reservation. Maishe had no need for it to be spelled out: he still was a "misguided socialist," and unless he could come to terms with the Bolsheviks, being shipped to Siberia was almost a certainty. What irony! Nicholas II, while still Tsar, had outlawed the Bund; if Bund publications were found in your home, the penalty was exile to Siberia. Yet here were the people's revolutionaries threatening Bundists with the same treatment.[11]

By the time Maishe got home, the news had already arrived, and Rose, meeting him at the door, her sleek black hair pinned loosely back, her violet-blue eyes shadowed with worry, simply took his hands in hers, laid her head against his shoulder, and wept.

By August 13 the Red Army was at Radimin, twenty-five kilometres from Warsaw, and the Bolsheviks were elated. Surely the workers in Poland proper would rise in support of the revolution now that the Red Army was there to help them. Lenin had said Russia was not trying to grab territory; it was trying to spread communism by helping sister revolutionary movements gain power. "We shall break the crust of Polish bourgeois resistance [to the rise of the Polish proletariat] with bayonets of the Red Army," he had declared.[12] And once the revolution had swept through Poland, the German proletariat would surely rise, for already, Lenin said, it was restive and militant.

To Bolsheviks across the western front it seemed that at last world revolution really was going on the march. Certainly that was the mood in Svisloch, where impatient, boisterous soldiers were charged with commandeering food, transport, billets for officers and administrators, and anything else that the Russian heartland, ravaged by hunger and shortages, could not supply. And when their impatience translated into intolerance and boisterousness into arrogance, Maishe told Rose that no longer could he remain silent.

"We did not fight one tsar just to get another." He said it quietly, with a tightness to his voice. He would talk to some of the new deputies tomorrow. Although they were Bolsheviks and political enemies, he had known them most of his life. They would understand his concerns. They would even share them. But they would resent his raising them and they would be bitterly critical; that, he knew.

Terrified, Rose begged him to say nothing. They were sitting alone in the kitchen, Maishe, with elbows on the table and hands, toughened from scraping hides at the tannery, folded in front of him; Rose, near him across the corner of the table, squeezing the bunched apron in her lap, her knuckles white. "They will never let you come home," she said. "They are more Bolshevists than old neighbours."

"Raisel, Raisel, Raisel," he said, putting a hand on her shoulder and gently shaking it. "What do you expect of me? I am what I am. If I didn't go, I would be someone else."

The next day he did go . . . and he did come home. But early in the evening, as soon as it was dark, a friend slipped in the back door. "Run, Maishe. Run," he urged. "They're coming for you."

"How do you know?"

"Don't ask. Run. They just decided," and as quickly as he came, he was gone, making sure the door did not slam behind him.

Maishe turned to Rose and without a word took her in his arms and hugged her.

"Maishke . . ."

"Shh."

"You must hurry." She was insistent, frightened, pushing nervous-
ly against him until he stepped back. "Hurry."

Once outside, he walked quickly away from the back of the house,
seeking the nighttime shadows where he could, cutting through yards
to the back of a row of houses, moving to the east and north until
in no time he had arrived at a garden at the rear of a well-kept, two-
storey brick house, one of the largest homes in Svisloch. It belonged
to Dr. Bittner, a medical doctor in his mid-to-late sixties.[13] He was
Polish and Christian and one of Svisloch's most prominent citizens.
His home was on the west side of Grodno Street, one of the town's
main streets, which ran northward from the east end of the square.
Years later the Poles would rename it Bittner Street.

"Maishe!" the doctor exclaimed as he opened the door. "Come in
quickly." They had long been friends and liked nothing better than
to argue the fine points in the writings of European socialists, especially
the German social democrats. After Maishe was released from his police
station cell, Dr. Bittner immediately sent for him and offered to hide
him if ever it became necessary. "But only you and I and Rose must
know," he cautioned. Not even his sisters or brother could be told.

Now he took Maishe down a darkened stairway and guided him
through the gloom to a corner of the basement where some unused
furniture and odds and ends had been stored. "You can stay here,"
he said, "but during the day you must make no sound. No one but
I must know you are here." The maid arrived at noon and left at eight
in the evening. "It is dangerous for her and it is dangerous for me if
she suspects," Dr. Bittner added.

Later that night, stretched on a child's narrow bed and staring into
the impenetrable darkness of the basement as he wondered about his
own children and waited for sleep to come, Maishe was unaware that
the tide of battle at Warsaw had reversed. Now it was the Red Army
that was overextended, weary, and on the run. Within days the Poles
would recover Brest-Litovsk and Bialystok. And once again Svisloch
would lie in the path of an advancing army.

• C H A P T E R   T W O •

Mead takes a long time to ferment, but then it bursts the bottle.

Old Russian proverb

Maishe Lewis and Lenin came into the world at roughly the same time. Maishe was born on March 23, 1888. Vladimir Ilyich Ulyanov — Lenin — was born eighteen years earlier. But on May 8, 1887, Alexander Ulyanov, his older brother, along with four other university students, was hanged for plotting to kill Tsar Alexander III, and that turned young Vladimir, a good but unassuming student just past his seventeenth birthday, into a revolutionary. He later chose the name Lenin as his *nom de guerre*.

Unlike Lenin, Maishe made no indelible mark on history, he did not write his name in the affairs of state, nor did he transform his society or add to Western thought. But because he was committed to a revolutionary ideal and because there were scores of thousands like him, the current of history was changed. Because he preached participation, because he rebelled against centralism, he became an enemy to Communists. And because he had a generosity of spirit, people honoured him long after he was gone.

Alexander Ulyanov, and the four students hanged with him, were children of despair. Before they died, they had shouted, "Long live Narodnaya Volya." Long live People's Will, the group that six years before had tried to assassinate Tsar Alexander II. They were part of a long and growing line of disillusioned idealists who had turned to violence.

The irony is that they they were among the more fortunate; they could have led comfortable lives. But they hungered for relief from the profligate and the privileged who ruled Russia, and in that hunger was embedded a psychology of violence that progressively, over generations of frustration, had come to accept assassinations, force of arms, terror, as depersonalized, necessary, and inevitable instruments of change. As no worse than, and as an answer to, the violence of poverty, deprivation, and squalour that the privileged kept rigidly in place. In the late 1800s the historical inspiration for this state of mind were the Decembrists, a group of noblemen who formed a secret society in 1816 to assassinate Alexander I, free the serfs, and abolish the autocracy. Alexander Herzen, Russia's first great socialist, traced his political lineage to the men of December. And Lenin himself paid them homage. (See Appendix A.)

In Canada, a hundred years later, it's difficult to understand the Russia struggling to be free without appreciating this psychology of violence. Because of it, words carried different shadings, debates had different subtexts. And in many cases they maintained those shadings and subtexts right through the Second World War.

The reign of Alexander III (1881–94), the Peasant Tsar, big and dull-witted, tremendously strong — he bent horseshoes with his bare hands — but forever fearful of assassination, was an interregnum between his reform-minded father, Alexander II, and his ineffectual, vacillating, and stubbornly autocratic son, Nicholas II, the last of the Romanovs.

However, lack of guidance from the Tsar did not mean lack of movement. Russia was lumbering inexorably into the industrial era with a momentum that might have been directed but never could have been diverted.

Maishe Lewis grew up in the conflict between that momentum and social structures that would not bend willingly to accommodate it. What it meant was that he spent the first half of his life embroiled in two revolutions, one within the other. In the larger revolution he struggled as a Russian and a socialist for the overthrow of capitalism and the end of the Tsarist regime; in the revolution within the revolution he struggled as a Jew and a member of the Jewish Labour Bund for the spiritual and economic emancipation of Russia's Jews, the overwhelming majority of whom were living in life-draining poverty: inward looking, passive, and intellectually inbred.

In this struggle Maishe turned his back on formal religion. His surviving family shy away from the word "atheist," preferring such words as "irreligious" and "agnostic." But in truth, he was a non-believer.

What he did believe in, and passionately, however, was Jewish culture. That culture had survived incredible assaults because it had developed an insulating self-sufficiency. But the insulation had hardened into an impermeable crust that locked in more than it kept out. Consequently the revolution within the revolution was a delicate affair, the dilemma being how to break that crust without defacing the luminous culture that it enclosed.

To break it meant to discard old viewpoints and practices, to challenge community authorities, and to propose new values — a ticklish and volatile undertaking, as Canadians who experienced Quebec's Quiet Revolution and the eventual transformation of a hidebound, priest-ridden community into a vigorous, disputatious, and sometimes outward-looking society, can begin to understand. However, the analogy is limited. The pressures on the Jews of Eastern Europe were far more intense and the release far more explosive than anything seen in Quebec. At best, understanding the one implies a sensitivity toward the other.

For Russia's aristocracy and its monied classes, the closing years of the nineteenth century were a time when fear of the Dark People — the illiterate masses, that hulking, brooding colossus that in their mind's eye lurked everywhere just beyond the last lamppost — hung like a grisly apparition at the edge of every thought and every action, colouring each perception and shaping each decision. It was an ancient, subterranean, tribal terror for this relatively small group sitting astride a vast land and a sprawling, diversified, exploited, devastatingly poor, and in many cases unassimilated population. The thought that this colossus might awaken and brush off its bonds like cobwebs, though verging on a preoccupation in the last half of the 1800s, had haunted Russia's rulers for at least 300 years, and a version of it continues to haunt them today.

It was a fear that knew more about aristocratic vulnerability than it did about peasant inertia. Nevertheless there was a historical basis for it in the hundreds of serf uprisings over the previous 125 years.[1]

Since at mid-century 103,400 private landowners owned 25 million serfs, the slightest tremor among those in bondage took on the proportion of a shock wave to those perched so precariously on top. (The remaining serfs were owned by the state, which included the imperial family and the Church, and the sense of unease prevailed there too.)

This sense of vulnerability increased through the last half of the 1800s because when Alexander I freed the serfs in 1861, he set conditions on their acquiring land that left them economically bound. So instead of generating stability, freeing the serfs simply unlocked a tremendous revolutionary dynamism. Peasant discontent remained; the aristocracy was undermined since its power was based on the ownership of land and serfs; the monarchy was weakened because the aristocracy was a bulwark in its own power; and illusory though freedom initially was, it created a sharper appetite for the real thing.

On top of all this came industrialization and the inevitable social dislocation that it bred. (See Appendix B.) In the twenty-five years from 1865 to 1890 Russia doubled its industrial production and doubled the number of industrial workers. This headlong plunge into industrialization brought familiar social ills: workdays of twelve to fifteen and sometimes as many as seventeen hours, flogging of workers who often lived in unheated, lice-infested, wooden barracks, child labour, and the Tsar's Cossacks to whip or even shoot protesters. One result was more strikes and, beginning in 1875, the creation of trade unions.[2]

All this was occurring during a time when the government was the Tsar. And the Tsar — whether it was Alexander II during his later years or Alexander III or Nicholas II — was first and foremost an autocrat, out of touch with the times, out of sympathy with pleas for reform, out of temper with disorder, and out of patience generally. It was a recipe for conflagration.[3]

Even so, through most of the 1800s, revolutionaries living in Russia posed no immediate threat to the empire. When serfs reared up in inarticulate pain, they struck and were struck down. When intellectuals revolted, it was in cloistered dissent. They wrote or they expounded in discussion groups, and although they could be articulate, the people who read their tracts or who attended the discussion groups were those least likely to effect change, namely members of the establishment or those with no power base. However, as historian Bertram Wolfe describes, in the latter part of the century, "Almost involuntarily they were forced into open enmity to the old order that had no use for them . . . and driven into open rebelliousness, a mood so general that the very word 'student' would finally become synonymous with revolutionist."[4]

Then in 1878 terrorism as a systematic undertaking began. The St. Petersburg chief of police was shot and wounded. The chief of the Tsar's secret police was assassinated. Alexander II was killed. The chief of police in Odessa was assassinated and the chief of secret police in St. Petersburg was clubbed to death. However, instead of fomenting rebellion, the terrorism only spurred more repression and the closing of universities until by the mid-1880s the police had destroyed the groups responsible for it. Lenin's brother and the four other students who were hanged in 1887 were not part of any ongoing organization. They were strictly a haphazard collection of individuals. What they were part of, however, was an ongoing — and growing — hunger for revolution. (See Appendix C.)

This was the larger world into which Maishe Lewis was born: a world of widening horizons and burgeoning expectations brought about by emancipation of the serfs and industrialization but also a world of dislocation, anxiety, and frustration; a world of enormous disparities with swaggering wealth jostling against excruciating poverty; a world of still unyielding class structures where the educated, awake to Western ideals of liberalism and democracy, were divided on lines of self-interest, fear, and reform-mindedness, and the uneducated, especially the factory workers, were beginning to sniff the heady air of organized power; a world of increasing strife; a world of increasing polarization; a world where the revolutionary spirit was spreading wider afield while all the time the Tsar, stewing in his own frustration, turned increasingly to repression to restore a society that he didn't realize was already gone.

It was a world in which no one was content and no one was at ease.

The smaller world, in which the revolution within the revolution occurred, began for Maishe in the tiny town of Svisloch. The origins of the town are lost in the mists that rise from the swampy meadowland at its edge. There are no memories, there is no written record. All anyone can say is that it is very old. Twice in the 1800s it burned to the ground and in 1910 fire demolished half of it again. Even the ancient minute book of the Jewish Holy Burial Association was destroyed in one of the fires, and in the older of the two Jewish cemeteries the tombstone inscriptions weathered away so long ago that no one can remember anyone who could recall whose grave was where.

One of the more gifted sons of another Svisloch, which was located southeast of Minsk, was Shmarya Levin, who became one of the more prominent orators of his time and a member of the 1905 Duma, the first Russian parliament. He was born twenty years before Maishe and was one of the last to pass a boyhood to the measured pace of an almost medieval town. Precarious though that pace might be at times, he describes it in his memoirs with a fondness for its sensuous pleasures, such as the "ocean of green" that was the summer hay covering the surrounding meadowlands, and beyond them "the wheatfields of the peasants . . . fat, rich fields, soft to the foot, breathing an odour of fruitfulness and sustenance," and yet farther from the town and on either side, forests "scores of miles deep; in fact, no one knew where they really ended, . . . primeval, virgin, thickly tangled." It is a description that almost perfectly fits Maishe's Svisloch, 300 kilometres to the west.[5]

The winters were hard and Levin tells of high winds that would tear off the roofs of "houses, or rather hovels of the poor," and how, "under

the mad rage of the winter blasts . . . , doors were sealed . . . and life
was suspended, congealed. Then Svisloch looked like a town of the
dead, half buried under the snow, with the wind howling a dirge over
it [and] within the howling of the winds we heard the howling of hungry
wolves. . . ."[6]

The 1847 census counted 997 Jews in Maishe's Svisloch. Fifty years
later, according to Abraham Ain writing his recollections after immigrating to Montreal,[7] the town had 3,099 people of whom 2,086
were Jewish. At the turn of the century it was one of the larger towns
in the district of Grodno. "Two of the larger streets, the market [area]
and the synagogue yard were inhabited by Jews," says Ain. "[On] the
other large and most of the small streets both Jews and non-Jews lived.
The non-Jews were White Russians, Poles, a score of Russian civil servants and a dozen or so Moslem Tartars."

Because of the fires that kept destroying the town, homes were
periodically rebuilt so that by 1900 "many of the houses were substantial
two-storey brick structures adorned with balconies."[8] Some even had
hardwood floors and, luxury of all luxuries, papered walls. But that
kind of high living came with the prosperity brought by the leather
industry.

The first factory opened in 1870 and, "from 1900 to the German
occupation in 1915, the leather industry was the decisive factor in the
economic life of the town. [By] 1900 there were eight leather factories
employing between 40 and 50 workers each, and a dozen or so smaller
shops employing from six to twelve workers."

In all, about 70 percent of the Jewish population was directly or in-
directly involved in the production and sale of leather and leather
goods. The other major activity was lumbering since "the district around
the town abounded in forests." Better logs were floated down the nearby
Narew River to Germany; others were used for railway ties, and the
rest became firewood. There were about sixty shops in town and a
busy group of artisans, three-quarters of whom were Jewish —
shoemakers, men's tailors, women's tailors, blacksmiths, joiners,
coopers, tinsmiths, shoe-stitchers, bookbinders, bricklayers, dyers,
harness makers, glaziers, carpenters, bakers, watchmakers, capmakers,
locksmiths and potters — serving not only townspeople but farmers,
peasants, and villagers from the surrounding countryside.[9]

In 1906, when the railway through Svisloch opened, bringing easier
and wider access to markets, it seemed that despite the ongoing political
turbulence, the future was assured, troublesome though it might be
— but nothing could have been further from the truth.

CHAPTER THREE

I remember the love that poured out of the Losz family in
Svisloch. A very loving family. All of them.
                              Doris (Lewis) Andras
                              Ottawa, September 1985

"Hear O Israel, the Lord our God, the Lord is One. Blessed be His name whose glorious kingdom is for ever and ever. And thou shalt love the Lord thy God with all thy heart, and with all thy soul, and with all thy might . . ."

The five-year-old boys stood around the bed where Maishe lay cradled in his mother's arms and in their high, silvery voices chanted the *krishmeh*, the ancient prayer taken from Deuteronomy. Early in the evening for seven days, the week of his mother's traditional confinement, they gathered at the bedside, the beginners in the local *kheyder*, the elementary religious school, to recite the prayer that Maishe himself would say every evening as soon as he was old enough to remember the words. It was the time-honoured ceremony that marked the birth of a boy and introduced him to the world of learning and religious study.[1]

It was only the beginning of the ceremonies. On the Friday night after he was born, friends and relatives arrived after dinner for *ben-zokher*, the gathering to acknowledge the arrival of a male child, offering congratulations, joining in discussions of the Torah, eating small cakes and sipping tea.

On the next day, the Sabbath, there was open house to celebrate *sholem-zokher*, a day of peace and welcome to the new male child; brandy, cake, and cold, boiled chick peas were set out and all day long people dropped in to talk, recite psalms, sing songs, and discuss parts of the Torah.

The night of the seventh day was "the watch night," when mother and child dared not be left alone. All night men stayed in the room praying so that Maishe would be protected from the evil afoot in the world before his circumcision the following morning. The circumcision would be his Covenant with God, his *bris*.

The Covenant would be a reaffirmation of the commitment made by Abraham who had pledged his soul and those of his descendants to God and undertaken to be holy in all deeds according to God's will. Abraham's circumcision, the first of any Hebrew, was remembered as a sign of his readiness to comply with God's will. His name, before his circumcision was Abram, but to comply with God's wish, he changed it after the circumcision to Abraham. Following in that tradition, Maishe was given his name at the circumcision ceremony.

In 1888 Svisloch was still a pious community, even though the young had been scrambling out of its cloistered piety in a rising groundswell of eagerness. Nevertheless, groundswell or no groundswell, at Maishe's birth all the old traditions were observed. To his parents the cloister was their home and their refuge.

On the morning of his circumcision his godmother took him from his mother's bed, dressed him with new clothing she had brought, and took him to the House of Study where she handed him to his godfather. He, in turn, passed him to the *sandeke*, the person who would hold him while the ceremony was performed. The *sandeke*, wrapped in his prayer shawl, placed Maishe on "the chair of Elijah" brought from the synagogue for the occasion, and recited the lines: "This is the throne of Elijah. May he be remembered for good." Then he dipped a piece of cotton in brandy and put it between Maishe's lips so that he would fall asleep easily.

The men of the community crowded around and as the circumcision was performed, Maishe's father recited the prayer of dedication that formally gave Maishe his name and his acceptance into the community of Svisloch: "Our God and God of our fathers, preserve this child, his father and mother. . . . And it is said, He hath remembered His Covenant forever. The word which He commanded to a thousand generations: [the Covenant] which He made with Abraham, and His oath unto Isaac, and confirmed the same unto Jacob for a statute, to Israel for an everlasting Covenant. . . . This little child, Maishe, may he become great. And as he has entered into the Covenant, so may he enter into the Law [the Torah], the nuptial canopy [the *khupa*], and into good deeds."

Maishe's father, Ezekial (Chatskel in Yiddish), was one of several small grain dealers in Svisloch, buying grain from landowners and well-to-do peasants, grinding some of it to flour for sale to bakers, and selling the rest to wholesale merchants. His house, which had been his father's and one day would be Maishe's, was brick, weathered to the colour of old rust with the upper bricks still bearing faint marks where the roof had once burned, and, as Doris proudly points out, it had floors throughout. The front room was a combination of entrance and kitchen. To the right, a staircase led upstairs to what the family called the attic, which was where the children slept. Farther back was the main room with its large brick oven that heated the house in winter taking up the right-hand wall. Here were the dinner table, chairs, and couches. Finally, at the back of the house was a bedroom. Like early Canadian houses that had to cope with severe winters, windows and rooms were small.

"It was really three rooms and an attic," explains Doris, and in Svisloch it was one of the better homes.

Svisloch was a shtetl, which, to the Jews of Eastern Europe, meant a small town or village but, above all, a community. There were thousands of shtetls in a broad strip of territory about 500 kilometres across and 1,700 kilometres long called the Pale of Settlement,[2] running from the Baltic Sea in the north to the Black Sea in the south and from the Sea of Azov on the east roughly to what is now the border of Romania on the west. It also included as a westward bulge about two-thirds of what is now Poland.

For the most part, Jews in the shtetls were dirt-poor. Zborowski and Herzen wrote about their homes in a 1952 study:

> A few buildings may have two stories, the others will be shabby, unadorned, one-story structures, some with a yard and perhaps a small vegetable garden surrounded by a fence, often broken down.
>
> . . . The poorest [non-Jewish] peasant spends his spare time puttering about his home, repairing the door, the fence, the whitewashed walls. The impoverished [Jew] accepts the condition of his house as part of the state of things, beyond his jurisdiction.
>
> The general appearance of neglect declares . . . that the house is viewed as a temporary shell. "My shtetl" is the people who live in it, not the place or the buildings or the street. "My home" is the family and the family activities, not the walls or the yard of the broken-down fence. . . .
>
> Doctrine teaches that only the mind and the spirit endure — "life is a hallway to heaven" — and even the least soulful Jews of the shtetl, through force of circumstance if not of conviction, treat their physical dwelling places in accordance with this teaching.[3]

Svisloch was a cut above the normal shtetl, at least in the time of Maishe and his parents, because of its tanning factories, which gave it a degree of prosperity other small towns lacked, and its Russian state "seminary" for training elementary school teachers which brought to it about fifty teachers and staff and 300 students from the district of Grodno.[4]

The test of being really poor was whether there were shoes for the children and, again proudly, Doris says, "We were never barefooted. We always had shoes."

But food?

"It was like the Yiddish song: Monday potatoes, Tuesday potatoes, Wednesday potatoes, and then the melody changes, Thursday potatoes, and Friday potato pudding. Friday was the novelty."

Abraham Ain had similar memories:

> "Like every other town [Svisloch] had a nickname: *sislevicher krupnik*. The town fully deserved that nickname. For there was not a day, except the Sabbath and the holidays, when *krupnik* was not on the menu of every Jewish home in town. What is *krupnik*? It is a thick soup of barley or groats mixed with potatoes. In the winter time, when meat was cheap, a slice of lamb or veal was added to the mixture. In the summer time, when meat was expensive, only the wealthy could afford to season their *krupnik* with meat. [Most people] had to be content with a little beef fat in their *krupnik*, to which onions were added as a preservative. . . .
>
> Another popular dish was *lekshlekh bulve*, peeled potatoes thinly sliced and boiled with meat. The dish was prepared in the morning, placed in the oven, and eaten for lunch or supper. [Also] popular were potatoes boiled in their jackets (*sholekhts bulve*). The wealthy ate potatoes with herring; the rest of [us] with herring sauce.[5]

To which Doris adds, "And some days we would make a little cheese."

Shmarya Levin talked in his memoirs about going to Minsk around the time that Maishe was born, and he recalled an area of the city where Jewish shopkeepers worked. The city was a long way from a village shtetl, but the closeted atmosphere of the Jewish section was the same:

> The sun never came that way, except toward evening, when a dying beam entered briefly as if in conscious pity. In this pent and dark prison the Jewish shopkeepers passed their lives. It was a semi-subterranean world in whose perpetual twilight families were raised, marriages celebrated, and social distinctions established.
>
> In Minsk, as in every large Jewish city, there were countless such burrows, and the moles that inhabited them lived literally from day to day: the earning of each day decided the character of the family "dinner." Very often the "shop" consisted of half a barrel of herrings, a few thin loaves of bread, a dozen cheeses, a box of nails and a hunk of soap from which the shopkeeper sliced pieces for a kopec (half a cent) or half a kopec.

I have seen with my own eyes a customer enter such a shop, in Minsk
and in Svilsloch, and buy a herring for a kopec, and half a kopec's worth
of herring juice, called lyak. The herring was wrapped in a piece of paper
and for the herring juice he brought a cup. The lyak would be the staple
of the family dinner that evening. The mother would add a lot of water
and throw in pieces of bread.[6]

There were about 47,600 Jews in Minsk at the time of the 1897 census, and throughout the Pale there were other cities with heavy con-
centrations of Jews: Odessa on the Black Sea in the south with 139,000;
Yekaterinoslav (later named Dnepropetrovsk by the Soviets) on the
lower reaches of the Dnieper River with 40,000; Kishinev near the
Romanian border not too far from Odessa with 50,000; Berdichev about
100 kilometres from Kiev with 42,000; Vilna, northwest of Minsk, with
64,000; and Vitebsk, northeast of Minsk, with 34,000. And in what
is present-day Poland, Warsaw with 219,000, Lodz with 99,000, and
Bialystok with 42,000. In addition Dvinsk, Kovno, Grodno, Mogilev,
Brest-Litovsk, Pinsk, and Gomel in the north; Lublin in present-day
Poland; and Zhitomir, Kiev, Kremenchug, and Yelizavetgrad in the
south all had between 20,000 and 30,000 Jewish residents — in all about
1.1 million Jews.[7]

But within the Pale there were more than five million Jews, which
gives an idea of how many thousands of shtetls were scattered across
it. And within Eastern Europe, which encompassed the Pale of Settlement and included Hungary, Romania, Bulgaria, Latvia, Lithuania,
Estonia, and those parts of Ukraine and White Russia that extended
beyond the Pale, there were seven million Jews — about one-half of
the Jewish population of the world.

This was no random sprinkling of Jews, as the West has come to
perceive its Jewish populations. This was the largest reservoir of Jewish
culture anywhere in the world, where everyone spoke a common
language, Yiddish, as a mother tongue, where a single religion was the
dominant force, where there were common customs, where synagogues
and Jewish schools and libraries were everywhere to be found, and
where each Jewish community had its own council to administer
religious and local affairs, including commercial and other disputes
among Jews.

In many ways it was a nation spread among nations: unique, self-
sufficient, culturally homogeneous, and to a significant degree
self-administering.

It was just exactly what Russian rulers in the nineteenth century
didn't want. They wanted assimilation, not cultural independence.

THE PALE OF SETTLEMENT WHEN THE JEWISH LABOUR BUND
WAS FORMED IN 1897

St. Petersburg

RUSSIA

BALTIC
SEA

Riga

Dvinsk
(Daugavpils)

Moscow

Kovno
(Kaunas)   Vitebsk
Vilna
(Vilnius)

GERMANY

Grodno   Minsk
Mogilev
Bialystok

Warsaw   Brest-Litovsk   Pinsk   Bobruysk
Lodz   (Brest) Northern
Gomel
Poland   Provinces
Lublin

Zhitomir   Kiev
Berdichev

Central Provinces

AUSTRO-
HUNGARY

Kremenchug

Yelizavetgrad   Yekaterinoslav
(Kirovograd)   (Dnepropetrovsk)
Kishinev
Odessa   Southern Provinces

ROMANIA

0   400
kilometres

BLACK
SEA

BERNARD BENNELL

Within the Russian Empire, Jews accounted for 4 to 5 percent of the total population of
Russia, but within the Pale they accounted for 11.6 percent and within cities inside the
Pale it was much more. In the northern provinces they represented 57.9 percent of the
urban population; in the central provinces, 38.1 percent; and in the southern provinces,
26.3 percent. In Poland (then occupied by Russia), almost half of the Jewish population
lived in cities. The centres shown within the Pale all had Jewish populations greater than
20,000.

Cultural differences were tolerable (indeed, under Lenin they were declared desirable), but only if cultural independence was abandoned. Differences could be controlled, independence could not, and the distinction was perceived with an excruciating anxiety rooted, as always, in fear of the Dark People.

It was not just the separateness of the Jews that tugged at the Russian subconscious; it also was their religion. Russia had known no Reformation, but history was full of the monumental repercussions that heresies and religious "deviation" could bring. The Albigensian Heresy, Wycliffe, Luther, Cromwell, Calvin, the Anabaptists, the Hutterites — the names sent shudders down the spine of the Russian Orthodox Church. And then, of course, there were the Freemasons, who were flourishing again following a decline during the later years of Catherine the Great. Many of the Decembrist leaders in 1825 had been Freemasons, but what bothered the Church most was their connection with Freemason lodges in the West, especially in Paris and Berlin, which were seen as sinister hotbeds of anti-religious ideas.

And here were the Jews, nonbelievers, brazenly defying the Russian Orthodox faith, with each passing year, like Freemasons, more caught up in the secular liberalism of the West, more vigorous, more clamorous, more outspoken, breaking out of the old ways with electrifying excitement. In short, threatening to offer an alternative to the Church's authority, or at least an example of dissidence, to any Russians who might be growing restless. And just to tweak the Church's anxiety, there were the Zhidovstuiyvishe, Russians who already were leaning away from Orthodox dogma toward the Jewish faith. They were part of a religious movement that focused on coming closer to Judaism as a means of getting back to original Christianity.

So, in their refusal to assimilate, not only were the Jews an affront to the spirit of Russian nationalism; they were seen by both church and state as an example of indomitable and hazardous intransigence that had a potential to set off the Dark People.

And to assess that potential, all that church and state had to do was look at the heavy Jewish participation in the German revolutions of 1848–49. There, for priest and prince, was proof of their lack of loyalty.

The paradox is that in trying to combat this supposed threat, Russian rulers guaranteed not only its continuance but its increasing strength. Their solution was two-pronged: the first was to keep Jews penned within the Pale of Settlement, which strengthened their culture by keeping them together; the second was to enact discriminatory laws, which encouraged them to look inward even more, drawing support and sustenance from their culture and in the process, supporting and sustaining it.

Catherine the Great created the Pale of Settlement by ukase in 1794 in response to pressure from the Orthodox Christian middle class, which was worried about competition from Jewish merchants and traders. Up to then they had not been unduly fretful because the Jewish population of Russia had not been very large and, from the late 1400s onward, Jews had been prevented from crossing its western borders to settle. However, the partitions of Poland in the last twenty-five years of the eighteenth century, and especially the partition of 1793 and the dissolution of Poland in 1795, had incorporated Poland's Jewish population into Russia. All of a sudden the Russian middle class discovered that it had a lot of Jews as countrymen, and promptly decided it had a problem.

The ukase, which forbade Jews to live beyond the Pale, was a predictable response by Catherine. At the time restrictions on movement were normal. Everyone — serfs, merchants, and townspeople — were confined to their areas of residence. The difference was that over the years, as the restrictions on others were eased, on Jews they were increased.

Obviously something far deeper than a newly awakened fear of competition was at work. Not even Jewish separateness or the dread of touching off the Dark People or Christianity's characterization of Jews as Christ-killers explains it all. Deep within the makeup of White Russians and Ukrainians[8] was a feeling of distrust, an inarticulate sense of grievance dating back through 200 years when Poland occupied much of Russia and Jews were employed by a Polish nobility that was bent on exploitation. (See Appendix D.)

When Catherine the Great created the Pale of Settlement, its eastern border almost coincided with what had been the Polish border 200 years earlier when Poland had pushed its frontier to the Dnieper River and a little beyond in the upper reaches — just short of Smolensk in the north and including Kiev in the south. The Pale's inner border was just to the east of that, providing a bit of an extra buffer for old Russia. Beyond the Pale, Catherine felt she didn't have to worry about Jews because there weren't many.

What happened then, however, was the explosive growth in the Jewish population and that accentuated everything — the strength of the Jewish community and its culture as well as Russian fears and prejudices. In 1775 the Pale held a million Jews; in 1875, before large-scale emigration began, there were 5.5 million.[9] Then, to top off Russian apprehensions, the Pale became a breeding ground for Jewish revolutionaries and that gave real cause for imperial indigestion.

Police statistics on political arrests show that in 1875 about 4 percent of all Russian radicals were Jewish — less than the proportion of Jews in the population. By 1905 that figure was 37 percent and the real figure could well have been closer to 50 percent because government officials, not being able to speak Yiddish, were hampered in their detective work — and this level of radicalism at a time when Jews numbered only 4 percent of the population.[10]

Pogroms where Jews were killed, their women raped, their homes and shops destroyed, and often their neighbourhoods burned — with the implicit approval of government authorities — resumed following the assassination of Alexander II after an interlude of relative quiet for thirty years or so, and the spiral of unrest and discontent tightened.

Svisloch, however, had never seen a pogrom, possibly because Jews were so much in the majority that even the surrounding peasant farmers couldn't muster enough men to feel safety of numbers. But the fires that periodically swept the town? No one now can say what set them off. Regardless of whether they were deliberately set, Jews in the town had to live with the realization that any day their turn might come.

In the meantime life went on as usual. Maishe reached age three and it was time for him to begin school. There were about twenty *melamedim* — teachers at the elementary level — in Svisloch, some operating a *kheyder* for beginners, some for intermediate students, and some for advanced.[11] On a Sunday morning his mother Deborah, or Dvora as she was known in Yiddish, woke him earlier than usual so that Ezekial could take him to the synagogue for morning prayers and, to mark what a special occasion it was, let Maishe sit next to him. Afterward Ezekial introduced him to his new teacher. Throughout the shtetl world a *melamed* was looked on by young boys with fright that varied according to how handy he was with the switch.

In the *kheyder*, beginning students learned the alphabet and the elements of reading and the prayers. It took no special skill or learning to be a *melamed* for beginners, and for this reason he was rarely held in much respect in the community.

After prayer services Ezekial and Maishe, together with a crowd of relatives and friends, returned home where Dvora had laid out sweetmeats and drinks. Maishe was given the seat of honour. When Shmarya Levin went through the same rite of passage he recalled that: "To me was handed a prayer book. Two of the pages had been smeared with honey and I was told to lick the honey off. When I bent my head to obey, a rain of copper and silver coins descended about me. They had been thrown down, my grandfather told me, by the angels; for the angels, he said, already believed in me, knew that I would be a diligent pupil, and were therefore prepared to pay me something in advance. I was immensely pleased to learn that my credit with the angels was good."[12]

The family celebration over, Ezekial wrapped Maishe in his *talis*, his prayer shawl, while Dvora, as much to shore up Maishe's spirits as to prevent her own tears, kept telling him how grown up he was. "A big boy, already my little man, going to learn his letters."

The *kheyder* was nothing more than a room in the *melamed's* house furnished with a rough wooden table with benches on either side and a chair at the head for the *melamed*. And in the corner, the switch. Neither Ezekial nor Dvora would complain over the inevitable whippings. As with the father, so with the son. Like other mothers, Dvora might "peer through the windows, weeping in agony as her child [was] beaten for failing to know his lesson, for speaking while another was reciting, for laughing when he should have been deep in Holy Writ. But she [would] not raise a finger or say a word of protest."[13]

On that first morning Ezekial sat with Maishe as he went through his first lesson, occasionally dropping a candy or a penny on the open prayer book from which he was to learn his letters as an inducement, and passing around candies and cakes to the seven or eight other boys in the class.[14]

From then on, Maishe was on his own: classes half-days, from nine to four in the first term, and then full days, from nine in the morning until nine at night with an hour for lunch which the boys brought with them. Lunch, says Levin, was "usually a piece of unbuttered bread, the tail of a salt herring and perhaps a bagel for dessert.[15]

It was here that Maishe acquired the habit that was to remain with him to the end of his days of rocking gently as he read and chanting, sometimes almost inaudibly. The first months "demanded tremendous intellectual effort of a child who is almost a baby," say Zborowski and Herzen: "The only guides . . . are dingy, tattered prayer books with incomprehensible letters and words and old Bibles used over and over again. The process of learning is endless repetition of unfamiliar Hebrew words, memorizing each letter, each syllable, the rote meaning of each word, translated separately without reference to grammar or derivation.

". . . Like praying, reading a sacred text is accompanied always by incessant rocking forward and back, forward and back; and the words are read aloud in a low-voiced chant that rises and falls. 'It's easier to remember when you rock.'"[16]

At age five Maishe entered his second *kheyder*, where he began studying the Pentateuch, the five books of Moses (Genesis, Exodus, Leviticus, Deuteronomy, and Numbers), and once again friends and relatives were invited to a ceremony at home. Dvora had set out pastries, wine, and nuts, and when the time came, Maishe, dressed in his best clothes, climbed to the centre of the table and stood up. Four older *kheyder* students, wearing prayer shawls, climbed after and stood around him. Ezekial and family friends, all men since this was a male ceremony, sat around the table as the four boys, placing their hands on Maishe's head, recited blessings. As they finished, Dvora and the other women showered the boys with candies and nuts.

Then Maishe sat down next to his new *melamed*, and after a ritual discussion, it was time for the pastries and wine.[17]

In this *kheyder* Maishe gradually passed into translating whole sentences and then into memorizing elementary commentaries on the Pentateuch. Finally, at age eight, he passed into his third *kheyder*, where learning by rote was gradually replaced with "the principle of independent study under the guidance of the *melamed*," and examination of the Bible gradually gave way to study of the Talmud. Now he had entered on "continuous discussion, commentary and interpretation with the help of innumerable commentators and interpreters . . . [and] the study [of such matters as] the holiday ritual in the Temple of Solomon, the ethics of man-to-man dealings, the laws of divorce or the rules governing connubial behaviour during menstruation."[18]

There was no formal celebration when Maishe entered this third stage, just a special dinner with a plump chicken that Ezekial obtained by making a special deal with a local farmer and Dvora cooked to a golden brown. It would be seven years before he would finish his studies; it was customary to keep a boy in *kheyder* until he was fifteen. Now Maishe called his teacher "learned man," and no longer was the switch the engine of inspiration nor was the teacher looked down upon. The *reb* was a man of learning and respected for it.

The intellectual discipline demanded of a boy was enormous. Shmarya Levin gives a vivid idea of just how enormous: "By the time I was nine years old the foundations of my Hebrew education had been laid. I knew the Bible by heart and stood up under all the weird tests that were devised for us. Here is one of them: . . . we used the Letteris edition of the Hebrew Bible, issued by the London Bible Society. The book would be opened at a given page, a word would be chosen, and then a pin would be driven through pages as far as it would go. I would then be asked what words the pin had passed through on the various pages; and with the rarest of exceptions I would be able to name every one of them."[19]

Unquestionably, Levin was an outstanding student; certainly his accomplishments were beyond those of Maishe. Nevertheless, his description evokes a dramatic image of the level of accomplishment set as a goal. However, it had its darker side, as he also described:

> I cannot stress too strongly the dominating, the exclusive role that the kheyder played in the life of a young Jewish boy. He saw his parents only for half an hour in the morning before first prayers and then for an hour in the evening before he went to sleep. . . .
>
> Thus it came about that there was little intimacy between parents and children, or even between brothers if they happened to attend different kheyders. Between brother and sister there was even less opportunity for the ripening of friendship and affection. A wall stood between boys and girls — the latter did not go to kheyder and had nothing to do with studies. The brother looked upon his sister as another kind of creature, belonging to another world.[20]

That doesn't mean there was no love and affection. On the contrary, there was a great deal, especially in the Losz family. There just wasn't all that much time to be together, to talk, and especially to listen. The priority for boys was learning — twelve hours a day. If it had one unhappy consequence it was in heightening the generational gap that every family encounters but which in times of deep and rapid change, such as the Losz family would experience over the next thirty-five years, could be painfully wrenching.

• C H A P T E R   F O U R •

*To be Jewish is our only way to be human. . . . To find
the essence of Jewishness in all places at all times, in all
parts of the scattered and dispersed world-folk; to find the
soul of all this and to see it lit with the prophetic dream
of a human future — that is the task of the Jewish artist.*
I.L. Peretz, quoted in
Milton Meltzer,
World of Our Fathers[1]

"This is my son Maishe. One day, God willing, he'll be a rabbi."
Ezekial and Maishe were standing in the doorway of a
second-floor flat in a brown brick building in Volkovysk.[2]
"Come in, come in," said the man, shaking both by the hand and
leading them to the kitchen. "Sit, please. I'll get Bella," and he stepped out to the wooden stair landing at the back. "Bella," he called.
"Come. The Loszes have arrived."

Coming back into the kitchen, he grinned at Ezekial. "She likes to
talk at the water pump." And turning to Maishe, "So you'll be coming to eat with us, my wise young man?"

Maishe smiled.

"What will be the *tagh* [the eating day]?"

"Thursdays, I hope," Maishe replied. "Already Mr. Artzer said he
would take me on Mondays, Mr. Shochor on Tuesdays, and Mr. Pakess
on Wednesdays."

"So," said the man, "you have a week of *tegh* [eating days] almost?"
He was in his late thirties, a good ten years younger than Ezekial, his
sleeves rolled up, his boots off, *Di Arbeter Shtime* (The Workers' Voice),
the Yiddish underground newspaper put out by the Central Committee of the Bund, open on the table — a factory worker relaxing after
dinner. "Your cousin" — he nodded at Ezekial — "said he was a good
boy. Thursdays are fine."

For a time they talked and then Ezekial and Maishe left to visit the
next family that Ezekial's cousin said might help with a *tagh* for a stu-

dent at the Volkovysk yeshiva, the rabbinical school. Volkovysk was a town of about 14,500, of whom 8,000 were Jewish, located about thirty-three kilometres northeast of Svisloch.[3] In any yeshiva town, Jewish families offered dinner and scraps for the next day's lunch one day a week for students who had no money to pay for meals — and this was always by far the majority. It was a *mitsva*, a good deed, and it would count in the final assessment on the Day of Judgement.

Ezekial's cousin gave Maishe a place to sleep. Not a room. A place in a room with his own children, and meals with the family on the Sabbath. But that was all he could afford.

Maishe was fourteen. He had been quite a good student in *kheyder*, showing the characteristics that David would later describe in his memoirs as spending "every spare minute reading, his brown eyes thoughtful and contemplative. . . . He had a logical mind, sympathetic ear, and an arresting manner of speaking that invariably held one's attention, whether in private conversation or from the public platform."[4]

Like all yeshiva students, he was up before dawn and, as the sun was breaking over rooftops he would enter the House of Study next to the city's main synagogue. Except for an hour away to have dinner, he would be there studying until past midnight. "A yeshiva boy," say Zborowski and Herzen, "customarily sleeps no more than four or five hours a night. . . . The general principle of the yeshiva is independence and self-reliance. The program of study allows for infinite variation. The basic study is exhaustive analysis of the Talmud and its commentators. In addition, each student is privileged to spend a large share of his time on the part of Jewish wisdom that appeals to him the most. . . . In all cases, the approach is the same: commentary, interpretation, referring to the different texts on the biblical quotation that is their ultimate source."[5]

However, it was not all poring over books. The yeshiva teacher would pose a problem, and after students had analyzed possible solutions, "drawing on a vast array of commentators," there would be a general discussion which, more often than not, became a general free for all: ". . . students often jump up on the benches in their excitement, or leave their seats in order to crowd around the teacher. Their great reverence for him is no deterrent to the vehemence of the arguments they hurl at each other and against him."

Nor did independence mean lack of supervision. A teacher was always present, and sometimes a rabbi, and under their stern and unyielding eyes "infinite variation" did not include dallying with rabble-rousing writers who were preoccupied with secular issues such as organizing workers to unite against unfair working conditions, or discussing the nature of man as a rational being in a universe governed by rational principles, or arguing whether Jews should create a Jewish homeland in Palestine or fight for equality at home. At the heart of any preoccupation with secular issues was an attitude that religious authorities felt was anti-religious and hostile to traditional values. It was dangerous. It was a viper at the breast of Judaism.

But for students this was exciting stuff. It had all the romance of idealism and all the adventure of the forbidden. They read pamphlets and essays, novels, poems, underground newspapers, tracts, and treatises, anything they could get their hands on, modern writers as well as thinkers of the past; they read it in Polish, in Russian, in Yiddish, in Hebrew, and especially in German. They read it in nooks and crannies, they read it before going to school and after coming home, they even read it between the covers of the Talmud under the very eyes of their teacher.

And when they were caught . . .

"Maishe! What is this!" There was real shock in the teacher's voice.

Maishe had been lost in the essay *What is Enlightenment?* of Immanuel Kant. Even though it had been written more than a hundred years earlier, it so stirred his imagination that he heard nothing, sensed nothing. The teacher had been scanning the damning words over his shoulder: "Do we live in an *enlightened* age? No; but we live in an age of *enlightenment*. Though certainly much is lacking, the obstacles to the general enlightenment are gradually being reduced. Men are releasing themselves from self-imposed tutelage and learning to deal freely with religious and other matters. . . . Eventually it will have an effect on the principles of government, for rulers will find it to their own advantage to treat men in accordance with their dignity as rational creatures."

Words that thundered down the years to enthrall a boy born in the airless confines of a shtetl. Like all shtetls in the Pale, it had been increasingly buffeted by winds of change, but family, synagogue, and *kheyder* had tempered their power. However, here in Volkovysk they were gale force.

"It is Immanuel Kant, my teacher."

"So I see. Come with me."

The rabbi to whom he brought Maishe was not a man without sympathy. But he also was not a man to underestimate the dangers of "anti-clericism."

"You know young Mordecai was expelled just three weeks ago for just what you were doing?"

"Yes, Rabbi."

"And why was he expelled?"

"Because he lacked sufficient discipline and devotion to learning."

"So why should you not be expelled?"

"Because, Rabbi, as it is said in Proverbs, 'A foolish son is the calamity of his father.' I have learned a lesson."

It was a double-edged answer: correctly put yet capable of several meanings. The rabbi almost smiled despite himself. He loved the intricacy of language. Maishe was a promising student. He would not admit defeat so soon. Maishe could remain, "but if there is another occasion like this, you will be expelled."

From then on Maishe became the model student. But outside the yeshiva he read voraciously, some nights barely sleeping at all as he pored over the controversial authors by candlelight at the kitchen table.

"Maishe, you'll burn out your eyes," the wife of his father's cousin used to say. During the day he spent every free moment dissecting with fellow students the arguments he had read the night before.[6]

At last he was tasting freedom. For years Maishe had been hostage to yearnings he didn't understand. Half-formed thoughts of a different life that stirred vague feelings of disloyalty. Whispers of other worlds as he lay in bed reaching for sleep. Feelings bordering on dismay as he studied older men in the synagogue and wondered whether he would be like them. The twinge of guilt when his father said how proud he would be when Maishe became a rabbi. The wanting something, he didn't know what, but something . . . *more*.

He was exhilarated when the Bund called the first strike in Svisloch leather factories just a few months before he left for Volkovysk. It was less than a year after a branch of the Bund had been formed in town and owners thought the strike was little more than a boyish prank. But the workers were serious. The working day was fourteen to fifteen hours and wages were low. They wanted higher wages and a twelve-hour day with an hour and a half for breakfast and an hour for lunch. When not a man showed up for work and when owners failed to break the strike by offering higher wages to older workers, they quickly settled on the Bund's terms.[7]

Why did Maishe feel such admiration for the workers? His father had always said it was better to work with your head than your hands. The Bund said the place to seek strength was in unity, not in the prayers of the patient, and it seemed to work; but was this a sacrilege that would lead ultimately to failure? Why should owners be so reluctant to help their workers? Weren't they both Jewish?

He was tormented with whys and he could find no answers in the Talmud. But in these secular writings he began to see a framework, a pattern, a history of thinking, that led up to the things the Bund was saying. His own yearnings began to take a form and a texture and he began to see the interplay of forces behind them. As he did he began to realize that taking control of his life was not a disloyalty to his past, that believing he could shape his destiny was not an affront to God, and the revelation was electrifying.

He had begun to taste the fruits of Haskala, the period of the Enlightenment.

The Haskala marked one of the great epochs of Jewish history, a time when wave after increasing wave of Eastern European Jews burst from the claustrophobic cocoon where they had wrapped themselves in resignation and religious preoccupation for 200 years. When the spirit of the Age of Reason finally reached the Pale of Settlement after travelling eastward for seventy-five years or so from Western Europe, it hit shtetl attitudes with the force of a colliding galaxy. Here for the sampling were the ideas that had transformed the Western world: Montesquieu, Rousseau, Diderot, Kant, Voltaire, Schiller, Goethe, Hume. By mid-century the influence of the Haskala was limited to small groups of intellectuals; by the time Maishe entered the yeshiva it had produced a yawning gap between anyone under twenty-five years of age and his elders, and only tattered remnants remained of the old, medieval-type Jewish world.

The Age of Reason offered three basic assumptions: that the universe is governed by rational principles; that people can understand these principles; and that they are capable of acting on this knowledge. It resulted in a spirit of enterprise that was laissez-faire in character but based on a sense of self-respect, decency, and the dignity of man. Its social philosophers demonstrated "a spirit of reasonableness, sanity, democracy, and optimism about the capacities of human nature."[8] In the Pale, it was a recipe for adventure of mind and spirit so catalytic that when it was introduced into the backward and repressed world of the shtetls it touched off an incandescent hunger that drove Jews to accomplish in single lifetimes the kind of intellectual liberation that it took West Europeans generations to achieve. And it was a liberation of the illiterate as much as of the literate.

David Rome, eighty years old at the time of being interviewed, is a historian and the former archivist of the Canadian Jewish Congress Archives in Montreal. He emigrated from the Pale when he was ten. He discusses the metamorphosis of shtetl Jews into Canadian citizens with the affection of a man who loves the interplay of ideas the way artists love the interplay of light — seeing how textures change, realities shift. It is his consuming delight. He talks of worlds within worlds within worlds and cautions incessantly against the dangers of looking back with "outside" eyes.

The shtetl world was self-contained, he stresses. To understand the people who came from it, you have to understand it; and to under-stand it, you have to guard against seeing it as a part of the ebb and flow of Continental politics. It was not. It was hostage to those politics, but its people did not gaze beyond their shtetls until Haskala freed them to look up . . . and out.

He leans into his words physically, his white hair combed back flat, his brown eyes fixed on the distance, trying to pierce the barrier of time: "This vast, multi-form revolution that hit the shtetl was really one blow. It was a blow against the old and it had many forms. One group said the key to the whole thing was education: formal education, systematic education, vocational education, proper teaching methods, establishing institutions of learning. And for thousands, maybe millions, of Jews this concern for education as a response to the challenge of the Enlightenment was their whole life."

In Svisloch there were practical results. A Hebrew elementary school was established in 1900 and in 1915 a secular Yiddish school was open-ed. By 1919 the old-fashioned *kheyder* was all but extinct.[9]

"Then you came to the thing called the class struggle, which as a term didn't exist. Suddenly . . . [workers] adopted a certain attitude toward employers. . . . [It was at the level of] the carpenter and his apprentice. That's where the battlefront was. Sometimes it resulted in action by the employee, sometimes in the reaction of an employer. . . . [The employers' weapons] were mostly social-religious sanctions, for instance the boycott of the restless employee. He could be blacklisted and never get another job as an apprentice. It's just as good as killing a guy, you know. So bit by bit you have the beginning of the Jewish labour movement."

In addition, he says, between the initial awareness of class differences and the creation of the Bund, a concept of profound importance developed. It was the idea of social justice. "Justice — fairness — was a word out of the Bible. However, don't think of the Bible as a manual for social justice. It wasn't. But the word was there: *yosher* [in Yiddish: *yaisher*]. And these people suddenly pulled it out. No one had noticed that the word 'justice' was there and could be used in this sense until this period in history. . . . I wouldn't know how to translate the phrase 'social justice' in the Hebrew of that age. Or in Yiddish."

In the shtetl, justice — *yaisher* — meant correcting the wrong done to an individual, and in the correcting, the criterion was fairness. For instance, in the Torah and the Prophets there are injunctions against harming widows or orphans or strangers in the land. And if any were harmed, they were entitled to redress. But the focus was on righting a wrong, not on curing a social ill. Just as it was on aiding the indigent or assisting the underprivileged, and not on ending indigence or terminating privilege. The emphasis was on protecting those who were socially weaker, not on looking for the cause of social weakness and trying to do something to correct it.

With the growing awareness of employer-employee classes, a sense of cause and effect began to develop. It was an idea that said individuals aren't alone; they are linked with others just like themselves — orphans, workers, the aged, the poor, the disabled. And when an entire group ends up weak or vulnerable, something has caused it. Yes, one widow may have a problem. But when all widows have the same basic problem, something must be at the root of it. And what used to be a problem concerning individual disabilities quickly became a problem concerning group inequalities.

So people in shtetls got a frame of reference for seeing cause and effect — class conflict. In the beginning it was not class conflict in Marxist terms. It was more a recognition that groups had identities and that groups had common interests and common complaints. It was a recognition that society was more than a collection of individuals; it was a collection of groups with competing interests.

Even with this new perception, however, a change in attitude was needed if anything was to be done about the common injustices they identified. This they got from the Enlightenment. They had been taught by rulers and rabbis to accept their lot in life because God's rules were immutable and the state's rules they could not change. What the Enlightenment brought was the notion that reason, not God, could be the source of moral law. It didn't preach a rejection of God; God could still be the voice of reason. But it did preach that people could look beyond narrow religious and secular codes; that general, rational principles should prevail — if general, rational principles could be identified.

That's where the old biblical concept of fairness came into play. It was expanded to deal with this newly defined set of wrongs — social wrongs; wrongs done to social groups; class wrongs. What developed is what we recognize today as the idea of social justice. It implied a system of fairness independent of existing laws that people, as members of a group (orphans, workers, the aged, the poor, the disabled, and so forth), should be entitled to expect of their society as a fundamental right.

It was an absolutely revolutionary notion. It was never called social justice in the shtetl. And it wasn't a concept that jelled overnight; there was a lot of groping toward it. But even the groping mobilized people.

It was an idea that was bound to offend authorities. Within the shtetls, says Mr. Rome:

> I come to something very complicated and very subtle: the reaction to the Haskala. The response to it was all religious. Solidly. Universally. We don't have to this day in Jewish history a single group or a single movement or a single person who was religious and who found it possible to be religious in his thinking and in his conduct who still felt positively about this social motif. . . .
> Now it's not true of Catholicism. It's not true about Protestantism. Look at all the Protestants who were in the head and certainly were in the body of the social justice [movement] in Canada and elsewhere. We don't have that in Jewish history. The Jewish Orthodoxy — and that's the only religion there was, there were no Conservative or Reform [branches] or anything in the shtetls — was solidly anti-Enlightenment.
> They were against education in a moderate sense. They were against vocational training. They were against learning the geography or history or languages of the country. They were against moving from the shtetl. They were against going to the city. They were against going to Montreal. They were against Zionism. They were against literature. They were against using Yiddish and Hebrew as literary vehicles. They were against everything and everything and everything.

But let it be said in defence of the Orthodoxy that it was just this kind of opposition that had maintained Jewish communities through thousands of years and endless pressures and persecutions. "When, for example," says Irving Howe, "Jewish reformers . . . proposed changes in the schooling of the young, the rabbis resisted such schemes on the grounds that even a partially secularized education would deprive Jewish youth of traditional ways of life without really enabling them to find a place in the gentile world. Motives apart, the rabbis were speaking to a reality."[10]

Within the Yiddish world that Haskala was laying siege to, religion was inseparable from daily life, from identity. God did not rule from on high. God was a constant Presence. Someone to argue with, to debate with, to berate if necessary. To walk with in the sun and to muse with in the dark. "He was a plebian God. . . . Because the east European Jew felt so close to God he could complain to him freely, and complain about Him too. The relation between God and man was social, intimate, critical. . . . The despair with which a Kafka knocks on the door of the Lord suggests that he does not expect the door to be opened, whereas the rasping impatience with which Yiddish folk writers of the Hasidic period appealed to the Lord leaves no doubt that they knew He would respond.[11]

God, then, was part of being. What Haskala seemed to threaten was loss of that relationship. And that could only mean loss of identity, loss of being. It could only lead to that most dreadful of all fates, assimilation. But the traditionalists were no match for the new ideas that were being generated. By the time Maishe left for the yeshiva in Volkovysk, the banner of social justice had been unfurled and legions of shtetl youth were brandishing it aloft. Even if they hadn't yet put the name to it, even if they didn't understand its intellectual roots, they still grasped its spirit — and there was more than enough injustice to fuel the fires of their idealism.

And to the injustices of the present they could add the injustices of the past. The history of repression. The persecutions. The expulsions. The pogroms. As they began to grapple with everyday inequities they began to see the past as part of an ongoing pattern of oppression, and as that became clearer and clearer, they began to focus on the need to change the system . . . and that changed many of them from activists to potential revolutionaries.

Nicholas I (1826–55), the Iron Tsar, lived in their memories like the Demon of Darkness. Their grandfathers told stories of life under Nicholas that curdled the blood. Alexander Sergeivich Pushkin, Russia's greatest poet, called him, "an execrable sovereign, but a remarkable colonel."[12] In Jewish annals he is remembered most for military conscription of children. It was an attempt to force assimilation of Jews. In 1827, the year after he was crowned Tsar — and a year after hanging the Decembrists — he ordered that the minimum age for conscription of Jews be lowered from eighteen to twelve, and made sure that youngsters who were conscripted were sent to the interior of Russia, far from any Jewish communities. The term of military service was twenty-five years.

Alexander Herzen, while in internal exile, described a group of such children. He questioned the transport officer:

> "Whom are you escorting and to where?"
> "As you see, a horde of damned little Jews, eight to ten years old. . . . Not half will reach their destination. They just die off like flies! A Jew boy, you know, is such a frail weak creature . . . he is not used to tramping in mud for ten hours a day and eating biscuit . . . being among strangers, no father nor mother nor petting; well, they cough and cough until they cough themselves into their graves."

> The children were lined up in proper formation. It was one of the most terrible sights I have ever witnessed. Poor, unfortunate children! Boys of 12 or 13 might somehow have survived it. But these little ones of eight and ten! . . . No brush could create such horror on canvas. . . .[13]

Milton Meltzer adds a further description:

> Every means was tried to induce them to convert. . . . A favourite method was to make the child kneel on the barracks floor when bedtime came. If he consented to be baptized, he was allowed to sleep in his bed. If not, he was kept on his knees all night until he collapsed. The stubborn ones were beaten or tortured. If they refused to eat pork, they suffered more beatings. They were fed on salted fish and then denied water unless they agreed to baptism. Most of the younger ones gave up and were baptized. The older children often endured the whippings, the hunger, the thirst, the sleeplessness, refusing to betray their faith. Some who would not yield were whipped to death, some were drowned.[14]

The Iron Tsar had entered his reign in 1825 with his father having already banned Jews from holding leases on land and having stripped them of some of their major occupations: selling liquor and operating taverns, saloons, and inns. It had been partly a means of extending the Russian system of state monopoly to the newly acquired Polish territories, where the liquor business was in private hands. Nevertheless, 40 percent of the Jewish work force was engaged in these occupations and the result was to expropriate their livelihood.[15]

He toured Russia shortly before his father died, and concluded that the Jews were nothing but "leeches." As Tsar he saw them as an "internal enemy," and during his thirty-year reign he enacted more than 600 anti-Jewish decrees, among which: Jews were forbidden to wear their traditional clothing; men were ordered to cut off their earlocks and women to stop shaving their heads before marriage; Yiddish and Hebrew were banned in commercial documents; the Pale of Settlement was reduced in size and Jews outside the new borders were ordered to relocate inside; Jewish books were heavily censored and foreign editions were burned by the cartload; efforts were made to force Jews into the cities where they would no longer form the majority in their community; and, most odious of all, child conscription was launched.

When he died in 1855, men hugged one another in the streets.

Most of his major anti-Jewish initiatives were undone, or at least modified, by Alexander II during the early, more liberal, part of his reign but, with the exception of child conscription, which Alexander II stopped shortly after mounting the throne, they were largely restored under Alexander III (1881–1894) and Nicholas II (1894–1917).[16]

In addition, Alexander III and Nicholas II gave their implicit support to the revival of pogroms, the most terrifying indicator of their race hate. Nineteenth-century Russia had never been without pogroms, but under Alexander II they had abated. However, when he was assassinated in 1881 they resumed immediately. And since Konstantin Pobedonostzev, procurator of the Holy Synod and chief adviser to both Alexander III and Nicholas II (and described by Turgenev as the "Russian Torquemada"), had said that the only way to deal with the "Jewish problem" was to create conditions where one-third of the Jews would assimilate, another third would emigrate, and the final third would perish, there was really only one way for Jews to look at the pogroms.[17]

Alexander was assassinated on March 1. In mid-April the pogroms erupted, first on Easter Sunday in Elizavetgrad where 15,000 Jews lived. A government commission, whose report was never intended for publication, described the onslaught:

> The city presented an unusual sight: the streets were covered with feathers and cluttered with broken furniture; doors and windows shattered; an unruly throng rampaging in all directions, yelling and shrieking, pursuing its task of destruction unhindered; and as a supplement to this scene — complete indifference on the part of the local non-Jewish residents toward the pogrom in progress.
>
> The militia called upon to restore law and order had no definite instructions, and . . . had to wait for orders from its own superiors or those of the police. Under such an attitude of the militia, the anarchial mob — smashing houses and shops in full view of the passive garrison — could only conclude that its destructive progress was not illegal, but rather authorized by the government. . . . In the evening the disorders intensified because a mass of peasants had arrived in the city from neighbouring villages in hopes of confiscating some Jewish possessions.
>
> On April 17 an infantry battalion restored law and order in Elizavetgrad.[18]

Over the next few weeks pogroms raged through 160 cities and villages in the southwestern Pale. The pattern was the same. First accusations were made that Jews had killed the Tsar, then newspapers repeated the charges, and then rumours would spread that the new Tsar had allowed "three days to plunder the Jews" — and indeed, the police did stand aside for three days while the killing and plundering went on.[19]

In some towns pogroms were prevented either by the local authorities or, in rare instances, by Jewish defence militias. But quite often the consequence was fire sweeping through the wooden houses of Jewish settlements. In Minsk, for instance, where two-thirds of the 50,000 residents were Jewish, fire destroyed 20 percent of the city: "In a few hours, 1,000 of the wooden houses burned down and 21 of the synagogues [and] 10,000 men, women and children were left homeless."[20] By 1882 there had been pogroms in 225 communities.[21]

In his memoirs, Shmarya Levin recalled his reaction and, even though he had drunk deep of the Enlightenment, his response remained that of the old shtetl resident, the passive fatalist:

> No pogrom took place in [the other] Svisloch, but the terror of the pogrom was suspended almost visibly over our heads. There were times when we envied the towns that had already suffered the pogrom, "Better an end with terror than a terror without end."
>
> . . . And then, the shame and the degradation of it! It is not easy to say which was the greater affliction, the terror or the shame. A Jew was ashamed to look his gentile neighbour in the face; as far as possible he would avoid meeting his look; he feared to catch in it the first glimpse of the first fires of hatred. And he was afraid to let the gentile catch his own look because of the shame that was in it. He was ashamed of his own shame and humiliated again by his own humiliation."[22]

It is difficult in today's world to comprehend such an attitude. Why shame? Why a feeling of humiliation?

Where was the anger? Where was the fighting back? Where was the kind of stance that David Lewis would take ninety years later, the kind of stance that we are accustomed to in the modern world? In his 1972 booklet called Louder Voices: The Corporate Welfare Bums, David says with a heady anger, after recounting a litany of inequities: "Justice is not blind. Justice comes only to those who work for it, demand it, shout for it and proclaim its worth above other considerations."[23]

Granted, David was speaking on the other side of the century, on the other side of two world wars. On the other side of the Holocaust. But that was still the voice of the Haskala, the voice of a Jew, born in 1909 and raised to age thirteen in a shtetl.

Further highlighting the contrasting attitudes, Levin described the message of "wandering preachers — the maggidim — those troubadours of the Jewish exile" who travelled through Svisloch in the summer of 1881 as "the 'comforters of the people' whose task was to prevent the spirit of the Jews from sinking into depths from which it might never rise again."[24]

They spoke, as was their wont, obliquely . . . what sense was there in mentioning, in terror and trembling, the name of Alexander III, Emperor of Russia, when it was just as easy to speak fearlessly of Pharaoh, Emperor of Egypt? . . .

What need to say "Ignatiev"[25] or "Pobedonostzev," the two bitterest persecutors of the time, when the Bible had so thoughtfully given us Haman as a symbol and so provided us with countless legends about him? . . .

They dragged from their graves the ancient enemies of Israel. They reminded the Jews of the fate of Pharaoh; they recalled how Haman had ended up on the gallows and how Nebuchadnezzar had eaten the grass of the field for seven years. And the Jews understood. Patience. Patience. There are still seas enough for all the Pharaohs, trees enough for all the Hamans, and more than enough grass for all the Nebuchadnezzars.[26]

This was the attitude of the old cocoon, the shtetl before Haskala, where hope rested in God and not in the power of an individual to wreak change; where the solution lay in patience, not in initiative.

But the pogroms of 1881 did bring a change in Levin: "To the crystallizing effect of my own growth was added the crystallizing effect of the epoch. The pogroms had opened my eyes; I understood that I was forever bound to my people, my persecuted and tormented people."

Twenty-two years later Maishe Lewis experienced the same crystallizing experience and for him it meant leaving the yeshiva, rejecting the prospect of becoming a rabbi, and taking up the life of a worker and organizer.

Nicholas II was now Tsar. A small man in every sense of the word, invested with enormous power that he had neither the wit nor the strength to cope with. So excruciatingly polite that people rarely knew what he thought and sometimes couldn't understand what he meant. A frightened man-child in a fearsome, overly large suit of armour whose only means of displaying manliness was to clank awkwardly about the Imperial stage waving the banner of the autocracy. The agony for Jews, and for Russia, too, was that each clank, each wave of the banner, was law.

He was enveloped in anxiety, fearful for his throne, resentful of Jews who, he was constantly being told, were at the centre of all revolutionary plots. He so blamed them for everything that he called anyone who opposed him a Jew. Jews, of course, made up the largest single group arrested for political crimes and the Bund seemed everywhere. By 1902 Nicholas felt beset at all sides. In Vilna, on May Day that year, the Bund held a demonstration, the governor called in troops, and a number of workers were arrested. The next day twenty Jewish and six Polish prisoners were publicly flogged. In retaliation Hirsh Lekert, a Bundist shoemaker, shot but failed to kill the governor. He was immediately hanged and thousands of Jews were imprisoned or exiled to Siberia.

Lekert's hanging followed by days that of a Socialist Revolutionary who had assassinated D.S. Sipyagin, minister of the interior.[27] Nicholas's reaction was portentous; he appointed Vyacheslav K. von Plehve as the new minister of the interior. This was the same Von Plehve who, as director of state police during the terrible 1881 pogroms that followed the assassination of Alexander II, had never lifted a finger of restraint. Where a generation earlier he had had to deal with sporadic street demonstrations involving only handfuls of activists, now Von Plehve was facing gatherings of 50,000 in St. Petersburg's squares with red banners waving and revolutionary speeches defiantly shouted. It was all the work of the "foreigners," the Jews, Von Plehve maintained. He would, "drown the revolution in Jewish blood," he promised.[28]

On the day of Passover, April 6, 1903, in Kishinev, a city of 125,000, of whom 50,000 were Jewish, a raging mob plundered and raped and killed Jews for two days as policemen watched — and even disarmed those Jews who rallied to the streets with clubs. At the end of the second day there were forty-seven Jews murdered, eighty-six seriously injured, 500 others injured, 1,500 homes and shops looted or destroyed, and 10,000 people homeless.[29]

A week later Alexei Nikolayevich Kuropatkin, the war minister, noted in his diary: "I heard from [Minister of the Interior Von Plehve] as I had from the Tsar that it was necessary to teach the Jews a lesson, that they were putting on airs and placing themselves at the forefront of the revolutionary movement."[30]

The pogrom had not been slow in coming. The local tax collector, a man named Krushevan, had started an anti-Jewish newspaper called *Bessarabetz* in 1897. It was Kishinev's only newspaper and operated under a government subsidy with government officials writing for it. When Jews sought permission from Von Plehve to open a second newspaper they got nowhere. "The *Bessarabetz* is good enough for Kishinev," he told them. Krushevan preached that Jews were at the root of all the problems facing Russia and they were especially dangerous because they dominated the revolutionary movement. As Milton Meltzer describes it, the non-Jewish townspeople — officials, police, military, ordinary people — gradually absorbed the idea that Jews were outside the law's protection. After all, wasn't this newspaper a mouthpiece for the Government?

Then, in early April 1903, leaflets appeared all over Odessa declaring that a Tsarist edict had allowed the slaughter of Jews at Easter. That did it. April 6 was also Easter Sunday and as the church bells rang out at noon to celebrate the Resurrection, gangs of men began rampaging through the Jewish community.[31]

The Jews of Odessa sent the poet Chaim Bialik to Kishinev to discover what had happened. His poem, "The City of Slaughter," was read in every Jewish home in all of Russia:

> She saw it all, and she's a living witness,
> The old gray spider spinning in the garret.
> She knows a lot of stories — bid her tell them!
> A story of a belly stuffed with feathers,
> Of nostrils and of nails, of heads and hammers,
> Of men, who, after death, were hung head downward,
> Like these along the rafter.
> A story of a suckling child asleep,
> A dead and cloven breast between its lips,
> And of another child they tore in two,
> And many, many more such fearful stories
> That beat about the head and pierce thy brain,
> And stab the soul within thee, does she know.

It was more than a recounting of the horrors. It was a railing against the same kind of reaction that Shmarya Levin had experienced in 1881. It was a denouncing of a sense of shame, a fury with passive attendance on God's will, and a wild, angry call to action:

> Can you hear? They beat their breasts, "Forgive us!"
> They call to Me I should forgive their sins!
> How sins a shadow on the wall, a dead worm?
> A broken pitcher?
> Why do they pray? Why do they lift up their heads?
> Where is their fist? Where is the thunderbolt
> That would settle accounts for all the generations
> And lay the world in ruins, tear down heavens,
> And overturn My Throne! . . .
> Your unwept tear bury within you,
> Immure it in your heart, build up there
> Of hate and wrath and gall for it a fortress,
> And let it grow, a serpent in its nest,
> And you will suckle from each other,
> Yet always hungering and thirsty you will be.
> Then when the evil day comes upon you,
> Break your heart open, liberate the snake.
> And like a poisoned arrow send it
> Ravenous, with burning venom,
> Into the very heart of your own people.[32]

Galvanized by the poem, young Jews in towns and villages armed themselves and formed defence militias.

And in Volkovysk, Maishe Lewis, now sixteen years old, knocked on the door of the rabbi's study.

"I cannot stay," he said with a simple finality.

• C H A P T E R F I V E •

When we are attacked . . . it would be criminal on our part to bear it without resistance. In such cases we must come out with arms in hand, organize ourselves, and fight until our last drop of blood; only when we show strength will we force everyone to respect our honour.

Di Arbeter Shtime,
Bundist newspaper,
October 1902

Ezekial looked more tired than Maishe had ever seen him. Grey age seemed to have leaped on his shoulders and weighed him down. He walked, eyes downcast in thought, hands clasped behind his back. He had no arguments left.

The dream he had cherished for so very long lay shattered. And for what? That was what he could not comprehend. For what? For a job in the factory that any young man could do. The dullest, the most inarticulate, the least favoured. A strong back, that's all that was needed. Yet here was Maishe, a good brain, a fine speaker, a scholar! One of the best students in Svisloch. Promising, so the rabbi said. And what did he want to do? Work in the factory. Like any *proster mensch*, like any common drudge.

Nor would he come into the grain business with Ezekial! Why? Did he think it was something to be ashamed of? That his father had soiled his life working so hard to build it up? There was no *yikhus*, no status, no respect for a labourer. You worked with your hands when that was all you could do. Why, Maishe? Why, why, why?

He wouldn't come to the synagogue for prayers. Him who was studying to be a rabbi! Saying things like, "It is not God who shapes the future but us." Blasphemy! He was not bad, Ezekial knew that. But this! For this God would ask payment.

Ezekial mourned the son he had lost, and did the best that he could to live with this strange young man he couldn't understand but to whom he was tied so closely in blood and memories and love. He never did understand. He died not understanding. Although they remained close, it was different. There was a gap, a chasm, between them that neither could bridge, so that interwoven with the love and the closeness was a wariness. A wariness of the hurts that lay at the bottom of the chasm, should one push the other into it. Which meant that much of the intimacy that comes with sharing was no longer theirs. And for Ezekial especially, it left an emptiness that sometimes startled him, so intense could it be; like trying to use the part of a limb that had been amputated, forgetting that it was gone, and, in a flash, reliving its loss. That's when it pained the most.

Maishe was not unique. Thousands like him had gone through the same experience and thousands of parents, like Ezekial, had been distressed.[1]

There were eight leather factories in town, each with forty to fifty workers, and about a dozen smaller shops with six to twelve workers each. Maishe went to work in a tannery owned by Mintz on the north side of town.[2] His job was scraping the hair from hides after they had been chemically treated. On the eastern outskirts of Svisloch there were other large tanneries owned by Finestone, Medviediev, Vigonsky, Meisel, and Finklestein. Near Mintz's tannery was the large slaughterhouse that served all tanneries.[3] Maishe was wiry — some would say skinny — and the years of prodigiously long hours of study did not serve him well in the factory. For the first weeks he came home exhausted, his hands blistered and often bleeding.

But he had joined the future. He had made his choice. By now he had come to see the world in terms of class. Them and us. The *them* were capitalists and reactionaries; *us* were the working people. If he had not already reached that point, the Kishinev pogrom and the pogrom in Gomel four months later would soon have pushed him there.

In fact, it would be hard to imagine how a Jewish student could resist being radicalized, what with the pogroms coming on top of cutbacks in university quotas, the intransigence of Nicholas II, the blossoming of the spirit of Enlightenment, the abominable conditions — 50 percent of Jews depended on charity in the last years of the 1890s and 40 percent of Jewish families were those of *luftmenshn*, people without skills, capital, or specific occupations[4] — to say nothing of the meteoric growth of the Bund and the swelling number of radical writers, speakers, and organizers in the Pale.

It was a period of mass emigration. Between the assassination of Alexander II in 1881 and the outbreak of war in 1914, about two million Jews, almost one-third of Eastern European Jewry, departed. Most went to the United States. The peak year was 1906 when 153,748 arrived in New York City. Most stayed there. In 1870 the city had 60,000 Jews;

in 1880 it had 80,000, by 1910 there were 1.1 million out of a total population of about 4.8 million.[5]

However, Maishe never gave emigration a thought. Svisloch, the Pale, Russia: this was the crucible of tomorrow. This was where justice for all would be forged, for workers, for Jews, . . . for posterity. This was where his world, the Jewish world, could be transformed; where Jewish workers could wrestle capitalists, Jewish and non-Jewish, to the ground; where social justice could triumph. This also was a world where Jewish history could be changed. It was the centre of Jewish existence, where a new awareness of energy, of strength, and of mission could write an end to the ostracism that had existed since the destruction of the Second Temple 1,800 years ago.[6] Finally, this was the world of Russia, second in size and strength only to the British Empire, where the future of nations could be cast.

History was full of wandering Jews; this was the time to stay put and create change.

Maishe joined the Bund in his first days home, and once he recovered from the daily exhaustion of working in the factory, his days were as long as they had been in the yeshiva. He was up before dawn, but where his father went to morning prayers at the synagogue, he remained at home poring over books, journals, newspapers, and essays until it was time to go to work. After work it would be meetings, study circles, discussions, delivering pamphlets and copies of *Di Arbeter Shtime (The Workers' Voice)* or *Der Yidisher Arbeter (The Jewish Worker)*, seeking new members for the Bund, and then, once home, reading, reading, reading.

For the most part Ezekial kept his views of these activities to himself. But when Bund members pasted leaflets to the synagogue walls on Friday nights — where they would remain through the Sabbath until Sunday when work could be resumed and they could be removed — it was too much.[7] It was always too much.

"Maishe. The synagogue was desecrated again."

"I know, Papa."

"By your friends."

"I know, Papa."

"Why do you do this? It is an insult to the House of the Lord. It is to spit on everyone who goes there to pray. Do you know what pain you cause? Do none of you care?"

"It's because we do care. I didn't put up the leaflets, but I defend it. Papa, the revolution can come only . . ."

Ezekial cut him short. "Only if you act like barbarians? Who wants a revolution of barbarians?"

"People need to understand. They need to see."

"See? See what? How to despoil what good there is?"

And so it would go, often for hours. And always, mixed in with Ezekial's anguish over the path Maishe had chosen, was the fear that his son would be arrested and that easily could mean inner exile to Siberia. By the Bund's own reckoning, police had arrested 2,180 members in the two years between April 1901 and June 1903, and in the year ahead, June 1903 to July 1904, they would arrest 4,467 — double the number in half the time.[8]

The police had been a constant threat to the Bund from the very beginning. In July 1898, barely nine and a half months after the organization was founded, they arrested fifty-five key members, including the entire Bund Central Committee, and closed down the only two presses it had. It was an almost fatal blow. The Bund survived only for two reasons: first, in the short time that it had existed, it had built a sturdy organization out of the solid framework bequeathed to it by earlier activists; and second, there was no leadership cult.

Throughout its years there was a strong sense of community within the Bund. Self-effacement was characteristic, both for security reasons and, more importantly, as a personal preference. As it was put years later by A. Litvak, one of the more prominent Bundist writers whose real name was Khaim Yankel Helfand: "As far as I can recall, there never was a single leader in the Bund . . . who looked on himself as the boss of the party and was so regarded by others. The leadership of the Bund was always a collegial one. . . . One had an idea, others seized on it, added to it. . . . When it finally became a decision, it lost its individual character and became a collective work."

Even the Central Committee would not presume to make decisions on important problems. Instead, it would call a conference to discuss the issues. According to Litvak, the Bund tried "to draw as many people as possible to the leadership so the voices of the masses could be heard as clearly as possible."[9] This gave the organization tremendous staying power in the face of police crackdowns. It meant that, regardless of whom the police arrested, the organization would survive.

Nevertheless police could seriously harass the organization — and they did, especially in 1903 and 1904. They had spies everywhere. Landlords were penalized if meetings were held on their property; houses were searched for evidence of meetings; demonstrations were attacked with unbridled ferocity and suspicious-looking people were put in detention; such minor activities as smoking on Saturday, the Jewish Sabbath, was enough in police eyes to mark a person as a radical who should be detained.

For Maishe the year went by rapidly as he gained a reputation for hard work and a level head. Then, in the summer of 1904, Svisloch had its second general strike in the leather factories. The war with Japan was under way and business for the factories was booming. But with the boom came higher costs of living and demands for higher wages. The tannery owners were prepared to give a small increase that was nothing near what the workers wanted, so one day the Bund passed the word that there would be a general assembly in Vihshnik forest right after work.

The forest was about one and a half kilometres from town. "Your job, Maishe," they told him, "is to organize the lookouts."

He was thrilled to have such a trust. It was an honour. During the afternoon he contacted about a dozen young workers and that evening, as soon as they were out of the factories, they raced to the forest to hide by footpaths and likely entry routes. Maishe went deeper into the forest, to the edge of the clearing where the meeting was to be held, so that he could double-check all who arrived.

All were in place with about an hour left of that mellow, end-of-the-day sunlight that turns green things olive and ushers in the cool night air. They came in ones and twos, most of the men still wearing their factory clothes, the sprinkling of women in their long skirts, some from shops, some from home, until there were about 250 in the clearing talking quietly in small groups. Then one of the older workers moved to the base of an old oak where the ground was a bit higher.

Brothers, sisters [he said as they gathered around], you all know why we're here. We're here because it's time for action. It's time to fight for our rights. It's the only thing our little capitalists understand. . . .

Talking has got us nowhere. We have a right to fair wages. We have a right to go to bed and not fear tomorrow. We have a right to be sick and not have our families starve.

We're not plough horses to be whipped through the fields for the privilege of resting in a leaky shed.

We're not serfs. We're not pieces of machinery that are dumb and blind and deaf.

We're honest workers. We don't have to beg for justice. We don't have to plead for favours.

If we don't get what's rightfully ours, if our little barons say no, if our belly-worshipping little capitalists refuse us, then I say smash the fist of greed. Strike.

Maishe was caught in the emotion of the moment. "Yes," he yelled from his position at the edge of the clearing, joining the others. "Yes.

Yes." Then the speaker introduced the Bund spokesman from Volkovysk to present the list of demands that the Bund had prepared. They were: wage increases of about 35 percent; reduction of the working day from twelve to nine hours extending from 8 A.M. to 5 P.M.; job security (no firing without sufficient cause); and medical security (employers to pay all medical bills).

There was little discussion and, unlike the 1901 strike, there was no swearing on a pair of phylacteries not to work until the demands were met.[10] There was no need. Solidarity within the Bund had gone a long way in the short space of three years.

Looking at the determined people in the clearing, Maishe felt a surge of kinship and pride, and when one of the women began to sing the Bund hymn and they all clasped hands, he ran to join them and they stood defiantly hand in hand, sending their militant battle song ringing through the forest:

> Brothers and sisters of work and need,
> All who are scattered like far-flung seed —
> Together! Together! The flag is high,
> Straining with anger, red with blood,
> So swear together to live or die! . . .
>
> We swear our stalwart hate persists,
> Of those who rob and kill the poor:
> The Tsar, the Masters, Capitalists.
> Our vengeance will be swift and sure. . . .
>
> To the Bund our hope and faith we swear
> Devotedly to set men free.
> Its flag, bright scarlet, waves up there,
> Sustaining us in loyalty.[11]

The strike committee left immediately to confront the owners. There was no waiting until the morning. They sent three young workers running ahead to call on the owners to meet at one of the factories, and then they filtered back into town.

On wages and working hours the owners were prepared to negotiate. But job and medical security were out of the question. The demand for job security especially angered them. So there was a strike. It lasted three weeks and then the owners gave in completely. The four demands were met in full. For seventeen-year-old Maishe it was proof that things really could change — if there was a will; if there was organization; if there was solidarity.

By now the Bund was more than just a labour organizaton of a radical socialist cast. It was a full-fledged political party, one of the biggest and most powerful among the radical left-wing parties in Russia, even though it was restricted almost entirely to the Pale of Settlement.

The formal move from being an organization that focused primarily on working conditions to an organization dedicated to full-scale revolutionary action came with the Bund's Fifth Congress in June 1903. Partly it came from realizing that limiting action to economic issues was too constraining — although the Bund had 30,000 members by mid-1903, it had been able to involve only 7,000 members in strikes over the previous two years.[12] But partly it also resulted from increased police crackdowns and pogroms.

When the Congress convened, not only did it redefine itself in terms of a revolutionary political party; it put itself on a war footing. It resolved that "Committees and other organizations of the Bund should take all measures to see to it that at the first signs of an impending pogrom they are in a position to organize armed resistance."[13]

Armed resistance. That was no idle phrase. It was not rhetoric. It meant taking up arms. It meant blood. It meant the Bund was placing itself even further outside the law than it already was. But it was not a call to rebellion — not yet.

These were not frail, retiring people the Congress was addressing. These were workers. Hardy. Tough. Draymen, carpenters, butchers, factory employees, shoemakers. They also were people who by now knew very well how to organize, and organize they did into self-defence units, arming themselves with knives, clubs, cleavers, axes, which they called cold weapons, and hot weapons: bombs (often called *knaidlekh*, or dumplings) and revolvers.

And so was established, says Tobias, "A tradition of a fighting Jewish proletariat, with the Bund playing a major, and often the only, role."[14] Throughout the Pale there were reports of pogroms averted. And when they were attempted, they often were curtailed, as was the case in Gomel in September 1903: "What occurred . . . was a fight rather than a pogrom," *Der Fraind* reported with some satisfaction.[15]

The result of the Bund's shift was dramatic. Comparing the period May 1901 to June 1903 with the period from June 1903 to July 1904, the frequency of meetings increased almost four times and the 74,162 people attending in the one year was double what it had been in the previous two years. In demonstrations it was the same story. The frequency doubled and the 20,340 people who went out in the one year doubled the number of the previous two years.[16]

In the period 1905-07 membership in the leading radical parties was:

Bolsheviks	46,000	Poalei Zionists	16,000
Mensheviks	38,000	Jewish Socialist Workers	
Bundists	33,000	Party (SERP)	13,000
Polish Social		Latvian Social	
Democrats (SDKPL)	28,000	Democrats (LSDRP)	13,000[17]
Zionists			
Socialists (SS)	27,000		

These were not large numbers, given that the total industrial labour force was about three million and the population of Russia was about 140 million. But in the turmoil of the times, this many people dedicated to forcing change made a potent force.

Up until 1903 left-wing Zionism posed no great competitive threat to the Bund. But after the Kishinev pogrom, the horror of what had happened galvanized left-wing Zionists, and from that point onward, the competition between the Bund and left-wing Zionists became increasingly intense.

General Zionists, following the lead of Theodore Herzl, rejected not only socialism but political action of any sort in Russia. But left-wing Zionists turned to battling the regime and to self-defence while still holding fast to their commitment to establish a Jewish homeland abroad. Initially they were little more than a series of unconnected groups, but in 1905 they began crystallizing into political parties: the Zionist Socialist Workers Party (SS) was formed early in 1905; a preliminary conference of Poale Zion (Poale means "Labour") was held in February 1906; at the same time, the Jewish Socialist Workers' Party (SERP) evolved out of a group called Rebirth (Vozrozhdenive) that had been formed in the fall of 1903 in Kiev. Poale Zion and SS saw themselves as Social Democrats and orthodox Marxists; SERP was ideologically closer to the SRs (the Socialist Revolutionaries).[18]

Their membership figures when added to those of the Bund show dramatically how Jews predominated on the left. Jewish radical parties had a total of 89,000 members, while the Bolsheviks and Mensheviks had only 84,000 and, even then, many of them were Jewish — in fact, about 11 percent of the Bolshevik leadership was Jewish, as was about 23 percent of the Menshevik leadership. Jews at this time comprised only 4 to 5 percent of the general population, which again emphasizes the degree to which the world of the shtetl had become radicalized.

The Bund — its proper name was Der Algemeyner Yiddisher Arbeter Bund in Lite, Russland un Poiln, the General Jewish Workers League of Lithuania, Poland and Russia and it was known as The League or

Der Bund — was created in October 1897 in the cellar of a one-and-a-half-storey plastered frame house that squatted behind a rickety fence in Vilna, "the Jerusalem of Lithuania."[19]

Its beginnings were in what was called the Vilna Group, formed around 1890, and when the Bund took it over it acquired an already existing structure and shape from which it unleashed on the revolutionary movement a discipline and an organizing skill never before seen.

One of the secrets to its success was that it never forgot the fundamental lesson that the Vilna Group had learned through its work with *kases* — embryonic trade unions that Canadians today would describe as mutual benevolent aid societies — that "a real revolutionary movement must have its roots . . . in its own environment."[20]

It was a lesson that Maishe never put aside; when he came to Canada he brought it with him. David applied it coast to coast as national secretary for the CCF, hammering it relentlessly into the party psychology, and Stephen took it the next step, to individual ridings, honing and refining it still further.

It was a lesson that the Communists under Stalin never learned. They destroyed the international Communist movement by trying to turn it into a tool of Russian foreign policy.

As a corollary to focusing on local concerns, the Bund developed a perspective that for most of the other radical parties in Russia, dominated as they were by intellectuals, was even more revolutionary. Bundists argued that "It is better to go along with the masses in a not totally correct direction than to separate oneself from them and remain a purist."[21] This, for Bolsheviks, Mensheviks, and even Poalei Zionists, was heresy, at least up until 1905.[22]

It is a credo that David applied to Canadian politics, as did Stephen, and it has been at the heart of the most troubling internal debates within the CCF and the NDP. It is the point of difference between ideological missionaries and power pragmatists, raising that most volatile of issues, compromise. It has dogged the party from the beginning and it continues to this day.

Bundists arrived at this viewpoint when they saw Jewish workers, unlike non-Jewish workers, continuing to strike during the depression that began in late 1899. No doubt it was because Jewish workers were better organized under the Bund. Nevertheless, it drove home the point that workers were a potent force and even if they were untutored, their allegiance was more important than ideological fidelity.[23]

In March 1898, half a year after the Bund was created, the Russian Social Democratic Workers' Party was formed in an effort to unify all Marxist groups in Russia, and the Bund joined immediately as an "autonomous" organization of Jewish workers. From it, half a decade later, were to spring the Bolsheviks and the Mensheviks.

Creation of the Russian Social Democratic Party, as it came to be called, was the crowning achievement of Georgi Plekhanov, founder of the Russian Marxist movement and the dominating influence for more than twenty years. He founded the first Marxist party in Russian history — Liberation of Labour — in 1883, the year of Karl Marx's death. Lenin, who first read him in the late 1880s, said many years later that "never, never in my life, did I hold for any one man such respect and honour."[24]

Plekhanov held much sway even though in person he was strangely colourless — but then so was Lenin. In the case of both men, it was the intellect that commanded: Plekhanov with well-crafted, often eloquent argument; Lenin with fierce determination and an out-standing ability to reduce complicated issues to simple terms — and, said N.N. Sukhanov, the habit of "hammering, hammering, hammering them into the heads of his audience until he took them captive."[25] Comparing the two, Vera Zasulich, one of his close associates, described Plekhanov as a greyhound, Lenin as a bulldog with a "deadly bite."[26]

It was one thing to cobble together the Russian Social Democratic Party out of splinter groups. It was quite another to make it work, so for three and a half weeks in August 1903 the party met in its Se-cond Congress. Out of it came three significant results: the party split into two wings, the Bolsheviks and the Mensheviks; Lenin drove a wedge between himself and Plekhanov that spelled the eventual eclipse of Plekhanov; and the Bund, in a wrenching decision, renounced its membership in the party.

The dominating issue at the conference was how to organize the par-ty. Would it be an open and democratic structure, as Plekhanov, the Bundists, and others argued, allowing anyone, including those who were not full-time revolutionaries, to join and insisting that members be able to participate in debate and party business under a system that emphasized equality?

Or would it be a structure that was authoritarian and highly cen-tralized, as Lenin argued, with power focused in a small group at the top and strict discipline descending through a membership that would be restricted to dedicated, full-time revolutionaries?

Underlying this issue were two conflicting views of the working class, one populist, the other elitist. Vladimir Medem, a leading speaker for the Bund, voiced the populist view: "A workers movement cannot be created from the top down . . . [it] must arise from below. . . . The task of the . . . intelligentsia is only to illuminate this massive current . . . to remove obstacles, to help, to serve."[27]

Lenin delivered the elitist view. "Social Democratic consciousness among the workers . . . could only be brought to them from without," he said.[28] Thus the working class could not be trusted on its own to come to the right decisions, to do the right things. He pressed for an organizational framework for the party that concentrated enormous power in a central leadership.

"Blind, bureaucratic centralism," the Bund called it. Medem was even more explicit. It was monstrous, he said, a power so great that it could destroy local organizations instead of guiding them. Later he would say of the Bund's departure that "we felt much as if a piece of flesh was being torn from a living body."[29] The depth of his feeling underlined then, and for generations to follow, how central to being a Bundist was open participation and how implacable must be the opposition to what later became the Communist Party.

There was another, more personal side to the Bund's fight with Lenin which the Bund saw as a battle over the future of the Jewish community. The issue was whether revolutionary ideology should call on the Jews to assimilate or whether it should recognize the concept of a Jewish culture that was as separate and distinct as any of the nationalities in Russia, such as the Tartars, Ukrainians, Poles, Georgians, Azerbaijanis, Poles, or Uzbeks.

Jews like Trotsky thought there was no problem for the Russian Social Democratic Party to represent Jews. There were Jews within the party who could speak for the Jewish proletariat. But Trotsky himself was assimilated. He had grown up in Ukraine, in the southern Pale, in one of the few Jewish families that farmed for a living, and consequently he had little contact with other Jews in his formative, younger years. He thought that integration was the solution to the problems faced by Jews.

Trotsky and others like him spoke from a perspective which said that the party would provide equality of representation for all, that only unity of purpose should prevail. Bundists listened from a perspective which heard that their special interests would be subordinated to larger concerns, that theirs would be a small voice in a big crowd, that equality of representation meant compromise would be forced upon them.

(These concerns are familiar to all Canadians. Riel went to battle over them. Quebeckers almost separated because of them in the 1970s; Albertans angrily invoke them. In another variation, native peoples have demanded not only cultural autonomy but aboriginal rights to vast areas of land. They are concerns that have bedevilled Canada throughout its history. Having cut his teeth on the Russian-Jewish version in Svisloch, David Lewis felt at home when facing them in Canada.)

Had Jews been allowed a status in Russia — what in the terms of the day would have been called a "nationality" — they would have been better equipped to defend their culture. However, the idea of nationality was inextricably bound up with the idea of a homeland. All the other groups had a territory that historically was theirs: the Tartars, the Azerbaijanis, the Uzbeks, or what-have-you. Consequently they had nationalities and that meant the irrefutable right to a cultural identity. The only "homeland" the Jews could claim was Russia itself, and therefore, taking this line of reasoning through to its logical conclusion, what right did they have to cultural separateness?

None, said Lenin. The whole idea of Jewish nationality was "absolutely false and essentially reactionary." The tests for nationality were language and territory and the Jews had neither. And race, he said, was not a criterion. The aspirations of Jews could be settled only in one of two ways, he said: "assimilation or isolation."[30]

If everybody else could flourish under laws to protect equality, why couldn't Jews, Lenin asked? Why did they need to be separate?

Because, said Medem, Lenin was talking about civil rights and they protected only common rights; they did not protect differences.[31] They focused on such things as the right to free speech, the right to equal treatment before the law. They did not focus on what made people different, such as identity and culture. Only national self-rule in such matters as education could do that.

Shmarya Levin, who was not a Bundist but a Zionist, explained in his memoirs what nationality meant: "England, France and Germany were almost homogenous units in the matter of population . . . [in] England, for instance, the concept of nationality did not differ from the concept of state. The bearer of a British passport was known to be, and thought himself to be, British by nationality too. In Russia, on the other hand, no Jew, and for that matter no Tartar, would ever have conceived that he was of Russian nationality — not even if he had assimilated."[32]

In other words, a Tartar would see himself as a Russian citizen and a Tartar national. However, Jews were not allowed to officially make that kind of distinction. They could offer themselves only as Russians — which, of course, they never did. And their intransigence, their insistence on seeing themselves as culturally separate, which meant they refused to assimilate, gave Russia's rulers heartburn of the worst order.

You can almost see Minister of the Interior Vyacheslav K. von Plehve in 1903, gritting his teeth in displeasure as he outlined the perspective in which he put the Jewish "problem." The four most serious issues plaguing Russia in order of their importance, he said, were the need for land reform, the Jewish question, intellectual radicalism for which the school system was responsible, and unrest in the working class.[33]

Bundists, therefore, went to the 1903 Congress deeply concerned about the status of Jews in Russia and the status of the Bund within the Russian Social Democratic Party. On top of everything else, this was barely more than three months since the Kishinev pogrom. So when Lenin blocked their efforts to gain autonomous, federative status and belittled their concerns, it doubled their reasons for leaving and doubled their animosity toward the Bolsheviks.

Zionists were not nearly as threatening to Bolsheviks because they wanted to leave the country. They wanted to create a Jewish homeland in Palestine where never again would they be under pressure to submerge their culture in someone else's; where at last they would have worth.

In his famous quip after the Bundists quit the Russian Social Democratic Party, Plekhanov called them simply Zionists afraid of a sea voyage. However, the fact that it was the Bundists he singled out for his derision indicates whom he saw as a greater threat to his ambitions for the party.

Bundists were internationalists. They saw themselves as part of the flesh and blood of the international workers movement. They were out to change not just the lot of the Jews but the lot of the world. Their aim as Jews was to transform each country in which they lived into an egalitarian society where Jews would enjoy respect, equal citizenship, and the right to control their cultural destiny. Their aim as socialists was written in hard-line Marxist terms: to foment the revolution, to overthrow the capitalists, to put workers in control of the means of production, and to bring equality to all.

Zionists they saw as misguided. As far as Bundists were concerned, it would be "unethical . . . for a socialist to leave Russia" as long as he was not being hunted by the police.[34] Moreover, creating a Jewish homeland in Palestine or anywhere else was tactically wrong. It would just be creating a ghetto on a larger scale; and it would do little to combat discrimination in the countries where it existed. In short, Zionism was a selfish movement aimed at improving life for its own adherents instead of improving society.

From the point of view of both General Zionists and left-wing Zionists, the Bundists were preaching integration, and that meant betrayal of their heritage and the eventual death of Jewish culture. Moreover, they saw a tremendous gap between reality and the Bundist vision of an egalitarian society.

To be sure, the Bundist approach did mean a higher degree of integration. But culture was to be their bulwark against absorption. Perhaps because it would be their only bulwark, they became the great defenders of everything Yiddish: the language, the theatre, the literature, the newspapers, the folklore.

Their message was one of pride and of confidence, and regardless of whatever else, it was a message that stood them in good stead in the revolution within the revolution — in their efforts to tear away the last shreds of the 200-year-old cocoon in which the shtetls had lain gasping for air.

But for culture to be their bulwark of the future, it was absolutely necessary for Bundists to win acceptance for their argument on nationalism. It was an argument that Zionists of all stripes rejected. Partly it was a matter of definition: if the idea of Jewish nationalism was accepted in Russia, what need was there for a separate Jewish state elsewhere? But more fundamentally, Zionists were overwhelmingly convinced that it was a pipe dream. Anti-Jewish sentiment was too strong; the regime was too antagonistic to the idea; international proletarian brotherhood would never transcend national selfishness; and too much suffering would have to be endured during the interminable wait for people to become enlightened.

Only if Jews had their own territory, their own homeland, could they be assured of dignity.

Bundists could abide these arguments from General Zionists because they countered that they were the arguments of establishment Jews. Of capitalists and their hangers-on. Of bourgeoisie. And not just that, but bourgeoisie who co-operated with the state. These were not people who were in competition for the allegiance of the workers who formed the Bund's constituency.

But when the same arguments were made by Poale Zionists, SERP, and the Zionist Socialists, it drove Bundists to a fury. These were Marxist-oriented groups. These were direct competitors. And the agony of it was that they had a far simpler solution to offer: self-rule in a national homeland. By comparison the concept of nationalism and an international proletarian brotherhood was infinitely more complex and difficult to promote.

The Bund fought back. *Der Bund*, a new newspaper that appeared in January 1904, declared that:

If our ancestors had come with swords . . ., then the land would have been their "own". . . . But since our ancestors came as peaceful dwellers, and in the course of a thousand years, together with the surrounding population, aided in the cultural development of the land, watering it with their sweat, soaking it with their blood, and covering it with their bones, now the Jews are "not in their home." As "aliens" can we, the proletarians, accept that point of view? No! The land where we have been living for hundreds of years and to which we are bound by thousands of threads — this land is our home. It belongs to us just as it belongs to the Poles and Lithuanians, and all other peoples who inhabit it.[35]

The Bund insisted that the revolution and the establishment of a democratic republic would bring an end to discrimination. As Tobias analyzes it:

Where the Zionists saw a still undeveloped working class composed of backward artisans, the Bund saw a rapidly developing Jewish proletariat. Where the Zionists saw the exclusion of Jewish workers from modern industry as a function of national hatred, the Bundists saw the workings of a set of legal restrictions that would be eliminated in the future. Where the Zionists saw enmity between Christian and Jew as a bar to joint employment as a permanent condition, the Bund saw merely the lack of necessary class consciousness, especially on the part of the Christians. . . . Where the Zionists saw anti-Semitism as [barring] Jewish employment, the Bundists saw residential restrictions that barred Jews from working in new industrial areas outside the Pale as well as a strong class consciousness that made the Jewish worker troublesome to employers.[36]

The Bund played its greatest role in the eight years leading up to 1905 Revolution, all of it as an outlawed organization, all of it focused on spreading revolutionary awareness among Jewish workers. For some of those years — 1897 to 1899 — it was the only revolutionary organization working among Jewish workers, winning three out of four of the 237 strikes it sponsored. After that it had competition, and as soon as it did, S.V. Zubatov, head of the Moscow secret police, sought to undermine it by giving support to the competition.

This was the same Zubatov who almost destroyed the Bund in its first year by arresting many of its members, including the entire Central Committee. The same Zubatov who conceived of the plan to give covert support to tame unions, hoping in this way to create a "legal" trade union movement that would head off the recruiting of workers by radical unions.

After 1900, as labour consciousness began to spread among Zionists, Zubatov did what he could to support them, having police protect strikers, on occasion intervening with employers. To the degree that it split the Jewish community, the strategy worked. As Tobias reports: "The greater and the more obvious the aid given by police to non-Bundists, the farther apart the Bundists and the Zionists moved and the more certain a complete rupture became. The Fourth Congress of the Bund finally drew the line, resolving that 'under no circumstances' were Zionists to be allowed 'into either our economic or our political organizations.'"[37]

So the Bund was battling on all sides: against the state, against the police, against the Bolsheviks, Mensheviks, left-wing Zionists and General Zionists, against spies and informers, against capitalists, against the bourgeois middle class, against industrialists and factory owners as well as many small businesses, against the Black Hundreds, against pogromists, against the generation gap within the Jewish community, against the Jewish religious establishment, against discriminatory laws, against oppressive working conditions, against Jewish conservatism, against the army, and most important of all, against ignorance.

The eye that did not see, the ear that did not hear, the mind that did not comprehend — these it saw as its greatest challenge. It poured forth information — a deluge of leaflets, pamphlets, articles in underground newspapers, discussion groups, speeches, lectures, classes, reprints of everything from great literature to the latest political tracts, theatrical performances, poems, plays, short stories, novels — all aimed at fostering awareness.

And for those already aware, news of current developments, news from Europe, news from other parts of the empire, attacks on other ideologies, ongoing dialogues on current issues, debates, analysis, polemics — and practical advice, as when Bund newspapers published articles on how to build a proper barricade following a street battle in Lodz in June 1905 where more than 1,500 people were killed or wounded battling police.[38]

And strikes and demonstrations everywhere.

More than any organization in all of Russia, the Bund identified with workers. They were its inspiration, its family, its mass base, its army. This was no intellectual preoccupation. This was the gritty business of day-to-day involvement. It became, says Tobias, "something of a state within a state. . . . Divorce, dowries, a falling out between business partners, a swindled speculator, a shamed girl, a family dispute, the complaints of a servant girl about her employer — all sorts of matters were brought to [the Bund], and it was impossible to refuse help, to say that it would be better to go to the rabbi."[39]

A. Litvak, a dedicated Bundist whose opinions must be seen in that light, reflected the feedback the Bund was getting: "The authority of the Bund in Warsaw and in all Poland [in 1905] was very great," he said. "It was regarded as some kind of mystical being, with fear and hope. It could achieve everything, reach everyone. . . . The word of the Bund was law; its stamp worked like hypnosis. Wherever an injustice, wherever an insult, even when it had no relation to the workers' movement, . . . one came to the Bund as to the highest tribunal. . . . It was legendary."[40]

Trying to peer through the Holocaust to an assessment of the Bund, especially for anyone whose experience lies entirely on this side of the Second World War, is to flirt with an almost absurd ambition. Nazi death camps colour everything. They cannot be banished from the awareness, even when you're looking at the early years of this century, and they tend to taint perceptions of that wild, exuberant idealism of the Bundists with heavy qualifiers — such as misplaced, or misguided, or deluded, or even irresponsible. Bundists persuaded people to stay where they were and to work for change, and those who stayed ended up finally as prey for Hitler's death squads. So many Bundists and their sympathizers were slaughtered that the Bund never survived the war except as the feeblest echo of its former self.

There's no doubt that Bundists can be accused of over-optimism. But to ask whether they were right or wrong, or whether they were irresponsible, is to ask the wrong kind of questions. It throws a shadow across their accomplishments and gives no credit to the heroic proportions of what they attempted and what they achieved. It is one of the most poignant tragedies of all time that such a shining faith in the ability to convert nations to a mutual, international dedication to social justice, democracy and the brotherhood of all, should have been drawn into the void of genocide.

Since the war, the Western world has seen other groups similarly dedicated, but none that match the skills and the political clout of the Bundists in those years leading up to 1905.

All that can be done now is to look at what they accomplished and to ignore the question of whether their idealism was one of mankind's greatest follies, for regardless of the answer to that question, this is the kind of idealism that inspires. This is the kind of idealism that can transform societies. Without it, the world is a meaner place.

• CHAPTER SIX •

And I looked, and behold a pale horse . . .
Revelations 6:8
And a poem by Valery Bryusov[1]

Maishe was a young seventeen and Rose an old nineteen when they discovered each other in that wild and tumultuous year of 1905. Maishe had been aware of Rose, and she of him, since childhood. But being two and a half years younger, he had existed somewhere below her line of vision and she somewhere beyond his. That changed when they worked together in a Bund presentation of a Yiddish play in Svisloch that for the first time used women actors. Until then young men had played the female roles.[2]

Rose, in the full bloom of womanhood, with long, dark hair and eyes so violet that Maishe said they were as beautiful as hope, and he, taut with young manhood, dark and lean, yet with a gentleness and vulnerability that he would never lose — they met in the old barn on the edge of town where the play would be performed, Rose sewing costumes, Maishe preparing posters.

It was characteristic of the Bund that in the midst of that revolutionary year, with everything else that was happening, with everything else that it was doing, it should be putting on a play. But in the Bund's eyes, the revolution was not just about power; it was about attitudes. It was not just a revolution against the Tsar; it also was a revolution against the old ways. It was the long-standing struggle for a revolution within a revolution. If Jews as Jews could be liberated, then Jews as Russians could be liberated too.

For the Bund, doing the play with women was basic. Social justice meant not just equality among men; it meant equality between men and women. From its earliest roots in the Vilna Group, women played a significant and equal role. Indeed, because traditional Jewish life so circumscribed the role of working-class women — marriages were arranged for them, education was out of the question, they were decidedly of secondary importance in religious rituals, the linking of menstruation to uncleanliness was so emphatic — that once a woman joined the Bund and rejected such strictures, rejection by her family became a very real possibility. Where that happened, the Bund often became her new home.

As Henry Tobias describes it: "Many [women] came to regard references to their physical appearance as out of place and frivolous, and security considerations as more important than personal emotional considerations. The idealism of the initiated and the almost religious mood in which they approached their work bred a kind of purity — in speech as well as in personal relationships. . . . The sense of belonging was reinforced by the use of a special form of address — *bekante* (acquaintance) in the early years, *khaver* (comrade) in later times. At May Day celebrations the young revolutionaries began to use the distinctive colour of the revolution, proudly flaunting their red blouses, red flowers and red flags."[3]

Rose's family was more sympathetic than many, and although her membership in the Bund caused a strain, it did not cause a breach. The play was just one more trial among many that her parents endured. So brazen for women to flaunt themselves on stage! It set Svisloch humming. The orthodox were upset; the liberals were elated; almost everyone was curious. And almost everyone noticed that Maishe had taken to walking Rose home.

As it turned out, the play was a welcome diversion, slicing as it did through the tensions that had never let up since January 22, that awful morning in St. Petersburg which shook Russia to its core and marked an end and a beginning.

Bloody Sunday.

Hundreds of workers were shot dead by the Tsar's troops; hundreds more, perhaps thousands, were wounded; and the Dark People, who beyond almost all understanding had held to their faith in the Tsar, the Little Father of All Russia, believing it was not Nicholas but his evil subordinates who were responsible for their miseries, at last began to lay that faith on the funeral pyre of their despair.

That Sunday evening Maxim Gorky, the writer and Russian correspondent for the New York *Journal*, cabled New York: "The Russian Revolution has begun."[4]

The carnage was the act of a weak and floundering despotism, out of touch with reality, armed to the teeth, and spastic with fright. Local police and at least one or two of the Tsar's ministers were aware that the march would be peaceful, but the Tsar, his confidants, and most of his ministers were feeling beleaguered and harassed, and gnawing like a rat at their subconscious was the old dread of the Dark People rising in blood lust. To be sure, the Dark People were on the rise; there were 140,000 to 150,000 workers on strike in St. Petersburg.

Two deadly catalysts seem to have been a bunker mentality within the palace and troops trained for cavalry charges, not crowd control. Estimates of the dead and wounded varied widely. Government authorities put the dead at 130 and the wounded at 299; a group of journalists settled on 4,600 dead and wounded. Regardless of the numbers, it was a wanton slaughter that seared memories across the empire.

The die was cast. Now there was no alternative but revolution. The last recourse, the last hope, the Tsar, had turned on his children.

From its secret headquarters in Dvinsk, the Central Committee of the Bund churned out within days 115,000 copies of a leaflet. It was a call to the battlements: "The great day has come. The Revolution is here. . . . Now we must conquer or die. . . . Break into the arsenals! Seize rifles, revolvers. . . . To Arms!"[5]

However, the Bund was in no position to lead a headlong rush into insurrection. Powerful though it was among Jewish workers, there was no conceivable way it could begin to confront the Tsar's armies, and there was such disarray and lack of co-ordination among the other radical parties that there was no hope of any kind of united action.

A month later, from February 24 to March 2, the Bund held its Sixth Conference in Dvinsk and took a much more realistic line. It was still brimming with revolutionary fervour but it focused on practical things that it could do. It ordered local institutions strengthened, leadership improved in many of its organizations, and an increase in the number of meetings and armed demonstrations. And "it suggested that local organizations obtain arms, teach their members to use them, and urge them to resist not only the police, but even the military. As in the past, it advocated the building of special forces to lead the resistance."[6]

It was, by any definition, a call to revolutionary confrontation. But armed force was to be defensive, not offensive. It was a call to hack away at the regime's remaining foundations and to shoot back, if necessary, to prevent interference.

At the same time, assassinations across Russia increased. By the end of the year 1,500 government officials had been killed, including, on February 17, the Grand Duke Sergei Alexandrovitch, governor of Moscow, uncle to Nicholas, brother of Alexander III.[7] Most of the assassinations were carried out by the Russian Social Revolutionary Party, political heir to Narodnaya Volya — the SRs, they were called. They had the greatest support among peasants because of their promise of land reform that would turn over all land to "the nation as a whole."

But there were also counter-revolutionaries at work, secretly supported and encouraged by the regime, and chief among them was a new organization called the Black Hundreds, as vile a collection of racist hate mongers as Russia had seen. They denounced Jews as being responsible for all Russia's troubles, including the war against Japan (Port Arthur had fallen to the Japanese in January and in May the Russian Baltic Fleet was destroyed). They flooded the Pale with inflammatory leaflets. A typical one read: "Soon, soon a new time will come, friends, when there will be no Jews. The root of all evil, the root of all our misfortunes is the Jews."[8]

At Easter the Black Hundreds struck in pogrom after pogrom, the worst at Zhitomir, which followed the now-familiar pattern of unhindered attacks on Jews into the third day. Fifteen Jews and a Russian student who fought with them were killed and sixty were seriously injured. But bad as the attack at Zhitomir was, two things prevented its becoming a second Kishinev: the indifference of much of the Christian population toward the Black Hundreds and the strength of armed resistance among the Jews.

The Bund saw the Zhitomir pogrom as fundamentally different. The regime had used earlier pogroms to divert dissatisfaction from the state, but in the spring of 1905 it had so little public support that not even accusations against Jews could divert anger. This, concluded the Bund, accounted for Christian indifference toward the Black Hundreds. Instead, the Bund saw Zhitomir as an effort to draw its fighting forces into the open where they could be destroyed. But the regime miscalculated the strength of those forces. (Conservative estimates place the Bund's permanent force at about 1,100 armed men spread through various communities in the Pale and backed up by reserve forces of 7,000 to 9,000.)[9]

In the face of the pogroms, even liberal and conservative Jews began to get politically involved. In April the Alliance for the Achievement of Complete Equal Rights for the Jewish People of Russia was formed which, according to Simon Dubnow, one of the founders, was "the first attempt at a struggle for freedom *as a Jewish nation* rather than as a religious group."[10] That was a rather florid overstatement, considering what the Bund had been doing for the past seven years. Nevertheless, petitions began to pour in from Jewish communities requesting equality, many of them also calling for national and cultural self-determination. Then the Jewish Democrats were formed; and the Jewish People's Party (which Simon Dubnow headed).

The coming on board of the Jewish establishment was perhaps the final and greatest testimony to the Bund's success in winning the revolution within the revolution, in breaking the Jewish community out of its cocoon. Regardless of what happened to the 1905 Revolution, this revolution had been won. Irredeemably.

Never again would the world of the shtetl rule. Never again would Jews be their own prisoners.

Meanwhile, across the land, demonstrations increased. In Lodz, for example, there were 2,316 strikes, compared with 1,861 in St. Petersburg, which was the principal hotbed of revolutionary activity outside the Pale.[11] Everywhere there were Bundists, they were imposing levies on Jewish taxpayers to raise money for strikers. They even had committees to collect and distribute food. No longer was the first priority education of the masses. Now they were urging people to "square accounts" with the Tsar — Nicholas the Last, they called him.[12]

On August 19, in an attempt to cool things down, Nicholas signed a new law establishing the Duma, Russia's first parliament. However, its powers were paltry and the franchise was strictly limited. The law had no impact.

Then it happened. Like a string of firecrackers going off, strikes exploded across the land with such force and rapidity that the regime was forced to its knees. It was a revolution without a battle, a victory without a bloodbath. That it slipped between the fingers of the victors shortly afterward was a comment not on the achievement but on their failure to prepare for it. Energy has its limits; so does concentration. Like everything else, the public needs to rest and restore itself in a race toward change. How far it races before it rests depends on how clear are the goals and how determined the pace setters. On this occasion goals differed from group to group, as did the sense of urgency in reaching them, and the result was that Russia rested too soon and the first to recover was the regime. It was a mistake Lenin never made in 1917. He learned his lesson well.

The revolution began in earnest when workers at the large Sytin publishing house in Moscow went on strike on October 2 and the next day the city's entire publishing industry walked out in sympathy. They were followed by workers at the city's bakeries, and from there demonstrations multiplied. Fifty thousand workers singing the Marseillaise marched under red banners. The shipbuilding plants, steel factories, and naval works all went on strike. And soon railway workers were walking out. Before long, rail travel throughout the empire, the "veins of capitalism," was at a standstill. Food became scarcer in cities. Prices shot up. Banks cut off credit. In Moscow and St. Petersburg workers established councils that they called soviets and the Mensheviks joined them enthusiastically — and gained valuable experience in how to orchestrate control.

Finally, what existed was a total general strike. There was no electricity because the power workers had struck. Doctors, postmen, even stockbrokers, were on the streets.

On October 30 Nicholas capitulated. He issued his Manifesto purporting to establish constitutional government.

The very next day the Black Hundreds went wild and for a full week Jews were savaged in pogroms that spread across more than 700 cities, towns, and villages in the Pale and beyond. More than 200,000 Jews were victims; 900 were killed, 8,000 were injured, thousands of homes, shops, and synagogues were destroyed. The worst hit was Odessa where the pogrom lasted four days and left 302 dead, 5,000 wounded, 1,400 businesses destroyed, 40,000 homeless, and 3,000 artisans reduced to beggars.

On November 21, three weeks after the Manifesto had been posted, Lenin stepped from the train at Finland Station in St. Petersburg. He was too late to have any real impact. It was the Mensheviks who had seized the opportunity, not the Bolsheviks, and the reigning star of the Mensheviks, the power within the St. Petersburg Soviet, was Lev Davidovitch Bronstein, better known as Leon Trotsky. If Lenin was a bulldog and Plekhanov a greyhound, this proud, volatile, and acid-tongued orator behind the pince-nez was a Russian wolfhound.[13] Lenin would spend the next twelve years regaining pride of place from the Mensheviks, ultimately winning Trotsky to Bolshevik ranks and appointing him foreign commissar and, during the civil war, commissar for war.

Within two weeks of signing the Manifesto, the Tsar was complaining that his magnanimity seemed to have gained nothing. Unrest not only continued; it increased — until the crack Semyonov Guards were sent to Moscow where badly organized, poorly armed workers' battalions had congregated in the Presnya district. Trotsky figured there were only about 200 armed men with eighty guns and revolvers,[14] but for two days the artillery bombarded the district and for two more days the troops moved through it burning, blasting, and shooting until all of Presnya was in ruins. The toll was a thousand casualties including a hundred troops and police and eighty-six children — and the end of the 1905 Revolution.

For months afterward, Nicholas sent troops ravaging city and town, carrying out 100 to 160 executions a week. The shadow of the gallows lay across the land. Lenin went underground, hunted constantly by police, and two years later slipped out of the country to Switzerland.

The Duma assembled for the first time during May 1906 in the Tauride Palace in St. Petersburg, and among the first items of business was a demand that the government explain its role in the pogroms that followed the Tsar's Manifesto. From the beginning the Tsar had shown where his heart lay: he was greeting official delegations from the Black Hundreds within ten weeks of the Manifesto.

Pyotr Stolypin, then minister of the interior, promised an answer within a month. However, before he could give one, there was at Bialystok, in the words of Shmarya Levin (then one of twelve Jewish deputies to the 497-member Duma), "an orgy of beastliness after the fashion of Kishinev." Even soldiers joined in it. Eighty Jews were killed and hundreds wounded. In his memoirs Levin remembered "bellies ripped open, heads with nails driven into them, children with their brains dashed out." The Bialystok pogrom, he said, "acted like a cold shower on Jews and Liberal Russians alike, and many had begun to feel that the Duma would not live much longer."[15]

Deputies called on the Tsar to dismiss his cabinet in order, said Levin, "that the rulers of the country might dissociate themselves from the disgrace of the pogrom." The Tsar responded by dissolving the Duma.

It was July 22. The Duma had sat for seventy-three days.

During the next ten years the Tsar would repeatedly dissolve the Duma, and although revolutionary activity was stalled — the Bolsheviks had been almost eliminated, the social democratic parties were ineffective, and the SRs were largely confining their efforts to the Duma — people were fed up with the autocracy and unrest had spread to the army. And so everyone waited for the final revolution but no one knew how to make it happen. "The revolutionaries were not ready but it — the revolution — was ready," V.V. Shulgin, one of the Duma's Kadet deputies, was to say years later.[16]

Svisloch was spared the pogroms that swept the Pale before and after the 1905 Revolution. The Jewish residents had formed a defence militia, and since the town was so predominantly Jewish they had nothing to fear from inside. As for the countryside, well, stories still circulated about what had happened to the chief of police in 1903, the year of the Kishinev pogrom.

He had been newly appointed and brought to the job a determination to squelch the "subversive" elements in town. As Abraham Ain recalled it:

His zeal knew no bounds. Once, encountering on the outskirts of the town two young men reading a book he had them arrested and questioned for two weeks. Subsequently they were released. Another time, he raided a meeting of the clandestine Jewish Labour Bund in the forest and arrested ten young men and three girls. The arrested maintained that their gathering was . . . a harmless outing and, as no forbidden literature was found on them, they were released.

The young bloods of the town decided to teach the chief a lesson [so] on a dark night they set fire to the woodshed of a school on the outskirts of town. The regulations called for the chief to be present at a fire. A group of young people lay in wait for him and gave him a good thrashing. This experience considerably diminished his zeal for discovering conspiracies.[17]

Apparently it also diminished whatever zeal people in the surrounding area might have had to attempt a pogrom, especially in the face of an organized defence "militia" and an obvious determination by the factory workers and Bundists of the town. Beating up a chief of police was no little matter, especially since he was an official of the Tsar's government and was under the administration of the provincial governor in Grodno. News of the beating flew from lip to ear like birds to their nests, and the message to area toughs was clear: stay away.

The fact that there was no attempt to punish the Bundists who delivered the beating signifies something else: the ability of the central government to exert its will in outlying areas had crumbled to the extent that the police chief felt he no longer could rely on it if he pressed the matter any further.

Nevertheless, when the pogrom swept Bialystok in the late spring of 1906 it shook Svisloch[18]. Bialystok was about sixty-five kilometres away. Almost next door.

"Maishka, I'm frightened." Rose had been using the affectionate diminutive of Maishe's name for several months now.

"I'm frightened, too," said Maishe, "but we're ready. They won't find it easy."

As soon as news of the pogrom had arrived, the Bund had called meetings to review all plans for defence of the town: how the women and children would be protected, how the various fighting squads would operate, how fires would be put out, how the injured would be cared for.

They were days of almost unbearable tension. It was like living under a sword suspended by a thread: would it fall or wouldn't it? It hung there by day, by hour, by minute, interrupting sleep, overlaying conversations, jangling against every thought, rearing up every time children went outside to play; and all the time there was the struggle to hang on to decent instincts, to keep from suspecting people who were regular acquaintances, especially the peasants and farmers who came to town in droves on market days.

The insidious thing about waiting was its corrosiveness, the way it could gnaw at restraint. So the Bund doubled its meetings. There were more speeches, more readings, more discussion groups. They talked not only about socialist issues but also about the merits of various literary works. Gradually the weeks passed and turned into months and, as nothing happened, a sense of normalcy came straggling back.

But it never fully arrived. The dissolution of the Duma passed a signal to factory owners that hope for the old order was not lost, so in Svisloch they began to dig in their heels. They started adopting a kind of management militancy. They began to see less need to discuss, more need to exert their authority. Finally, in November 1907, they called a general assembly of workers and told them they wanted a 35 to 45 percent cut in wages, an end to company-paid medical aid, and an end to job tenure. If there was no agreement, they said, they would close the factories.[19]

The demands were intolerable. Russia was entering an economic boom and there was no need for such drastic measures. In the years 1906 to 1911 harvests were exceptionally good and heavy industries broke all records in production. In 1907 the market for leather was strong and the prospects for Svisloch factory owners were excellent. The intention obviously was to break the power of the unions and the Bund and for the owners to retrieve all that they had lost in the 1904 strike.

But the Bund was ready and at its head was Maishe Losz. Nineteen years old. Representative from the Minz plant. Chairman of the Svisloch praesidium.[20]

One of the most striking features about the radical movement was its youth. The average age of members in the Russian Social Democratic Party (which at this point once again included the Bund) was said to be eighteen.[21] Although this almost certainly was an exaggeration, by far and away most members were young, many were in their mid-teens, and within the Bund it was not at all unusual for the head of a branch in a small town to be nineteen or twenty. Besides, Maishe had been in the Bund for four years.

His two great strengths lay in organizing and in settling differences. He had a talent for recruiting newcomers, especially younger workers, and since Poale Zionists, SERP, and the Zionist Socialists were now seeking the same recruits, it was a talent highly valued. As for settling differences concerning everything from domestic disputes to worker grievances, Maishe had a skill that would have served him well in earlier days as a rabbi and in present times as an arbitrator or conciliator.

Already he had developed a style of speaking that was brief and to the point. And he was developing a platform style that had a cadence much like that of wandering *maggidim*, preachers who for centuries crossed the Pale. Those who remember him today recall his analytical clarity, and the few who recollect the rare occasions in Canada when he spoke publicly, remember cadence and an eloquent command of Yiddish.

Being a good speaker in Yiddish means something more than expressing thoughts well and vividly. It means manipulating the language itself so that the structure of phrases and sentences are used to emphasize points. It means observing not only a logic in argument but a logic in language. Maishe's was a cadence that immigrants from the Pale, now in their seventies and eighties, found traces of in David's speeches and, in some cases, even more so in Stephen's.

As soon as they heard the owners' demands, Maishe called a meeting of the general strike committee, made up of Bund officials and representatives from each of the factories. They agreed: a strike was the only answer. That night in the same clearing that he had guarded for the 1904 strike meeting, at the base of the same old oak where the 1904 leaders had stood, Maishe faced the workers, many of whom were half again as old as he, some double his age — collars up, hands in pockets, breath steaming in the chill evening air, feet rustling in the fallen leaves, watching him in his first big test.

We know what they want. [Maishe's voice cut across the clearing.] They want us on our knees. They want us on our knees and afraid. They want us on our knees and powerless.

They're not doing this because they're short of money. They're not trying to scrap our doctors because we're always healthy and don't need them. They're not trying to cut our wages because business is bad. When have we seen business so good?

They're doing this because we demand fair treatment. They're doing it because we stand united and strong and they want to break us. They're doing it so they can turn back the clock to when they ruled like sultans.

This is what the revolution was all about. This is what people died for. Did we work so hard, did we fight so hard, did we suffer so much, just to give it all away now?

Both arms were stretched out. He was appealing to them.
"No, no!" Their responses rang like cheers. "Never!"

"Then vote to strike!" he shouted, and to a person they did.

It was obvious from the start that this was to be no ordinary strike. It was a test case for the entire district. If the owners won, other factories throughout the district would follow.

The Tanners Union from the district surrounding Svisloch provided one of its ablest organizers to help, mainly by canvassing district workers for contributions. The strategy of Maishe and the strike committee was to hold out until promissory notes issued by the owners became due in the hope that this would create enough financial pressure to force them to back away from their demands.

It didn't work. Two months after the strike started, the owners began shipping half-finished hides to raise cash, and when the workers tried to prevent the loading of the hides, Svisloch police stopped them, firing a salvo into the air to make their point. So the workers marched to the homes of the owners, and in the arguments that followed, one of the owners was beaten. Immediately the chief of police called in troops to patrol the streets. Charges and counter-charges flew, but as Abraham Ain recounts: "Fortunately, the strikers' committee kept cool heads. An ultimatum was presented to the factory owners to effect a withdrawal of the police and the military from the factories and the streets, or they would bear the responsibility for the consequences. Soon the military were recalled and the strike again assumed a peaceful character."[22]

One of those cool heads was Maishe's. In the fever of the moment all his skills in conciliation were needed, especially a few days later when the owners succeeded in getting a shipment of half-finished hides through the workers' blockade.

"You see," angry workers shouted at him. "You see what happens when you let go their throats? You see? In the middle of the night, like thieves, they sneak out hides." They were all set for another march on the owners' homes. However, Maishe prevailed. "Wait," he counselled. Find out where the hides had gone.

It was no difficult task. The Bund had contacts with railway workers throughout the entire district, and before long the hides were traced and workers in the town where they were located refused to work on them. It was a far more effective response. There were no more attempts to ship out hides — buyers didn't want the risk of paying for hides from Svisloch that no one would work on — and the strike extended into its tenth week.

But some of the workers were beginning to waver. It was deep into January's cold. Household supplies were running low, and with no paycheques and only a trickle of funds coming in from workers in neighbouring towns, people were hurting. Maishe had seen to it that whatever supplies people could spare had been pooled so that the more needy families could be helped, but it wasn't nearly enough. There were nights when he would come home despairing after scraping and scrounging to get one more family through one more week.

"They're almost starving, Raisel. Almost starving." Slumped over the table, head in hands, he was weary from the inside out. "I tell them to hang on because we must win, but I'm not sure we can. And if we don't, what misery have I caused?"

Rose poured some hot tea. "Drink this," she'd say and Maishe would drink the tea and they would talk and slowly brick by brick he would rebuild his determination. However, it was obvious that something must be done to break the impasse, so, after discussing it with the strike committee, he called a conference of the Tanners Union for the districts of Bialystok and Vilna — and that gives an indication of the importance placed on the strike. It had assumed a provincial character.

The conference was held at Svisloch during the twelfth week; it lasted three days and in the end decided that the strike should continue. However, by the fifteenth week — mid-March — spirits were flagging. Financial aid from the district was dwindling, Passover was pending, workers were broke.

But the strategy had worked. Owners had reached the end of the line. They couldn't hold off creditors any longer. A week later, after four months, the strike was settled. Workers took a cut in pay but not anywhere near the 35 percent the owners wanted, and the owners dropped their demands for an end to company-paid medical aid and job tenure.

The strike was over, but the cost was high. Customers in the meantime had turned to other suppliers, and as a result several factories in Svisloch closed and others had heavy losses. There was no rejoicing among the workers. How could you rejoice when men lost their jobs? As Maishe said to Rose, "Everybody lost. But if we hadn't fought back, it would have been worse. We can only be thankful it's over."

But it wasn't over. A few weeks later, after they had some breathing space, the owners renewed their demand for an end to job tenure. According to Ain, "the workers were exhausted by the previous prolonged strike. After three weeks of lockout, [they] capitulated and accepted all the demands of the owners.

"The workers were quite demoralized. Since several factories had closed, a number of them were unemployed. Furthermore, the large factories began selling their products in half-finished form. This meant that the workers in the dry factories were left without work. Dry factories that had previously employed forty and fifty workers reduced that number to fifteen or ten."

He concludes: "A large number of workers decided on emigration to the United States and Canada."[23]

It was the beginning of a bad time for socialists. It was the beginning of a bad time for radicals. The number of strikes across Russia steadily fell while the percentage that employers won rose. By 1910 there were only 226 strikes involving 46,623 workers.[24] There was the beginning of a return to militancy in 1910, however. Strikes more than doubled. Then in 1912 they quadrupled and by 1914 there were 3,534 strikes in which 1,337,458 workers went out, a number equal to nearly half the three million industrial work force.[25]

Paralleling the drop in strikes after 1906 was a decline in the membership of the radical parties. They all but disappeared from the face of Russia's political map, and that included the Jewish radical parties as well as the Bolsheviks and Mensheviks. Of them all, the Bund was best able to hang on because of its close links with workers and the community services it had established.

The economic boom from 1906 to 1911 was part of the reason for the decline in unrest — although decline is a relative word; unrest still prevailed. Perhaps the most important factor was the land reform brought in by Pyotr Stolypin, who was appointed prime minister by the Tsar in 1906.

Of course, the monarchy's worst enemy was still the monarch himself: limp, vindictive, untalented, irresolute, insensitive, and obtuse. It didn't take him long to dislike Stolypin, but he had no one as able to put in his place. Then, on September 14, 1911, Stolypin was assassinated and the last remaining moderating influence on the Tsar was gone.

So Russia entered 1912 with strikes violently in the upswing, Stolypin dead, the Bolsheviks and Mensheviks in a shambles, Rasputin scandalizing the country with his hold on the Tsarina and his debauchery, the Duma stumbling, tripping, falling, trying desperately to learn how to make parliamentary democracy work in one quick dash from the doorway of feudalism, and all the while the stench of decadence that was rife in Russian high society wafted across the land. As Harrison Salisbury describes it:

It was a strange time. In a leading St. Petersburg whorehouse the portrait of one of Russia's best known writers (and most honoured guests) was hung — in order to attract the trade of others. Another house catered to husbands and wives, the same courtesan often serving both husband and wife, each in their preferred manner. In another, young women of good families, having sworn an oath of secrecy, appeared naked before men and ravished them. It reminded Andrei Bely [the mystic poet] of Goethe's famous dictum, that from boundless romanticism to the whorehouse is but a single step. . . .

Scandal filled the air. One evening at the Yar, Moscow's most luxurious restaurant, as the band played a tango, the city's newest, maddest passion, a young man walked up to a table where a beautiful woman sat with several older men, all in evening dress . . . [and] emptied a revolver at his former wife. His trial, the Praslov case, became the sensation of Russia. The young man and woman had been bright stars in Moscow's decadent night life. They had met at the "Suicide Club". . . . After 28 days of gaudy testimony and violent silence (several who were called killed themselves rather than testify) Praslov was acquitted by a jury. The defence attorney had quoted Goethe: "I have never heard of a crime no matter how gruesome, which I could not have committed myself."

A few days later the newspapers had another sensation. Two young Petersburg students of titled families planned a champagne supper at an expensive restaurant. When their parents refused to give them money for the meal, they broke into the flat of a prominent actress, stabbed her to death and made off with her jewellery. A newspaper columnist commented: "A real gentleman is obliged to keep his social engagements at no matter what price."[26]

And so it went, with the race between reform and revolution mired on both sides in confusion, self-indulgence, and myopia — until the war began in 1914.

•CHAPTER SEVEN•

*A fryeh velt, a nyeh velt, a yaisherdikeh velt, a velt foon
gleichheit — a free world, a new world, a world of justice,
a world of equality.*

The Bundist ideal

Whin Maishe and Rose were married in the late summer of 1908, the town talked.

"Bohemians," they said.[1] There was no malice in it; Maishe and Rose were too well liked for that. But there was a degree of uneasiness. And in some cases concern.

In other towns there had been couples who had rejected the old ways, or so people had heard. But not in Svisloch.

"Maishe, you must think of Rose," Ezekial had said. "People will say she won't be a proper mother with no respect for tradition."

But Maishe and Rose would not waver. "What people will think is their business," Maishe said. "We can't do what we don't believe. It wouldn't be right. That's not how we want to start our marriage."

Their decision not to have a religious wedding deeply hurt Rose's father, Usher Berel Lazarovitch. He was a profoundly Orthodox man who saw the decision as a rejection of the values to which he had dedicated his life and as a blasphemy that he could not comprehend. Marriage was a holy institution that should be performed in God's house before His eyes and with His benediction.

"As you reject His ways, you reject Him," he had said to Rose. "And as you reject Him, you will live in shadows and leave the door open to evil."

Rose was sitting on a stool close to his armchair by the window. As a child she would ask him to read from *The Five Megilloth* and then draw the stool close so that she could lay her head on his arm as he read. Her favourite was Solomon's Song of Songs although she would thrill to the language of all five books.[2]

"But Papa, I don't reject God, and neither does Maishe. He says the path to God should never be through a toll gate run by the bourgeoisie."

"Bourgeoisie? So now I'm a bourgeoisie?"

"Oh no, Papa. Not you. Never. It's just that's the way things are, and Maishe and I don't believe it's right."

"Oh child, child, child." He said it with such sorrow that tears started in Rose's eyes.

David described him in his memoirs as he was when he met him twenty-five years later:

> His house of worship was the most modest of the three in Svisloch, for he was a poor peddler. He owned a tired horse and a small covered wagon with which he travelled through the countryside buying and selling goods of all sorts to farmers. He eked out a meagre living and always walked stooped, as if burdened with worry, but he was one of the most honourable men I have known. He was devout in his faith and believed that if his lot were to be hard work and small return, it was perhaps regrettable but must be accepted without complaint because it was God's will . . . his simplicity and humility were those of a saint.[3]

Doris's memory is of a kindly man with a large beard "who was always sitting in the synagogue. You know, that Orthodox sitting and praying all day long." To help make ends meet, her maternal grandmother sold vegetables that she grew.

For generation upon generation, weddings in Svisloch had been the same. They would be held at one of the synagogues, and men and women would be divided by a curtain called the *machitza*. The actual ceremony would take place under the *khupa*, a canopy held aloft on four poles, located at the end of the curtain. The bride would come up the women's side of the curtain, the groom up the men's side, and they would meet under the *khupa*. There the rabbi would pronounce the betrothal benedictions. Then the mother and mother-in-law would walk the bride seven times around the rabbi to get rid of any evil influences, and finally the groom, placing a ring on his bride's finger, would declare the simple oath of marriage: "Behold, thou art consecrated unto me, according to the Law of Moses and Israel."

The curtain would remain in place for revelries that would last well into the night. Men would dance with men on their side of the curtain, women with women on theirs. Each group would sit down to supper on its own side of the curtain. The only thing to cross the barrier would be the singing and the laughter.[4]

Rose and Maishe were married in the big room at the back of her home. The day before, Rose had picked the flowers that filled the room — purple wild iris and orange lilies from down by the river, wild roses from the forest edge, white daisies and yellow buttercups from the open fields, blue-and-yellow asters, delicate, lacy wild carrot, and the brilliantly coloured orange hawkweed (which in Canada is called the devil's paintbrush). The spare, dun-coloured room with its massive oven sang with colour. The table had been moved from its commanding position near the centre of the room to the side, and Rose's mother, Henye, had piled it with food and cakes. Glasses and sugar were set out for the pots of tea to come. Friends and relatives stood quietly around the edges of the room while a rabbi presided over the barest minimum of a wedding ceremony. Then the fun began. They danced, they ate, they sang Bundist songs, they told jokes, well into the night.

Although he didn't approve, Rose's father was gracious to the guests, but when they started singing Bundist songs, he quietly excused himself and walked to the synagogue where he prayed and meditated for the rest of the evening. Maishe's father stayed until later, but then he, too, retired to his synagogue. Both mothers remained, and although they didn't sing the Bundist songs, they did join in the others.

The next morning Maishe reported for work at Mintz's factory. This was no time to be away from work. This was the painful aftermath of the 1907–08 strike that saw the Bund defeated, the workers forced into humiliating and crippling concessions, the wholesale loss of markets and the slashing of work forces. He was lucky to have a job.

Mintz was doing him no favours. Maishe, now twenty years old, worked hard and well. He was the kind of experienced worker Mintz needed to get maximum production with a skeleton crew — a quarter of the men who used to work in the factory.[5]

The mood among workers had changed in Svisloch. They were battle-weary and dispirited; unconvinced they had strength to mount still another assault; soaking up time off like parched earth takes in water. They had lost their battle against employers. Jobs had been wiped out by the scores. Those who hadn't emigrated concentrated simply on staying alive and making ends meet. The revolution was dead, or so it seemed. The Duma was a failure. The Tsar still reigned supreme. His armies were still tramping the countryside trailing a hangman's noose.

Even the mighty Bund had been brought low. Vladimir Medem recalled in his memoirs the last days of September 1906 while he was still working on the editorial staff of *Di Folks-Tsaytung* in Vilna:

The number of people under the sway of our movement had begun to decline. The prevailing mood was one of depression.

. . . we were supposed to celebrate the tenth anniversary of the Bund . . . and I was asked to do a festive article. But I was unable to. I remember going to the Bernadine Gardens to clear my mind. . . .

I sat on a bench and tried to gather my thoughts. . . . I was far from losing my faith at that time, but an anniversary article should perforce be cheerful — and I was without any feeling of cheer. . . . So I went up to the editorial office and told our colleagues that I would not write."[6]

He could not write falsehoods, he said. As a member of the Bund's Central Committee, "I had occasion to spend frequent evenings at the *yavka*, i.e., an apartment to which representatives would come from the Bund's provincial centres to meet with a representative of the . . . Central Committee for discussions on various party matters. . . . Earlier — as recently as the year before — people from various cities and towns had come by the dozen. . . . It was an endless clatter, a constant seething.

"But now things had grown quiet, subdued. Very often only a single person would arrive; at most two. And we frequently found ourselves waiting there a whole evening while no one arrived. Bitter, sad times. . . ."[7]

A. Litvak put it more succinctly: "Through the entire summer of 1907 . . . there was talk of crisis. . . . By 1908 there was nobody left to talk of the crisis. One after another, the units folded up. . . . The first to leave were the fellow travellers and sympathizers. Fashions changed; interests shifted elsewhere. . . . A little later, the ranks of active workers began to get thin. . . . Then the veteran workers began to leave, those who had devoted their entire youth to the movement. . . . That was the tragedy."[8]

The Bund was not the only organization to suffer; all the radical parties did. In fact, their losses were even worse than the Bund's. Poalei Zion, its official report said, "has entirely collapsed. . . . The total number of workers is about 400."[9] The disintegration of the Zionist Socialist Workers' Party was much greater than that of the Bund, said B. Gutman in his memoirs. "Not only rank and file members abandoned it; a number of prominent leaders likewise left."[10] Even the Russian Social Democrats fell to pieces, said Lenin's wife, Nadezhda Konstaninovna Krupskaya, in her *Reminiscences*: "The police, with the aid of agents provocateurs had arrested the leading party workers [and] left without . . . leadership . . . the fighting squads degenerated."[11]

Lenin himself commented on the "appalling chaos" early in the spring of 1910 when he saw, "tremendous decline among the organizations everywhere, almost their cessation in many localities. The wholesale flight of the intelligentsia. All that are left are workers circles and isolated individuals."[12]

Zionist Socialists had established a branch in Svisloch in 1905 but it closed in 1907. There also had been an anarchist club in town, but its leader left during the bad times following 1907, and that was the end of it.[13]

The Bund, however, stayed. There was no point trying to urge strikes or demonstrations. People weren't listening. So Maishe and the small cadre that remained turned to cultural activities and organized "symposia, lectures, discussions and similar enterprises."[14] And they maintained as best they could the Bund's assistance programs. Many were the times that Maishe, a sack over his shoulder, trudged to outlying farms, "gathering a couple of potatoes here, a couple there . . . so the Bund could give them to poor people in the town."[15]

At the heart of the Bund's problem throughout the Pale was its failure to recognize that people were prepared to give the Duma a chance. The Bund saw in the Duma only what the Tsar said it would be — a totally powerless "consultative legislative establishment" — and so it decided to boycott elections. The Bund was fiercely uncompromising. The old order had to be liquidated. Totally. Co-operation with this flimsy substitute for a representative assembly would betray the workers and delay the day of their freedom. Therefore, the Duma had to be destroyed.[16]

It was a fateful error. The First Duma, which sat from May 10 to July 21, turned out to be far more representative and far more independent-minded than anyone had expected. As Medem put it, "the Duma was [an] actual fact, and whether we liked it or not, the focus of general attention and the centre of political life. The stream of events flowed not past but through the Duma."[17] The Bund had lost a lot of political ground.

It made the same mistake toward conventional, non-party trade unions, refusing to co-operate with them and even setting up formal Bund unions in opposition. The choice, as the Bund saw it, was between organizations preoccupied with self-interest and those dedicated to social justice. When members were accepted without regard to their political views, a union's vision could extend no further than its members' paycheques. Such unions would be politically impotent and would end up reactionary. They needed to be tied by ideology and organization to political parties. Then they would be outward-looking; then they would be forces for change. Then liberation of the working class could proceed.[18]

By the fall of 1910 the Bund again realized it had made a mistake and declared that independent unions "ought to enjoy a status of equality within the family of the working class."[19] However, once again, it had lost the ability to influence.

In an effort to halt declining membership after 1905, the Bund decentralized and passed even more powers to the rank and file. And in May 1906 it rejoined the Russian Social Democratic Workers' Party, in the process gaining the concessions that had been refused in 1903. It won full organizational autonomy and the right to work for Jewish national, cultural independence.[20]

But, like lifting the boycott on the Duma and reversing itself on independent unions, rejoining the party came too late to make any difference. The revolution lay gasping, its momentum spent. The left remained splintered, liberals were lost in fuzzy thinking, people fled from struggle to the delusion that freedoms for newspapers and unions and political speech were harbingers of democratic change, and that great pacifier, an improved standard of living, began appearing now that the war against Japan was out of the way.

After they were married, Maishe and Rose lived with her parents in a house that was arranged much like that of Maishe's parents, except that it was smaller and the floor in the front room was earthen. They were lucky. They had the second-floor attic all to themselves and so had more privacy than most newly married couples. Rose was so radiantly happy that her mother would hug her just for the joy of it.

"You shine into all the dark corners," Maishe used to tell her. And in those days there were many.

"Fishl has gone," he told her one evening. They were strolling to the outskirts of town, hand in hand, Maishe having the after-dinner smoke that he loved but wouldn't take around the house because he knew Rose's father would not approve.

"Where?"

"To New York."

Rose held his hand tighter. Fishl was a boyhood friend. He and Maishe had gone to *kheyder* together. They had joined the Bund together. They had worked together, argued together, studied together. But Fishl had been laid off.

"It's like a piece of me is torn away."

"Him, too, I'm sure."

Maishe nodded. "I gave him some of our money."

"I'm glad." She squeezed his hand tighter still, raised it and held it against her cheek, and for a time was silent.

"Will it never end?"

He gazed across the greening fields. "It has to," he said finally.

David was born in late October the following year, 1909.[21] (In Canada his birthday is officially listed as June 23 because, says his daughter Janet, it was the first date that popped into David's twelve-year-old head as the family — excited, apprehensive and non-English speaking — was being interviewed in the Halifax immigration sheds.)

It was a simple affair, unattended by the rituals that surrounded Maishe's birth. There were no *kheyder* boys chanting the *krishmeh* during Rose's confinement, no *ben-zokher* celebration on the Friday after birth, and no *sholem zokher* on Saturday, the Sabbath. And there was no watch night, when men prayed with Rose and the baby until dawn of the next day, the day of circumcision.

But there was a day of circumcision and it was attended by a rabbi and Maishe did recite the prayer of dedication when giving David his name. It took place in the big room at the back of the house and in addition to grandparents, aunts, and uncles there were friends of both Maishe and Rose, and afterward there were cakes and tea and even a little singing, but, in deference to the grandparents, not of Bundist songs.

Rose was four months pregnant with her second son, Charlie, when the great fire swept through Svisloch in early July 1910. Half the town was destroyed.[22] No one was sure how it started, but in the back of everyone's mind was the question no one wanted to ask: was it deliberate?

Rose awoke first. "Maishe." Her voice was sharp and tight.

"Mmm."

She was looking out the tiny window at the end of the attic. "It's fire!"

He was out of bed in an instant. He could see the soft peach-coloured light flickering on Rose and on the sloping roof by the window.

"Take the baby and your mother. Hurry! Make sure you stay outside."

The state seminary had a pump wagon. Already there were men filling it at the river. Maishe and other men got wagons and every barrel they could find and rushed them to the fire as soon as they could be filled with water. Almost all the houses had wooden shingles and they were tinder-dry. Hour after hour they rushed back and forth, wetting down roofs, filling up barrels, losing first this house then that, to the flames. People had piled belongings in the street, and when they didn't have time to move them they soaked them with water — mattresses, bedding, clothes, couches. Several of the barns in town were infernos sending bits of flaming debris roaring skyward. They were much smaller

than the country barns; some merchants had them for their horses
and equipment, some used them to store grain they were selling, some
people kept a cow, some stored hay. It was almost impossible to prevent their catching fire. They were generally made of unpainted,
weathered planks just waiting for a spark. Most of the horses were
too terrified to be of any use, so men pulled the wagons of water
themselves. People worked kitchen pumps where they could, set up
lines to pass pails of water, struggling without words, their faces blacken-
ing in the ash, then streaking with sweat, sometimes with tears, hearing the snap of wood splitting in heat and the hungry soughing of
the fire, the shouted directions, the clatter that comes with rushing,
eyes stinging in the smoke, the air hot and dry, yellow flames streaked
with red and barbaric with excess.

By noon the worst was over. The fire was contained, but half the
town lay black and smouldering.

For the next four months Maishe and Rose shared their attic with
another couple and their two children while their house was rebuilt.
The fire had swept through the east end of town, pushed westward
by the night breeze, and it had finally been stopped at the town square.
The houses of Maishe's parents and Rose's parents lay not far beyond.

Maishe and other members of the Bund immediately began organizing
work parties to help rebuild the houses that had been destroyed. Maishe
also got in touch with Bund members in other towns asking for help
in collecting money and building materials, and within two weeks
wagons loaded with lumber and bricks and doors and used furniture
and clothing began trundling into Svisloch, where they were directed
to a yard set up as a depot. Maishe and his comrades parcelled out
the materials as even-handedly as they could, trying to tend to the
needs of the elderly first. Workers from other towns also came to lend
a hand in rebuilding. Some came for weekends. Some stayed a week
at a time. By early November, when the snows began, almost everyone
had shelter and would be secure for the winter.

Charlie was born that January 1911 and Doris in May 1913.

But in early 1912, before Doris was born, Maishe's mother Dvora
died. Ezekial, following the old ways, called in the elderly women of
the Khevreh Kadisha, the burial society, so that just before she died
she could repeat the final confession of sin as one of the women read
it to her.[23]

"Blessed be the True Judge," Maishe murmured in the traditional
response when one of the women emerged from the back room to say
his mother was dead. The women then sewed the shroud and after
washing and purifying the body, placed Dvora in it and lay her on

the floor, feet toward the door, a candle at her head. All day people from the village came to pay their respects and to "ask pardon" for affronts or offences that they might have committed over the years, and Ezekial, wearing his white *kittl*, a short, pull-over, gown-like garment, and his prayer shawl, received them one by one as they stripped off their heavy winter coats.

In the late afternoon everyone trooped through the rutted, snow-covered streets, a throng of weeping, wailing neighbours, many of whom had known each other and Dvora since childhood. The whole town was implicitly invited because, as Zborowski and Herzog have pointed out, it was one of the most important of the good deeds, the *mitsvos*, to accompany the dead since, "as many people accompany the dead body, so many angels will greet the soul."

She was buried at the edge of town in the House of Eternity. Instead of a fence, there was a ditch surrounding the area, but all that could be seen of it now was slight depression in the snow.[24] To Christian eyes it was a cemetery, but that word was never used for Jewish burial places. It was always the House of Graves, the House of Life, the Good Place, the Holy Place, or, as here, the House of Eternity.[25]

As the years had passed, Maishe had grown in stature. Now he was twenty-five years old, a father twice over, a steady worker, a Bundist who had continued tirelessly in the party's service for almost ten years and had been chairman in Svisloch for six. He was a person to whom people came with their problems. He had a way of putting them at ease. There was a gentleness and a sympathetic interest. He cared. That always came across. But he also had the knack of getting to the heart of a problem, peeling back the layers of hurt and anger until people almost solved their difficulties themselves, the answers became so obvious.

Where there were things to be done, he did them. If it meant talking to a difficult neighbour, he would do it. If it meant dealing with a family member whom others were reluctant to approach, he made the approach. If teenagers were causing a problem, people discovered that Maishe could talk to them. If documents needed to be arranged, if contacts had to be made in another town, he knew with whom to get in touch.[26]

At its Eighth Conference in the fall of 1910, the Bund sensed that bad times were bottoming out. Since the fires of revolution remained banked, it took a different tack from its usual exhortation to organize and agitate. It called on local party organizations to "proceed with the active pursuit of all kinds of legal associations, from trade unions to dramatic circles, cultural clubs, choirs, historical and educational societies."[27]

In a less euphemistic phrase, it was a call to infiltrate all organizations in which people were taking an interest. And Maishe did just that. But it was not infiltration for subversive reasons. Maishe worked hard and long to help each organization succeed on its own terms. In the process, the Bund remained visible, it helped to meet community needs, and it maintained contact with workers.

By the middle of 1911 workers in Svisloch were beginning to regain their confidence and spirit. Work was steady, the factory owners were regaining lost markets, and the Bund was recovering some of its old strength. Maishe was as happy as Rose had ever seen him. Once again he was talking agitation and was helping organize strikes in smaller shops, and once again they were winning concessions.[28]

Then in April 1912, at the Lena River gold mines in Siberia, a dispute broke out between workers and management. Soldiers were dispatched and a number of workers were shot and killed and more were injured. Immediately it was dubbed the Lena Massacre and widespread protests broke out.

For the first time since the 1905 Revolution was smothered, Jewish workers in the Pale demonstrated. On May Day, 6,000 marched in Warsaw; 3,000 (including non-Jews) in Vilna; 400 in Minsk; 500 in Bobruysk.[29] Nothing to match demonstrations in the days leading up to the revolution; in fact, not much more than a tiny puff in revolutionary sails that had been slack for almost six years. Nevertheless, something was stirring. Across Russia the number of strikes had shot upward over the past year and a half. Workers were growing restless again. Obviously the Lena Massacre had touched off a rising level of defiance that was brewing just below the surface.

Brewing or not, however, it didn't disrupt the surface calm for long. The year 1913 dawned: the 300th anniversary of rule by the Romanov royal family. There were lavish balls and state processionals and ballets and special operatic performances; dinners that were feasts almost beyond imagination; commissioning of paintings and music and ceremonial masses; and Nicholas riding through the streets of Moscow alone and unprotected at the head of a triumphal procession that included the Tsarina and the royal children in an open carriage. Nicholas's gesture was more than a personal declaration of victory over the revolution. It was an affirmation of the divine right of the Romanovs.[30]

But 1913 also brought widespread attention to the trial of Mendel Beilis, who had been charged with murdering a Christian boy in a

Jewish religious ritual in Kiev. Beilis was a simple labourer who was entirely innocent, but the trial had dragged on for the better part of two years with government experts testifying about Jewish blood rituals. As the proceedings ground on interminably, it became apparent that local Black Hundreds, acting in collusion with local police, were behind it all.[31]

The Bund and the other radical parties reacted angrily, party newspapers thundered condemnation and anti-Tsarist expletives, speeches resounded in the Duma, and even the liberal press took up the issue. Meetings were organized and, for the second time since the 1905 Revolution, mass demonstrations broke out in the Pale. In September 1913 about 20,000 workers went on strike in Warsaw, and within days 50,000 Jewish workers in seventy communities went out in sympathy. Beilis eventually was acquitted for lack of evidence but, like sludge that leaves a residue, the affair stuck in the awareness and demonstrated that nothing had changed and that nothing would change as long as Nicholas the Last remained. As long as the proletariat lay under the heel of the bourgeoisie.

But, as Raphael Abramovitch described it, "at precisely the moment when the revolutionary currents began to attract increasingly wider support, the war broke out . . . [and] was of special significance to the Jewish labour movement. The war zone comprised the entire Jewish Pale."[32] A year almost to the day after war broke out between Germany and Russia, decisive battles on the Eastern Front were fought as the Germans tried to trap the Russian armies in the Warsaw salient — and Svisloch, on the doorstep, hunkered in its cellars as soldiers fought door to door on the streets above.

In early May 1915 the Germans, under Field Marshal August von Mackensen, had smashed across what is now southern Poland, driving the Russians before them, until by June 22 they had reached Lvov in Ukraine. They then turned northward, sprinting to meet the forces of Field Marshal Paul von Hindenburg, who was driving southeast from what is now northern Poland. Mackenson was stopped at Brest-Litovsk and Hindenburg at the Narew River, and this left a gap through which the Russians were able to escape eastward. The Narew ran close by Svisloch; Jewish lumbermen used to float their logs down the river. And Svisloch was almost directly north of Brest-Litovsk, about 100 kilometres distant as the crow flies.

By the end of August 750,000 Russians had been captured, but in failing to close the gap in time, the Germans had missed their chance to cripple the Russian defence. By fall the Eastern Front had settled into a line that ran roughly fifty kilometres to the east of what is now

Poland's most easterly point, stretching from just west of Riga on the Baltic Sea to Chernovtsy, near the Romanian border, on the south. Svisloch was on the German side of the line and all the Polish provinces that had been in Russian hands for 100 years now were held by Germany.

It was with mixed feelings that the Jewish residents of Svisloch peered into the streets after the firing stopped. There had been widespread indifference toward the plight of the Tsar's armies. Russian propaganda early in the war had accused the entire Jewish population of being spies for the Germans, and on that pretext, late in 1914, close to a million Jews in border areas, but primarily in Poland, were driven from their homes and, facing starvation and exposure, forced to find their way back into Russia.

On the other hand, as the invaders advanced, German newspapers trumpeted the need to liberate the Jews from the scourge of the Russian Tsars, and German officials, following the lead of Hindenburg and Erich Ludendorff, chief of staff of the German 8th Army, proclaimed their friendship. Obviously these were attempts to neutralize an occupied population — and Jews knew it. But they also knew that Jews enjoyed a status in Germany, and especially in Austria-Hungary, far superior to what they had in Russia.[33]

So as they emerged from their cellars to stare dumbly at the first dead bodies they had ever seen lying in the streets of Svisloch and at the craters in market square and the handful of houses that had been ripped by exploding shells, and as they studied the foreign uniforms and the alien faces with the realization sinking in that now they belonged to someone else, there was little sense of allegiance one way or the other. There was only a gnawing uncertainty about which would prove the lesser of two evils.

Ezekial died shortly after the Germans occupied Svisloch. It came as no surprise. In the three years since Dvora's death he had become old.

"Come, Papa, we'll go for a walk," Maishe would say when he visited in the evening and they would amble along the market square in a comfortable closeness, able at last to ignore intimacies that were out of reach, nodding to neighbours, stopping to exchange a few words, sometimes pausing to look at something, a German soldier across the square perhaps, sometimes pausing longer as Ezekial's inner eye took over and he stared, sightless, into the distance. It was a world grown strange to him and he had stopped trying to subdue it to his understanding. They talked of the here and now. Household things, the weather, friends. And when they parted he would go to the synagogue where now he spent almost all his time.

Maishe gave him the traditional funeral he would have wanted, and wept as much for what they had not shared as he did for him.

Not long after the funeral Maishe, Rose, and the children moved into the Losz house. Two of Maishe's sisters, Sarah (Soreh in Yiddish) and Ida (Chaiya), and his brother Zebullen (Z'vullen) were still living there. Sarah had taken over the running of the grain business from Ezekial before he died. Another sister Fanny (Faiche) had married Rose's brother Max (Motke) Lazarovitch and was living away from home.

On their first evening there, sitting in the back room with Rose and Zebullen after the others had gone to bed, Maishe let them talk while he drifted into the memories that each chair, each cup, each corner of the room, evoked.

Finally he spoke. "It's good to have *something* stay the same," he said softly.

• C H A P T E R   E I G H T •

The uncompromising attitude of the Bolsheviks
[will] mean the crushing of the Revolution.
                                    Henryk Erlich
                                November 8, 1917
                        Ten Days That Shook the World[1]

When the Germans seized Svisloch, David was almost six years old. Many of the early memories that he would carry through life would be about war and struggle. First the German army, then the Polish, then the Russian, then the Polish again, always against a background of manoeuvring by the Bolsheviks and Mensheviks and Bundists and Poalei Zionists and Zionist Socialists and SERP and the SRs and the Kadets and the Social Democrats and the Reds and the Whites and all the other splits. And all the factions in Poland as well.

Already one of his favourite pastimes was listening to grownups talk politics around the dinner table in the soft glow of the kerosene lamp. "I didn't understand what was being said but I could sense that it was terribly important," he says in his memoirs. "That I was permitted to stay up and listen for a while before bed made me feel part of it all. I didn't know what the terms meant but justice, working class, democracy, equality, peace, were words that became as familiar to me as school, teacher, bread and water."[2]

And equally familiar became the magic names of Plekhanov and Medem and Liber and Marx and Mill and Abramovitch and Litvak and Portnoy and Martov and Izenshtat and Kremer and Dan and Axelrod and Shulman and Alter and Erlich and so many, many more. Names that became like family to him. And names like Trotsky and Lenin and Zinoviev and Lunacharsky and Radek and Valentinov and Kerensky — not family, but real and alive and striding past his mind's eye larger than life.

He had been in school for a little more than a year, attending a *kheyder* as Maishe had instead of the Russian public elementary school or the Hebrew elementary school, both of which had been established around 1901. Doris would get no schooling until the family moved to Canada; education for women was not a priority in the Pale.

Then, early in 1916, the new Yiddish school opened[3] and Maishe took David and Charlie to their first day of classes, one small hand in each of his, tears of pride welling in his eyes. Pride for his sons, pride for the school, pride for the Bund that made the school possible, and a torrential happiness in what he was helping to give. Establishing the school had been a heart's desire. Here, children would be able to learn in their mother tongue. For the first time classrooms would be an extension of their world at home, a workers' world, a world where childhood fantasies stretched beyond legends and tales and droll stories to a mystical thing called brotherhood that their parents talked about. Here they could read the books that to Maishe had been forbidden inside classrooms.

To an outside eye, the two boys looked like any Russian boys their age. "We were dressed like the Russians," Emanuel Goldberg recalls. "And if you had come to our town [Svisloch] you wouldn't have been able to distinguish between a Russian little boy and a Jewish little boy."

And, speaking in particular about the Losz family when he knew them shortly after the war, "One has to be extremely careful in saying it, but they were in a way Russified. Unknowingly Russified. You can say they were unaware of it and they would be the last ones to accept it. But there were strong Russian influences: Tolstoy, Dostoevski, Pushkin, all the Russian literature. Turgenev. They had a powerful influence. Of course I am speaking about those Jews who read and were interested in literature."

And most Jews in Svisloch were interested. They were *misnagidim*. The entire town was *misnagid*.[4] It was a tradition that prized intellectual rigour and especially an unrelenting, uncompromising logic. Unlike the Hassidim, the other great tradition among Russian Jews, there was nothing lighthearted in the process. Shmarya Levin was *misnagid*, coming from the other Svisloch in the area of Bobruysk, a short distance southeast of Minsk. In his memoirs he recalled his impressions in the late 1800s:

> Russian Jewry . . . [had] three huge divisions: Polish Jewry, northwestern or so-called Lithuanian Jewry and southern Jewry which included New Russia, Ukraine, Bessarabia and the Crimea. Each of them had between one and a half and two million souls. Each of them also had its own character.

> There was a great difference between the Lithuanian Jew and the southern Jew. The northwest was a poor district; the earth is lean and the peasant can barely wrest a living from it. . . . Ukraine, on the other hand, is blessed with a marvellously fertile soil. . . .
>
> The Lithuanian peasant, then, was a depressed, worried creature; when he sang it was of want and hunger. His brother of the Ukraine was well-fed and carefree and he sang of joy. The difference . . . was reflected in the Jews. The Lithuanian Jew was a pessimist, his brother of the Ukraine an optimist. The former sought refuge in speculations on a world to come; the latter found joy in this world. Lithuanian Jewry produced the Gaon of Vilna, the pure intellectualist; Ukrainian Jewry produced the Baal Shem Tov, the founder of Hassidism and the mystic lover of this life.
>
> And yet the difference between these two groups was minor compared to that which divided both of them from Polish Jewry. Poland was a conquered country, yet it had always remained foreign. . . . The same foreignness was felt by the Russian Jew among Polish Jews. Even their pronunciation of Yiddish was so different they often had difficulty in understanding each other. . . . The line of division did not lie between *Hassidim* and *Misnagidim*, but between Russians and Poles.[5]

Lithuania, Levin says at another point, "was looked upon as the nest of the skeptical, over-intellectualized scholar; the south was the home of the ecstatic religionists."[6]

The Svisloch of Maishe Losz was on that blurred dividing line between true Russia and true Poland, geographically more toward the Russian side, linguistically more toward the Polish side, and culturally as much within the orbit of Vilna as within the orbit of Warsaw. The appearance of a *Hassid* was so rare, Emanuel Goldberg recalls, that "if one of them appeared in Svisloch the young Jewish boys and girls would surround him and follow him to get a look at something out of this world."

For David and Maishe before him, the dispute had little relevance. For them, the divisions within Jewry were not between religious factions or intellectual traditions but between bourgeoisie and proletariat and between Zionists and Bundists. Where they bore the mark of the *misnagid* was in their logic. It, too, was unyielding. In the hands of earlier *misnagidim* it led to intense dissertations on microscopic theological issues; in the period of the Haskala it provided a discipline with which they assimilated vast stockpiles of knowledge with astonishing speed — imagine what the intellectual discipline of a *misnagid* such as Shmarya Levin could accomplish, a man trained from age four to study at least ten hours a day and as an adolescent at least fifteen hours, who at age nine could tell you what words a pin pierced when thrust through the pages of a Bible. In the hands of a politician such as David Lewis it became a weapon to be feared and respected and sometimes, unfortunately, to be avoided rather than confronted.

The Yiddish school that David and Charlie entered was in a converted home. There were only three or four teachers and at first only junior grades were taught. It was a far cry from the Hebrew school, which offered seven grades and had its own building with about fifteen teachers. It was supported by the well-to-do Jewish factory owners and merchants and by student fees that lower-paid workers and the unemployed had no hope of paying. Students of poorer families could send their children to the public school, of course, but instruction was in Russian or German or Polish, depending on which regime occupied the town. And there were still a few *melamedim* — conducting *kheyders*, but their instruction remained focused on religious works and didn't include subjects such as mathematics, science, history, and contemporary literature.

Maishe had dreamed of a Yiddish school for years. Dreamed of it, organized support for it, raised money for it, worked on renovations to the building, scoured the area for donated furnishings, and, most important of all, he had been in constant touch with the Bund's Central Committee for Yiddish schools in Polish-speaking areas. The committee, which was located in Warsaw, was financed largely by expatriate Bundists, primarily those in New York, and in the beginning was allowed to operate freely by the occupying Germans. Without money from the committee and without Bundist teachers who worked for next to nothing, Svisloch workers could never have afforded the school.[7] Even in good times they lived in a poverty that by contemporary Western standards was wretched beyond belief.

Those who could, contributed modest fees. But many were unemployed and many with jobs had nothing to give. After a brief return to prosperity, Svisloch was again on hard times. In 1914 the town had fully recovered from the lean years following the revolution. The leather business was booming, "with every worker employed." But once the German armies occupied the town, Svisloch was cut off from Russia, its major market for leather, and the Germans would not allow penetration into Western markets. So the backbone of Jewish economic life was snapped.

People scrabbled for a living as best they could, helped out by remittances from abroad, from Svisloch emigrants living mainly in England, the United States, Canada, and Argentina. But after April 1917, when the United States entered the war, it became next to impossible to get money to families in German-occupied territories, and for the next year and a half, until the armistice in November 1918, the poor in Svisloch lived on the brink of starvation.

The event that convinced Svisloch Jews that the Germans were no better than the Russian Tsarists was the closing of the schools. It took a while for the German occupational forces to settle in, but once they had, they decreed that the only schools in town would be German. It was part of a policy of "Germanization." It made a mockery of all that the people of Svisloch had heard about liberal German attitudes toward Jews. What the Germans wanted was assimilation. For Maishe the decree was especially shattering. His beloved Yiddish school was consigned to oblivion before it was a year old.[8]

When the Germans left in 1918 and the Poles took over, factory owners tried to resume leather production. However, Svisloch remained cut off from Russian markets, the supply of hides was limited, and new markets were difficult to find. Several small shops started producing fine leather from calf skins but, "on the whole . . . the leather industry . . . never regained its former position."[9] But remittances resumed and the Yiddish school reopened.

When the Yiddish school closed, David and Charlie switched to an underground *kheyder*. Literally. "I remember attending [it] surreptitiously," David says in his memoirs. "My parents were not anxious for me to attend a religious school but the secular one would not be opened for some time. The *kheyder*, on the other hand, was functioning only because it was carried on in a cellar. The rabbi who taught us was devout and brave."

He was eight years old "when the Russian revolution broke out, but I was interested enough to listen eagerly to every discussion. . . . I didn't know how the adults learned that the Tsar had been overthrown, but there was rejoicing in our home and even in the streets. I heard about the government of Kerensky and how at last Russia would become democratic. Then Kerensky's name was replaced with those of Lenin and Trotsky. I could sense that my parents and their friends were not entirely happy at this development, but they still rejoiced that Tsarism and capitalism were finished."[10]

The war, crashing across the land, uprooting, denuding, like the ravening storm before the flood, brought the country to revolution. Within nine months of the outbreak, soldiers were being slaughtered because they didn't have the means to fight. Ammunition was scarce. Firing of artillery was limited to two and a half shells per gun every twenty-four hours, while the minimum needed to hold a line was five and at least seven or eight were required for a successful offensive. By the fall of 1915 the supply of rifles had run out. Cartridges were in meagre supply. Half the Russian forces retreating from Warsaw had been killed or captured. "In a year of war," said Gen. A.A. Brusilov, one of Russia's best commanders, "the regular army had vanished. It was replaced by an army of ignoramuses."[11]

Food was so scarce that soldiers and horses grew ravenous on half-rations. Behind the lines a government survey found food shortages in 500 of 659 cities. By June of 1916 more than ten million peasants had been called from the land to war and, as a result, crops had been cut by 25 to 30 percent. Even so, there was enough grain to feed the cities, but there was no way to get it to them. Rail transportation had been commandeered for the army or had been destroyed. Grain shipments to cities dropped by a third. And in the cities speculators prevailed. Inflation ran rampant. Meat prices had jumped 332 percent over 1914. Butter was up 220 percent; flour, 265 percent. The 142 percent increase in industrial wages had been savaged by a 69.8 percent crash in the gold ruble. Rents in St. Petersburg were up 200 to 300 percent. By the end of the year thirty-six blast furnaces had closed down for lack of fuel.[12]

The front was full of foreboding, the cities full of want, the farmlands full of mourning, the forests full of bandits. Everything was out of joint. The peasants had had enough of war, their women enough of death. The nobility had had enough of Rasputin and his scandals, enough of his strange hold over the Tsarina, enough of her manipulations of the Tsar and, while he was at the front, of his ministers. Soldiers had had enough of fighting futile battles on empty stomachs for fancy officers they didn't trust. Workers had had enough of sweating through impossible work schedules for wages that bought them less and less and less.

Then on December 30, 1916, Rasputin, symbol of the gangrene reaching to the heart of Russia, was murdered. The aristocracy rejoiced. The peasants grew still more surly, saying aristocrats had killed him because he was a *muzhik*, a peasant, one of theirs. And in the army, according to an Okhrana report, soldiers were saying that the murder was only "the first swallow."[13]

Yet things continued to get worse. St. Petersburg needed 120 carloads of grain a day to feed itself, but in the last ten days of January 1917 it got only twenty-one. Mikhail V. Chelnokov, chairman of the Union of Cities, reported that "there won't be any bread in February. We have grain for mills that have no fuel, flour where there are no freight cars to haul it and cars where there is no food for the population."[14]

The revolution began, just as it had in 1905, with a strike. This time it was at the Putilov steelworks in St. Petersburg, the largest military factory in Russia with 26,700 workers. Several workers in the gun-carriage shop were let go, and the shop committee demanded their reinstatement and a 50 percent pay increase. It was refused and the next day, March 3, 1917, the shop walked out. Two days later four other shops joined them, and on the evening of March 6 the entire factory decided to support them. The next morning management declared a lockout.

Few thought they were bellying up to the revolution. It just turned out that way. All of St. Petersburg left work and swarmed through the streets. In the end, with almost no bloodshed, a Provisional Government was formed under Alexander Kerensky on March 15, the date of Nicholas's abdication.

During the eight months of its life the Provisional Government had the trappings of power, but power itself rested with the St. Petersburg Soviet of Workers' and Soldiers' Deputies, formed within hours of the Provisional Government, the only body that could claim support of the masses.[15] Throughout much of that time it was the Mensheviks who effectively controlled the Soviet. Yet never once did they try to push aside the Provisional Government. Instead, it was the Bolsheviks who did it. Why the Menshevik reluctance? When, before or since, has a group ushered in a revolution, steadfastly refused to take over the reins of government, and then let them pass to opponents?

There were 2,000 to 3,000 deputies in the Soviet and at the outset the Bolsheviks' independent "fraction" commanded no more than forty deputies. Control was held by a coalition of SRs and Mensheviks, and although the SRs were the largest single group in the Soviet, the Mensheviks dominated the coalition because they were better organized, more experienced, and had more talented politicians.[16]

Right beside the Mensheviks were the Bundists. In fact, "there was such intimate collaboration . . . that several men prominent in the Bund were also leaders of Menshevism."[17]

To people of the television era it seems inconceivable that revolutionaries should not take over government once a revolution has succeeded. Theirs is an age of revolution. Every couple of months a new revolutionary leader somewhere in the world appears on their screens to announce victory and a new government. It seems absurd — foolish, unintelligible — to have a revolution and then turn down power. But that's what the Mensheviks did.

To understand why they did it is to understand how they saw the world. If perceptions differ, actions differ.

This was 1917. A very great many Mensheviks were Jewish. A very great many of them, like Maishe Losz, grew up in the tail end of

Haskala, which, in addition to offering concepts of liberty, social justice, and the spirit of enterprise, deeply imbued them with a belief in a secular universe that Western science could dissect and render intelligible. It was a belief bred by the works of people such as Charles Darwin and Karl Marx and confirmed by the works of men like Emile Durkheim and Max Weber, who were laying bare the roots of social action, and Sigmund Freud, who was uncovering the roots of individual action.

It was a time of astonishing insights in the social sciences. A time of faith in the ability to discover how everything worked. A time of conviction that everything was controlled by a mechanism of some sort — a mechanism of chemical reactions, of historical relationships, of interplays between id and ego, of economic cause and effect.

There was a perception that everything moved to a kind of organic logic in the sense that it moved in a sequence peculiar to itself. Given the same sequence, it would always develop in the same way. All that was needed was the right methodology and people could discover the rules guiding that iron logic. And once they had the rules, they could forecast the future.

Mensheviks believed in their scientific explanations as completely and fervently as people of the television era believe that technology can fix the ills of the world.

As Darwin had done for the evolution of the species, so Karl Marx had done for the evolution of society. He had discovered the rules and they declared that the collapse of capitalism was inevitable. Capitalism, he argued, constantly needed more mechanization and specialization to keep its profits up and that would produce growing alienation among workers and increasing unemployment until eventually, workers would rebel.

Consequently, before there can be a revolution, there have to be enough workers who are alienated, and radicalized by unemployment and the cyclical collapsing of the economy — in other words, a proletariat big enough and angry enough to carry off a revolution. Otherwise the revolution would fail. The mechanism would be missing a few parts. The universe would be prevented from unfolding as normally it should.

The problem in Russia was that the proletariat was comparatively small. In spite of its large industrial output, Russia was basically an agricultural nation. So during the mid-1880s Plekhanov evolved the theory of a two-staged revolution. First there would be the overthrow of the Tsar — the bourgeois revolution — and then, after the proletariat had grown bigger and angrier, the overthrow of capitalism — the socialist revolution. It was an approach that Pavel Axelrod, the leading Menshevik theoretician after Plekhanov, urged right up to the day Lenin seized power.[18]

So there was in Menshevism a perspective that believed that the organic process of revolution required two stages. This was no airy theorizing. Mensheviks bet their lives on it.

They believed that the first stage of the revolution had occurred in March but that the proletariat had not yet developed sufficiently for the second stage to be undertaken — and if it were attempted prematurely and against the rules, it would fail. Consequently they were prepared to let the bourgeoisie keep control of the government through the Duma while they and all other socialists prepared the proletariat for the second and final revolution. At the same time, they thought they could keep the Duma in line by exerting democratic pressure.

From the perspective of 1917 that was not altogether unreasonable, given the turmoil, the war, the difficulty of reading political tea leaves, and the fact that there was indeed no large, politicized proletariat — provided, of course, that the Mensheviks had clear objectives and strong leadership. In fact, they had neither.

Nevertheless, the Duma was doing some things right so that, in the beginning months at least, people did not want to do away with it. For instance on April 4, with Alexander Kerensky as minister of justice, it passed a decree granting free and equal rights to Jews throughout Russia and, as Raphael Abramovitch put it, "For the first time in the history of Jewish emancipation, a Jewish community received not only civil and political but also national recognition. . . . For the first time they felt that they were on a par with all others."[19]

As a result a majority of the Bund rejected radical calls such as Lenin's for an end to the war and supported the Duma in its determination to continue the fight against Germany. At this point only about half of the Jewish workers were in Russian-controlled territory. The rest were behind the lines in German-occupied areas. The Poalei Zionists reacted in the same way as the Bundists and, says Abramovitch, in the early months of the revolution the Bolsheviks "attracted but a negligible part of the Jewish working class."[20]

In the end, Lenin leapfrogged the entire issue of whether the proletariat was large enough and ready enough. He turned directly to the peasants, who were not part of what had been defined as the working class and certainly were not "politically educated," and won the so-called Bolshevik Revolution with farmers, especially those turned soldier and sailor, and whatever workers were available. But it was no grand heroic undertaking. It was as confused and stumbling, as chaotic and semi-accidental, as everything that had gone before.

The keys to Bolshevik success were the single-minded, even fanatical, determination of Lenin to head straight for power whatever the price, and the slogan he had given the party: "peace, bread, land."

While the fighting for the Winter Palace in St. Petersburg was carrying into the early hours of November 8, the Bund, led by Henryk Erlich, was trying desperately to preserve the Provisional Government.[21] A meeting of the All-Russian Soviet was in high swing at the Smolny Institute, the select school for daughters of the nobility which had been taken over by the Bolsheviks as their headquarters. It was the meeting that elected Bolsheviks to control of the praesidium.

In the hall were 650 delegates, "workers in black blouses . . . soldiers in rough dirt-coloured coats . . . packed immovably in the aisles and on the sides, perched on every window-sill, and even on the edge of the platform . . . [with] no heat in the hall but the stifling heat of unwashed human bodies . . . and a foul blue cloud of cigarette smoke [hanging] in the thick air."[22] It was past three in the morning and Erlich, "his eyes snapping behind thick glasses, trembling with rage," had the floor: "What is taking place now in Petrograd is a monstrous calamity!" he said.

"Our duty to the Russian proletariat doesn't permit us to remain here and be responsible for these crimes. Because the firing on the Winter Palace doesn't cease, the Municipal Duma together with the Mensheviki and Socialist Revolutionaries, and the Executive Committee of the Peasants' Soviet, has decided to perish with the Provisional Government, and we are going with them! Unarmed we will expose our breasts to the machine guns of the Terrorists. . . . We invite all delegates to this Congress. . . ."

But at this point, according to John Reed, "The rest was lost in a storm of hoots, menaces and curses which rose to a hellish pitch as fifty delegates got up and pushed their way out. . . . And Trotsky, standing up with a pale, cruel face, letting out his rich voice in cool contempt, 'All these so-called Socialist compromisers, these frightened Mensheviki, Socialist Revolutionaries, Bund — let them go! They are just so much refuse that will be swept into the garbage heap of history!'"[23]

It seemed, in the civil war that followed, that the country was disembowelling itself. The deprivation was far greater than that which underlay the March 1917 Revolution, worse than what confronted the country when the Winter Palace was stormed. Industry was in ruins; peace with Germany had stripped Russia of 33 percent of her manufacturing industry, 27 percent of her arable land, and 26 percent of her population; with what Germany took, what was controlled by counterrevolutionary armies, and what areas declared independence, the nation was reduced to the size it had been almost 500 years earlier; unemployment was rampant — 70 to 80 percent of St. Petersburg workers were without jobs; inflation went wildly out of control — the number of paper rubles in circulation increased forty-two times from the end of 1917 to 1921, by which time each ruble was worth 800 times less; and the endless fighting kept generating the hate and starvation and death. Brother against brother. Peasants in the dead of winter selling corpses for food.

Cleaving compulsively to power like the bulldog he was — and haunted by the failure of the Paris Commune that collapsed in 1871 because, he said, "it showed too much humanity toward its enemies" — Lenin unleashed Red Terror.[24]

Instead of the guillotine, he would use the revolver.

As he had once said: "Revolution is a dirty job. You do not make it with white gloves."[25]

There can be no arguing that force was necessary to maintain the barest minimum of order and to preserve what remained of the state. Lenin expected Red Terror be a fearsome retribution for acts against the state. But his secret police, the Cheka, had no inhibitions about extending it far beyond that.[26] Its 31,000 employees would look only for the mark of Cain: membership in the capitalist class. Retribution would be carried out for being, not for doing.

The Cheka killed something like 50,000 people and "This . . . would not include insurgents who were shot with arms in their hands or people who were killed by mobs or by uncontrolled bands of soldiers and sailors."[27] According to an estimate of the Patriarch Tikhon, 322 bishops and priests were executed from 1917 to 1920.[28]

In the end, Lenin arrived where Trotsky predicted he would when Trotsky chose the Mensheviks over the Bolsheviks following the 1903 split in the Russian Social Democratic Workers' Party. Lenin's centralism was really "egocentralism," he said, and one day it would lead to a situation where "The organization of the Party takes the place of the Party itself; the Central Committee takes the place of the organization; and finally the dictator takes the place of the Central Committee."[29]

In the beginning Red Terror was not aimed at Bundists and Mensheviks simply because they were Bundists or Mensheviks. After all, they were workers and socialists and they had not tried to sabotage the revolution. Nevertheless, no love was lost. These were people who, like Henryk Erlich, remained unrepentant in their support for parliamentary democracy. Their opposition was voiced through whatever democratic means was left to them. Whatever newspapers were not closed down, whatever meetings they could still address.

At the end of 1917 there were about 40,000 Bundists in almost 400 branches.[30] Delegates met in March 1919 at the Eleventh Conference of the Bund in Minsk, and after passionate debates accepted the "platform of a soviet government." At the same time, however, they condemned Red Terror and called for freedom of speech, freedom of the press, and democracy in the soviets.

Over the next three and a half years there were splits in the Bund. Some members joined the Communist Party, but the core remained, vociferously condemning the Soviets for Red Terror and authoritarian rule.

Finally Lenin had enough. In March 1921 he ordered the suppression of the remaining socialist parties. Mensheviks and Bundists were special targets because they still enjoyed popularity in trade unions.

The Cheka needed no urging. Some Bundists were liquidated, some followed predecessors into the Communist Party, most of the remainder fled the country. Mensheviks fared no better. Although a few lingered on, that was the end of them in Russia.[31]

As Abramovitch sadly commented: "Thus ended the eventful existence of the Bund in Russia. The centre of the Jewish labour movement shifted to [independent] Poland."[32]

• C H A P T E R   N I N E •

With all the disappointments — with the First World War,
Red Terror, Stalin, the Second World War, the Holocaust
— God forbid that people should give up hope of
improving this world. That's why I'm still a Bundist.
                    Israel Falk, Survivor of the Warsaw Ghetto
                    and two years in German concentration camps
                                        Montreal, July 1985

"**W**e've come to see Maishe Losz."
Rose had never before seen the two men in the doorway.
"He's not here," she managed to say and failed totally
to look calm.

"Then you won't mind, comrade, if we take a look," said the smaller
one, brushing by her and heading toward the back of the house. It
was the same evening that Maishe had disappeared into Dr. Bittner's
basement.

All the next day the Bolsheviks searched for him. They were
reasonably sure he hadn't left town and they wanted him. He was a
key member of the Bund in the Svisloch area and he was proving
troublesome.

"He is accused as a saboteur. He has been plotting against the Revolutionary Working Class," they said when asked.

But on the second day they dropped their search.[1] Other, more
momentous matters took precedence. The turning point in the battle
for Warsaw had come, it was August 16, 1920, and the Soviet army
was in full rout. It was, says Viscount D'Abernon in a book on the
subject, the eighteenth decisive battle of the world. "Had the Soviet
forces overcome Polish resistance and captured Warsaw, Bolshevism
would have spread throughout Central Europe and might well have
penetrated the entire continent."[2]

By the 19th the Poles had recaptured Brest-Litovsk; by the 23rd they
were in Bialystok. In the south, at Zamoste, southeast of Lublin, the once-
fearsome Budenny and his mighty cavalry charged forward in a final
attempt to snap the Polish spinal cord, but he was soundly defeated.

Dr. Bittner was shouting as he came down the stairs on the morning of the 25th: "Maishe. Maishe. They've gone. They've left. They retreated."

They met in the middle of the darkened basement and threw their arms around each other.

"You're safe, my friend. Safe."

Maishe was hugging him fiercely, grinning through the ten-day-old beard he was growing as a disguise.

"Safe," he said, holding Dr. Bittner at arm's length, "thanks to you." And he hugged Dr. Bittner again. He started to say something more but Dr. Bittner interrupted.

"Come. A celebration. A quick celebration," and led him upstairs and poured two small glasses of clear, almost oily Polish schnapps.

"To free Poland," said Dr. Bittner.

"To a new world," said Maishe.

The next morning grim-faced Polish cavalry marched into Svisloch, seized five young Jewish men, and buried them up to their necks on the outskirts of town. Guards were posted until they died. It was punishment, they said, for being spies and helping the Soviets in the battle that had been fought seven weeks before.[3]

Maishe and a number of townspeople, including Dr. Bittner, went as a delegation to plead with the officer in charge. They couldn't imagine what spying had been done, or what spying would have been at all useful to the Red Army in the battle that was fought. But to no use.

"This is what happens to spies," was all the officer would say. "Let it be a lesson."

Maishe was aghast. Svisloch had never seen a pogrom, had never seen man at his most brutish. He could understand anger. He could understand hate. But how to understand the sullenness of a soul that would design such a slow, horrible death and then wait impassively for it to arrive. It clung to his consciousness like a leech. Loathsome and gorging on his anguish. He could hear nothing else, feel nothing else, think of nothing else — be nothing else. Weeks turned into months as still he struggled to find a footing.

Finally, one evening, he told Rose he thought they should leave for America.

It was a painful decision — a choice between a safer, more promising future for his children and his Bundist commitment of staying and fighting for a more promising future for all.

On the one hand, leaving could be seen as an act of selfishness. Was it not self-indulgent to want a life for his children that was certain to be far easier than that facing those left behind? Fathers who stayed also had loved ones and their love was no less than his. Why should his private love take such precedence over his public obligation? No one ever said the battle for human betterment would be easy, and that battle needed people like him. Moreover, as chairman of the Bund in Svisloch he carried a heavier obligation than most. A decision to leave would mean not only abandoning that obligation but providing an example hurtful to the Bund.

The Bund had lost in Russia. That much was certain. But Poland was another matter. First of all, its new borders included much of what had been the old Russian Pale of Settlement. Svisloch now was within Poland, about 200 kilometres from the new border with Russia.[4] Second, the Bund was a significant party in the new, independent Poland. There had been a strong Polish Bund within the old frontiers, and after the acquisition of territories in the Pale and the flight of Bundists from Lenin's Red Terror, it was stronger still. Already it had control of the national council of Jewish Trade Unions within its reach.[5] The future that Maishe would have in Poland would not be without problems, but it would be a future with vitality and meaning.

On the other hand, must his children be denied the opportunity to seize a better life? A better chance to pull themselves out of the poverty he had known? Free of pogroms? Free of cavalry units that buried people alive? Would it not be more selfish and self-indulgent to stay? Would he not be catering to his own desires at the expense of his children?

Whatever the decision, it carried its own burden of guilt.

Rose also wrestled with the decision of whether to go or stay, and in the end agreed with Maishe that they should leave. As Doris remembers, it was "entirely for the sake of the children. The decision was made because he [Maishe] was very worried about what the boys would do, where they would end up. . . . [It was] should we, shouldn't we, and if we should go, whether my uncles should go along with him [Maishe] . . . and when the rest of the family should come. But we had to go because the children were going to get a better education. . . . And I heard him [Maishe] say in the discussions that we had no choice. 'We've got to go.'"

One of Rose's brothers, Eli, had emigrated to Montreal twenty years earlier and eventually had become a partner in a men's clothing factory. (In Canada he changed the family name from Lazarovitch to Lazarus.) He could offer work. So the decision was made that Maishe and Rose's brother Max should sail for Canada, work in Eli's plant, and, as quickly as possible, save the money to bring over the rest of the family. In addition to being Rose's brother, Max had married Maishe's sister Fanny, so the two couples were extremely close.

Maishe and Max left Svisloch in May 1921 and by the end of August Rose, David, Charlie, Doris, and Fanny stepped ashore in Quebec City. Maishe and Max had saved a little money and had borrowed the rest from Eli to pay for their passage.

About three weeks before they left Svisloch, Rose's father took David aside and as David recounted it, told him:

> "You will soon be thirteen, but knowing your father, you will not have a bar mitzvah, and if you follow your father's ideas you will probably never learn how to put on and wear phylacteries. Would you mind coming with me to morning services until you leave? I will teach you how to wear phylacteries even though you are not yet thirteen."
>
> He sounded so concerned that I agreed instantly. What struck me at the time and what I have always respected is that he did not say a critical word about Father, although his tone expressed regret at my father's agnosticism. Nor did he lecture me on what I should do in the future. He simply did what was necessary to make sure that his grandson experienced a tradition of Jewish religious practice which he believed to be important.[6]

Fanny and Max lived with Maishe and Rose in their first home at 5170 rue St-Dominique in the Jewish section of Montreal just off "The Main" — Boulevard St-Laurent. They had the second floor. There was no central heating and only a coal stove, but David remembered "walking about the small flat with my brother, switching electric lights on and off, turning faucets, pulling the chain in the toilet, asking permission to light the elements on the gas stove, and exclaiming with wonder and admiration. In Svisloch, and on the ship, I had begun to feel grownup, as a 12-year-old can when given responsibility, but as I walked through the flat I felt like a child again, born into a marvellous and unknown world."[7]

The two families lived in the flat for two years, until Fanny and Max found a place of their own, and then Maishe and Rose moved closer to downtown to 4370 rue Coloniale, still beside The Main, still in the Jewish section, near the public baths, again taking a second-floor flat. They made two more moves, both to second-floor flats: the first after about four years at rue Coloniale to 4385 Clark Street, where they lived for eight years (until 1935), and the last to 4607 rue Esplanade. Again, both were near The Main in the heart of the Jewish section.

The Lewises came to Canada in the great surge of Jewish immigrants who arrived between 1901 and 1921. The first Jews to arrive in Montreal were Sephardic, coming in a trickle from Spain and Portugal from about 1760 to the mid-1800s. Next came Jews from England and Germany, especially after the failed 1848 Revolution in Germany. The surge of which the Lewises were part came from Eastern Europe after the resumption of pogroms that followed the assassination of Alexander II and continuing through the Russian revolutions.[8]

Maishe's life, especially in Canada, poses something of a mystery. He is remembered as an outstanding figure. But there is nothing in the public record that stands as a monument. Not in Svisloch; not in Canada. And no one points to an achievement that looms above those of other men. There are even some who say he was nothing special.[9] Yet in Svisloch he was vividly remembered for his work in the Bund twenty-five years after he had left.[10] And in Montreal generally it's the same. For instance, Maurice Silcoff, seventy-eight years old at the time of being interviewed in 1985, president of the Headware, Optical and Allied Workers Union of Canada and Canadian director of the International Plastics and Novelty Workers Union, and his wife Beatrice say that in fifty years they never came across anyone to equal him. Moreover, a branch of the Workmen's Circle has been renamed in his honour.

Why, then, was he so highly thought of if there is no record of achievement?

The key to understanding Maishe lies in understanding what David Rome calls Mr. Anonymous, and if Rome is right, the reason why people have honoured Maishe lies more in what he was and what he represented rather than in offices he held, edifices he erected, or official acts he performed. Perhaps the best place to see Mr. Anonymous is in the Yiddish stories of I. L. Peretz so loved by Maishe. There are many stories portraying Mr. Anonymous. One of the best known is called "If Not Higher":

EVERY FRIDAY MORNING, at the time of the Penitential Prayers, the rabbi of Nemirov would vanish.

He was nowhere to be seen — neither in the synagogue nor in the two Houses of Study nor at a *minyan* [a quorum of ten males required for communal religious services]. And he was certainly not at home. . . .

So where can the rabbi be?

"That's not my business," said [a] Litvak, shrugging. Yet all the while — what a Litvak can do! — he is scheming to find out.

That same night, right after the evening prayers, the Litvak steals into the rabbi's room, slides under the rabbi's bed, and waits. He'll watch all night and discover where the rabbi vanishes and what he does during Penitential Prayers.

Someone else might have got drowsy and fallen asleep, but a Litvak is never at a loss; he recites a whole tract of the Talmud by heart.

At dawn he hears the call to prayers.

The rabbi has already been awake for a long time. The Litvak has heard him groaning for a whole hour.

Whoever has heard the rabbi of Nemirov groan knows how much sorrow for all Israel, how much suffering, lies in each groan. A man's heart might break, hearing it. But a Litvak is made of iron; he listens and remains where he is. The rabbi — long life to him! — lies on the bed, and the Litvak under the bed.

Then the Litvak hears the beds in the house begin to creak; he hears people jumping out of their beds, mumbling a few Jewish words, pouring water over their fingernails, banging on doors. Everyone has left. It is again quiet and dark; a bit of light from the moon shines through the shutters. . . .

Finally the rabbi — long life to him! — arises. First he does what befits a Jew. Then he goes to the clothes closet and takes out a bundle of peasant clothes: linen trousers, high boots, a coat, a big felt hat, and a long wide leather belt studded with brass nails. The rabbi gets dressed. From his coat dangles the end of a heavy peasant rope.

The rabbi goes out, and the Litvak follows him.

On the way the rabbi stops in the kitchen, bends down, takes an axe from under the bed, puts it in his belt, and leaves the house. The Litvak trembles but continues to follow. . . .

The Litvak follows him into the forest where the rabbi chops down a small tree, cuts it into logs, ties the logs into a bundle, and carries the bundle back to town.

He stops at a back street beside a small broken-down shack and knocks at the window.

"Who is there?" asks a frightened voice. The Litvak recognizes it as the voice of a sick Jewish woman.

"I," answers the rabbi in the accent of a peasant.

"Who is I?"

Again the rabbi answers in Russian. "Vassil."

"Who is Vassil and what do you want?"

"I have wood to sell, very cheap." And, not waiting for the woman's reply, he goes into the house.

The Litvak steals in after him. In the gray light of early morning he sees a poor room with broken, miserable furnishings. A sick woman, wrapped in rags, lies on the bed. She complains bitterly, "Buy? How can I buy? Where will a poor widow get money?"

"I'll lend it to you," answers the supposed Vassil. "It's only six cents."

"And how will I ever pay you back?" asks the poor woman, groaning.

"Foolish one," says the rabbi reproachfully. "See, you are a poor sick Jew, and I am ready to trust you with a little wood. I am sure you'll pay. While you, you have such a great and mighty God and you don't trust him for six cents."

"And who'll kindle the fire?" asks the widow. "Have I the strength to get up? My son is at work."

"I'll kindle the fire," answers the rabbi.

As the rabbi put the wood into the oven he recited, in a groan, the first portion of the Penitential Prayers.

As he kindled the fire and the wood burned brightly, he recited a bit more joyously, the second portion of the Penitential Prayers. When the fire was set he recited the third portion, and then he shut the stove.

The Litvak, who saw all this, became a disciple of the rabbi.

And ever after, when another disciple tells how the rabbi of Nemirov ascends to heaven at the time of the Penitential Prayers, the Litvak does not laugh. He only adds quietly, "If not higher."[11]

Irving Howe and Eliezer Greenberg emphasize in the introduction to the collection of stories from which this tale was taken that Peretz focused on writing about "this-world saintliness,"[12] and "saintly" is a word that a number of people turn to when speaking of Maishe. But Beatrice Silcoff says it is the wrong word to use. She met Maishe in 1939 when she was nineteen years old. Now in her late sixties, she smokes incessantly and talks passionately about Maishe in a husky, deep-throated voice. Dressed entirely in black with red hair, plum-coloured nails, and a silver and gold rope necklace, she is a dramatic figure. Maishe, she says, became the grandfather she never had:

> We developed such a relationship. He could ask me to do anything because his sincerity and honesty were there at all times and his whole being was geared toward helping people — notwithstanding the fact that calling him a saint was nonsense.
>
> I thought he was a religious man, not in the [conventional] way of looking at things. . . . But in the broadest sense of the word "religion," he was a very religious person in the highest sense. . . .
>
> He never wanted to play the role of a leader because, first of all, his humility didn't permit him to be forceful [although] he could be forceful in other ways. And it wasn't a phony humility. It was a very sincere thing. He was a very, very honest individual and he had no patience with people who weren't honest. This was one of his fortes. . . .
>
> His whole philosophy of life was to help his fellow man. I can't think of any other way of putting it. It's simplistic, but it's true. Because he lived it, notwithstanding the odd time when he'd blow up or something. . . . He was a true idealist, a true humanitarian.

Time and again people paint the same picture of a man forever giving and never claiming credit. For instance, Israel Falk of Montreal, one of the prominent Bundists from the Old Country, remembers him as "a wonderful man, a wonderful character and that was why people came to him for all kinds of favours, because they knew he was always ready to help if he could help."

And there is Steve Perkal, also in Montreal, the retired secretary of the International Ladies Garment Workers' Union and manager of the Cloakmakers' Union, whom Maishe helped to immigrate in 1947 when he was thirty-three years old. He had fled eastward from the Nazis through Russia and Siberia to Japan, and when Japan joined the war, to Shanghai. "I was a recipient of his help. . . . He was a very simple man in the sense that he was very modest. He wouldn't let anyone tell him about his achievements, about the great things he was doing for people like me. . . . I kind of grew to make him my father confessor and adviser and what-not."

And Kalmen Kaplansky, seventy-four years old, who has had a distinguished career promoting civil rights. He says, "Most Jewish immigrants in those days . . . believed the world was divided between *menschen* and those who were not *menschen*. A *mensch* was a person who had concern for others, who was kind, who was given to good deeds, who felt that we can't live by bread alone. All these attributes were described by one word and it was *mensch*. Maishe was a *mensch* and he wanted to live like a *mensch*. For Maishe it meant things [beyond the usual good deeds to others]. Books to be read. Keeping up with what's going on in the world. It's a duty to know what's going on. . . . He read everything. He was well read. He was a very erudite person in a sense, you know."

But underlying Maishe's humility was the hard core of his beliefs. According to Kaplansky:

> He was a very realistic person, down-to-earth. Not one of those street-corner orators. But whenever he spoke, it was always A *fryeh velt, a nyeh velt, a yaisherdikeh velt, a velt foon gleichheit*. A free world, a new world, a world of justice, a world of equality. Other speakers would conclude their hour-and-a-half or two-hour speeches with this rousing vision of the world. But Maishe believed in that, you know, he really believed in that.
>
> He was not a fanatic. That's one thing about him. He was never fanatical. He just believed. . . .
>
> He was a proud man. He was no shrinking violet. He stood up for what he believed in.

...rg), sung
...ircle Choir,
May 1943[1]

T   ...nt — chief artery of Montreal's
J...   ...than fifty years, running northwest
fro...   ...ng so close to Mount Royal's east side
you can count   ...that burn out on its illuminated crucifix.
A person could ...   ...etime and never have to pass beyond. Here
were the butchers, t.. bakers and the delicatessens, the furniture shops,
drapers, ladies' boutiques and men's wear shops, the drugstores, the
fish stores, the jewellers and watch-repair shops, the bigger grocery
stores, the milliners and hatters, the hardware stores and corner garages,
the lawyers' offices, soda shops and restaurants, the pool halls and pawn
shops, the sporting goods and shoe stores, the odd bar. A noisy, jostling, old-time market square squeezed oblong until it fit a city street
and then lured into New World waywardness. Dusty in summer, slushy
in winter, lined with faded, graceless buildings tarted up with florid
invitations to sample BEST BARGAINS, FANTASTIC PRICES, DISCOUNTS!
DISCOUNTS! DISCOUNTS! A place to meet neighbours, to gossip.

"Something for all our appetites," was how Mordecai Richler saw
it during the forties in his book, *The Street*. "Across the street from
the synagogue you could see THE PICTURE THEY CLAIMED COULD
NEVER BE MADE. A little further down the street was the Workman's
Circle and, if you liked, a strip show. Peaches, Margo, Lili St. Cyr.
Around the corner there was the ritual baths, the shvitz or mikva,
where my grandfather and his cronies went before the High Holidays,
emerging boiling red from the highest reaches of the steam rooms to
happily flog each other with brushes fashioned out of pine tree

branches. Where supremely orthodox women went once a month to purify themselves."[2]

And on either side of The Main — to the east, St-Dominique, Coloniale, and a handful of lesser streets; to the west, Clark, St-Urbain, Waverly, Esplanade, and Jeanne Mance — were the crowded, working-class homes standing shoulder to shoulder in what would have been formidable stoicism had it not been for outside staircases to second floors, some curving, some straight, some wrought-iron, some wooden, some rusting, some painted, some peeling, but taken together, giving the streets a slightly roguish air, the way a slight tilt of the hat can change a sombre look into a rakish. And on each corner, says Richler, a grocery store and a fruit man — necessities in the days before refrigerators — and a cigar store.

This was the town within the town that Maishe Lewis immigrated to, a largely self-contained world that from 1921 to 1946 was concentrated in a one-mile radius from the Davis building of the YMHA at the corner of Avenue du Mont-Royal and rue Jeanne Mance, right by Fletcher's Field at the eastern edge of Mount Royal park and four blocks west of The Main.[3]

After the First World War, as times got better and people more well-to-do, the community shifted around the northern edge of Mount Royal to Outremont's gentle, tree-lined streets, completing a journey that had taken it from south of rue Ste-Catherine before the turn of the century, then up The Main centring on Duluth and Coloniale Avenues by 1911, Mount Royal and Esplanade Avenues by 1926, and Fairmount Avenue and Jeanne Mance by 1941.[4] A journey from poverty to prosperity. As Richler recalled it, "We were always being warned about The Main. Our grandparents and parents had come there by steerage from Romania or by cattleboat from Poland by way of Liverpool. No sooner had they unpacked their bundles and cardboard suitcases than they were planning a better, brighter life for us, the Canadian-born children. The Main, good enough for them, was not to be for us, and that they told us again and again was what the struggle was for."[5] They all had the same dream, Irving Layton said in one of his short stories: "to grow rich and move away to a better neighbourhood."[6]

There are a few monuments to the old Yiddish community that still remain along The Main. The odd store, the occasional snatch of Yiddish overheard on the street, and still standing at 4848 rue St-Laurent the Workmen's Circle building, now with Don Quixote and Sancho Panza on a maple leaf painted above the door. For twenty-one years it has been a centre for the Spanish community; immediately before that it was owned by Les Grands Ballets Canadiens. In the gymnasium upstairs, which used to echo to rousing speeches against capitalism and, during the Hitler years, to impassioned fund-raising rallies, the crash of flamenco dancing now resounds.

"We started building that building in 1930 with no money," says Faga Falk, born in 1906, a Bundist all her adult life, and now something of a matriarch among the Bundists who remain in Montreal:

> But . . . the people, the members of the Workmen's Circle contributed. Everybody gave a hundred dollars. At that time a hundred dollars was a lot of money. If they didn't have a hundred dollars they paid out every week five dollars. I remember my husband came home and he told me that he made a pledge for a hundred dollars . . . so I started to laugh. He says to me, "Why are you laughing?" I says, "Where are you going to get a hundred dollars?" So he says, "Where do we get the money for the food and to pay the rent? Whatever I make we will take off from the food and the rent five dollars every week and we'll pay our hundred dollars." And that's how we paid our hundred dollars.

When it was finished in 1934 the building was the pride of The Main, or more correctly, that part of The Main which was radical, non-Communist, non-religious, and emphatically working-class. It was the crowning symbol of twenty-seven years of activity: the first Workmen's Circle branch had opened in Montreal in 1907.[7]

The Workmen's Circle became Maishe's synagogue. He went there every night. It was always within walking distance of wherever they were living. Doris remembers that he even went there on religious holidays: "The religious people went to the synagogue on the Day of Atonement; my father went to the Workmen's Circle. And he met some of his comrades there. And he felt just as good a Jew as the ones who went to the synagogue. Definitely."

There were discussions about politics. Always. And the odd game of cards. And there was the business of the club: it operated a soup kitchen during the depression; it administered what was called the Workmen's Circle Loan Syndicate in which members could buy shares and from which they could borrow money; through individual branches it maintained cemeteries for members; it allotted office space to various unions; it provided relief to the needy. It had a medical plan that provided a doctor's services to members who paid a premium; it had a group insurance plan; it brought in speakers from New York and elsewhere; it held rallies and workshops and open forums and discussion groups; it had a sixty-voice choir; it raised money for various causes, especially labour causes; it contributed to strikes; it put on dinners and teas; it got involved in election campaigns, assisting the CCF; it was the home of the Farbund, the Yiddish-speaking socialist organization; it staged plays and concerts; and it began a youth section that in six years blossomed from a membership of 430 to about 3,500.[8]

For its sons and daughters it followed the pattern of "such successful capitalist youth organizations as the Community Centres, YMCAs and YMHAs" said J.L. Afros in a souvenir booklet published at the time the building was dedicated. "So we too, in the Young Circle League, have [resorted] to athletics, socials, dramatics and parties to attract and interest our youth. But whereas these activities, along with so-called 'character building' are the objectives of the various Ys and Community Centres, in the Young Circles League, the social, athletic, and dramatic activities are only a means of interesting the young people; our real purpose is to develop a consciousness of current social and political problems in our members, and to imbue them with a passion to work co-operatively for the elimination of capitalism and the substitution of Socialism."[9]

Listed prominently in the booklet were Doris Lewis, a member of the three-person Youth Committee and "Leader" of the Challengers Club, and the man she was later to marry, Andy Andrashnick (who was soon to change his name to Andras), a member of the Youth Committee and the person in charge of science activities for the Red Falcon Club No. 2 as well as a member of the executive committee of Labor Corner Branch 1018.

Youth sections organized baseball and hockey teams; they held sleigh rides, tobogganing parties, and ski outings; they sponsored tournaments for Ping-Pong, badminton, checkers, and boxing; there were dances and bowling; and always, there were lectures and debates on subjects such as The Origins of Superstition and Religion; Propaganda of the Movies; What Is Fascism?; Who Owns Canada?; Crime and Socialism; Spain Today; Resolved That Mercy Killing Should Be Established; and Resolved That an Education Is More Beneficial than Experience.[10]

In short, the Workmen's Circle was a temple to socialism, and this new building would be the altar. It even had a small second-storey balcony, built only for standing, directly above the front door; its builders must have had visions of fiery speakers rallying The Main from that tiny vantage point, urging on throngs of workers in the march to the socialist millennium.

The seven years since Maishe's arrival in Canada had been good. He was earning $37 a week at Eli's garment factory where he worked as a cutter, laying out patterns on a pile of material and then cutting through the pile. Maishe and Rose helped to cover expenses by having roomers — at one time a couple, at another a woman and her daughter. In those days roomers were the norm, not the exception, and there would be roomers through the thirties and forties — until Maishe and Rose became too ill to cope.

During those good years the children galloped through school. Doris and Charlie both skipped grades twice. For Doris, school was a treat since girls never got the same opportunities as boys in the Old Country. David, the eldest, did the eight years of public school in three but, as he recounted in his memoirs, not without an initial confrontation with Maishe. After his first few days in class, unable to speak the language and laughed at because he couldn't answer the simplest question, he decided to quit school and study English at night. "My parents listened patiently and sympathetically, but my father said no to my scheme. He put the counter-arguments carefully to show his respect for my reasoning. We argued back and forth for a long time while I became more and more obstinate and cried bitterly. Finally, my father called an end and deliberately slapped me across the face. This was the first time my father had hit me. Corporal punishment was against his principles, but I had left him with no alternative, so he left me with none. School it had to be."[11]

He bought a copy of Charles Dickens's novel *The Old Curiosity Shop*, a Yiddish-English dictionary, and several notebooks, and for more than a year he never went out to play. "Or almost never." It was straight home after school to do homework and then to plough word by word through *The Old Curiosity Shop*. By the fall of 1922 he was entering Grade Four with a vocabulary larger than most of his classmates and English that was on the way to becoming impeccable but with a distinct Welsh accent. One of the teachers at Fairmount Public School who spent extra time helping him learn English was Welsh, so he learned not only the language but an accent the traces of which would stay with him the rest of his life.

(One of the ways the accent showed up was in his pronunciation of New Democratic Party. For most Canadians it seems to come out "Noo Democradic Pardy." David enunciated every syllable. It came out crisply: "New De-mo-crat-ic Par-ty." Listen to Ed Broadbent pronounce the party name today. Or Gerry Caplan. Or Stephen. Or any number of other people. You'd swear David was speaking. The old Welshman must be grinning — wherever he is.)

By June 1924 David had graduated from Grade Eight, three years after arriving in Canada, and in the summer of 1927 he had finished the fourth year of senior school and graduated from Baron Byng High School.

In this breathless rush through public school, he was rarely out of doors, studying at the kitchen table while Rose tiptoed about her chores, "lifting pans and dishes with the noiseless care one bestows on expensive china,"[12] and, says Doris, helping his mother around the house, scrubbing floors and so on. Charlie was the one for outdoors. Even though he was eleven months younger than David, he was David's protector, always standing up for him in the street confrontations that are inevitable with young boys. "He was a terrific athlete," says Doris. "He was on the YMHA lacrosse team and they used to go to Caughnawaga and play the Indian team, and every time he came home he had a wound in a different spot, and my mother would just, you know, faint. He had scars, several scars. I remember he had a big one on his forehead. . . . And David was not athletic at all. Never was. He could barely swim. I don't know if he swam at all."

Fay Ain, or as she then was, Fay Mletchkovitch (which her parents shortened to Mars), used to love going over to the Lewises because of the warmth of the family: "Mr. Lewis used to cuddle Doris, and I used to see that and I thought my father was warm on the inside but he'd never show emotion on the outside, and I used to sit there and say, 'Oh, if this man could be my father.' I worshipped him because he was all the things I ever dreamed of in a father. The relationship between Doris and her father was very, very close."

And on Friday nights especially, and often on Saturday and Sunday nights, members of the family would drop in — Max and Fanny; and Zebullum, who remained single and immigrated in the mid-twenties; Ida, the youngest, who immigrated in 1925 and married Harry Kula in Canada; and Sarah who arrived in 1927, the last of the family to immigrate, and her husband Abraham Krashinsky. Occasionally they'd be joined by others such as Fay and sometimes Kayleh Ain, who wrote a memoir of Svisloch, and her husband Herschel. The small flat would be filled with adults and children and the contented buzz of familiar conversations, and Rose would make tea and put out whatever she had baked for the weekend. "She baked every Friday, as most Jewish mothers did," Doris recalls. Maishe would hold the centre of attention, telling stories or talking about politics. "It was always fascinating," says Fay. "He held me spellbound."

Maishe became a member of the Amalgamated Clothing Workers of America shortly after he arrived, and before long he was invited to take an active leadership role. It was a natural turn of events: he had obvious organizing skills; he was a committed socialist; he was intelligent, well read, personable, and tough enough when need be. But he refused. He turned down the invitation even though he probably knew, as Doris speculated years later, that it would have opened the way to a much more secure life and would have provided the opportunity to play a far more prominent role in public affairs.

So why did he turn it down? According to Doris: "He refused because he didn't like the look of the Canadian or American trade union movement. It wasn't idealistic to him. It wasn't as socialist as he thought it should be. I remember his talking about it . . . it was a mistake, you know. He would have had a much easier life with a better income, and maybe not even have had his heart attack. I don't know. But he thought very strongly about that. He didn't want to, and he was wrong. There was a lot of the trade union movement that was good and idealistic. But it didn't appeal to him and he decided not to enter [it] as an activist."

Whatever idealism existed in mainstream unions in the 1920s, it was much less politically focused than what Maishe had been used to. The Bund in Russia was a working political party as well as a labour movement. It had always drawn a line between unions preoccupied with economic self-interest and those dedicated to altering the system. Always it tried to focus on the cause, not the symptom, and if pay was low and working conditions were harsh, fighting for higher wages and better conditions was only a step in the battle to change the political and economic system that produced them in the first place.

The primary goal was to liberate workers. It was to revolutionize society. That would put an end to exploitation for everyone, not just the members of one union. Business unionists, as Bundists called the mainstream union members, were basically self-centred and selfish, and if they succeeded in their objectives they would become an adjunct to the bourgeoisie and be equally reactionary.

There were some radical and politically committed union movements in Canada, such as the remnants of One Big Union in the West; but the conservative legacy of Sam Gompers, who reigned over the American Federation of Labor (AFL) for thirty-seven years until his retirement in 1924, extended across the border to many of the international unions. That legacy called for no political affiliation, no radicalism, and concentration on economic goals — all epitomized in his famous slogan that glorified a non-philosophical, ad-hoc approach to problems: "Reward your friends and punish your enemies." It was an approach that had some practical usefulness in the United States where individual congressmen could vote as they pleased. But in Canada, with its parliamentary system and strict party discipline, it made much less sense. Individual members of Parliament might be friendly but they had to abide by party policy. You could reward them all you wanted, but if party policy dictated that they vote against you, they voted against you.

The Amalgamated Clothing Workers was more activist than many of the craft unions in the AFL, and in 1935 would break away to help found the Congress of Industrial Unions (CIO), in 1923. But it was a far cry indeed from the Bund.

However, there was more to it than that. Maishe wasn't longing for a transplanted Russia in Canada. He was fully aware that it was a land of different traditions, different structures, different ways of doing things. Probably a combination of things were at work. Decisions rarely are one-dimensional. More often, they're spooned from a mixture of rational and irrational, compatible and incompatible, weighty and trivial.

Maishe was out of step with this New World. He had spent a lifetime in an emotional and intellectual war zone with the enemy plainly in sight; here the enemy was more vapourish, seducing with glitter instead of threatening with truncheons. His home had been a village; this was a bulging metropolis and the metropolis had bold, staccato ways. Here his culture, his Jewishness, was under siege from the Lorelei of North American culture, and it was more menacing than assimilationist policies in the Pale had ever been. In Svisloch he had worked as a tanner for seventeen years and was an experienced and valued employee; here he was working at a new trade in which he was adequate but without flair. On top of everything else, he still carried some sense of loss for having left the battle back home.

There is no denying that by emigrating he sacrificed much. Although no one recalls him ever complaining, he must have missed greatly being at the centre of the Bund's activities in Poland. But on the other hand, seeing David weld the CCF into North America's only successful socialist party gave him boundless pleasure. As a Bundist he was an internationalist, and to him it was supremely important that the ideals of the Bund should take root in North America, if not through him, then through his son. And indeed, through David they did take root. Had Maishe not come to Canada, would the CCF have survived with no David Lewis to guide and shape it? Walter Young, whose book *The Anatomy of a Party* is the most authoritative history of the CCF, claims that "unquestionably, without Lewis the party would not have maintained and developed its contact with labour. Indeed, it is not an exaggeration to say that without Lewis the party might have subsided into nothingness altogether during the dark days of 1945, if not before."[13]

Donald MacDonald, former leader of the Ontario party, won't go as far as Young. He says it weakens the point to say that the CCF might have collapsed without David. The reality is that David "was the main force in holding the party together. He . . . was the main architect of the party. . . . He shaped its sense of direction."

But all Maishe's pride could never fill up the void of knowing that his days in the thick of political action were over. Still, he was a Bundist and as always, at every level, there was much to be done. Bundists from Eastern Europe, says Irving Howe in *The World of Our Fathers*,

> . . . played a vital role in the immigrant community. They grasped, better than anyone else, that the problems of the immigrant Jewish working class were not merely the problems of organization but, still more, of morale. They grasped that it was necessary to forge a Jewish working class that would have a sense of its own worth. Too many Jewish workers still lived under the sign of fear, too many still bore the stigma of shtetl passivity, too many still thought of self-exploitation as a strategy for escaping exploitation. The Bundists understood that they had to confront a major problem in collective self-regard.[14]

Many of them confronted it through unions, says Howe, especially in the garment industries, winning victories that were "not merely for workers who happened to be Jews but for *Jewish* workers."

Maishe chose to do it by helping immigrants in their private lives. Sixty-three years later his grandson, Stephen's brother Michael, would make much the same kind of decision, eschewing a high-profile, public role to work more closely with workers on the street — and he would make that decision not knowing of the choice his grandfather had made.

Maishe spent the rest of his days helping immigrants, initially in his spare time and finally in a full-time job. First he became president of his *landsmanshaft*, a society of immigrants from the district of Grodno, his region of Russia. It was organized about the same time that he received the offer from the Amalgamated Clothing Workers. It took up a lot of his time, says Doris. *Landsmanshaftn* were welcoming committees; centres for aid, advice, and assistance; introduction services; counselling agencies; burial societies; social clubs; co-ops for handling medical expenses and sometimes life insurance; job placement centres — organizations that by and large fell under the heading of benevolent societies. Except they were also something at once more intangible but in many ways more important: an emotional sheet anchor for people who were leaping, not just from one culture to another, but in most cases from one era to another. From shtetls still stumbling out of the nineteenth century to the hustling downtown of a busy North American city in the turbulent twenties.

In 1928 Maishe joined Branch 151 of the Workmen's Circle,[15] the one that was established in 1907 and now bears his name, the Maishe Lewis Branch. The *Arbeiter Ring*, as it was called in Yiddish, had branches across North America. It was like an infinitely bigger *landsmanshaft* with the added dimension of socialist fervour. "They used to call themselves the left cross of the labour movement," says Kalmen Kaplansky. Born in 1912, Kaplansky is scrappy and surprisingly agile, with the sturdiness of a welterweight. His pure white hair is combed straight back and when he speaks he stares directly at his listener, poised combatively. A verbal counterpuncher. He arrived in Canada from Bialystok in 1929 and after the Second World War became executive secretary of the Jewish Labour Committee in Montreal, where he led the committee's initiatives in the field of human rights over the next three decades. "Left cross of the labour movement is a little exaggerated," he says, but there was always labour political action of some sort going on.

There was even a Workmen's Circle school for children to attend after normal school hours, he says, and, "they had an ongoing lecturing program [that] would attract several hundred people. . . . I knew many people who, after they came home for supper would walk for fifteen or twenty minutes to the Workmen's Circle and spend the rest of the evening there. Fight, argue, insult each other, you know, like all meetings. . . . But they enjoyed every bit of it. It was their environment. Their ambience. It was, in Yiddish, very *svide*. You lived on that. That's where you met, you got married, you brought your children. It was a very important fraternal organization."

From his first day with the Workmen's Circle, Maishe held what were called open forums for immigrants and for students. Joe Ain, the semi-retired millionaire partner in the firm of Montreal developers Ain and Zakuta Ltd., attended Maishe's lectures in 1930 which at that time were held in rented rooms above a restaurant: "We were about eight or ten or twelve in class, I forget now," says Ain. "Kids about seventeen, eighteen, nineteen, and he would lecture to us about Yiddish literature, about the socialist movement, a little bit of Jewish history, a little bit of politics, about the working-class movements. I didn't attend it for too long because . . . I wanted to learn English."

It would no more occur to Maishe to hold open forums in English in Montreal than it would occur to him to hold them in Russian in Russia. Knowing, understanding, and maintaining Jewish culture was just as important in Canada as it was in the Old Country. He continued the open forums into the late forties until he became too sick to continue.

There were other competing attractions as well. In the late thirties, "To be honest with you," says Bea Silcoff, "I always resented the fact that the Communists were smarter than the socialists in getting youngsters in because they used to have dances and so on."

The Communist youth club dances, it seems, were more frequent and less restrictive than those of the Workmen's Circle. Usually the gym at the Workmen's Circle wasn't available for big dances because dancing left black scuff marks on the floor. That, for the older guard, was a cardinal sin. Maishe was always fighting to get permission for kids to use the gym, says Bea. "He had a feeling for kids." But to little avail.

So his efforts were beset at every side: by the siren calls of the new world, by Communists on the left who, regardless of everything else, constantly proved themselves very able organizers, and on the right by the old guard. "They were the . . . nineteen-fivers," says Kaplansky. "still living in that 1905 tradition. You couldn't tell them anything."

"He used to tell them, 'You're out of date,'" says Doris. "'You're living in Canada now, you know. Change your approach.' . . . But they didn't agree with him. There was no animosity or anything. They just thought they were doing the right thing."

Before the Second World War there were very few Bundists in Montreal, probably no more than twenty-five.[16] With the wave of immigration after the war, the number rose to about 250.[17]

However, even if there were twenty-five before the war it's unlikely that there were any like Maishe, says David Rome, historian emeritus of the Canadian Jewish Congress archives. At best there would be only two or three. Although a Poale Zionist himself, Rome greatly admired Bundists and after the war used to attend their meetings out of interest and respect. He speculates that up until the mid-forties there were no other Bundists in Montreal at Maishe's level of moral commitment. To begin with, he says, think back to Eastern Europe:

> . . . to Warsaw in the 1920s. . . . You would have found . . . a class of persons which . . . was the most numerous . . . in Eastern European Jewry. I'm speaking . . . about the large society called the Bund. . . .
>
> Now not all [lived a life that was] the essence of [Bundist] ideology . . . just as, shall we say, not all Catholics are priests, not all priests are like St. Thomas Aquinas and not all St. Thomas Aquinases are like the Apostles or like Jesus. . . .
>
> Among the leadership of the Bund in Europe there were several people who were — and let me use this as a straight word — saintly people. Let's use the phrase "highly moral," with an excruciating kind of morality that [they] wanted to make sure was very, very perfect. . . .

> Now here a man comes from Eastern Europe. Ideologically and in
> his heart a full-fledged [Bundist] . . . and if he found five, six, eight,
> ten like him, he might form a . . . Bund committee in Montreal. But
> [before the war] there never was one because there were never enough
> of these people to form one. However, there was this peripheral group
> called the Workmen's Circle, where at least he could find other socialists.
>   He would be comfortable only with people like him, whom he didn't
> find many of. I don't have a list of Messrs. Anonymous. . . .

This man from Eastern Europe is how Rome reconstructs the Maishe
he never met but heard so much about. If he is anywhere near correct
in the image he has painted — and by all acounts he is, at the very
least, quite close — it is a portrait that for all the warmth of family
and friends, for all the joy that came in helping others, is tinged with
an enduring loneliness.

And that would be inconsolably deepened, given Rome's final assessment of the Bund after the Holocaust where "the word 'Bund' has
been wiped out of existence. . . . You have only a memory of the Bund
because [in Eastern Europe] they've been wiped out. So what you have
left are survivors, mourning remnants, without any mass or membership, no geographic area that can be the fulcrum of anything. They're
finished. There's no more Bund thinking. . . . And the legacy of the
Bund is zero. The nearest thing you have [aside from] a kind of nostalgia
. . . is what might possibly be passed on to grandchildren. Heritage,
an atmosphere, preferences, whatever you want to call it. That I don't
dismiss at all."

It's a harsh assessment, at first blush too harsh. But when you look
to see what remains in the forefront of contemporary affairs, it's close
to the mark. There are no institutions or parties carrying on Bundist
traditions. There are no prominent figures on the international stage.
No great Bundist centres of learning. No Bundist writers influencing
major events. No movement in the Jewish community with the Bundist
drive for parity of Jewish nationalism and international brotherhood.
There's not even much of a Jewish workers' movement left.

There are the Bund archives in New York. Some local organizations
have their own archives. There are small groups of Bundists here
and there. And in libraries there are the books — the histories,
treatises, discourses; the plays, poems, novels, stories. But, as Rome
says, these are remnants. There is nothing that is even a faint echo
of that dynamic, brawny organization that existed up to the Second
World War.

But the heritage, that sense of social justice, the identification with
workers, the focus on organization, the commitment to equality and

democratic procedures, the fierce anti-communism, the secular humanism, the multi-culturalism, the sense of international community, the anger with exploitation — in these things the genes of the Bund live on. What departed with the Bund was the revolutionary fervour, the absolute conviction that the only way to secure lasting advances was to rip out the existing system and replace it.

While David was still in public school, Maishe would take him to political meetings:

> In 1922 or 1923 I accompanied my father to a meeting held in the Monument National Theatre on The Main, south of St. Catherine. Mother refused to come because she was certain there would be trouble. To Father, trouble was a necessary ingredient in socialist activity. . . .
>
> The meeting was addressed by a well-known Jewish Menshevik [and Bundist] called Abramovitch. He had been a member of the Kerensky government and for a short time also a member of the Soviet government. . . .
>
> The theatre was packed to overflowing. Abramovitch was a very distinguished looking man, and he spoke like a prophet of old, his carefully trimmed grey beard bobbing in harmony with his indignant gestures. He spoke in Yiddish and held the audience spellbound. Suddenly there was an agonized shriek from the balcony, followed by a thud and a commotion as a number of people appeared to carry a woman to an exit. . . . This occurred at regular, brief intervals throughout the rest of the meeting. . . . These performances had been prepared and organized by the Communist Party to disrupt the meeting. . . .
>
> Abramovitch persisted for a very long time. Between bouts of noise he got many of his points across to the audience . . . and our anger with and contempt for the Communists grew. [18]

This was the decade when reform groups of all kinds — socialist, labour, Communist, union, farmers, religious — swarmed across the political landscape, eager to buck a system they didn't like. A time when none of them had ascendancy. When the rich were getting richer and the poor be damned. When emotions ran high and rhetoric higher.

It started off mean and ended up profligate. It began with war industries closed down, world-wide deflation, high prices, low wages, heavy unemployment, strikes and lockouts, a wheat glut, dust storms, grasshopper plagues, a bank failure — in a word, hard times. (See Appendix E.) In its last half, it was a glorious few years for the fast and the frantic — in the big cities where the factories were, in the mining towns and oil boom areas, for some great athletes, for dance halls, for flappers, for big bands. American money flooded in. (By 1925 about half of all investment was American.) Cosmetics and the movies had begun to remould reality. (In 1917 only two people in the United States earned enough from "beauty culture" to pay income taxes; by 1927, 18,000 did.[19]) For most workers it was a far cry from prosperity, but at least they could get a job and take care of a family — unless they happened to live in the Atlantic Provinces.

And then there was October 24, 1929. Black Thursday on the Winnipeg Grain Exchange. Wheat prices went through the floor and thousands of speculators were wiped out in just a few hours. Five days later came the Wall Street Crash.

This was the decade before the Regina Manifesto and the creation of the CCF.

This also was the decade still smarting from the Winnipeg General Strike, which culminated in Bloody Saturday, June 21, 1919, when Mounties, shooting randomly, charged into a crowd of peaceful demonstrators, leaving one person killed and thirty injured — including sixteen policemen. The strike, and the police action that would have done credit to Nicholas II, defined the enemy more graphically than any speech. For J.S. Woodworth it was a straight class conflict "essentially between the producers and the parasites."[20] It convinced those who wavered. It goaded those who were lagging. It inspired those who were committed. Across Canada it aroused "intense interest"[21] and set the mood on the Left for the next twenty years. (See Appendix F.)

In the scramble for prominence on the Canadian left, Communists and democratic socialists had battled ever since 1919 when Lenin convened the Third International of socialist parties or, as it became better known, the Communist International or the Comintern. Lenin saw the Comintern as playing Svengali to the world's radical left. But he realized that if the Comintern were to do that, he would have to prevent the kind of factionalism that had bedevilled the Russian Social Democratic Party. So he called for a "rupture" in the socialist movement that would create a clear division between revolutionary communism and social reformism — by which he meant democratic socialists. Communists, said Lenin, must engage in ceaseless ideological warfare against social reformism. Reformists, he said, were "the principal social bulwark of the bourgeoisie."[22]

So the tactics of disruption that young David encountered in the Abramovitch meeting were not new. They simply had intensified and become part of a coherent plan of attack over the past couple of years.

However, Lenin was not long for the world. Barely was the Comintern established than, in May 1922, he had his first stroke and by January 1924 he was dead and Stalin was firmly pushing Trotsky aside. That meant the Comintern would end up being governed not by

Trotsky's more flexible theories of permanent revolution but by Stalin's theories of "socialism in one country" and his malevolent dictatorship. (See Appendix G.)

In practical terms, it meant that for a time in the early twenties when the Comintern was still largely under the influence of the Russian Communist Party and not the Politburo, it was outward-looking — giving active support to the Chinese Communists in 1922 and making an abortive attempt to encourage revolution in Germany in 1923. But with Stalin's growing strength, Comintern policy became parochial. Stalin, unlike Lenin and Trotsky, had never lived abroad — his roots were in a backward part of what, at the turn of the century, was a backward country — and it showed. It was a disastrous approach for the Comintern, and forced the Communist Party of Canada to flip and flop time and again, usually incoherently.

Nevertheless, what the urgings of Lenin and Stalin did in Canada was to heat up the struggle on the left.

Over the years Communists were elected to city councils and to provincial legislatures. But none made it to the House of Commons until the 1940s, and that irked them no end because Woodsworth was there, elected as MP for Centre Winnipeg and member of the Independent Labour Party. As such, he had a stature and a national presence far outstripping that of anyone they had. He was "one of the most dangerous elements in the working class," fumed Communist leader John MacDonald in 1929. ". . . a large number of workers look upon him as a real champion of the workers."[23]

Caught in the midst of all this turbulence was Montreal's Jewish community — Quebec's third solitude. French Montreal and Quebec as a whole were cool to socialists. The Church saw them as an extension of anti-religious Bolshevism. But in Montreal's Jewish section there were 51,000 Jewish immigrants who had arrived between 1901 and 1931, many of them, like Maishe, left-leaning, most of them workers, a good proportion of them class-conscious, all attuned to English-language North America — prime recruits for a socialist struggle. And within the Jewish community there was the Workmen's Circle, home to Jewish socialists, an ideal target for takeover or, failing that, for forcing a "rupture" that would create the clear division that Lenin wanted between revolutionary Communists and social reformism.

The tactics were familiar. Lenin had used them repeatedly: do everything that will assist your supporters; do anything that will disrupt your opponents — and never sleep.

Among potential supporters it meant working tirelessly to gain better working conditions on shop floors, assiduously recruiting anyone with the slightest grievance, getting supporters into influential positions in key organizations, holding demonstrations and meetings, publishing political tracts, sponsoring cultural events, organizing help for the disadvantaged, holding social and athletic events for teenagers. In short, working without stop to educate, organize, and confront.

Among opponents it meant disrupting meetings if that was the only way to prevent opposition gains, dragging out meetings until people who had to work the next morning went home and then passing resolutions supporting Communist positions, shouting down opposition speakers if need be, being reasonable if it served your ends, otherwise being obstructionist, and hammering away relentlessly, endlessly, until the opposition began to crumble out of sheer weariness.

It was a potent mixture. In 1926 the Communists forced a split in the Workmen's Circle from which it didn't recover for fifteen years.

The battle in Montreal was only part of a continental attack on Workmen's Circles that lasted from 1921 until 1930.[24] It began in earnest with the formation of the Communist Party of Canada, which was clandestine at the time, in May and early June of 1921; its public arm, the Workers' Party of Canada, formed in February 1922, and its U.S. counterpart, the Workers (Communist) Party, formed in New York in the last week of December 1921.[25] Workmen's Circles weren't the only targets, of course. Equally in the Communists' sights were the garment trade unions.

Initially Communists made little headway because Workmen's Circles already were friendly to the Soviet Union and it was difficult to paint them as reactionary. The headquarters in New York had cabled congratulations to Kerensky in February 1917; it had called for the removal of the blockade of the Soviet Union in 1919; during the famine of 1921 it provided relief to Jewish communities in the Volga region; and to celebrate the fifth anniversary of the revolution it had raised money to establish a hospital in the Russian town of Gomel.[26]

But by the time of the Twenty-Third Congress of Workmen's Circles in Toronto in early May 1922, battle lines had been drawn. Branches were polarized into Left Wingers (the Communists) and Right Wingers, and the Left Wingers were harassing the generally Right Wing leaderships. At the Congress, delegates voted 111 to 26, with 22 not voting, to warn Left Wingers against creating parallel committees within branches "with the objective of capturing the Workmen's Circle."[27]

The Left Wingers paid no heed, and later that year the National Executive Committee in New York "warned against the attempt to create a status in stato, an organization within an organization."[28] Still, the Left Wingers persisted and at its Silver Jubilee Convention

in May 1925 Workmen's Circle delegates passed a "discipline resolution" by a vote of 834 to 171 authorizing the National Executive Committee to expel Left Wingers if necessary to stop what the convention
saw as subversion.[29]

The only effect of the "discipline resolution" on the Left Wingers
was to goad them into calling a "national protest conference" in January
1926 that resulted in a clamorous demonstration in front of the order's
national office in New York. That did it. The National Executive Committee disbanded sixty-four branches and the Left Wingers retaliated
by seizing twenty New York Workmen's Circle schools whose school
boards they controlled, as well as a summer camp whose management
they controlled.

In Montreal the Left Wingers departed the Workmen's Circle with
nothing. "They couldn't take anything along with them because they
were a minority in the organization," says Norman Massey, born in
Lodz, Poland, in 1908 and until 1984 a member of the Communist
Party. He left the party because of the "anti-Semitic policies" of the
Soviet Union. Massey is his "pen name," he says. His real name is
Noah Puterman. "We formed the Canadian Labour Circle, bought
our own cemetery, and rented our own hall. . . . We had to build from
scratch."

Left Wing opposition in the Workmen's Circle arose, he said, because
". . . of changes in the world situation. The Russian Revolution. Most
of our members came from Eastern Europe. Many of our members
were friends of the revolution. They were for the revolution. . . . The
leadership was against. They were Mensheviks. Social Democrats. And
they didn't want to tolerate members who were for the revolution and
that's why they expelled entire branches."

In Toronto the expelled Left Wingers formed the Labour League,
and in April of 1945 the Montreal and Toronto organizations united
with similar groups in Winnipeg, Vancouver, and Hamilton to form
the United Jewish People's Order.[30]

Massey is genial and articulate — and personable. But occasionally
the glint of a hard edge flickers through his conversation. After the
split, relations were "not very friendly," he says:

> We didn't fight. We didn't go around with knives in our pockets. We
> carried on extensive cultural activities. We had every week lectures from
> prominent people from the States, mostly in Yiddish — 80 percent of
> the Jewish people were Yiddish-speaking in those days — and also in
> English. The Workmen's Circle were in their own shell with their pro-
> gram of hatred against the Soviet Union and hatred against the

Communists. . . . [The Abramovitch lecture] we interrupted not because
he was a member of the Workmen's Circle but because he represented
the Mensheviks and the enemies of the Bolshevik revolution. He was,
if I'm not mistaken, a minister in the Kerensky government. . . . They
[the Workmen's Circle] were always against the Communists, but we
weren't always fighting because they weren't much of a voice during
the depression. The people weren't following them very much.

With the split the Communists "almost broke the Workmen's Circle
that time," says Arnold Greenfield, for seventeen years recording
secretary and for another five years financial secretary of the Montreal
branch to which Maishe belonged. "There were fights, you know. . . .
They wanted everything. It took us years and years to build back what
we'd lost. The members. It was different afterwards. Some of them,
not all of them, but some of them came back."

In fact, it was only with the surge of immigrants after the Second
World War that the Workmen's Circle in Montreal fully recovered
its membership.

What happened with the split was that instead of the struggles continuing internally, they continued externally — between the Workmen's
Circle and the Canadian Labour Circle and its counterparts elsewhere
in the country — in print, in demonstrations, in recruiting, in heckl-
ing and disruptions at meetings, in election campaigns.

Maishe's chosen battlefield was not the public auditorium. Not the
speaker's platform nor the heckler's barbs. It was the field of quiet persuasion — within his union, among new immigrants he was trying to
help, in his *landsmanshaft*, which, like any other immigrant organization, was a target for Communist takeover, and finally as a member
of the Workmen's Circle. He talked to the unsure. Explained.
Reassured. Swayed with his logic. He was trading on eighteen years
of fighting Communists in Svisloch, and the Montreal variety were
not all that different. Most were from the Old Country in any event.
Where they hammered, he exposed. Where they recruited, he interced-
ed. Where they denigrated, he upheld. Where they accused "reformists"
of betraying the socialist cause he talked about Communists betraying democracy.

"Mr. Lewis was a socialist that came from the other side," says Steve
Perkal, a Bundist originally from Poland. "The fantastic thing about
these people is that their devotion was so great that all through the
years, from the twenties when he came here to Canada until the forties when we started coming in, they kept the faith in the things that
they were doing. Communism was the enemy that destroyed the

socialist dream. Erlich and Alter were not the only ones that were killed by the Communists. I remember as a youngster the pain that we went through, we were so close to the [Stalinist] purges."

In the twenties and thirties the issues were not nearly as clear-etched as they are today. No one realized how deep in the blood of his country Stalin was wading. The very occasional journalist, such as Malcolm Muggeridge, gained an inkling. But prominent people such as Beatrice and Sidney Webb, weaned to the Soviet cause in the mid-thirties to the point of publishing *Soviet Communism: a new civilization?*, kept rattling on about the marvels of the great experiment, oblivious to mounting atrocities. It took the Khrushchev revelations of 1956 to confirm Stalin's "ethnishcidal" frenzies[31] and to put an end to the debate, still lingering from pre-war years, that, however stern the measures, they were necessary to preserve an infant revolution from sabotage by capitalism.

The left was thronged with people who refused to let their faith in the revolution die. Given the hard times of the depression, the unsympathetic face of capitalism, and conflicting and confusing reports of what was going on in the Soviet Union, it was small wonder that the issues were clouded. According to Massey, most of the Left Wingers were not out-and-out Communists: "As a matter of fact, 90 percent of the Canadian Labour Circle were not Communist. They were left-wing-minded, but they were not members of the party. They followed some of the lines of the Communists but not all along the line."

Maishe, having barely escaped with his life from the Bolsheviks, had no illusions about the nature of the Soviet regime. He was forever trying to dispel uncertainties.

"Raisel," he would say some nights, "if they should be so eager to see as to believe, then we might get somewhere." It was a never-ending struggle.

The struggle with left-of-left was one that David would continue through most of his adult life. It was one that Stephen would engage in with the Waffle in Ontario. In fact, the parallels between the Left Wingers' attempts to set up an organization within an organization in the Workmen's Circle and the Waffle's attempt to do the same thing within the NDP — with the same results — is striking. The Waffle wasn't Communist, although there was a sprinkling of Marxist-Leninists and Maoists and Trotskyites among its members. But it certainly was a faction of "Left Wingers."

•CHAPTER ELEVEN•

Democracy . . . is something we want badly and have not got. To get it, we must expand our present freedom to include economic and social democracy.
David Lewis and Frank Scott,
Make This YOUR Canada[1]

The year 1932 should have been just about the best of Maishe's life. David had won a Rhodes scholarship. Doris had graduated from the Montreal Commercial High School and, at age eighteen and in the midst of the depression, had managed to get a job as a bookkeeper. Charlie, who worried Maishe because he didn't seem settled, had begun his first job as a novice designer with a clothing manufacturer after a brief stint as a cutter — and a good thing, too, because Maishe had moved Doris out of her tiny bedroom at the back of the flat so that he could put in a large table and hire a man to teach Charlie designing.

Maishe himself was earning $37 a week, and even though there were reduced hours at Eli's clothing factory, at last he and Rose had a tidy sum in the bank which gave them the first real sense of security they'd had. What's more, he was chairman of the City Committee at the Workmen's Circle, which was the central decision-making and co-ordinating committee. ("He was very active and very respected," says Norman Neslen, a former member now living in Toronto. "He devoted most of his time to it. He was always in touch with the general office in New York.") And the new Workmen's Circle building was coming along nicely.

But then his world collapsed. In late September, two months after David sailed for Europe and Oxford University, he had a massive heart attack on the cutting-room floor of the factory. Doris and Rose were there when they brought him home on a stretcher ashen and barely able to whisper.

"Oh, Maishke. Maishske. Don't talk. Don't try, my Maishke," Rose kept repeating, almost crooning, as she got him to bed.

For almost four months Maishe lay there and when at last he could get up, he discovered the attack had left him so weakened he would never be able to return to the garment trade.

He was forty-four years old. Middle-aged and disabled in the middle of the depression. He went looking for jobs but it was hopeless. Even old acquaintances turned him away and their embarrassment pained him because he realized they had nothing to offer. No one had anything to offer. Writing of that time, Irving Layton remembered walking down The Main, "or one of the streets just east of it and you feel the terrible Depression in your bones and marrow. You feel the hopelessness and pain, the bewilderment and panic. The gilt put on during the boom years had rubbed off. From storefronts and houses, from the sidewalks and asphalted streets, the shine was peeling away. Everywhere, there was evidence of decay, plain as the bare wood from which the paint has been scaled off. . . . Soon, the neighbourhood became dotted with soup kitchens and columns of people lining up to receive their daily meal."[2]

Early in the Spring of 1933, when he had gathered sufficient strength, Maishe opened a small concession booth selling pop, fruit, and sandwiches in an old building on rue Notre Dame near the foot of The Main. "I used to run down on my lunch hour and help him make the sandwiches and gather the empty bottles and then run back to the office," says Doris. "He couldn't bend under machines to pick up the empties. It's all a penny business, you know, so all the empties were money. He'd close up about four or five in the afternoon.

"We were unusually close. Any help I could ever be . . . ," she pauses and swallows. "I loved him. He was a nice, nice person. He wasn't just a father to me, you know. He was just a really nice individual."

Maishe kept his booth going for about three years. He didn't earn enough to make ends meet, but with help from Doris and income from roomers, they got by.

> I helped out in a way that the boys never knew what was happening [says Doris]. I would give my mother my pay, whether I earned $10 a week or $20 a week — by the time I stopped [when she married in November 1936] I was earning the magnificent sum of $25 a week.
>
> If I needed a skirt, I would ask my mother for the money and I would go and buy it. My parents never asked me for it. I never felt that my parents were starving and I was giving them the money to live on. . . . There was always food on the table and always the house was clean. I gave it to them and they thought it was theirs to use.

Later on in life, when my father had no earning power, David contributed some. Neither of us contributed big sums.

These were anxious years. They marked not only the depths of the depression; they were the years when Hitler was coming to power in Germany. In January 1933 he became chancellor of the Republic. In February the Reichstag burned to the ground and Hitler blamed the Communists. In March he headed a coalition government following elections that left him just short of a majority. Immediately the coalition was formed, he engineered passage of the Enabling Act, which gave his government power to issue decrees independently of the Reichstag and of the president, Field Marshal General Paul von Hindenburg. In April Jews were dismissed from government jobs, from universities, from museums, from academies, even from private employment. Lawyers and doctors were allowed to practise only in proportion to Jewish populations. In May trade unions were suppressed and, shortly after, so were all political parties except the National Socialists (Nazis). Joseph Goebbels became minister of public enlightenment and propaganda. Hermann Göring replaced former chancellor Franz von Papen as commissioner for Prussia. Virulent newspaper campaigns against Jews were unleashed. The first concentration camps were established in Germany. By the new year about 70,000 Jews had fled and Germany was thoroughly en route to a dictatorship.

A year and a half later, in September 1935, the Nürnberg Laws were proclaimed, stripping Jews of their civil rights and forbidding marriages between Jews and "true" Germans. And then came the pogrom of November 9–10, 1938, when the SS confiscated the majority of Jewish property and confined surviving Jews to ghettos. Jewish refugees flooded into Palestine, bringing its Jewish population to almost 500,000 by the end of 1939 from about 60,000 at the time of the Balfour Declaration in 1917.[3] Then came the war, the mass rounding up of Jews, and finally the death camps.

In New York, late in 1933, a group mainly of labour leaders from the needle trades and activists from the Workmen's Circle who were alarmed at Hitler's progress, formed the Jewish Labour Committee "to combat the menace of Hitlerism, Facism and Anti-Semitism" and "to waken the consciousness of the labour movement generally to the growing threat to humanity resulting from the rise of Hitlerism abroad and his Fifth Column on this Continent."[4]

In 1936 a Montreal "division" was established and Maishe was offered the job of secretary.[5] First, he talked it over with Rose. The pay was only $8 a week — not enough, by itself, to live on. But neither of them had the slightest doubt that he should accept.[6] At last he could pack away his booth. No more selling sandwiches. No more scouting for empty pop bottles.

Instead, there was digging out the real story in Europe. Helping to smuggle aid through underground channels to European Jews. Sketching the venomous face of Hitler's National Socialists to Canadian audiences. Wrestling with reluctant Canadian authorities to allow just one more Jewish refugee into the country. And beating the bushes for money. That was the committee's job. Most of the money went to the New York headquarters, which was the conduit to Europe. It was a conduit that remained during the war. As soon as the war began, the committee in New York,

> organized an international coordinating committee of the labor underground, comprised of representatives of labor and social democratic groups in countries that had been overrun by the Nazis. . . .
>
> The Jewish Labor Committee was uniquely equipped to undertake this dangerous but vital effort. David Dubinsky (head of the International Ladies' Garment Workers' Union), Sidney Hillman (head of the Amalgamated Clothing Workers of America), B. Charney-Vladeck (president of the Yiddish-language Jewish Daily Forward, one-time New York City alderman and Socialist Party leader), and Joseph Baskin (of the Workmen's Circle in New York) had each been associated with the Jewish socialist movement in Poland — the Bund; each had fled repression in Eastern Europe. Their organizations had maintained links to labor and socialist movements of Europe through international labor and social democratic confederations. . . ."[7]

Writing about the Nazi occupation of Poland, Emanuel Scherer says that it was "quite natural" for the Bund to be the first to organize an underground Jewish movement. "The Bund's cherished tradition of clandestine work in Tsarist Russia was an invaluable experience for the revival of underground struggle. . . . Subsequently, other political parties, particularly various Zionist groups and, after 1941, the Communists, also joined the ranks of the underground movement."[8]

However, so profoundly did Bundists still believe that it was wrong and selfish to leave the struggle for human rights that they stayed in Eastern Europe even in the face of Hitler's march toward war and his unequivocal hatred for Jews.

"The Bundist ideology of 'Doykeyt,' poorly translated as 'hereness,' emphasized the right of Jews to full equality and cultural autonomy in their country of residence," says a Jewish Labour Committee publication. "Consequently, the JLC opposed emigration and sought to stem anti-Semitism as it did in Poland, for example, by supporting the Bund's struggles during 1937–1939. Only the advent of World War II and the obvious danger it represented to Polish Jewry, reversed the JLC's stance. During the war, it became the primary advocate for loosening the U.S.'s [and Canada's] tight quotas for entry."⁹

The Jewish Labour Committee and the Bund also helped Jews escape — sometimes, as was the case with Steve Perkal, by helping him to flee eastward through the Soviet Union to the Pacific. Perkal managed to work his way from Poland to Vilna in late 1940 where the committee provided him with money to travel to Japan early in 1941. "There was someone in Vilna that had money and wanted to send it to America. And the Jewish Labour Committee wanted to send money to Vilna. So there was an exchange." The committee invested money in New York in the name of the person living in Vilna, and the person living in Vilna gave the equivalent amount to Perkal and other refugees. "I understand that it was a very high-risk operation. But it was managed over a period of many months and a large group of people, I don't know exactly how many but there must have been more than a hundred people in our group that managed to survive this way."

There was nothing that Maishe could have turned to that would have been more fulfilling. This was the Bund as it should be, at the forefront, leading the struggle.

Finally, after fifteen years in Canada, he felt at home.

And to his everlasting pride, David, by then working for the CCF, was able to use his contacts on Parliament Hill to assist the committee, especially in helping refugees get around Ottawa's immigration barriers.

For David, those fifteen years had been a time of single-mindedly crafting his political skills. Day by day. Reflex by reflex. Subject by subject. He never questioned the commitment he brought to Canada. His most formative years had been spent in the hurricane's eye of revolution and war. Endless political discussions around the kitchen table in Svisloch had convinced him of the need to "ride the whirlwind and direct the storm."¹⁰ Until David left Canada for Oxford, his father remained an inspiration.

H. Carl Goldenberg, former senator and arbitrator extraordinaire, knew David as a student at McGill University in Montreal. In fact, he seems to have known just about everybody at one time or another. He's like a plump bantam rooster — he's got the size, the energy, the pride . . . except he's also a shade puckish. The world might have been constructed of foibles mainly for his gentle amusement. Perhaps that comes from years on labour arbitrations and royal commissions. His

Sherlock Holmes pipe, clamped straight ahead, never leaves his mouth except as a stage prop to stab home a point. In three and a half hours he relights it twice. Most of the time it's dead. His book-lined library has copies of what appears to be every book written on contemporary Canadian politics, all signed by the authors, and his political credo is probably best summed up by the four busts spread evenly about his library: John F. Kennedy, Franklin Delano Roosevelt, Abraham Lincoln, and Stephen Leacock. "David and I were both active in the mock parliament," he says. "I was a Liberal and he was Labour. We had some pretty tough debates. . . . He was always extremely eloquent. One of the most articulate speakers. . . . His father had a great influence on him. He'd say, 'My father told me this,' or 'My father told me that.' He had a great respect for his father's left-wing views. He wouldn't say this in a public address but when we were talking in a group."

David entered Baron Byng High School in Montreal in the fall of 1924. At that time the student body was predominantly Jewish, so much so that Christians were rare, says Josephine Malleck, who went to school with David. A doctor, she now lives in Vancouver in a waterfront townhouse that won an award for architect Arthur Erickson, and as darkness thickens across the bay and lights begin to people the opposite shore, she recalls those days. She was Josephine Schacher then. She speaks quickly, robustly, an opinion forever at hand — one of those people for whom life is a marvellous carnival.

Protestants? There'd be one in a class. Maybe two. I think we had one in my class. Actually . . . it was a real ghetto because even if you didn't live in the district for the school, they wouldn't let you go to another school. I lived closer to Montreal High but I wasn't allowed to go there. This [Baron Byng] was the Jewish school. I'm quite sure that any non-Jewish kids in that area who wanted to go to another school could. But if you were Jewish and wanted to, they wouldn't let you.

There were practically no Christian children in Baron Byng. . . . Mind you, the non-affluent Jewish population was concentrated there. The affluent Jewish population wouldn't have anything to do with the kids from Baron Byng. . . . If you came to university from there, socially you were scum. . . . There was a lot of snobbery at that point. And the elegant children, the children of people who thought that they were somebody, all lived in Westmount. And the ones that didn't quite make the grade, they lived in Outremont. And anybody that lived anywhere else was just not socially acceptable. And most of us lived somewhere else. . . . At that time, it just was definitely, actually, positively the wrong side of the tracks.

Her mother and father were both doctors and practised on Sherbrooke Street.

> I lived on Sherbrooke Street. . . . 159 Sherbrooke Street. It's a rooming house now. As a matter of fact, across the corner from our house a couple of prostitutes lived. This was when things began to go downhill. We used to entertain ourselves as kids to sit and count and see how good business was. This little lady would come out and confront all the men that came by, and she'd pick one up and we'd say, well, this is one, you know, and we'd count them for the night.
>
> Then she'd disappear for a while, so we'd figure she must have been caught or picked up. And then she'd come back. And this went on for years. This is how we grew up. I think they worry now because prostitutes park across from the school. [But] it didn't hurt us. It was very interesting. We were fascinated.

Josephine Schacher graduated from high school at sixteen in 1928. For the first couple of years she was in the same year as David, but not the same class. Then David skipped third year and went directly from second year into fourth. As David explains it in his memoirs, he was going out with Sophie, who was a year ahead, as were his best friend, Abe Klein, the poet, and his girlfriend.

"That bothered me a great deal. If anything were to be done about it, it had to be accomplished while I was in my second year; clearly I couldn't skip fourth year or catch up in university. After agonizing for days, I finally screwed up my courage and went to see the principal. Mr. Campbell was an intimidatingly large man, but kind and caring. I told him my problem frankly and asked to be promoted directly from second to fourth year. He queried me pretty thoroughly for a considerable time and finally agreed to my request, with the proviso that I would be on trial for the first month in fourth year. . . . I left on air."[11] Malleck's memory of David is of someone distant:

> I don't remember him ever being a boy. I thought he was a grown-up man. Always. And not particularly fun, you know. He always had this lady that might as well have been a wife. I mean, he was just grown-up. He never was silly. . . .
>
> He and Klein were close, close, close friends and they both were going out with the women they married. So they never flirted. And they never partied that I know of. They may have, but certainly not that we knew. We had a social club at high school that went on for a couple of years at university, and he belonged as long as he was president. If he wasn't president, he never came until the next year when there was another election. I mean, he was either the boss or he wasn't. Not that he ever did anything great about it, but the point is that unless

he was the chairman or something I don't think he was terribly interested.

He certainly was the valedictorian of the school because I can still remember the speech. It was a very interesting school. A very nice school. Very much on the wrong side of the tracks. On St. Urbain Street.

Her impression of David as being grown-up, mature, was common. Willy Victor, who also went to Baron Byng with David, comments that "if you had told me that he was five years older than me at the time, I wouldn't have questioned it." (David was one year older.) And even though Senator Goldenberg was two years older than David, he remembers him at McGill as being "more mature" than his classmates. Not more mature than Goldenberg himself, mind you. "I was too conceited. I felt we were on a par."

In high school David never played marbles. Or handball against the wall, as did Willy Victor. Or traded hockey cards. Or did any of the usual things that students did. "I remember him especially [because] he spoke beautifully," says Victor. "That I remember."

David and Abe Klein first met at the Sholem Aleichem Club during David's first year of high school. Klein, who was to become one of Canada's great poets, founded the club with a group of friends in 1924 and named it after the famous Yiddish storyteller. Klein, says Doris, "was a brilliant man. He was very tolerant and very intellectual. He had a tremendous intellect. There were lots of discussions . . . around the kitchen table as a rule. He'd come in at the end of a meal or something and start talking."

And Maishe, David, and Klein would go on sometimes for hours on politics or religion or great literature.

I have no doubt about [Klein's] important influence on me [says David in his memoirs]. Because I had started reading English literature only a year or two before I met him, [his] incredible range of literary knowledge at age fifteen, and the depth of his interpretations of prose and poetry, could not fail to enrich my mind and my imagination. All my experiences as a boy, combined with the influence of my father, had committed my thoughts almost exclusively to the social struggle and the instruments needed for political victory. . . . Klein's erudition staggered me when I first got to know him. He constantly produced gems from Greek, Roman and Hebrew mythology. He delighted in quoting from the Talmud, a compilation of Jewish law and custom, with intriguing interpretations by learned rabbis, written mostly in Aramaic. He sat for hours reading a dictionary with the same pleasure that I read a novel.[12]

David introduced another budding poet to Klein: Irving Layton — rebellious, raven-dark, scrambling up the tree of life ravenous for the lush fruit at the outer branches of experience. In 1930 he had been expelled from Baron Byng and David, then at McGill, urged him to write his junior matriculation exams regardless of his expulsion.

> It was Lewis who persuaded A.M. Klein to coach me in Latin for my matrics exam. . . . Klein and I met once weekly at Fletcher's Field just across from the YMHA on Mt. Royal Avenue, and I vividly recall the first lesson: Virgil's Aeneid, Book II: I[13]
>
> . . . hearing Klein roll off the Virgilian hexameters in a beautiful orotund voice that rose above the traffic, I think it was then that I realized how lovely and very moving the *sound* of poetry could be. I must confess my Latin wasn't sufficient to appreciate the sense that Virgil was making with his marvellous hexameters, but Klein's zeal and enthusiasm, his forceful delivery, his very genuine love of language, of poetry, all came through to me at the time. And I think that was most fortunate for me. . . .[14]

It also was David who loaned Layton the $10 fee he had to pay to write his matriculation exam. "He was no more flush than I was," says Layton; "he had borrowed the money from his girlfriend Sophie Carson."[15]

Goldenberg remembers how much David lacked money: "The students in my time used to have lunches at the McGill Union Building, it's the McCord Building now, where we could get a lunch for 15 cents and sit around and talk with people . . . but David every now and then was hard up and would ask me if I could pay for his meal, and he would say, 'I'll repay you,' and the amount would usually be from 16 cents to 25 cents and he never repaid me. I was so sorry for him. I mean, here was this fellow who was so brilliant and couldn't afford to eat at the student's cafeteria."

David did earn some money from private tutoring and from working as a "spieler" or guide on sightseeing buses. But there was little left over after paying for tuition and books and helping out with the family.

David's relationship with Klein left him with a lasting love of poetry. Murray Weppler, David's executive assistant when he was leader of the federal NDP from 1971 to 1974, remembers that on the campaign trail David would read for relaxation: "It was pretty wide-ranging. I can remember Yeats, and Dylan Thomas as well. He used to read a fair bit of Yiddish literature. He always had something totally unrelated to the campaign. I can't recall if it was always poetry. But at least a half-hour of reading something totally unrelated to the campaign and quite often poetry."

And in 1978, more than fifty years after he met Klein and after he had retired from politics, David took a trip to the Soviet Union with Joe Ain to see Svisloch once more. Ain remembers that "every night David had two books of poetry with him and he always fell asleep on his poetry book."

It was at the end of his first year at Baron Byng that Abe Klein introduced David to Sophie Carson, fifteen years old, her soft, dark hair worn long, aggressively intelligent, with "dancing brown eyes and . . . outrageously coquettish gestures."[16] Klein used to tell the story that as the two of them walked home after that first meeting, David dreamily proclaimed, "That's the girl I'm going to marry."[17] And, ten years later, on August 15, 1935, they did marry.

Sophie, in turn, introduced Klein to Bessie Kozlov, the woman he later married:

> I didn't like the boyfriends she had at the time. They were older but less refined. When I suggested she might like to meet the group of young men I had met recently, she scoffed at first. But one Friday evening in August, I persuaded her to come along with me. We gathered around the bandstand in Fletcher's Field, and the moon was shining. That was the night that Klein was first introduced to her, and one could see the look on his face — he was so enraptured, so thrilled. He was — for him — speechless. He fell in love with her at once.
>
> But to begin with she didn't feel the same way about him. When we returned home — we lived right next door to each other and used to converse across adjoining balconies — I asked her what do you think of Klein? "Oh," she replied, "I don't like some of the things he says, he's so cocky! So arrogant! I'm not interested in him!" I said, "Give him a chance. He's so brilliant." "Well," she answered, "I don't like some of the things he says, and he just makes us all feel very inferior." I said, "He doesn't make *me* feel inferior; just answer him back!"[18]

The two couples became fast friends. As Sophie recalled:

> When the weather wasn't that good, we would go either to Bessie's home or to mine. The girls would play the piano, David would play the fiddle, and we would sing songs — Yiddish songs, popular songs of the day, songs from school — and invariably we noticed that Klein never joined in. He was quite self-conscious that way — we also could never teach him to dance. Once we questioned him about it: the poet, the man of rhythm, unable to sing? "Oh, no," he said, "I can't keep a tune." I said, "You do sing, I've heard you humming something." "Oh," he said, "there's only one tune . . . Yes sir, that's my baby. No sir, don't

say maybe. . . ." And at the end of every one of our singing sessions, up would pop his voice with Yes sir, that's my baby.[19]

When Sophie met David, "I had the impression of a young man with very, very startling blue eyes. Later on I said to myself, 'They are really cornflower-coloured eyes,' and a shock of black hair. He looked sort of pale and thin and he looked very much like the poet Abe Klein. . . . But it turned out that this fellow was a different kind of poet. He was in what those years was termed a revolutionary. He wanted to change the order of things."[20]

Sophie came from an orthodox Hassidic family. Her father was a deeply religious man who, says Sophie's sister-in-law Rose Carson, "always had his nose in books." He had two children from a previous marriage and Sophie's mother had three from her previous marriage. Together they had four more children, two boys and two girls of whom Sophie was the older girl. In January 1926, after a long illness, and a year and a half before Sophie graduated from high school, her mother died. With financial help from Sophie's older brother Sam, who had established a successful business, a housekeeper was hired. As soon as Sophie finished high school in 1927, she took a job as a bookkeeper.

What her life was like at home is difficult to say. Rose Carson says Sophie's family was far from affluent, but whose was any different in those days? And her father and mother were loving. But it's equally true that her father was very strict in insisting that religious laws be obeyed. And it's obvious that Sophie rebelled against that strictness. In her later life with David she would have absolutely nothing to do with religion.

She had a flair for dramatizing life, exaggerating some would say, and that has to be taken into account in considering her recollections, especially when they come second hand.[21] But however dramatized, they at least represent a perception and it would be that perception which guided Sophie in her later years.

Michele Landsberg, author, journalist, feminist, remembers Sophie, her mother-in-law, talking about her early years. As she speaks, Michele is in the sitting area of the ambassador's residence in New York that goes with Stephen's UN posting, an area the size of a single's tennis court that is outfitted in the creams, pale blues, and beiges that so delight the foreign service, and she is enshrouded in endless white crepe from which a foot or an elbow never appears. As she settles into a cream-coloured couch — with swirl upon swirl of white as she arranges and rearranges and arranges again — it is impossible to focus attention anywhere else. An Ethel Merman, a Sophie Tucker, a Queen Medb of Connacht, could do no better. It is a defiant celebration of ample as attractive — and at the epicentre: expressive brown eyes and a face that is open and warm and, like her conversation, hearty.

Much of Sophie's life, Michele says, was in reaction to the religious restrictions of those early years:

Sophie hated Jewishness because of her father. . . . [He] insisted on the laws of *kashruth*, keeping kosher and so on, and forcing all these religious observances on her. . . . A lot of David's distance from Jewish observance and Jewish organizational involvement came — though the family never talks about this, but I knew them long enough to figure this out — came from her berserk hatred of Jewish observance. Berserk. When David died, my children wanted to say Kaddish for him that same day, and she screamed at them for wanting to say Kaddish. So that's how extreme her feelings were on this.

Many times over [during] David's life, I got the feeling that he had a yearning for some of the old ways, but she wouldn't let him. That was a bone of contention and [to avoid a scene] he just went along with it. He placated her in all these things.

That's what a traditional marriage can be like. He placates her, but he has to bottle up all this rage because she is a defenceless little woman according to the mythology. So I think it's worth saying, and I wouldn't want to say anything mean or horrible about Sophie, but the Jewish community certainly always misinterpreted David's distance from them.

David rejected religion on ideological grounds, just as Maishe had before him. But it also was part of his culture, and to that aspect of it he had no ideological opposition. "At Elena's bar-mitzvah," says Michele, "David was called up to the Torah to say one of the honours and he stumbled through the prayer, which he hadn't said since he was maybe twelve years old, and afterward he took me aside privately and said with great emotion, tears were coming to the front, 'I haven't done that since I was a youngster. It brought back so many memories.'

"But that was the sort of sentimental, emotional thing he could never say about Jewish observance to Sophie because she hated it so much. So he just kept it to himself."

As far as Sophie's father was concerned, David was just about the last person he wanted seeing his daughter. It was bad enough that David was anti-religious. But he also was an immigrant, a socialist, and poor. He forbade Sophie to see him. Kalmen

Kaplansky tried to explain the mindset that existed among those who had become established in the New World:

> He didn't like this heretic, this young punk David hanging around his daughter. He thought it was a come-down for her. What the hell, [what if] she married this guy without a future, without a penny to his name. An immigrant and the son of an immigrant. In those days if you were a greenhorn that was the worst offence. A person who was in the country for ten years was looked down on [as] a newcomer, a greenhorn.
>   One has to understand the mentality. . . . My first job was for a Romanian Jew — Simenovitch was his name — also in the east end of Montreal. His favourite name for me was "you green arsehole" and he'd do it in Yiddish — *du greener tokhes*. And he thought it was funny. . . . He resented the fact that I would buy the Montreal *Daily Star* because I learned English that way. Why didn't I continue reading the Yiddish newspapers? So this was the mentality of the people.

Sophie ignored her father's prohibition and, as David says, went right on seeing him: "I couldn't visit her home so she came as often as she could to mine, where my parents accepted her with open arms. I never had any doubt that her family would eventually come around, and by the end of my first year in university her father and brothers began to soften somewhat. . . . To see Sophie's independent spirit stand up to the opposition at home was a delight."[22]

So it took three years of forbidden meetings, of relentless scrutiny of her comings and goings, of shouting and tension and pain and words better left unsaid, before the pressures on Sophie "began to soften." And then only soften, not end. Whatever were her other complaints, it's little wonder that Sophie came to harbour an intense dislike of religious observance since it so dominated her father's life, and through his, hers, and since he so adamantly set himself against David — and especially since her love for David and her confidence in him were so profoundly justified.

When David left for England and Oxford University, Sophie went with him. "Unusual for those days," says Doris, "Very unusual. That's why I think her brothers objected a little. Her father, being an Orthodox man, objected a lot." But Maishe and Rose raised no objections. After all, hadn't they been a touch "bohemian" in the eyes of Svisloch?

Sophie was a natural rebel. In her later years she revelled in telling the story of refusing to curtsy for the Queen. David was leader of the NDP at the time and her refusal threatened to blossom into one of those incidents that makes royal equerries and protocol officers blanch.

"I would curtsy to a Casals or a Picasso or a Chagall. They had done something. They had earned respect. But the Queen! I should curtsy to her! For what? I said no. There is no way I would curtsy to her."

David was at his wits' end and the NDP caucus was tying itself in knots over how a slight to the Queen would appear to a largely royalist electorate. David finally decided he wouldn't attend the reception at the Governor General's. But that in itself would cause a problem because only twenty-two people and their companions had been invited and the absence of the leader of the party would certainly be noticed. "He came home and said, 'Sophie, is curtsying such a big thing? Can't you find a way to give her a curtsy?' I said no. I would not budge. He said, 'Isn't there some way to compromise? Isn't there anything you can do?'"

There was. When Sophie was introduced to the Queen she simply nodded her head slightly, "like you do when nodding to an acquaintance on the street."[23]

So Maishe, who had no truck or trade with anything that required a bended knee, was much to the liking of this mutinous teenager. And equally attractive was his outlook — and all the more so because it was independent of scriptural cant. In its place he stressed decency and honesty, integrity and tolerance. "*Menschekeit* — decency — was the first. I can always remember that," Doris says. "He never talked about being good the way a religious person would. . . . To learn to have relationships with people, most of the time in our discussions about growing up, that was very important to him. For me to know how to relate to people. Friendships and whatever came after them, you know, integrity. He used to preach that [to us] all the time, to be honest in [our] political activity."

People would come to him with their problems — small businessmen, parents, couples — and always he would lay the emphasis upon integrity in relationships. "I can give you an example," says Doris:

> There was a Mr. Lachinsky who was in a partnership for years . . . and got along beautifully and then one day they didn't get along. Mr. Lachinsky came to the house and . . . put his case on the table and said where do I go from here? My dad . . . brought the two partners together and negotiated and they ended up staying together until Mr. Lachinsky died. . . .
> There were a lot of small business people [like that]. He couldn't help if they had financial problems. But if there were problems in the relationships within the business, that's where he advised. . . . I think in most cases they took his advice.

> Then there was another man who had trouble in the family . . .
> daughter and wife trouble. . . . My Dad was just logical and considerate.
> It wasn't that he was a lawyer; he didn't [give] legal advice. What a
> rabbi in a European shtetl used to do, it was very much that role.

The difference was that he didn't extol divine acceptance; he preached
the brotherhood of man.

When David began to get involved in socialist politics, Maishe felt
the same exhilarating joy that he had felt when, with the Bund, he
helped open the first Yiddish school in Svisloch. On leaving high
school, David helped found the Montreal branch of the Young People's
Socialist League. Yipsels, it was called.[24] The organization began in
the United States with the support of the more moderate wing of the
U.S. Socialist Party with which Norman Thomas was allied. "It was
centred in the Workmen's Circle," recalled David, "and was composed mainly of sons and daughters of immigrant Canadians. It was
resolutely anti-communist in an area of Montreal where the Communist
Party and the Young Communist League enjoyed their greatest
popularity. Energetic and militant, the 'Yipsels' participated in
demonstrations, picket lines and other such activities, the members
dedicated to the point of fanaticism."[25]

Montreal Communists, young or old, during the twenties and early
thirties were a far cry from the bloody-fanged monsters portrayed
through the McCarthy era and right up to the presidency of Ronald
Reagan. They were militant, yes; they were disruptive and often
obstreperous, yes; they preached the violent overthrow of capitalism,
yes; they were too servile in hewing to Moscow's line, yes. But they
also had another side that made them daunting opponents, as Irving
Layton describes:

> Though I never became a member of the Communist party, I was sym-
> pathetic to the heartbeat of communism, to its idealistic vision of man
> and society, and to the militancy Communists were exhibiting
> everywhere. They were becoming prominent because they took part
> in trying to organize the unemployed. The socialists did not.
> Householders were evicted for non-payment of rent. Services were cut
> off for non-payment of utility bills.
>
> The Communists organized groups that would immediately put the
> furniture back into the house from which an unemployed family had
> been evicted. Some of the landlords took to hiring idle men to help
> in the law's enforcement. There were bloody fights, and one
> householder, an out-of-work Ukrainian who protested his eviction, was
> shot and killed by the police. Of course the Communists made a big
> howl about that and staged a protest rally at his funeral and I remember
> filing past Zynchuk's bier along with hundreds of other mourners.

I made comparisons between Communists and the weak-kneed intellectualism of the socialists whose Marxism more and more struck me as emasculated and academic. Nevertheless I still believed the capitalist system could have its carious fangs pulled by Parliamentary reform.[26]

Norman Massey was one of the Communists who participated in fighting evictions. He described a favourite tactic: "When people couldn't pay rent, landlords called in the bailiff [to] sell their goods. The left wing — I wouldn't call them all Communists, you know, there was a trend toward the left, mostly fellow travellers — they filled up the house where there was a bailiff's sale and they bought all the furniture for ten cents. Where it was very expensive furniture, it was for one dollar and [after buying it] they gave it back to the owner [the tenant]. The bailiffs couldn't sell it again because it was sold already. . . . And this was [done] . . . all over Montreal. This is how the [Communist] movement was built. From below."

David continued in Yipsels during the early part of his five years at McGill University — four in arts and one in law. Again, Irving Layton remembers — this time the Sunday morning lectures David used to give to Yipsel members:

> He became our mentor in the economics and politics of socialism. Terms like "monopoly capitalism," "class struggle," and "historical materialism" . . . acquired substance and definition for me.
>
> [David] had a clear, logical mind and was a convincing speaker but he lacked the fire and disciplined passion to be an orator. There were no flashes of wit or humour. There were no imaginative assaults on the senses. He was too cool, too self-possessed to ever let himself go, too fearful of the unknown, too literal-minded to venture very far into that dark thicket. Listening to him, I felt he carefully planed his sentences as a carpenter might plane door jambs. . . .
>
> He always gave his listeners the feeling that he knew where he was going, that he had the blueprints for the future safely tucked away in one of his pockets and that they would be doing the greatest service to themselves should he convince them to walk stolidly after him.[27]

When she was seventeen, Doris also joined Yipsels (and there met her husband-to-be, Andy Andras, who was president), but by that time David had departed, returning only occasionally to give lectures. Already, says Fay Ain, he had built himself a name.

At eighteen years of age he was secretary of the Montreal Labour Party; in his first year at McGill he won the Talbot Papineau Cup for debating and later became president of the McGill Union debating society; he became president of the McGill Labour Club, secretary of the Quebec Labour Party, and an officer of the Menorah Society. He even got involved with the Student Christian Movement along with Eugene Forsey and King Gordon. ("The religious aspect of the SCM was irrelevant to me," he says in his memoirs. "What was important was the commitment of so many to the struggle for social change."[28]) For a year he also joined Young Judea, a Zionist youth group, and served as a director. ("I studied the approach of Zionist socialists as never before, but I remained unconvinced."[29] And in his third year he and Abe Klein founded *The McGilliad*, a campus magazine that "published a broad range of essays on politics, philosophy and the arts, as well as poems and book reviews." In his final year of arts, David took over as editor, Klein by then having graduated.[30]

Klein and David debated quite often as a team. "I hugely enjoyed the way they polished off their opponents," says Layton. "Klein with his extraordinary wit and gift for repartee and Lewis with his invincible logic that cut like a sharp knife."[31]

In his days at McGill David's outrage at injustice was so unbridled that it seemed any enemy of capitalism, even the Soviet Union, must be treated with some tolerance. In the 1980s there seems to be a strange inconsistency in his rejection of communism and his willingness to see Soviet Russia as a grand experiment that should not be criticized too harshly. However, it was an attitude that was prevalent at the time.

Capitalism was still the most prominent enemy of working people and the Soviet Union was still the only country that had rejected it. There was no contradiction in being a Marxist and being anti-Communist. In fact, communism was seen as a deviant strain of Marxism and an excess brought on by the excesses of capitalism itself. The hope was that it would, in time, return to democratic socialism — especially if democratic socialist regimes could be established elsewhere as living examples of what socialism was all about.

It's worth remembering that Marxism did not always call for the violent overthrow of established order, as communism did. That certainly was Marx's position in the late 1840s and the early 1850s. However, by the late 1860s — after the second Reform Bill of 1867 in England — he was saying that a peaceful evolution toward socialism was possible in England, the United States, and a number of other countries. So a Menshevik-Bundist insistence on democratic procedures was thoroughly in keeping with Marxist doctrine. (Lenin, however, disputed this. He claimed that Marx regarded the situations in England and the United States as an exception and the exception was no longer valid because, since the time of Marx's writing, monopoly capitalism had developed in both countries.[32])

It's also worth remembering that, at the practical level, an accurate profile of Stalin's perfidy had not yet been drawn. And Malcolm Muggeridge would not leave for Russia to write for *The Guardian* until the spring of 1932.

In the February–March 1931 issue of *The McGilliad* David wrote:

> I am afraid I have lost all faith in our law-givers, nominal and virtual. . . . Faith, Confidence, Trust, these should be the powers behind a young man's spirit. It makes me shiver, this piety. . . . One must inevitably come to the conclusion that the present social machine is breaking down. All that we can do is look into the future, and build something finer to replace it.
>
> What else can we do to make the present system work? We have oiled the machine again and again; we have repaired it with our last despairing ounce of strength and, frequently, when it has refused to work of itself we have applied our shoulders to it until we became one with it. But so far of no avail. With an unheeded shriek it invariably clogs, and thousands of lives are caught within its wheels still shrieking and still unheeded. . . .
>
> I am convinced . . . that all small improvements and palliative legislation can accomplish little, very little indeed. A complete change is necessary, a radical alteration in the entire structure is essential. . . .

In another issue of *The McGilliad* (December 1930), he applauded the Russian Revolution, called for a greater understanding of what was happening in the Soviet Union, and at the same time declared that he was no friend of communism:

> In 1789 a people struggled for freedom in France. The whole world was in sympathy with them. About 1830 a people fought for liberty in Greece, and Shelley, Byron gushed forth in music. In 1917 a people rebelled for justice in Russia, and very few have exhibited sympathy or appreciation. One really wonders why.
>
> You may not agree with the economic doctrines enforced; you may strongly condemn the political system of terrorist dictatorship. You may find fault with every thing and every body connected with the Bolshevist regime. You . . . have every right to maintain your stand. But need this preclude an appreciation . . . that in Russia now a great experiment is under way . . . to evolve a better and more equitable system? Certainly not. . . .
>
> I am not advocating the adoption of communist views, I do not hold them myself. But I do suggest that there might be a great deal more intelligence shown in the analysis of Russian conditions. . . . One might then understand the reasons for the economic outrages that the Russian government is forced to perpetrate. . . . One might learn . . . to distinguish between the doctrines of the western socialists and those of the communists.

David himself recognized this early leaning toward a "brand of socialism of the rather harsh medicine variety, the only cure for an increasingly sick system": "My socialist ideas had derived from the rather closed Bundist circle of which my father was a leading spirit. . . . It was of working-class origin and had nothing but contempt for 'hypocritical bourgeois morality.' It was hard-nosed, derived from Marxism of the revisionist kind, and concentrated more on strategies to smash the capitalist systems than on programs to build a more humane one."[33]

Under the influence of Frank Scott, King Gordon, and Eugene Forsey, all former Rhodes scholars and all teaching — Scott and Forsey at McGill, Gordon at United Theological College — and through others he met at the League for Social Reconstruction, especially Professor Frank Underhill, he began to reach less for the throat of capitalism and more for bindings that, Gulliver-like, would restrain it.

And then, in the late fall of 1931, he won the Rhodes scholarship. "He didn't win his scholarship because of his outstanding work as a student because his work was not outstanding," says Senator Goldenberg. "I don't think he ever worked hard at his studies. In fact, I know he didn't. But he managed to get through. He always did a great deal of reading, outside reading, you see. And he didn't have time to waste on ordinary courses on the examination. . . . Nor [did he win it] as an athlete. It was his qualities of leadership, which is one of the requisites of a Rhodes scholarship. He had those qualities."

Senator Forsey confirms that David could have done much better in his studies: "David was a student of mine and he wasn't a particularly brilliant student because I don't think he was terribly interested in the subject he was taking from me, which was the government of Canada. . . . He was unquestionably brilliant, but I don't think he applied his mind much to this. He went through all right, but he didn't produce anything that was very remarkable or worthy of his power. He was just an average student as far as I can recall. . . . I was surprised that he didn't do better."

All of which means that the Rhodes selection committee's assessment of his leadership abilities must have been very favourable indeed. Not lost on it, obviously, was the cocky assurance with which he responded to Sir Edward Beatty, chairman of the committee, president of the CPR, and chancellor of McGill University. "Lewis," asked Sir Edward, "if you became the first socialist Prime Minister of Canada, what would be the first thing you would do?"

"Nationalize the CPR, sir," David replied.[34]

Sir Edward, says David, smiled.

David's reponse recalls a comment he made a year before in the same issue of *The McGilliad* in which he wrote about the Russian Revolution. He was tweaking Mackenzie King and he wrote: "To me the difference between the Liberals and the Conservatives is only a difference in degree, and not in kind. In fact, if I had my way. . . . But I haven't — yet."

That "yet" was to carry him through the next forty-five years.

• CHAPTER TWELVE •

They dance best who dance with desire
Who lifting feet of fire from fire
Weave before they lie down
A red carpet for the sun.

Irving Layton,
"A Red Carpet for the Sun"[1]

David Lewis was once described by Sir Carlton Allen, warden of Rhodes House at Oxford, as the most outstanding man of his generation at Oxford.[2] And Lord Lothian, secretary of the Rhodes Trust from 1925 to 1939 and then British ambassador to Washington until his death in December 1940, said during a visit to Ottawa that David "was the most brilliant young man to come up to Oxford in my time."[3]

Such statements are outrageously controversial. David's brilliance was admitted. But to single him out as the most brilliant of his time is an invitation to debate. And to describe him as the most outstanding of his generation begs dispute. Even among his admirers there are those such as Sir William Nield, a former student colleague and the retired vice-chairman of Rolls Royce, who say it is impossible to pick anyone of that time as the most outstanding of his generation. The field is too broad, the interests too diverse. How, for instance, would one compare a great oarsman with a great debater or a fine poet or a brilliant philosopher? And since Sir Carlton Allen spoke of the "most outstanding man," not the "most outstanding student," what are the criteria of judgment?

However what's important is not whether the judgments were accurate but that they were expressed — and expressed by people who were themselves eminent. Whether correct or incorrect or simply irrelevant, at least they indicate the context in which David was perceived.

He was, says Michael Foot, former leader of the Labour Party, "the most powerful socialist debater in the place. I don't think with any rival. . . . He had a very powerful influence indeed amongst students, partly because he'd had so much more experience than the rest of us, but partly because he had brilliant debating powers. I mean one of the best I've ever heard. If you talk of tough political debate, well, he was absolutely unbeatable. . . . I knew him [at Oxford] when I was a Liberal [and] he played a part in converting me to socialism."[4]

He was also one of the principal reasons why the Communists did much more poorly at Oxford than at Cambridge. These were the years that Kim Philby, Guy Burgess, Donald Maclean, and Anthony Blunt — the notorious Soviet spies — were being recruited at Cambridge. However, at Oxford the Communists had no comparable success — with the possible exception of Roger Hollis, who was there only for two years a decade earlier. One of the three or four major reasons for this lack of success was the alternative presented by the Oxford Labour Club. And within that club it was David, the dominant personality, who led the battle against the Communists.[5]

David arrived at Oxford in the fall of 1932. Philby went up to Cambridge in October 1929, Burgess in 1930, and Maclean in 1931. Blunt entered Cambridge in 1926, was elected to a Trinity Fellowship in 1932, and in November of that year sponsored Burgess's membership in the Apostles Club, the secret society that became such a focus of Communist recruitment at Cambridge.

Writing in 1979 in his book *The Fourth Man*, Andrew Boyle comments: "The year 1933 may well be regarded by posterity as a watershed in the political history of Britain. Among politically conscious undergraduates, in particular at Cambridge, it was a year when the cult of Communism established itself openly as something more pervasive and sinister than a passing fashion. By skilful propaganda and individual proselytizing, the movement consolidated its hold and eventually succeeded in forcing the once-dominant Labour Club to capitulate and close its doors."[6]

At Oxford, on the other hand, the university Labour Club flourished. It had a membership of about 400 when David arrived; when he left in the summer of 1935 it had more than 650 members — about 14 percent of the student population.[7]

The path to the "watershed" that Boyle identifies extends back through the First World War. England, after the war, was emotionally mazed. It knew it had become different, but the war had fractured the mirror and it could no longer see itself whole, or even in complementary parts. And principal among the broken shards were the alienated at Oxford and Cambridge. Not until the Second World War, when Churchill restored a sense of national purpose, was the mirror repaired.

Over a twenty-five-year period the key mood at the two universities changed radically, and nothing evokes those changing moods better than the poetry written at the time by three promising young poets — the first in a pre-war voice that cherished the order and grace of old England; the next in a disillusioned post-war voice that escaped into the world of the aesthete as a defence against becoming part of the old England that had sent its best and brightest to such a grim end on foreign battlefields; and finally the third in an even more alienated voice of the thirties, appalled at the frivolities of the twenties and angry with what it saw in the thirties.

Rupert Brooke's is the first voice and his "Grantchester" poem, written in 1912, speaks of the untrammelled security of pre-war home:

> God! I will pack, and take a train,
> And get me to England once again!
> For England's the one land, I know,
> Where men with Splendid Hearts may go; . . .
> Say, is there Beauty yet to find?
> And Certainty? and Quiet kind? . . .
> Stands the Church clock at ten to three?
> And is there honey still for tea?[8]

In the 1920s, dandies — outrageous, wanton, feverishly flamboyant — presided over Oxford and Cambridge undergraduates and, especially in their sexual effrontery, declared their secession from a society that had spawned the Great War. They were particularly prominent at Oxford, where Harold Acton, Brian Howard, Evelyn Waugh, John Strachey, Alan Pryce-Jones, Randolph Churchill, Cyril Connolly, Peter Quennell, John Betjeman, and others like them created a legend in their time and left an imprint on the university for generations to come. It was a world that Malcolm Muggeridge saw at Cambridge in the mid-twenties and viciously denounced:

Public schoolboys, whatever their particular school . . . had a language of their own which I scarcely understood, games they played which I could neither play nor interest myself in, ways and attitudes which they took for granted but which were foreign to me — for instance, their acceptance of sodomy as more or less normal behaviour. . . . The University, when I was there, was very largely a projection of public school life and mores, and a similar atmosphere of homosexuality tended to prevail. There was also a hangover of Wildean decadence, with aesthetes who dressed in velvet, painted their rooms in strange colours, hung Aubrey Beardsley prints on their walls and read *Les Fleurs du Mal*.

Cambridge as a whole, he said, was a fraudulent, second-rate institution; a "place of infinite tedium, of idle days, and foolish vanities, and spurious enthusiasms".[9]

But for those of that life and that time, university was a place of anarchic hedonism, airily dismissive of the values expressed by Rupert Brooke which had led only to war, and Betjeman, who in his later years was to become England's poet laureate, wrote "The 'Varsity Students' Rag," the chorus of which went:

> *We* had a rag at Monico's,
> *We* had a rag at the Troc.,
> And the one we had at Berkeley
> Gave the customers quite a shock.
> *Then* we went to the popular,
> And after that — oh my!
> I *wish* you'd seen the rag we had
> In the Grill Room at the Cri.[10]

By the early thirties John Cornford had arrived, later to become the first Englishman to enlist against the Franco rebels in the Spanish Civil War, killed the day after his twenty-first birthday in December 1936. He went up to Cambridge in the fall of 1933, a brilliant student, a magnetic personality, already a poet of great power, and a committed Communist who detested dandies. He could write tender love poems in addition to "As Our Might Lessens," in which he reviled the old men — old in age, decayed in spirit — who sent young men to war:

> These carrion men that fear our power,
> The heroes of the pogrom hour,
> Who measure virtue by the strength to kill,
> Because they know their time is near,
> Would hold us down by murder's fear.
> The dying crucify the living still. . . .
>
> We cannot hope to ease life's itch
> Gleaning the harvest of the rich.[11]

His solution: seize the harvest; divide it fairly.

The dandyism that Muggeridge saw, and that has been seen by innumerable writers commenting on England's great spy scandals of recent years, has generally been viewed as a phenomenon of the British public school system in which boys inhabited an almost exclusively male world that produced a hothouse eroticism. Certainly that was a factor. For instance, Cyril Connolly tells of Cecil Beaton's female impersonations at St. Cyprian's preparatory school during the war where, at Saturday night concerts, he would sing, "If you were the only boy in the world," in imitation of Violet Lorraine, and was so charming that "the eighty odd boys in the audience felt there could be no other boy in the world for them." And at Eton, Brian Howard was a great success acting female roles. Connolly thought he had a "distinguished, impertinent face, a sensual mouth, and dark eyes with long eyelashes," and said that he became "the most fashionable boy in the school."[12]

But there was much more to it than that. The dandies were direct lineal descendants of Charles Baudelaire, Beau Brummel, and Oscar Wilde and were part of a broader grouping that even had a name, "Children of the Sun," or, to use the German word identifying them, *Sonnenkinder*. Within the Sonnenkinder there were: aesthetes, naïfs, and rogues. The aesthetes — the dandies, who, as Baudelaire put it, were interested in neither money nor love but in style and fantasy and refinement — were represented by people such as Connolly and Beaton and Howard and Harold Acton and John Betjeman and Osbert and Sacheverell Sitwell, and who generally were homosexual. The naïfs — the limpidly sensitive — were eternally in search of their potential such as Lord Jim in the Joseph Conrad novel or, in real life, Christopher Isherwood, Stephen Spender, Philip Toynbee, Alan Pryce-Jones, and John Strachey, and more often than not they were homosexual, at least until they left university. And the rogues — rougher and often coarse and careless but sexually as narcissistic as the dandies and often their counterparts and companions — were represented in literature by Rudyard Kipling's heroes and in reality by people such as Randolph Churchill. Generally, they were heterosexual.[13]

The hallmarks of the Children of the Sun are the exaltation of young men as the most sublime expression of life and an unremitting rebellion against their fathers and what their fathers represented. In the twenties it was the aesthetes, especially at Oxford, who set the tempo. They were determined to create for themselves a world of sybaritic glamour; should divine intervention have allowed them to step alive into the pages of Aubrey Beardsley's *Yellow Book*, their ecstacies would have set the heavens sparkling. Diaghelev was their god, Nijinsky their Christ figure, and Jean Cocteau their prophet.

When Kim Philby, Guy Burgess, Donald Maclean, and Anthony Blunt reached Cambridge, the glitter of their predecessors was still resplendent. Blunt was a true aesthete, Maclean a naïf, Burgess a rogue and a homosexual, and Philby a rogue and a heterosexual. But all were

Children of the Sun, and that is of more core significance than homosexuality or any other factor linking the four.

Even when they were revealed as traitors, they were not likely to be reviled by other Sonnenkinder. Writers such as Graham Greene, Evelyn Waugh, and Rebecca West have all made the case that there are higher goals than patriotism and even that treason can be a higher form of patriotism.[14]

It should be no surprise that fealty to country did not rank highly among the Sonnenkinder when "country" meant a nation run by the old men of stock exchanges, factories, and countinghouses to whom fantasy was impractical, style was frivolous, and youth was a memory. It should equally be no surprise that most careers outside the artistic were unpalatable. Only a few offered a dandy scope. Journalism was one. The aristocratic army regiments was another. A third was a career in the foreign office or the foreign service and a goodly number gravitated there. Martin Green described the result in *Children of the Sun*: "The embassies established private worlds, exempt from the laws obeyed by the greater society. . . . While Harold Nicolson was in the British embassy in Berlin, around 1927, David Herbert was sharing an apartment with Christopher Sykes, also an attaché at the embassy, and Cyril Connolly wrote for them a series of "Oriental" plays, in which Herbert played a seductive slave girl, Connolly a pimp, and Sykes a carpet seller. These entertainments were performed in the Nicolsons' apartment before an audience that included the British ambassador. The mingling of moral anarchy and political authority was very intimate."[15]

David was as far a cry from the Children of the Sun as it was possible to imagine. He stood four square, not for fantasy and eternal youth, but for practicality and the world of men. For maturity, political reality, and military strategies, for hunger marches, for union halls and smoke-filled conventions, for historical materialism and the balance of payments, for coal miners and factory workers and people who had never heard of *Les Fleurs du Mal* and would trumpet their displeasure if they had.

Jean Cocteau thought the greatest struggle of 1917 was the controversy over his ballet *Parade*, and he was quite serious in that belief — just as for Sonnenkinder of a generation earlier 1905 was the year of Diaghilev's great exhibition of Russian eighteenth-century art; for David and the world of men, 1917 and 1905 could mean only the Revolutions.

Yet for all those students at Oxford still hovering between the world of Peter Pan and the world of men, intrigued by Sonnenkind glamour and disillusioned by events they saw happening around them, David had a glamour of his own. He, too, was in rebellion and he, too, had a magnetism with his burning eyes and cocky assurance and, for an Oxford student, his extraordinary past amid the sacred fires of revolution in Russia. Other students could travel to Eastern Europe to appraise its results, but David had been *there*. Not until the Spanish Civil War in 1936 would similar opportunities arise for young Englishmen. What's more, David knew poetry, and loved it. He was articulate and his merciless skill in debate lent him an aura of dark power. And, with Sophie at his side — bright, vivacious, irreverent Sophie — flaunting, as it were, their affair, he, too, was insolently scorning convention.

He was talked about, he was pointed out, he was written about. In the winter term of 1934, a year before he was to win the presidency of the Oxford Union, the university debating society, David's college journal, *The Lincoln Imp*, published a profile. The tone was lighthearted, the message was clear: "When four hundred 'blessed damozels' lean over the balcony of the Union . . . is that not evidence enough as to who is Oxford's idol? Who is this man with craggy brows and granite jaw, whose flashing eye bores inexorably into the soul of every honourable member? Who, four hundred fluttering hearts ask, who? When four hundred hungry marchers [the unemployed hunger marchers who passed through Oxford] hungered in helplessness and marched in misery, who bought butter? Who fried fish? Who served soup? Who?"[16]

This "who" — this David Lewis — cast a long and lively shadow.

In a very real sense David stood between the worlds of the fathers and the sons, the captains-to-be of society and the Sonnenkinder. Each could see characteristics to admire and, as a result, each was open to the force of his personality and convictions.

The Sonnenkind temperament supplied only part of the impetus for communism that David confronted at Oxford. The other part was the second, even deeper wave of disillusionment that came sweeping in with the Great Depression, alienating non-Sonnenkinder and even furthering the alienation of the Sonnenkinder themselves. That second wave, breaking upon Oxford and Cambridge in the early thirties, had been given an extra push by teachers in the public schools many of whom were disenchanted Sonnenkinder from the early twenties.

The General Strike of 1926 probably marks the beginning of that second wave although, as with everything else, there are overlaps. That also was the year that Louis MacNeice arrived at Oxford, in October, and commented: "Oxford in 1926 was just at the end of its period of postwar deliberate decadence — the careful matching of would-be putrescent colours. At the first party I went to there was no drink but champagne, a smart young man played by himself with a spotted stuffed dog on a string and the air was full of the pansy phrase 'my dear.' I discovered that in Oxford homosexuality and 'intelligence,' heterosexuality and brawn, were almost inexorably paired. This left me out in the cold and I took to drink."[17]

The General Strike, although it lasted only a week, shocked the entire nation into a realization that all was not well with the economy; it created a sense of unease that continued through to the depression, which brought unemployment that, for England, lingered at agonizingly high levels throughout David's stay at Oxford. (David, in fact, arrived at the peak of unemployment.)[18]

What deepened the disillusionment so dramatically was the decision by Prime Minister Ramsay MacDonald — who was unable to cope with the financial pressures of the depression — to dissolve the government and, in August 1931, to set up a national coalition with the Conservatives and Liberals. On the left, it was seen as an absolutely disgusting action, a total betrayal of the socialist cause. This was the man who had become England's first socialist prime minister, and here he was in bed with socialism's sworn enemies. Worse still, he had invited them to bed.

To undergraduates at Oxford it appeared that nothing was working. Capitalism was wheezing what apparently was its last and English socialism had proved untrustworthy. And globally, order and reason were succumbing to dumb, brutish force. In September 1931 the Japanese invaded Manchuria. In Europe, Fascists were on the rise. Mussolini, who had staged his coup d'état in 1922, was having great success with the Italian economy. Hitler would be chancellor by January 1933, and two months later the right-wing Austrian chancellor, Englebert Dollfuss, would declare parliament unworkable and begin ruling by emergency decree.

Less than a year later, in early February 1934, Dollfuss would send his troops to smash Otto Bauer's socialist enclave in Vienna — which by its very success was challenging the existing system — where public housing had been created for 200,000 of the city's poorest; health clinics and public baths were free; electricity, gas, and water were available at cost at workers' estates; schools and kindergartens were flourishing; and sports and cultural institutions had been organized. Artillery would be used to blast workers out of flats. At least 300 men, women, and children would be killed, 1,000 wounded, and Bauer driven into exile.

The year 1934 would also be a year of political murders: Ernst Röhm, chief of Hitler's storm troops, would be seized and shot by Hitler; Kurt von Schleicher, the last chancellor of the Weimar Republic, would be murdered in his Berlin flat on the "Night of the Long Knives"; Englebert Dollfuss, who had established a dictatorship after destroying Otto Bauer's socialist enclave in Vienna, would be assassinated by Austrian Nazis in a raid on the Chancellery; and Sergei Kirov, who was emerging as a powerful rival to Stalin, would be murdered; and when Stalin was suspected of being responsible, he would claim there was a widespread conspiracy to assassinate the entire Soviet leadership, and would launch a purge that saw hundreds executed and thousands deported. It also would be the year that Italians and Abyssinians began fighting on the Somaliland frontier.

So, when David arrived at Oxford in the summer of 1932, England was in a mess. The world was in a mess and the situation was to go from bad to worse. Nothing seemed to work and at that point only Marxism seemed to have the answers.

To Oxford undergraduates, England's political leaders were either inept or uncaring. Or both, says Sir William Nield:

> What a great many people believed and what a great many people feared was that the ultimate crisis of capitalism was upon us. There was an economic cataclysm [coupled with] the current Establishment either not knowing or not caring what to do about it; there was the inadequacy of the preceding reformist doctrines; and there were the beginnings of the questioning of that in Oxford [which was] the centre of opinion and ideas and proudly so. And suddenly there appears this little man, David Lewis, very, very, very Marxist who appears to know all the answers.
>
> He appears with great maturity and with his Russian background, and he has this great certainty in a situation which is favourable to the views he holds and the effect was catalytic.

Nield is not a man given to excesses, in speech or otherwise. The interview, at his request, is at the Farmers' Club, a respectable but modest club in the City, a shade tatty around the fringe, like so many of London's old clubs, but with a good menu. He is retired, a former deputy chairman of Rolls Royce (1971) Ltd., former secretary to the cabinet, under-secretary of several government ministries, including the Department of Economic Affairs, and from 1937 to 1939 employed in the Labour Party's research and policy department. At seventy-three years of age (when interviewed in November 1985) he still has the relentless, analytical mind of a tough senior civil servant.

During David's stay at Oxford, Nield was a Marxist, but in 1936, Nield's final year at Oxford, J.M. Keynes published his *General Theory of Employment, Interest and Money*, and Nield, "from that moment onwards, ceased to be a Marxist." It was, he says, an absolutely revolutionary concept. It called for deficit financing when times were tough — make-work projects to get the economy going — and in good times socking enough away to cool off inflation and pay down the accumulated deficit. The theory declared that it was totally unnecessary for the state to own the instruments of production. For the first time, Nield says, "we had an answer to the inevitable collapse of capitalism and the destruction of the bourgeois state."[19]

David recruited Nield to become active in the Oxford Labour Club. Nield hadn't been much interested in the club, "The prestige of the labour movement was at rock bottom because the MacDonald government was seen as a failure, which it was." But David

was very quick to pick up people who were sympathetic and give them something to do. He gave me the job of looking after the literature stall at meetings. It had been very slackly run.

He did a lot of that and in an undergraduate body that kind of initiative — coming from a mature, senior chap, especially one who was almost in a paterfamilias role — has a tremendous effect. . . . It was an injection of life. An injection of urgency. An injection of purpose. . . .

[Before that] the club had been very — I'm going to use David's terms — very bourgeois. Petit bourgeois. Things were done in a reformist way, in a slightly half-hearted way. There was no thrust in it, virtuous people being perhaps somewhat futile. . . .

Hence, you see, when the hunger marches came through Oxford, the university Labour Club was the body which received the marchers and helped them through. More than the Oxford City Labour Party did. This was the sort of thing that he advocated. . . . People were to spread the word generally that the club was to be livened up. We got better speakers and we [undertook] more public relations activity.

He was *far and away* the most powerful personality in the Labour Club. Tremendously powerful . . . through force of personality, experience, maturity, and this fact that he was riding one of the waves of the future, you see, which is the way anyone gets to be prominent.

And he had this girl Sophie with him all the time and that in itself was a tremendous thing at Oxford . . . and even if you had views that this was somewhat improper, to be unmarried and to go around the way they did, you hardly felt you could criticize it because . . . they were so devoted. She was tremendously charming and was an immense foil to him.

This, *eruption* [of David] into the situation at Oxford was very considerable. [The emphasis throughout is Nield's.]

Michael Foot arrived at Oxford a year before David. He is the same age as Nield. In his office he comes briskly around the desk to give a cordial handshake and to sit in an armchair opposite the one obviously reserved for visitors, and it is not until he takes off his enormous glasses with the side shields that are like translucent blinkers that you realize how big he really is — probably because the glasses change the scale of things. Without them you're immediately struck by how large his head is, made even larger by a thick mane of white hair brushed back and a nose that suddenly appears twice its former size. He twists and turns restlessly in the armchair, leaning forward, shifting his feet, twisting to lean on one arm of the chair and then the other. He seems to be trying to squirm into the interior of each question to see what it looks like from the inside. He speaks with no pauses. No "ahs"; no "umms." And when he has to search for a memory, he goes silent — and still — staring intently at the far side of the carpet until he has found it. He speaks in a rich baritone that actors must envy:

Oxford [in the early thirties] was more politically conscious than it had ever been before — on a bigger scale and more fiercely and dramatically than ever before — and David Lewis was one of the leaders, pretty well *the* leading figure who expressed that. . . . The overthrow of the Labour Government was a very deep, traumatic affair. People didn't know whether the labour movement was going to survive and how it was going to survive and, of course, there were furious controversies on how it should survive. [The emphasis is Foot's.]

The Communist Party at that stage thought that it was going to be taking over as the lineal descendant of socialism in Britain. . . . I think most of us thought that there was going to be a transformation in our society, just as there had been in the Soviet Union. It wouldn't take the form of communism, but we thought it would happen, and I think David expressed that and that was the mood in Oxford. . . .

David was a bit older than most of us and he was much more expert and was already an absolutely accomplished and skillful and devastating debater, and so when he came to the Union or spoke at the Labour Club he was really better at it, I would say, than anybody else. Partly because he had more experience and knowledge. But he put the socialist case more formidably than any other student debater, or near-student, or ex-student debater if you would like to call it that, and the impression was a very powerful one. . . .

He was a most attractive chap, you know. Most of us knew him and Sophie right from the beginning, so we associated them together.

[And then as an afterthought:] There was still a tendency at Oxford to lapse into some kind of dilettantism, or something like that. . . . But after 1931 the debating of the Union became more and more serious.

(Indeed, the thirties grew increasingly unfriendly to dilettantes and dandies. But the Children of the Sun remained. The Sonnenkind temperament found its outlet in people such as W.H. Auden and Christopher Isherwood and in the image of radiant young men, their eyes fixed fervently on the future, shirts open on bronzed chests, heroically discarding the world of their fathers — the typical portrait of the revolutionary worker in the art of social realism so favoured by Communists. And the perfect picture of a Sonnenkind naïf.)

"Catalytic" as David was, and vigorous as the Oxford Labour Club came to be, they still were only partial reasons why the major spies came from Cambridge and not from Oxford. But even as partial reasons they take on a global significance, given the Philby–Burgess–Maclean–Blunt accomplishments and what counterparts at Oxford might have achieved had they ever been allowed a foothold.

T.E.B. Howarth, who, in addition to writing *Cambridge Between Two Wars*, attended Cambridge as a student from 1933 to 1937, stresses that among the other possible reasons and perhaps the most basic, was that Oxford was more worldly than Cambridge — more conscious of practical politics, more versed in analyzing political ideologies, more activist. "The atmosphere was so much more politically sophisticated at Oxford." At Cambridge the emphasis was on economics, science, and mathematics — and even the economics was basically algebraic; at Oxford the emphasis was on philosophy and history. Howarth underlines his point by noting that British prime ministers Clement Attlee, Harold Wilson, and Harold Macmillan came from Oxford, not Cambridge — as, at a later time, so did Ted Heath and Margaret Thatcher.

As a second reason Howarth points to the Apostles Club, the now-notorious secret literary society that functioned as an incubator for the budding spies. The lack of a comparable secret society at Oxford may be significant, he says. However, he lays great stress on the homosexuality of the club. "You see, they did have this feeling of superiority, of this not belonging to society. It was not possible for [homosexual relationships] to be open and so it seems to me that if you developed a conspiratorial lifestyle of that sort, you were quite likely to fall prey to another form of conspiratorial lifestyle. The two go together psychologically."

But his description of the members, their sense of superiority, their feeling of not belonging to society, is a description of the Children of the Sun, and while he may be right in his view of conspiratorial lifestyles, the key factor with the Children of the Sun was their alienation and disillusion, not their homosexuality. Oxford had its quota of Sonnenkind too. And homosexuals. They also met together, although not within the confines of a secret society. So if the Apostles Club was a factor, it was marginal.

A third factor was the presence of influential dons with opposing views at the two universities: Maurice Dobb at Cambridge and G.D.H. Cole at Oxford. Dobb was an out-and-out Communist who was constantly extolling the virtues of communism and, in fact, probably was the first academic to carry a party card (it was dated 1920). Cole was equally persuasive in promoting guild socialism of a kind that could be achieved through constitutional means. In the early thirties, Cole was seen as the most influential socialist that Oxford had ever had.[20] Howarth relates both men back to the basic difference he sees between Oxford and Cambridge, "Cole as a characteristic Oxford politics tutor . . . Dobb in a sense not respectable because he was so overtly political, which you shouldn't be as a pure economist." So the third factor may not be independent but simply an aspect of the greater political worldliness of Oxford.

Another consideration, and this again may be another aspect of Oxford's worldliness, is that there was a line of eminent socialists who were extremely influential at Oxford and who, over time, imbued a sense of perspective. People such as William Temple, later to become Archbishop of Canterbury, who lectured before the First World War at Oxford; Richard Tawney, author of *The Acquisitive Society* (1920), who also lectured at Oxford before the war and then became a noted author and professor at the London School of Economics while still remaining influential in Oxford circles; and Richard Crossman, an Oxford tutor in the thirties who later had a distinguished career as an author, Labour MP, and member of the cabinet.

Another consideration, as Ted Jolliffe points out, is that the city of Oxford was itself worldly. It was a county seat and an industrial centre. (The Morris motor car company was located at Cowley, just outside the city.) Jolliffe was at Oxford with David and later became the first Ontario leader of the CCF. "There were trade unionists all around us. Not that we saw much of them, but you couldn't help rubbing shoulders with them. . . . Cambridge, as you know, is a rather isolated place out in the country."

Then there was John Cornford, David's counterpart at Cambridge, if counterpart there was. Cornford was not just a poet. He was brilliant, a dynamic organizer, a crusading natural leader, and a lineal descendant of Charles Darwin. His mother was Frances Cornford, the poet; his father, the Lawrence Professor of Ancient Philosophy. In his three undergraduate years at Cambridge (1933–36; he graduated with a BA

First Class with Distinction in History) he was credited with boosting the membership of the Socialist Society (which was Communist) from 200 to 600.[21] According to Steven Runciman, "younger son of the Liberal statesman Viscount Runciman, who as an undergraduate carried a parakeet on his heavily-ringed fingers and who later became a historian. . . . 'There is no doubt in my mind that Anthony Blunt was one of twenty people who were morally converted [to communism] by John Cornford, who was relentless about recruiting people. I have no doubt that Cornford made an impact on Burgess first and then through Burgess on Blunt.'"[22]

Just as there was no David Lewis at Cambridge, so there was no John Cornford at Oxford.

Finally, there is even the theory that Cambridge has a messianic approach to reform in its blood which dates back at least to its support for Cromwell and the Roundheads, in contrast to Oxford's support for the Crown and the Cavaliers. Maynard Keynes alluded to it when he saw so many turn to communism at Cambridge, especially within his beloved Apostles Club. His biographer says Keynes "attributed it to a recrudescence of the strain of puritanism in our blood, the zest to adopt a painful solution because of its painfulness." Keynes probably was referring to the English in general, but he certainly was referring to the situation at Cambridge in particular.[23]

No doubt there are a dozen other theories. But equally there is no doubt that David was a major factor in denying Oxford as a recruiting ground for Soviet moles.

He embodied the alternative. He was the barrier against which the Communist wave broke. Among students, he was the specific embodiment that expressed the difference between the two universities. He was, says Nield: "as impressive in his way as G.D.H. Cole or Richard Crossman."

A prominent professor and Labour Party member, Crossman was responsible for the good conduct of the Labour Club — all university clubs had to have a monitor — and as such he participated in the affairs of the club. Consequently, says Nield, there was a highly charged atmosphere, with Cole preaching Marxist socialism through a prism of guild socialism, David preaching "Bundist-Menshevist" socialism, and Crossman preaching revolutionary socialism through a Hegelian prism.

David was not the easiest person to get along with, says Nield. Despite his magnetism, he seemed to have a chip on his shoulder, possibly because of his "background of oppression in Eastern Europe"; possibly in part because he was Jewish; but also it might have stemmed from "the fact that he was a little man."

> I don't know what you experience, but in my experience I've automatically gone on my guard when a little man has appeared in my life because they compensate. And so David was small, he was Jewish, and he had this appalling thing that happened in Eastern Europe quite apart from its outcome as a Bolshevist regime. The event itself must have been horrendous. The retreat from Moscow in Poland's time must have been terrible. He had all that.
>
> So he was devoted to the Cause. And nothing was to be allowed to interfere with the Cause. No momentary deviation. This is where the Bolsheviks got some of their stuff from, of course, this kind of doctrine. No deviation. So however friendly you got with him, you might have stayed with him for a day or two at a country cottage and whilst you were there as his guest you would get blasted if what you said was out of line. And I mean blasted.
>
> Now he didn't mean it to be a blast at you; he meant it to be a blast at the heresy that you had just uttered. But it was very assertive. . . . [In fact] he invited confrontation. And enjoyed it. And he expected you, his confronters — I think to be fair to him — to be able to undertake the argument in its full rigour and for its own sake. And then to resume a friendly thing afterwards, which is not easy to do.

Irving Layton also comments on David's size in his book *Waiting for the Messiah*. But he sees a different David. One just as assertive, but without the chip on his shoulder:

> [He] was only three years older than myself but gave me the impression of being much older than that. The self-assurance that had so impressed me on our first encounter derived not only from the possession of an acute mind but also from his abbreviated stature. Perhaps because short people are closer to the ground they develop the feeling in others that they stand more securely on it. Sometimes when I looked at him, he put me in mind of a tree stump — solid, firmly rooted in the soil, immoveable. Whirlwinds might come and go or for that matter the blasts of history, of wars and revolutions, but come back and you'd find the stump exactly where you'd last seen it. Precisely because I was a young enthusiast whom impulse bent this way then that, his tree-stump solidity impressed me.[24]

David and Sophie arrived in England at the beginning of August 1932 and, after making a few preliminary arrangements, left immediately for Svisloch, arriving five days later on August 7. It would be the last time David would see his relatives. His grandfather, Rose's father, died a few years later and his grandmother may have died before the Nazis arrived; no one is sure. But the rest of his relatives, two aunts and uncles and five cousins, and all the other Jews in Svisloch — all 3,000 to 4,000 of them — were shot in a mass killing by the Nazis during the Second World War.

In the little town David and Sophie found "desperate poverty," every leather factory closed by the depression and every worker unemployed. People survived on what money relatives abroad sent home and on what vegetables they could grow behind their houses. But "what they could not hide was the despair in [their] eyes. Sophie and I felt all this keenly because we were being fêted with tea and cookies and occasionally even schnapps in many homes. Both of us felt that our hosts needed the cookies more than we did."[25]

Every night David's grandmother would pray for the well-being of relations in Montreal: "O Lord, don't weaken the hands that feed us," she would implore.[26]

The townspeople were fascinated with David, eager to see if he could match their memories of Maishe in public speaking and proud to see that he did. But they were entranced with Sophie. And when she spoke with them in Yiddish — which she had learned in the Lewises' kitchen, not at home — she captivated them forever. When they left after two weeks, schoolchildren gathered at the railway station to sing labour songs, and half the town turned out to say goodbye. They had become celebrities. David, one of the town's own, was going to the greatest university in the English-language world. On a scholarship. For the people of Svisloch, locked in such devastating poverty as they were, this was miraculous. Almost beyond imagination. Like the biblical David being invited to the court of King Saul. And Sophie was his chosen.

From Svisloch, David and Sophie travelled to Warsaw and Paris before returning to London. Their stays in Svisloch and Warsaw toughened still further their socialist resolve. In Warsaw they were sick at heart over what they saw — the slums and the squalor, the crowded needle-trade sweatshops, the families squeezed into airless rooms where they lived and worked, the beggars and prostitutes, ragged hungry children, people scavenging in the garbage of the well-to-do. They visited a cemetery where I.L. Peretz, the Yiddish storyteller; S. Ansky, author of the play, The Dybbuk; and others were buried, and that evening, when they were asked how they had spent the day, Sophie replied, "We've seen the cemetery of the living and the cemetery of the dead."[27]

As he was to do for the rest of his life wherever he travelled, David met with local socialist leaders. In Warsaw he visited the headquarters of the Bund, and through Bundist leaders he met prominent figures in trade unions in the arts and in politics — including members of the Polish Socialist Party and the Labour Zionists: "Many of [the people I met] had been active in Russia before the Revolution and had worked with Lenin, Trotsky, Bucharin, Plekhanov, Kamenev, Zinoviev and Martov, and all the other revolutionaries whose names are in the history books. Most of these had spent some years in prison, some in Siberia. From them, and from their experiences at the hands of the Bolsheviks, I learned a great deal about the conditions in the Soviet Union and about the Communist International and Communist parties, and what I learned confirmed my anti-communist convictions."[28]

However, even though he saw himself as anti-Communist, he still had the ambivalence that he expressed in his days on *The McGilliad*, remnants of which would remain with him throughout the thirties:

> My new socialist friends complained bitterly about the disruption which communists caused in their ranks. This was the period when the line of the Communist International referred to social democrats as fascists to be excoriated and smashed. . . . I was somewhat skeptical about the complaints. During those early years my main concern was the need for unity among the working class. It took me a while to learn that communists rejected the standard of behaviour which governed socialists and that there really were no autonomous local communist parties outside the Soviet Union. There were only agents serving the foreign policy and ideological papacy of Russia. During the fatal days of the thirties this was a calamity for the working class and for democracy throughout Europe.[29]

From Warsaw it was off to Paris where David met Paul Faure, general secretary of the French Socialist Party; Jean Zyromski, a member of the party's executive committee; and other French socialists. When he wasn't caught up in politics, he and Sophie, like lovers from time immemorial, wandered hand in hand through the City of Light.

Back in London, early in September, David immersed himself in the affairs of the Labour Party, which had just been split by the departure of the Independent Labour Party. The ILP had been affiliated with the Labour Party and had been its "socialist conscience." David's reaction to the split came right out of his Bundist roots. He was impatient and intolerant of schisms. His attitude was identical to that attributed to Vladimir Medem, quoted as an epigraph to this book, namely, "It is better to go along with the masses in a not totally correct direction than to separate oneself from them and remain a purist."

> I was almost impolite in my lack of sympathy [David said]. They thought they would be able to influence events more effectively because they would be free to state the socialist and pacifist case without regard for the compromise which the Labour Party leadership forced on members of the party, particularly those of the parliamentary caucus. . . .
>
> Separate, purist groups never appealed to me, even in my earliest years of socialist activity. The exclusiveness of such groups always seemed to me self-indulgent futility and even recklessness, for the objectives of democratic socialism can only be achieved by a united mass party. And this was my governing interest from the start.[30]

Before going up to Oxford, David and Sophie were to sit in on meetings with, as David described them, "some of the labour giants . . . Stafford Cripps, Harold Laski, G.D.H. Cole, Nye Bevan, William Mellor, Ellen Wilkinson, and Barbara Castle."[31] Right off the bat, he was at the heart of socialist affairs in England.

When David stepped into the Front Quadrangle at Lincoln College, Oxford, with its clean fifteenth-century Gothic lines — and its ambiguously austere "sashed" windows that replaced the Gothic-arched windows in the eighteenth and nineteenth centuries — and was ushered to his two modest rooms at the top of a staircase on the third floor, his timing, though unintended, was impeccable. At that very moment John Strachey, the Marxist theorist, was publishing his book, *The Coming Struggle for Power*, which maintained that "there is no force on earth which can long prevent the workers of the world from building a new and stable civilization for themselves on the basis of common ownership of the means of production."[32]

Probably more than any other book, it would be responsible for the large swing to the left among British intellectuals in the thirties. What the disillusionments of the previous fifteen years did to inflame the emotions, Strachey's book did to channel them politically. Strachey himself was one of the Children of the Sun — a naïf — at least during his Oxford days (1920–23), writing poetry, playing cricket in a ribboned woman's hat, breakfasting at noon on chocolate cake and crème de menthe, and all his life maintaining the somewhat effete manners of the aesthete.[33] He also was a closet Communist. He denied any Communist connections in the mid-thirties, but in 1946 while visiting Ottawa as a minister in Clement Attlee's government, he admitted to David that he had been working with the Communists in the thirties and had been instructed not to take out membership. He would be of more use to the party if he was able to claim that he was a nonpartisan social theorist, he said.[34]

A year and a half after David's arrival, Julian Bell testified to the extent of the change in attitudes at the universities. In his celebrated letter to the editor of *The New Statesman* in December 1933 he wrote:

> In the Cambridge that I first knew, in 1929 and 1930, the central subject of any conversation was poetry. As far as I can remember we hardly ever talked or thought about politics. For one thing, we almost all of us had implicit confidence in Maynard Keynes' rosy prophecies of continually increasing capitalist prosperity. Only the secondary problems, such as birth control seemed to need the intervention of the intellectuals.
>
> By the end of 1933 we have arrived at a situation in which almost the only subject of discussion is contemporary politics, and in which a very large majority of the more intelligent undergraduates are Communists or near Communists. . . .
>
> If Communism makes many of its converts among the "emotionals," it appeals almost as strongly to minds a great deal harder. It is not so much that we are all Socialists now as that we are all Marxists now. . . . It would be difficult to find anyone of intellectual pretensions who would not accept the general Marxist analysis of the present crisis.[35]

Of course, Julian Bell was caught up with the Communist cause at this point, so his remarks have to be read with a dash of salt. And just to add another perspective, in the summer of 1929 and for at least another year or so, he was having an affair with Anthony Blunt. However, Bell was never an uncritical Communist and he was soon to become fed up with the Marxist dialectic, which he found rigid and smothering to free discussion within the Apostles Club. Howarth, in *Cambridge Between Two Wars*, accuses Bell of overstating the case, saying that it was not until the Spanish Civil War that communism reached the level of attraction that Bell claimed for it in 1933.[36]

Nevertheless, overstated as it may be, it's like trying to describe the speed of Olympic sprinters. Those who are slower than the leaders are still breathtakingly quick. So if you were to excuse Bell his overstatement, you would still be left with a rate of change that could accurately be put as "breathtakingly quick." And as it was at Cambridge, so it was at Oxford — with the qualification that Oxford's more worldly restraints altered the texture of change while not appreciably slowing down the rate.

Rhodes scholarships did not permit marriages, or even countenance a fiancée living near the university. Too much of a distraction to serious minds. So Sophie took a flat in London with room for two, and since it was little more than an hour's train ride away from Oxford, it didn't pose much of an obstacle to their being together. In London, Sophie "tried to do things which in a sense, without my consciously realizing it, would prepare me for being the wife of a man who would be immersed and working in politics his whole life. I went to the London School of Economics. I joined what they called the Socialist Party and participated in protest marches which took place, and spent time with people who were working in the field of English literature, which, of course, I had always liked. This is what I always wanted to do, really."

In fact, it was the opportunity to attend university that she'd been denied in Canada because after her mother's death she'd had to get a job and run her father's household. And what made the dream-come-true even more exciting were the museums, theatres, concert halls, and art galleries that are sprinkled around London so generously — and especially the Old Vic, Sadler's Wells, Covent Garden, and Albert Hall, which were her favourites. "The last year, the third in England, I went down to live in Oxford with the approval of the warden of Rhodes House and that was really a first because I was the first official fiancée to be recognized by Rhodes House."[37]

Despite the air of supreme confidence that David projected, there were moments of misgivings. In a November letter to Maishe he explained that studying law really didn't interest him. "Law is the thread, not the sewing machine." The theory of law was interesting, but the details bored him. He felt like a deserter to the cause and maybe he should chuck it all and jump wholeheartedly into the movement. Then, on December 15, he again wrote Maishe and recalled that it was exactly one year since he had received the scholarship. It must have meant that "I possess something worthy. . . . This frightens me a little. Perhaps people are making a mistake; perhaps I don't possess what I appear to possess. . . .

"Here, too, in England, people are prophesying about me, await achievements by me. . . . It is not easy to believe but it is nonetheless true: all these expressions of confidence, belief in my potential, don't evoke in me feelings of egoism but feelings of fear. What if people's judgment about me is wrong, what if I don't and can't deliver? I must accomplish so much to justify the expressed confidence in me. It frightens me, this responsibility."[38]

But by year's end he was well settled in, and in the final days of January 1933 he made his first appearance in a debate at the Oxford Union, arguably the most prominent university debating society in the English-language world. Two months earlier, Michael Foot had been elected treasurer of the Union. The debate was on the resolution "That the British Empire is a menace to International good will" and, after the four opening debaters, David was the first to participate from the floor in support of the "Ayes." The Ayes lost, 85 to 122.[39]

A week later he was again for the Ayes in a debate over the resolution "That this House demand the abolition of the means test and an immediate increase of 10% in the rate of Unemployment Benefits," and this time the Ayes won 153 to 123.

And then, a week later on February 9, came the debate that made the front page of newspapers around the world. It was on the resolution "That this House will under no circumstances fight for its King and Country." The Ayes won 275 to 153. There were five opening speakers, followed by nine others supporting the motion and ten against. David was the eighth of the nine speakers in favour and "informed the House in tones of ringing satisfaction," said the report carried in *The Isis*, the weekly student magazine, "that a class war does exist. It is charming to think," the reporter concluded, "that such a simple fact can give Mr. Lewis so much innocent pleasure."[40]

The British were thunderstruck. So were Canadians and citizens of other countries in the empire. Not fight for King and Country! This was tantamount to treason. Cowardice. Betrayal. This was the work of "woozy-minded Communists" or "sexual indeterminates." No word was too foul to describe this effrontery.

The Times of London, scrambling to stand above the fray, declared that "to those . . . who are determined to take the result of the debate *au grand sérieux* let it be some consolation that the Union is in no sense representative of the University; that (despite the eminent persons in every generation who have used it as a training-ground for Parliament) it has always been liable to fall into the hands of a little clique of cranks; and the great body of undergraduates live their life at Oxford without ever concerning themselves about its activities. There is not the slightest reason to regard its latest resolution as a symptom of universal decadence."[41]

Two days later *The Isis* responded to the barrage of comment in an editorial of its own:

> We may grant at the outset that the motion was tactlessly and controversially phrased: 'That this House will *in no circumstances* fight for its King and Country.' The emphasis is ours. But we venture to assert that if it had put the issue of pacifism in a less arbitrary form, there would have been nothing to debate about. The verdict would have been unanimous. It is the duty of a President to make possible a vivid debate.
>
> The real significance of the verdict . . . is not that Oxford is disloyal, or Communist — the latter is a very ancient and fish-like red-herring by now — but that it has with no uncertain voice declared the futility

and immorality of war. It is not necessary to have a leaning towards Moscow to realise that war never settles anything. . . .

To say, then, that the verdict of pacifism does not represent the opinion of Oxford as a whole is not true. To say that it was due to the preponderance of Communists in the Union is ridiculous: for the Oxford Communists were not in the Union that night at all. They were holding a meeting of their own elsewhere, listening to Mr. Wal Hannington. . . .[42]

To David, war was an abomination, a consequence of monopoly capitalism with its competition ethic and its limitless greed; it was something to be opposed at every turn. But he was no pacifist. How could he be, having lived among the pogroms of Eastern Europe as a child and seen first hand the necessity for the Jewish defence militias that the Bund established in Svisloch and across the Pale? He knew that in the end Jews had only two choices: resist or be victims. So if all else failed and war with Hitler was inevitable, he would support armed resistance. Consequently, in a 1946 article, he saw the King and Country debate differently than did the editors of *The Isis* — and probably unwittingly touched on a part of the Sonnenkind creed: "The young men at the Oxford Union that evening . . . declared they wanted higher things than narrow nationalism to live and fight for. They were neither pacifist nor unpatriotic. They were simply distrustful of the old men and the old slogans. In the war against Fascism, the same men fought bravely on all fronts."[43]

One of the more thoughtful comments made at the time came from a Communist, R. G. Freeman, who was a founding member of the October Club, Oxford's Communist club. He wrote an essay that was published in 1934 in a collection entitled *Young Oxford and War*. His was one of four essays from student leaders representing different political parties. He said of the resolution debated that the

wording from our point of view was not very satisfactory; it was a negative, pacifist motion with the disadvantage of a motion of such a type having a score of interpretations which could be ascribed to it. . . . Yet even with its limitations the motion was important . . . in that it finally destroyed the belief that those undergraduates who would be anxious to combat war were to be found only amongst the members of the October and Labour Clubs. By the support that the motion received in Oxford it was made clear that the case against imperialist war could get far wider sympathy than we had previously imagined.[44]

A month later, on March 2, the "Noes" tried to reverse the vote in a second debate but failed, and a week later David was elected one of five members of the Union's Library Committee. Twenty people had submitted their names for election. During David's three years at Oxford, again and again *The Isis* commented on his debating skills, calling his speeches "excellent," "devastating," worthy of "The Isis palm," "best of the term," "devastating," and remarking that he had met his match only against Aneurin Bevan, then a Labour MP who had visited Oxford to deliver a speech to the Labour Club.[45]

The thought of going for the presidency of the Union came to David about this time, although it's unclear whether it was before or after his election to the Library Committee. In his memoirs he says only that it was in the spring at a tea for Rhodes scholars at the home of Carlton Allen. When others were talking about sports they were playing, "I quietly asked Dr. Allen whether becoming president of the Oxford Union would be an adequate equivalent since, as he knew from my dossier, I could not win a blue [an Oxford sporting colour]. He was obviously taken aback but laughed and suggested that it would be very nice indeed to have another Rhodes man a Union president, particularly a Canadian because there had never been one from my country. Although he was very polite and chose his words carefully, he seemed rather doubtful about my being able to carry it off."[46]

That fall David stood for election as treasurer, the second-highest office, but lost. A week later, at the end of November, he topped the polls in being elected as one of five members of the Union's standing committee. On his second try for treasurer, at the end of March 1934, he was successful, winning 214 votes to 121 and 35 for his two rivals. In June he ran for the presidency and lost, but finally, in late November 1934, he won it in a two-way race 209 203. That meant he held office for the Hilary Term, from the beginning of January to the end of April — and that summer he sailed for home.

When he made the obligatory candidate's speech for the presidency he was ill with a fever and severe abdominal pains. The doctor said it was chronic appendicitis and afterward David remembered nothing of what he had said. As was customary, *The Isis* published a profile of the new president:

> When David Lewis steps into the Union presidency next term he will be, beyond question, the least Oxonian person ever to lead the Society. In appearance, background, and intellectual outlook he is a grim antithesis to all the suave, slightly delicate young men who for generations have sat on the Union rostrum . . .
>
> Aside from his continual participation in Union debates, Lewis has given most of his time in England to helping build up the University Labour Club into a powerful machine with 700 paid members. Twice

Librarian of the Club, he has refused higher office on the grounds that the organization should be guided by British students . . .

When he has taken his Schools in June, he plans to plunge again into Socialist politics on the other side of the Atlantic. . . . For a person who has grown up in the shadow of war, poverty and economic oppression, no other path is open. It is, perhaps, because his social theory is such an integral part of his personality that neither his friends nor his enemies have ever questioned his sincerity and disinterestedness. The almost ferocious energy with which Lewis defends his convictions is, however, the root of his most dangerous fault. Tolerance comes hard. He cannot help attacking hypocrisy, snobbery and muddled thinking with a scathing, merciless sarcasm. His forthright earnestness has antagonized many of the more timid and soft-spoken Oxonians.

At the same time, it has won their respect.[47]

Among the students David met soon after his arrival at Oxford was John Cripps, who had come up the year before David and had become active in the Labour Club. David made an instant impact on John, who was impressed with "his maturity. He lived in the real world in a way that most of us hadn't. And with the definitiveness of his views. He had a much deeper philosophical basis for his ideas than we did. We were sort of playing a part, really. He had thought the whole thing through and . . . seemed to have worked it all out."

Soon John was inviting Sophie and David to the family home at Filkins, not far from Oxford, where his father Stafford took a liking to David. Stafford Cripps, in the words of Michael Foot, was the greatest barrister of his time in England. "He was really magnificent. When you heard him in the courtroom, or in the House of Commons, the authority with which he would present a case was absolutely stunning."

Stafford Cripps became David's mentor, taking the place that until then had been occupied solely by Maishe. He opened doors for David, introduced him to people, took Sophie and him to see Shakespeare at Stratford-on-Avon, talked politics with him endlessly, sometimes on strolls through the fields of his estate, sometimes before a roaring fire at Filkins, sometimes, as one photograph shows, sitting in the sun on a patio with Anuerin Bevan.

No doubt David sooner or later would have met most of the people that Cripps introduced him to. But the level of immediate intimacy that was available through Cripps was something else again. It was pretty heady company. Cripps himself was a bit of a conundrum. A brilliant student in chemistry, he switched to law and was made a King's Counsel in 1927. His father was Lord Parmoor, a cabinet minister in the 1924 Labour Government. His uncle was Sidney Webb, one of the founders of the Fabian Society. But in spite of his political heritage, Cripps didn't become active in politics until 1929 when, at the behest of some friends, he joined the Labour Party and in less than a year was appointed Solicitor General by Ramsay MacDonald. He was elected to Parliament in 1931, but when MacDonald formed his national coalition he refused to serve. In 1932 he helped found the Socialist League and throughout his career resided on the far left of the Labour Party.

According to Michael Foot, he was, certainly in the early years, "a political innocent. He knew little of the Labour movement, less of its history and amid all his other preoccupations had little time or inclination to repair the deficiency by a reading of Socialist literature. His Marxist slogans were undigested; he declared the class war without ever having studied the contours of the battlefield."

But, he possessed virtues "in abounding measure . . . the faculty to stir great masses by his burning sincerity combined with an even more evident capacity to subdue other assemblies by sheer intellectual power. More successfully than any great political lawyer of that age or most others, Cripps carried his skill undiminished and his reputation untarnished from the Courts to the Commons."[48]

He was to serve as chancellor of the exchequer in Clement Attlee's government (1947–50) and to be credited with righting the British economy under his austerity program. And on the way there, he served as ambassador to Moscow, a member of the War Cabinet, and as special envoy to India attempting to rally disparate political factions against the Japanese in 1942. But he also advocated a united front with the Communists in 1936 — a year after, it should be remembered, his uncle and aunt, Sidney and Beatrice Webb, had published *Soviet Communism: a new civilisation?* in which they rattled on about the wonders of the Soviet Union. (Among their earlier achievements, the Webbs had founded the London School of Economics and the *New Statesman* and had been leaders of the Fabian Society.) Cripps, along with a few others such as George Lansbury, is credited by Michael Foot with saving the Labour Party after the Ramsay MacDonald debacle in 1931: "Stafford threw himself into the whole of this situation in the thirties. He was the number-one socialist political leader as far as the students went. . . . But he wasn't trained in socialism like David was. David knew much more about Marxism than Stafford would ever know."

Despite the difference in their ages, David and Stafford became close friends. Cripps obviously enjoyed the cut and thrust of discussion with David — the sharpness of his mind, the depth of understanding of Marxist thought that he could bring to bear — and David equally relished the older man's incisive, adversarial mind and the windows to Fabian socialism that he could open for him.

The insights into Fabianism that he obtained, his encounters with members of the British Labour Party, his association with G.D.H. Cole, his trips to the Continent to meet European socialist leaders, his activities with the Oxford Labour Club, all added to the modifying process begun by Frank Scott, King Gordon, Frank Underhill, and Eugene Forsey at the League for Social Reconstruction in Canada.

But the core of his socialism remained Marxist — primarily in his economic analysis of society — and it remained so to the end. But Marxism comes in many shades and sizes. What was David's?

In trying to measure the shade and size of any version, a litmus test is a person's opinion on the necessity of violent revolution and the need for a dictatorship of the proletariat. David rejected both and always had, and that rejection sprang out of his Bundist roots.

Through his youth in Svisloch, the Bund had insisted, to the point of obsession, that the revolution should be sought through democratic means, as Marx had judged possible in the late 1860s, and that democratic procedures should continue to prevail for everyone after the revolution. And that was the position Maishe continued to take.[49] The Bolsheviks, at the other end of the spectrum, espoused both revolutionary violence and the proletarian dictatorship. And in between, but closer to the Bund, were the Mensheviks, denying the necessity of violent revolution but supporting the need for a somewhat restrained dictatorship of the proletariat.

Lenin called those who insisted on full democratic procedures "liquidationists," meaning that they had fallen prey to reformism and bourgeois tendencies.[50] And Stalin, as he was consolidating his power, took to calling them social fascists.[51] Little wonder that David had an undying antagonism toward Communists.

As sharp as were the differences among Bundists, Mensheviks, and Communists, they had one thing in common: they were revolutionary.

Fabian socialism on the other hand, was not nearly so confrontational — or so muscular. In fact the word "Fabian" was taken from the name of the Roman general Fabius Cunctator whose tactics of harassing and delaying Hannibal's armies — a strategy of attrition — gave Rome time to recover its strength and to take to the offensive. His name came to be linked with policies that were gradual and cautious — and gradual and cautious is exactly what Fabian socialism was. It preached "the inevitability of gradualness." H.G. Wells called it "evolutionary collectivism."[52]

Its emphasis was on educating the public about socialism by publishing books, periodicals, and pamphlets; by sponsoring meetings, lectures, conferences, and discussion groups; and by conducting research into economic, political, and social issues. The idea was not to strive for power itself but to win over the minds of those with access to it. Sophisticated this might be, but a call to revolution it most emphatically was not — not even to a quiet revolution. In 1900 it helped form the Labour Representation Committee, the predecessor of the Labour Party, and it has been affiliated with the party ever since it took the name in 1906. At its height in 1946 the Society had about 8,400 members.

Now that's a far cry from the militant socialism that coursed through the veins of David Lewis. Nevertheless, because its research was so expert, its approach so humane, and its focus on issues so practical and immediate, he was, of course, influenced. But the influence was in policies that could be implemented and in procedures that underlined democratic practices, not in his determination to lay siege to the power structure.

On the other hand, the Labour Party did focus on the pursuit of power, and in its practical experience David found much to interest him, much that he could appropriate, much that resounded sympathetically with the organizational side of his Bundist heritage.

So what he ended up with was a modified Bundist interpretation of Marxism. Call it, if you will, Parliamentary Marxism. It was a Marxian analysis of economics and a parliamentary approach to politics. And if David had ever been forced to choose, he would have chosen the Parliamentary over the Marxian.

Compared to its European counterparts, the Labour Party was a pretty tame affair. It had its left wing, to be sure — its Aneurin Bevans and Jennie Lees — but basically it was stolidly reformist. In fact, in all of Oxford socialism there was little to challenge David's basic ideology. It had never sunk roots into hard-core Marxism. Its roots were in Christian activism or in the non-ideological pragmatism of unionism or in the not-quite-so-scrappy socialist theories of people such as R.H. Tawney, whose famous pamphlet, *The Sickness of the Acquisitive Society*, was originally presented to the Fabian Society (and then incorporated into his book, *The Acquisitive Society*). In fact the challenge went the other way; one of the reasons for the vitality of the Labour Club was the shaking up it was receiving from David.

For instance, by October 1933 David had succeeded in organizing study groups throughout the entire university under the sponsorship of the Labour Club. There were ten groups, each comprising members from two or three colleges. Only Balliol College didn't participate. "The whole is centralised under the control of Mr. David Lewis," noted *The Isis*, adding, "The energy of these young University Socialists is almost unbelievable. If the Socialist movement as a whole is anything like as active as they are, then a Socialist victory at the next election is inevitable."[53]

The greatest challenge to David's revolutionary impatience came from G.D.H. Cole, who had come to Marxism through a background as the chief exponent of guild socialism, which argued for a decentralized approach emphasizing self-government for major economic and social groups. It was a philosophy in direct opposition to the centralized, albeit democratic, thrust taken by David and by the Fabians. "He was my economics tutor and had labour relations as a special subject," says Nield:

> His was a nice, gentle Marxism from a comfortable member of the British upper middle class . . . a very kindly man indeed. A most civilized man. Brahms was his favourite composer. He had gone a little further than Beethoven and required something a little more. Very interesting. Listen to Brahms and you know about Cole.
>
> His influence was tremendous. He wrote this great history of the working-class movement that appeared at the time. More than looked askance at; almost sent to Coventry by the more respectable elements. A tremendous influence among undergraduates . . . quite a considerable popularizer of the Marxist doctrine. It was a great honour at Oxford to be invited to Cole's seminar.

David and Cole were very friendly, says Ted Jolliffe and Cole's informal seminars, noted *The Isis*, were "composed of some twenty leading members of the Labour Club (and was) the most exclusive" group on campus.[54] "A number of us were invited," says Jolliffe. "David was a faithful attendant at those meetings. They took place in the late afternoon, once a week . . . Cole would just talk and toss questions back and forth." They were times of good sherry and good conversation, and what Cole's probings did more than anything else was force David to a deeper understanding of working-class movements — in short, to take off more of his rougher edges.

The first impression of Ted Jolliffe, on walking up to the farm that has been in his family for 150 years at Rockwood, Ontario, is that it isn't him at all, this smallish, unpretentious, slightly stooped, and white-haired man in baggy trousers and a mauve shirt — not him at all but perhaps some old retainer. But the moment he begins speaking, walking up the wide sloping lawn to the old farmhouse, there's no mistaking him.

Some people capture you with their eyes, some with craggy looks or an air of conviction. With Joliffe it's his voice, somehow as weatherbeaten and crevassed as his face. Bass baritone. Gravelly and commanding. He pulls two wooden lawn chairs to an ancient tree stump that serves as a table for mugs of tea and a repository for spent matches used to light his pipe and tap down its contents. It's a fine, breezy summer day in the shade of a large maple, with a view across fields that dip away and rise to his fence row half a kilometre away. By the end of the afternoon there is a pile of thirty or forty used matches on the stump with no end in sight. Born in 1909, the same year as David, an old war horse relishing the glory days, recalling his time at Oxford, his years as the first Ontario leader of the CCF and his legal battles as partner in Jolliffe, Lewis and Osler in Toronto fighting for trade-union clients. He is still working as a labour arbitrator.

> I think David spent far more time at Oxford talking with people than he did studying. At least that was certainly the impression I had. Most of us didn't go to lectures very much. Most lectures at Oxford were very poor. We all had a tutor and the tutor was supposed to guide us on our way. For those of us who already had four years of university, that didn't seem out of the ordinary. If a lecturer was outstanding we'd go and listen to him. . . .
>
> People went to Oxford with may different intentions, some of which they carried out. Many had the intention simply of cultivating important connections, like the American boys who arranged tea parties or sherry parties for Felix Frankfurter [who was lecturing at Oxford at the time and "was very dull; a very big disappointment"] because they knew it might help them on their way later. You know, that sort of thing.

One of David's main intentions was to acquaint himself with European socialism — with the people, the organizations, the policies — and this he did with boundless energy, travelling with Sophie to Europe as often as they could, establishing relationships with the bright lights of the British Labour Party. "We had very lengthy vacations," says Jolliffe, "and David was always hobnobbing with these people. . . . He was very friendly with Harold Laski . . . and Nye Bevan, although Bevan was a bit too much of a character, I think, for David's taste. Colourful, but not David's type. . . . And Hugh Gaitskill. David was very close to Hugh Gaitskill. . . . He and Hugh were very much of one mind about many, many things."

And there were Léon Blum from France; Pietro Nenni, exiled from Italy; Otto Bauer from Austria (before the destruction of Vienna's socialist enclave); and one of David's most thrilling encounters, Henryk Erlich, member of the St. Petersburg Soviet at the time of the 1917 Revolution and, along with Victor Alter, a leading Bundist in Poland. David met him at the last full Congress of the Second International, which was held in Paris in August 1933. He was, says David, "particularly friendly and helpful. He had attended many international meetings, knew every leading delegate, and went out of his way to make introductions and to fill me in on personal and political backgrounds. He was very knowledgeable and terribly worried about Germany and the Jews. Contrary to the wishful hopes some others were expressing, he had no doubt about Hitler's intention to eliminate the Jews and all political opponents, as *Mein Kampf* spelled out in detail."[55]

In March of that year, in another display of his Bundist roots, David became impatient with the policies of the Labour Party in England and the Social Democratic Party in Germany for their lack of resolve in dealing firmly with left-wing members. He wrote home, echoing Medem. These people, he said, "were more interested in the purity of their souls than in the building of socialism," and so were causing tensions and splits at a time when socialism needed all the strength it could muster in the fight against fascism. A month later, in another letter home, he paused to wonder whether he was being egotistical in persuading himself that he was right and the leaders of the parties were wrong since the leaders were all people he respected. However, it was a short pause.

David and Sophie spent the summer of 1933 in France, despite Sophie's desire to go home for a visit, because, said David in a letter home, they needed to improve their French. "I need it in Quebec," he said, both for a law practice and for participation in the labour movement. In that same letter he despaired over the "shameful capitulation" of German trade unionists to the Nazi regime. In the end it had done them no good because two weeks before he wrote, Nazis had arrested union leaders and had confiscated all union property.

"So where is there light?" he asked. "Only God knows and he doesn't exist."

The spring of 1934 marked the point of no return for David at Oxford. He was almost two-thirds through his scholarship and was still desperately unhappy with the study of law. If he were to shift direction, this was his last chance to do it. So he went on the spring vacation that year troubled and anxious, trying to sort out his next step, and immediately involved himself in two undertakings that must have strengthened the emotional underpinnings for his decision to switch — if they didn't, in fact, actually precipitate the decision.

One proclaimed what could be, the other what must not be; one inspired, the other inflamed; one spoke to hope, one to anger.

One dealt with birth, the other death.

The Regina Manifesto was at the centre of the first; the smashing of Otto Bauer's socialist enclave in Vienna was the subject of the other.

The Regina Manifesto had been adopted at the CCF's first national convention the previous July, and for the spring vacation David and Ted Jolliffe organized a weekend conference for Canadians studying in England to discuss it. Bob Bryce came from Oxford where he was studying economics under J.M. Keynes. (He would later become secretary to the federal cabinet, secretary of the panel that screened civil servants following the Gouzenko spy revelations, deputy minister of finance, Canadian executive director to the International Monetary Fund, and chairman of the Royal Commission on Corporate Concentration.) W.L. Morton from Oxford (who would become a distinguished professor of history at the University of Manitoba), James Coyne (who would become governor of the Bank of Canada), Fred Kurgen (destined to become one of Canada's leading surgeons and medical superintendent of Toronto General Hospital), Herbert Norman (who was studying at Cambridge and would become a top-ranking diplomat — and who would commit suicide in Cairo in 1957 in the face of accusations that he was a security risk because he had been a Communist in the 1930s, despite continued expressions of confidence in him by Lester Pearson, who was then Minister of External Affairs), Jack Stewart (who was to serve as a colonel on staff for the D-Day invasion and later became a prominent lawyer in Toronto), and fifteen or twenty others. Sir Stafford Cripps was the only non-Canadian to participate.[56]

"David," says Jolliffe, "had no sympathy, of course, with Woodsworth's attitude that Oh, we mustn't have a political party; all we can have is a movement and a co-operative commonwealth. . . . He thought [this attitude] was too much to the right; and he thought some of [the Manifesto] was a little too utopian and too far to the left such as [the provision that called for the 'eradication' of all vestiges of capitalism]."

It was an exciting weekend. Cripps was the only guest speaker and the discussions were made the more lively because everyone knew they no longer were talking theory. Back home a major development actually was happening.

The second event, the trip to Vienna, was less than a month after Dollfuss had overrun the socialist enclave. It was a visit to a battlefield where brethren had died for the beliefs David shared. Blasted by artillery. Cut down by snipers. David wrote letters home full of admiration for the heroism of Bauer and his comrades. And he described the aftermath in *The Oxford Forward*, a journal published that November:

> Before February, I was told, [the workers'] houses often carried the air of a club. For there was always some activity of interest animating most of the inhabitants. Now these activities were forbidden, but they were carried on secretly with a determination which had all the more strength because it was silent and bitter. But the results of Fascism have begun to be felt in other ways too. The rent has been universally raised from 50 to 100 per cent. Many of the February fighters have lost their jobs without any hope of finding another.
>
> The many workers' libraries have been purged. A comrade gave me a volume of Karl Marx as a souvenir. He had saved and hidden away some thirty volumes from their local library. What he intended doing with them? "Keep them until these houses and libraries again belong to us."
>
> Millions of Austrian schillings were spent on beautifying Vienna during some fifteen years of Socialist rule . . . But above all, that money went towards the building of workers' homes, towards the construction of kindergartens, schools, libraries, clubs, theatres, parks. This enraged the bourgeoisie which had been so mercilessly taxed to make these achievements possible. For the present it has been victorious. Cannons have arrrested further progress. . . . But the visit to Vienna . . . forced me to share the faith of the comrade who presented me with the volume of *Das Kapital*.[57]

One of the first things he did when he got back to Oxford was attend a meeting of the Labour Club, and when members sang "The Red Flag," the official Labour Party song, as they always did on adjourning, emotion flooded his voice, almost cutting off the words, as the song once again took on new meaning:

> The people's flag is deepest red,
> It shrouded oft our martyred dead,
> And ere their limbs grew stiff and cold
> Their heart's blood dyed its ev'ry fold.
>
> *Chorus:*
> Then raise the scarlet standard high!
> Within its shade we'll live or die.
> Though cowards flinch and traitors sneer,
> We'll keep the red flag flying here.
>
> . . .   .

With heads uncovered swear we all
To bear it onward till we fall.
Come dungeon dark or gallows grim,
This song shall be our parting hymn.[58]

The realities that he had been dealing with over the vacation made continuing in law doubly irrelevant, so, with only four terms left out of the nine in his scholarship, he determined to quit law in order "to broaden my knowledge in the social sciences and in philosophy." In a letter to Abe Klein written on August 24 he explained why:

> . . . I was faced with another year of law in Oxford. That almost made me physically sick. I had already wasted two years on the bloody subject without there being the slightest prospect of its being of any use to me, since I would have to study for and write the bar exams anyway, and I was damned if I was going to waste another year at it.
> I sat down and thought: . . . I have all the time wanted to do the Modern Greats course (i.e. philosophy, politics and economics). If I change immediately I will just have sufficient time to do it well, if I read a great deal.
> There was a terrific battle with the Rhodes people and the College authorities; my tutor was annoyed and felt personally insulted. He argued that I was certain of a second-class in law and I was foolish to abandon it for a possible third in Modern Greats. The College authorities argued that it was impossible to do Modern Greats in one year. The course was too wide. . . . The Rhodes Secretary argued that it outraged his every sense of propriety; to have studied a subject for almost two years, to have made fairly good progress, and then refuse to take a degree in it! By dint of calm insistence, I won them over to the idea.
> Result: For the last five months I have been joyfully reading books without wanting to destroy them. . . . My father, I am afraid, was rather upset about it, and there is certainly no lack of concern or understanding in his case. But I am so happy about it that right or wrong, I am glad I did it.[59]

Like father, like son. Maishe abandoned rabbinical studies in Volkovysk because they were too remote from the working-class movement that was forming at the turn of the century. Of course he understood why David was quitting law. But he also was an immigrant father with the intense desire that his son do well. After all, that's why he had emigrated. So it's no surprise that he was at the same time upset. It was a large risk David was taking, trying to do a three-year course in one. However, he was not coming to Modern Greats bereft of background. He had done a lot of reading on his own during the previous year, mostly concerning Marx, but also including Kant, Hegel,

Spinoza, and Ludwig Feuerbach (a moralist who wrote extensively on the nature of God and Christianity and who had strongly influenced Marx). Still, three years in one. . . . But not only did David succeed, he got a high second-class in his examinations.

The summer of 1934 David and Sophie again spent in Europe — in Paris, Cologne, Liège, Brussels, Antwerp, Rome, Florence, Genoa, Turin, Padua, Venice, Vienna, Linz, Salzburg, Berlin, Munich, and Nurenberg. In Vienna he met Hugh Gaitskill, who had lived through the attack by Dollfuss on the socialist enclave and had been horrified by it. Interestingly, Kim Philby had also been there at the same time, working with underground Communists. However, Philby left shortly afterward and was not in Vienna during David and Sophie's visit. Philby had graduated from Cambridge the preceding summer and Maclean that same summer of 1934. Burgess graduated in 1935. Blunt did not leave until 1937, having become a don in 1934.

While David and Sophie were in Vienna, Dollfuss was assassinated. "When we walked back to our [lodgings] soldiers with bayonetted rifles and armed police were everywhere and heavy artillery was in the streets," David wrote home. "There were rumours that those involved in the putsch had also captured the radio station but the Government recaptured it. The putschists are believed to be Nazis . . . the real objection of the Government was not to nazism as such but rather because it wanted to maintain an independent Austria, or, at least, that was the line."

In Vienna they opened their lodgings to members of an illegal social democratic group preparing to flee to Czechoslovakia; in Berlin they accompanied an underground courier, a woman, delivering documents that would have brought her "certain death" had she been found out; also in Berlin, David mingled with workers and was aghast at the support they voiced for Hitler; in addition, he and Sophie met with underground groups, dodged Gestapo agents, and learned with horror of the atrocities that were being committed against Jews, socialists, Communists, and trade unionists. "It was hard to believe that a people as cultured as the Germans would indulge in such uncivilized and inhuman behaviour," he commented in his memoirs.[60] But there was no denying it.

England, of course, had its own fascists, led by Oswald Mosley. When they came to Oxford on their first visit in November 1933, there was a terrific brawl. Calling Mosley's blackshirts hooligans, *The Isis* reported, "Knuckledusters were used; a chair was thrown from the gallery; members of the audience who rose to ask questions were seized, brutally mauled and finally thrown down stone stairs."[61]

Three months later they came back and rented a dance hall for a meeting that was addressed by William Joyce, the infamous Lord Haw-Haw of the Second World War. "Lewis and I and others in the Labour Club organized something which worked," says Jolliffe. "The dance hall had a wooden floor. And moveable chairs. So we wrecked the meeting simply by getting up and leaving in twos and threes. There was no provocation to assault and there was nothing they could do about it."

The Labour Club members were strategically located in the middle of rows throughout the hall and when they left, the scraping and clattering of chairs on the wooden floor caused such a distraction that Joyce couldn't command the attention of the audience. "Then the townspeople got the same idea. They thought it was a bore, so they got up and left too. The meeting was a complete fiasco. The blackshirts were furious. Well, that resulted in street fighting. I guess it was about the only time in recent years that there's been street fighting in Oxford, for which a number of us were gated by the [university] authorities because we participated."

It was a night he'll never forget, Jolliffe says: "The Labour Club was entirely there. But the Communists were nowhere to be seen."

The Isis pronounced itself "heartily sickened by the appalling nonsense" expressed by Joyce. And of the proceedings before the meeting dissolved in shambles, it noted that "(A)ll the oral questions fired at [Joyce] came from members of the Labour Club, chief amongst whom were Mr. David Lewis, Mr. Rutherford, Mr. Bob Gerard, Mr. Hunt and Miss Betty Morrison."[62]

By December 1932, half a year after David had arrived at Oxford, the Labour Club had 484 members, the highest number in the club's thirteen-year history, and Communists from the October Club, which by then had about 300 members, were constantly trying to infiltrate — and throughout David's time at Oxford they never gave up trying.[63]

> There were some almighty rows about that [says Jolliffe] . . . and the dominant figure throughout these debates was David Lewis. Much of the debating turned on the events in Austria and Germany. This was the crucial period, you know, 1932, 1933. Very crucial. David knew the story very, very well. He knew what the Communists had done in Germany to frustrate the socialists and, as a matter of fact, to facilitate Hitler's accession to power. . . .
>
> In debates, when the October Club spokesmen tried to get the floor, he was devastating. Absolutely devastating. He had the facts. He was far more familiar with the whole subject than they were, and there was

not much that they could do. Many of them were just spouting what they'd been told anyway.

I cannot recall a single individual of any intellectual stature, like David, who spoke for the October Club. They were weak. Or, at least, they were no match for people like David. . . .

There was a difference between his speeches at the Union and his speeches at the Labour Club. His speeches at the Union had more humour in them; the atmosphere was entirely different. But his speeches at the Labour Club were deadly serious. . . . His influence at the Labour Club, more than anyone else's, I think, explains the failure of the Communists to make any headway there. There were so many naïve people around who could have been taken in.

Figures for club memberships are a little misleading because many people joined simply for appearances. As Nield points out: "If you had rooms, you had cards on your mantelpiece, which was a sign of social prestige. Every club, political or anything else, had a card. You had a card for your college cricket club, for your college soccer club and rugby club, you had a card for the Labour Club, October Club, Tory Club, for the John Oldham Society, which was a literary society. . . . Lots of people had both the Labour Club card and the Tory Club card, and a few even the Liberal Club card. And not everybody had an active relationship. And you even had the October Club card as well. The more cards you had, the brighter [your social star]."

In any event, the membership of the Labour Club increased three-quarters over its original size in the three years that David was there and "a great part of that was the influence of David in the club and in the Union," says Nield.

Despite the escalating fear of fascism and the growing anti-war feeling, the Communists were not yet ready to push for a popular front. The focus was not on co-existing with the Labour Club but on destroying it. The Comintern portrayal of socialists as social fascists was still in effect — so much so that in Germany the Communists concentrated on attacking the Social Democrats and united with the Nazis, whom they said they feared less, to bring down the Weimar Republic. But then in 1935, at the Comintern's Seventh, and last, Congress, the policy changed. The defeat of fascism now became a prime concern and Stalin was looking for allies against Germany. So the call went out to seek popular fronts. *The Isis* reported the result in its issue of May 15, 1935. The biggest bombshell of the term, it said had come from the October Club, which proposed fusion with the Labour Club. There was going to be "a first rate political controversy on a question of principle" such as Oxford had not seen for some time, it said.

The debate in the Labour Club came little more than a week before David was to take his "schools" — the compulsory written examinations held prior to oral examinations — but he threw himself into it with abandon. In the end there were only twenty members of the Labour Club who voted for fusion with the October Club. It was a humiliating defeat for those seeking union.[64]

However, the matter did not end there. In June, shortly before David's graduation, *The Isis* noted that: "The Labour Club may have rejected fusion but the matter is not yet settled. An interesting thing is the dearth of what are technically known as 'promising people' in the ranks of the Labour Club. For years the Labour Club has been turning out a Geoffrey Wilson, a Frank Hardie, a John Cripps, a David Lewis, each year; but this [coming] year there seems to be no figures as outstanding as these."[65]

It proved to be a perceptive comment. The following December, with David long gone and with no one approaching his stature to lead the fight, the Labour Club amended its constitution to remove impediments to fusion with the October Club and shortly after, the actual affiliation took place.[66] At its pre-war peak in 1938 "or thereabouts," the Labour Club had a membership of more than 1,000 and, according to some accounts, approaching 1,200 — which, considering that Oxford's total student population was 5,023, was impressive indeed. Of the total membership, Communists made up something less than 200.[67] The year 1938 also saw the Union acquire its first Communist as president in the person of Philip Toynbee, the son of historian Arnold Toynbee.[68]

In his final days at Oxford, David arrived at the most dramatic crossroads of his career. He could stay in England, enter the most prominent firm of barristers in London, become a member of Parliament, be assured of a cabinet post when Labour took power, as it did immediately after the Second World War, and after that, who knows what else? Or he could return to Canada to a socialist movement that was struggling for survival with no promise of anything but hard work, low pay, and perhaps little thanks or recognition.

A British general election was planned for later that same year, and Labour Party officials offered David a safe seat if he would stay and run for office. And Stafford Cripps offered him a job as a barrister in his chambers. David chose to go home. As he said in his memoirs: "I felt a deep gratitude to Canada for the opportunities which had opened up before me almost from the day I first arrived in Montreal fourteen years ago."[69]

Hard on the heels of this decision came a handwritten letter from J.S. Woodsworth dated June 19, 1935. David was jubilant. It confirmed for him that he had made the right decision.

> Dear Mr. Lewis, [it said]:
> At a little meeting of the LSR [League for Social Reconstruction] of Montreal, we were discussing the situation at this coming election, and someone suggested that you might possibly be free. We were all unanimous that if this were the case, there was a wonderful field for your activities here in Canada. I had heard . . . that you might enter public life in Great Britain, and I can well understand the openings that there would be there, but if you have any pull in the direction of Canada, we can assure you plenty of hard work and more or less uncertainty, but at the same time, a great opportunity to wake up and organize this young country of ours.[70]

David's last official function at Oxford was as valedictorian at the farewell dinner for Rhodes scholars — the first time where there was only one speaker; in other years, representatives of each country had said a word or two — and at the end of July he and Sophie sailed for home. It was the end of his salad days, a time when he laid siege to the imagination of a great university, creating an aura of excitement and promise that he would not again engender to the same extent until thirty-seven years later, when he laid siege to the imagination of a country with his denunciation of "corporate welfare bums" in the 1972 federal election campaign.

It also closed a chapter on a love story that had touched all who had met them with its tenderness and devotion.

On April 24, Sophie wrote a chatty letter to Bessie Klein, who by then had married Abe in Montreal, that describes as well as anything can what their life had been like. She and David were staying at a cottage in Somerset during the spring vacation:

> Paul Engle, an American poet (Iowa) and Rhodes scholar, spent 4½ weeks with us. He is a fine fellow, very congenial and possesses a marvellous sense of humour. I wonder whether Klein or you saw his book *American Song*. . . . It has had a magnificent sale and he has already had $1,800 in royalties up to the end of 1934 only. . . . He wrote 1,000 lines of poetry while here, worked like the devil. It was good fun having him here and we enjoyed ourselves greatly.
> While he was here, the English poet Cecil Day Lewis came down to the cottage and spent two days with us. Day Lewis and Paul are broadcasting on May 2nd in London and will be heard in America as well. . . .

Paul had to leave to practice rowing for Merton — he was genuinely sorry to leave — and Brian Farrell came to take his place and is staying with us until we leave, which is this coming Friday. Bill Nield, an Englishman (last term's chairman of the Labour Club) came down to spend a week with us. His girl friend lives in Bristol (nine miles from here) and so he found it rather convenient to be so near to her. . . .

We have been very fortunate in that we have had spring weather. I have picked masses of primroses, daffodils, violets, forget-me-nots, polyanthus, wallflowers — and lately cowslips have come out. Everything seems alive. Newly born lambs blink on the hills, sheep and cows munch the grass and refuse to budge. Many delightful walks have we taken and run through fields wild with gorse.

David is working hard, harder than I have ever seen him work before. But he looks very well, almost got a double chin, I feed him that well. And this spot has proved most conducive to his work. Another six weeks of devilishly tiring work and then his schools arrive — ten days, about, of hard grind, then three weeks holiday followed by the "viva" — oral exam. Results in a day or two and then HOME.

We do hate going away from here. Again a bachelor and spinster existence. Rather disturbing and quite undesirable. But so it must be. I do wish I didn't have to go back to Oxford. David will be so busy. All the people I'm friends with are taking schools and I'm afraid life will be a bit trying. . . .

Tomorrow marks three years of my father's death. The time has flown. There are moments when I still find it hard to entirely forgive him. How hard I must be, you say to yourself? Perhaps "honest" would be a better word. Very often, I wish my life had been a different one. It might have been possible. He made it impossible.

I have managed to do some reading in spite of domestic responsibilities. At present I'm reading *The Rise of Modern Industry* by the Hammonds. What a beastly lot, the capitalists of the 18th Century in England were! I've read *Peace or Property?* by H.M. Brailsford and *From Locke to Bentham* by H.J. Laski. I discovered that John Locke was born in Wrington (three miles from here) over 300 years ago and went looking for his grave but found none. Also read John Strachey's *Literature and Dialectical Materialism*. There is a new book which came out about two months ago called *Our Young Barbarians or Letters from Oxford* by Barbara Silver which I should like you to get hold of and read. It was quite typical of three years in the life of a girl student in Oxford . . . It's very amusing and would really be a masterpiece if it were intended as a satire. But alas, I think the woman is very serious. . . .

I must say good night and go to bed. It is 1 a.m. and David is waiting for me and reading the last few pages in his chapter (doing Kant).[71]

On August 15, less than two weeks after they arrived back in Montreal, David and Sophie were married. It was a simple ceremony performed by a rabbi but without the wedding canopy, the *khupe*. In fact, so simple was it that it was more a civil than a religious celebration, held in the living room of the Lewis home at 4607 rue Esplanade, the new flat that Maishe and Rose had moved into just six weeks earlier.

• CHAPTER   THIRTEEN •

*Christ, we're dyin' by inches. For what? . . . Joe
said it. Slow death or fight. It's war!*
                    Agate *in* Waiting For Lefty,
                                    Clifford Odets

Everyone was there for the homecoming. Crowded into the little flat were aunts and uncles and cousins and friends; the table
was laden with food; the air was thick with pride and admiration. There were kisses and hugs and laughter and toasts, little jokes
and little speeches, everyone huddling around success as they would
around a bonfire on a cool evening, even to the back of the room
where Charlie was standing with his wife Katy — they had been married in April 1933, shortly after Charlie had turned twenty-two. And
they all sang David's favourite song, "A Dudu" — *Du* in Yiddish means
"You," referring to God, and the song declares that God is to be found
everywhere.[1] The Lewises sang it as a folk tune, not as an expression
of religious belief, like people sing spirituals today, and Charlie joined
in happily as he always had, from the fringe where always he had stood.

It was yet another celebration for David, yet another occasion to
cherish, yet another reminder to Charlie of what had never been his.
In a family preoccupied with politics, with one son who had accomplished the unbelievable, Charlie was the odd person out. "[He] never
gained the recognition he should have," says Fay Ain. "Nor the outward affection and attention. For everyone in that whole family —
aunts, cousins, uncles — David was their god. And this young man
was talented . . . and not recognized by anybody but Doris. . . . The
one thing I always held against [Maishe] was that I thought he didn't
give Charlie enough credit."

"The two boys were so *totally* different," says Doris. "My poor parents
couldn't cope with the two, you know, so they chose, . . . " and she

pauses, glancing down at her hands, "well, they coped with Charlie in their own way, but David was closer to their life style."

Yet Doris, who has always defended Charlie and saw him as "warm, engaging, and talented," still to this day can't quite shake the image into which he was cast, referring to him as unrealistic, someone always dealing in fantasy. And perhaps he was. But on the other hand, perhaps his realities were not those of other people. Perhaps his was a different world.

Every family has its darker sides — none escape — and the puzzle with the Lewises is how a family so committed to the idea of individual worth could spare so little attention for a boy whom people repeatedly referred to as jolly and kind and giving. Even David, whom Charlie helped so much — it was Charlie, the athletic one, who protected David on the streets during their youth even though he was the younger; it was Charlie who left school after Grade Eight to go to work in the needle trade helping to bring in the money that kept the family going and helped free David to pursue a university education; it was Charlie who lived at home with Katy helping to pay expenses, as did Doris until she, too, married in 1936, while Maishe struggled with his sandwich stand and David dazzled Oxford — despite all this, even David gave Charlie only one three-line reference in his memoirs.

Charlie's elder son Sheldon is philosophical about it all. (Sheldon is fifty-one years old and a high school teacher in Ottawa; Barry, forty-six, the younger son, is a helicopter pilot in British Columbia and several years ago finished a master's degree in the history of religion.)

"There is only so much affection and attention to go around in any family," says Sheldon. "It is a highly sought-after commodity. And if someone is getting the lion's share, then someone is getting a little less. . . . But more important than anything else, Charlie was more North American in his impulses and desires than maybe any other member of the family . . . contemporary literature is much more about people like my father than people like David."

Charlie grew up in the streets, in the rough-and-tumble world of other immigrant boys, not at the kitchen table bent over books like David. But at the same time he loved to sketch and never was far from pencil and note pad. "Politics wasn't his world," says Fay Ain. "He loved sports. And he especially loved music. . . . Once he was working and moved into his own apartment, he had whole cabinets full of records . . . a library of music second to none . . . all the classics. Not so much jazz but all the classical music and Yiddish music and folk music."

But even that ran him afoul of the family, says Doris. "He spent a lot of money [on records] which, of course, was criticized too." Today, says Sheldon,

> . . . it would be quite common among people who cared about records to have a collection like his, but in those days it was quite unusual. . . . [He also had] a good book collection. We had books all around. . . . When I grew up there were a couple of guys who liked to baby-sit for me at my place because they liked to browse through the books. It was unusual. . . . Oh, I know other people had books, but they were political books or religious books. He had modern literature, the best that was being written at the time. Faulkner. Steinbeck. I can remember art books.
>
> My father was also interested in sports. When we got together we often talked about sports. We went to hockey games. He was much more typical of the people who grew up in that time. . . . [When] he was a kid they boulevarded, they went out in the country together. [When] the first cars that they could get their hands on came out [they bought them]. And they had their girlfriends. . . .
>
> My father used to take me to steam baths on Sunday. The men went together to the steam baths and talked about things, and then they went out for bagels and coffee together. Or went down to the YMHA to listen to a speaker. . . . There was a guy [at the Y] who made a name for himself holding recorded symphony sessions. Not everybody had a record collection. He would introduce the records and people would listen avidly to Tchaikovsky or Chopin or Beethoven and this would go on on a regular basis.

At sixteen Charlie graduated from public school, having skipped grades twice, and went to work as a cutter in a garment factory. But he wasn't in that job more than a few years before Maishe came home one day and told Doris she had to move out of her bedroom behind the kitchen. "He said he wanted the back room to set up a cutting table so that he could get a teacher to teach Charlie designing and so [Charlie] would be able to use his artistic ability," Doris says.

Throughout his boyhood, Charlie had sketched and this was Maishe's way of recognizing that ability while at the same time trying to launch him on a more upscale career. To a degree it worked. Charlie ended up selling his designs to Simpson's in Montreal under the label "Cindy Lou Blouses." Each year he would go down to New York to scout the latest fashions and then return home to duplicate them, and Simpson's would unabashedly sell them as copies.[2]

But even as a designer Charlie never felt that he was on track, certainly not as compared to David. The frustration, says Doris, was immense. It wasn't until he was almost thirty years old, when he discovered acting during the late thirties, that Charlie felt that he had found a place of his own. He was a good actor. In fact very good. But not good enough to earn a living in the days before theatre began to flourish in the late fifties.

The depression and the advent of talking motion pictures meant that commercial theatre almost disappeared during the thirties and forties, and initially there was nothing to take its place. From the mid-1800s, when grand and impressive opera houses began to spring up across the provinces, English-speaking Canadians had been heavily dependent on British and American touring companies to provide them with drama, so that when the tours were curtailed, there was precious little to take their place. There were amateur groups but no professionals to fill the gaps.

Herb Whittaker, retired drama critic of *The Globe and Mail*, sometime set designer, sometime director and enthusiast extraordinaire, was in Montreal at the time as critic for *The Gazette*. He is tall and courtly, with a conjurer's long, expressive fingers and eyes slightly protruding as if in a headlong rush to take everything in. His knowledge of theatre is encyclopaedic, his love for it unrestrained, his treatment always gracious. He witnessed the demise of road shows and the conversion of great old theatres into movie houses. For a while it looked as if it would be thin gruel indeed for theatregoers. "Instead of that, people rallied and made their own theatre and it was a much more significant move than we recognized at the time. Nowadays we tend to think, well, it was just amateur theatre. But it actually was preserving a link in an age when electronic substitutes were being presented on all sides. Radio was flourishing in Montreal under Rupert Caplan, and films that had learned how to talk were challenging a centuries-old tradition. But it turns out that there is no substitute for theatre and when people have to make their own, they do."

In 1913 the Ottawa Drama League was formed; in 1919 the Hart House Theatre at the University of Toronto opened; in 1930 the Montreal Repertory Theatre started up; and in 1932 the Dominion Drama Festival was established. Before the thirties were out, every major city and a good many smaller centres had at least one established amateur group. Then came CBC radio to provide a base for professionals, especially with Andrew Allan and his CBC Stage series, which produced more than 400 dramas and ran from 1944 until 1956. By the early fifties there was an impressive list of Canadian actors of professional calibre. What they lacked were professional stages. The response began with the Stratford Festival in 1953 and Toronto's Crest Theatre in 1954. Alive to the challenge, the National Theatre School in Montreal opened in 1960. At the same time CBC television was just getting off the ground, so there was the possibility for actors to earn enough from TV drama and advertising commercials to pay the rent.

But the real turning point came with Vincent Massey's 1951 *Report of the Royal Commission on National Development in the Arts, Letters and Sciences,* which led, in 1957, to the creation of the Canada Council and its mandate of funding professional theatre. From that point on, permanent regional theatre was assured and Canadians at long last could begin to use the stage with some promise of consistency to examine the texture of their society. "In those [intervening] years," says Whittaker, "some remarkable theatre was produced. In Montreal, the dominant theatre was the Montreal Repertory Theatre run by Martha Allan. All the actors from the various groups in Montreal and its outlying areas were very honoured to play in Martha's MRT productions. It was like a flagship above all the others."

That flagship sometimes brought in actors from other groups for specific parts, and among those invited was Charlie — which testifies to the respect for him as an actor. One of the plays he did for MRT was Clifford Odets' *Waiting for Lefty,* a workingman's howl of protest, and what makes it interesting was the audience's reaction. The play is a series of vignettes depicting the savage exploitation of working people and their attempts to fight back which end with the exhortation in the final line of the play to "STRIKE, STRIKE, STRIKE!"

The response was tumultuous. Parts of the audience stormed out midway through to register disapproval. But, says Whittaker, "some of the Jewish press thought it was sentimentalized. Soft and not harsh enough." The view from The Main, then, was a view from a world entirely different from that of the middle-class patrons of MRT. A world of meaner streets. Of outsiders. More radical. More angry. More determined. The Jewish community in Montreal was a Third Solitude in more ways than one.

Charlie's home base was the little theatre group at the YMHA/YWHA. Whittaker reviewed him there in Lillian Hellman's *Watch on the Rhine* in 1942 and commented: " . . . perhaps the most worthy thing that can be said was that they brought us the truth of Miss Hellman's writing, held down hard and fast to its quietness and strength, believed in every word they spoke.

"It was not easy. The restraint it calls for, the throwing away of strong emotional scenes for the sake of stronger ones, is easy for no amateur group. . . . [This] production is the best they have done, a thing to be proud of and a tribute to the director. . . . Charles Lewis as Muller, the anti-Fascist worker, played with quiet strength throughout and held your heart in each of his great scenes."[3]

The list of plays that the Y group performed was long and impressive and included *Golden Boy, There Shall Be No Night, The Cherry Orchard, Morning Star, Thunder Rock, Winterset, Skin of Our Teeth*, together with Yiddish plays such as *Riverside Drive, Hidden Roots*, and *Tzurich Tzu Zein Folk*. Charlie directed several of them as well as playing lead roles in most, and consistently received good reviews.

There were many theatre groups in Montreal, Whittaker says, enough to keep him reviewing two or three nights a week — church groups like the Trinity Players, school groups, university groups. Madeleine Sherwood, who moved to Broadway, came out of one of them. So did John Colicos and Christopher Plummer, who came out of Montreal's Canadian Art Theatre. Charlie's YMHA group was among the top four or five, says Whittaker. "Not quite as strong as the Trinity Players which was the oldest, but close behind it for consistency of standard. They had a fairly good auditorium at the Y and a lot of talent. . . . Charlie Lewis was what you might call the president. He was the most active member and the leader of the group."

And being the leader was no mean feat, given the outspoken, argumentative nature of the group. "Charlie had strength. He was not afraid to speak up. If he had been the least bit soft, he probably would have been steamrollered and banished. Instead, he was the leader in a good strong way."

The highlight of his acting career was probably the role of Willy Loman in Arthur Miller's *Death of a Salesman*, performed in January 1953. Sydney Johnson of the *Montreal Star* concluded that

> The Salesman itself is an exhausting virtuoso role in which I frankly expected Charles Lewis to go down fighting valiantly, a martyr to the worthy cause of the Y's drama group. Instead, Mr. Lewis, overcoming all his natural physical handicaps for the role, gave a moving and convincing performance. It is true that he was better in the present-day scenes than in those of the conjured-up past, better at lamentation than invective, and more the beaten dog than the loud-mouthed, joke-telling American salesman who has finally been clubbed into pitiful defeat by business and domestic failure; nevertheless, Mr. Lewis's Salesman was an acceptable and well-sustained characterization in which there were many moments of pathos and surprising vigour.

Whittaker's successor at *The Gazette*, and the critic for *The Montreal Herald* also were complimentary.[4]

The physical handicap that Johnson was referring to was Charlie's voice. It tended to the harsh rather than the mellow; but far more important, he never quite lost his Yiddish accent. "That kind of accent," says Whittaker, "had started to become in radio terms a comic one, largely because of the number of Jewish comics who popularized, 'Vas you dere, Charlie?' and all of that. It wasn't ghetto-inflicted. It was them using their own language to make fun.

"We had an example at Stratford a couple of years ago. A splendid actor from the Habima National Theatre in Israel came to play *Othello* and was practically laughed out of court on the opening night because of his accent. . . . It was a very tragic situation."

Shortly after *Death of a Salesman*, Charlie moved to Toronto to try his luck in the theatre that was starting to burgeon in Ontario. But Tyrone Guthrie wouldn't have him at Stratford because of his accent. And neither would Andrew Allan for his radio dramas. Allan had recruited a band of superb actors such as John Colicos who could do any accent required. Colicos had come from Montreal, the son of Greek immigrants, out of a milieu similar to Charlie's, but he had worked diligently with a voice teacher for years. Charlie never underwent the same intensive training. Had he arrived in Toronto fifteen or twenty years later, he might well have been able to support himself in theatre, Whittaker says. "He had a striking face, a good face. . . . He was not an exceptional actor [but] he was a good actor . . . his emotional intensity was great and he could be very moving. He welcomed scenes where he could express emotion and passion. He was not what the English theatre calls a throwaway actor. . . . Charlie might have arrived if the theatre had been more developed. . . . If [he were acting today] he might have worked from place to place, always in roles that could stand the accent."

Instead, he started up a small clothing manufacturing business, employing eight or ten people, that could produce his designs and earn him a reasonable income.

Right to the end, Charlie was seen as a problem by his parents. He separated from Katy in the mid-fifties, when Sheldon was seventeen years old and Barry was twelve, and that, says Sheldon, "was an absolute no-no in the world we lived in," Yet this was not a separation of bitterness and rancour; the relationship between Charlie and Katy remained "decent and affectionate. . . . There was a lot of dignity in it," says Sheldon. "My mother, even today, has fond memories of my father."

By then Maishe had been dead for about five years, but he had witnessed the strains leading up to the separation long before he died, and it was as if one last sorrow had been piled on a load already too heavy to carry. In Svisloch he thought he had known Charlie;

certainly he was proud of him — as much so as of David, but in a different way. If one were beauty and the other truth, it would explain the love and the difference. But almost from the day they set foot in Montreal a gulf had opened between them. Beauty had turned its face to a different sun, a sun whose warmth Maishe couldn't feel, a sun he couldn't even see, certainly never in its full radiance. But Charlie basked in that radiance. Loved it, understood it, wanted to be part of it. It was Coca-cola, Tinseltown, pulp magazines, and Ford coupes; it was hanging out with the guys at the corner talking dreams; it was Jack Benny, Amos 'n' Andy, Benny Goodman, and Artie Shaw — and women who wore slacks and smoked in public. It was New York, neon, and those of their own who had made it, like Norma Shearer and Fifi D'Orsay.

It was a world where theories of dialectical materialism did not press heavily on the consciousness. Its gods were not Abramovitch and Martov and Medem and Erlich. Nor were they the likes of Clement Attlee, J.S. Woodsworth, Meyer London (the socialist Congressman from New York last elected in 1920), and Jacob Pat (the Bundist who came from Poland in the late thirties to become executive secretary of the Jewish Labour Committee in New York). They were more like Cecil B. DeMille, Howie Morenz, George Gershwin, Fiorello La Guardia, Joe Louis, and John Steinbeck. The goal was not so much to change the world but to get where you could enjoy it. The object of making money was to spend it, not squirrel it away. The aim was to get aboard the Chattanooga Choo-Choo like everybody else, not to stand separate and apart — culturally, politically, or in any other way.

It seemed to Maishe that everything that was holy to him, everything that he had sacrificed for, was peripheral as far as Charlie was concerned — the dreams for which he had come close to dying in Svisloch, the struggle for social justice to which he had dedicated a lifetime, his intense sense of Jewishness — Yiddish Jewishness — and success for his sons, which was why he had left Russia in the first place. This is how he defined himself. This is how he saw himself as part of a 5,000-year continuity of Jewish history. How well he passed on that continuity to his sons would be how he assessed himself. David understood the dreams, the dedication. David heard the same drummer. But Charlie . . . Charlie seemed to hear siren calls and they kept luring him from the true path.

So, although neither wanted it, the gulf between them grew. To Maishe, Charlie was irresponsible — frivolous in the way he spent money, frivolous toward politics, frivolous toward his job, frivolous toward his heritage, and frivolous toward his obligations. To Charlie, Maishe simply didn't understand the new world.

Charlie was Maishe's greatest disappointment, and Charlie knew it. It was not that Maishe was harsh. Just that Charlie knew he never measured up. The irony was that by working and helping to meet family expenses while David was at school, he was helping David toward achievements against which he himself would be compared. And those continuing, spectacular achievements made the frustration of not meeting his father's expectations that much more intense.

He tried to do what his father wanted. He went to work in the garment trade. He learned designing. He did his best to be a skilled and responsible worker. But the passion, the ability to let himself be carried away on emotions made larger than life that would bring him applause on the stage — that could never be tied down to a garment cutting table. It kept seeking outlets and Maishe, not understanding, kept trying to discourage it.

Had he tried instead to encourage it, had he suspected theatrical talent early on and encouraged Charlie to seek it out, what then? If he had seen voice lessons as an absolute necessity instead of another frivolity, what then? If Charlie had received the kind of support David got . . . what then?

It was not as if the stage was foreign to Maishe. On Saturdays he and Rose would take Doris and sometimes Charlie to the Yiddish theatre — and Maishe's brother Zebullum, Doris's favourite uncle, would take Doris every Wednesday night as well. "The Yiddish performers would come from New York," says Doris. "Comedies. Melodramas. There'd be Menashe Skulnik. And Maurice Schwartz. And the Hollanders, a husband-and-wife team. There was Nathan Goldberg." And there were the Adlers, Jacob and Sarah. "I loved it," says Doris. Maishe loved it too. But he loved it because it was Yiddish, because it was part of his culture, because Bundists had always supported it, and because, simply, he enjoyed it. But it was no place to earn a living.

It would never occur to him that someday Charlie might want to make at least part of a living in its English-language counterpart. Theatre had its place in the struggle for a better world; Maishe knew that. The Bund knew that. But what did it have to do with security? And raising a family? And day-to-day discipline and responsibility?

Like his own father before him, when faced with Maishe's decision to leave the yeshiva to work in a leather factory, it was something totally outside his experience, something he had no possibility of understanding. And so he grieved for Charlie and never understood his artistic temperament. And did his best to encourage him in the precise things that Charlie never should have been doing. "That's the one error, in retrospect, that my father made," says Doris. "It was not letting him loose to go to drama school or whatever he wanted to do. To my father bread and butter was the first consideration, and it was to that whole generation. Charlie was the one with talent. Really."

By 1961 Charlie was dead from stomach cancer. He was fifty-one years old.

David's arrival home in 1935 came at a time when his parents were still struggling through the difficult times that had followed Maishe's heart attack. It would not be until the following year that Maishe would become secretary of the Jewish Labour Committee and could close down the sandwich concession booth that he set up each day on rue Notre Dame. Being reduced to running the little booth merely confirmed for Maishe that Charlie should never end up like him. These were the years when Charlie was in his early twenties. So focusing on "bread and butter" instead of Charlie's artistic leanings could be explained even if not excused in the eyes of later generations.

What the Jewish Labour Committee offered Maishe was a job with a purpose — and pride. But it didn't improve his financial situation. And the work, although different, was just as strenuous as running his concession booth. "He did whatever was necessary," says Bea Silcoff. "He went out canvassing from door to door. Anywhere. And how many times did he have the door slammed in his face. . . . When I'm talking about trying to collect money, I'm not talking about thousands of dollars, I'm talking about two dollars or one dollar and five dollars and ten dollars. Sometimes it was only as much as the carfare. And there was no such thing as a car to drive around in. He went shank's mare. . . . If someone would've had to be the cook, he would have been the cook."

The bond that developed between Maishe and the young, newly married, stylish Bea Silcoff, who saw him as the grandfather she never had, was open-hearted, enthusiastic. She learned how to speak Yiddish so she could be of more help by relieving him "of the everyday things he used to have to do," such as recording the minutes of the committee.

She remembers the Jewish Labour Committee's response to the first group of refugees that arrived in Montreal fleeing from Hitler's terror. They had travelled from Poland across the Soviet Union to Japan and had sailed from there to Vancouver, arriving in Montreal at the end of August 1941.[5] Among the thirteen who arrived were Sofia Erlich, wife of Henryk Erlich, leader of the Bund in Poland.[6] With David

Lewis's help in Ottawa, the committee had managed to obtain landed immigrant entry visas for the group. It was, says Kalmen Kaplansky, a "substantive and concrete achievement . . . and proof of the organization's potential".[7]

Maishe organized a *hunge* banquet — a hunger banquet — and about 400 people turned up at the Workmen's Circle building to eat herring, potatoes in their jackets, black bread, and tea and to listen to speeches and raise money to help other refugees.

> [The menu] was in commemoration of the people who didn't even have that [says Bea Silcoff]. They were lucky even to get a piece of black bread. The herring and potatoes were the staple in Poland because during pogroms and thing like that they couldn't get anything else. But they could get herring and potatoes. . . .
>
> Maishe had tears in his eyes seeing these people. He was very, very happy. He wasn't too demonstrative other than these tears. They just came by themselves. It was very moving.
>
> As time passed and we brought in more people, the banquet was no longer a *hunge* banquet. I remember once when we served something different to a new group of refugees and Maishe said to me, "Do you think we're doing any better now giving them this instead of herring and potatoes?" and I said, "No, but that's life."

It was only a few months later, on December 18, 1941, that Sofia Erlich learned that her husband and Victor Alter had been arrested again by Soviet authorities.[8] Mrs. Erlich was at a meeting of the Bund executive gathered around the dining room table at Faga Falk's home in Montreal when the news came. "Everybody got numb when they heard that [says Falk] because we knew, all of us knew, that if they were arrested again they were finished . . . but Mrs. Erlich calmed us down. 'Don't worry friends,' she said, 'nothing is going to happen to them in Russia.' . . . But we were all convinced that it was the end of them." They were never released and a year later they were shot.

By coincidence, Steve Perkal of Montreal was with Alter when he was arrested before. Both were fleeing eastward from the Nazis in late September 1939 and had reached the Polish–Ukranian town of Kovel':

> "We had only been in Kovel' one day when Alter, being the kind of man he was, already had formed a Bund group in the city and we were politically active. . . . I remember the night before he went to see the commander of the [Soviet] garrison. . . . One of us said, "They'll kill you." But he said, "No. They can shoot me but they can't kill me." He went the next morning to the commander of the garrison and had an hour-long meeting with him and said, "We [the Bund] don't

consider you as enemies, . . . " and the commander said, "You go home and we'll be in touch with you." Well, sure enough, that same night they came and took him away and we never saw him again.

Perkal is seventy-two years old at the time of the interview in 1985, his face rounded from the cortisone treatments necessary to keep a blood disease in remission, frustrated by the physical limitations the disease imposes. But his eyes shine when he talks about socialism: "It's like a religion. My mother and father never took me to a synagogue. Our belief in a better world came through socialism, and I still find it possible to believe that someday, somehow, we'll have a society where people will contribute according to their ability and receive according to their need."

He stops for a moment and shifts in his chair.

"Not in my lifetime — but someday."

Outside the living room window an autumn breeze is stirring leaves on the lawn — red and yellow and brown — frisking them into little whirlpools of colour and he watches, quiet and still. Finally he turns from the window.

"Someday," he says and his eyes still shine.

Late in February 1943 when the Soviets finally acknowledged that Erlich and Alter had been executed, David took the matter up with the national executive of the CCF, urging that Stalin be condemned. However, the executive, in what must have been one of its most ignominious hours, placed expediency over conscience. It passed a resolution and placed it before the CCF national council regretting the executions and recording "its disappointment at this recent evidence that the dictatorship in the Soviet Union remains unchanged." But added, "the National Executive is also cognizant of the urgent need to maintain and extend co-operation with the Soviet Union for the purposes of victory and of building a post-war international organization and is aware of the reactionary forces at home ready to use every opportunity to destroy this necessary co-operation.

"It therefore resolves not to make any public protest on this matter."

Not only was there to be no public protest; the very making of the resolution was to remain a secret from the public because, as David later noted, the resolution was placed in the minute books of the national council and "These minutes are supposed to be private."[9]

By any standard it was an astonishing resolution, on the one hand acknowledging cold-blooded murder and on the other resolving to keep mum about it. Worse still, when the resolution was placed before the national council, there was substantial opposition to approving it. A majority of the non-executive-committee members voted against it, although with the executive committee members voting, it carried.[10]

It was a paltry gesture, and in no way was it going to satisfy David. For the first and only time during his twelve years as CCF national secretary, he refused to abide by a National Executive decision. If the CCF wouldn't condemn Stalin publicly, he would. Erlich and Alter were Bundists, they were Jews, they both were friends. He took level aim at Stalin in the CCF's *News Comment* and spoke at protest meetings at the Workmen's Circle in Montreal and the Labour Lyceum in Toronto.

Typical of some of the reaction was a letter from Hilary Brown, a member of the executive of the CCF in British Columbia, to David, in which she said "it appears to us that you are seeking to plunge the CCF movement into the most complicated psycho-political imbroglio in Europe with no thought to the fact that we are engaged in a fight for survival with Fascism, a struggle in which, incidentally, the Soviet Union has already lost 10 million lives."[11]

David's response came in a letter he wrote to Frank McKenzie of Vancouver, asking him to pass on the letter to Ms Brown. McKenzie had complained that condemnations of Stalin had become a large campaign. "This is just a communist lie and I am surprised that you people swallow it so unquestioningly," David said. The so-called campaign had consisted of his activities and a resolution passed by a local CCF club in Ontario. "To my positive knowledge, not a single other national officer of the CCF, except myself, took part in any meeting or said any word about the matter in public . . . what there was of [a "campaign"] came from the communists who showed themselves as dirty and unscrupulous in this instance as in every other."[12]

In his memoirs David says that "colleagues on the executive understood and supported his actions." That may have been the case — the vote on the executive had been unanimously in favour of the resolution — but if members supported his speaking out, it is, at the very least, odd that no one said so publicly.

Throughout the forties Maishe and David worked as a team to help Jewish refugees — David by arranging approvals in Ottawa for such things as direct relief shipments to Polish refugees in the Soviet Union[13] and by constantly drumming away at the Immigration Department to ease quota restrictions (and, once they were eased, by arranging for visa approvals[14]); Maishe by raising money, publicizing the cause, and arranging for refugee sponsors.

One of his sponsors was Joe Ain in Montreal:

"I once had eighteen people that Maishe got me to sign for as being responsible for jobs and housing. An immigration inspector called up . . . and said, "I know you have a fairly large construction company but how do you manage with housing?" So I said, "Come . . . and I'll show you" . . . and I said see, "Here's my home. We have six rooms on the ground floor, we have three rooms downstairs and we have another six rooms upstairs." I didn't mention that the upstairs was already rented to somebody. "Well," he says, "that is a big house. That's fine. I'm perfectly happy." Now that was only myself. How many other people was Mr. Lewis involved with that signed for immigrants?"

But this was in 1948, after the creation of the state of Israel, when Canada had nudged its door ajar to Jewish immigrants. The door had been all but closed for fifteen years, especially during the thirties when Jews could have escaped from Europe if they had had somewhere to go. But there was no place that would have them in numbers that offered a real alternative. As the Jewish Labour Committee in New York observes in a classic understatement, European Jews had little room to manoeuvre.[15]

So the committee concentrated on raising money to help the New York office smuggle Jews out of Nazi territory to wherever they would be safer, and on trying to awaken the world to the horrors of what was happening in Europe. It recalls that "At the end of May, 1942, the Bund Report was smuggled out of Poland and brought to London. It unequivocally stated that the Nazis had murdered 700,000 Jews and intended to kill the rest. The BBC and several newspapers in London covered the details."[16]

But, says the commitee, when it tried to publicize the report in North America, it was met with lethargy. Sometimes, in trying to break down that lethargy, it went too far, as it did in Montreal one night when Jacob Pat, the New York committee's executive secretary, addressed a large group in a synagogue. He was a flamboyant speaker and at one point during an eloquent appeal he picked up a small box from the table, opened it, and reverently held aloft a bar of soap made by Nazis from the remains of Jewish inmates of one of the death camps. Bea Silcoff remembers:

I'll never forget that meeting. It was an absolute disaster. People were fainting. Some were screaming. . . . It was just too much. . . . [Maishe] was furious . . . it was a terrible thing. . . . These people were starving for information. They didn't know whether their families were living or dead or what was happening to them. We didn't need this kind of a reminder. We knew that [the Nazis] were doing all sorts of foul things. . . .

I can't even describe how shocking it was. . . . The only thing I could think in retrospect was that things were pretty rough at the Jewish Labour Committee and we were desperate, desperate for money.

Maishe didn't get into a shouting match with Pat. His was a cold, hard anger. He thought it was more than just bad taste. He thought it was senselessly cruel, and from then on there was a coolness between the two men.

After the war the focus of the committee began shifting from immigration to the wide field of human rights and in mid-1946 Kalmen Kaplansky was made the new director of the committee and charged with reorganizing it. One of the first things he did was to double Maishe's salary from $8 a week to $16 a week. Kaplansky was hired at the same $60-a-week salary that he had been earning as a linotype operator.

At first Maishe refused the increase, saying that the committee couldn't afford it. "I remember his coming home and saying that the executive had offered him an increase and he refused it and it was one of the few times that I got annoyed with him," says Doris. "'How can you refuse it?' I said. 'Mother has so little to live on.'

"'I can't take the money that I knock on office doors to collect for my salary,' he said. And I said, 'Mom hasn't even got a refrigerator. How can you refuse an increase?' And he said well, that was the thing to do."

In the end Maishe relented and accepted it, but looking back at the incident, Doris still feels the exasperation: "Very often, among men who are dedicated to their work, there's a selfishness about the dedication. . . . My husband had it because of the way he worked, so hard, so long, never said no. During the time I didn't object but in retrospect, in my grief [over his death], you know, there was a bit of selfishness. The satisfaction they got out of their work made up for whatever else they were neglecting. But whatever was being neglected remained neglected."

Kaplansky was more than a new director. He was a new breed. An ambitious mandate meant an ambitious program and that meant efficiency. Organization. Streamlined fund-raising techniques. Spending money to make money. Building contacts with academics, politicians, and labour leaders outside the Jewish workers' movement. And, beginning in early 1947, helping to organize the tailors' project, a plan to bring in groups of Jewish refugees from the concentration camps as workers for the needle trades under the government's "bulk-labour" program that allowed labour-intensive industries in Canada to recruit displaced persons in Europe. All this, Kaplansky could do and could do well. But it meant that the old ways, the ways of Maishe Lewis — the Maishe Lewis whom Kaplansky can only remember as speaking Yiddish although he could get by in English — were out of favour.

Trying to explain, Kaplansky tells a story, and he tells it, not only to illustrate how the old ways could no longer work because they were time-consuming and inefficient, but also to illustrate Maishe's courage because by now he had leukemia, which was diagnosed in the summer of 1947.

> I'll never forget one day when he was very sick, at the start of the afternoon we dragged ourselves on a streetcar from St. Joseph Boulevard and St. Catherine Street out to Hochelaga at the east end of St. Catherine. It took us an hour just one way in order to get $50 or $100 from a supporter . . . who was a former Workmen's Circle member, who became a rich man. . . .
>
> A taxi wold have cost us $2, maybe $3, return. The bus fare was . . . a dollar for the two of us [return]. . . . On the way back I looked at Maishe. I was thirty-three or thirty-four years old; he must have been almost sixty at that time, already racked with this leukemia. But still he would not take a taxi.

He also tells of attending a Trades and Labour Congress convention in Windsor and, at Maishe's behest, staying at the home of a CCF supporter. "The fact is, I had to go from his place by streetcar to the hotel. In the evening when it's most important to circulate and meet the delegates, I had to worry about the streetcar. But we saved money that way. It was his generation. Money was a public trust. The kind of money we raised was not to be spent lightly."

As the leukemia progressed, Maishe became increasingly weak, but still he went to work. The committee had offices in the Workmen's Circle and Steve Perkal used to see him every day.

> For months I remember him coming into the office. His face was swollen and he could hardly walk, and we all felt that he was coming into the office because this was one of the things that kept him alive. He never complained. . . .
>
> He had an ability of getting people to love him, to be loyal to him. People . . . always felt they had to be around to do the things that he could not do any more. To help him.

When he went to the hospital, and these were the last months or weeks of his life, we used to line up to give blood to him. We considered it a great privilege if we were allowed two minutes to be in the room where he was. He had this radiating ability of attracting people to him. For people to love him.

And oh, the dreams he had! He had dreams of peace. He had the dreams of the old Russian socialist. He believed, right to the end, it will come one day.

For the last nine months of Maishe's life Doris returned to Montreal from Ottawa where she was living, bringing Lorne, her young son, with her and she looked after Maishe and Rose. David was in Ottawa and Charlie was in Toronto, so by herself she moved her parents into a ground-floor flat because the doctor didn't want Maishe climbing stairs. It was on the same block of rue Esplanade as they had been living. To make matters worse, Rose was experiencing trouble with her heart and was bedridden much of the time too.

When Maishe no longer could leave his bed, Kaplansky made a point of bringing to the flat, and later to the hospital, cheques for him to co-sign. Signing authority could have been changed, but it was Kaplansky's way of paying his respects. "I went to that street entrance apartment [where they had moved]. You went in a corridor and then the living room and then to the left was a bedroom and he was lying in one bedroom and Rose was lying in another room. Poor Doris looking after them. He could hardly breathe. It was a very debilitating thing. Dignity disappears under those circumstances."

Not long before he died, Maishe passed the word that he would like Israel Falk, Faga's husband, to visit him in the hospital. Falk is a Bundist who survived the Warsaw ghetto uprising and two years in a series of concentration camps. He had immigrated to Canada after the consolidation of Soviet power in Poland in 1949, and had first met Maishe in 1947 during a five-day stopover in Montreal en route to a Jewish Labour Committee convention in New York that both of them attended and at which Falk was a featured speaker.

When he walked into the hospital room Maishe beckoned him to the bed. "It was hard to hear him he was in such pain," Falk remembers. He bent over the bed so he could hear and, speaking barely above a whisper, pausing between phrases, Maishe asked him to take over his job at the Jewish Labour Committee. He wanted to ensure that the tradition of the Bund carried on. "I was inclined to say yes, but they had hired someone in the meantime and I didn't want them to fire the man. But Maishe [said] I shouldn't have any qualms and finally the man left the job and I took it."

For ten years he remained with the committee. To Falk, Maishe is a person to remember and to honour. "He was a soft man, a very idealistic man. He was an idealist par excellence. Among the Jews of the Old Country, being soft meant not sitting down at your own table before you made sure that your neighbour, who is very poor, can also sit down to his table and eat. Here you call it soft-hearted or good-hearted. Over there it was a way of life. Maishe was very soft. Not everybody was like him. He believed not only to preach but to practise."

As Maishe's final days drew near, Rose developed blood clots in her legs and also was hospitalized until the danger passed. Both were in the Victoria Hospital but in different wings. Through his illness Maishe had been angry that he was so ill. Now that had subsided, but his hope for a final cure never faded. Days before he died, a doctor at the hospital thought that a new drug might help. "It had just come out and hadn't been used," says Doris. David spoke to Paul Martin, who was then minister of health, and Martin arranged for special approval to experiment with the drug.

When the day came to try it, Doris had some nurses help put her father in a wheelchair and, before taking him for the medication, wheeled him to Rose's bedside. "He was looking very, very ill." Neither spoke for a moment, and then Maishe slowly raised his hand and placed it on Rose's. "I'm going to the Tree of Life, my Raisel," he said quietly in Yiddish. "If I get to it, I'll see you again. If I don't, this is goodbye." He caressed her hand gently and Rose, her lips so tightly compressed that they went white, said nothing. The vein at her temple throbbed visibly and her eyes, brimming with grief, never left his face.

Not another word passed between them, and when Maishe gave a final squeeze to Rose's hand, Doris wheeled him from the room.

Rose never saw him again. He died February 5, 1950. He was sixty-two years old.[17]

To honour Maishe, the branch of the Workmen's Circle that he attended in Montreal was renamed the Moishe Lewis Branch, and in October 1975, at the biennial national convention of the Jewish Labor Committee in New York City, the Canadian committee announced that it had established the Moishe Lewis Foundation, "to actively educate the public with respect to human rights and, in doing so, assist in ending discrimination based on race, colour, creed, nationality or ethnic origin." It was created, the committee said, to "continue the work [Maishe] started and preserve the memory of his name."

•CHAPTER FOURTEEN•

There are establishments in the city of Toronto where, in the last ten or fifteen years, the owners have made their hundred thousands and their millions, while the workmen measure their prosperity by the smallness of their mortgage on their little homes. Both owners and workmen have put blood and life and heart into the business, and the owner has pocketed the earnings, allowing food to the workman on the same principle as he allows oil to the machine.

"That is his right," declares the law; "That is his right," admit the people; "That is his right," moan the workmen; "That is his right," proclaims the Church; and the owner, sustained by this universal verdict believes it to be his right. . . .

[But] that, in the direct language of Scripture, is theft.
Albert R. Carman
General Superintendent
Methodist Church
1891[1]

I t was overcast but balmy on the day the CCF was conceived, that Thursday afternoon on May 26, 1932. The temperature was hovering around 23 degrees Celsius. A light shower, barely a sprinkling, had speckled the sidewalks along Wellington Street, raising the damp-musty smell of new-mown dust. Once through the main gate leading up to Victoria Tower — it would not be renamed the Peace Tower for another year — the fresh green lawns added an earthy luxuriance to the air. This being the Great Depression, not much had been added to the grounds since reconstruction of the Parliament Buildings had been completed in 1928, twelve years after the great fire. About all that Mackenzie King's Committee on Beautification had been able to install were new light standards. As yet there were no flower beds.[2]

Inside Parliament's Centre Block on the sixth floor, Room 607 to be exact, a group of men had gathered. It was three in the afternoon. J.S. Woodsworth was there, already fifty-eight years old, his trim, pointed beard now almost white, member of the Independent Labour Party (ILP) from Winnipeg North Centre. Bill Irvine was there from the United Farmers of Alberta (UFA), the member for Wetaskiwin in east Calgary. A.A. Heaps, the battle-hardened union activist representing the ILP and Winnipeg North, was there, growing a little impatient with what he thought was Woodsworth's overly idealized concept of socialism, but showing a guarded enthusiasm nonetheless.[3] Heaps, like Woodsworth, was one of the great heroes of the Winnipeg General Strike — charged with but acquitted of seditious conspiracy. And also with the ILP from Vancouver South, there was Angus MacInnis. These were the so-called Labour MPs.[4]

All the rest of the sitting members present were remnants of the Ginger Group — those who, beginnning in 1921, had sided with Woodsworth and Irvine on left-wing issues. In 1921 there were eleven of them; now only seven remained in Parliament. No records remain of who was at the meeting, but it's a pretty sure bet that six and possibly all seven were present. Undoubtedly there was Robert Gardiner, leader of the UFA representing Medicine Hat in the riding of Acadia, and probably all the other Ginger Group members from the UFA: E.J. Garland (Bow River), D.M. Kennedy (Peace River), H.E. Spencer (Battle River), and G.T. Coote (Macleod). Agnes McPhail (Grey South East) certainly would have been there representing the United Farmers of Ontario and the seventh, who could well have been there, too, was M.N. Campbell (Mackenzie) still sitting as a Progressive.

There also were some outsiders, but again it's unclear who they were. A pamphlet published by the CCF in 1942 on its tenth anniversary says only that there were "additions from Toronto and Montreal." The two most likely would be Frank Scott from Montreal and Frank Underhill from Toronto, but there is considerable doubt that they attended.[5]

So there were at least thirteen people, a sizeable group to squeeze into the fourteen-by-sixteen-foot room. Most would have had to stand; there wasn't all that much space, what with the marble washbasin attached to the wall on the right as you came in and the desk and side table and bookcase. There were a few chairs, but not enough for everyone. Probably one or two sat on the edge of Irvine's desk—it was his office (and is now part of Stanley Knowles's two-office suite and has been renumbered as Room 630C[6]). Another could have sat on the window ledge that still looks out on the greying sandstone walls opposite that angle northeastward into a bleak central courtyard pointing in the direction of the stone towers of the Senate that jut above the far roof-line.

Forty minutes was all the meeting took. The minutes say simply: "Much consideration was given to the matter of dominion organization. A motion was moved and seconded that a committee be formed to consider ways and means of carrying out the wishes of the group as expressed during the discussion — that is, drafting a tentative plan of organization for future action thereon. Carried. Moved by D.M. Kennedy, seconded by Angus MacInnis, that J.S. Woodsworth and R. Gardiner be a committee with power to add to their number."[7]

They had taken the first step in creating the Co-operative Commonwealth Federation. From that flowed the Calgary Conference — a joint meeting of the Western Conference of Labour Parties and the UFA — on August 1, 1932, at which the CCF was formally created, and the convention in Regina beginning on July 19, 1933, which adopted the Regina Manifesto.

It was to be an odd union. That first meeting in Room 607 brought together three quite distinct groupings: the social gospel, the farmers' protest movement, and labour. And the most compelling of these, certainly in the persons of J.S. Woodsworth and William Irvine, was the social gospel.

From the beginning, even as there is today, there was tension between farmers and labour. Even in the West where prairie populism prevailed and the spirit of mutual assistance produced the great farming co-operatives, there was a spirit of rugged independence that distrusted the power of organized labour. The farmers' protest was not a movement based on working-class solidarity, as in the labour movement. Nor was it wedded to socialist philosophy. If anything, the farmers were entrepreneurs, business people who risked their own capital every growing season, mortgaging their properties, buying equipment, fertilizer, seed, and stock, following market prices, watching the futures markets, betting their livelihood on the sales that they could make. They would band together to ensure orderly markets and to fight exploitation by giant feed companies. But they shrank from talk of throttling capitalism and taking over the means of production. They weren't against a market economy. They just wanted a market where they had a more effective voice.

So in Ontario, where manufacturing was centred and unions would mushroom, farmers soon dropped their commitment to the CCF; in Saskatchewan, where the situation was reversed, and farmers did not feel threatened, the CCF was elected a mere twelve years later as the first socialist government in North America.

Basically, there were two things that kept the CCF afloat through its first few years, buffeted as it was by these tensions and by the warring brands of socialism that ranged all the way from the hard-driving Marxism of the West Coast to the soft Fabianism of Ontario universities. The first was the loose structure of the CCF — it was a federation only; a relatively mild-mannered association of self-governing bodies without any whip-wielding central authority. Consequently, few were forced into the position of either conforming to a central policy or getting out. The second was the combination of inspiration that could be traced back to the social gospel and an absence of a well-defined theory of socialism — which meant the CCF could be a house of many mansions.

What's interesting about the social gospel as far as David Lewis is concerned is how well its outlook blended with that of the Bund: this meant that David could feel quite at home with it and with people like Woodsworth, even though David's socialism was Marxist-based and theirs was not. In fact, the affinity was so great that when Stanley Knowles first met David he said it was like meeting his own brother.[8]

This convergence of belief was pivotal. If the social gospel was a fundamental inspiration to the party, and if David's skills in organizing and directing the party were indispensable — if, as Walter Young says, the party might have subsided into nothingness without him or if, as Donald MacDonald says, he was the party's main architect and he shaped its sense of direction — what a tremendous source of energy this ethical symmetry must have been to the party and to David. And what a legacy from the Bund must reside within the fabric of the party.

It's a legacy that's almost unrecognized. And small wonder when no one called attention to it. Tommy Douglas could give speeches resonating with images and messages from the social gospel and everyone knew what he was talking about. But if David had mentioned the Bund he would have drawn only blank stares — except maybe in Cartier riding. Or in Winnipeg North. Instead, if he had to call forth antecedents, he opted for those that audiences could relate to, such as the British Labour Party. Or the Fabians. Or Crosland or Gaitskill or Attlee. Better them than Marx or Bundists nobody ever heard of.

So how did the philosophy of the Bund and the social gospel compare?

The social gospel was a vision. An exultation. An exhortation. A sounding trumpet declaring that the way to sing the Lord's song in a land made strange with hunger, poverty, and inequality was not to sit by the rivers of Babylon and weep, not to curse the present or extoll the hereafter. It was to rise up and build anew. Create a heaven here on earth. A society of sharing. A place of human dignity and universal grace of spirit. Forget about waiting for reward in the afterlife. Change the system *now*. Tommy Douglas, calling upon audiences to "build a new Jerusalem in this our green and pleasant land," was calling on them to join in a mighty mission, to take up the hammer and saw of Jesus and erect a dwelling where all could live in peace and equality and prosperity. And he said it in the militant tones of William Blake's great poem "Jerusalem," which, more than a century after it was written, caught as well as anything the spirit of the social gospel:

> Bring me my bow of burning gold!
> Bring me my arrows of desire
> Bring me my spear! Oh clouds, unfold!
> Bring me my chariot of fire!
>
> I will not cease from Mental Fight,
> Nor shall my sword sleep in my hand,
> Till we have built Jerusalem,
> In England's green and pleasant land.[9]

In inspirational terms, the social gospel was as described by the U.S. social critic Henry George in his 1879 book *Progress and Poverty*:

> With want destroyed, with greed changed to noble passions; with the fraternity that is born of equality taking the place of the jealousy and fear that now array men against each other. With mental power loosed by conditions that give the humblest comfort and pleasure; and who shall measure the heights to which our civilization shall soar? Words fail the thought. It is the Golden Age of which poets have sung and high raised seers have told in metaphor! It is the glorious vision that has always haunted men with gleams of fitful splendour. It is what he saw whose eyes at Patmos were closed in trance. It is the culmination of Christianity — the City of God on earth, with its walls of Jasper and its gates of pearl. It is the reign of the Prince of Peace![10]

Four years after George's book came out, the social gospel landed in Canada in the columns of the weekly publication of the Hamilton Knights of Labor, *The Palladium of Labor*;[11] and from then until it lost its steam during the late 1920s — in the distractions of church union, the Temperance fight, a preoccupation with pacifism, and the gradual transferring of social services from the churches to the state — the social gospel was indeed a bow of burning gold.

Christianity had always taught that social action was a religious duty. But individual salvation came first; saving society came second and only as a consequence of individual salvation. What the social gospel did was to reverse the order. As historian Ramsay Cook puts it so nicely, the aim of the social gospel "was not born-again individuals but born-again societies."[12]

Like any movement, the social gospel had its conservative, progressive, and radical wings, and it was from the radical wing that the early CCF got its energy. However, common to all wings was the concept of social salvation which had spread rapidly in the closing years of the nineteenthth century. So in 1906 Woodsworth was expressing a widely accepted view when he proclaimed: "Jesus said very little about saving souls — He spoke often about the establishment of the Kingdom."[13]

It was a theology of service to mankind, a dedication to the idea of brotherhood among all peoples, and it made — and still makes — personal salvation as a first and dominating concern look selfish and self-centred. S.D. Chown, secretary of the Methodist Department of Temperance and Moral Reform, described social salvation in a slightly different way in a 1905 lecture (and to give an idea of the acceptability of such an attitude, it should be noted that he went on to be elected general superintendent of the Methodist Church in 1915): "The first duty of a Christian is to be a citizen, or a man amongst men. We are under no obligation to get into heaven, that is a matter entirely of our own option; but we are under an obligation to quit sin and to bring heaven down to this earth."[14]

There are hundreds of other examples, mainly from Methodists and Presbyterians, but also from Baptists, Congregationalists, and the occasional Anglican. Nevertheless, it was a leaping-off point for those who were really radical. Among the foremost were Woodsworth, William Ivens, A.E. Smith, and Salem Bland, all Methodist ministers, and William Irvine, a Presbyterian minister. Their radicalism, however, widened the gap between radicals and conservatives in their churches and eventually led to their departure.

Irvine resigned from the ministry in 1916 and Woodsworth in 1918; Salem Bland was dismissed from his post of teaching church history at Wesley College during an economy drive in 1917. Smith resigned in 1919 and that same year Ivens was prohibited from practising as a minister. Ivens had established the Labour Church in June of 1918 as a special ministry of the Methodist Church, and after the prohibition he continued to preach in it. What the prohibition meant, however, was that all ties were severed with the Methodist Church. Smith's radicalism carried him further than the others, and in January 1925 he joined the Communist Party, proclaiming that Christ was the first true Communist.

All were principled men of strong will. With the exception of Salem Bland, who vigourously fought against his dismissal, all found the conventional church too restricting. All had battles with conservative blocs within their congregations that led to inquiries by superior church bodies. But those superior bodies turned out to be remarkably tolerant, and, much as it might be tempting to read class warfare led by conservative business interests into their exodus, that seems not to have been the case. Warfare there was, of course. But, with the exception of Ivens, it did not force their ouster nor did it lead to intolerable conditions being imposed. Basically, they wanted to move farther, faster than they themselves felt would be consistent with church doctrine.

They had been part of a broad current of social reform in the church and part of that current had always run swiftly. Their going did not necessarily slow the current where it was swift; it allowed the swiftness to be diverted more easily — away from causes and toward effects. Away from trying to overthrow the system and toward such specific evils as liquor and war.

Nevertheless, in or out of the church, they were in notable company. In 1887 Phillips Thompson, a prominent satirical journalist and, to use Ramsay Cook's phrase, "hot gospel social reformer," maintained that labour was the source of all value — hitherto a purely Marxist outlook — and was not something to be bought and sold in the marketplace like onions at the prevailing rates. " . . . [P]olitical economy needs to be rewritten from the standpoint of the Sermon on the Mount and the Declaration of Independence," Thompson said.[15]

In 1891 the Reverend Albert Carman, the most powerful Methodist in Canada, the church's general superintendent for thirty-two years until his retirement in 1915, a theological conservative but a social reformer, declared:

> Should the suddenly rich, the monopolists, those who have filched the savings of the people, all who live by the labour of others, meet in secret council to frame a religion under which they would like the world to live; what better could they enact but that the oppressed would bear with Christian humility their oppression, and that the wronged would live with silent lips, looking for right only beyond the grave? And yet that is in practical effect the gospel heard today in many an upholstered pew — the gospel of charity on the part of the rich and humble gratitude on the part of the poor — of exhortation to the rich to give, that they may evidence their goodness, and of promises to the poor of a fairer distribution of God's mercies in the future life. And then we wonder, wonder, wonder at the awful perversity of the poor who will spend the Sabbath in God's sunlight, having taken us at our word that the Gospel has nothing particular for them until after death.[16]

J.B. Silcox, a Congregationalist, delivering a sermon to Canada's first Brotherhood group in 1895, said that the resurrection of Jesus proved "that humanity shall rise . . . into higher, nobler and diviner conditions of life," and that meant world-wide revolution in the twentieth century: "This uprising of the people is divine in its source . . . God is in the midst of it. . . . To the ecclesiastical and industrial Pharaohs of today, God is saying, 'Let my people go.'"[17]

In 1898 Alexander Sutherland, a prominent Methodist minister and activist, was only one among many in the church calling for profit sharing between owners and employees.[18]

By 1909 the view of Jesus as the world's first labour leader was being espoused. By 1913 Salem Bland was declaring that real estate speculation was as great an evil as liquor. And by 1916 William Ivens was preaching in favour of industrial democracy.[19]

A year later, with a little more than a year left in the First World War, Presbyterians and Methodists were calling for conscription of wealth as well as conscription of men, and the Presbyterian commission on the war found that men *and their corporate structures* must accept their implication in social guilt and stand under the radical judgment of God; otherwise progress would be impossible.[20]

By 1918, with attention turning to reconstruction in the closing days of the war, social gospellers of all stripes were pretty much of a mind about one thing: the fundamental evil was competitive individualism; the specific remedy was industrial democracy; and the over-all salvation of society was to be found in the "Kingdom of God conceived as a co-operative commonwealth."[21]

The Methodists, in the first General Conference they had held since the beginning of the war, adopted a program that almost completely rejected capitalism. It remains the most radical social program approved by a national church body. "The present economic system stands revealed as one of the roots of war," it said. Business was to be encouraged to organize more democratically and to involve labour as much as possible in plant operations. How business was to be encouraged and how this industrial democracy was to function were not spelled out. Nevertheless, the theme was unambiguous: "[T]he triumph of democracy, the demand of educated workers for human conditions of life, the deep condemnation this war has passed on competitive struggle, the revelation of the superior efficiency of rational organization and co-operation, combine with the undying ethics of Jesus, to demand nothing less than a transference of the whole economic life from a basis of competition and profits to one of co-operation and service."[22]

At about the same time, the church-dominated Social Service Council brought out a new publication called *Social Welfare* that demonstrated to readers how the Lord's Prayer should be interpreted:

> We are one and all to "Hallow our Father's name" and to pray and work for the new social order in which His will is done "as in Heaven"; in which His children have "bread" (all needed material good), shared on a basis of brotherhood which will be according to the need of each, love — not selfish competition — governing the distribution; in which each shall be so disposed to all, that he shall seek forgiveness from God and grant it to his brethren; in which each shall prayerfully seek to shield all from temptation and evil; in which there shall be "universal righteousness and social justice throughout the evangel of Christ."[23]

1918 was also the year that Ivens established the Labour Church in Winnipeg. It was in June and of those who attended the first service, 200 or so signed a card saying: "I am willing to support an independent and creedless Church based on the Fatherhood of God and the Brotherhood of Man. Its aim shall be the establishment of justice and righteousness among men of all nations."[24]

The Church had an open pulpit, even though Ivens occupied it most often and sermons usually had a social theme under titles such as "The League of Nations," "The Immorality of the Profit System," "Reconstruction and the Reconstructionists," and "The Resurrection of Democracy."[25] Returning soldiers loved the open pulpit. It gave them a respectable platform from which to express their hopes and fears and criticisms. A year later it was one of the rallying points in the Winnipeg General Strike, and it was then that Woodsworth attended his first Labour Church meeting: "It was the third week of the strike. The vast congregation, estimated at 10,000, filled Victoria Park. For nearly two hours I talked — I could not but talk! Dixon talked, Canon Scott talked, Robinson talked, Ivens talked. The people stood it — in a double sense of the word, and then gave a collection of $1,500 for the relief of the girls on strike. The police detectives reported us as Bolshevist spellbinders and a dangerous crowd of illiterate foreigners. Some of us thought we felt the spirit of a great religious revival."[26]

The Winnipeg General Strike, said A.E. Smith just days before he resigned as a minister of the Methodist Church in the final days of the strike, "was just as religious a movement as a church revival."[27] Four years later, two years before he became a Communist, he elaborated on his views to the People's Church in Brandon:

> What is Jesus? Who is Jesus? Theology has misrepresented him and the church has misrepresented him. He has been represented as a wandering

evangelist travelling about playing upon the emotions of people by "heal-ing" and trying to "save" souls from "sin" and "hell." This is the very thing he did not do, and if he did he was a real failure at the business. Jesus was a deeply convinced and well informed leader of the Communist order of thinkers and teachers that had been extant for many years in the Hebrew race . . . until it was perverted by individualist theologians and politicians.

I am standing with Jesus the Communist, the Religionist, the Social Leader, the Saviour of Society. I have no place for the invention created by false theology, Hymnology and Sentimentalism.[28]

Contemporary reaction to Smith's views has been coloured by the fact that he became a Communist and therefore suspect. But take out the references to communism in this statement and it would be a view that Woodsworth or Ivens or Irvine or any of the radical social gospellers could have embraced.

Although the Labour Church did not last many years beyond the strike, it was immensely popular during it. Jesus Christ, people kept pointing out, had led the way: He was one of the best-known agitators the world had ever seen.[29]

In early June of 1919, while the Winnipeg strike was still going on, the Presbyterian Assembly, meeting in Hamilton, declared that capital and labour owed a joint obligation to ensure that industry existed primarily for service. Because of this, and because of the need to observe human dignity, labour should have a share in the control of industry and an equitable reward.[30]

Within the year Ernest Thomas had declared that class consciousness was a vital part of "God's proclamation of a mighty spiritual fact which has almost faded from Protestant consciousness." Thomas was a Methodist minister and the newly appointed field secretary of the Methodist Board of Evangelism and Social Services. Richard Allen says in his book, *The Social Passion*, that Thomas was "in all probability the finest mind that was to do the social gospel service in Canada."[31] Workers who were not class-conscious were often "unsocialized," Thomas said. They would stand by, accepting the sacrifice and strug-gle of others instead of joining them in solidarity — and that was not what the Bible had in mind.

1920 was also the year that Salem Bland brought out his book, *The New Christianity, or the Religion of the New Age*, in which he said that to attack public ownership was to attack Christianity. Public owner-ship taught people to think socially, and that was the purpose of Chris-tianity. The distinctive task of the age, he said, was the abolition of capitalism. It bred competitiveness and individualism instead of brotherhood and democracy.[32]

(The book, incidentally, caught the perturbed eye of the RCMP, the Royal North-West Mounted Police as it was then known, and in a confidential letter to prominent Methodist T.A. Moore, Lieutenant-Colonel C.F. Hamilton expressed concern that the book would "lend to the revolutionary movement an air of religious sanction." Moore told him not to worry; a statement would be made. And sure enough, a review by Moore appeared in the Methodist weekly newspaper, the *Christian Guardian*, panning the book and saying that it was "not a logical and reasoned advocacy of the rights of Labour."[33])

Finally, in December 1921, the social gospel achieved one of its greatest triumphs. The Progressives elected sixty-five members to Parliament, second in number to the Liberals, who formed the minority government. The Progressives were not a party *of* the social gospel; they were a party of people shaped *by* the social gospel. In truth, they weren't a party at all. They were a "group" — farmers protesting maltreatment, ex-Liberals seeking free trade with the United States, industrial workers seeking social and industrial cures, ministers preaching brotherhood, and ordinary people seeking the new dawn of civilization.

Some were articulate and dynamic; some, angry and groping. Not all wanted to abolish capitalism; not all wanted free trade; not all saw liquor as one of the world's great evils. But prominent and influential among them were leading figures in the social gospel.[34] As a whole, they believed in "group politics" and were aiming at "group government" mainly because tensions inside the group made creation of a cohesive political party impossible. Eventually those tensions tore them apart: by 1930 the Progressives' share of the vote had dropped from 61 to 12 percent. But in their hour of glory they were formidable.

For the social gospel the next political step, after the disintegration of the Progressives, was to the CCF. However, it was a step taken by individuals, not by a movement, for there no longer was anything cohesive enough to be called a social gospel movement. It had scattered its energies running after too many different goals. Nevertheless, it had left a legacy, its moral outlook, and that legacy individuals took with them into the CCF and the CCF became the new movement.

Woodsworth and Irvine led the way, but over the years there were other men of the cloth in whom the message of the social gospel reverberated, extending from Tommy Douglas (Baptist) and Stanley Knowles (United Church) in the early years to Dan Heap (Anglican) and Bill Blaikie (United Church), who currently are NDP members of Parliament, and Jim Manly (United Church), who retired as an NDP member of Parliament with the calling of the 1988 election. Interviewed in 1988 before he retired, Manly said he very definitely was in the social gospel tradition. When he was studying theology in the 1950s, "the phrase was out of favour," but "it was something I was desperately looking for. I picked up more about it outside theological training than I did inside. I worked in a logging camp for two years right after theological school. . . . The tradition has continued in the United Church, and especially in the Board of Evangelism and Social Services."

In recent years, he adds, messages similar to the social gospel have found expression in such doctrines as the theology of hope in Germany, liberation theology in Latin America, and the Iona Movement in Great Britain.

Bill Blaikie sees himself as "very much in the tradition of the social gospel," although he cautions that it has changed over time. In the early days there was much less skepticism about modernity, about such things as the consequences of technology and environmental change, and much greater acceptance of the doctrine of progress.

At the 1987 NDP convention in Montreal a Christian Socialist Caucus was organized and Blaikie was enthusiastic about the turnout: "A lot of people in the NDP had been looking for an opportunity to be explicit about their politics and their faith. Partly this was because religious language had worked its way out of social discourse. You wouldn't know that the person who had just spoken was in the tradition. The caucus was a sort of sharing of where we were at."

Among prominent nonclerical members in the early CCF there were such people as Woodsworth's daughter Grace MacInnis who shared her father's moral convictions. And Ted Jolliffe, bequeathed a sensitivity to social gospel values by his father, who had been a missionary in West China and, says Jolliffe, "an apostle of the social gospel." And Charlie Millard, who was a lay preacher in the United Church in the early part of the depression. Although he came to think that the organized church was irrelevant, he held a deep Christian belief in the need for social action, his son Allan says. And in later years, Andy Brewin, a son of the Anglican manse. "His theology led him into the CCF," says his son John, stressing that although the Anglican outlook differed slightly from that of the United Church, the basic message of Christian social action was much the same.

Then there was the League for Social Reconstruction (LSR), that early think tank for the CCF, also reverberating from the outset with the message of the social gospel — especially in Montreal where there were three of the LSR's top six personalities: Frank Scott, King Gordon, and Eugene Forsey. (The other three were Frank Underhill and George Grube in Toronto and, once he had returned from Oxford, David in Ottawa.) Gordon, a United Church minister and son of a Presbyterian minister, had studied at Wesley College in Winnipeg, as had Douglas and Knowles, and with Forsey was a member of the Fellowship for a Christian Social Order. Forsey, the son of a Methodist minister, describes the influence of the social gospel on the CCF and in the LSR as "considerable, although to some extent indirect." Gordon acknowledges the influence of the social gospel in his early days, but by the time he reached the LSR he had come firmly under the sway of the Christian socialist thinking of Reinhold Niebuhr. Frank Scott, son of an Anglican minister, was brought into the social gospel tradition not only through his father but, says Gordon, by R.H. Tawney, author of *The Acquisitive Society* and *Religion and the Rise of Capitalism* and a member of "the committee of archbishops which, I think in 1919, produced a statement called *Christianity and Industrial Problems* [which] influenced Frank Scott's thinking very much."

So how did David Lewis and his Parliamentary Marxism fit with this Christian socialist tradition? He was there at the beginning of the LSR. King Gordon recalls that he attended the earliest meetings of the Montreal section of the LSR, before the founding of the CCF — and before he left for Oxford — along with Scott, Forsey, Gordon, and two or three others. "David was in that group," says Gordon, "as head of the McGill Labour Club."

In the first place, his Parliamentary Marxism did not appear strange or untoward. As Gordon explains:

> Niebuhr once classified Marx as the last of the great Hebrew prophets. In other words, he thought Marx drew a lot of his critical social and moral thinking from the tradition coming up today through the Jewish faith. It's difficult today to appreciate the extent to which at least a kind of second-run Marxism influenced the thinking [in the thirties]. The writing and thinking of Marx was much more common then than it is now.
>
> We are apt to identify Marx with a tight kind of doctrinaire orthodoxy, and it's been vulgarized, of course, by the right-wing moral majority which [thinks] anything that is not a 100 percent Americanism represents a dangerous Marxism. But in those days, while certainly your traditional establishment forces would brand you a Communist — as I was branded a Communist and the whole CCF crowd in Quebec was branded Communist — there was an acceptance among our group that, while we certainly didn't go along with Marx's particular historical analysis or his revolutionary prescriptions, nevertheless, as an analyst of society, he was to be taken into account.

In the second place, there were great similarities between the tradition of the Bund, out of which David sprang, and the social gospel.

The parallels are obvious in such matters as attitudes toward class consciousness, labour as the only real source of value, industrial democracy, public ownership, and changing the system as the only means of ending social evils. But such parallels would exist between the social gospel and most other groups espousing socialism. For instance, they existed within the CCF between people with a social gospel background and the hard-line Marxists in British Columbia; but they were never really comfortable with each other and the relationship was marked more by clashes than by a sense of shared vision.

With David it was different; there was a shared vision:

WHERE the social gospel progressed out of a rejection of the concept of Christian submissiveness that looked to the afterlife for rewards instead of concentrating on changing a system that was oppressive, the Bund's attitudes had evolved out of Haskala, the Jewish Enlightenment, which taught the same thing regarding Jewish religious submissiveness.

WHERE the social gospel assumed the perfectibility of man through the exercise of reason and persuasion in the service of God, the Bund inherited from Haskala a view that assumed the perfectibility of man through the exercise of reason and persuasion in the service of humanity — and this is what separated the Bund's Democratic Marxism from Lenin's brand of elitist Marxism.

WHERE the social gospel insisted on linking morality and socialism in opposition to what some called materialistic socialism, the Bund was permeated with the Jewish concept of *menschekeit*, striving to become a good person — an implicit system of morality — and, as Maishe had demonstrated in refusing office in the Amalgamated Clothing Workers, rejecting commitments that did not have a higher social purpose than material improvement.

WHERE the social gospel taught that industry should exist primarily for service and that corporate action would be placed before God's judgment, the Bund inherited from the Jewish community of the late 1800s in Vilna the view described by Shmarya Levin that the reward for businessmen should be service to the community, not profit.[35]

WHERE human brotherhood was the most important principle to the social gospel,[36] it was even more important to the Bund because for Jews it was more than a principle to be applied to others; it was crucial to their own safety and to their recognition as a nationality. Having rejected the call to establish a national homeland in Palestine, Bundists could rely for protection only on emphasizing a sense of kinship, understanding, and tolerance among non-Jews in whatever country they happened to be.

WHERE the social gospel stressed the need for social justice, even interpreting the Lord's Prayer in that context, the Bund's whole existence was based on applying the concept of social justice that emerged out of Haskala.

That shared vision was the nucleus that locked into orbit so many varied parts of the CCF. But what has to be recognized is that it brought other things to the party as well — other aspects of David's heritage that are consistently and mistakenly attributed primarily to his experiences with the British Labour Party.

Murray Cotterill comes close to recognizing what it was, although he does so in a combative and highly critical way that gives voice to what many of David's critics thought. Cotterill, now retired, is the former public relations director of the United Steelworkers of America. He is hearty with a ready and resounding laugh. "Stalwart" is the word that jumps first to mind. Big workman's hands, a broad build, a determined viewpoint — a guardian who would defend unto death. In the end, however, the description doesn't fit. Cotterill's conversation is solid, blunt, what you'd expect, heaving propositions into place like rugged Easter Island totems. But behind those totems a shadow suddenly flits from one to the other. You catch it out of the corner of your eye and aren't sure you really saw it. A trick of perception perhaps? But there it is again. And again. And soon you begin to realize that working in the background, and kept from open display, is a quick mind — probing, anticipating, testing.

The trouble with David, as he sees it, is that he was too much a European socialist — and Cotterill has no use for European socialists. "Canada simply doesn't operate under the same rules as one of those bloody little townships they call countries across the water," he says. European socialists were too doctrinaire, too inflexible, too chary to proceed with North American pragmatism, too much given to the rhetoric of the socialist struggle:

> I don't think they tended to be more radical, they just had less exposure to the Industrial Revolution and, except for [the French, the British, and the Germans], they were much later in getting rid of the bloody feudal part of their society. Let's be blunt. They were backward and their radicalism couldn't possibly be as radical, as up-to-date, as the

radicalism of a British worker who had probably been a member of the working class for several generations. . . .

I think that, if anything, European socialists were less radical. They loved making revolutionary speeches. They used to roll it around on their tongue, the word "revolution." . . .

David was a European. His background was that of a European socialist which was based on the assumption that the socialists had to lead the working class if, as, and when they could find one to lead. . . . Basically, I would say he was a socialist who believed that the ultimate salvation of the working class came from a socialized economy under a socialist government and that unions were a step on the way. The problem with that point of view is that the unions, no matter what they sounded like or what their structure was or what their leaders were like, were formed by workers, and in very few cases had the workers been led by intellectuals.

People like David thought nothing good came out of the United States, Cotterill says as he launches into a defence of the Gompers approach to politics:

I'm a good Canadian nationalist, but I think you're a damned fool when somebody comes up with a technique that works not to use it. The fact that they now make Buicks instead of McLaughlins doesn't mean that you should refuse to drive a Buick. . . .

Gompers believed in fighting his political enemies and supporting his political friends [which in his case was] within the framework of a political system that was not the same as the parliamentary system. There was nothing wrong with that. . . .

I can remember once I had called a meeting of shop stewards of all the unions in Vancouver to discuss political action; and we had them there from the Seafarers and the Longshoremen and the Teamsters and all the business unions as well as all the good socialist unions. . . . Dave, George Gruba, and a couple of others dropped in . . . and this little guy got up and he says, "What I can't figure out is, if we have to have a government to introduce legislation that involves spending money, why the hell did we pick the CCF? Why didn't we pick the goddam Liberals or Conservatives? Christ, we can get them elected and you can't get the CCF elected."

Dave and George and the rest were at the back and I said, "Well, brother, there is a simple reason. Our bosses had enough bloody brains to buy the Liberals and Conservatives first. We can't afford them. The only thing we can afford is the CCF."

Jesus Christ, Dave was so fucking furious! He was just incredibly furious. I said, "Well, Dave, it's true."

Cotterill still says that Gompers could have worked and can still work in the very different Canadian system.

Let's be equally blunt. Cotterill is talking nonsense when he talks about the backwardness of what he calls European socialism and by which he later acknowledges he means East European socialism. There is a grain of truth to give his analysis credibility, but his over-simplification is staggering. What he says is important because it represented a very definite perception within a part of the labour move-ment, a perception that looked with some satisfaction on the fact that North American unionists were better off than their European counter-parts. And when he speaks in disparaging terms about socialists see-ing unions as instruments in a political campaign to change the system, he is right in his observation, though wrong in his opinion that this made socialists somehow elitist. In response it need only be noted that most of the industrial unions in Canada were founded by people who were politically motivated.

What Cotterill doesn't accept is that, had his view prevailed, there probably would be no New Democratic Party today. Nor would there be the equivalent of the British Labour Party. Had Canada followed the Gompers tradition, there would not have been a commitment broad and fervent enough to sustain the party through its troubled times. And a labour party on the British model would probably have withered, as had been happening before the formation of the CCF.

All that aside, what Cotterill and others sensed about David was accurate. He was very much the son of his beginnings. What they didn't realize is that they should have been talking about a very particular kind of East European socialism: that of the Jewish Workers' Bund — a trade union that was, at the same time, a political party. A trade union that was ideologically committed and politically active. That's where David's roots were. He had no sympathy for a union move-ment that wanted to play off one political party against the other for its own advantage; he had grown up in a household where the union was a party battling to change society for the benefit of all.

Kalmen Kaplansky points out that, in Yiddish, even the language stresses this dual role: "'Bund,' in its literal translation, is 'union' — Jewish Workers' Union, you know. So it was both a trade union and a political party. And David carried with him the language, the con-cepts [of the Bund]. It's very important, you know, when your mind gets used conceptually to issues. . . . A neutral trade union in a European sense is almost like a capitalist . . . what is it they call it? A yellow dog union, a company union?"

David realized that the Bund model would not work in Canada. The Bund was unknown. Its traditions were foreign, even to most immigrant workers who were radical, such as the Finns and the

Ukrainians. Moreover, One Big Union had tried to create something similar and it had failed, not least because it aroused such intense hostility among other unions that prized their identity and independence.

However, there was another model that Canadians could relate to: the British Labour Party, and David made the most of it. But in doing so, his hand was guided by the link with his own personal past. That link influenced him in several distinct ways:

HE remained, in the deepest recesses of his heart, a Parliamentary Marxist — even though he came to discard certain Marxist notions as being inapplicable to Canada, such as the need for full ownership of the means of production and to modify others, such as the insistence on talking about class differences. He doubted "the validity of the term 'class' in Canadian society" and preferred instead to talk about working people who were at the mercy of the corporate structure.[37]

HE was virulently opposed to the Moscow line of communism — after all, these were the people who almost killed his father, who instituted the Red Terror, who murdered Erlich and Alter, who sought to strangle democratic socialism with the dictatorship of the Central Committee and, under Stalin, the dictatorship of the individual.

HE was determined, from his first day with the CCF, to see labour united with the party, and by labour he meant unions — it was an article of faith that traced back to the Bund, says Kaplansky, who, besides being David's lifelong friend, has an intimate knowledge of the Bund and Eastern European politics that goes back to his youth in eastern Poland.

HE was equally determined to establish a disciplined structure for the party — or as Kaplansky puts it:

David's greatest contribution to the CCF was . . . to protect the organizational structure while at the same time allowing for [the party's] ideological development. He was one of the few people active in the CCF who understood that without structure there cannot be ideological blossoming. A healthy structure has to face the problem of eliminating, or at least making it difficult for, those who want to use that structure for their own narrow partisan purposes, while at the same time retaining the possibilities for democratic discussions and democratic decision-making. It's something that faces all parties on the left. It has to do with the breakup of the socialist movement and the very essence of the Communist movement. And I think David understood this from the lessons he learned from his father and his time in Svisloch and then his years in the United Kingdom [at Oxford] and his trips to Poland

and the European countries [while he was at Oxford]. I think all of his life he tried to do this.

But the emphasis on organization goes deeper than even Kaplansky suggests. It was the strength of its organization that enabled the Bund to survive underground during the Tsarist years; that enabled it to withstand assaults from the Bolsheviks prior to 1917; that served it so well in the Warsaw Ghetto. David grew up learning that the first rule of political survival is to have a strong organization.
FINALLY, in the tradition of the Bund, David was determined to compromise if it was necessary to remain in touch with the broad body of would-be party sympathizers.

Sir William Nield recalls meeting David almost twenty-five years after he had known him at Oxford, and despite the compromises and adjustments that came with the years, found him at heart to be little changed:

> About the time that he was either founding or taking part in the founding of the New Democratic Party, I heard he was coming to London and I was invited to meet him, and so I went along to the hotel for some coffee in the morning and found a dozen or more people there and David was expounding. He was telling them about how the New Democratic Party was going to further nationalization and all that sort of thing.
> He didn't take any notice of me until the end . . . and then he said, "Well, you heard all that, Bill. You know a bit about Labour Party policy, what do you think about it?" I said, "I've got one thing to say to you and that's, for God's sake, don't disregard market prices or it will be absolutely disastrous because it will cost you billions. The coal mines are costing us a thousand million a year."
> David's answer was typical. He said, "There's no such thing as market prices." And I said, "Don't be bloody silly." And I didn't intervene any more . . . because I knew what he meant. He meant that it was all [controlled by] bloody entrepreneurs and capitalists and that sort of thing. . . .
> This capacity of his to be scathing and the extent to which he insisted on the letter of Marxism are what made him very seminal at Oxford and certainly influenced a lot of us for varying amounts of time.

Stephen also is emphatic about the abiding influence of the Bund on his father:

> Yes, he brought the intellectual reservoir of the Bund to the party. It was almost unconscious, however; it simply suffused his being and made him what he was without any reference to it.

The social gospel, on the other hand, was a constant reference point. . . . No speech was without it. No carrying cards without it. No party meeting was without it.

It would never have occurred to David to say, "Back in the Bund, chaps, . . . " Whereas with Tommy and Stanley and Andrew and Coldwell I can remember . . . strong biblical references, great evangelical motivation.

I am just saying that, yes, of course, they overlap.

Stephen, ambassador to the United Nations at the time, is speaking over lunch at a stylish French restaurant a stone's throw from the United Nations plaza. Even as a diplomat, he would never make anybody's best-dressed list. He makes even a well-cut, suitably dark business suit look a touch proletarian. But the waiter knows him and hovers with Gallic deference. Stephen is in his best oratorical stride, intrigued by the question: "From 1961 to 1963 the word 'socialist' had disappeared from the public documents of the NDP. . . . The question that comes up is whether deep in his heart of hearts David still held to the old socialist theme while, at the same time, realizing that he would never be able to implement it or get elected on it. Is there a contradiction?"

I'm not sure [Stephen says]. I think I may be helpful on this because I think we shared it. I think it is the legacy he left very deeply with me. I understood him and we talked about it. In fact, we didn't have to talk about it. It was like a code. It's where I think — and this is the son talking — it's where I think the world underestimated David. Writers, journalists, and others who never gave him his fair due, historically.

Yes, he was a pragmatist. Yes, he would have loved to see the CCF or NDP in power, although he never imagined it possible. Privately. Just as I never imagined it possible and thoroughly accepted that. Accepted his analysis that there's an awful lot to achieve on the road to utopia. You don't have to inhabit utopia. You don't have to be the one who ushers it in. . . .

And yet he could be tough and intellectually brutal with what he regarded as silly arguments at conventions or in caucus and, because he built the party in very real terms, with all the organizational strengths that that required. Fortitude and immersion. People could see him as, not arrogant, but overly single-minded. Authoritarian.

You had in David a combination which in a sense was forced on him and was not entirely embraced by him. When you are going to be both the organizational force in the party as well as the intellectual, ideological force, you are assuming everything from the cost of membership cards to whether there should be public ownership. You know, do you hire this hall or do you nationalize the banks?

The world forgets this. You are bridging such absurd opposites in your daily activities that the impatience with the one, at any given moment, manifests itself as a sort of peremptory action with the other. I saw that time and again because, in fact, the party surrendered to him, just as it did to me sometimes, the organizational emphasis because [it appeared that] the Lewises just sort of loved that, naturally, by doing it, even though they were equally satisfied with other things.

It was absolutely true of David that he had, to the point that it overrode everything else, this sustaining intellectual conviction in the goodness of the cause . . . and in the juxtaposition of the cause with workers. In a class sense. And this, I think, is a Bundist inheritance. That ultimately the workers have the right to inherit the earth. And that's what it's all about. And when pressed, David instinctively and naturally reverted to those prescriptions of life. Under any moment of pressure or emotion or test of conviction, back David went to the fundamentals, even if it wasn't put in stark class-struggle terms, although there were moments when he did speak in class terms.

That was the way he saw the world. When you stripped away all the excretions of the political apparatus — functioning as a politician, standing in the House of Commons, protocol, dealing with health care one day and sanitation systems the next, and regional economic planning — when his convictions were tested, he instinctively reverted to a classic democratic socialist credo where the workers were the meek who would inherit the earth and you could express it in class terms and you could lacerate capitalism and lacerate communism and find your role.

It absolutely sustained him. It made his eyes water when he talked about it. Tears came to David's eyes more naturally when he was talking about the benefits and glories of democratic socialism, of the quest for justice. That's when he became most emotional. That was in his heart. That was what he was all about. . . . That was his whole life. In one sense, his magnificence. Sometimes he was a little hard on capitalists, of course. But, by God, it was real and it explained so much of him.

It was the wellspring of an implacable determination. It was the rock on which to build a workers' party.

Today, when people trace the lineage of the party, they usually point to the social gospel, protest movements that ranged through the early years of this century and the Great Depression, Fabianism, the British Labour Party, and an Anglo-Saxon heritage. But that's only one bloodline. The other reaches back to Haskala, Parliamentary Marxism, the Russian revolutions, the Jewish Workers' Bund, and the heritage of the Pale of Settlement.

David never talked publicly about the Bund legacy. Most people would have been mystified by talk of Haskala and shtetls and *misnagidim* and *menschekeit*. And they would have been alarmed by the mere mention of the word "Marx." So he phrased his thoughts in terms of Fabian socialism and the British Labour Party and traditions to which most Canadians could relate, and day by day, over forty-five years, he fashioned the character and structure of the party, and the injunction, "Clear it with David," became the standard response to anyone with a proposal for the party to consider.

• CHAPTER FIFTEEN •

*I fear that the present rather innocuous attitude of the
Communist Party may lull our people into a sense of false
security. Really, it was disgraceful and dangerous to see
how that small handful at the Convention was able to turn
the whole affair into a beargarden in no time.*

Grace MacInnis
letter to David Lewis,
May 1944[1]

"**D**avid Lewis! That goddammed sonuvabitch was all over the place at Port Colborne."

Mike Solski speaking.

Port Colborne — from 1948 until 1961 the site of repeated efforts by the Steelworkers to oust Local 637 of the International Union of Mine Mill and Smelter Workers from the INCO refinery. In December 1961 Steel finally succeeded.

Raids, Solski calls them. He was president of Mine Mill Local 598 in Sudbury. With more than 17,000 members, it was the largest local in Mine Mill's international organization, and it had 61 percent of the total membership in Canada. In effect, it ran Mine Mill in Canada and could thumb its nose, if it wanted to, at the international.

In 1962 Steel finally got the Sudbury local too — and in 1967 all other Mine Mill locals in Canada except for Falconbridge — by forcing Mine Mill to merge into Steel.

Freeing Mine Mill of Communist control was how Charlie Millard, head of the Steelworkers, described Steel's actions. Undoubtedly that was a motive. But in a 1987 interview his secretary of the time confided that this was only a second priority. Millard's prime motive, said Margaret Lazarus, was to capture Mine Mill's membership for Steel. He wanted Steel to control all metal industries — from mining through to manufacturing. The Steelworkers controlled iron ore mines and steel production. But Mine Mill had the nickel and copper mines, smelters, and refineries. It stood in the way of his dream and his ambition.

Lazarus is, in everything, spare. In action as well as in appearance. If something is to be said, it should be said directly and to the point and accurately. That becomes apparent before the end of the first question is reached. If things are to be done, they should be done the same way — and that's how she prepares a pot of tea and sits you down at a kitchen table. And if you survive under her rules, then there's a slight softening, a hint of acceptance, a touch of pleasure in returning to struggles long ago. She is married to Morden Lazarus, who was provincial secretary of the Ontario CCF from 1949 to 1953.

In the early days, when there were just a few people in the Steelworkers' national office, she made sure it ticked precisely on beat. "She ran it," says Lorne Ingle, the CCF national secretary who succeeded David. "I can recall Charlie getting a call from I.W. Abel [the Steelworkers' international president] in Pittsburgh and Margaret, after she had told Charlie that Abel was on the phone, she went and stood at his door and told him what to say."

Margaret also was secretary-treasurer of the Ontario CCF Trade Union Committee, the agency the party had created to combat Communists and build support in unions. She was efficient and impatient with delay — and renowned for a tart tongue by any who were inefficient or tardy.[2]

David had a different motive from Millard's for taking on the Communists, and he never made any secret of it. Communists were blocking a CCF alliance with unions. David saw support from labour as the key to power. But to get it, Communist opposition in unions had to be removed. So it was a two-step process: first, get rid of Communists; second, win over the unions. The two steps weren't mutually exclusive. Campaigns at both levels could go on simultaneously. But both were necessary. In a September 1942 letter to Bert Leavens, CCF provincial secretary in Ontario, David stressed that until the CCF won over organized labour, "we shall not be a mass movement capable of achieving power in this country. . . .[3] But before it could win labour's allegiance, he added in his memoirs, "the first step had to be to wrest control from the Communists wherever possible."[4]

It was not just Mine Mill that was seen as riddled with Communists. It was the United Auto Workers (UAW), the United Electrical Workers, the International Woodworkers of America, the Fur and Leather Workers, the Canadian Seamen's Union, the United Textile Workers, the Lumber and Sawmill Workers, and the B.C. Shipyard Workers. It was a fight with few holds barred, as demonstrated by Eamon Park, a Steel staff representative and chairman of the Ontario CCF Labour Committee, in a March 1946 letter to Oliver Hodges, an organizer for the Ontario CCF Trade Union Committee. Park was discussing strategies for an upcoming international convention of the

UAW and the delicate balancing act that George Burt, Canadian director of the UAW had been performing between the Communists and
the anti-Communists in the UAW. Park thought most of the balancing had been done in favour of the Communists.

> Burt is not a Commie. I'd be interested to see his record on the Inter-
> national Board. I don't like the louse and would be very happy to dump
> him any time it would not do damage to the union. He is essentially
> a weak sister who will go wherever he is shoved. I am frankly fearful
> he might double-cross us if he is re-elected and yet I can't see a man
> who could take his measure and hold the union together.
>
> The best thing for the time being, it seems to me, would be to have
> men like Poole and Shultz call on Burt and lay it on the line. That
> is the only talk he understands. . . . He must be told that he will be
> re-elected only if he gets rid of men like [Harry] Rowe, [Drummond]
> Wren, Cohen [the legal adviser], and key CPers in the field. He must
> himself go along with the executive of the [Canadian Congress of
> Labour] on matters of policy and quit playing the role of Commie tool
> in that executive. He must stop his palaver with Jackson and Harris
> of the UE and co-operate with Steel. It should be arranged that cer-
> tain persons like Poole, MacDonald and others can be placed on the
> international pay-roll in place of dismissed Communists. No
> Communists must handle publicity or education for the union. If at
> all possible these spots must go to a CCFer. Unless a significant number
> of these guarantees are forthcoming then he should be told we will not
> suppport him and take a chance. If the Commies run [Roy] England
> for the Board he should be told we don't give a damn if England is
> elected because we'll get him a year from now. If Burt will meet part
> of this program then I think we could support him and start now to
> get ready to give him the boot a year from now.
>
> If our gang can show strength Burt will wilt. If [Walter] Reuther can
> make the international presidency then I am not worried about Burt
> and Canada. If on the other hand Reuther does not make the grade
> then no matter what is done in Canada, Burt will be on the fence, and
> we'll have to hold him in check by local action. . . .
>
> Notwithstanding this letter, I think a war of nerves on Burt would
> be very advantageous. It might put him in the proper frame of mind
> to receive a delegation. You'll get your rumours about a change. I've
> got a line into Canadian Press which can do the trick. . . .[5]

Reuther did become international president of the UAW at the 1946
convention, and after the next convention in November 1947 he won
control of the board, and from that point on Communists on both
sides of the border were on their way out of the UAW. Burt, wily union
politician that he was, settled into the CCF camp and remained head
of the Canadian Autoworkers.

A folklore has grown up around the battles with the Communists
in the thirties, forties, and fifties that embellishes the victor's version

of history. It says that the Communists were ousted from unions (1) because they were so disruptive to the union movement, (2) because they opposed national policies such as support for the Marshall Plan that restored a war-ravaged Europe, (3) because, given the opportunity, they would use unions to the political ends of the Communist Party, (4) because Communists had repeatedly demonstrated, especially under the leadership of Tim Buck and Sam Carr, that they would subordinate an independent policy for Canada to the policies of Stalin's Comintern, and (5) because without a unified labour movement Canada would be subjected to the divisions and bitterness that had made Europe bleed.

All this is true.

But equally true is the fact that CCFers wanted to enlist unions in the pursuit of their own political goals. And non-Communist union leaders wanted to expand their turf. And both gave as good as they got. And where CCFers didn't give, they benefitted from those who did without demurring. The singular truth behind all the manoeuvring, all the political broadsides and name calling, all the secret intrigues on both sides, is that a gargantuan struggle for power was under way that rivalled anything Canada had seen.

So there was no holy side in this struggle. Only the level of sin varied. Power was the issue; unions were the battlefield. On both sides there were visions of a better society with exponents who were idealistic and highly motivated. Among Communists, for instance, who would want to criticize as not being humanists Norman Bethune or A.E. Smith or Joe Salsberg, who became an Ontario MP, or Becky Buhay, the orator, or the fiery Annie Buller, the Red Boadicea as she was called, or C.S. Jackson, Canadian president of the United Electrical Workers, or Winnipeg Alderman Jacob Penner, or, coming back to Mine Mill, Weir Reid, who ran the local's social programs? Who, on the other hand, would want to raise similar objections to Frank Scott or Andy Brewin or Frank Underhill or M.J. Coldwell or Tommy Douglas or Angus MacInnis or David Lewis?

Who would care to dispute that Mine Mill or the United Electrical Workers deserved tremendous praise for winning recognition for their workers? Or, on the other hand, that the Steelworkers or the Amalgamated Clothing Workers greatly improved working conditions for their memberships?

What made all the difference, what was the greatest sin of all, was the slavish adherence of principal Commmunist leaders to Stalin's policy of the moment; and, as policy contradictions multiplied and the curtain began to be drawn back on the horror of his purges and his grisly repression of Ukraine that left some 10 to 12 million Ukrainians dead — starved, shot, or perished in labour camps — CCFers were increasingly buttressed in the rightness of their cause and Canadian Communists increasingly lost support and lost faith.

In the year David arrived back from Oxford — 1935 — three profoundly important events occurred:

JOHN L. LEWIS, president of the United Mine Workers in the United States, spearheaded creation of the CIO, then called the Committee for Industrial Organization, to establish unions among the new mass-production industries. At the outset the CIO was a committee of the American Federation of Labor (AFL). It was enormously effective at organizing, but the old guard in the AFL was unhappy with the upstart unions in their midst and after a year the AFL suspended them. Two years later they were expelled and established the Congress of Industrial Organizations, with Lewis as president. The consequence for Canada was that the organizing zeal of the CIO set off a stampede to organize industrial unions in Canada.

THE COMINTERN abandoned its ultra-left policy of labelling social democrats as social fascists and reversed its policy on union membership. Formerly it had decreed that Communists must work only in their own unions. Now it ordered them to abandon their unions and join mainstream unions. (This was the same policy switch that impelled the October Club at Oxford to try and "fuse" with the Labour Club just as David was leaving the university.)

The first result in Canada was that the Workers Unity League (WUL) — a Communist organization which had been formed in January 1930 as an alternative to the Trades and Labor Congress (TLC) and the All Canadian Labour Congress — was jettisoned and its affiliated unions were absorbed into the TLC. (The WUL was such a scrappy union organization that it won praise from the League for Social Reconstruction (LSR) in its 1935 publication *Social Planning for Canada*. The LSR called it the most active group of unionists in the country and said, "Their militancy at a time when most orthodox unions are in a state of coma has nearly doubled their membership in a single year."[6])

The second and more far-reaching result was that, with the elimination of the WUL, Communist organizers were freed to work in main-line unions and, since they were experienced and good organizers, the CIO put them to work.

THE ON-TO-OTTAWA TREK took place. It was the most potent expression of working-class discontent since the Winnipeg General Strike.

As the well-disciplined trekkers passed through town after town, it became apparent that they had wide public support. The country was primed for change; the trek focused desire.

Canada, in 1935, was a land of tensions, nervous and often ill-tempered. The Great Depression may have peaked but misery hadn't and communism, with its promise to end the system that produced the misery, had great appeal for many who had suffered. There still were about 600,000 people searching for jobs out of a total work force, including farmers, of 4.4 million, and there were still more than a million on relief.[7] Public welfare spending was continuing its upward surge: in 1926–27 the cost to all governments was $99 million, in 1933–34 it was $230 million, and by 1939–40 it would be $317 million.[8] Most of the provinces still had more than 200 labour camps each, run with military efficiency by the Department of National Defence — Prime Minister R.B. Bennett's solution to keeping men off the streets where they might breed trouble — and to that point more than 170,000 had passed through them earning 20 cents a day and board.[9]

In the camps Communists had organized the Relief Camp Workers Union, and in April they led an exodus out of the camps in British Columbia to the streets of Vancouver, the exact thing that Bennett feared most. They snake-danced through department stores, distributed leaflets, made speeches, and, asking for donations on street corners, raised $22,000 for food and shelter.[10] In early June, 1,200 boarded railway boxcars and began the On-To-Ottawa Trek. By the time they reached Regina there were 1,800, and there the Trek ended in one of the worst riots the country has ever seen. Bennett was determined that the trekkers would never ride the rails into Winnipeg, home of the 1919 General Strike, where 1,200 more were waiting to join up. So in Regina they were stopped by Mounties. Everything remained peaceful up to Dominion Day, when police decided to break up a rally and arrest the speakers. The result was one dead — a policeman — seventy-eight injured, half of whom were strikers and local citizens, and of them, half were suffering bullet wounds, "not a store with a window left in it," and the disbanding of the Trek.[11]

Across the country there was widespread support for the Trek, and in the House of Commons especially by the CCF, but even so, there still were a lot of people who were frightened by radicalism. A lovely little ditty, "Tea Time Tattle in Toronto," published in The Canadian Forum in 1931 and still applicable in 1935, offered an airy perspective:

> Little old ladies as sweet as can be,
> Sitting and knitting and sipping their tea,
> Lowered their horrified voices and said,
> My dear, there are Bolsheviks under the bed![12]

However, if one were to believe the chief justice of Ontario, at any moment Bolsheviks might spring from beneath the bed and murder any innocent they could lay their hands on. In an after-dinner speech Sir William Mulock described them as conspirators, atheists, destroyers of the family, "who would rob all citizens by any degree of force, up to that of murder, of all their worldly goods and leave them penniless."[13]

For an establishment that basically still hailed back to the British Isles, the country had become dreadfully unruly and overrun with foreigners who did not have the best interests of the nation at heart. The antidote, declared *The Globe* of the day, was a stern response. In the face of an upcoming demonstration it lectured police that, "The menace of [communism] grows in proportion with the degree of gentleness with which it is handled. . . . Any group that seeks to promulgate atheism among people, disobedience among children, sabotage among workers, and revolution among all, is a canker on society."[14]

But then most of the press couldn't tell a Communist from a cannibal. When the CCF was created, *The Mail and Empire* wrote approvingly about an accusation that the United Farmers of Ontario had sold out to the Reds.[15] In 1937 *The Globe and Mail*, sounding uncannily like Tsarist organs in the early 1900s, declared that although not all Jews were Communists, in all probability most Communists were Jews.[16] And as late as 1938 John W. Dafoe, the redoubtable editor of the *Winnipeg Free Press*, was sure that David — of all people! — was a Communist.[17] Meanwhile, in Quebec the Catholic Church fumed that even the CCF was communistic and should be run out of town.[18]

In Ottawa, with Bennett as prime minister — a millionaire who ran a one-man government, lived alone in a magnificent suite at the Chateau Laurier, "dressed himself with foppish care . . . [and] usually consumed a pound of chocolates every night"[19] — there was little reason to expect empathy on Parliament Hill for the plight of the unfortunate, or even understanding for the radical currents sweeping the country, regardless of the long and diligent hours the prime minister worked. And indeed, he had little empathy or understanding. His election promise to relieve the depression proved hollow, his policies were largely ineffectual, proposals for social reform tended to irritate rather than engage him (until, on election eve, he recanted), and before long he began to look indecisive, soon becoming a favourite of cartoonists and the butt of jokes. Mackenzie King and his Liberals threw him out of office in the October 1935 election.

However, Ottawa was not the only place where changes had been brewing. Clambering on stage were powerful provincial premiers, impatient to deal with regional concerns, who soon would be yanking at the trusses of strong central government: Duff Patullo for the Liberals in British Columbia (1933–45), Bible Bill Aberhardt introducing Social Credit to Alberta (1935–43), Mitch Hepburn for the Liberals in Ontario (1935–42), and, starting off slowly in Quebec for the Union Nationale, Maurice Duplessis (1936–39 and 1944–59) — all of them bolstered by a long line of decisions favouring a shift in power to the provinces handed down by Canada's highest court of appeal, the Judicial Committee of the Privy Council in England.

Into this political whirligig stepped David. A centralist in a nation that was decentralizing. A socialist in a country that voted solidly capitalist. A campaigner for a party with no money, facing two parties each of which was big, powerful, and affluent. A labour supporter for a party with no union support. A professional in a party of amateurs who mostly thought of themselves as a movement, not a party. An anti-Communist at a time when Canadian Communists were about to enter their heyday.[20] A publicist seeking a unified voice for a party riven with dissent. An organizer whose leader, J.S. Woodsworth, really didn't believe in organization, thinking that the CCF should remain a loosely knit, co-operative association and believed this so implicitly that when it came time to appoint David full-time to the job of national secretary he resisted, fearing the CCF would lose its spontaneity.[21]

That David not only survived, but prevailed is a testament to his skill and perseverance.

The best recruiters that the Communists had were Bennett in Ottawa and Hepburn in Toronto. In the years leading up to the On-To-Ottawa Trek, Bennett made a hero out of Communist leader Tim Buck, and in the years after, Hepburn made heroes out of Communist organizers in the industrial unions.

In the late twenties and early thirties police and Communists battled with mutual loathing. To the Communists, the police were agents of oppression. Bullies. Thick-headed thugs in blue. To the police, the Communists were subversives. Poisonous vermin out to destroy the country. Weapons for the Communists were mass rallies, parades, and street-corner orations. For the police, horses, billies, hard-toed boots, jail, and deportation.[22]

As the depression gathered steam, the Communists had growing success. Throughout the twenties they had worked diligently among immigrants helping them through the ins and outs at City Hall, showing them how to apply for relief, representing them where necessary. And they had been equally diligent in forming unions in coal mining, lumber, and the needle trades. In the early thirties the WUL set out to organize any shop with seventy-five to a hundred employees — shoe workers, furniture makers, rubber workers, transport employees, poultry workers, lumbermen. "It was unions [in the WUL]," said the LSR in 1935, "which, against tremendous odds, fought with complete or partial success the furniture workers' strikes in Stratford and Toronto, and the poultry pluckers' strikes in Stratford in the summer of 1933. Less successful in the lumbermen's strikes in Ontario and Quebec in the winter of 1933, their action nevertheless undoubtedly helped to secure some legislative protection for the lumberjacks in Ontario, Quebec and New Brunswick."[23]

By the time of its dissolution in 1935, the WUL had organized about 40,000 workers.[24] These were not numbers large enough to challenge the established labour organizations, the TLC and the ACCL, but they offered a good enough platform to confront a system insulated by privilege and defended by bombast. In 1933 Communists were claiming leadership in 75 percent of of the 122 strikes begun that year and 58 percent of the 189 strikes in 1934.[25]

In 1931 they began their campaign for a non-contributory unemployment insurance plan with 76,150 demonstrators hitting the streets across Canada on February 25: 13,000 in Toronto, 12,000 in Winnipeg (the biggest demonstration since the General Strike), 5,000 in Montreal, and 5,000 in Vancouver.[26] Two days before the demonstrations, but well aware that they were being organized, high-ranking police officers met with the federal justice minister pleading for the go-ahead to smash the Communists. If they didn't get it there could be riots beyond their control, some said. They got it. The justice minister wrote the Ontario attorney-general offering him the full co-operation of federal authorities and of the RCMP if he ordered a crackdown.[27]

The crackdown came, but not for several months, and in the meantime, on April 15, a delegation of twenty-four Communist leaders travelled to Ottawa and presented the prime minister with a petition signed by more than 94,000 people calling for non-contributory unemployment insurance. "Never," Bennett huffed, "will I or any government of which I am a part, put a premium on idleness or put our people on the dole."[28]

Four months later the police swooped and Tim Buck and eight other Communists were arrested. Buck and seven of the others were sentenced to five years in Kingston Penitentiary and the ninth received a two-year sentence.[29] The weapon used against them was section 98 of the Criminal Code, the infamous law passed immediately after the Winnipeg General Strike that made it an offence punishable with up to twenty years in prison to be linked with an association that proclaimed a belief in violent revolution. (See Appendix H.)

For the unemployed and the radical it was not too hard to draw a line from a law that was passed because people went on strike to get the right to form unions, to demands for unemployment insurance, to arrest and conviction and jail. The message coming from the establishment was clear. It would offer no quarter. And then there was the attempt by prison guards to assassinate Buck in Kingston Penitentiary eight months after he was imprisoned. (See Appendix I.)

The attempted assassination caused such a furor that Buck and his seven companions were released midway through their prison terms. When Buck walked into a mass meeting at Massey Hall in December 1934, within a month of his release, 17,000 people roared their welcome and the 8,000 who couldn't get in roared in spirit.[30]

The campaign for Buck's release had been conducted by the Canadian Labour Defence League, led by A.E. Smith, which saw its membership go up from 25,000 in the spring of 1932 to 43,000 early in 1934.[31] Without a doubt, Tim Buck had become one of the most popular figures in Canada. And when Norman Bethune, freshly returned from the Spanish Civil War, toured Canada in 1938, his reception surpassed even that given Buck.[32]

In the United States, John L. Lewis was an aggressive anti-Communist, but he also was a tough, pragmatic trade unionist, and so when he began his organizing drive for the CIO, he immediately set out to get the best organizers he could — and some of the best were Communist. Two he hired on to his personal staff, others he persuaded newly formed CIO unions to hire, and by April 1937 the CIO had acquired a membership of almost four million.[33]

This explosive growth south of the border dazzled Canadians and, as Irving Abella tells it in his *Nationalism, Communism, and Canadian Labour*, "On their own, without informing the CIO, scores of ex-WUL organizers began organizing CIO unions in Canada. The director of the Communist Party's trade-union section, J.B. Salsberg, travelled to New York and Washington and begged CIO leaders to launch campaigns in Canada. He returned empty handed . . . [so] Salsberg and other party stalwarts accelerated their efforts on behalf of the CIO.

Within months these men, and a handful of others, had organized hundreds of new workers and scores of new CIO locals."[34]

The event that embedded the CIO in Canada was the strike against General Motors in Oshawa in the spring of 1937. It wasn't organized by the CIO; it wasn't financed or led by the CIO. Nor was it organized by Communists. It was a spontaneous reaction to a speed-up by the company, and it resulted in the creation of Local 222 of the UAW, with Charlie Millard, even then a CCF supporter, as president. However, the CIO gave the fledgling local its blessing, and a couple of advisers and the strikers were able to use the threat of American CIO help toward gaining a contract. It was a modest contract that was signed, but the fact that it was signed at all, signed despite Hepburn's determination to break the new union, signed despite his Sons of Mitches, or Hepburn's Hussars — the special squad of anti-strike provincial policemen recruited to strengthen the company's defiance and later used against strikers in the gold fields — and signed under CIO auspices, put fire in the bellies of organizers across the country. If the CIO could bring the biggest company in the world to terms, who could withstand them?

There were ups and downs. The Communist gains in 1935 had almost been wiped out by 1937. After the Oshawa strike, gains in Northern Ontario's mining industry were subsequently lost. But still the Communists took the initiative. They had the organizers, they had the organization, and they had the will. Two days after the Oshawa strike they began their successful drive to organize electrical workers under the UE. They hit the gold fields in the north, the textile, steel, and rubber plants in the south, smelters in British Columbia, a few small plants in Montreal.

Graham Spry, editor of *The New Commonwealth*, vice-president of the Ontario CCF, and chairman of its executive committee, wrote David a "personal" letter in December 1936 describing the situation before the strike:

> The situation now is that the Communists are powerful in the unions, slowly becoming as powerful almost as they are in some of the foreign language associations. Even where they are not powerful in numbers, their representatives constitute a voting block that trade union officers have to consider if they want to hold either jobs or offices . . .
>
> I think the situation is difficult, and might be serious. And especially so because we have not got the people to do the work of visiting and explaining the situation and generally helping the [CCF] clubs, whereas the Communists have not only their scores of publications (I mean scores) starting with a daily through to the trade union organizing

sheets, hammering away at us, but they have 50 to 60 full time organizers in the South Central Ontario region. In a word, the CCF is in second place so far as providing leadership to labour is concerned.[35]

Four months later, and a week after the Oshawa strike, Spry wrote David again, exulting at the opportunities and despairing that the CCF could do anything about them: " . . . everywhere there is the demand for union organizers, everywhere there is the cry 'labour party', everywhere there is a new attitude, a new public opinion, and everywhere the CCF is almost totally ineffective."

Galt, Guelph, Brantford, Hamilton, Kitchener, all were ripe for organizing, but local CCFers were out of touch, almost useless, and their groups were, "for practical purposes dead," He would have to quit, Spry said. "I simply cannot carry on any longer; every cent I manage to scrape up goes into the CCF — for the radio, the New Comm[onwealth], the Stafford Printers — I am up against it . . . Margaret Sedgwick [who was to become Margaret Lazarus] feels as I do — as long as we are ready to go on like this, nothing will be done to correct the situation."[36]

He was disgruntled over not having been re-elected chairman of the executive committee. That was the real reason for wanting to quit. But that detracted not at all from his despairing analysis of the state of the CCF in Ontario.

In June he left. Toward the end of the month he and David had lunch and as David wrote Sophie, "While it is probably in the main his own fault, it is nevertheless tragic. He sacrificed a great deal, but he wasn't quite big enough. And the movement wasn't quite big enough to provide for him in some job where he could really do good. And there are many such jobs, for he has great ability. The result? He has to start life all over again with a terrific psychological disadvantage. It's too bad."[37]

The Communist Party, taking advantage of the shambles in which the CCF found itself, flourished. According to party figures, its membership increased from 5,500 in July 1934 to 16,000 early in 1939.[38]

Total union membership went from 385,000 in 1938 to 664,000 in 1943, the biggest growth in Canadian history. Most of it was in CIO industrial unions, and Communists were responsible for a good part of it.[39] In 1939 they pushed Charlie Millard out of the UAW and George Burt, not a Communist but much more accommodating, took his place, and for the next eight and a half years Burt's balancing act, though it held the UAW together, was a constant thorn in the side of the CCF.

In his determination to purge the labour movement of Communists, David was facing a formidable task.

CHAPTER SIXTEEN

*David was arguably the best labour lawyer that Canada's
ever seen.*

> Gerald Charney,
> Toronto labour lawyer,
> January 1989

W ally Ross, an organizer for the Steelworkers in the sixties
in Ontario and now retired in Terrace, British Columbia,
tells a story about David, "just to show you how single-
minded he was." Ross was B.C. campaign manager for David during
the 1971 leadership race and they were driving back to Vancouver
after attending a meeting. It was winter — snow was piled about six
feet high on either side of the road — and it was about three-thirty
in the morning. Ross was driving. David was intent on a point he was
trying to make. All of a sudden a mule deer leaped the nearest bank
and landed directly in front of them. Ross spun into the bank, careened
off, and miraculously missed the deer "by about two inches."

"Christ!" he shouted. "Did you see that?"

"Yes," replied David. "Now as I was saying . . . ," and he continued
with the point he was making, barely missing a beat.

It was this ability to focus concentration with such determination
that had served him so well in learning English, that had eased his
way through university, that made him such a devastating debater.

"His powers of concentration were unbelievable," says Murray
Weppler, David's executive assistant while he was party leader. "I don't
know anyone that briefed as well as David. . . . What always amazed
me about him was that he could recall verbal briefings, whereas a lot
of people with great recall have to read it." He'd only have to hear
it once and "in most areas I don't think he would ever lose it. In all
the three or four years that I worked there, rarely would he lose
something."

David launched himself at the CCF's problems with the same single-mindedness. In the beginning he also worked for the Ottawa law firm Smart and Biggar and had to divide his time between law and politics. In August 1938, three years almost to the day that he began with both, he quit practice and began working full time as CCF national secretary for a salary of $1,200 a year.[1]

He had been impressive as a lawyer dealing in the highly technical field of patents, trademarks, and copyright. Mowatt Biggar, a senior partner in the firm, once said that no young man he had ever known showed greater promise before the bar than David. According to Ted Jolliffe, "If he'd stayed, he'd have become a senior partner. . . . David had the kind of mind which had no difficulty in absorbing a very technical brief. It was his meat; he had that kind of mind.

"He explained to me once that he did not have a pictorial mind. He did not visualize things the way many lawyers do . . . seeing pictures all the way through . . . what the jury will look like, what the judge will look like . . . visualiz[ing] the kind of scene which will be staged in the courtroom. And even in the preparation of a factum and things like that, memory tends to be visual. At least that's been my experience."

In another testament to David's single-mindedness, Jolliffe adds, "David was a great chess player when he was young . . . [but] he gave up chess because he felt it would take up too much of his time and exhaust too much of his ability. So he quit deliberately when he was in his teens. By all accounts he was an excellent chess player. I don't believe he ever played chess again. He just put it aside as irrelevant to what he wanted to do. He was like that."

These characteristics served David well in stitching together an organization that, with its emphasis on being more movement than party, was so loose-jointed it was ungainly and sometimes perverse and which, in Ontario, was still dishevelled from that March day in 1934 when Woodsworth summarily disbanded the Ontario party. Its labour section had been supporting A.E. Smith's Canadian Labour Defence League in its campaign to free Tim Buck and the seven other jailed Communists, and Woodsworth would have none of that. Especially since Smith had accused Woodsworth of instigating the sedition charges that were laid against Smith for speaking out against the assassination attempt on Buck. Woodsworth would have no compromising on his stand against any dallying with Communists. If action was to be taken, if protests were to be made, the CCF would do it independently — and the party did protest the jailings independently. The effect of Woodsworth's action was, in Gerry Caplan's words, to destroy in ten short minutes "much of the original CCF. . . . Leadership went as precipitately as structure."[2]

The Ontario party regrouped after Woodsworth's ultimatum, but it was anaemic and a good seven or eight years passed before it began to show muscle. And for most of those seven or eight years it was David who had to carry out the repairs.[3]

Not only was David single-minded and determined; he had a stamina remarkable in someone with no physical abilities whatever, whose younger brother had to protect him in the streets. In fact he was so physically inept that Murray Weppler says when he was party leader they had to watch him carefully to make sure he didn't get "too involved" in anything inappropriate. These were the days when the devastating photo of Robert Stanfield bobbling a football appeared in every newspaper in the country, adding to the impression that the Tory leader was maladroit.

> David could hardly run [says Weppler]. I don't think he had ever run in his life. . . . [But] he had unbelievable physical and mental stamina. . . .
> He walked a lot . . . [especially] during campaigns. We'd get off for a long walk quite often. He didn't drink much but he smoked a lot throughout his life. I suspect that one of the things [that helped him stay reasonably fit] is that he probably did learn to eat carefully. . . . He knew how to relax. And like almost everything else he did, it was a conscious effort where he said, okay, this is put aside and now I'm going to relax.

Sometimes he did it reading poetry, sometimes seeking rapport with friends. Whatever the means, the result was he could drive himself mercilessly, hour upon endless hour — week after month after year.

There is a kind of valour to commitment of this sort, but as David's sister Doris alluded to earlier, there is a kind of selfishness too, a dark side to the single-mindedness, and the person who had to live with that dark side was Sophie. She revelled in David's successes, she was ecstatically proud of his achievements and she was exultant in her love of him.

It was a love that shimmered, not like moonlight across quiet lakes, but like heat waves rising from a summer road. This was no passive love. Sophie was vibrant, strong-willed, and demonstrative, and so was her love. But it was a love that needed to celebrate itself. In England it was possible. They went to plays and concerts and all kinds of functions. They took long walks. They went on trips and vacations together. They held hands. They discussed books they were reading. They talked sense and they talked nonsense.

They rejoiced.

In Ottawa it wasn't so easy. David worked as hard at both jobs as most people do at one. Even when he was in town he was more often at a law library on evenings and weekends, or at a meeting, than he was home, and he was out of town a lot. Vacations together became a weekend here, a couple of days there when he could join Sophie at Val Morin or somewhere else in the country.

Stephen was born on November 11, 1937, and David barely made it home in time from Montreal that day. Michael was born on January 26, 1945, and David couldn't get home from the office in time to take Sophie to the hospital because of a snowstorm. In the spring of 1948, when Sophie was stricken with a pulmonary embolism following minor bone surgery on her foot and narrowly escaped death, David was away on a speaking tour for an Ontario election scheduled for June 7. When the twins, Janet and Nina, were born prematurely on November 13, 1948, once again David was out of town. It was Sophie's third delivery and David's third absence. She never forgave him.[4] In 1950 when David left his position as national secretary to return to the practice of law with Ted Jolliffe's firm in Toronto, he bought their first house but, "As happened so often in those years, I had to leave Sophie with the major part of the job of settling in. I had time only to put up the beds with Stephen's help and to push heavy pieces of furniture and cartons out of the way before leaving for the national convention and meetings of the National Council in Vancouver."[5]

And so it went. For a political family, David's absences weren't all that unusual. And the argument is made by some party people that Sophie knew beforehand that she was marrying David's commitment as much as she was marrying David, so why should she complain? But the reality of living with this commitment was something else again. As almost the entire responsibility for raising the chidren fell on Sophie and as it grew more demanding, she found her world shrinking to that of a house-bound nanny.

Rarely were there long walks or concerts or outings together, or the extravagant pleasure of letting a whole afternoon, dappled in intimacies, drip slowly through their fingers. Her outside activities, like taking university courses, as she did in London, or working in the CCF office, as she did in Ottawa before Stephen's birth, dwindled. The evenings alone multiplied.

As her isolation increased, she began to look more and more to David to bring home the texture of living — not just by his presence but with news of what he was doing and what was happening in the party and who was doing what, and when and with whom. She had forceful political opinions of her own and enjoyed, indeed relished, acting as critic, sounding board, and inspiration. But in the end David's successes became her successes; his excitement, her excitement; his life, her life. And slowly she began to fold her identity into his. Her identity never disappeared; she was too strong a person for that. What happened was that she insisted on occupying part of David's identity as her own territory. Sometimes demanding. Sometimes clamouring.

Tensions inevitably grew out of this — times of argument and anger that in later years came to be witnessed by party intimates who sometimes saw Sophie as a trial for David. But what these people saw were incidents. They weren't looking through the long lens of the years the two had spent together. And they saw Sophie outside the aura of profound love that she and David shared even though, in its frustrations, it sometimes drove them to wound each other.

David always used to refer to Sophie as "my Sophie." He speaks that way in his memoirs,[6] and even when he was sixty-seven years old and retired, he would respond to a formal invitation by saying "my Sophie and I do intend to be at the affair."[7] There is a haunting loveliness about the way he used the phrase, full of tenderness and caring. There also was another side, as Stephen mentions, and for Stephen it was not so touching:

It tells you everything about possession and not autonomy. It really does. . . .

I don't want to romanticize it, on the one hand, and I don't want to understate it on the other. They had an incredible love affair in England during the Rhodes days, an unbelievable love affair, and they were enormously attached to each other through life. No question . . . but there was also something a little unsettling that the possessive implies. . . .

Sophie subordinated herself so completely to David, in every single aspect of his life — intellectual, cultural, ideological, personal — that what didn't reflect him was not pursued by her. . . . Everything that he cared about, she cared about. What he didn't care about, she didn't care for. . . . It was a relationship of such massive dependence that when he died, her life ended, in the classical, novelist way. Just the next day it was over. If she could have died the next day you never would have found a happier person. And her regret at not having died is one of the saddest things about it. . . .

She was an amazingly bright person, you know . . . very descriptive, and intuitive as well, and had a lovely sense of what was going on in the world and could wander through a valley and be moved while my father pondered Marx. I often regretted all of that never quite emerged for her because I think it would have given her great pleasure.

Their letters tell much and, in David's case, they sometimes vividly described his work in the party:[8]

Sophie to David: from Montreal
January 19, 1937

My darling,

... I haven't told you everything — not about the many times a day I've thought about you and how I feel that I love you so much. I wonder what the feeling really was when I said I thought I loved you many years ago. . . .

David to Sophie: from Toronto
May 21, 1937

My own Wife,

... I am the principal speaker at tonight's opening session. This is really the first major speech I shall have made in Toronto, and I'd like to do well. Now I must have some breakfast and rush to the CCF office. They have already phoned me. The Provincial Council is meeting and they want me.

... I think of you all the time. But we must not become impatient. After all, this sort of thing is the least I must do for the movement, and I know that you really want me to. . . .

David to Sophie: from Ottawa to Montreal
June 28, 1937

My darling wife:

... I could not help thinking quite a lot about what you told me. It's caused me unhappiness. Please, please don't let it continue. I say it's up to you. People like yourself and myself who have had, have, and have reason to hope that we shall continue to have so much out of life must be sympathetic with and tolerant to those who have failed. And that's the secret in the change in Dad. He has failed. And because he once had ambitions and believed he had the ability to realize them, the failure has for him been all the harder.

Mother is undoubtedly one of the best women in the world and it is understandable that just because of her goodness and simple strength she was not able to help him find himself when he began to slip. I love father, and my heart bleeds for him. It's not that I excuse his present behaviour, but it is my duty also to understand it. And I refuse to set myself up as judge. Even at some cost to ourselves we must not, not you, not I, not anyone of us, add to the moral and psychological tragedy which is there. Please, please, my darling, my own sweetest wife, try to understand, and act as I have always seen you act. Good, understanding, generous. You and I have no right to be selfish. Life has been too good to us. We have had much happiness. I love you so very dearly. People are so vicious. Most of them deliberately; some of them unwittingly. We can't be vicious deliberately. We must not be so unwittingly. . . .

David gives no indication in his letter, and neither does Sophie in hers, what happened to cause David to make these remarks about Maishe. The intriguing question is, how much did his belief in his father's failure fire David's own determination, and for that, there is no ready answer.

Sophie to David: from Val Morin (where Sophie was spending the summer of her pregnancy at a cottage) to Winnipeg
July 23, 1937

My Own,

What to write? My heart is so full of love for you, words alone are inadequate. Our few days together were so happy, it was very much like living a lifetime together, so much joy did we crowd in. I wonder whether some people pack in so much happiness in an entire lifetime as we did in four and a half days. I love you. I am buoyed up and filled with a new zest for living after our little interlude.

David to Sophie: on the train to Winnipeg
July 23, 1937

My Own Darling:

. . . Try not to be too lonesome, my darling wife. I must be honest with you and tell you that although my heart aches that you are not with me, I am, nevertheless, quite excited about the trip. I am looking forward to meeting a number of new people. This is only natural, and I know that in spite of her lonesomeness, my sweet wife is glad that I have this experience which, otherwise, would have to be postponed for quite some time. . . .

David to Sophie: from Winnipeg
July 27, 1937

My Own Sweet Wife,

This is the first breather I have really had so far. The convention reassembles in 15 minutes, and I want to talk to you. I love you my darling.

I received your letter yesterday, and it warmed me so I was revived. Discussions so far, particularly at National Council meetings, have depressed me to some extent. King Gordon and I have been bucking most of the rest of the Council on several important matters. The details I shall tell you about when I get back. The general approach was discouraging as indicating an essential failure on the part of most of our leading people to understand the present situation, a sort of narrow surface comprehension. It was very difficult to break through this, to inspire a conception of the sweep of the political situation and the imaginative action required. Before the National Council meeting ended . . . we did succeed to some extent.

King is a great fellow. We work together very well. He is a fine head, really first rate, and a fine personality. . . .

I presented my National Council report this afternoon. It was very well received. I was quite a little hero. I really think it was well done.

The fifteen minutes are up. Good-bye my darling. I love you very much.

Sophie to David: from Val Morin
August 10, 1937

My Own,

. . . In that last moment of parting I felt the inadequateness of words. I don't seem to be able to capture those words which I want to tell you. I just feel, I regret, I feel anguish. I am tormented by all the nasty things I have said (and which I shall probably repeat in the future). I am torn with sorrow at the thought of the words I might have said to tell you how much I love you, all feeling — feeling, rush of feeling — and words won't come.

To me nothing new has happened. We all retired early on Sunday. Yesterday was fiercely close. I fell asleep at 3 in the afternoon and slept until 5:30. Rose came to see us in the evening, we talked a while and I was in bed by 11 P.M. It sounds dull, doesn't it? And it was dull. . . .

P.S. Your poopsie has been carrying on and kicking like mad. Doris felt and Mama felt and they both giggled. "It's alive," the thought struck me suddenly today. I felt eager to see it — I hope it won't be disappointed in us, when it sees us!

Sophie to David: from Val Morin
August 17, 1937

My darling,

I write this letter before having received one from you. . . . Having you with me on Sunday evening and night was such a treat, to me it really was a distinct celebration.

I nag and I torment you and I find that I must be getting joy out of it, for life is so colourful and good with you near me. I love you so dearly, so much — I have twinges of conscience in retrospective thought — why do I tease you so? When I love you as I do? But this weekend past I really feel as though I behaved as well as I could!

I fell asleep about ten minutes and awoke, my body bathed in perspiration. A lightning had lit up the whole room and a lovely storm was on. I was trembling. I awoke Doris to come and sleep with me. I was awake until 5 A.M., terrified and shivering. I was never so bad, dear, really never. The pain in my side grew and swelled into a hard painful lump. I took my pills — it didn't seem to help. I awoke this morning weak and tired. Because of these storms alone, I feel it is time to go home — for a storm in the city is never so frightening as . . . one in the mountains, where every sound reverberates tenfold. . . .

David to Sophie: from Ottawa
August 17, 1937

My darling,

. . . I have heard from Toronto and am definitely going there this weekend. They are arranging a number of informal group meetings. I shall also lecture at the CCYM Summer School and, in addition, will probably address a public meeting on Sunday night. The weekend will, therefore, be pretty full.

So I shan't see you for two weeks. It makes me sad. But duty is duty. And I know that you're sweet and won't mind even though you will miss me, or will you, you crookler? You don't know how I am looking forward to your coming back home. I love you so.

David to Sophie: from Ottawa
August 18, 1937

My Own Wife,

. . . Last night I wasted the evening attending a meeting under the auspices of . . . the Friends of the MacKenzie-Papineau Battalion in Spain. . . . The speaker was a Bert Levy from Windsor. . . . His speech was not very good and consisted entirely of tales of horrors and atrocities — the sort of thing that makes an audience slightly uncomfortable. The meeting was very poorly attended, there were only about sixty people. This was probably due to the heat. . . .

I am just a little sad. The thought of not seeing you this weekend is — well, I love you so very much, my own. But both you and I must be ready to make this kind of small sacrifice for the movement. . . .

All week I have been thinking about father. As I worked through the sweltering heat my heart broke at the thought of what he must be suffering. When I was studying Ethics at Oxford, one of the problems of moral behaviour which attracted me most was the problem presented by conflicting duties. I did not quite realize how soon I would be faced with that problem in my own life. One thing is probably clear. I can't sacrifice father and mother for the movement, whatever I might do to us. If only I can find a way of helping them without sacrificing my work for the movement too much. We must find such a way. You must help me. When I look into your eyes, I know you will in spite of the things you sometimes say. . . .

David to Sophie: from Ottawa
August 23, 1937

My Own Sweet Wife:

I arrived back from Toronto this morning. . . . The weekend was full. I met with the Provincial Executive all Saturday morning and all afternoon. At about seven in the evening we set out to a place called Georgetown where the CCYM has its summer school. I lectured Saturday night, Sunday morning and Sunday afternoon. In the evening back to Toronto and another meeting with the executive and a number of other leading people. . . . The CCYM held its summer school in a camp out in the open in very lovely country. The weather happened to be glorious so that it was really a day spent in the country. . . .

. . . The meetings with the executive were much less exhilarating. They're a dead bunch, the smallest fry conceivable. Ted [Jolliffe] is the only one with any political sense or thought. As I wrote you, I went down to wake them up about the election, and they needed waking. Did I succeed? For the moment, yes. But it won't last. I am writing Angus today suggesting that he and Grace come to Toronto a soon as they can. . . .

Sophie to David: from Montreal
September 1,1937

My Own,

. . . This afternoon I had planned to see Eva, but — I had a peculiar attack of neuralgic pains in my arms, shoulders, back and chest. My arms particularly. I felt I was going mad with pain. . . . The pain [has now] left but I feel like a wet rag, so limp and tired out. . . .

How much I am looking forward to being home again with you, I cannot begin to express. I am looking forward to it as to a new life, a new beginning of better health. I am so tired of being ill. . . .

David to Sophie: from Truro, N.S.
October 2, 1938

My Darling:

. . . The CCF meetings in Moncton (they were all executive meetings with the Maritimes Council) were useful but rather depressing. The people are terribly confused, naive and most of them ineffective. There never will be a movement in New Brunswick if stronger people are not found. A few of them are quite hopeful, but they need at least a month of intensive training. The hope lies with Nova Scotia. If we can create a movement there, they may be able to do something in this province.

. . . I love you, my own. I hold you close and kiss you. Play with our little son for me. . . .

David to Sophie: from Glace Bay, N.S.
October 5, 1938

My darling wife:

. . . The organizing work is interesting and the experience is new and fascinating. This is all a completely working class district. Rough and ready miners. They drink like hell and they swear like troopers. They work hard and they live harder. Of nonsense there is none, of common sense there is much, but of intelligence very little.

Perhaps half of them are Roman Catholics, a large number of them are Scotch. The district does not look particularly squalid, but nor does it look cheerful. There is an absolute lack of any kind of cultural life — quite unlike the European workers. What little culture there is has emanated from the educational movement connected with the Extension Department of the St. Francis Xavier College and with the cooperatives and credit unions. This is fairly good, but is too closely connected with the church and too much under the influence of the priests.

From all this you will gather that it will not be too difficult to start a CCF movement here — the workers are pretty class conscious. But it will be tough as hell to keep it going, and still tougher to keep it from running amuck. It will all depend upon whether . . . we can find a dozen men who can be relied on to remain always sober and can be trained into an intelligent consciousness of what we're after. . . .

Normally I would be very happy at the prospect of travelling all through the Maritimes and really getting to know the people here. But I am so very miserable at being away from you and Sholem'l [Stephen] that I am looking at it merely as a job which must be done and must be done as well as possible. . . .

David to Sophie: from Toronto
March 28, 1939

My Darling Wife:
. . . Father had another fairly serious heart attack last Tuesday and was ordered to stay home and mostly in bed for three weeks . . . He and mother were almost in despair, even though they tried bravely not to show it. For it means that dad cannot undertake any work. They can't, nor can I, think of anything within his reach which would involve less physical exertion. What are they to do?

There was only one answer. Charlie and we must provide them with a minimum. If dad knows that mother has the few dollars she needs for her weekly expenses he will try to adjust himself. Perhaps he may be able to pick up an occasional dollar. Perhaps he may be able to strike something which his health may be able to stand. But in the meantime we must not let them be destitute. There just is no other alternative.

So I acted on it. I wished with all my heart that you could be there and I could talk the matter over with you. But I could not delay it because they need the money immediately but also because my heart broke. I could not have stood any delay.

I gave mother twenty instead of ten dollars and we shall give her twenty dollars every month. Darling, my own, I know that you may say to yourself that I should not have done this without you, that I owe it to you to discuss matters of this sort before acting. And you are right, my darling. I knew that and I know that. But it was important for them and for me that I act without delay. . . .

Charlie gave mother three dollars and promised faithfully to give her three dollars every week. This means that mother will get regularly $7.50 a week, which is as much as father could have made and enough for them to make ends meet.

. . . It's humiliating and heartbreaking for father but that's the situation. I cannot write much more. I have been crying inside me ever since Saturday night. Such an unhappy life for them. Dad is only just past fifty and to be a complete invalid. . . .

Sophie to David: from Ottawa
March 29, 1939

My Own,
. . . I had suspected that something might be wrong since Papa sent me a letter which arrived yesterday and he wrote that he didn't participate in the Sunday meeting as he hadn't felt well. But another attack — it took me terribly unawares and I cried until I couldn't any more. I feel terribly guilty. If we had sent mother more money, father wouldn't have felt that he had to do something in a hurry or else. . . .

Of course, darling, you did the right thing about the money. I blessed you inside me for being the man you are and wished a little for mother's sake that you were less the idealist and more concerned about making money. Only for mother, dear, honestly, not for me. I really am content, dear. . . . Bless you anyway, darling, your heart's in the right place and any man who loves his parents as much as you do — well, his love for his wife must be great indeed. . . .

David to Sophie: from Hamilton
March 30, 1939

My Own Darling:

I have about half an hour here waiting for my bus to take me to St. Catharines. . . . The lecture to the LSR Tuesday night went off very well. I did a good job and it was really appreciated . . . Yesterday I spent in Galt. . . .

I found exactly what I suspected: the people have never received the slightest suggestion or advice as to what they might do, what activities they might undertake. All of them hard at work at their jobs and they are at their wits' ends to figure out how to keep the organization doing things. Central direction, authority and advice could make the organization there three times as strong and alive in one month. Good, willing, devoted socialists without leadership.

Sophie to David: from Montreal
April 5, 1939

My Own,

Your letter written in London came today. You sound more tired than ever. I hope you return home alive and not in a hearse. . . .

David to Sophie: from Windsor
April 6, 1939

My Own:

A few minutes between appointments. . . . I am rather tired mentally. Nothing is more tiring than talking about big things to little people. (Don't you ever quote me.) But I am sure my trip will do a lot of good.

I have a Provincial Council meeting tomorrow night, the convention Friday and Saturday, and then a meeting of the newly-elected Provincial Council on Sunday . . . I've never in my life shifted people and things around so much. It's been a difficult but interesting experience. . . .

Sophie to David: from Ottawa
August 17, 1939

My Own,

. . . This morning's papers have me sick at heart. War seems on the doormat — and it looks like the elections will never take place this year. . . . Didn't you too find the news particularly disquieting? Thank God for Sholemke, he keeps me busy and happy. . . .

David to Sophie: from Toronto
August 18, 1939

My darling Own:

. . . I have been terribly busy. Office work, constituency work, finding a room and a car, learning to drive and, generally, getting settled . . . I was sitting down to write you early yesterday evening, before a meeting, when the organizer phoned to see me about a matter which had to be discussed before the meeting. The meeting, a constituency council one, lasted till close to midnight. I had to go to the other end of the city so I didn't get home until after one o'clock. At the moment I am also writing in a hurry. I have to leave in a very few minutes for another committee meeting in a section of the riding. It's going to be pretty awful.

. . . I must run. I am late already. Kiss and hug Sholeml for me. My mind is tired — too tired to find the words for the lonesomeness which fills me. I love you both so.

David to Sophie: from Toronto
August 27, 1939

My Own:

Sunday off. Believe it or not. Slept in. . . . [Went] to the CCYM summer camp where Emma Goldman was speaking. . . . Emma spoke on anarchism, interesting nonsense. . . .

Sophie to David: from Ottawa
November 30, 1939

My Own,

. . . Today is a red letter day. Mollie and Doris took Sholeml to Moe the barber, and he had his first haircut. It's very becoming and he looks like a real little man. . . . He sat in the chair, so they reported, as stiff and proper as could be; turned his head to left and right as instructed and not a peep out of him. He seemed terribly anxious to return home quickly and show off what had happened. I think you'll be pleased with the result.

. . . I find that he talks and understands more than I had dreamt he would. He counts up to ten, I taught him that today. He knows the different colours by name — blue, orange, yellow and red. That too I taught him. He's as fast as lightning . . . and here he is at two [three weeks past his second birthday] taking colours in his stride. I'm a little overwhelmed at his tempo. . . .

Sophie to David: from Ottawa
February 8, 1940

So, my dear,

It's Thursday and no word from you. I have changed from disappointment to anger and back to disappointment again. I will grant you that you're busier than I can possibly imagine — but there's always half an hour somewhere to write . . . I feel like a fool — asking for what you should have brains enough to do without any coaxing. And so I only say, I warn you — as from this letter — that if you won't find the time to write regularly, you will not hear from me at all. I will be more stubborn than you've ever known me. The only reason I'm writing now is that I'm going to give you the benefit of the doubt to think that perhaps you're not well.

. . . Good night. Your son is well. I'll write you news about him when I feel you deserve to hear it.

Sophie to David: from Montreal
February 13, 1939

My dear,

I am sorry that I wasn't home last night when you called. I had gone to a movie with Sam and Rose and had dropped in to Murray's for a bite. I felt awful when Momma told me I had just missed your call.

I had resolved not to write until you came on Thursday — just a mild form of punishment. But since you're not coming, I have relented.

You sound so rushed, you probably are not sleeping nights, otherwise there is no way I can work it out as to when you have time to push all that work in. I still don't know in any way how your campaign is progressing. Perhaps you can manage to stay awake a little longer one night and write me a little more detailed report of how things stand . . .

David to Sophie: from Toronto
February 13, 1939

My Own Darling:

. . . All morning I have looked for an opportunity to write you and haven't found one. I can only write a rush note now as I must run out to my constituency immediately and do some canvassing with a committee. I am already a little late.

. . . I am looking for a place for both of us since you will be here in about two weeks. Please darling, write me. Be understanding. I literally haven't had ten minutes to myself. I haven't rested an hour since I arrived. And work is all I do. . . . I love you, my own, more than my pen can say. But wait till you get here. You'll see.

Sophie to David: from Montreal
February 14, 1939

My darling,

I got your letter this morning and I'm getting awfully worried about you. . . . I'm looking forward to being with you and helping as much as I can. . . .

. . . I have finished reading *The Grapes of Wrath*, at long last, and I'm sick at heart and at the same time, just furious to the bursting point. . . .

. . . You write you're lonesome. We have really not seen each other for weeks, for you were too busy those last few weeks before we left Ottawa for us to have any time together. I am so lonesome I find it hard to fall asleep nights. I sometimes stay awake until 3 and 4 AM.

I simply can't sleep. And Sholeml is in the room and I can't turn the light on. So that I just lay there in the dark and remember and think and plan and hope and hope fervently and am happy and sad in turn as I lie and the thoughts race through my mind. And always I love you. And even when I'm annoyed at your not writing, my heart aches and I love you fiercely. . . .

> *David to Sophie: en route to Vancouver*
> June 15, 1941

My Wife:

We're in the foothills of the Rockies approaching Jasper Park. . . . A long trip. Time to think. . . . The first thoughts are always heavy. The problems so many; the solution difficult. Plans, policies fill one's mind. Always they come to grief on two rocks: lack of people and lack of finance; the first more serious than the second. Like all democratic socialist movements we are cursed with fine, honest, saintly ineffectuals. Christians without Christ's courage; Ghandists without Ghandi's cuteness; socialists without a sense of struggle. Hopeful, wishful, prayerful band of hope for the Kingdom to come. People trying to tame tigers with a prayer; closing their eyes and trusting in God or something. Oh, to administer hefty kicks in the pants before someone else does the kicking.

. . . I know how you must resent my long absence at this time. Don't be angry with the movement. Work must go on, whatever one is doing. . . ,

> *David to Sophie: en route to Victoria*
> June 30, 1941

My Own Darling:

I am on a boat on the way to Victoria. . . . Yesterday I worked as hard as every other day. In fact it was so typical, an outline of it will give you some idea of my normal program. At ten in the morning a committee came to see me regarding straightening out a mess in one of the Vancouver constituencies. At 12:30 lunch with Angus and Grace and a committee regarding the coming B.C. provincial election. At 2:30 a meeting with a committee of the CCYM regarding youth organization. At 5:30 a dinner engagement with a young couple who seem interested and who might be of help in organizing financial assistance. At 9:30 a large group at Mrs. Jamieson's, the place where I am staying. This was a little more in the nature of a social — people who wanted to meet me. To bed at about 1:30. Up at half past eight and down to the boat.

Add to this kind of daily program — membership meetings where all the authority of my position and whatever personality I may have must be exerted carefully, tactfully, with perfect timing in order to beat down disruption; public meetings the speeches at which must be really striking, so as to give the tone to our movement and at the same time obtain the right kind of publicity; hours with trade union leaders, middle class people, writing of memoranda; the constant mental and nervous strain — and you will get some picture of the range and tempo of my work here. Perhaps you will also forgive me a little for not writing more. . . .

. . . More than once suggestions I have made were adopted unanimously even when there were people who did not wholly agree with them. But they could not find an answer to the relentless arguments I outlined and were sort of cowed mentally. That's my main fear. The position I have taken which is, of course, the position of the movement is so sound that disrupters can't stand up against it. But they are still not convinced. Or worse, they are so convinced that they become much more unreasonable in their opposition. For nothing enrages some people more than to have been proven wrong; nothing makes them so furious as to have to bow to superior logic and knowledge. So that I am sure that after I shall have left and they will have realized the extent of their defeat, they will seek to strike back, fairly or unfairly.

However, I am sure that the good I have done will really last and have a lasting improvement, especially if followed up.

. . . Your letter written Friday sounded so sad and tired. . . . Oh, my wife, my darling, forgive me for all those mean moments. All this constant nervous strain of my work must be responsible for it. For my heart is full of love for you. . . .

David to Sophie: from Edmonton
July 13, 1941

My Own Sweet Wife:

I wrote you just two words on Thursday and haven't written since, in spite of my promise. It was impossible. Bill Irvine put me in his car on Thursday and we didn't get back to Edmonton till 3 o'clock this morning. For three days we wandered around the country, stopping in the evening to address a public meeting, sleeping at a farmhouse . . . and on again fairly early in the morning. . . .

I am sorry, my own. I know how empty the weekend will have been without word from me. But that's the battle. . . . I had three picnics in Saskatchewan between Monday and Wednesday. The first was a complete failure because it rained all day. The second was a partial success. There were about a thousand people. . . . The third was a great success. About 2,000 people and I spoke for almost 1-1/2 hours to shouts of approval and thunders of applause. There was quite a shower in the middle of my speech but when I suggested stopping until the shower ceased, they wouldn't let me. So we all got wet but I carried on, soaked but emphatic. It was quite a thrilling experience. . . .

Sophie to David: from Ottawa
July 14, 1941

My Own Darling,

I had your letter written yesterday in Edmonton. It left me more lonesome than ever. These last days have become unbearable — my nerves seem to be screeching on edge, and so I get into the car with Sholeml and get out of the house. . . .

Is it only ten days before you return? I can hardly believe it. I look forward to the cottage and the beach as to something I haven't anticipated now for years. I hope with all my heart that we'll enjoy it and benefit from it.

Good night my own. I long for you more than I can write. I plunge myself into work, into doing silly nothings at times, just because the longing is more than I can stand. . . .

Sophie to David: from Ottawa
October 10, 1941

My Own,

My first letter to you after a few days now. Your swamping me with two cards and a letter positively overwhelmed me. . . .

I'm still at Shirer's *Diary*. It seems to me the man matured very rapidly when war began and with it more serious contacts and experiences. I find his writing more solid and substantial. . . .

Sholeml is as disobedient as ever. I'm at my wits' end to know what to do about it. He answers back and yesterday told me to "Shut up and go to hell." I almost fainted. . . .

David to Sophie: from Creston, B.C.
October 13, 1941

My Own Darling:

. . . I have about half an hour free before supper and tonight's meeting and I have excused myself and retired to drop you a note.

The last few days have, in a sense, been the most tiring I have spent because of the unearthly hours at which I've had to catch my trains. Thus I arrived in Medicine Hat at 3 o'clock Thursday morning where I had to change trains. Friday morning I was up at about the same time. Saturday morning I arose at 2:30 to catch a train and got off it at 5 in the morning. This morning I caught the train at 4 and was off it at 6:30. If you add 2 or 3 meetings every evening, chasing about canvassing all during the day and to bed never before 1 o'clock, you will get the general idea. Pretty hectic.

. . . The CCF chances in the [B.C.] elections seem to be very fair. . . . Our movement has attracted the finest among the lowly folk. That's a stable foundation. Self-educated, intelligent, unassuming and sincere, they work hard without any thought or possibility of any personal gain. I do love these people. They are really so much finer, healthier beings than so many of our acquaintances who have become distorted sophisticates. . . .

Sophie to David: from Ottawa
October 19, 1941

My Own,

. . . I spoke to Mrs. Coldwell and said I'd be up this week to see her. She called us "political widows" which I thought was rather good. . . .

This is a poor excuse for a letter — but I have so little to tell. I wish you were home — the weekends are hardest of all. I am far too emotional by temperament to be left so much alone.

I love you — oh so much. And yet I quarrel with you.

David to Sophie: from Vancouver
October 21, 1941

My Own Darling:

Today is election day. . . .

I feel sort of pumped dry. Speech, speech, speech. Applause, ballyhoo, noise. The last couple of days I dreaded getting on the platform. The sound of my voice grated on my ears. The story sounded stale; the reaction of the audience mechanical. You know what I mean. I was glad when at about eleven last night I spoke my last word. . . . As if a huge weight had been lifted off me.

. . . Damn it's lonesome. And I can't help feeling a little anxious about your health. I love you, my own, so very much. And I am squeezed dry of words.

Sophie to David: from Ottawa
October 22, 1941

My Dearest One,

. . . The news today about the CCF landslide is terrific. You can't imagine what's been going on here. The phone hasn't stopped ringing all evening — everybody surprised and congratulating. . . . I'm so happy today, at last I'm glad you went out there. Everyone seems quite positive that your going turned the tide! What confidence they have in you! . . .

David to Sophie: en route to Winnipeg
October 24, 1941

My Own Darling:

. . . Well, I'm on my way back. And we were successsful. I know how thrilled you must have been when you read the news Wednesday morning. We all hoped to do fairly well. But we did not dare hope to do quite as well. [Liberals 21 seats, CCF 14, Conservatives 12, others 1] The movement throughout the country will get new encouragement.

I was awfully glad to be there. Not because I was so useful — although every additional help is of value — but because it was useful to me. It will help me in my work to have participated, as the national representative, in a successful election. I hope when you saw the results your lonesomeness was a little repaid.

. . . None of the parties has a majority. There is talk of a coalition between the Liberals and Conservatives. There is also talk of a union government of all three parties. We support the first. We reject the second. . . . Our only fear is the possibility of another election.

It's obvious that the old parties are afraid to leave the CCF in the strategically powerful position of Parliamentary opposition if they form a coalition. For in that case the CCF would be beautifully situated to win power at the next election. So they would like to drag us, too, into the government. But we won't go. In which case they might easily call another election and gang up on us i.e. have saw-offs in the ridings which we won. In that case it would be very hard to win them again. We can win them in a three-cornered fight but whether we can hold them in a straight contest is a different question. I don't think the situation will crystallize itself for a few weeks.

. . . Last night and today I am almost unbearably lonesome. Until I got on the train I was so busy I did not miss you in this way. And then I got into my berth last night and relaxed. And shut my eyes and saw you lying beside me, snuggling up to me. The pain was so deep and burning, I went off bed, smoked cigarettes and chatted with the porter.

I love you.

Sophie to David: from Ottawa
October 27, 1941

My Dearest,

I have about reached the stage where I detest the very physical movements necessary to sit down to write. How to relate of the many times when my heart stands still with pain and a voice that I hardly reconize rushes out of me and says, "Oh David!" . . .

. . . This trip of yours has done something drastic to me — something has died and I've been feeling terribly old. And to feel old and weepy at 32 is desperately wrong. Dull, dull, just dull. . . .

David to Sophie: from Winnipeg
October 28, 1941

My Sweet Darling:

Your yesterday's letter reached me today. . . .

My own, I have been most unhappy on this trip. I have avoided mentioning it in my letters but your unhappiness, so evident in all your letters, has been a most heartbreaking experience. I am sorry, my own. I must do everything possible to avoid being away from you for the next number of months. I have almost determined that if I have to go to New York, you come with me or I don't go. I shall not cause you so much pain again. . . .

David to Sophie: from New York
December 9, 1941

My Own Darling:

. . . Arrived here safe and sound Sunday morning and was met by King [Gordon] at the station. Spent the day chatting to King, talking my program over with the secretary of the Union for Democratic Action and listening anxiously to the radio news about the Jap attacks in the Pacific and discussing, conjecturing on the role of Germany in the new situation.

The United States is in the war. The third important phase has started; the war now covers the world. From our point of view it's a good thing. All the diplomatic shadow boxing is now ended. The forces are now definitely on one side or the other. . . .

David to Sophie: from New York
December 14, 1941

My Own:

I feel more guilty than I can say for having written you only one letter this week. . . .

It's been an awfully crowded time. . . . Meetings Monday, Tuesday, Wednesday, Thursday and Friday evenings and Saturday lunch. I have met most leaders of the unions. I have met newspaper people, particularly a man from *Time*, the editors of the *Nation* and *New Republic*. I spent time with the heads of the Workmen's Circle, the *Forward*, the American Labor Party, Jacob Pat and the Bundists. If you remember the size of this city, the time which I have had to spend in subways going from one appointment to the next, you will see how crowded the week has been. . . . I am exhausted as a rag.

I have had no relaxation except Wednesday afternoon and yesterday evening. On Wednesday afternoon I squeezed in a matinée to see *Watch on the Rhine*. Just between appointments. I was determined to see this play, at least. Last night I refused two speaking engagements. I just couldn't do any more. The Gordons and I went to dinner. . . .

I have regards for you from hosts of people. Emanuel (you remember Warsaw) who looks gray and worn . . . Mendelsohn who is as lively as ever and remembers meeting us. And — a great surprise! I walked into the Bund office yesterday and, to my amazement, there stands Gurfinkel! He has been here for about six months. Came here from a French concentration camp where he spent almost a year. He fell on me. We almost kissed each other. It was good seeing him. . . . He asked after you many times with obvious fondness. . . .

Many more people I'll have to tell you about when I return. . . .

During 1942 David wrote to Sophie from Welland, Niagara Falls, Campbellton (N.B.), Montreal, Halifax, Toronto, Windsor, and Winnipeg, where he helped secure the election of Stanley Knowles. As year followed year the pattern never changed — except for one thing. As David crisscrossed the country, organizing, campaigning, and speaking, letters from Sophie dwindled. Those that she did write were filled with sunny stories about the children. And occasionally, as in the following letter to David in Winnipeg, she would write of her endless loneliness:

Sophie to David: from Ottawa
December 28, 1943

Here I am again, Dear!

. . . Today, Doris (and Stephen and I) went off to Mrs. Coldwell's. . . . Stephen was very good there. He wanted to "do" his speeches, then he said when he got up to speak, "I don't know why I feel so shy suddenly. My heart seems to be jumping around inside of me. Perhaps I

could just sit down in this chair and we could have a 'dish-cushion.'
Just ask me questions and I'll answer them."

Mrs. Coldwell and Margaret were amazed at his eloquence and M.
hid her face in a magazine several times to stifle her laughter. She ended
up by saying, "That boy knows more about politics and world events
than I do." I can believe that for she seems very poorly informed. Well,
your son was a huge success. . . .

. . . Everyone wants to know what I'm planning to do on New Year's
Eve. I'm sure I don't know. Do you? You'll probably have a bit of fun
tucked away somewhere. I envy you, seeing so many people and being
away from routine. Or is what you are doing routine?

I sat down at the table in the kitchen on Sunday after you left and
had a good cry. I had wanted it all day. I hate this sort of life.

It's not that David was insensitive or uncaring. It's that he felt he
had no choice. The movement demanded and he gave. But he gave
not only of himself. He gave of his family and he knew it.

David to Sophie: from Montreal
October 23, 1947

My Darling:

. . . I don't know about dad. One of the lumps on his neck has become
hard and looks very angry. I don't like the idea of its playing up
again . . . I was strongly tempted to stay behind and go with him to
the doctor, but he objected vehemently and, since I couldn't really do
much, I didn't want to act in a way . . . suspicious to him. . . .

My family seems to be going to pieces. Avreml Krashinsky is in bed;
he had a heart attack in the middle of the night a few days ago. . . .
One feels dreadful about it. I guess their hard life in past years is taking
its toll.

I cannot help a deep feeling of sadness. How silly and almost criminal
it is, in the face of so much unavoidable illness and suffering, to be
responsible for causing oneself and one's loved ones unnecessary and
wilful unhappiness.

There were times, however, when his commitment stood naked to
the eye, and it was uncompromising.

David to Sophie: from Toronto
April 27, 1948

My Own Darling:

I have never been so sorry to leave home, even for so short a time,
as I was this morning. The children, particularly the little fellow
[Michael], rely on me; and not to see you for two days during your
hospital ordeal, is hard. I hope to see you tomorrow evening. . . .

. . . I love you, my darling. There are certain things that, if you like
— unfortunately —, I am not prepared and can't change. But if you are

ready to accept that, if not with pleasure, then as one must accept the colour of one's hair — we shall continue to live a happy and full life — even if often a hard one for you. At least you have the love of your husband and the respect of your friends. Perhaps they are most important.

But their love survived — or perhaps it is more appropriate to say Sophie's love survived because it was on her that the stress of David's commitment lay the heaviest.

> *Sophie to David: from Ottawa*
> August 16, 1948

My Dearest,

. . . My days are such monotonous repetitions of one after another, there is very little to tell. You know my routine pretty well by now, and the evenings, of course, are dull and lonely. I've phoned more people but I guess it's turned too warm for visiting, and in any case, I don't care much about seeing them.

. . . I, too, am so thrilled about the coming of this third child of ours [actually the twins, Janet and Nina], that if any complication should set in I'd be disappointed. My one concern these days is that I should be strong enough when my time is due to take an operation — and that there are no further worries at the time.

I try not to think about it but sometimes when it's quiet and I'm alone with myself I get a terrifying fear and I try hard not to cry or to harass myself. It's hard to prevent these thoughts from occurring and project- ing themselves in view of what happened in May and June [the pulmonary embolism that Sophie suffered] — and by now you know that I'm not a coward, not physically anyway — so that I really need you here to bolster my courage.

I think of you with such warm and tender feeling. Have you been aware, really, of how I've clung to you these months? In an almost un- natural and childish way? You must know too, because I've known how almost bankrupt I was inside and realizing my vulnerability and riddled morale, I've tried to put forward a front which didn't at all mirror my real self. I was really frightened about life and death for the first time in my life and I keep hoping that when I have to go for my operation for this child that I won't disgrace myself and break down.

I love you more than I ever have in our whole life together. For despite my silly bickering about small things, I am proud of the way you have been and acted these last months and I know that very few men could have been as patient and as good. Money, well, that you haven't to give — but without sounding silly and trite, your affection to me, to the children, your care of the whole household arrangement, has made me prouder than ever that I married a man. . . .

All of the children were delivered by caesarean section and all of Sophie's pregnancies were difficult. She had to lie still for weeks with each, and in the case of Michael she was bedridden in a nursing home for two months. The cost, in the days before Medicare, was nearly crippling. "I wanted those children and I fought to have them," Sophie would say later. But, in her final pregnancy, "when I discovered I was going to have twins, I wept bitter tears. Where was the money to come from? Where?"[9]

David to Sophie: from Winnipeg
August 19, 1948

My Own Darling:

This is the first time since Saturday that I have felt relaxed enough to write. I know that this is small consolation to you, and my sweet one, you can't imagine how bad I have felt about leaving you without a letter the whole week. But I have been under a terrific strain . . . [and] for the first time in my life I have not slept well.

. . . Your letter, darling, brought tears to my eyes, and since I read it while at a Council meeting, it was almost embarrassing. How sweet, how warm, how warming. I do love you so, darling.

A week has gone since I left. In less than another week I shall be back home. What will we have accomplished this time? I don't know. I have been so tired that I feel a little depressed. In the world context our show seems so small. And the Alberta results following on the Quebec ones make one wonder. It's hard to know. In spite of the stimulation of the convention I wish I were home with you and the children.

David began practising law in Toronto in 1950, and, although he did have out-of-town cases, he never was long or often away from home. However, in 1957 he acted as counsel for the Brotherhood of (Railway) Firemen before the Royal Commmission inquiring into the need for firemen on diesel engines of freight trains. The hearings lasted months as the commission travelled across Canada and also spent time in Europe studying European railways.

David to Sophie: from Calgary
July 4, 1957

My very own Darling:

The days grind on, but too slowly, far too slowly. . . .

The case gets tougher every day and more demanding and frustrating. What a silly, irrational world and how little understanding of real issues! Narrow profit seeking by the Railway and equally blind and selfish obstinacy by the Brotherhood. How difficult to make truth the master or even apparent to either side. Each sees only a part of the picture and denies the existence of the other part in spite of all the evidence.

So often during the case have I wished that I were only a lawyer, without social principles and conscience. But I am what I am, and the result is a feeling of futility and unhappiness because I see (or, at least, think I see) both parts of the picture, but my duty requires that I address myself only to one. So I keep on, consoled in part by vanity that the job appears to be appreciated and respected and in part that our financial position will be so much easier as a result. Since you know me so well, I don't have to tell you how little such consolation means to me.

. . . I love you so my darling. It's so deep, the roots are so overwhelmingly strong, that the occasional withered leaf is quickly replaced by a luxuriant branch. In the cycle of life, the wintry day is unavoidable but love makes it short and inconsequential. In simple language, I am dying to be home. . . .

David to Sophie: from Vancouver
July 13, 1957

My darling Own:

I start this note with a bit of good news. We have speeded up our trip, so that . . . I shall arrive in Toronto next Thursday. . . .

I feel as if I have been away from you for a year, and indeed, I have been away for five months. The snatched and hurried days at home since March can't be counted. Now we will, at last, have six weeks together. . . .

David to Sophie: from Paris, France
September 10, 1957

My Own Darling:

. . . I have an eerie feeling, as if I am only half here. . . . The explanation . . . is not far to seek. Paris is, in my mind, a part of our joint life. I walk the streets and I recall our eager sightseeing, our togetherness in parks and museums and art galleries, the pictures we took, the hotels and pensions we lived in. . . . I see the beautiful sparkle in your eyes, your aliveness and thirst for the beautiful.

I remember our walks through the Tuilleries, the Luxembourg, our visit to Versailles, our insatiable curiosity, our visits to the Louvre and Notre Dame and the other sights, the way me made friends and the eagerness with which we learned about the Socialist Party and the trade unions. And somehow — please don't laugh for it is terribly real and deep to me — I rebel against seeing these things alone, without you. I feel as if I am about to commit an act of injustice, even of sacrilege. This is ours, not mine alone.

David to Sophie: from Paris
September 12, 1957

My darling:

May I start this note by being a cat? I had dinner tonight . . . with Mr. and Mrs. Gilbert. And what do I find? Mrs. Gilbert has not found anything to do during the days. . . . The spirit of Paris, of the old world, is just so much garbage to her. She looks at it not only without appreciation but with actual, arrogant disgust. And the finance committee of the Brotherhood voted the president up to $5,000 as a special expenditure for this trip. . . .

Talk about throwing pearls — I wish this were all of my disappointment, but it isn't. I find that Mr. Justice Kellock and Mr. Justice
McLaurin show little, if any, interest in the things that mean Paris for
the culturally sensitive. [Roy Kellock, a justice of the Supreme Court
of Canada and Colin C. McLaurin, chief justice of the trial division
of the Supreme Court of Alberta were commissioners on the Royal
Commission.] I expressed regret yesterday that our program is so heavy
that they will find no time to see Paris except during the weekend. Oh,
says Kellock, his wife is visiting the art galleries and that will suffice
him. And McLaurin says the same and adds that it would only tire
him. . . . I could not help smiling and, with apparent jocularity, telling
them that they are a couple of Philistines. What price education and
professional eminence!

This will continue to be a lonely trip for me. . . . I am going to bed
with the Koestler book, which I have almost finished . . .

I wish I were an artist and could draw a symbolic and unforgettable
figure, say of something like a willow tree reaching sadly and droopingly
for the unreachable sky. I wish, I wish I were home. . . .[10]

Sophie to David: from Ottawa
September 20, 1957

My Darling,

. . . Well, another two weeks and you'll be home, and I do hope not
too tired. I can't bear this emotional separation and I don't seem to
be able to write down any more the same beautiful words that you do.
The change in me bothers me. I start writing and my heart is overflow-
ing and I become very sad. What do I do? I tell you about little things
that are happening to us — almost as though I'm afraid for you to lose
contact with our everyday life.

You write about Paris and where you've been and what you've done
and you remind me of things we did together. I feel that period belongs
to a stranger who was keen and alive, vivacious and excited — it doesn't
belong to me. This person has no relationship to me. As though I were
hearing about someone I had never met.

What has happened to me in these years? Does every middle-aged
woman ask the same question and not really want to hear the answer?

I know one thing that has survived and strengthened and that is my
love for you. With all my heart, with all my senses, with my whole
being I love you. Despite the differences, the quarrels, the heartaches
— I love you and I never want to live longer than you — that would
be worse than dying.

Maishe and Rose, taken while they were still living in Svisloch. Maishe emigrated in May 1921 when he was thirty-three years old. Rose and the children emigrated the following August

A secret meeting of a Bundist self-defence group in the woods outside Pinsk in 1905. Photo courtesy of the Bund Archives of the Jewish Labor Movement, New York.

Rose's father, Usher Berel Lazarovitch, and her mother, Henye, in Svisloch. The photograph was taken when David and Sophie visited in the summer of 1932, just before David entered Oxford University under his Rhodes scholarship.

David and Sophie in London, England, in March 1933, two weeks after the "noes" failed to reverse the vote at the famous "King and Country debate" in the Oxford Union. In the original debate five weeks earlier, David spoke in favour of the resolution: "That this House will under no circumstances fight for its King and Country."

At the Oxford Union on February 7, 1935, following a debate on the resolution: "That this House prefers Mr. Lloyd George's New Deal to socialism." Following the four Oxford debaters, Megan Lloyd George spoke in favour and Sir Stafford Cripps spoke against. As president of the union, David presided over the debate. The "Ayes" won by a vote of 266–261. In the front row, from the left are: Sophie, Sir Stafford, David, Miss Lloyd George, Lady (Isabel) Cripps, and Bill Shebbeare, an officer of the union.

David and Sophie on their way to England aboard the SS Alaunia in July 1932. David would take up his Rhodes scholarship at Oxford that fall.

Back row: Maishe, Sophie, and Rose; front row: Doris, David, and Bessie Kozlov, who married the poet Abe Klein in February 1935. Bessie was Sophie's best friend and Abe was David's.

Sophie and two-month-old Michael in March 1945 — the year that was the turning point in the battles between the CCF and the Communists in Canada.

David with Michael and Stephen in 1947. Michael was two years old and Stephen was ten. In the summer of 1947 the French ambassador gave a dinner for Léon Blum, the celebrated socialist leader who was visiting Canada, and during the course of the evening Prime Minister Mackenzie King tried to woo David into the Liberal Party with the promise of a cabinet post. David declined the offer.

A meeting at Woodsworth House in Ottawa in September 1947. Sitting under the picture of J.S. Woodsworth is his widow, Lucy. The others, from the left, are: David, Frank Scott, M.J. Coldwell, Angus MacInnis, and A.M. (Sandy) Nicholson.

From the left: Stephen, John F. Kennedy, then the junior senator from Massachusetts, and Gordon Coleman following a debate at Hart House on November 14, 1957, on the resolution: "Has the United States failed in its responsibilities as world leader?" Stephen, speaking for the affirmative, was one of the four University of Toronto debaters. Senator Kennedy spoke against the motion, which was defeated on a vote of 204–194. Photo courtesy of The Globe and Mail.

David and Stephen at the April 1971 convention, just after the final vote was announced that made David leader of the federal party. Stephen had been elected leader of the Ontario party six months earlier.

David and Sophie at the April 1971 convention of the federal party at which David was elected leader.

Stephen takes over the leadership of the Ontario New Democratic Party from Donald C. MacDonald in 1970.

Seated from the left: Sophie, Avram, Jennie, David, and Ilana. Standing from the left: Michele and Stephen, Michael and Wendy, David and Janet, Daniel and Nina.

Stephen and Ilana, then ten years old, taken on the campaign trail in Sault Ste Marie. This photograph was featured in the main NDP poster in the 1975 Ontario election campaign.

•CHAPTER SEVENTEEN•

The taxation system . . . puts a large portion of
[Canadians] at the mercy of . . . corporate developer
landlords. Government has recreated the feudal lords.
These modern barons control most of the land available
for housing. . . .

David Lewis
Louder Voices,
1972[1]

Superimposed on David's awareness of what his absences did to
Sophie was the feeling that he had not given as he should to
the children. It plagued him most of his married life, but he
locked away his remorse. He imprisoned it behind the steel doors of
his resolve so that it, too, was denied to Sophie. Had he not done
so, he would have had to deal with it. But all his life he had shut out
whatever impinged on his determination to serve the cause. It was a
habit learned as a youngster and a young man. Expected of him by
family and community. He was the vehicle for their aspirations. The
object of their pride. He was proof to the world of their rightful place.
Moreover, he had grown up in a milieu steeped in male values. Sacrifice,
however much it hurt, was honourable; preoccupation with emotional
turmoil was self-indulgent. So when Sophie came to pound on those
doors in loneliness and frustration he had not the key to open them.
He could acknowledge her need, he could sympathize, but he couldn't
cope with it.

So the doors remained locked on his own guilt and frustration, and
when Sophie, on the one side, turned increasingly to her sharp tongue
to prize them apart, David, on the other side, found frustration twisting
into rage. He couldn't bear the needling — here he was, a man of
considerable pride, of commanding intellect, respected and often held
in awe across the country, being treated like a simpleton. He hated
this. No one else would dare it. Yet he didn't know how to give Sophie
what she needed, and he carried the guilty conviction that he was

driving her to it. It was a mixture that could ignite the emotions. Rage with Sophie. Rage with himself.

For Sophie, his inability translated as denial. Not just denial of her need but of her worth. Although David never realized it, and maybe Sophie didn't either, he was denying her identity. If he was not prepared to confront the most unrelenting pain in her life, if he considered his own private feelings about her pain too personal to be aired, then he was saying that he wanted to deal only with part of her. The part that didn't hurt him. He was saying that he was not prepared to recognize her as a whole human being, and in doing so he was saying that what he did recognize was really not her. It provoked an inner scream that cut across all her sensibilities, pleading: "This is me, dammit! For God's sake, *look* at me!" But the male code decreed that her role was to accept while his role was to be brave, and he would avert his eyes. At times, it drove her to a frenzy. And her frenzies would set him to grinding his teeth to maintain self-control.

Michele saw it:

> I know how he endured it. I could read that, the stony face he put on. It was pure rage. He didn't dare say anything in front of other people because he'd explode if he let himself say one word. He spent so much of his life controlling this terrible rage he felt against Sophie. . . .
>
> It took me years to work all this out. . . . I saw how Sophie waged a guerrilla war on the whole family, needled people, made them frantic, made them miserable, put them down. It's impossible to describe all the things she did inside the family. And at first I spent all my time blaming her because, of course, I truly worshipped David, too, and I thought he could do no wrong. It took me years to figure out that very often he and the children would so isolate Sophie, or so ignore her, or so override and overrule her, that she would start needling and disrupting. You know, it worked both ways. So I can't pronounce finally on their marriage.

Lewis Seale saw it. He was David's press secretary during the time he was leader of the party. On the campaign trail the first few dinners would be fine, and then Sophie would begin whittling at his emotional anchor lines and David would simply endure it. Or, as Seale describes it, he would be "just terribly deferential to Sophie to the point she got away with abuse." He puts the deference down to "gross guilt going back to all the time [David forced] Sophie to spend on her own." Inevitably it ended up in a competition between Seale and Murray Weppler, David's executive assistant, to see who could escape the dinners.

Cliff Scotton saw it too. He was national secretary from 1966 to 1976. He is a smallish man. A greying pixie almost, but with an underlying sternness. A shrewdness. Like the original fairy-tale pixies before comics made them cute. The kind that had no compunctions about visiting you with boils if you failed to live up to expectations. In an interview at the 1987 party convention in Montreal he sits slouched in a chair, one leg over the arm, his worn, blue-grey cardigan an announcement that he needs no announcing. He is an oasis of slightly bemused tolerance in a disorderly world.

You haven't heard about Sophie's sickness during the 1972 election campaign? [It's not really a question; it's just Scotton getting started.] She was quite sick. Murray [Weppler] called from Vancouver and said, "Sophie is sick and David is almost completely obsessed with taking care of her and is just not functioning." And I said, "Why doesn't Sophie come home?" [But] oh no, Sophie insisted on being beside her man during the campaign. And Murray said, "I can't hack it any longer." "Well," I said, "you're there in Regina now, so I'll [leave Ottawa and] meet you in Regina."

So I called a friend of mine in Saskatchewan and I said, "Get a doctor for 12:30 tomorrow to see a patient. The diagnosis is exhaustion and whatever else you can think of, and the prescription is there should be complete bed rest in her own home with somebody to look after her."

I get to Regina and Murray is sort of flapping all over the place and I say, "I've got a doctor lined up, Murray." "Well we can't do this to David," he says. "I know it's for his benefit but she'll kill him. I mean she'll be furious about it." And David already is going around saying yes my darling and yes my sweetheart.

[Anyway] we decided not to wait. David comes in the door and I say, "David, this is what's going to happen. She's obviously ill. She obviously needs to go back and I've arranged for the doctor to see her. I think he can diagnose it and we can [get on with the campaign]." "Oh, you can't do that to my Sophie," he says. And I say, "The fates have ordained it."

So David says, ". . . how can she get back?" I say, "David, at great sacrifice I will travel back by train with her. I will see that she is installed at home. I will ensure there are twenty-four-hour nursing services." He says, "Oh my God, I can't do this to my sweetheart."

Then the impossible happened. It was like Lourdes. It was one of the most remarkable recoveries in medical history. Sophie recovered that very day.

Murray Wepler shakes his head recalling the incident. "I think she was just being extremely difficult," he says. Then he adds, "The history is understandable . . . but at that time it didn't make much sense." Especially in the middle of a tough election campaign.

Yet the love David and Sophie shared was real. Complicated, infinitely complicated, but real. "They depended on each other," says Michele. "It was a very symbiotic relationship. They had been together for a very long time and I think there was lots of affection and lots of rage. . . . There was a strong bond there that couldn't be broken."

The saddest part about David's denial is that it established a never-ending spiral of tension that ended up being so intense that Sophie, in an extreme demand for recognition from David, could drag the 1972 election campaign to a sputtering halt. The more he refused to deal with his own feelings, the more she felt ignored. And the more she reacted, the more obstinate he became. They were constantly reinforcing the pattern.

> David hated any talk of psychoanalysis or psychiatry [says Michele]. I don't think he wanted to look beneath any human surfaces. That was partly the set of his mind, being political, but also I think there was a personal element. He didn't want to explore those dark, terrible places that everybody has. You know, there are some people who set aside all that. They realize that to cope with their sadness or their grievous mistakes or the wrong they have done other people, the crazy way they are themselves, is going to take a lot of effort and energy, and David was not willing to expend that energy on personal salvation. So he just put a lid on it.
>
> All the personal he repressed. Anything personal. Which is a terrible and sad thing in someone's life.

On learning how Ted Jolliffe recalled that David never thought in images, Michele nods. "That's what I mean. . . . If you repress feelings, your feeling side, you repress the whole side of your being from which artistry springs. The whole feeling side of life underlies all art and all artistic expression. To come up with images you have to have free access into your unconscious. That's where images spring from and, boy, he didn't have free access into his unconscious. He was a pragmatic, ideological, ruthlessly logical intellect, and poetry and art did not grow in that ground."

But he loved theatre and poetry. Isn't that contradictory? Michele says no:

> I'm not saying that he didn't appreciate these things. But they weren't his mode of expression. . . . He was supremely rational. He was so lucid. I trusted him absolutely on political and legal judgments and very often on moral judgments. . . .
>
> He was so swift and clear and he was very unswerving in his personal values. That's something that always moved me very, very much.

A total lack of hypocrisy. David lived his life according to his values. He didn't have a public and a private set of values, and that was always extremely impressive and moving to me, even though we clashed on many things and I felt sorry for him in some of his life's circumstances. But I always respected and admired him tremendously, while you see, with some chauvinists, I wouldn't respect them at all.

It's interesting that Michele should say David was not prepared to expend energy on personal salvation because, of course, it was social salvation, the salvation of society that was his preoccupation. In Bundist ideology, social salvation might be a pathway to *menschekeit*, just as with the Social Gospel personal salvation might be a by-product. But in neither case were these the rewards. The reward was the new Jerusalem itself.

Michele calls David unswerving and it's true. When you look back on his public career, it's remarkable how consistent were his political views. One of the most persistent criticisms of David is that he sacrificed socialist ideology to the god of power. That he sold out. There's no denying he was prepared to compromise in order to attract a mass following. But if socialist ideology calls for revolution by parliamentary means, the ability to compromise is fundamental to success.

If the socialist revolution is to occur through a violent overthrow of the government, then it can be achieved by a relatively small elite, and that elite can cling to all the Marxist theories that pre-date the English Reform Bill of 1867, including a dictatorship of the proletariat that will impose socialism on recalcitrants.

But if David's brand of Parliamentary Marxism is the ideology, then violence is ruled out and the revolution must be won through persuasion. The revolutionists have to be elected to office and that means gaining mass support among electors. And that inevitably means compromise and change and adaptation. It means hammering the holy grail of socialist orthodoxy into a shape that will be acceptable to an electorate. The skill lies in retaining the values and programs that lie at the core of the orthodoxy. David should be judged on whether he had that skill, not on whether, in the hammering, he changed some of the peripheral features of the holy grail.

The irony in criticisms of David is that they take as the holy grail the two great icons of the CCF, the Regina Manifesto and *Social Planning for Canada*, which, on their faces, are the mildest of socialist documents. David subscribed to a much tougher, more militant Parliamentary Marxist version of socialism — and he never let go of it.

As a socialist document born of the troubled thirties, the Manifesto was singularly restrained. There has been much learned debate over the weight to be given to agrarian protest compared to industrial socialism in its makeup. But what these arguments usually missed was that it didn't matter. The importance of the Manifesto lay not so much in what it said as in how it was used. It was a talisman that could be shaped to the needs of individual leftists, whether they were radical or conservative.

Social Planning for Canada was the 524-page program for change produced by the League for Social Reconstruction that served as a policy blueprint for the CCF for thirty years after its publication in 1935. It was gentle, civilized, almost courtly in its language and approach. In an introduction to a 1975 republication, the six surviving signatories to the original edition commented that the program laid out "was more pragmatic — not to say reformist — and less socialist, than we might have admitted at the time."[2]

David and Frank Scott, on the other hand, published *Make This YOUR Canada* in 1943. In 197 pages, and with a couple of exceptions, it followed the policies outlined in *Social Planning for Canada*; but there the similarity ended. (See Appendix J.) It was an eloquent call to parliamentary revolution. Much of the eloquence was Frank Scott's; the muscular socialism was David's. It was a runaway bestseller: 25,000 copies were sold in less than twelve months,[3] an almost unheard-of number for a Canadian book at that time. By comparison, *Social Planning for Canada* sold out its first printing of 1,500 and a second edition was printed in 1936. After a brisk start, it did not sell out until the war years.[4]

Language distinguished *Make This YOUR Canada* from *Social Planning for Canada*. As it always does, it evoked images. Gave texture. Resonated. Language always paints what prowls across a page. It puts stripes on tigers — or reduces them to tabbies. Two people describing the same set of proposals can make them sound quite different, and they will be different. Language points to the ideology and passion of the speaker, and that, in turn, bears on how that person would implement the proposals — with what intensity, what compassion, what speed, what thoroughness.

The language of *Make This YOUR Canada* was Marxist — Parliamentary Marxist — and urgent. It referred constantly to class and class struggle; it spoke of the "masses" and "robber barons" and the "capitalist press" and "reactionary forces." And, most importantly, it talked about "the laws of capitalist growth," the Marxist belief in the scientific inevitability of capitalist decay. It was a brazen call to revolutionary change. It proclaimed that:

We face a new revolution. We must replace monopoly capitalism by democratic socialism. Let us plan this revolution like free men, and cease being the victims of a blind process. . . .

The fighting men and women themselves must realize that when, through bravery and sacrifice, they have won the war, there will still be another battle to win on the social and political front. In unity with the rest of their countrymen they will have to help complete the great people's revolution which the war has started. . . .

Everywhere democracy has begun to possess again something of the dynamic content that made it a revolutionary watchword in the 18th and 19th centuries. Democracy was once a fighting creed. It made men stand up against overwhelming odds, made them overthrow foreign invaders and domestic tyranny, and gave them a vision of a new society they were determined to create. In the revolutionary democratic tradition, enlarged by the wider horizons of today, lies sufficient incentive to evoke in people of all races the will to change the world. . . .

The democratic socialist society must replace the rapacious system of monopoly capitalism. Unless we advance to the co-operative commonwealth, we may be forced back into fascist darkness. . . .[5]

So up until 1943 at least, there can be no question of backsliding. And a look at David's speeches shows that he held fast to essential socialist views: for instance, that a class system existed and it bred all kinds of inequities; that out of that system grew attitudes that extolled the pursuit of material gain and stunted the spirit; that a society structured around the profit motive was immoral and cruel; that changing the system, not just changing a government, was necessary; that significant public ownership was needed to create a society that was equitable; that labour was the source of all value; and that only intensive social planning could give direction and predictability to the country's affairs.

None of those views have ever been shared by Liberals or Conservatives. They are quintessentially socialist.

In 1962 the same undercurrent of hard-core socialist zeal was still running through David's language. In a private interview he claimed that the ultimate aim of the party should be "a complete reconstruction of society wherein the means of production and distribution, et cetera, were publicly owned. . . .

"What will always distinguish our kind of party is that we do not believe that profit is the be-all and the end-all of life. On the contrary, we believe that the profit idea is immoral rather than moral . . . and that people are capable of being motivated by things other than profit in society, and that society ought to appeal to these other sources of motivation rather than to their self-seeking search for private gain."[6]

Then there was the 1972 federal election, David's first as party leader. That campaign said everything that needed to be said about class inequities in three words: "Corporate Welfare Bums." Not since the Second World War has there been an election that focused so precisely on ideology. It electrified the country and returned the New Democrats with thirty-one members, increasing the party's standing by 41 percent and giving it the most members it had ever had.

There was a fire in David. An anger not to be confused with the emotional turmoil he shared with Sophie. No matter how he banked it, no matter what the compromises, it smouldered — even to the public eye. It's part of what made him so compelling a public speaker. But it's hard to live with that kind of anger. It can twist and distort, turn sour to become bitter and cutting. It can become strident. It can tear a person apart. But if, as in David's case, it can be channelled, it can become a font of energy.

People marvelled at his durability on the election trail, at his fierce determination, at his mental toughness, at his sheer physical stamina — especially in his final years. Had they placed their hands closer to the coals of this anger, they would have understood. What fuelled it was the way people were betrayed by the capitalist system — even those who survived and profited because in doing so they had to suborn their better selves. If they were not broken, they were bent. And broken or bent, they were denied the beauty of life.

If they placed their hands still closer, they would see that the bellows that fanned the coals was the theory of historical materialism, Marx's belief that it was the system of production that fashioned people's attitudes and not their attitudes that fashioned the system of production. In a 1946 speech at Dalhousie University in Halifax that Walter Young says became a major part of the party's ideological equipment,[7] David was passionate in explaining just what this meant: "In addition to the material misery [that it produces, capitalism] represents, it seems to me, the most sordid kind of living — a kind of blind, ruthless pursuit after material security which nine times out of ten can be achieved only at the expense of someone else, and results in the concentration of one's entire mind, spirit and energy on that one objective. That, to me, is evil. I hate the capitalist system precisely for that, for that more almost than for anything else."[8]

At David's death in 1981 *Toronto Star* columnist Richard Gwyn wrote:

My sharpest memory of David Lewis was of interviewing him during the 1974 election campaign in the back of a school bus somewhere near North Battleford, Sask.

The election wasn't going well. Lewis was edgy. The circumstances of the interview were difficult because the road was bumpy and we bounced about, words sometimes flying sideways out of our mouths and my pen making chicken marks on my notebook.

He didn't relax at any time during the interview. He was far too serious for that. But just because he was so serious, you knew that he really meant everything he said.

My opening question took him by surprise. It had nothing to do with policy. . . . Why are you so angry, I asked, and aren't you aware that these angry vibes that radiate out from you scare voters away?

Here's what he said: "I've been angry all my life, angry at the difference between what society is and what society should be. I have an abiding anger in me at the way people are treated."

Then he addressed the problem of his image: "It's a danger, I recognize. But when I speak softly I'm uncomfortable because I know I sometimes do it for the image. When I speak in anger, that's how I really feel."

At [his] funeral . . . Frank Scott . . . remarked that the press had described him as "an angry man," but that "anger" isn't the right word; he was a concerned man.

I still think of him as an angry man, one of our last angry men. But after listening to Scott, I realize that a better description of Lewis is as a true believer, one of the last of our true believers. Now that he's gone, our politics will be less vivid, less passionate, flatter.[9]

Capitalism was immoral. A rapacious system that smeared its greed across the lens of society, distorting personal aspirations and deforming social objectives. That was the bedrock of David's belief. In *Make This YOUR Canada*, he translated this succinctly into: "Efficiency measured by money profit may be inefficiency measured by social needs."[10]

For instance, under a capitalist system, in order to maximize profits, it may be necessary for a developer to build houses for the rich and well-to-do instead of for working-class families. That's a skewing of priorities. That's how social needs get ignored. As in Metropolitan Toronto where the federal government sold seventeen hectares of public land just east of Downsview airport to private developers for housing. In the fall of 1988 houses were being built — behind an imposing and elegant brick wall. The developer Bramalea Ltd. said it would begin selling the houses during the summer of 1989 for prices ranging from $680,000 to $950,000.[11] Everyone down the line maximized profits, even the federal government, which sold public land to the highest bidder and imposed no requirement that affordable housing be built for those who needed it most, young couples and working-class people.

All down the line the virtues of financial responsibility were extolled and market forces were saluted and free enterprise was celebrated, and quite possibly no one realized, even fleetingly, that in the kingdom of the golden calf, greed comes in many guises. (See Appendix K.)

When David got back from Oxford, there seemed little need to rein in his views. The mood on the left was volatile. The Spanish Civil War had begun in July of 1936 with Franco's attack on the Spanish government, and every passing day seemed to confirm, as an American journalist was to put it, that fascism was simply capitalism gone nudist.[12] In that same year two-thirds of Canadians entering the work force couldn't find jobs, and in Toronto the May Day celebration was the second largest in North America, with 25,000 people turning out. Only New York had more.[13] In 1937 farmers in the West had their worst year yet — less rain, more grasshoppers, more army worms, more Russian thistle than ever before. By the time the year was out, the Depression had seen 21,000 people leave Alberta, 34,000 leave Manitoba, and 66,000 leave Saskatchewan.

In Ontario, the CCF provincial executive was militant. It declared, in a report to the 1936 provincial convention, that "in no sense is the socialism of the CCF mere reformism, mere gradualism. . . . A CCF government . . . must proceed promptly, drastically, thoroughly to liquidate the power of capitalist forces. . . . The CCF is on the uttermost left in objective and understanding or it is nowhere."[14]

But, as it turned out, the CCF *was* nowhere. The party didn't win a single seat in the October 1937 election. Worse still, it didn't even come second in a single seat.

The defeat made doubly persuasive Frank Scott's warning, in a July 1937 letter written to David, that, "the CCF is far too far left for most Canadians . . . and in the political arena we must find our friends among the near right."[15]

Up to that point David had not stressed ideology but organization and forging links to unions.[16] From then on, however, he turned to moderating the party's image and, like a mythical champion on a quest to confine lightning to a lantern, he set out to harness the CCF — no little task in a band of willful, loosely allied dissidents accustomed to hurling their opinions like thunderbolts. David set himself to corral that energy and channel it.

He had outlined the ideological rationale for reining in the party in a speech to the League for Social Reconstruction in Montreal in 1936, and it was reminiscent of the Jewish Labour Bund and its determination to sacrifice ideology for solidarity if necessary. Compromise was going to be necessary to create a mass labour party, he said. That's the way it had been in Europe and that's what people should expect in Canada. Theory would have to bend the knee to necessity. Adjustments would have to be made.

The Gazette reported him saying that: "Not even in the works of Marx or Engels was there . . . any treatment of the way in which the socialist society . . . would look and how it would work. . . . Most of their writings were polemic and it was necessary to read into their writings in order to get at the things which formed the basis of their thought. . . . In Europe [outside the Soviet Union], the Marxian revolutionary approach to socialism was accepted, but in practice the socialistic organizations became . . . mass social reformist parties rather than revolutionary parties."[17]

In other words, it was okay to apply a Marxist analysis to the ills of society and to hold to the conviction that the ills could be cured only with sweeping and fundamental change. But people with families to raise and obligations to meet would not respond in droves to a call to flip society on its ear overnight. It meant that dismantling the capitalist edifice had to be measured and methodical, not demolition in one thunderous blast. It meant a revolution that leaned more toward what would be Quebec's Quiet Revolution — at least in its early stages before it ran low on steam — than toward the French Revolution. This was not Fabian gradualism. The Regina Manifesto and *Social Planning for Canada* already had established a program that, in David's hands, meant introducing socialism in significant chunks, not in a slow dilution of capitalism.

Year by year, the moves toward moderation did not seem large, but over a ten-year period they changed the thrust of the party. In 1935 the party was putting out pamphlets declaring that "Bank Robbers get Billions but the BIG-SHOT BANKER IS A BIGGER CRIMINAL THAN THE GUNMAN because the bankers' greed hurts all the people all the time."[18] By 1945 its pamphlets were stressing industrial democracy and security in homes, farms, health, old age, education, and unions and saying, "Monopoly capitalism, through its controlled press and parties would have you forget that which you should remember to fear. It wants you to fear the CCF instead of fearing poverty, unemployment, frustration and war. . . ."[19]

The switch was greatly aided by the Beveridge Report, published in England in 1942.[20] After the war the British Labour Government used it as a blueprint to produce the country's first welfare state. The Beveridge Report completed the journey from the Dickensian concept of charity for the poor to that of ensuring a minimum standard of living for everybody. Its author, Sir William Beveridge, who did not regard himself as a socialist, set abolition of want as the main objective. He saw no need to deal a death blow to capitalism through public ownership. His device was to apply insurance principles — which meant that people could receive benefits as a right instead of on sufferance — and his approach was to recommend universality, which meant that people would not have to prove need if they came within certain categories.

But even with the switch to moderation, David still talked of replacing the system, not housebreaking it. "Within the framework of a democratic system," he said in his 1946 speech at Dalhousie University, "a person searching for ways of improvement has only two alternatives: (1) to improve the capitalist system [and] (2) to build a democratic socialist system. . . . There is no way of which I know in which the capitalist system can be improved to achieve . . . obvious economic and social necessities in society."[21]

A year after publication of Make This YOUR Canada, — two years after the Beveridge Report — the party took a giant step in redefining what it meant by socialism, a step in which David played a major role. It said even large businesses could have a place in the party — if they behaved.

At its convention in November 1944, the party resolved, first, that it would limit nationalization to "key industries which are monopolistic in operation," and, second, that private enterprise would retain a bigger and better-defined field of operation than had been envisioned before. The resolution said: "The socialization of large-scale enterprise, however, does not mean taking over every private business. Where private business shows no signs of becoming a monopoly, operates efficiently under decent working conditions, and does not operate to the detriment of the Canadian people, it will be given every opportunity to function, to provide a fair rate of return and to make its contribution to the nation's wealth."[22]

The debate was long, heated, and "very severe," but with David leading the floor fight, it passed.[23] With its passing, the party abandoned any pretence of standing for pure socialism in the classic sense and proclaimed support for a mixed economy. As in the past, the list of candidates for nationalization didn't change much, so an argument could be made that the change was not all that significant. But it was significant because the party had changed fundamentally how it defined itself. The party had never got around to itemizing what would not be nationalized. Now, when it declared that it was narrowing its focus to monopolies and then took a hard look at what was excluded, it had to come to terms with the realization that a very large part of business indeed would be left in private hands and that capitalism would remain as a significant partner in the new society.

It surprised David when he discovered what the redefinition would mean, but it never lessened his commitment to see it adopted. He recalled in his memoirs that "Knowing that we would face a serious debate on the socialization plank, I asked Jamieson to ascertain, if possible, what proportion of Canada's work force would remain in the employ of private business on the assumption that all major industries were nationalized. His research showed that the answer was 'more than half.' This was a larger proportion than I expected. It made acceptance of the idea of a mixed economy important from the point of view of the welfare of the country's working class as well as politically desirable."[24]

With minor differences in wording, the formula for nationalization presented in the resolution was the same as in *Make This YOUR Canada.*[25] David had swung the party behind the version of socialism he thought Canadians would accept.

The swinging didn't always come easily. His code was strict: if it hurts the party, don't say it even if it is true; don't do it even if the motives are pure. He laid this out in a letter written in late 1940 to Angus MacInnis criticizing an editorial in the *Federationist*, the CCF's newspaper in British Columbia: " . . . what we say and do must be measured by the effect which it will have on our purpose of mobilizing people for action. If what we say and do will blunt or harm our purpose . . . then, we are saying and doing a false thing even if, in the abstract, it is true. . . . When, in Heaven's name are we going to learn that working-class politics and the struggle for power are not a Sunday-school class where the purity of godliness and the infallibility of the Bible must be held up without fear of consequences?"[26]

Little escaped David's attention, and when he came upon anything that was potentially damaging, he never was loath to point it out — and in doing so he invariably added to the legion of people in the party who over the years nursed a grievance against him. One small example: in late 1944 he wrote Dr. Carlyle King in Saskatoon because King had toured North Dakota on behalf of Norman Thomas, leader of the U.S. Socialist Party: "I write this note entirely personally and without the slightest intention of throwing my authority around, but merely as a comrade, quite informally." And then he as much told Carlyle that he was a fool. Thomas's anti-war position had no support and Thomas "is through as a socialist leader," he said.[27]

If that was less than subtle, David could be even more blunt if he thought it was necessary. Lorne Ingle, the the party's federal secretary from 1951 to 1958, recalls the 1950 national convention in Vancouver where a woman had set up a bookstall of Trotskyist literature outside the convention hall. David, about to enter the hall, saw it and told her in no uncertain terms to remove it.

"You don't have the power to make me move," she retorted. "Oh, don't I!" said David. "I'll show you whether I have the power," with which he marched into the convention, garnered a floor microphone, declared he had an urgent matter to raise, and proposed a motion that the stall be ordered removed. The motion carried "overwhelmingly" and the bookstall was removed. "I have never seen anybody that didn't wilt in front of David," says Ingle. "Generally he was considerate and mild-mannered when there were no problems, but God help you if he got angry and took you on. Oh boy! [He'd] cut you to shreds . . . [and] generally tell you what he thought of you and your arguments in a very persuasive, domineering kind of way."[28]

When people wanted to deviate from socialist first principles, David could be scathing. Murray Cotterill tells a story that occurred just after Tommy Douglas was elected in Saskatchewan in 1944. Recalling the popularity that had met William Aberhart's Social Credit proposal to pay state dividends to all Alberta residents, Cotterill suggested to Tommy that the publicly owned crown corporations in Saskatchewan should declare a dividend payable to all Saskatchewan residents.

"I didn't care if it was only $5.95. At least give them something," Cotterill remembers telling him. "Tommy liked the idea, but when David heard about it, he was absolutely furious." He phoned Cotterill and tore up one side of him and down the other. "Why? Because it didn't fit in with the classical approach of socialism."

To David, declaring a dividend would have meant embracing capitalist methods. Dividends come from profits. To have crown corporations declare them would mean acceptance of the profit motive — and profit, as a motive for "service" industries, would be immoral. End of argument.

There was another side to imposing party discipline, and it earned David even more people with a grudge to settle. He became the person for whom others left the dirty work. The person who had to tell someone he wasn't going to get an appointment. The person who had to explain the unpopular decision. The one who carried the bad news. "He was the son of a bitch in the party," says Kalmen Kaplansky. "All the others, oh, they were such nice people; they were the defenders of democracy. They wouldn't dirty their hands. He had to do it." It was the same even with Tommy Douglas. "Douglas was never the heavy," said Allan Blakeney. "Douglas said yes, and other people said no," And that's how it continued when Tommy became national leader in 1961. It was still David, by then fifty-two years old, who said no when it had to be said.[29]

Perhaps because David held himself on such a tight rein, perhaps because he had sacrificed so much of himself and his family, his anger had an Old Testament severity to it when he thought someone in the party was being self-indulgent and disruptive — and especially so if that person refused entreaties to stop. He had grown up amid the bloody warfare within the Russian Social Democratic Workers Party, familiar with every immobilizing argument, every self-immolating tactic. He had seen the British left tearing itself apart in the thirties. He had seen the Austrian left obliterated and had watched the German left erect its own gallows under Hitler. Criticism he accepted. When he thought it became self-mutilation he acted. And then he was pitiless — as he was in a squabble over Woodsworth House, where he would give the drubbing of his life to an old and valued associate, a person as respected within the party as he was himself.

In 1943 Charlie Millard came up with the idea (and the offer of $1,000 of his own money) to establish a home for the Ontario CCF. This resulted in the creation of a foundation, independent of the party, to promote and discuss socialist ideas. The party raised $25,000 for the foundation, and in 1945 the money was used to buy a house, which was christened Woodsworth House. In January 1947, with renovations completed, it was formally opened with great pride. As David said in his memoirs: "[It] was a defiant symbol of survival and permanence. The Liberals could filch our policies, the Tories besmirch our name, the Communists disrupt our activities, and editorialists and columnists misrepresent our ideas, but none could halt the work of democratic socialism, not even in temporary defeat."[30]

Frank Underhill, the person who, with Frank Scott, had conceived of the League for Social Reconstruction, whose pen had breathed life into the Regina Manifesto, who had been a source of inspiration and advice to the CCF since its birth, became the first educational director and vice-president — and, seven years later, the principal victim of David's wrath. His transgression, which he kept repeating with increasing loudness and disdain, was that the pursuit of power was turning the CCF into a party of rigid, dogmatic ideologues lusting to apply nostrums from the depression years that no longer were applicable. A man of hungry intellect, he was continually shifting territory. He had always been an admirer of liberalism in the tradition that dated back to Jeremy Bentham, and was embarked on a revisitation to liberalism that eventually would bring him to an admiration for the accomplishments of Mackenzie King.

Underhill, who saw himself as an intellectual provocateur, a gadfly — King Gordon, who conducted his funeral service in 1971, called him "a dissenter by temperament" — thought he was stimulating debate; David thought Underhill and his associates had become an ingrown clique, sneering, negative, and abusive — and, since their function was to educate, hurtful to the party.

The climax came with the intention of the foundation to sell Woodsworth House because it couldn't afford the upkeep. David maintained it was in financial trouble because of a publishing program that was too ambitious. He led the attack to unseat the board of directors while Charlie Millard led the organizing drive to sign up new members to support him. The Underhill forces never had a chance. Forever afterward, Underhill recoiled at the Lewis name, seeing a lust for power as David's only motive.

Two months after his ouster, he published an article in *The Canadian Forum* that says, as forcefully as anybody was ever to say it — and many tried over forty years — what was at the nub of grievances against David. As is often the case in politics, the vitriol had less to do with whether the grievances were true or untrue, justified or unjustified, but whether they stemmed from a severe bruising. If there is to be one major criticism of David over the affair, it is that he didn't head off the issue before it reached a critical stage. In an out-and-out political fight, which is what resulted, Underhill could never be a match for the combat-hardened resolve of David Lewis and Charlie Millard. The drive to unseat the foundation board, said Underhill,

> . . . was carried out . . . with an unscrupulous thoroughness that the Communists themselves could hardly have bettered. . . .
>
> The party leadership has fallen into the hands of a small clique who perpetuate themselves in party office regardless of the ups and downs in electoral results in the province. They have become adepts in the art of managing party conventions and in using democratic forms to centralize power in their own control. . . .
>
> The reformer in religion or in politics always has a certain amount of fanaticism in his make-up; and the end-result of pure fanaticism is likely to consist in redoubling your effort when you have forgotten your aim.
>
> This subtle corruption is one which peculiarly affects the leaders of reform movements. . . . It is the unworldly reformers, the children of light, who are specially liable to the kind of corruption I am talking about, the corruption which overtakes idealists who have concentrated too much on power.[31]

Underhill, who considered himself a realist and everyone who disagreed with him an idealist, never involved himself in the grinding toil of political organizing. He preferred instead the interplay of ideas, an equally valid pursuit that could be equally demanding but lacked the perspective that comes from sitting in bleak meeting rooms at the back of Chinese restaurants, in unions halls, at less expensive hotels in not-so-fashionable areas of towns where beer parlours were the main cultural outlet, trying to glue together local party structures.

His sense of grievance stayed with him. But his days of effectiveness within the party were over. David had stripped him of more than his position within the foundation. "Personally," Underhill wrote a colleague ten years later, "I think that the main threat to the New Party is Dave Lewis who will be the real power whoever the nominal leader may be. He is by instinct a communist commissar, and he hopes to have all the machine of the trade unionists to wield his purposes."[32]

Meanwhile David maintained that the Underhill forces had been intellectually dishonest and, that in his *Canadian Forum* article, Underhill himself had been inaccurate and unfair in his recounting of the events.[33]

Andy Brewin, responding to Underhill's article in a letter published by the *Forum*, dismissed his accusations as "sheer nonsense," and commented that: "Such [views] could only have been advanced by Professor Underhill because he has not been close to the conventions of the CCF or has been misinformed." Discussion and criticism were needed and were welcome, Brewin said, but Woodsworth House could hardly be effective "if it . . . alienated the sympathies of many loyal supporters of the CCF and permitted hostility to develop into complete separation or divorce. . . ."[34]

Like Underhill, David also was never to forgive. "[Even] the best of us," he wrote in his memoirs, "are from time to time *blinded* by prejudice and capable of unkind and ungenerous accusations."[35]

Not only friendship died. So did a fertile relationship between the party and a relentlessly probing intelligence. Underhill has been called Canada's first intellectual historian.[36] It was sad — for him, for David, for the party — that it ended. All were the poorer for it. But David had emblazoned on the party's consciousness as never before that discipline and solidarity were now inviolable characteristics of the organization, and that there were limits to discussion and tolerance: in the final analysis, "If thy right hand offend thee, cut it off, and cast it from thee."[37]

•CHAPTER EIGHTEEN•

*We . . . agreed in the Fifties to swallow any nonsense that
was repeated often enough, without examination of its
meaning or investigation into its roots.*

Lillian Hellman
Scoundrel Time[1]

June 1945 was a watershed — for the party, for David, and for
Communists in Canada. For the CCF it was a time of dreams
destroyed. Of near-despair. For David it was a re-enacting of the
venomous battles between socialists and Communists in Germany
that allowed Hitler to slip into power. For the Communists it was a
time of jubilation.

Most important of all, it was a time that gave final shape to an attitude that almost thirty years later would hammer the Waffle into
oblivion. Not because the Waffle was Communist. Not even because
it was perceived as Communist. But because by then it was a reflex
response — and the legacy of that response still lingers in the party
like a bad back in an old miner.

No one, least of all the CCF, realized that June 1945 was the turning point in the struggle against the Communists.[2] It was the occasion of the CCF's most excruciating defeat, the time, in David's words,
of its "crushing disappointment."[3] For a year afterward the party was
dazed — or as Frank Scott, then the national chairman, put it to the
national council, "It is as though we had lost faith in ourselves."[4] The
party, he said, was dormant — and the person upon whom this fell
most heavily was David, who by then had been steersman of the CCF
for a third of its lifetime.[5]

For David it meant rejecting plans to retire as national secretary and
explaining to Sophie that personal concerns would have to be put aside
yet one more time. He had been planning to retire, he says in his
memoirs, because "the financial burden on Sophie was becoming too

heavy and the long absences from home dangerously disruptive. These
personal problems became doubly pressing early in the year when our
second son was born."[6] But the party had to come first and it would
be another five years before he again would think of leaving his post.

This was no longer the cocky David Lewis holding the world by the
tail. This was a badly bruised thirty-six-year-old still trying to shake
off his humiliating defeat by Fred Rose, the Communist candidate in
the Cartier by-election two years earlier. Rose was elected; David came
last in a field of four.[7] Their confrontation flew in the face of
Communist proclamations about the need for a popular front to support the war effort. But David's attacks on Stalin, only weeks before,
for the murder of Erlich and Alter rankled Communists who saw it
as "CCF mischief-making and readiness to sow discord among Hitler's
opponents."[8] In the campaign, Rose played on racial prejudice. According to David, "Several of our canvassers were almost in tears as
they reported that Communist workers had persuaded Jewish voters
who didn't know me that, in view of my name I must be English or
Welsh, not Jewish. At the same time, they had underlined to non-
Jewish voters that, despite my name, I was Jewish and why should they
vote for a Jew?"[9]

And this even though Rose himself was Jewish and his name —
Rosenberg — also had been anglicized. It was a stormy campaign that
in addition to its racial overtones and vicious personal attacks left David
outraged and repelled over voting-list scandals, roving goon squads,
and violence.[10]

At the end of the campaign Rose brought in Sam Carr, the party's
eminence grise and a formidable debater to speak at an afternoon rally
in Fletcher's Field at the foot of Mount Royal in Montreal. It was on
a Sunday, the day before the election, and Abe Klein described it in
a detective novel about Communist spies that never was published.
He changed the names, but changing them back, the passage reads
like this:

> [The Communists] . . . figured it out that the big danger was the socialist
> *Lewis*, who although he couldn't win himself, might pull enough votes
> to kill *Fred's* chances. So he was it. They ran him ragged. Every day
> there was a new pamphlet, in two colours, showing what a dirty, double-
> crossing betrayer this *Lewis* was, betraying both the constituency and
> [Canada's wartime ally] the Soviet Union, how he was really in the
> employ of the big corporations, and how he was making himself the
> willing tool of the capitalist candidate to split the labour vote. *Carr* came
> down specially from Toronto, and devoted an evening at an open air
> meeting in Fletcher's Field to *Phillips's* lackey. [Lazarus Phillips was the

Liberal candidate.] He laughed at *Lewis's* academic distinctions, he mimicked his Oxford accent — for him that wasn't hard. He contrasted *Lewis's* career with *Rose's*. *Rose* sitting in jail because he dared to speak out for his class, and *Lewis* sacrificing himself for the workers by making two hour speeches. *Carr* made quite a comedy out of the fact that *Lewis* was a little fellow — "pint-sized" — although *Rose* wasn't bigger, only stouter. By the time *Carr* was through, *Lewis* was a Fascist done up brown. A good time was had by all.[11]

It was strictly an LPP rally and "several thousand" attended. David himself had a rally in Fletcher's Field three days earlier at which "upwards of 6,000" attended. On that same night the Bloc Populaire candidate held a separate rally at which "over 7,000 people gathered."[12] Obviously, interest and feeling were running high. Norman Penner, history professor and former Communist, was at the LPP rally and says that, except for the fact that the real rally was in the afternoon, not the evening, Klein's description is accurate. According to David, "[Rose] rode to victory on the heroism of the Red Army and the Soviet people in stopping the Nazi Wehrmacht at the gates of Leningrad and Moscow."

David had the chance to run again against Rose — in the 1945 general election. Had he run, Rose would have lost and the Liberal candidate would have taken the seat.[13] At the time David gave two reasons for not challenging Rose: first, he doubted the advisability of having a national officer of the party contest a seat held by a sitting Communist member; and second, M.J. Coldwell and the national executive had expressed the wish that if he were to run again it should be in a riding where he could win.[14]

But there was a riding with no sitting Communist member where David could have run and won — Abe Heaps's old seat in Winnipeg North. Instead, he ran in Hamilton West and again lost badly (11,439 votes for the sitting Liberal member, 9,250 for the Conservative candidate, 6,730 for him, and 1,053 for the LPP candidate).

Why didn't he run where he could win? Why did he pick a riding where he had little chance, contrary to his expressed view that he should run only where he *could* win?

In his memoirs he says: "The result of the [Cartier] byelection was a shocker to me: first that the Communist won and, second, that I came last. . . . [It] so affected me that when it was later suggested that I seek the nomination in Winnipeg North for the general election due in 1944 or 1945, I refused. My reasons were simply that I could not take another Cartier campaign . . . I said that, ' . . . it is my personal hope that if I should ever get to

Parliament I should do so as a Canadian socialist who happens to be Jewish and not in the opposite way,' and that I did not want to be 'plunk in the middle of a fight between the CCF and the Communists.'"[15]

Since he certainly had no compunction about seeking the Jewish vote in Forest Hill in Toronto when he finally won a seat in York South in 1962, his recoiling from "another Cartier campaign" must have had much more to do with not having the stomach for the kind of campaign he would face against another strong Jewish Communist candidate and much less to do with his philosophic rationale. In short, he had been emotionally flayed in Cartier and two years later he was still unnerved.

"In a sense, it was a pity that I [didn't run]," David says in his memoirs, "for Winnipeg North was obviously winnable — the seat had been held by A.A. Heaps for 15 years."[16] It was a momumental understatement. Had David run, he would have been elected and could have been a member of Parliament until he died.[17] Instead, Allistair Stewart ran in his place, dominated the polls, and held the riding for the next thirteen years, and after him David Orlikow held it — with one brief interlude from 1958 to 1962 — until 1988.

Having won Winnipeg North, Stewart made no particular impression on Parliament or on the party. On the other hand, both would have benefitted enormously, as they later did, if David had been elected instead.

The wounds inflicted by Rose were deep indeed. So David went into 1945 already prepared to give no quarter to Communists ever again. (See Appendix L.)

What dazed the party, destroyed whatever tolerance wartime alliances had raised for Communists, and committed the CCF to an implacable battle to the death against them was the successful Communist campaign to join with Liberals and defeat the CCF in the federal and Ontario elections held back to back in early June. The Communist strategy was to split the left-wing vote by running against CCF candidates. It worked. The CCF elected not a single candidate from Ontario in the federal election and in the provincial election it was replaced by the Liberals as official opposition. What made defeat doubly bitter was that the party's prospects had been so good. Tommy Douglas had just been elected in Saskatchewan and the party had been doing well in the polls.[18]

There was never any real doubt about the Communists' intentions. Six months before the election the editor of the *Canadian Tribune*, the LPP newspaper, was quite explicit in a full-page article:

The Social-Democratic "'parliamentary cretins" as Lenin called them, failed the working class precisely because they made parliamentary careerism the be-all and end-all of their activities without preparing the working class or proving capable of leading it in the many-sided activities and struggles demanded of it when the "peaceful" era of capitalist development had ended. . . .

It seems clear that nothing less than repudiation of the CCF by the labour movement and a resounding defeat of the CCF at the polls accompanied by the election of a powerful block of LPP, labor and independent MPs, together with any CCFers who take a pro-unity position and the reform Liberals, putting the Tories to a decisive rout, can assure the achievement of a progressive Parliament and Government in the next election.[19]

Liberals responded coyly to the LPP initiative. "We are glad of co-operation in putting into force the basic principles that are the real solution to want and the war. . . . [But] we're for co-operation, not coalition," declared Allan G. McLean, national director of the National Liberal Federation when the Communists proposed a formal Labour-Liberal coalition in May 1944.[20]

And Mackenzie King, who had pinpointed the CCF as a greater election threat to his Liberal government than the Tories,[21] responded with a reform platform the centrepiece of which was the Family Allowances Act. It was scheduled to come into force on July 1, 1945, so he called the federal election for June 11, two weeks before the cheques started flowing — $5 a month for every child up to six years of age and $8 a month for every child over six and under sixteen. As he confided to his diary following a meeting with J.W. McConnell, owner of the Montreal Star: "When I spoke to [McConnell] about family allowances and what they meant about letting the country see the determination of the Government to redistribute wealth, he strongly approved the policy. I pointed out to him that unless we were going to let the CCF sweep the country and take measures that would be extreme, how necessary it was that we should keep Liberal principles continually to the fore. He agreed entirely with this."[22]

So the CCF was caught in a squeeze play. The Communists kept up a steady barrage against the CCF on the left, hacking away at its policies, maligning its members, and decrying its refusal to join a popular front, while on the right the Liberals took the high ground, proposing the very kinds of policies that the CCF had been preaching for a decade. It was, said David, looking back in his memoirs, "an unholy alliance between the Liberals, who had no principles, and the Communists, who had no ethics."[23]

Part of the squeeze play involved the TLC, the more reactionary of
the two labour congresses. It invoked the Gompers tradition and gave
tentative but unmistakable support to the Liberals.[24] Here again, if
you went looking for it, was the hand of the Communists. TLC President Percy Bengough was a friend of Tim Buck — described by Buck
as a very close personal friend[25] — and in the powerful position of
TLC secretary-treasurer was Pat Sullivan, a member of the Communist
Party's central committee.[26]

It's always difficult to sell a message that sounds like a complaint,
and so it was for the CCF when it criticized what the Liberals and the
Communists were doing. As so often happens when there is squabbl-
ing on the left, voters shifted to the undemanding middle. Gallup polls
showed a steady increase for Liberals and a steady drop for the CCF,
with support for Tories staying in exactly the same place. A week before
the election, the Liberals had 40 percent of voter support; the Conservatives, 27 percent; and the CCF, 19 percent.[27]

The rest was history. It was the final metamorphosis for David and
the party.

However, trouble never walks alone. Rebuilding party support after
the election was undercut by two new developments: a drive by big
business against the left and the Cold War. Big business had been appalled at the vision of a new post-war industrial democracy painted by
the left during the latter years of the war and was determined to regain
its old supremacy. It turned on unions like a beleaguered bear on hounds.
With C.D. Howe as Liberal minister of reconstruction, wartime restrictions were being scrapped and the way was being cleared to reconvert
Canada to free enterprise. Strikes erupted across the country. Nominally
they were over the issue of wages, the fear of inflation, and the need for
international competitiveness. In reality they were a life-and-death struggle over the role that unions were going to play in society.

Three months after the 1945 election a blue-chip businessman laid
it on the line. He was Victor Drury, president and chairman of
Canadian Car & Foundry Co. Ltd. in Montreal and officer or director of a string of prominent companies — and father of Bud Drury,
president of the Treasury Board in the government of Pierre
Trudeau.[28] On August 31 he declared that, "The party is over. . . .
Not only will there not be enough jobs, but wages will have to be
brought down to former peace-time levels. If the employees won't take
a cut in wages, the plant will have to close down. We can't afford to
have our profits cut into by paying the high war-time wage levels."[29]

There was absolutely no way unions would agree to revert to pre-
war conditions and Drury undoubtedly knew it. When his message

was decoded, it translated as "The buggers have been having their way too long and it's time to show who's boss."

Hard on the heels of Drury's pronouncement came the 100-day strike at the Ford Motor Company of Canada, still the most important strike since the Second World War. Ten thousand workers marched out on September 12 and stayed out until December 20. Ford was determined to break the United Auto Workers, but in the end it failed and Mr. Justice Ivan Rand, appointed as arbitrator, established ground rules that were to revolutionize collective bargaining. However, as other unions fought doggedly to implement those rules, companies fought just as doggedly to escape them by crushing the unions they faced. The result was that 1946 turned into what would be the worst year for strikes for the next thirty years — until the mid-seventies when the country was struggling to adjust to the inflationary pressures introduced by the upsurge in world oil prices.[30]

So the CCF was left floundering, dispirited by the election, harassed from the left, and drained of union involvement by attacks from the right that forced unions to concentrate on their own personal defence. And then came the Cold War labelling as dangerous anything that was even vaguely left — and that put the CCF in quarantine. In the public mind it might not be diseased, but it had been in contact and so was suspect. Even without the debacle of the 1945 elections it would have been enough to convince the party to turn, snapping, on the Communists in an effort to free itself from false perceptions.[31]

Scare tactics were nothing new. In 1943 Fred Gardiner, the man who was to become Big Daddy, the first chairman of Metropolitan Toronto, then reeve of Forest Hill, was warning that "Socialistic rule in Canada would mean 'muscle men and gangsters,' who understand mob organization and the handling of machine guns, and they are already fomenting discontent in the belief that they will be commissars should the Karl Marx philosophy come to this country. . . ."[32] At the same time Ontario Liberals were claiming that: "If the CCF wins [the 1943 election] the light of democracy goes out in Ontario. . . . You give up the title of your farm, your business, your insurance, and you vote away your freedom for the regimentation of your life and that of your children."[33]

The difference in the late forties and early fifties was that more people were frightened. More people listened. And the scare rhetoric was even more frantic. By 1948 Dr. Watson Kirkconnell, president-elect of Acadia University in Nova Scotia, was conjuring up visions for audiences across Canada of Communist undercover agents, like plagues of locusts scrabbling to suck the life blood of democracies. They were

a fanatical fifth column of 12 million members, he told Toronto's
Canadian Club, and as a result the world was living "in an age fraught
with more immediate peril for more people than any since the dawn
of history."[34]

In this kind of scenario, socialists were pinkos and it mattered not
how fanciful this labelling was. It mattered not that from before the
time of the Red Terror socialists had battled Communists. The constant din of the Cold War — of the rhetoric of brinksmanship, of armies marking time, of patriotism ascending — pervaded everything,
like rain drumming on a tin roof.

Only three months before the 1945 election M.J. Coldwell, then the
party leader, indicated how remorseless the party would be in getting
rid of Communists. Writing to an official of the New Brunswick section of the CCF he said: " . . . if there are Communists boring from
within the CCF, they must be exposed and driven out, even if it means
wrecking the organization temporarily."[35]

In the trade union movement, that determination translated as usurp-
ing power where possible from Communists and, where it wasn't possible, destroying the union and replacing it with one sympathetic to
the CCF. (See Appendix M.)

Many of the campaigns against Communists succumbed to excesses.
For instance, the flimsiest of technicalities was used to boot the United
Electrical Workers out of the CCL. And the substitution of Hal Banks
and the goon-ridden Seafarers' International Union for the Canadian
Seamen's Union was an appalling chapter in the history of unions in
Canada.[36] The excesses can be explained in terms of frustration,
anger, and overreaction to the hysteria brought on by the the Cold
War — although the pros and cons of the methods used can be argued
interminably. However, the results had two important consequences
in the evolution of the party. First, the way was cleared to unite
mainstream labour behind the CCF, and that eventually led to the
creation of the New Democratic Party. Second, in some cases the struggle went on for so long, was so bitter, and became so all-consuming
that people were marked for the rest of their working lives, and when
the Waffle seemed on the verge of creating the same kind of disruption as the Communists, they reacted, as they eventually had with
the Communists, with no quarter. And that has left a mark on the
party from which it still suffers.

In that context, the campaign against the International Union of
Mine Mill and Smelter Workers stands out among all the others —
because it involved the Steelworkers and it was they who carried the
fight against the Waffle in the final days of that battle; because the

fight was so long and so dirty; because the consequences for the party were so drastic (it lost the heartland of its support in northern Ontario for the next twenty years, well beyond what Coldwell was contemplating when he talked about wrecking the party organization temporarily if necessary to get rid of Communists); because the party, including David, misread the North and misread Mine Mill so badly; and because it illustrated how intimately intertwined were personal ambition and ideology (the campaign against Mine Mill served extremely well Charlie Millard's determination to grab its jurisdiction for Steel).

In all the battles against Communists David was centrally involved. The difficulty is that so little of his involvement is recorded in writing. Despite the lack of documentation, however, it appears that David insisted on due process throughout. For example, in one instance that was documented, he disapproved of the way in which the Labour Relations Board stripped the Canadian Seamen's Union of its right to represent employees of a small shipping company. "That it is extremely desirable, in the present international situation to oust communist control from Canadian trade unions is obvious to every Canadian democrat," he wrote. "But whether it is wise to do so on grounds and by methods which are questionable in law and flimsy in fact, is another matter."[37]

It was characteristic of David to insist on due process, says Robin Sears, former national secretary of the NDP and currently principal secretary to Ontario leader Bob Rae. Son of a prominent journalist, grandson of Colin Cameron, one of the battling old men of the CCF's left wing, he has had more than his share of royal jelly. He is a gracious First Gentleman of the Bedchamber within the Emperor's Circle, or the EC, as Bob Rae's entourage is called by party members at Queen's Park. Like all political junkies, he arranges his knowledge by occurrences — the dates of campaigns and conventions, parliamentary votes, major events, and great debates. First he disarms, with his casual manner and seemingly ingenuous frankness, his boyish build and somewhat donnish good looks. His tie is loosened, his jacket off, his recollections flowing, his body language relaxed and proclaiming, "I'm enjoying this; you should too."

What he is, is an old hand. A political seducer whose strength is erudition, not guile; dialectics, not flattery.

He knew David from the time he was five or six years old. He served as assistant national secretary while David was party leader. David, he says, was meticulous — obsessively meticulous — in ensuring that no blemish stand against the party's record. That everything be done democratically. Legally. He was a "total loyalist," says Sears, "almost neurotically so."

> David had a very acute perception of the importance of making sure that what appeared in public about these enormously serious and difficult circumstances could not be held up to ridicule by either left or right, and revealed no more than was absolutely necessary about how painful the circumstances had been. And that, if examined subsequently by people who were enemies, would not reveal to someone in the near future another vulnerability which might be a future threat. That's why you find so little that's written by him that's critical. He was a working politician almost to the day he died and therefore he was keenly aware that whatever he said or wrote might subsequently be used against him or the party.

Undoubtedly Sears is right about David's protectiveness of the party. It's part of what makes it so difficult to track his actions through the final struggle with the Communists. The other part is that union leaders didn't want to commit their discussions to paper. As Ted Jolliffe explains:

> If [the CCL's A.R.] Mosher called [David] over to a meeting . . . to discuss a problem Mosher had with the Communists, there would be no record of it in the congress office or anywhere else. Mosher would be the last person in the world who would want to commit it to writing. That sort of thing very often happened. Union leaders in particular weren't very keen in putting on record the fact that they consulted somebody who wasn't even in the congress. Charlie Millard would go down to Ottawa . . . and the first person he would go to see would be David . . . and sometimes he would take David with him to Mosher's office.

Even before David began practising as a lawyer, Jolliffe says, labour leaders "frequently took advantage of his legal acumen. I know A.R. Mosher did. . . . One thing you have to understand about David, he was a great man to operate on the telephone . . . he was in touch with people in all provinces, in the labour movement and in the party." And in the struggle against Mine Mill, "David did most of this stuff by phone," Murray Cotterill says.

Over a period of more than twenty years, for instance, he was in touch with Charlie Millard almost daily, Jolliffe says. And in the years following 1950, while David was working as a lawyer in Toronto, Jolliffe could observe his daily schedules: "[Union leaders] were constantly running to us for advice, and particularly to David because he was good at that and they liked his strategic approaches. . . . Millard was not a good tactician. . . . [He] had a great drive for power, you know. He sometimes had to be a bit restrained. . . . That whole period, the forties, the fifties, and to some extent the sixties, was an organizing period. The labour movement was gaining in numbers. Not necessarily gaining in strength but they were certainly gaining in numbers. That took a lot of time and effort and a lot of sweat . . . endless battles before the labour board. David was very good at that. He was masterful."

David's emphasis on due process was more than just protectiveness of the party. It was bred into his bones. It was a hallmark of the Bund, which, even amid the excesses of 1917's revolutionary zeal and later during the Red Terror, clung passionately to a belief in democratic procedures, often at the peril of its members.

Nevertheless, attachment to due process didn't mean David would shy away from a frail reed as long as it met the criteria of being legal, at least minimally democratic, and effective in the battle against Communists. Sears explains in terms of the expulsion of the United Electrical Workers from the CCL. The union was kicked out for non-payment of per-capita tax even though the tax wasn't paid because of a clerical error and the UE tried to pay it once the error was brought to its attention.

The dilemma that party managers in those days were facing I have the greatest sympathy with [says Sears]. [W]hat the Communists typically did was to find an equally tangential kind of question with which to challenge the leadership and say, because you gave away so many pencils last year, the treasurer should be impeached. It had nothing to do with the fact that the treasurer was a right-wing sellout and that was really why they were challenging. So each side was using coded arguments to fight the other. . . .

I guess where I might have parted company with David and those who were most ferocious [would have been over the attitude] of my grandfather because he often defended . . . the Fourth International types, . . . on the ground that the party . . . and our democratic conviction [were strong enough] that we could permit this kind of thing and not take extreme, or excessively stern measures to deal with it. . . .

But my world is a much more civil and less threatened world than theirs was. We have all the power. Some pimply-faced Trot that wants to hand out leaflets that attack Bob Rae in our meeting is a nuisance. But they were dealing with the future of their movement. Sometimes the death of their comrades at the hands of Communism. . . .

[The grounds for expelling the UE] would be precisely the sort of manoeuvre that David would dream up. He was a master of that kind of procedural rug-pull and revelled in it. And among those who

respected and loved him, it was those types of procedural sleight of hand
. . . that gave him his reputation. . . .

Nevertheless, despite what Sears calls his ferocity toward Communists, David retained a sense of perspective, as witnessed this letter
to Oliver Hodges, organizational director for the CCF Trade Union
Committee in Ontario. The committee acted as a liaison between the
party and the trade union movement, with the objective of organizing support in unions that would neutralize the Communists.

> I do not think I have had the opportunity of mentioning at any length
> my concern at your concentration on the purely negative work of
> organizing anti-Communist factions in some of the unions. I am not
> saying this critically of you personally, because I know that it is the
> job which was assigned to you by the Committee. But I am certain that
> neither from the point of view of results nor from the point of view
> of your own interests, is it a good thing to concentrate on such work
> exclusively. If I were you, I would insist that the Committee review your
> functions and that you be given the opportunity to do a positive pro-
> CCF educational job in a trade union so that you can build something
> on a sound basis. I think the time has come for you to take a stand
> on this question and to think it out pretty clearly.[38]

In the campaign to take over Mine Mill it is next to impossible to
separate the Steelworkers and the CCF because most of the
Steelworkers involved in the struggle were also party members and
often party officials. In the beginning, most of Mine Mill's top people
also were CCFers and the signs that loyal CCFers in Mine Mill were
being misunderstood and alienated were there for all to see.

Mike Solski and Elmer McVey were two such loyalists. Both were
members of Sudbury's CCF Trade Union Committee. Solski was then
vice-president of Local 598 in Sudbury, the huge local covering the
operations of INCO and Falconbridge; McVey was the local's recording secretary and one of the North's CCF bluebloods. His father, Jack
McVey, had signed up for the party in 1932 before it had its founding
convention, and got his card directly from Woodsworth. Elmer still
has 1,941 application cards for people that his father had signed up
for the party by the early forties. His father also collected union cards
when Mine Mill was organizing INCO. "When the company goons
went in and broke up the union office looking for the membership
application cards [in 1942]," says Elmer, "one of the reasons they
couldn't find them [was because] they were in the filing cabinet of the
CPR station where my Dad worked.[39] The guys would come through

our back door . . . and give my mother the cards and then . . . she would put them in his lunch pail and I would carry his lunch down to the CPR station. . . . I did that for years. We got CCF cards as well. . . ."

Jack McVey was president of the CCF club for the federal riding in the early forties. Elmer looks much younger than his sixty-eight years. On a sweltering summer day in July 1988 he is wearing coral-coloured shorts, and sweat is trickling through chest hair that's barely turning white. He has the face of an ascetic, the body of an athlete, and the language of a hard-rock miner. He was never a Communist, nor was he ever a middle-of-the-roader: "My philosophy was socialist and that's where I belonged. I didn't belong in the Liberal Party or the Tories or the Communists or anywhere else. You can't be a fence-sitter, walk the goddammed fence like a Liberal does — you know, he's got legs twelve feet long to walk a ten-foot fence. It doesn't matter which side he falls on, he never scrapes his nuts."

However, loyal to the CCF as Solski and McVey were, their first loyalty was to their own union — as in February 1948 when they launched a bitter attack on Charlie Millard for accusing Mine Mill of being a safe haven for Communists fleeing the Taft-Hartley Act in the United States. The issue was incidental. What was at the root of the accusation and behind the harshness of the attack became apparent when Solski topped off his remarks with a swipe at the Steelworkers for suggesting to Mine Mill delegates attending a convention of the Ontario Federation of the CCL that they should "join a good union," namely the Steelworkers. Steel delegates claimed it was all said in jest, but their research director confirmed what was going on by saying everyone would be better off if Mine Mill merged with Steel.[40]

Solski and McVey were not unique. Thousands like them in Local 598 would attack their CCF colleagues from the South with unbridled fury if their union was reproached. Why? Why the intensity of the reaction?

What the CCF and the CCL leadership didn't grasp — or if they did they didn't acknowledge it — was that Mine Mill in Northern Ontario was not a Communist union. It was a radical union with its roots in the anarchism and syndicalism of the turn of the century. Mine Mill was a direct descendant of the Western Federation of Miners (WFM). Big Bill Haywood had been secretary-treasurer of the WFM and had brought it with him into the founding of the International Workers of the World — the Wobblies. He became general organizer and, as he had been in the WFM, the organization's dominant personality. In Canada, the first cousin to the Wobblies was One Big Union, which had an equally charismatic leader in Bobby Russell, the person who drew the heaviest sentence in the Winnipeg General Strike.

To understand the old Wobblies was to understand Mine Mill.

At the front of Mine Mill's handbook containing its constitution was a preamble, almost a replica of the preamble to the Wobblies' first constitution in 1905, that declared a defiant, militant radicalism:

> We hold that there is a class struggle in Society, and that this struggle is caused by economic conditions.
> We affirm the economic condition of the producer to be that he is exploited of the wealth which he produces, being allowed to retain barely sufficient for his elementary necessities.
> We hold that the class struggle will continue until the producer is recognized as the sole master of his product.
> We assert that the working class, and it alone, can and must achieve its own emancipation.
> We hold that an industrial union and the concerted political action of all wage workers is the only method of achieving this end.
> An injury to one is an injury to all. (See Appendix N.)

This was the credo of the miners and smeltermen who used to sing "The Ballad of Joe Hill" at their conventions. The ballad was their anthem just as much as "Solidarity Forever." Joe Hill was the Wobbly troubador, the Pete Seeger of his day, the writer of such songs as "Hallelujah I'm a Bum," "There Is Power in a Union," "Casey Jones — the Union Scab," and "Should I Ever Be a Soldier." He had been helping efforts to unionize copper when he was framed for murder, sentenced to death, and given the choice of execution by hanging or by firing squad. He chose the firing squad. U.S. President Woodrow Wilson pressed the Utah governor for leniency, as did the Swedish government. (Joe Hill was a Swedish immigrant to the United States; his original name was Joel Hägglund.) However, the governor refused. On the eve of his execution in November 1915 Joe Hill wired Big Bill Haywood: "DON'T MOURN FOR ME — ORGANIZE!" Twenty-three years later the song was written:

> "The Ballad of Joe Hill"
>
> I dreamed I saw Joe Hill last night,
> Alive as you and me.
> Says I, "But Joe you're ten years dead,"
> "I never died," says he. . . .
>
> "The copper bosses killed you, Joe,
> They shot you, Joe," says I.
> "Takes more than guns to kill a man,"
> Says Joe, "I didn't die,"
> Says Joe, "I didn't die."

And smiling there as big as life
And smiling with his eyes,
Joe says, "What they forgot to kill
Went on to organize,
Went on to organize."

"Joe Hill ain't dead," he says to me,
"Joe Hill ain't never died.
Where workingmen are out on strike
Joe Hill is at their side,
Joe Hill is at their side." . . .[41]

If you knew nothing else about Mine Mill in Sudbury but could feel the power of that song, you'd be a long way toward understanding the union. The men who sang it were Northerners. They were hard-rock miners working in the heat-drenched bowels of the Laurentian Shield who had little in common with and nothing good to say about, people from Toronto. They were men with the common experience of living through the bad days, the days when they were driven to exhaustion to meet quotas, when fear of being fired haunted every moment, when everyone was suspect because one out of every six or seven was a company informer — mucking (shovelling) tons of ore a shift, only to be fired if they didn't ante up the bottle of liquor the shift boss regularly expected; safety conditions so poor that rarely a week went by without someone being killed; going to work to find a dismissal notice clipped to their time cards, no reasons given; ventilation so bad that not even long underwear would soak up the sweat; sulphur gas so heavy in the Copper Cliff sintering plant that noses would bleed spontaneously; a shift boss at Frood Mine boasting that he liked to fire a man a day; 400 to 500 men hanging around the gates of the big mines looking for work with maybe one or two a day being hired; shift bosses removing safety measures to speed up production, like taking out grizzlies — the steel rails across ore chutes that prevented men from falling in — so that big pieces of ore could be dropped down the chutes without having to be broken up first.[42]

They were men in the spirit of the frontier, brawling in beverage rooms on Saturday nights, ripping a living out of solid rock with liner drills that left their ears forever ringing by their early twenties and deafness increasing by middle age, testing manhood in their teens lugging 100- to 150-pound timbers in stopes and tamping down dynamite, learning to step back from no one and nothing, proud of their union, proud of its past, hating Authority, distrustful of establishments, knowing mining companies wouldn't give them the spit from a dying dog, knowing they'd have to fight for anything they got — and now that times were better, now that their union had won them some dignity and decent wages, there was no goddam way outsiders, especially from the South, were going to tell them they had to get rid of a buddy who'd been through the bad times with them, who'd helped build the union with them, just because he was a Communist.

The power the song had in 1949 was demonstrated when radio station CHNO in Sudbury allowed Mine Mill to air a weekly fifteen-minute program only on condition that it never play a recording of the "Ballad of Joe Hill" sung by the great American bass, Paul Robeson.[43]

The Western Federation of Miners prevailed because it was tough, stubborn, and proud. In an era of violence those qualities served it well and provided a heritage that did the same for Mine Mill in its early organizing years. But they were qualities that didn't allow much room for bending, for compromise, for developing the political skills needed in a labour movement that was increasingly political, increasingly united, and increasingly ambitious.

At the turn of the century the WFM was pitted against mining companies from British Columbia to New Mexico, fighting for the eight-hour day. It was a brutal, violent struggle. Miners' homes were blown up. Strikers were shot. Families were evicted. Miners who supported the WFM were forcibly deported from their communities, leaving behind their homes, their wives, and their children. Organizers were beaten. Others were set upon by vigilantes and hanged. U.S. army units herded strikers into "bull pens," notorious stockades that held hundreds of men imprisoned without charge and without evidence of having committed any crime. Company spies and Pinkerton detectives were everywhere. At the same time, company equipment was dynamited. Mining tunnels were sabotaged. Scabs were beaten. Spies, when they were found, were manhandled.

Big Bill Haywood himself was framed on a murder charge following the assassination of Frank Steunenberg, former governor of Idaho, and was jailed eighteen months before his case was heard — and the charges dismissed.[44]

Not for Haywood, or for his miners, would there be the temporizing approach of a Samuel Gompers. In fact, Haywood detested Gompers and Gompers responded in kind. When mine owners blacklisted WFM miners, the American Federation of Labor (AFL) raised no protest.

When the Wobblies held their founding convention in June 1905, six months after Russia's Bloody Sunday, Haywood gave the opening speech, declaring, "We are here to confederate the workers of this country into a working class movement that shall have for its purpose the emancipation of the working class from the slave bondage of capitalism. . . . The aims and objects of this organization shall be to put the working class in possession of the economic power, the means of life, in control of the machinery of production and distribution, without regard to capitalist masters."[45]

Two and a half years later the WFM, under the increasing conservatism of its president, Charles Moyer, left the IWW with Moyer declaring that "if to be conservative means to stay out of prison, I am going to be conservative."[46]

While he led the WFM and during the years he dominated the IWW, Haywood had shaken a lumbering fist under the nose of the establishment. Fire us if you want, he said, but we'll damn well strike when *we* want. Term agreements, by which he meant collective agreements that committed unions not to strike while the agreement was in force, were wrong. "We have no right to enter into an agreement with the capitalist class," he said, " because it is the historic mission of the working class to overthrow the capitalist system. It is our only means of emancipation from wage slavery."[47]

The Wobblies set out to organize whole industries, not just trades, and dreamed of having power to enforce general strikes that could bring the country to its knees. They wanted to replace management and run the industries themselves. Eventually they wanted to do away with state governments and have a national congress composed of the different branches of industry.

The Wobblies had 200,000 members, and they confronted not only the owners and managers of industry; they confronted conventional unions. The Gompers unions. But they were doomed to failure. America was in no mood for a revolution. Even within the bulk of the union movement, there was no support. The Wobblies conducted many successful strikes, they put an end to many industrial evils — one company had gone so far as to sell its workers cocaine, heroin, and morphine in order to maintain a loyal, and addicted, work force[48] — and they won long-overdue rights for workers. But they were uncompromising and totally incompatible with the existing system. They bruised or bloodied anything in their path, and in the end they were beaten unconscious.

One of the main allegations against the Wobblies was that they were trying to create a government within a government. By 1917 the IWW was broken. By 1920 it was dying.

When the Western Federation of Miners abandoned the Wobblies, it returned to the mainstream of the U.S. labour movement. By 1916, when it changed its name to the International Union of Mine, Mill and Smelter Workers, it already had amended its constitution to reject Haywood's abhorrence of collective agreements, and it had rejoined Gompers's American Federation of Labor. However, the 1919 anti-Communist government raids in the United States spurred business and industry into a vigorous anti-labour drive, and that sapped Mine Mill's remaining energy. By 1926 it was drifting aimlessly, with only one full-time officer and little to sustain it but memories of its ginger days as the Western Federation of Miners. By 1933 it had only 1,500 members in six locals.

Three events revived Mine Mill. First of all, the United States under President Franklin Roosevelt passed the Wagner Act in June 1933 guaranteeing the right to collective bargaining, which gave union organizers protection. Then came John L. Lewis's Committee for Industrial Organization (CIO), created in 1935. Mine Mill was one of the founding unions and by 1938 it had recruited 50,000 members. At that point, with the inspiration of Lewis's success and the possibility of help from the U.S. union, the stage was set for Mine Mill's resurgence in Canada. All that was lacking was a better climate for organizing, and that came when Prime Minister Mackenzie King introduced National Selective Service in March 1942. One of the things it did was restrict the right of Canadian companies to fire workers as they pleased in an effort to make sure there was a stable work force for war industries. And that, coupled with a labour shortage that developed in 1942, meant that workers were much less afraid to join unions. What Mackenzie King had unwittingly created was a much more favourable climate for union organizing.[49] What it meant in particular is that Mine Mill organized INCO. A little more than a year later, the Sudbury local had become the largest in the international Mine Mill organization.[50]

Bob Carlin led the organizing drive. He had joined the Western Federation of Miners in 1916 and had worked in mines throughout Northern Ontario. Names like Big Bill Haywood and Slim Evans — the galvanizing Canadian organizer, a former Wobbly who led Mine Mill in establishing the union at Trail, B.C., in the late thirties and who had been the leader of the On-To-Ottawa Trek — were as familiar as his brother's. In short order Carlin was appointed Canadian representative on Mine Mill's international executive board and, in 1943, he was elected to Queen's Park as the CCF member for Sudbury. He won the election in a landslide with 15,169 votes to 7,582 for his nearest opponent, the Liberal candidate. He won again in the 1945 election, polling 13,627 votes against the Liberals' 7,552. It was the casting out of Carlin from the CCF in 1948 that ruined the party in the Sudbury basin for the next twenty years. The crime attributed to him was that he was soft on communism and would not take a firm stand against Communists within Mine Mill. In particular, he was accused of not co-operating in getting rid of Communist organizers in the gold fields, especially the ones that Charlie Millard and U.S. Senator Robert Taft had labelled as being driven out of the United States by the Taft-Hartley Act. No one accused Carlin himself of being a Communist. And indeed he was not, never had been, and never would be. His position was quite simple: Mine Mill had been built with the support of both Communists and CCFers, and he would not abandon Communist members. Mine Mill was more interested in being strong than in being politically affiliated, he said.

The fact was that Local 598, with 11,000 dues-paying members at that time,[51] contained relatively few Communists. Its executive committee from its inception in 1942 until Carlin's ouster was dominated by CCFers. More than half the members belonged to the party or supported it. On the other hand, the executive committee never had more than three Communists on it. From 1942 to 1944 there was one; in 1945, two; in 1946, none. In 1947 there were three; in 1948, two. At no time did a Communist hold one of the key offices of president, vice-president, financial secretary, or recording secretary. The size of the executive committee went from nine in 1942 to eleven in 1948.

Moreover, a count of men prominent in the local — members of the executive committee, sub-committee chairmen, delegates to conferences, and members of negotiating teams — shows there were only nineteen out of ninety-three men who were Communist, and three who were from sympathizing Finnish or Ukrainian organizations. Again, more than half were CCF party members or supporters, far and away outnumbering the Communists. Among eighteen committee chairmen, twelve were CCF; one was Communist.[52]

In Carlin's view, to give in to the CCF demands would be to betray the people who had helped him build the union, to undermine an organization that was much more than just a rein on INCO's worst excesses. Mine Mill was adding a whole new side to life — ironically as far as David was concerned — in much the same way that the Bund used to do in Russia.

In the old WFM tradition it was going beyond union business and involving itself in the cultural life of the community. It built union halls where the miners were — in Sudbury but also in Garson, Coniston, Creighton, and Chelmsford. It engaged in community help — an iron lung to the local hospital, a mobile therapy unit to the Canadian Arthritis and Rheumatism Society. It established a theatre group, the Haywood Players (named after Big Bill Haywood), that competed in drama festivals and in 1958 won the Quanta Region Dominion Drama Festival award for best direction. It ran ballet classes in the Sudbury union hall. It brought in entertainers such as Pete Seeger, The Travellers, Doc Williams, the Wheeling Jamboree, and the Barnard and Barry Circus. It bought property on nearby Richard Lake and established a large and very popular children's summer camp. It brought in Paul Robeson to sing. It would have brought in the Royal Winnipeg Ballet one year except that the U.S. State Department forced a cancellation by threatening to cancel performances scheduled in Washington if the company performed under Mine Mill auspices. It held dances, often several nights a week, and put on Saturday morning movies for children. It held track and field competitions and trained competitors. It sponsored senior athletic teams in hockey, basketball, fastball, and women's softball that won championships in Northern Ontario and sometimes nationally.

"I never regarded the ouster of Communists as the real problem," says Ted Jolliffe, then the Ontario CCF leader. "The problem was not so much Carlin and the Communists as it was the rivalry between Steel and Mine Mill. Steel was determined to take over and the argument they used was that too many people in the union were affiliated with Communists.

"Charlie Millard always took the position that if you're not with me, you're against me. It was a complicated situation."[53]

On April 13, 1948, Carlin was called before a special meeting of the full Ontario CCF executive plus the CCF legislative caucus to answer allegations that he was giving a bad name to the CCF and to labour in general by co-operating too closely with Communists. The two serious issues discussed at the meeting were his opposition to the Marshall Plan, which paralleled the position taken by the Communist Party, and his refusal to comply with a CCL request to support deportation of the Communist organizers sent up from the United States to help in organizing the gold fields. When Carlin refused to recant on both issues, the CCF executive council ruled that it would not endorse him in the upcoming provincial election.[54] He responded by running as an independent. The Conservative candidate won the riding by 8,892 votes to Carlin's 8,613, and the CCF candidate came in fourth with 5,861 votes.

There was outrage in Sudbury when the news flashed north that the executive council would no longer endorse Carlin as a candidate, and Einar Johnson (Johannson), secretary-treasurer of the Sudbury CCF club, sent a telegram to Toronto asking that a representative be sent to Sudbury to discuss the matter. The council responded by turning to David, giving him "wide discretionary powers" to once again handle a difficult situation. The day before the meeting it decided Professor George Grube should accompany him.⁵⁵

When he got off the 6:25 train in Sudbury on Sunday morning, May 2, David was met by Johnson, at thirty-seven two years younger than he was and with a solid streak of Swedish stubbornness. Johnson was to take David to his hotel room; but they hadn't left the station platform before they were at it, toe to toe, breath steaming in the cool dawn air, Johnson shaking a thick finger under David's nose, David with his jaw out, his eyes flashing, his voice clipped and cutting, a small knot of people still in their winter coats watching, the engine hissing steam like an out-of-breath bystander, snowbanks past the end of the platform a fretwork of icy remnants glistening in the rising sun. Part of the encounter was described by Johnson days before he died. The remainder is not hard to imagine.⁵⁶

> Johnson, his voice getting louder, is standing bullish in front of David:
> "You damn Toronto people, you think you know best."
> David unbudging, as always: "In this case we do."
> "To hell you do." The words are laced with anger. "This is wrong, what you're doing."
> "Listen to me, Einar, Bob won't stand up to the Communists."
> "So what! You got no business coming from Toronto telling us who's our candidate. Let things alone and he probably won't get nominated anyway. He drinks too much. People don't like that."
> "That's not the point. Drinking's not the point," David's voice rising too. "Don't you understand? Communists want to destroy the party. They want to destroy democracy. Carlin helps them."
> "You! What d'you know about democracy? Who made this big democratic decision? People in Sudbury? People who voted for him? No. You did. You big brains in Toronto. You . . . "
> "Rubbish." David's wave is short and irritated. "You know who made the decision, the Provincial Council made the decision and you're represented on the council."
> "Hah! Big deal. And who controls the council?"
> "You do if you get the votes."
> "Fat chance with Charlie Millard and all you guys there." Johnson makes "you guys" sound like dirty words.
> "Don't complain to me," David is pressing both hands to his own chest, "if you alienate the council. Don't complain to me," repeating the gesture, "when Mine Mill attacks the congress, attacks other unions, attacks party policies, attacks the Marshall Plan. Don't complain to me" — the gesture again — "that you're unhappy they don't want Bob Carlin. What in God's name d'you expect?"
> "Just don't tell me it's so democratic."
> "Don't tell me democracy is being irresponsible and destructive."

It was, said Einar Johnson thirty years later, one "big chewing match," and it was just a prelude to what was to come. Grube arrived on a later train that day and both attended the meeting in the old St. Anne's Hall. It was raucous. There must have been 1,500 people there, Elmer McVey remembers. Carlin loyalists accused Lewis forces of packing the meeting, and McVey tried to get new members disqualified. He said Lewis forces had scoured the town looking for people who had a grudge against Carlin and had even signed up some in a beer parlour the previous Friday night. He was ruled out of order.

Carlin loyalists said the club should nominate him anyway, and the provincial council be damned. David told them that even if Carlin was nominated, the CCF would never permit him to stand as a party candidate. Loyalists said that would destroy party support in Sudbury. David said he didn't care if it broke the Sudbury organization wide open; there would be no backing down.

"That was one of the roughest sessions I had seen for a long time," Eric Johannson, Einar's brother, recalled many years later.[57] In the end the meeting approved Carlin's suspension, and, "So," says McVey, "from that moment on, a helluva lot of people were very upset, particularly about the number of people who were brought in to vote because they knew the majority of people in Sudbury would have supported him [Carlin]."

After the election Carlin was expelled from the party for having run as an independent, and six others were suspended for helping him in the election. They were Mrs. Florence Riley, president of the Sudbury CCF Women's Council; Nels Thibault, president of Mine Mill Local 598; Elmer McVey, recording secretary of Local 598; Carl Nielsen, member of the Local 598 executive board; and Milan Pilja and Larry Jorgensen, prominent members of the local.[58]

Ted Jolliffe expected there would be an exodus after Carlin was expelled. "I was quite sure it would take a long time for the bitterness to subside . . . but I never anticipated the full extent [of the departure of party members]."

Even Jack McVey left, Elmer's father, probably the most dedicated CCFer in the Sudbury basin, and he never returned. Elmer subsequently rejoined the party, worked for the Sudbury CCF candidate in the 1953 federal election, ran himself in the 1959 provincial election, became a member of the provincial council, and then was elected to the provincial executive.

From the day of Carlin's expulsion membership plummetted and there were thousands of people who were party supporters although not formal party members and their support was wiped out too.[59]

After 1948 the CCF didn't win a federal or a provincial seat in the Sudbury basin until 1965 when Norm Fawcett won the federal riding of Nickel Belt. Then in 1967 Eli Martel won the new provincial riding of Sudbury East, and in 1971 the provincial ridings of Sudbury and Nickel Belt were won by Floyd Laughren and Bud Germa.

As for the Communists, they never were a force in area elections. On the three occasions that they ran between 1943 and the early 1970s, they came last twice and second last once. In the 1988 federal election Rhinoceros candidates won almost as high a percentage of the vote in several ridings as the Communists did in those days.[60]

Mike Solski, vice-president of Local 598, also left the party, eventually became a Liberal, and ran for election against Eli Martel in Sudbury East — and lost — in 1967. Born in October 1918, he still lives in the compact, two-storey home that once was his father's in the shadow of the two smokestacks of the Coniston Smelter, just half a mile away across the blackened, rounded rocks where he used to hunt rabbits as a boy, long since stripped bare of life by sulphur gas but now sprouting new growth — scrub trees whose twisting roots spread fierce clawholds that make Solski grin in a kind of perceived brotherhood. He still wears a dapper pencil-thin moustache, and when he unfolds his lanky six-foot-three frame he walks rhythmically, a little stiffly, making you think, absurd as it sounds, of a great blue heron. Making no excuse, he holds out a maimed right hand for you to shake, explaining only much later when asked, that he'd been shot ten years ago, when he was mayor of Coniston, by a deranged man who burst into the council chambers and shot him three times, failing to kill him only because an address book in a pocket over his heart stopped a bullet.

He was vice-president of Local 598 from 1948 to 1950 and then president until 1959 and he had no use for Carlin: "He was such a pain in the ass. . . . He would go to [international] board meetings in the United States and he would be drunk from the day he arrived. . . . He isn't the goddammed guy who organized INCO. He was the figurehead. He went into the hotels and bullshitted a whole pile of people and became the hero. Before he had a chance to do anything he went down to the States to attend board meetings. . . . The guy never negotiated a goddammed contract in his life, though his signature is on the first contract. I was on the first bargaining committee and I know what he did."

Nevertheless, Solski was loyal to Mine Mill and when that meant being loyal to Carlin, he was. When Carlin ran as an independent, "I was in charge of his campaign headquarters."

Ousting Carlin was the first step in the CCF-Steel-CCL strategy of getting rid of Mine Mill; the second was kicking Mine Mill out of the CCL; and the third was for Steel to raid Mine Mill and capture the right to represent INCO workers. Expelling Mine Mill from the CCL was accomplished in October 1949. First it was suspended for printing an article critical of Charlie Millard and Aaron Mosher of the Canadian Brotherhood of Railway Engineers. Then it was expelled for refusing to abandon locals in Timmins and Port Colborne until the CCL could sort out a dispute between Mine Mill and Steel. Once Mine Mill was out, the CCL authorized Millard and Steel to raid Mine Mill in the two areas.

The battle lines were now drawn. Mine Mill was outside the pale. Carlin was discredited. Attacks on the union's rich locals were approved, and the most vicious Red-baiting assault imaginable began. Outlandish newspaper attacks were published, senior U.S. government officials got involved, the Roman Catholic Church in Sudbury provided training, rooted in a virulent Cold War ideology, that was key to ousting the left-leaning Solski leadership of Local 598, and the Steelworkers kept hammering, hammering, hammering, until they finally defeated Mine Mill and took over representation of INCO workers. Both the Church and the Steelworkers, each for its own ends, condoned and profited from the smear campaign against Mine Mill. There were reasons to fight the union. But this was a dirty campaign and it dirtied all who supported it — publicly or privately. (See Appendix O.)

Solski and the old, WFM-styled leadership were ejected in March 1959, and three years later Steel succeeded in raiding Local 598, winning the workers' vote by fifteen ballots — 7,182 to 7,167.[61] Mine Mill, with the exception of the Falconbridge local, merged with Steel in August 1967. Don Gillis, who replaced Solski as president, ran as a Conservative in the federal riding of Nickel Belt in the 1962 election — and lost badly. The Liberal candidate received 16,440 votes to his 8,059 and more than doubled his margin of victory from the previous election.

The interesting thing is that by the end of 1956 Communists across Canada —and in Sudbury — were a spent force. Soviet Premier Nikita Khrushchev's revelations of Stalin's "wanton killings" were made public in February 1956[62] and disenchanted Canadian Communists began abandoning the party, leaving it, before long, the skeleton that it remains today. So the claim that Steel needed to take over Mine Mill to put an end to Communist control was even more insupportable.

During the 1950s and until his election to Parliament in 1962, David was practising labour law and Steel was a major client. Mike Solski cursed him for representing Steel in its successful takeover of Port Colborne — which, in view of the narrow success Steel had in Sudbury was a crucial test because winning Port Colborne established a momentum going into Sudbury.[63] And Ray Stevenson has bitter memories of him in Kirkland Lake in the early fifties.[64]

Wally Ross, who was working as an organizer for Steel in Elliot Lake in 1958-59, has vivid recollections of David's power in the kind of legal battles Steel faced. Ross and other Steelworkers were trying to get workers for Consolidated Denison to switch from Mine Mill. It was Mine Mill's last outpost in Ontario outside Sudbury, and Consolidated Denison was the biggest mine in Elliot Lake. The raid lasted a year. By June 1958 Steel had eighteen staff organizers working on it and by July there were thirty.[65] There were about 1,400 Denison employees living in bunkhouses at the mine, Ross says, and "It was very important to us that we [win]. I was in charge of the attempt to organize. . . . It was a steppingstone into Sudbury."

The company had banned Steelworkers from the area, which, says Ross, was quite large — about eight or nine miles around the perimeter. So they used to sneak onto the property at night and talk to men in the bunkhouses. He goes on:

> The company played right into our hands by arresting us. They took us to jail, which was a joke because the fine for trespassing was $10. . . . The company laid a total of 180 charges for trespass and the case came up in magistrate's court in Elliot Lake in the spring [of 1959].
>
> The problem was that there was no question but that we were guilty of trespassing and if we were found guilty, then the company would have had a better reason for asking for an injunction prohibiting us from going on the property to organize. If they got an injunction, then we would be guilty of contempt of court if we did trespass. So it was imperative [to prevent that].

In other words, the name of the game was to prevent the judge from making a decision on the trespass charges until after the workers' vote was held. Otherwise Steel could have been hamstrung in signing up workers.

> We got David as our counsel and he came up to Sudbury, and I picked him up there and drove him up to Elliot Lake. And he explained on the way that there was no way we could win the case but that he could cite a lot of precedents and hopefully delay the judgment. So on the appointed day of the trial, David put on a brilliant defence, which took up the entire day. There was really no argument about the facts. They had all kinds of evidence. They had our snowshoes, and when we were

handcuffed, sometimes we would saw off the handcuffs and take them back and throw them at the feet of company officials.

David's first citation was somewhere in the year 1300 and he traced the whole history of trespass law from then up to the Canadian and provincial statutes. There were lawyers there who came from Sudbury and Sault Ste Marie just to hear David Lewis. [David argued that the court had no jurisdiction to hear the case.[66]] At the end of the day he packed up and left.

That evening I ran into the magistrate . . . [who] happened to be a good friend who came from Manitoulin Island, where I came from. . . . He said he'd have to check the authorities David had cited in his arguments, but all his books were back in his law office in Gore Bay. And he said, "Unfortunately, I don't think I'll be able to render judgment before your vote."

And I said, "Well, that's all right."

And he said, "When do you think the vote will be?"

I said, "Well, it'll be by the end of August or the early part of September." This would be in April or May.

And he said, "I may be able to come down with a decision about the fifteenth of September. How does that sound?"

And I said, "That sounds just fine."

So, to complete the story, the vote was held right around the end of August and we won.[67]

Then came the trial. I was the first guy up . . . [and] I said I wanted a jury trial and a separate trial on every charge . . . and the magistrate said the equivalent of "For Christ's sake!"

Jury trials on every charge for every accused Steelworker would have taken months. They all settled, Ross says, for a fine of $1.

Seventeen years elapsed after those fateful 1945 elections until Steel finally won in Sudbury. During that time it was a pressure cooker inside Local 598. Steel was constantly trying to divide the membership. Loyalties became divided. Families split. Friends became enemies. Feuds developed and never were forgotten. Brawls erupted. Meetings became shouting matches. People were arrested. The Riot Act was read. And the Local never matured, never seemed able to get its affairs on a stable, workmanlike plane. Instead of having the opportunity to grow confident and outgoing, it turned inward and paranoid.

Elmer McVey puts it in more earthy language: " . . . it was get rid of this guy and get rid of that guy, so they kept getting smaller and smaller in their thinking until there was no place for them to go. It's like running around in circles until you run right up your own arse."

In the final days before the votes in Port Colborne and Sudbury, all the stops were pulled out. In May 1961 U.S. authorities reopened proceedings to declare Mine Mill "a Communist-infiltrated organization."[68] In September, George McClelland, RCMP director of security and intelligence, urged more support for Steel in its battle to help workers within Mine Mill "lift the yoke of communism off their backs."[69] Three weeks later Justice Minister Davie Fulton supported McClelland's comments.[70] In early October U.S. Secretary of Labor Arthur Goldberg, visiting Ottawa, declared that he hoped the Steelworkers would win over Mine Mill.[71]

There were many who believed David had orchestrated Goldberg's visit and his comments. The two knew each other well. Goldberg had been the Steelworkers' main lawyer in the United States. However, David's involvement was never established.

In November a U.S. Senate subcommittee on internal affairs decided it would be appropriate to investigate Mine Mill.[72] In December the Subversive Activities Control Board in the United States recommended that Mine Mill be declared a "Communist-infiltrated organization." (The recommendation was adopted in May 1962, two months after Steel had won in Sudbury.)[73] And federal and provincial governments gave unmistakable support to Steel just before the Sudbury vote.[74]

In the end, David had his dream. Communists were no longer a concern. Except for one or two instances, which were not particularly troubling, Communists had been driven out of the labour movement, or neutralized, and labour had sided with the CCF/NDP.

Charlie Millard's dream of expanding Steel was realized and — victors can be magnanimous — the Steelworkers hired on staff the principal Communists who were with Mine Mill, people like Ray Stevenson and Harvey Murphy.

And in Sudbury, with the battles over and divisions within the union ended, Steelworkers turned their attention to political organizing and three years later, Norm Fawcett won Nickel Belt riding for the NDP.

As for the NDP, it allowed itself the vindication that comes with victory and created a doxology in honour of its labours. There was to be no questioning the necessity of what had transpired. Without doubt, the party was stronger for the struggles it had gone through. But in rationalizing its actions in the name of necessity and power, it had stored its emotional reflexes without ever examining them or putting them on a leash.

Finally, for the workers it was an end to the frenzy of division.

At last they had a stable, businesslike union. But there was almost a total end to community involvement. There would be no summer camp for the children. No theatre group, no ballet classes, no great artists to bring in, no top-flight sports teams to support, no union halls other than the one in Sudbury. No circuses. No Saturday programs for children. No dances for teenagers. What they got instead were solid training programs within the Steelworker organization. The support of a large and powerful union. A return to the Canadian Labour Congress and to the mainstream of the labour movement. And for those who wanted it, a welcome back to the New Democratic Party.

"The Ballad of Joe Hill" they would sing no more. And in the NDP, especially among Steelworkers, the emotional reflexes that had been stored would return to haunt Stephen.

•CHAPTER NINETEEN•

It is man's duty to aim at performing acts that observe the proper mean, and not to desist from them by going to one extreme or the other.

Maimonides[1]

Who is Stephen Lewis, this man whom Dic Doyle, former editor of *The Globe and Mail*, once said "is the only person I've ever known that speaks in perfect paragraphs, with commas and semi-colons already in place"? This man that Alan Borovoy, head of the Canadian Civil Liberties Association, still calls by the nickname, "Jesus." This former ambassador to the United Nations, this socialist, who outraged official Washington with his attacks on the Heritage Foundation, the right-wing lobby group, for its anti-UN diatribes, saying it was guilty of "inspired sophistry" and of publishing "a steady stream of sleazy accusations"?[2] And then delighted that same Washington and electrified audiences across the United States with his speech in the General Assembly assailing the Soviet Union for its invasion of Afghanistan?

This is a man who as leader of the Ontario NDP was so commanding a figure that opposing politicians used to fill the chamber just to listen when he was scheduled to speak. Still the country's best living orator in a long tradition that extends from D'Arcy McGee through John Diefenbaker and Tommy Douglas. Who still is special adviser to the UN secretary general on African recovery, the most significant new undertaking of the United Nations since it launched into peacekeeping at Suez in 1956.

Who became Ontario party leader at age thirty. Who destroyed the Waffle. Who taught school in Africa. Who was there when the first black students, passing through crowds of half-berserk whites, walked up the steps of Little Rock Central High School in Little Rock,

Arkansas. Who flew into the Biafran War to check its horrors for himself. Who debated Senator John F. Kennedy when he was a student at the University of Toronto. Who, at age fifteen, was elected president of a model UN General Assembly, the first ever held in Toronto, staged in the Queen's Park legislative chambers, and at sixteen won a trip to the United Nations in a high school debating contest. Who was tasting his first political campaign when he was six years old and next to his brother Michael was probably the best organizer the NDP had. Who was so bright in public school that his school principal agreed he could stay home up to two days a week, otherwise he'd be bored stiff in class.

And what of the other side of this man who never graduated from university? Who quit as Ontario leader most abruptly? Who was entangled in the John Brown affair? Who at intervals drove his closest political associates to near-frenzy with his agonizing over whether he was doing the right thing in life? Who, after leaving active politics, vowed vehemently, sincerely, and repeatedly that he would never return — never, never, never — and for twelve years never once considered it, even remotely?

Who is he?

Does Stephen Lewis know?

It's the kind of inquiry that sits uncomfortably with Stephen. He offers no insights. Most of his youth he says he can't remember. When he first consented to be interviewed, he said the only reasons he agreed were that the book would deal with his father and it would look at roots. They, he says, are important.

He voices no objections to inquiries of this sort. He simply skates away from them. Gracefully. Lampooning himself.

Do they invade the boundaries of privacy? There's no denying they herald a journey into hurts and fears that most people would oppose. But should people in whom public trust has been vested be spared them? Equally pertinent, do such inquiries have any real use? Or do they simply open the door to impertinent or amateurish speculation?

In Stephen's case, if they are not raised, how is his departure from politics to be judged? It was a major event for him and a major setback for the party when he quit. He left abruptly, immediately after the 1977 Ontario election that saw the party bumped out of its position as official opposition. By Stephen's own admission it was his blundering that cost the party its standing, and he blundered because he was so distraught with his life in politics. With his going, the party in Ontario lapsed into disorder, despondency, and stagnation.

Two questions arise and, put in their most severe form, they are: "How could he allow his personal problems to afflict the party?" and, "Once the damage was done, how could he walk out, leaving others to pick up the pieces?" There have been harsh judgments made. Robin Sears, next to Bob Rae the top party figure in Ontario, says his quitting "was profoundly irresponsible" even though in the next breath he praises Stephen's accomplishments as leader. "I was reflecting on the impact on the party yesterday morning," he says — and he is speaking two months after the 1987 Ontario election. "I was walking in the front door [of Queen's Park] . . . finally returning to [official] opposition status again. The party went into ten years of turmoil, stagnation in some respects, decline from that night. We have only now begun to claw ourselves back up to a point that's even close to where we were. You can't lay it all at Stephen's door, although some do. It's not fair to do that. Part of it was circumstances and the times and other events. [But these] certainly were triggered by, and had a very unhelpful initiation from that decision [to quit]."

If judgments such as this are to be made, should not there be an effort to look beyond the simplistic arena of gladiatorial politics? To try, however tentatively, to understand the spider's web of impulse?

To enter the inquiry is to deal with paradoxes. Here is a man of vaulting ambition, supremely capable at anything he turns his determination to, so bright and so quick of mind that it staggers people, so outwardly confident that people have commented on it for all of his life. A compelling personality.

Yet here also is a driven man who as a boy had already chewed his fingernails into deformities painful to see. Here is a man forever restless, always excelling but for whom success rarely seemed satisfying. A person for whom good was never good enough and outstanding was only passable, who would drive himself to the brink of collapse in pursuit of the superlative. A person haunted by moral obligation; guilty that he could never do enough; tormented by sins of omission.

On the other hand, here is a man whose private passion is collecting children's books.

Judith Golden, who attended high school with Stephen, remembers that shortly before he was appointed ambassador to the United Nations in 1984, he was invited to read from his children's books at the annual convention of the Ontario Association of Marriage and Family Therapists, of which she is a member. "He was wonderful," she says. "He just sat and laughed and introduced his books and read from them and he loved it. I've never seen him so relaxed. I've never seen him just so comfortable . . . I couldn't believe it was the same person."

Which turns attention to Stephen's own childhood, remembered briefly by him during a 1976 CBC radio documentary while he still was leader of the opposition in the Ontario Legislature:

> The whole atmosphere at home was very strongly political. All of my growing up was immersed in the CCF. . . . I naturally, of course, was greatly swayed in everything I believe because of my upbringing, because of things discussed at the meal table and discussed when I got up in the morning and when I went to bed at night. And, therefore, my natural bent was toward politics. I have recollections of animated conversations at breakfast, lunch and dinner. I have recollections of famous politicians and people forever visiting the house. My parents are always making the point that there wasn't much pressure applied to any of us and I guess that must be true. . . . If we had been pressured, bullied, brainwashed, whatever the words are, presumably one or the other would have opted out and not become so political.[3]

A year and a half after saying that, Stephen Lewis opted out. Aged thirty-nine.

Is it trite to ask if he ever had time to be a child? To take the journeys of fancy that children take? He never wanted to be all the usual things young boys dream of. Was David such a compelling figure, so distantly perfect, that Stephen entertained no other fantasies than meeting or surpassing the exacting standards set by his father? "It won't be me, David, and it won't be you," Sophie proudly recalls M.J. Coldwell saying to David one evening when he was over to the Lewis home and young Stephen had climbed on his knee. "This is the one," he said, bouncing Stephen. "He'll be the one to be prime minister."[4]

Even the private name Sophie and David gave to Stephen, his Hebrew name, the name of endearment, had political reverberations. To them he was Sholem — from *shalom*, meaning "peace" — a reminder that he was born on Armistice Day.

Talking about his childhood in that same CBC documentary, Stephen expressed a strong sense of loss: "I spend all my time now compensating for what I consider to be childhood deprivation by making sure that my own kids are protected. I would want . . . to spend a lot more time with my family. My priority is definitely not the party. Maybe that is the kind of thing one shouldn't say publicly or otherwise. My priority is my family, period. . . . I regret what I feel were gaps in my own childhood. I am absolutely determined that they won't happen with my kids and, therefore, I am not as politically centred as David."[5]

Sophie, also interviewed in the documentary, remarked that "I can't remember one holiday when [David] was home, very simply because he was out somewhere in the country. Speaking, organizing, getting groups together, building. . . . When David came home, it was like Santa Claus arriving. Everything was ready. Everything was perfect.[6]

And Michael's recollection was that when David came home, "he would sort of be the good guy because he wasn't around so much to discipline us and therefore we were much more resentful towards Mom because she was always the one who guided us, the one who disciplined us."[7]

So David, when he was home, was celebrated. And when he wasn't there, his example, his vision, and his dreams were, all of them larger than life and all of them underscored by Sophie's pride.

And for seven years during the time when David was struggling to build the party — right up to that disastrous political year of 1945 — Stephen was an only child and for much of that time the only company his mother had. In her growing loneliness when Stephen was not quite two years old, Sophie would write to David, "Thank God for Sholemke, he keeps me busy and happy."[8]

Until Stephen was twelve years old, the Lewises lived in Ottawa's Lowertown on Friel Street, a block below Rideau Street toward the river, about seven blocks east of Parliament Hill, five blocks from what is now the farmer's market. Their upstairs flat was at the back of York Street Public School, a stolid three-storey, yellowish-brown brick institution with a cornerstone announcing that it was erected in 1921. It was a small flat — when the twins Janet and Nina were born, the landlord created a new room for them by cutting a doorway into an unused bedroom in the flat next door — and, except for all the books, sparsely furnished; so much so, in fact, that Maishe was forever fretting because his son, the lawyer, the brilliant Rhodes scholar, didn't have enough money to put a rug on the floor. Not only that, when Janet and Nina were babies there wasn't enough money for cribs. Sophie put them to bed in dresser drawers that she pulled out.[9]

It was strictly a working-class area. Next door lived a trucker who, much to Sophie's dismay, would rev up his truck at four or five in the morning before setting off for work. And often would arrive home at midnight with crates of geese or chickens, all of them, it seemed, honking and clucking their displeasure at being moved and stored in his henhouse in the back yard.[10]

There were three synagogues in the area — not that David or Sophie ever went to them — including what is now the Jewish Memorial Chapel on King Edward Avenue, two blocks away, where funeral services for David were held in 1981, a modest brick building erected in 1932, painted a brick red, with cream-coloured, Russian-like cupolas at the two front corners.

And for anyone walking past King Edward and looking ahead westwardly along York Street, there, rising at the far end of the street like a symbol of enduring aspiration, was the Parliamentary Library, still today the most noble building in all of Ottawa.

The Friel Street flat is no more. In its place, and that of the neighbouring houses, is a cheerless, grey, six-storey public housing apartment. Also gone are the Irish, Jewish, and French Lilliputian warriors who used to stalk each other across competing schoolyards; the Irish from St. Bridgit's elementary school, the Jewish from York Street Public School, and the French Canadian from Brébeuf, a Jesuit school. Brian Doyle recalls those days in a delightfully extravagant children's book called *Angel Square*, after the real Angelsea Square. It's a story of a mystery that gets solved by a boy named Tommy, otherwise known as The Shadow.

Doyle himself went to York Street Public School, a couple of years behind Stephen. "I was in a very small minority because I wasn't Jewish," he says. "York Street Public School was known as the Jewish school because 90 percent of the students were Jewish. By rights I should have been at St. Bridgit's, being Irish Catholic, but I guess my parents didn't want me proselytized."

In the book, taking minor liberties with geography, Doyle has Tommy saying:

> There are three schools in Angel Square.
> On the one side is The School of Brother Brébeuf where all the French Canadians go. But nobody calls them French Canadians. Everyone calls them Pea Soups.
> On the second side of Angel Square is York Street School where Sammy and I go. Most of the people who go to York Street School are Jewish. I'm not.
> I'm not anything.
> But nobody calls them Jewish. Everybody calls them Jews.
> On the third side of the square is St. Bridgit's School of the Bleeding Thorns where all the Irish Catholics go. But nobody calls them that. Everybody calls them Dogans.
> So four times a day most of the Pea Soups, Jews and Dogans try to get home or go to school. . . .

Getting home or to school was never easy. Tommy, writes Doyle, had to cross Angel Square to get to school:

> I watched the groups of Jews running for their lives across the square. Who was chasing them this time? It looked like a vicious gang of Dogans.

In the distance, away across the other side of Angel Square, a terrified gang of Pea Soups was scattering. Moving in on them was a very serious-looking bunch of Jews.

In another place on the square two Dogans had a Pea Soup down and were beating him with their hats.

Over there, two Jews were tying a Dogan to a post.

Over here, two Pea Soups were trying to tear off a Jew's arm.

Over there, three Jews and a Dogan were torturing a Pea Soup with bats.

In the centre some Pea Soups were burying alive a Dogan in a deep hole in the snow. . . .[11]

Michele knows *Angel Square*. "Magnificent. I loved that book," she says. But she never knew that Stephen had gone to York Street Public School. "Isn't that funny? Stephen never mentioned that to me." She pauses, and then adds, almost musing, "He's lost his whole childhood."

Fred Cogan of Ottawa went to school with Stephen and says, yes, making allowances for Doyle's exuberant exaggeration, the book catches the way it was: "It's kind of funny now, but when you were a kid it was scary. If they caught you alone in the park you were dead. Ten guys would jump you. Lowertown was interesting. When we weren't fighting the other groups, we'd be fighting with ourselves. We were on the streets all the time. I guess there wasn't anything else to do.

"But Stephen was never part of our gang. When we left school we went right and he went left."

Since Stephen lived right next door to the school, he didn't have to negotiate ambushes all the way home. But even so, he still didn't get involved with the other children. Cogan can't remember him ever playing in schoolyard games. Not even alleys — marbles, people call them now. He was bright and articulate, Cogan says; he just didn't seem to mix much with the other kids.

His Grade One teacher, Miss D.A. Gilhuly, described him as "a little perfectionist in everything he did. He took great pride in his printing. He was a real little gentleman. He was immaculate in his dress. He spoke just as articulately as he does today. . . .

"He certainly was a teacher's delight. He was so polite I sometimes wondered whether he really enjoyed school, since he was almost too perfect. He seemed almost like a little adult."[12]

This is the boy who, at three years of age, was reading.[13] It's also the three-year-old boy Fay Ain, Sophie's childhood friend from Montreal, remembers with a proprietary admiration: "I used to come to the Lewis household and Sophie used to stand Stephen up on a chair or on a little table and she'd say to him, 'Now talk. Go ahead,' and he'd spill out speeches. He comes by it very naturally."

The little speeches — they could go on for fifteen or twenty minutes — would be, of course, political. And they'd make sense. But then Fay says what he'd be doing would be talking about what he'd heard David saying. Or, adds her husband Joe, "whatever Sophie talked about. I'm sure Sophie practised with him."

This again is the boy who, at six, participated in his first election campaign, accompanying his father around Cartier in his struggle against Fred Rose, Lazarus Phillips, and Paul Massé.[14]

Mostly what people remember about Stephen in his public school years is that he loved to talk. "But conversation had to have a point. There was no use talking trivia," says Saul Gunner, a doctor with the federal department of health in Ottawa. Gunner was in Stephen's class. "What I recall," he says, "is that even in those early days he was the most articulate among us. He had that enunciation that is characteristic even in his speech today. . . .

"I'll never forget once we had to do a project . . . where the kids were asked to get up in front of the class and we all picked some kind of subject. But Stephen picked something that was really esoteric. It was a learned dissertation on Audubon, the bird man. . . . He was really well versed on what Audubon had done and on his contribution. It was marvellous."

Gunner had his battles getting across "Angel Square." But, again, Stephen was never part of them — or of much else that was going on:

> We used to play baseball and soccer and things like that. I'd be out there every day when I was that age playing baseball, but I don't recall seeing him somehow. . . . [What I do recall] is that he played the piano . . . [because] you see, in those days I played the violin. . . . I wasn't bad, actually. I'm a part-time musician now. . . . It's my therapy.
>
> If my memory serves me correctly, I think he played a decent piano. But then again, you would have expected that anything he would have done would have been at a certain level of competence.

Indeed he did play a decent piano. He performed often with the Ottawa Junior Music Club, receiving complimentary comments in *The Ottawa Journal* and *The Evening Citizen* for his imagination and expression and "excellent control" and, in one clipping that he presented to David made up as a Father's Day card in 1946, for displaying "great promise and exceptional talent."[15]

All the Lewis children played the piano, but Janet says Stephen "was the most musical of the bunch, a really fine pianist." Stephen, however, sees his musical talent in a more modest light: "People tend to exaggerate. I was all right. I could have been maybe a good accompanist but never a serious concert pianist. For example, I didn't read music well. I had to work terribly, terribly hard at it. I had none of the natural affinities. I couldn't play by ear. I think those are things that most serious people are able to do. . . . I just played not badly. But I remember with great joy the music lessons which were the centre of my life for several years."

The piano was an old upright and, says Janet, "We all played it from the age of about five. There was a lot of practising, a lot of talking about it, a lot of listening to classical music."

When the family moved to Toronto, Stephen and the twins studied with Boris Berlin at the Royal Conservatory of Music. Berlin remembers the twins much more vividly than Stephen, describing them as very conscientious. Janet obtained her Grade Eight diploma and her Grade Two in theory from the Conservatory. Of Stephen his memory is only that he was "quite musical . . . but being able to practise is something else." He disagrees with Stephen's assessment of what skills a serious musician needs. The most important thing that a good musician requires, he says, "is six to seven hours of practice a day," and that, Stephen was not prepared to do. He dropped his musical studies when he was sixteen years old.

Gordon Shore, well into his seventies now, still working as a furrier, comes around a cutting table in his shop in downtown Ottawa, his shoulders slightly stooped from so many years working over garments, gesturing to a chair and saying oh yes, of course he remembers Stephen. He settles into another chair and with fondness tells of all those evenings in the late forties, after he had returned from the war and lived next door to the Lewises, when he and Stephen used to sit on the front steps after supper watching the day decline and talking politics. He was a Liberal. "We were always Liberal, my father and his father. And me." Stephen, he says, "was quiet. He'd rather sit and talk than maybe run around playing ball. . . . Whenever he said something, it had meaning to it. He didn't say anything just to talk, you know. . . . And you know, I never could get the best of him."

The Lewises were special, he says, and there's still a touch of wonder in his voice when he tells of the day when the secretary of the British Labour Party came to see David at home and rolled up "in a big limousine. Right there on Friel Street. Right in front of us!"

It was in July 1950 that the family moved to Toronto — and David was heavily in debt. Not only had he bought a house in Toronto, at 95 Burnside Drive, a quiet lower-middle-class street near Bathurst Street and St. Clair Avenue — "The guy across the street was an electrician. The guy beside us owned a fast food diner. The guy on the other side, a clothing store," says Janet — but he was bringing with him what remained of the crushing medical bills that had accumulated during the past several years. Maishe had died in February and, in addition to his long illness, there had been his mother's illnesses and Sophie's difficult pregnancies. (Thanks to a "benevolent fund" raised by party treasurer Sandy Nicholson, most of the medical bills relating to the pulmonary embolism that almost killed Sophie two summers previously had been paid.[16]) After Maishe's death David's mother moved to Ottawa to live with Doris and her family.

It would take several years, most of Stephen's high school years, before they could breathe easily, even though David made so much money practising law that after his first year the income tax he paid was twice his annual salary as the party's national secretary.[17]

At the time of the move, the twins were going on two years old and Michael was five and a half, a gentle, affectionate child. "I remember him as a little fellow playing when the family was in Ottawa, says his aunt Doris, "and as soon as the other kids would start fighting, he would step on the verandah and just stand back and watch them. He didn't like the noise. He didn't like the roughness."

"Soft." That's what Fay Ain still calls him today in the English translation that doesn't quite fit the Yiddish. It's the same word that was applied to his grandfather, Maishe. "Very soft," she says — very good-hearted, *un homme doux extraordinaire*. After the difficulties Sophie had with a headstrong Stephen, Michael was a dream, as she wrote David in August 1948, when Michael was three and a half and she was almost six months pregnant with the twins: "I am sitting out on the front balcony and listening to Michael's chatter with Sandy. He's a little darling and everyone who passes greets him with such warmth. He is really very little bother and hasn't been much worry during the night."

Between the lines there is a sense of ease that's missing when, in the same letter, she spoke of Stephen who, she said, "is not behaving too badly. He gets his spells as you know but on the whole I can't complain."

Nevertheless, it wasn't an easy childhood for Michael, growing up with a brother of Stephen's accomplishments on the one side, Stephen who by the time he had moved to Toronto was taking on his father heatedly in arguments and calling him David to boot — not Dad or Father . . . David — obviously the favourite son even though he and later the twins protested that it wasn't fair to Michael. And on the other side twin sisters, adorable as only infant girls can be, and one of them — Janet — just as bright as Stephen. In fact today it is Janet, not Stephen, who is most likened to David by close family friends for her penetrating logic.

She operates a labour arbitration firm and shares office space with the law firm of Sack, Charney, Goldblatt and Mitchell in Toronto. Her firm is called MS Consultants — "My former partner was Macdonald, so it was Macdonald and Solberg [Janet's married name], but it was also an all-female firm, so there was the Ms connotation." She sits as a labour nominee on arbitration boards.

> She's very bright [says Gerry Charney, a senior partner in the law firm]. She's got an absolutely first-class mind . . . I think she has a better legal mind than Stephen has. . . . I don't think she's as good with people. I don't think she's as good at compromising. A lot of things Stephen understands instinctively that Janet doesn't. But I think in the strict sense of logic and a legal mind that Janet would be a great lawyer. . . .
>
> She's extremely good. She doesn't have the extraordinary influence Stephen had [when he was doing the same thing prior to being appointed to the United Nations], because Stephen was able to get things that no one else ever got. But she's the equivalent of the very good lawyers on management side, even though she hasn't been train- ed as a lawyer. She's very, very smart. And she's persuasive. And creative. And you know, she's a tough person.

She's a briefer version of David, more to the angular as he was in his Oxford days, more to the ordered, not tending to the baroque like Sophie, smaller than both, straightforward, dwarfed by the boardroom table at MS Consultants. She is the one who tends the family pathways, making the telephone calls, maintaining the contact, watch- ing over Sophie now that she is incapacitated. Even the sound of her voice is more angular than round, and her words carry David's familiar inflections and have that same arching simplicity — unadorned and inevitable and symmetrical. "People say Stephen is David," Sophie once said in a 1971 interview, "but Janet is David. Stephen is his mother."[18]

In one respect at least, Sophie is right and that's in Stephen's use of language. He has her feel for words. Except he goes beyond, play- ing with them as with those hard, rubbery-plastic balls for children that bounce unpredictably, always higher, always farther than you ex- pect. Of Janet's similarity to David, Stephen says, "It's like transference. I just love it. Janet has his mind. His voice. . . . The intellectual rigour is what Janet inherited. I still don't have it. I know my own strengths and weaknesses . . . but that cutting through to the core, seeing instantly what the issue is and going for it, that's Janet. I sit and talk to Janet and I think, 'Jesus Christ, he's alive. He is incarnate.'"

Each of the twins had a special name, "Itie" for Janet — from Etkeh, the Yiddish of her name, and "Nuchell" for Nina from Ninotchka, which she was dubbed by a Russian woman who helped out while Sophie was not well following the birth of the twins. Michael never had a special name. His Yiddish name is Mordecai, "but we never got around to calling him anything but Mikey," says Janet, whose childhood memories of him are dear. "I remember vividly we didn't have a dining room set, so there was a big empty room, or a room with very little furniture, and it became the playroom. . . . I remember playing with Michael. He was really a very gentle older brother and he would read to us. He taught us how to read; he taught us how to write; he taught us how to do our numbers. [I guess] it was because he liked to be a teacher and these two cute little twins would sit there and lap it up."

The two girls loved sports, playing ball-hockey and baseball on the street, touch football on the lawn, and "taking a tennis racket and banging balls against the wall" at Hillcrest Public School on the other side of Bathurst Street from their home. A former gym teacher remembers that they were the first girls on boys' teams in the city, playing baseball and soccer. When they reached Grades Seven and Eight, and then in high school, they played girls' basketball and volleyball and entered track meets in Christie Pits.

Stephen, who played no sports in Ottawa, went out for football in high school and was quarterback of the Harbord Collegiate team for three years. He spent his first year of high school at Oakwood Collegiate, where classmates remembered him as "a little skinny guy who looked as if he had jaundice."[19] He switched to Harbord in the middle of Grade Ten and went out for football the following year. "My mother claims Stephen took up football because he didn't want to be seen as just an egghead," says Janet. "Actually, he was quite a good athlete."

Maybe so. But Harbord never won a game. Ray Stancer was a high school friend and, as it turned out, an actor of some talent at the University of Toronto. Now a lawyer in North Toronto, he is sheep-dog hairy with a full beard and moustache, a tousled head of hair from which it seems not a strand has gone missing, and bushy eyebrows — all of them grey. Crevices for laugh lines radiate out from the corners of his eyes. He lolls in the leather swivel chair behind his desk, compact in the way middle-aged men are who stop short of being portly, remembering Stephen's great moment in football. "He not only was the quarterback, he was the punt return man . . . and I think in those days he was about twelve pounds soaking wet." Stephen of the matchstick legs, he calls him. "There was an exhibition game at Varsity Stadium for the Red Feather campaign, Community Chest it was called in those days . . . and we elected to receive. So the ball was kicked off, he caught it, ran up the field, was tackled, a bunch of guys piled on, and when they got off Lewis was still lying there. A stretcher comes out, he disappears, and that was it for the game." He laughs uproariously. "He wasn't a great athlete. I don't think he had the size for basketball or the heft for football. But he was *very* gung ho."

For Michael it was music — music and the Oakwood Collegiate newspaper. He wasn't interested in sports; his classmates remember him as "unathletic," and until he was in Grade Eleven he was "very small." When he is asked about high school, the memory that comes most quickly to mind is of organizing students to protest compulsory cadet training — and it was ended. The memory still warms him. But he was bored with school. Paradoxically, school was not enough and too much at the same time. Not enough because the horizons it offered he found uninspiring; too much because he needed help to broaden them but never got it.

Florence Silver was his best friend. They co-edited the school newspaper — and wrote the stories for it at the Lewises' "because Michael had the typewriter." Now a stylish and self-confident woman, a mixture of warmth and practicality, living in a renovated home, all beige and fabric and half-hidden spaces in Toronto's fashionable Moore Park, she is a former public school principal, currently administrative assistant to North York's Superintendent of Community and Adminstrative Services.

Michael didn't feel like a brilliant student and he didn't feel particularly successful. He felt that if you were really bright it would be okay. But he said he struggled and he didn't get the support from teachers that he was looking for. Not that he was a poor student. He wasn't. . . . I found him bright. I found him interesting to talk to because he knew things that none of the rest of us knew. . . .

I'm an educator now and I have a sense that we can do a much better job with students like Michael. We don't expect the same from everybody.

He was very articulate. I remember him arguing very well with some teachers. His political sense was much more sophisticated than mine, and it got in the way of him accepting some of the stuff that we got from the teachers. . . . If I were looking at that class today, I'd say Michael should have done better because he challenged. Showed some original thinking and some sense. But that wasn't rewarded in the fifties and sixties in our school.

Where Michael shone was in the school orchestra. Oakwood had then, and still does have, one of the top orchestras in the province. He played the oboe and, says Silver, he played it well. "You had to be good to play in the orchestra because if you were a wind player [there were so many that] they had lots of choices. Everybody got to play in the band. But only the best got to play in the orchestra."

Silver, at the time she was interviewed in January of 1989, was chairperson of Toronto Workshop Productions, one of the more prominent theatre groups in Toronto although immersed in problems and closed for the season. And on the board was Michael. He had been recruited about a year earlier by the artistic director who met him while "trying to get some money out of the Steelworkers to support a play." He's "an extremely astute board member," says Silver. He has a way of taking complex issues and boiling them down and putting on the table a reasonable solution. We on the board have been in turmoil, financial problems and political problems and infighting, and his skills as a negotiator and as a peacemaker, and his wisdom, are very evident. He's very valuable. . . . Without a doubt, everyone on the board, no matter what side, the right or the left, has valued him. . . . He's wonderful."

Time and again such references to Michael call his grandfather to mind. This ability to mediate, even though he has no knowledge of theatre and no financial expertise to speak of, to alienate no one, and to win the attachment and often the affection of opposing sides, is exactly what Maishe is remembered for.

What made Michael very special for Silver while she was in high school with him was that "he cared about things that are important. He cared about people. He talked about issues. He didn't care about all the things our friends in school cared about, which were cars and going out and having parties and getting drunk and the other girls with fancy clothes and jewellery. Michael was understated. . . ." As for what he would be most proud of, "I would have said it was his music."

When Stephen was at York Street Public School in Ottawa, Sophie says she used to let him stay home when he wanted to as long as he maintained an A average. Many weeks he went to school only three days a week. The principal, she says, agreed with the arrangement; in fact he initiated it by writing to David and Sophie expressing concern that Stephen was finding school boring. When he was at home

Stephen spent most of his time reading or practising the piano or cover-ing the schoolwork that was being taught in class.

The other children had the same opportunity to stay home while they were at Hillcrest Public School. Their report cards show that, not counting the time they were taken out of school by their parents to participate in election campaigns, about two-thirds of the time they missed an average of about a day a week of classes, and for the other third about a day every two weeks. Michael had a more normal report card, missing about a day a month.

Many times my mother would come to the bedroom and say, "Are you kids going to school today?" And you'd say, "No, I don't think so. Not today." [Janet laughs delightedly at the memory.] You know, you'd want to play or practise the piano. . . . Certainly during election periods it would be five days a week that we'd be away. . . . The first campaign I ever worked in — and I mean worked in: our parents took us out of school and we worked full time — I guess I was nine. It may have even started a bit earlier than that.

[We would be] stuffing envelopes, walking door to door distributing leaflets. When you got a little older, so the handwriting wouldn't look too childish, addressing envelopes. Looking up phone numbers in the days when we used to phone that way.

It was weeks and weeks at a time. And there'd often be two or three elections in a year and we'd be pulled out each time for the full time. It was great. It was a whole new education. . . .

[Attending school] was optional all the way until the end of high school. . . . I'll be frank about it, I remember most of the time going to school only because there'd be a great soccer game at lunch. Or at recess. And that was a really nice place to see my friends and to play. It wasn't because I enjoyed going to school, because none of us did that.

Nina was different from Janet in that she found technical subjects, especially mathematics, difficult. "Unlike Janet who avoided school because she was bored and for whom nothing was difficult, I avoided school because I was bored and everything was difficult," Nina says. "School was just a torment for me. It was the greatest delight in the world when I could stay home. My parents were desperate and [in high school] they used to drive me to school. I used to go in the front door and then walk out and go to a shopping centre and read for the entire day." There was a seemingly endless line of tutors until she passed Grade Twelve and left. It wasn't until she went to Simon Fraser Univer-sity after working for a year that she discovered how enjoyable schooling could be "because I was allowed to read on my own and to think and talk." However, she left after two years to get married.

For Michael, there was always Stephen's long shadow. At music, at public speaking, he was good but Stephen had always been better. When he was thirteen and in Grade Eight, Michael won his school's public-speaking contest and placed fifth in the Metro Toronto regional semi-finals. And at graduation he was school valedictorian.

That same school year Stephen had debated with John F. Kennedy at the University of Toronto. Three years earlier, he had graduated from Harbord Collegiate with the first-place public-speaking award for Metro Toronto. Earlier in the year he had been elected president of a model United Nations General Assembly held in the Queen's Park legislative chamber which had delegates from each of twenty-four public and private high schools in the Metro area. And the year before that, he had won a trip to New York to visit the United Nations for being one of four to win a public-speaking contest.[20]

Throughout high school Stephen was a voracious reader. "He loved history," says Ray Stancer. "Absolutely adored it. I can't name the specific titles, but he just loved volumes on people like Napoleon. That's one thing I remember him reading. Every time I'd go over to his house, there was always a new book. Always." And, since he was Stephen's closest companion at the time, he was always over at Stephen's house.

When Stephen transferred to Harbord Collegiate from Oakwood he came as an unknown and made no immediate impact — which may explain in part why he went out for football when he entered Grade Eleven. Judith Golden was in the same year as Stephen, but she didn't even know he was there until he went after the presidency of the Students' Council in Grade Twelve. "It's interesting to me [now] because I was president of the Girls' Club and I was really involved in the school. I knew everybody and everybody knew me, and I didn't know Stephen."

Although her comment about knowing everyone and everyone knowing her looks imperious in print, in conversation it's not. There's a gentleness to bar such thoughts. No doubt she knows it; she is, after all, a therapist. And no doubt she knows she can weave a spell with her voice, a delicate web of intonation, dropping subtly when she wishes to make a point so that you find yourself straining forward lest it waft out of reach too soon. She sits so still — straight-backed, hands in lap — that what she is saying replaces all else in the room.

Harbord had a class that was called Form A in each year which, in Golden's words, was the "brain form." She was in it. Stephen wasn't. She also was a member of the Students' Council in Grades Eleven, Twelve, and Thirteen.

In Grade Twelve Stephen decided he wanted to be president of the Students' Council. "[He] had never served on the Students' Council," says Ray Stancer. "He just decided that he wanted to be president. So he ran and he won and I'll never forget his [campaign] speech. . . . He talked about taking the wheel of education and sending it spinning. It was a wonderful metaphor. But, of course, the Students' Council had no power whatsoever. I mean, it ran dances. That was it. And the fact that anyone thought that they could [send the wheel spinning] was extraordinary."

The person whom Stephen defeated in the election had spent years on the council, had worked his way up to vice-president, and was in line to become president. It displeased a lot of students that Stephen should suddenly make a lunge for the office, and one of those people was Gerry Caplan, a year behind Stephen. "I voted against him," he says. "I thought he was very pretentious. I thought he was very excessive."

So did Judith Golden, who was elected secretary of the council in the same election with Stephen.

> After the election I told him how dismayed I was. That he had taken the presidency away from [the person she thought had earned it] who was devastated.
> He won it because of the way he spoke . . . he was quite an electric speaker. Nobody had heard anything like that before at our school. . . .
> [But it turned out that] I liked him because as soon as I told him how angry I was at him . . . his answer to me was, "I understand why you're so angry at me and I like your loyalty to [his opponent]. Please just give me a chance.". . .
> I'm a sucker for that. There was no defensiveness on his part. And I mattered to him and I liked that. I think people do matter to him. . . . I don't think I ever heard him bad-mouthing or talking down to other people.

The picture of Stephen that fellow students at high school paint is of a person who did not fit easily into larger social groups; who, at that time of life when everyone, as Judith Golden says, was "gooky and gawky," was "skinny and pimply" and perhaps gawkier than most; who had difficulty developing friendships but who inspired great respect and loyalty among a relative few who, as he did, loved to talk about bigger things. "There wasn't a joining with Stephen," says Golden. "Stephen was different. Old before his time. . . . There wasn't a way of being just plain friends or one of the guys with him. He was always tense, sharp, somewhat arrogant." And by sharp she means "fast. You know the way he is. A wonderful skill. In high school it was a way to set yourself apart."

At home, his relationship with David was, in Janet's word, "tempestuous." But it was tempestuous at a political level, with Stephen arguing fiercely with his father over issues such as whether Canada should be in the North Atlantic Treaty Organization. (Stephen argued no. Now, says Janet, he thinks it has value as a multilateral forum for discussion on any range of issues, and the irony is that he was one of the people who originally pushed to get the anti-NATO position into the NDP policy books.)

Today Stephen can chuckle about the constant intellectual grappling with his father that went on right up to David's death. "The relationship that we had over the years, and in particular over the last years, . . . was that we would fight like tigers over issues and and I would yell and scream and call him an old fogey and a socialist of another generation and a man who hadn't thought a new thought in twenty-five years, et cetera, all the time choking inside that the son of a bitch understood so much better than I did what was involved."

Michael also saw in his father an impatience with any argument he thought was not well based. "He'd say to us as a group or as an individual, 'Cut it out.' That was one of his favourite phrases. Or, 'That's nonsense,' and then give you a very logical explanation. Usually you knew in your heart he was right, but it would bother you and you would feel sort of angry and humiliated and frustrated because you knew he was right; but by Jesus, you know, you had a right to be irrational and see things differently."

But the frustration was not all one way. Stephen could make life just as difficult for David. He was furious when David bought a cottage at Jackson's Point on Lake Simcoe. During their early years in Toronto, David and Sophie rented a cottage for the summer at Jackson's Point, and nearby there was a cottage, vacant and tattered with neglect. The twins called it the haunted house. It belonged to a doctor who had built it for his wife; when she died, he had stopped using it. When Sophie explored it one summer with the two girls she immediately saw its possibilities and once the doctor learned of her interest, he sold it to David, "for a song." It was Stephen's last year of high school. "He was apoplectic," says Owen Shime. "This was an extravagance that was unworthy of a socialist. Stephen was really indignant and he attacked David."

David already was embarrassed over the amount of money he was making as a lawyer, and Stephen knew it;[21] so no doubt he twisted the blade and no doubt David did his own internal fuming.

In those days, says Shime, Stephen was a utopian socialist, but he uses the term to mean someone idealistically searching for a new age, not in the traditional sense as it was coined by Marx to refer to the early nineteenth-century activists who wanted to ban all private property but who had no concept of class struggle or the materialist interpretation of history that Marx was to introduce. There's no disputing that Stephen was more doctrinaire then than now, but the inner core of anger that so characterized David to this day still burns within Stephen with an intensity that turns his language uncharacteristically ripe: "I think one of the nice things I've inherited from David," he says, "is that same sense that the way this goddammed world works is fucking awful. . . . What sustained him was not merely a vision of a better society but an outrage with present society which was fearsome and unrelenting. It was extraordinary."

On the other side of David's anger, Michael found a "warmth and sensitivity. . . . I guess what I remember most about my Dad are the times we walked down the street together discussing a matter of particular concern. . . . We did it very seldom. I remember those chats, I guess because he was away so much. There was so little opportunity, in a way, to be close, to be like an ordinary family. So little opportunity to be alone with him. . . . So the memory of those few minutes with him walking down the street, having a very personal, close discussion. . .are what stick in my mind. I always found them so useful and so loving."

And even when David's logic was most unrelenting, Stephen discovered it was rooted in caring about people. "I used to yell at him that he was so cold-bloodedly realistic, so damn pragmatic; why wasn't he emotional and why couldn't he go irrationally berserk, and where were the juices flowing through his veins; where was the milk of human kindness? In fact, it was an informed rationality, a rationality that never overlooked the human considerations. It was just the expression of the position. It had no time for other considerations. It just knifed to the centre. . . . It was thrilling to have known him that way."

As it turned out, the Jackson's Point cottage was a sanctuary for the family. David would read Shakespeare to Michael and the twins, preparing them for plays that were scheduled at Stratford. "Every Saturday or Sunday when he'd come up to the cottage he would go over the plays very carefully with us," says Janet. "My mother claimed that we used to know the plays so well that Nina especially would point out when somebody missed a line. These are very precious memories, very precious times."

It was a side of David that others saw as well. Ray Stancer says David was "very important to my growing up."

> He showed me that I counted. That my opinions counted. Even though I was a fifteen- or sixteen- or seventeen-year-old kid, and even though he may have thought that my opinions weren't worth shit, he didn't make me feel that way. Because he was who he was and because he made me feel I was important, I felt a lot better about me. . . .
>
> I remember meeting Jennie Lee there, in the living room of the house on Burnside. Here she was, the wife of Aneurin Bevan, visiting David. I was some little smart-ass kid and he and Sophie brought me in and introduced me to this woman. Now that's significant. They were saying something about me. It was like they weren't ashamed of me. They were inviting me into this room and were saying here, we want you to meet our friend. This is our friend Ray. . . .
>
> It was extraordinary to me because normally . . . [adults would say] you kids go out, or downstairs, and keep quiet, don't make any noise because we don't want to embarrass this person. We don't want to be embarrassed by you. But there was none of that.

During the summers he was at Harbord Collegiate, and for one or two while he was in university, Stephen worked at a Muskoka summer camp for "well-to-do, middle-class Jewish children" on Fox Lake, a small lake near Lake Vernon about fifteen kilometres from Huntsville. At least he worked there when he wasn't off helping in election campaigns. It was called Camp Ogama. He was sixteen years old when he was recruited in 1953 by Alan Borovoy, four years his senior, now head of the Canadian Civil Liberties Associaton.

Borovoy is one of those people of contrast — whose eyes peer through tangled, looping eyebrows as through the jungle of a Rousseau painting, artful and artless; whose mind is acute and orderly but whose humour is manic; whose arguments are precise and uncluttered but whose battered office desk is hidden under a six-inch pile of vagrant files and decomposing newspapers topped with a Walkman radio and earphones; who runs one of the country's most formidable institutions out of a set of cramped, paint-chipped, and plaster-cracked cubbyholes across from the palatial Eaton Centre, using the narrow, fourth-floor public hallway as a reception room from which you communicate over a Dutch door with a harassed secretary inside.

He comes to public advocacy through Sidney Hook, John Dewey, . . . and David Lewis. He is a lawyer and articled for two years with David.

> He was an inspiration for me [he says], because he was one of the few highly accomplished people, recognized for his great accomplishments,

who had himself consciously chosen a vocation [that for so long earned] him a fraction of what he could earn elsewhere. For me it was an inspiration to work with somebody like that because I had those kinds of interests apart from David. But David gave legitimacy to them. I was ready to do it anyway, but he made it respectable for me and he gave it clout in my own life that otherwise I might not have had.

One of the things that so impressed me in articling with David was the reasonableness about the positions he took. How non-doctrinaire he was. I expected him to be much more doctrinaire than in fact he was . . . and that contributed immeasurably to his advocacy skills. Because he would walk into court . . . and begin some of his arguments by making strategic concessions . . . by defining the issues so narrowly that the judges would experience a welcome reduction in their insecurity levels. He did it beautifully . . . and as I got to know him, I thought that a lot of that reflected his thinking about things. He was a much more practical person than his public image often led you to believe.

Borovoy and Stephen both began working at Camp Ogama in the summer of 1953, Borovoy as a section head, Stephen as a kitchen boy. But most of the counsellors, whatever their specific jobs, were left-wing. "I think to find a right-winger there you'd have had to turn the place upside down," Borovoy says. There were about 200 campers aged six to sixteen, boys and girls. The owners, says Borovoy,

. . . somehow got left with a camp. They didn't know anything about camping so they hired young people to run it for them. And by some series of coincidences we found ourselves on the head staff, holding positions like program director, head counsellor, and section head. . . .[So] we found ourselves with a summer camp, an opportunity to do creative and interesting things, to express our developing social consciences, and it was irresistible. So if we had a program at camp, it wasn't a colour war. It was a Geneva peace conference, a Hungarian Revolution. . . .

It wasn't an exercise in indoctrination. I remember saying so often to staff people, "I'm not interested in what the kids think; I'm interested *that* they think."

Marshall (Mickey) Cohen was on staff, later to become deputy federal finance minister and now president and CEO of Molson Cos. Ltd.; so was Owen Shime, now chairman of the Ontario Grievance Settlement Board, which arbitrates disputes between the Ontario Government and its employees; and Gordon Wolfe, executive director of Metro Toronto's Jewish Family and Child Service; Gaby Warren, a senior diplomat in External Affairs; Millie Rothman, later to marry Owen Shime and become an inspiring teacher before her untimely death; David Lewis Stein, the writer; and Gerry Caplan, Stephen's closest adviser when he was Ontario leader, former teacher at the Ontario Institute for Studies in Education, former co-chairman of the federal task force on broadcasting appointed by Flora MacDonald, former federal secretary of the NDP, and now freelance consultant and commentator.

> We'd get kids from those luxurious homes [says Borovoy — "Forest Hill homes," Stephen calls them] singing songs from the Spanish Civil War like "*Freiheit*" and "*Viva la Quince Brigada.*"[22] And "Solidarity Forever" and "Joe Hill." . . . From time to time Stephen and I would do a sing-song together. He'd stand at one end of the mess hall and I'd stand at the other, leading the kids. And I'd get excited by the way he was doing it and we'd just go out of our minds. It would be an orgy of singing. [He laughs at the memory.]
>
> And the kids, in turn, used to kid with us. On visitors' day, while the parents were coming in, they'd stand up in the mess hall and sing, "We are Communists forever 'cause Borovoy told us so." They were always needling us.

The programs that the staff organized would last two or three days. Some programs would be for the entire camp and some for individual units. And each cabin would have its own program too. "If I walked by Millie's camp at night," says Borovoy, "I could hear her reading Shakespeare to her kids, and they were loving it. And these were not easy kids. These were tough kids who had ridden other counsellors out of the place. . . . One program in my unit in 1955 I remember calling 'A Visit to Heaven' where the kids were greeted by Socrates, who taught them the message of free speech; Lincoln, who taught them the message of brotherhood; Einstein, world peace; and Maimonides, who taught them giving."

There would be the usual camp events — swimming, canoeing, land games, arts and crafts, dramatic pageants — but they would be tied into major themes and that would lead to discussion groups in cabins at night.

> Stephen was very imaginative, very creative. He'd always come up with interesting ideas and approaches. . . . He was a terrific organizer. . . . One of the things [he would do] is create a sense of emergency. I happen to agree with that. . . . Unless you can inspire people with a sense of urgency, nothing gets done. . . .
>
> We gave him the nickname of "Jesus." Partly because of his physical appearance — if you can imagine in the middle of summer to be gaunt, when the sun is out and we're all sporting tans and he looks as if he's come straight from a Siberian slave labour camp. And partly because his own personal test of whether he was doing a good job required that

he stay up half the night and vomit several times. . . . [Borovoy is chuckling again.] And only if he did that could he really have a sense that he was doing a good job.

His last program — he was the senior unit head in 1958 — was the Hungarian Revolution. It began with someone bailing out of a plane. Literally. We hired someone to parachute out of a plane, land in the water, and shout to shore, "Fellow Hungarians, the revolution is on!"

The kids didn't know what was going on. . . . After the parachutist, the kids were herded up and driven by truck to Budapest, which was . . . on the other side of the lake, and they were divided into workers, peasants, and students. Then they had water games, land games, creative pageants, and things like that — all with the theme of the Hungarian Revolution.

Now when Stephen was running a program like that, he'd be up all night planning it.

A highlight of all the years was in the summer of 1956 when David participated in a skit, a dramatization of the case brought in Dresden, Ontario, against a restaurant owner who refused to serve blacks. "David played his own part; he had been counsel to the blacks in Dresden. . . . The kids loved it. To this day those who were in the skit with him have never forgotten the experience."

Stephen recalls those summers as being "terribly, terribly important" to him.

Summer after summer from the time I was sixteen to twenty, that group of us who were very close used to wrestle with the question: "Do you make your contribution by dealing on an individual, human level, or by going into politics and fighting it out at a large level, affecting legislation and social change that way?" It seems awfully banal, putting it in those terms now, but we really used to wrestle with that. And we all decided on different approaches. . . . This was a group of young Jewish intellectuals of the left who were struggling deeply about how to use life. I guess I was the most politically committed, although they all were, in those days, CCFers.

Some may have changed parties in later life, but their essential efforts to change society remained. And that was the great debate: how do you do it. . . . I guess I was the ideological one, and I suppose that [it] was David that had deeply ingrained such commitments. So I tend to see a thread of what I wanted out of life, which was just to be useful. To be a part of the struggle. To identify causes and fight them.

But lots of people do that. . . . I've always thought the social-conscious columnists like the Ron Haggarts and Pierre Bertons were also devoting their lives to effect social change. . . . When I wrote for [the *Toronto*] *Star* . . . it never occurred to me to write descriptively, lyrically. It was always to find some cause or an issue or an aggrieved person that I could use to make a point, and I'm sure that's the influence of my family and my father particularly.

By the time he was fifteen years old, Stephen also was turning into a hardy campaigner. During the summer after Grade Eleven he went to live with Mel Swart, then deputy reeve of Thorold and after 1975 an NDP member of the Ontario Legislature, and, in his words, he went pounding around ridings in the Niagara Peninsula selling memberships where no one had tried. He also did that for part of the next two summers. And he was forever involved in campaigns — municipal, provincial, and federal.

Norman Penner remembers him in the June 1955 provincial campaign in Toronto–St. Andrew when Joe Salsberg lost his seat in the Legislature to Allan Grossman. Penner was working for the Communist candidate in neighbouring Bellwoods riding and also was helping Salsberg. Stephen was constantly touring the garment district in the back of a pickup truck with other enthusiasts singing "Solidarity Forever" and, says Penner, hectoring Salsberg. "Every time Salsberg got up to speak," says Penner, "up popped Stephen with a megaphone and drowned him out. 'The duty of workers of St. Andrews is to defeat J.B. Salsberg,' he'd yell."

Penner gets no little satisfaction from the results. Although Salsberg was defeated, 5,019 to 4,276, the CCF placed a distant third with only 1,420 votes.

The fall of that same year there was a federal by-election in Spadina riding, which covered roughly the same area of Toronto, and once again Stephen was out working for the CCF candidate. There, he says, he learned the canvassing techniques that were to become the mainstay of CCF election battles in the years to come and were to be dubbed "the Riverdale system" — the intensive and highly systematic method of canvassing voters in every poll of a riding.

The "system" got its name from the Riverdale by-election in 1964 in which Jim Renwick came from behind to win the Tory seat and, in the process, to beat Charles Templeton, the glamorous Liberal candidate. It was a turning point for party fortunes in Ontario.[23] Stephen and Marj Pinney were in charge of the campaign, and they and Ken Bryden, who had been provincial secretary from 1954 to 1961 and had worked on the system over a number of elections, finally perfected it. Stephen says the credit for perfecting the system goes to Marj Pinney.

During the Spadina by-election Stephen was irrepressible, says Ray Stancer, whom Stephen recruited into helping. "There was a fellow named Samuel Godfrey [running for the Liberals] and he had a big canvas sign stretched between two houses," says Stancer. "So Stephen got at it with his scissors. And the next morning" — and Stancer starts laughing so hard he can hardly finish — "the next morning the sign says, 'Elect God in Spadina.'" He laughs till he's out of breath.

And on another night they were tearing down signs — until they were spotted and chased by police,

> . . . and I said, "Enough." So we drove up one street and there was this big sign on a private garage and Stephen says, "Wait a minute. I want that one."
>
> And I say, "Stephen, it's a house. It's the guy's."
>
> "No. I want it." He goes into the guy's garage. Gets a stepladder. Sets it up in front of the garage and starts climbing to take the sign off. As he's doing it, two people walk by. It's eleven o'clock at night or something.
>
> "Stephen," I whisper, "there're people!"
>
> And Stephen says loudly, "I told them not to do this." Rip. "I told them not to put the sign up." Rip. "I told them I wouldn't stand for it." Rip. "The sign will come down." Rips the sign down. We put the thing in the car and take off.

Again he's laughing until he's out of breath. It was a Tory sign. The Tories win the by-election. The CCF comes last and once again Joe Salsberg beats them out, coming third.

In the spring of 1956 Stephen headed west to Saskatchewan, "to get a sense of the party in the promised land," worked for a while at the Economic Planning Board, and then with the Saskatchewan Power Corporation. Then he "went travelling with Tommy Douglas" during the campaign for the June election that Tommy called. In the course of their travels Stephen met Kim Thorson, the twenty-one-year-old candidate in Souris–Estevan and stayed on to manage his campaign. "I had the chastening experience of canvassing farmers in their fields who knew so much more than I did about every issue that I had to race back to headquarters and read up. In Saskatchewan everybody listened to the debates on radio. And everybody voted. Votes of 85, 90, 93 percent were not uncommon. They knew the whole thing, and I didn't know what the hell I was talking about. . . . I had to stop for several days until I learned what I was talking about."

It was his first election as a campaign manager and his first success. Thorson was elected. Before the summer was out, Stephen was managing his next campaign for a September election in Salmon Arm riding in the Okanagan Valley of British Columbia. That one the CCF candidate lost. The following summer he was managing Andy Brewin's losing campaign in the federal riding of Davenport in Toronto.

Next came Manitoba. At the end of the university term in the spring of 1958, Stephen, Gerry Caplan, John Brewin, and Bill Tepperman from Windsor were off to Winnipeg to work in the June election. Stephen managed the campaign of the provincial leader, Lloyd Stinson; Caplan managed the campaign of Donovan Swailes; and Brewin managed Alvin Mackling's campaign. Both Stinson and Swailes won.

They arrived four or five weeks before election day and to their horror found that Stinson had absolutely no organization in his own riding. Redistribution had done away with the old four-member sections into which the province had been divided, and had substituted single-member constituencies. Stinson had made no effort to adjust and had no constituency organization whatever. So, says Brewin,

"[Stephen headed] out to the CN rail yards talking to the railway workers, recruiting them to work in Stinson's campaign. . . . Within a week he'd begun to build the embryo of an organization. Within two weeks he had all the polls covered and he was driving people to knock on doors. He had a very successful campaign. . . .

He was extraordinarily persuasive. . . . He was bright, he was incredibly articulate and he had this very impressive will power which he tended to train and hone and in that sense he was an ascetic. . . . I never did get into any philosophical discussions with him about it, but I do remember . . . he talked about the need to develop his own will power, and, in some sense, imposing his will is what an organizer has to do. He also tested himself . . . by pushing . . . to the extreme, which was something he talked about and observably did.

For example, he was always being beset with wisdom teeth problems and pains of various kinds, which he clearly regarded as something that he should suffer in an attempt to develop and strengthen his will power. If he could overcome this terrible toothache for twelve hours, that . . . helped him develop will power, which in turn helped him to achieve things.

I remember him talking about his approach to getting people to work in elections. His view was that you had to . . . ask people to do . . . more than they could conceivably do. In doing that, they would do more than they would otherwise do. . . . That people . . . like to be challenged and responded well to that. And he had to do more than anybody else in order to justify making these demands on them.

That was his style. . . .

Owen Shime is another person who remembers Stephen consciously working on his abilities, in this case building his vocabulary. "Whenever he'd come across a word he didn't know, he'd look it up in the dictionary, and then for days afterwards he'd painstakingly use sentences that he could use the word in. . . . Now, of course, he's very eloquent."

By August 1958 Stephen had been appointed as an organizer to the Ontario CCF even though he was still going to university.[24]

Gerry Caplan begins verging on the rhapsodic when he talks about Stephen's campaigning ability: "One of the reasons why he's such an impressive person is that he does a whole lot of things better than anybody else. Not only is he one of the all-time great speakers, but he truly has . . . a wonderful analytic mind when he wants to use it. And he does have this fabulous memory. . . . And he was a splendid organizer. Meticulous, tenacious, very systematic, very highly motivating to other people. He was just great. Among the best."

Stephen's teen-aged involvement in campaigns began a long period of time when he was "notorious," says Ted Jolliffe: "He would go around from constituency to constituency, particularly when there was a by-election or a general election going on, telling them exactly how they should organize their polls and what they should do about the voters lists and all the donkey work of political organization. And he was first-class at it. Absolutely first-class. People began by resenting it and they wound up full of admiration for what he had taught them.

"It was later on, when he was more mature, that he became political rather than organizational."

John Brewin, his taffy-coloured hair going whitish, his complexion still pinkishly fresh, a good street campaigner, openly friendly, asking after aunts and daughters and pet projects and even pets of constituents he meets, was portrayed through all his youth as a kind of rival to Stephen. John had his own youthful achievements to point to, but on top of that he was the son of another formidable public figure who sometimes rivalled David in his accomplishments. His father Andy, like David, was a labour lawyer, but his representation of the West Coast Japanese who were dispossessed during the war won him a national recognition as a lawyer that David never received. Where David had unsurpassed connections within the labour movement, Andy had equally unsurpassed contacts within the establishment. Both gave unstintingly to the party. Both served as MPs. Both fancied foreign affairs. Both worked well together. Both even were built alike — close to the ground.

"[They had] different backgrounds and different cultures, which is an interesting part of the whole David Lewis story," says John. Andy, he says, had connections every bit as good as David's — in England and in Canada.

My grandfather had been educated at Oxford and sent my father back there when he was age eleven to go through the English public school system . . . and when he had finished his education in England he came back to Toronto and went directly into law, . . . articled with J.C. McRuer [later to become chief justice of the High Court for Ontario] and was junior to him right up until McRuer went to the bench in 1942 or whatever. My mother was Toronto upper middle class and all that kind of stuff. Havergal College. . . .

When I went through David's memoirs I found what really staggered me was the extent to which he wanted to be part of the WASP world, for lack of a better term. The Canadian mainstream. I read that into the book. That David was far more impressed with the Canadian mainstream than it deserved and than I thought he would ever really admit to. He was less secure with his relationship to the mainstream than I thought he would be and had needed to be. . . .

My father, on the other hand, felt somewhat jealous of David's higher profile and that irritated and frustrated him.

Peggy Brewin, John's mother, remembers "tensions," that were "not very severe. But, you know, I'd sort of resent sometimes that David got the attention when I thought Andrew should. These sorts of silly things. The same with relationships between John and Stephen. . . ."

Originally, she says, Andy concentrated on fund-raising for the party "because he had contacts. He knew people like Walter Gordon and those sorts of people who did give financial help. But there were always very good relations on the whole."

Contrary to what others say, Peggy is sure that Sophie never resented the party. "She was genuinely devoted to it." It was the way David gave it such overwhelming precedence over her that rankled.

I remember the first time I met Sophie. Andrew was going with David to meet some people in Rosedale and Sophie was going to be there, so I said, "Invite them back to dinner," and I put a roast in the oven. But they were later and later. Finally Sophie came in absolutely furious.

David and Andrew had left her outside parked in the car while they went into this house. It was quite a nice house and she could see them through the window having a drink. I was pretty irritated, too, because my roast was spoiled. However, we all remained friends and laughed about it later.

Looking back, John says the relationship between the families tended to be a little more competitive than it needed to be. John, short like his father, walks chest-first, as though midway through a breast stroke while standing upright. He talks of Stephen with great affection, even though in the now-distant past there was a slight hesitancy between them, especially after John vigorously supported Walter Pitman against Stephen in the race for the provincial leadership in 1971. He speaks of Stephen's ability to persuade: "Like all very persuasive people, Stephen had extremely good antennae for what the listener wanted to hear. And it would be almost instinctive, as I'm sure that some of the time Stephen wouldn't even know consciously that that's what was going on. But he could read what people wanted to hear, and he would feed it back to them in a very persuasive way. That's where he sometimes gets caught appearing to say different things to different people. It's been a criticism that has been tossed around about him. I think it emerges from that almost extra-sensory skill that he has."

However, says Brewin, there's a trap in talking too much about Stephen honing his political skills because it places him in too narrow a context. Makes it sound too much as if he were being groomed for high office, like a starlet pushed forward by stage parents. Too much as if he saw few options.

> By age fourteen or fifteen Stephen was his own master, out of his parents' control in a fundamental way. . . .
>
> Clearly, he must have thought of a political career, but it wasn't a single-minded expectation. I don't think he saw his particular, single goal in life to be the first socialist prime minister of Canada or anything like that. In fact, I can remember him once saying — and I guess we were in our teens before university — that he wasn't the kind of person who should be the leader. It was an interesting sort of calculation of the political climate of Ontario. . . . He had analyzed himself as someone who would not be completely acceptable to the voters of Ontario. He tried to persuade me that it was my role rather than his. Without him actually saying so, what he was speaking about was that I was the WASP kid who could be put up to win the support and his Jewishness was going to cost him and he was recognizing that.

But, says Brewin, by the time Stephen was partway through university and running in elections for the University of Toronto model parliament, "he was beginning to see that it was perfectly legitimate for him to aspire to the leadership. And in that group [of CCFers at university] he was the dominant figure. I would like to think that I was important to the group in many ways, but he was the stronger personality, and my part in the realtionship might have been somewhat similar to that between my father and David."

The year 1956 brought the Khrushchev revelations about Stalin; Soviet troops marching into Hungary; Churchill resigning; Lester Pearson pivotal in the dispatch of United Nations peacekeeping troops to Suez — for which he won the Nobel Peace Prize the following year;

C.A.R. Crosland, one of the intellectual leaders of the British labour movement, publishing *The Future of Socialism*; the great pipeline debate; the TLC and the CCL merging into the Canadian Labour Congress; the adoption of the Winnipeg Declaration.

It was a heady year for Stephen's political coming of age. His first election as a campaign manager, the end of his first year at university.

It also was a year when David began to itch to return to active politics.

It was a year that opened, says Walter Young in his history of the party, with David and others as "leaders of a movement of aging zealots and a party of defeated MPs . . . unable to revitalize the CCF as it then stood."[25]

It's a harsh description. Even inaccurate. This was no band of zealots, aging or otherwise, although zealots could be found in its midst. These people were weathered. They had prevailed through the almost endless struggles where they had seen their youth spent, their enthusiasms tempered, their resolve hardened. By now they were mostly pragmatic, having learned that no one emerges from a struggle unscathed, no one emerges pure. If their emphasis in the winter of 1956 was on moral and ethical criticisms of society, as Young says, instead of on standard socialist critiques, that's hardly surprising at a time when few in Europe or in Canada knew what socialism had become.

What Young missed was their sense of determination. What they had achieved at such sacrifice they would never jeopardize. In years to come, it would be difficult for younger generations to understand this. They would never fully appreciate the revulsion, the anger, at any prospect of endangering those hard-won advances; the intensity with which they would react against anything they saw as a return to factionalism.[26]

In a sense, sacrifices came more easily during the Great Depression and the war. The evils were so manifest that opposition was more natural. But after the war, when prosperity returned and the vision blurred, these were the people who held fast. They had clung to their faith with few resources and incredible stamina through those eleven long, lean years since 1945 as party strength dwindled, and in the process they had defeated the Communists, withstood the McCarthy years, stabilized the party, maintained and expanded the confidence of organized labour, and now were about to play discreet handmaid to the unification of labour and to undertake the difficult process of formally redefining the party itself. Little did they realize that, with the Diefenbaker sweeps still to come, there would be several more lean years before times changed.

In all this, David was central. According to Donald MacDonald, former Ontario leader, "David was involved in every major political development in the trade union movement from 1940 on, and even leading up to 1940. On the CCL side or the All Canadian Congress side — and increasingly even with the TLC."

Among the industrial unions, says MacDonald, David was an "honorary, de-facto member of every CCL union in existence. . . . They would be calling him for direction and David was never hesitant about giving directions. . . ."

However, he says, on the TLC side there is not a great deal in writing to document his work.

> David played a very careful role in developing support for the party. . . . Let me put it in specific terms. The CCL had political education committees. In the TLC unions you had unofficial trade union committees or unofficial CCF-supporting committees. They had to be unofficial because their union constitutions in many instances forbade it. And certainly the union leadership opposed it.
>
> But I know as the education director in the period from 1946 to 1950 I was working with people in many of those unions. Maybe one person. And he had maybe another half a dozen people that he could work with who were out on the shop floors. I suppose [he says, laughing] that in Communist terms it was a cell.

The merger of the two labour organizations occurred in April 1956 and that, coming in tandem with the ouster of the Communists from the labour movement, meant that, at long last, the party could concentrate on the road ahead and not be forever diverted to protecting its flanks.

On October 26, 1955, David delivered a lecture at Woodsworth House in Toronto entitled "A Socialist Takes Stock." It was a consolidation of his experience over the previous twenty years and was distinctive in the intensity of its focus on "giant corporations . . . without heart and without soul," the "evils of the concentration of wealth," and the "battle of the common man against the privileged." However, by then he had long rejected the old socialist solution of ownership of the means of production. He stressed that developments, especially in the Soviet Union, had "shattered . . . the assumptions" that "nationalization of industry would automatically bring with it greater social and political freedom." Some public ownership could still help end injustice — but no longer could it be seen as a panacea.

What he was saying, in effect, was that it no longer could be used as the definition of socialism.

So what was socialism? He listed goals, he listed means, he offered guidelines for public ownership, he dealt with the struggle to create a society without classes, he talked of universal brotherhood and equality and freedom and peace and economic and social security; but in the end there wasn't a sense of definition. All these things flowed from something else. They were cures or they were symptoms.

It was only when he touched on the old Marxist concept of historical materialism that there was once again a sense that here at last was the wellspring. It was from this that all else flowed. Here he could identify the legacy of capitalism and see that the the fundamental mission of socialists should be to reverse it.

> The growth and power of private corporations [he said, and the context shows that he meant big business only] have imposed on society a standard of values which perverts the best ideals of man. Wealth has become the major mark of success and he who dares to inquire into the ways used to accumulate that wealth and to question the ethics employed, is a wild-eyed agitator. All the precepts of the highest human morality expressed in religion or in the philosophies of great men are ignored even when they are praised, and perverted even while they are proclaimed in high-sounding phrases. Human co-operation, tolerance, charity, humility, sympathy, the idea that one is his brother's keeper, the notion that one owes a duty to live his life without hurting anyone else and the concept that one's rights are no higher than those of any other person — all these moving human ideals are derided and ignored by the daily practices of capitalist behaviour. And this attitude stems directly from the hungry drive for ever larger accumulations of wealth, of profits and of private power.

At the same time as this, Crosland was putting the finishing touches to his extremely influential book, *The Future of Socialism*, which proclaimed: "Marx has little or nothing to offer the contemporay socialist, either in respect of practical policy, or of the correct analysis of our society, or even of the right conceptual tools or framework. His prophecies have been almost without exception falsified, and his conceptual tools are now quite inappropriate."[27]

His definition of socialism was to say, in effect, that a definition was impossible: "It simply describes a set of values, or aspirations, which socialists wish to see embodied in the organization of society. . . . But exactly what degree of equality will create a society which does sufficiently embody them, no one can possibly say. We must re-assess the matter in the light of each new situation."[28]

He listed only two aspirations that were clear enough to be relevant. They were a "wider concern for social welfare" and "a belief in equality and the 'classless society' and especially a desire to give the worker his 'just' rights and a responsible status at work."[29] Among his conclusions was the belief that the more prosperous Britain became, the more tolerant and compassionate it would be. He quoted Keynes in support of this belief: "'When the accumulation of wealth,' Keynes once wrote, 'is no longer of high social importance, there will be great changes in the code of morals. . . . I see us free to return to some of the most sure and certain principles of religion and traditional virtue — that avarice is a vice, that the exaction of usury is a misdemeanour, and the love of money is detestable, that those walk most truly in the paths of virtue and sane wisdom who take least thought for the morrow. We shall once more value ends above means and prefer the good to the useful.'"[30]

Crosland was more humanist than socialist, and in the late 1980s he seems not only naïve in his assumptions about the continuing eradication of poverty but wrong in his basic approach. As Bryan Gould, a British Labour MP and shadow trade and industry secretary, argued in December 1987:

> It was . . . a failure of economic analysis in the early 1970s which ushered in the domination of the Right and the wholesale change in political attitudes and values from which the Left has suffered so grievously.
>
> That failure began . . . with the oil price shock of the early 1970s which seemed to demonstrate that the old Keynesian nostrums could no longer work. The consequences for the Left were apocalyptic. We suddenly found that our traditional lack of interest in ideas was costing us dear, and that reliance on a gentle Keynesianism and the Croslandite notion that socialism was simply a rather pleasing exercise in distributing the fruits of affluence were no longer enough."[31]

But in the mid- and late fifties, Crosland's was a powerful voice, and the sentiments he was articulating were widespread. Within the CCF the feeling had long been brewing that a new statement of party principles was necessary and work on it began in 1950.[32] It resulted in the Winnipeg Declaration passed at the party's convention in Winnipeg in August 1956.

Of course there was opposition. Bill Irvine declared that "We were born in the manger of the poor and the old capitalists are still the same." So why change the Regina Manifesto?[33] In 1952 the president of the Saskatchewan section of the party accused supporters of "a-whoring after the Bitch Goddess." Seeking power instead of public enlightenment.[34] There were scores of others. And on the other side there were some who went to the opposite extreme. Andy Brewin announced that with the Winnipeg Declaration the party had affirmed that "it has become . . . the effective inheritor of the liberal tradition."[35]

Dozens of analysts since then have declared that the Winnipeg Declaration was a watershed. That it marked the shift from public ownership to public control. That with it, the CCF ceased to be a movement and became a party. That it substituted social planning for the annihilation of capitalism. That it promised more property for more people in an effort to make the party more meaningful. That it was a monument on the road that turned the CCF into a liberal, reform party, albeit a distinctive liberal, reform party.[36]

Whatever version was accepted, everyone knew that the declaration signalled an official change in image — self-image and public image — and the debate was heated.

Unfortunately, the Winnipeg Declaration was a pedestrian document. There was no Frank Underhill to give it the lilt of the Regina Manifesto. No Frank Scott to make it sing. It went through six years of committee gestation until in desperation David, Lorne Ingle, Omer Chartrand, and Morden Lazarus hammered a final draft together for presentation to the convention in Winnipeg. It was perhaps one of David's greater lapses as a power within the party that he didn't ensure the convention was presented with a document that offered a vision. It could have been done. But it needed a spellbinder to write it. And none of the four was that.

Even so, it was not Croslandite. And the reason it was not was that at its heart there was, once again, the same theme that rested at the core of David's "A Socialist Takes Stock." In a section entitled "Capitalism Basically Immoral," it declared that "A society motivated by the drive for private gain and special privilege is basically immoral.

"The CCF reaffirms its belief that our society must have a moral purpose and must build a new relationship among men — a relationship based on mutual respect and on equality of opportunity. In such a society everyone will have a sense of worth and belonging, and will be enabled to develop his capacities to the full."

It was historical materialism wearing the robes of Judeo-Christian morality. It was the strongest statement in the Declaration and distinguished it radically from the chummy optimism of Crosland because it so obviously was the psychological starting point for everything else. Had it been made more the textual centrepiece of the Winnipeg Declaration, had it been more expansive, had it been expressed in more ringing tones, much of the concern over selling out socialist principles could have been dampened. It would have evoked more strongly the connections reaching back to roots in the Social Gospel and in Marx and, although most would not have recognized it, the Jewish Labour Bund.

But the prime concern of David and others was to break the public image of the CCF as wanting to end private ownership. To make the party more acceptable to the middle classes. His accomplishment was that he resisted the global trend pushing socialist parties toward a Crosland approach and held fast to the socialist belief that deeply imbedded in the capitalist ethic was a terrible sickness. His failure was in not producing a document that could inspire at the same time that it altered.

In late 1955, with the CLC forming and the Winnipeg Declaration coming up for consideration, David began to get restless. Out of politics, practising law, he had always felt diverted. Peripheral. That he was marking time even though he continued to hold office in the party and continued his involvement.[37] "When he came to Toronto to practise with us, he gave almost undivided attention to the work," says Ted Jolliffe, emphasizing the word "almost," "and I wondered how long it would last. Then I began to see signs that he was getting restless. . . .

"He had paid very close attention to his practice for four or five years. Then he became quite active again. . . . I was a little surprised because he had been so terribly busy. In great demand as a lawyer. . . . I think he felt that he had established himself sufficiently as a lawyer . . . and he wanted to start the party moving in the direction it eventually took."

The year 1956 turned out to be one of the most hectic of David's career, and it was not without cost. In May, a couple of weeks after the CLC merger convention and ten weeks before the Winnipeg convention that approved the Declaration, he collapsed at his law office desk. A heart specialist ordered him to bed. "I can still remember the anxiety in Sophie's face and the look of sheer terror in the eyes of our children," he wrote in his memoirs. "After a week or so of examinations, tests and cardiograms, the doctor released me with the conclusion that my collapse had been due to exhaustion."[38]

He was forty-six years old.

CHAPTER TWENTY

This is the age of the conditioned reflex rather than the reflective condition.

David Lewis, 1960[1]

"We spent a good part of our undergraduate lives at university talking about Stephen and what would happen to him and where he would go, and if he would get in so much trouble that he wouldn't go anywhere. . . . We spent hours and hours and hours. I still remember. People sitting around and talking about Stephen."

This from the person who says, "Stephen's been the most important person in my life" — so he speaks from a certain allegiance. This also from the person who was Stephen's closest confidant during his time as Ontario leader — so when he speaks of those years he speaks with intimate knowledge. But, in the way that relationships can be tangled affairs, this also from a person who felt a kind of skittish rivalry with Stephen, not for political office but for intellectual prominence — so when he turns to those leadership years and tosses in the occasional florid description, it's a factor to keep in mind.

"Leaders are very difficult people," he says. "I've now worked with lots and I've studied others that I haven't known intimately, and they are just very difficult people. And I think that is probably true in any world. In return for what makes them successful as leaders, they have a battery of personality idiosyncrasies that are at best awkward and at worst intolerable and the issue becomes when the balance is out of skew."

The speaker is Gerry Caplan, of whom Stephen now says. "I don't think in a million years I could have survived that whole period [of the leadership] without Gerry. Not in a million years. . . . It is an unusually and terrifically important relationship." To which he adds, chuckling — and a touch skittish himself — "although executive assistants are also very difficult people."

It was Stephen who brought Caplan to politics. Caplan entered the University of Toronto in 1956, a year after Stephen, and toward the end of the year when the two of them were at a meeting of Hillel — a campus organization sponsored by B'nai Brith to foster a deeper understanding of Judaism — "out of the blue" Stephen asked him to come to a meeting of the campus CCF club. Six months later, Caplan says with a touch of self-depreciatory surprise, Stephen had him working full time in Andy Brewin's federal election campaign. Up until then, his "biggest goal in life had been trying to get girls into the front seat of a convertible." So, in six months he had gone from "nothing" to "working full time for a kind of socialism that I began to live."

Unlike Stephen, Caplan is the person on the corner you always notice but never point out. Whatever the neighbourhood, he looks as if he's part of it. It's his talent. His conversation matches the level of the moment; his dress is without statement without saying so; at a meeting, on a television panel, he doesn't strain for attention, he waits for it to arrive. Where Stephen bounces language off the walls, Caplan rolls it to you across the floor, simple, straight and clear. Medium height, medium dark hair, medium build — he could be anybody: the branch manager of the nearest bank, the man behind the till at the corner variety store, the city clerk. Yet as he walks toward the doors opening onto the main floor of the party's 1987 convention late on a cold March afternoon in Montreal, Hugh Winsor, national political editor of *The Globe and Mail*, turns and says, "There goes the brightest person in the building."

For all his managerial skill in threading his way among the hungry egos of politics, he can't quite suppress his. He has had his differences with party leader Ed Broadbent and is no longer on the innermost councils, and everybody knows it. So at this family affair he walks with a casualness that is a little too casual. And he has slung his sweater across his shoulders, the arms tied loosely on his chest, as if he had just come off a tennis court. In this gathering of union jackets, rumpled tweed, and institutional non-statement, it's a touch too princely. Still, he manages it so well it doesn't seem all that much out of place. Even on this cold March afternoon.

All through university Stephen was a centre of attention, Caplan says. Even professors treated him as different — and with that, Professor Kenneth McNaught agrees. McNaught arrived at the University of Toronto in 1960 and taught a senior undergraduate seminar on

American Progressivism that Stephen attended. It was one of the best seminars he had in his entire teaching career, he says, even though it was his first venture. Now retired, his conversation still as rich as he is lean, he relaxes in a high-backed chair in a nook off his living room, his fingers interlaced across his chest, elbows on armrests, discoursing with the benevolent assurance of an Anglican priest discussing the intricacies of holy communion.

> In that seminar were Larry Zolf and Stephen Lewis and Gerry Caplan and Harvey Levenstein — now a well-known professor at McMaster. All Jewish, with that same kind of North Winnipeg outlook. Real sparky kids. . . . The seminar turned out to be . . . an ongoing analysis of why socialism failed in the United States and we kept on making Canadian comparisons.
>
> It was really fascinating. . . . I remember coming home and telling my wife, "I got a chance to say two sentences today." [Delight at the memory of those lusty sessions sets him chuckling.] We had lots of history and lots of good solid work. It happened that it was the political theme that was uppermost in Stephen's mind at the moment . . . so he did a *lot* of reading and he never missed a thing and gave good reports. I gave him a first-class mark at the end of the year.
>
> But in all the other [subjects] he had been attending in a desultory fashion, such as in Willard Pietenburg's classes on seventeenth-century England which he should have been attending because you have the foundation there of the Levellers and all kinds of things that would have been equally interesting [in relation to] Darlington Hoopes and the American Socialist Party. . . .

It was mutual admiration, in a way, says McNaught. Stephen liked the seminar and McNaught had a "great admiration" for his student activism. As to how good a student Stephen could have been, McNaught says "He had all of the abilities to become absolutely first rate. But it's not just ability. It's motivation and the bent of your character and background and inclination. . . . [Stephen] just wanted other things. He wanted the useful knowledge and the thoughtfulness that comes along with academe. But he wanted to pick and choose. Always.

"If you're going to become an academic you've got to be able to study things that you're not inherently interested in because they're part of a total picture. And he wasn't prepared to do that."

Stephen's university record was far below expectations. He failed second year. Repeated and passed it the next year. Took his third year at the University of British Columbia. Returned to the University of Toronto for his fourth year and never wrote the final examinations.

In later years he twice tried law school, once at the University of Toronto, once at the University of British Columbia, and dropped out both times. Always, politics came first. Always, he was off around the country on political campaigns of one sort or another.

> I don't know how to account for all that [he says now]. What is important, I think, is that I loved and valued my university years and probably got more out of them that most people did. And I think that's true even intellectually. . . .
>
> I read and thought and argued and cared and was stimulated. People like Ken McNaught had enormous influence on my subsequent thinking. . . . Of all the courses . . . [his] most influenced my life in terms of my conceptual view of the North American continent and American society. . . .
>
> And at UBC . . . I read Karl Popper's books, *The Open Society and Its Enemies* and so on, and Marx and Hegel were on the course, and for the first time I came to grips with the sort of Marxist left-wing thought which I had always dallied around with and fashionably espoused but didn't know what I was talking about. For the first time I seriously read all that stuff.
>
> I really feel I benefitted from university in the way universities are supposed to benefit people — make them think, excite them intellectually.
>
> I was a hopelessly crummy student. I always got things in late. I was lousy at examinations. I got preoccupied and fascinated by subjects and never had enough self-discipline to do what was required. . . .
>
> I didn't graduate because didn't have a pass French . . . and a pass philosophy. I suspect I was capable of both, but I never had enough *sitzslaish*, as the Yiddish is, enough glue on the bottom, to sit and do the work.

As might be expected, David was crushed over Stephen's failure to graduate. He had his heart set on his taking law and joining the Jolliffe, Lewis and Osler law firm.[2] Unknown to Stephen, he even went so far as to approach university officials to see if there wasn't a way for an exception to be made for Stephen. He got nowhere.[3] "I think he was always deeply disappointed at the hapless academic careers of all his children; certainly mine," says Stephen. "It was the ultimate sacrilege. I mean, next to becoming a Liberal, this was the worst thing that could happen.

"If defiance had to be shown, why couldn't I take drugs or steal or something? Why did I have to screw around at school? I think he was totally bewildered by that, by the lack of discipline, the irresponsibility, by what he saw as a bright kid gone wrong."

Now, of course, Stephen holds honourary degrees from twelve Canadian universities.

Michael made a far more dramatic rejection of university. He entered the University of Toronto but dropped out two-thirds of the way through his first year. He found it disappointing and uninteresting — except for managing the CCF club's involvement in the model parliament elections and other similar activities. After dropping out, he was off to help Stephen, Marj Pinney, and Ken Bryden in the September 1964 federal by-election in Riverdale that perfected "the system" and elected Jim Renwick. "Right in the middle of it, when I was really under great pressure," he says, "my parents . . . said, 'Michael, you've got to go back to school. We think the reason you dropped out of U of T was that it was too large, too overwhelming. Maybe you need to get away from home and go to a smaller university. We think Queen's would be terrific. Why don't you go to Queen's?'

"I think if I hadn't been under the pressure of a campaign and wanting to sort of push it aside, I might have given it more thought and said, no. But I said, 'Okay. Register me and I'll go.'"

He lasted three months. Quite wonderful months, he says, because he ran a classical music program on the local radio station for which he spent an "endless amout of time preparing. Not just playing the music but giving background and trying to have a theme running through the program."

As well, he prepared some special public affairs programs for the station. And he organized anti-apartheid activities on campus. All of which meant he largely ignored class work. By Christmas he was in Sudbury working as a full-time organizer for the party. Sophie predicted disaster for him without an education. David was more tolerant.

I remember my Dad and I walking down the street together and he handled it the way he handled everything else. He just said, "I wish you'd stay in school, but I understand what you are saying and maybe you are making the best decision for yourself and if this is how you feel, then you should do it and you have my support."

That was how he was with so many things. We talked it over rationally. He was objective and logical and ended up saying, "I think you'll be sorry later on," and he was right. Sure, today I wish I had the discipline.

[It would have helped] in a number of ways. I'm not very well read. I do not write or speak easily. I'm not trying to compare myself with Stephen because he is terribly unusual. But in my line of work, over the years I've had to do a certain amount of speaking, and where I feel comfortable and can give some time to preparation I do not badly. But writing things never comes easily. . . .

The B.A., the piece of paper, didn't mean anything to me then and doesn't mean anything to me today. So I'm not talking about that. I'm talking about certain things it would have done for my development.

When he stepped off the train in Sudbury, a skinny twenty-year-old who looked like sixteen, Michael was met by Doc Ames, the party's long-time organizer in Northern Ontario, and a companion who, the moment she spied him, turned to Ames in dismay whispering, "My God! What have they sent us!" Still, he was a Lewis, so people gave him a chance. But everywhere he went, says Michael, he was introduced as "our new organizer, Michael Lewis, David Lewis's son, Stephen Lewis's brother. Of course," he adds, "that still goes on today, but then it went on every hour of every day."

Elmer McVey remembers his arrival: "We wanted a full-time organizer so bloody badly . . . it didn't matter if he knew what he was doing or not. . . . Doc Ames took him under his wing and the Steelworkers took him under their wing and so did staff guys that came up frequently — Kenny Valentine and Murray Cotterill and Eamon Park — and we just kept building the party up and building it up.

"There was a pretty strong executive at that time, too, you know. Most of them were Steelworker reps or Steelworkers like myself. . . . We worked pretty hard."

Michael threw himself into expanding the party membership, recruiting candidates to run for office, raising money, generating publicity, running training sessions for workers on a variety of topics, bringing in speakers — and learning how to hang out with miners in beer parlours and talk their language. "I remember coming home one weekend after being up there six or eight months and sitting down at the dinner table and without realizing it, saying, 'Will someone pass the fucking peas.' I thought my mother would have a heart attack!

"I loved it up there and will always remember it and feel that it did, in so many ways, so much more for certain aspects of my education than I ever would have gotten in university."

Michael won't say it, but what he was doing was organizing the party's march out of the wilderness that had been the Sudbury basin ever since Bob Carlin's expulsion in 1948. Success came with the election of Norm Fawcett in the federal riding of Nickel Belt in November 1965. "He sure earned his stripes," McVey says.

Then it was organizing in North Bay and then Sault Ste Marie, and then Michael was off to British Columbia, well on his way to a career in the party.

Nina took some law courses in New York after she left Simon Fraser and was married but "absolutely never felt the need or urge to go back to university." Janet took a year off from schooling after graduating from high school and then "went into second year of an honours English course [at McGill University] and hated every minute of it. It was the most pretentious group of people I'd ever been involved with. . . . [They] were finding profundities in poetry that I never found . . . so I didn't finish the year." Two years later, married and in Vancouver, she entered second year at the University of British Columbia, studying sociology, politics, and anthropology, and thoroughly enjoyed it, but after two years left without a degree because she departed for England where her husband "was getting a master's. So for the third time I went into second year — in England — and finished, thank God, in an honours program in politics, anthropology, and sociology. And that was it" — the only one of the four children to receive a degree.

When Stephen failed his second year at the U of T, he was deliberate about it. He sat down, read the examination paper, paused for a few minutes, and then got up and walked out.

> It was like a knife for me [says Barbara Frum who was in the same room]. We knew he was losing his year. He was saying there's no point in my sitting here. I can't write this exam. And we knew it wasn't just the exam, because in those times you didn't take a summer course and catch up. You lost your year. . . .
>
> We were impressed because he didn't lie. He didn't sit there. We knew in our hearts . . . he could have faked it. You can see it in the way he can speak today. He can fake anything. He can sound erudite even when he doesn't know anything that he's talking about.
>
> So there was something kind of direct and honest about standing up and saying, "I didn't do the work . . . and I won't fake this." It wasn't an act of political defiance. He wasn't a defiant person.

Frum, the most prominent personality in televised daily journalism in Canada, is between tapings. Her dressing room is down a narrow, zigzagged hallway of scuffed white walls and tiled floors, next door to the makeup room where people are readied for the cameras. Across the hallway is a dimly lit room set with a few chairs, a table, and a chesterfield. A lounge, it's called. This is where outsiders wait. Workmen clatter by with wagons of resounding metal. Someone down the hall bangs feverishly at something. The area has all the charm of a locker room, but she is a study in personal magnetics. In the dimness she is wearing black — leotards, skirt, sweater. Her face is the only relief

from the gloom inside the room and the blight outside. In real life
her voice still has that measured lack of cadence that sprawls across
your attention on "The Journal."

"He was a marked man," she says of Stephen. "He was marked off
from us. . . . It was a very easy job market in those days. A very upbeat
economic climate that we were moving into. But Stephen was in
another stream. He was going to paddle up a different river. A very
narrow river where the rules were very severe. Where you had to succeed in a very predetermined way. All the rest of us had the world
as our pool. But not him. He had to swim up a certain stream. He
had to excel in a certain way and he had to succeed in that way."

The university could be an exciting place in the late fifties. This was
the breeding ground of the new nationalists who in years to come would
move into the arts, into the academic disciplines, into the media. Into
politics.

It was a time when change was not always racing straight ahead.
Sometimes it leaped wildly, unpredictably, to the side; sometimes it
simply mushroomed. Marshall McLuhan already was grappling with
the impact of television although his *Understanding the Media* would
not be published until 1964. And although Allen Ginsberg was writing
Howl and George Grant was turning his pessimistic eye on the new
ideology of technological progress in *Philosophy in the Mass Age*, working his way up to writing *Lament for a Nation*, and Jack Kerouac was
intently slouching around; throughout the universities there was a sense
that everything was possible. And events seemed to confirm that it
was. The birth control pill was developed. Roger Bannister broke the
four-minute mile. The first nuclear power plant opened in Schenectady,
New York. The Soviets blasted Sputnik into orbit. Montreal won the
Stanley Cup for five consecutive years. A U.S. submarine sailed around
the world under water. The Soviets landed a rocket on the moon. Polio
vaccines were developed. The first weather satellite began transmit-
ting TV pictures of the earth. The Crewcuts, graduates of St. Michael's
Choir School in Toronto, singing "Sh-boom, Sh-boom," sold more
than a million records.

The Cold War was still raging, but Joe McCarthy was discredited
by December 1954 and was dead by early May 1957. In Canada,
everywhere you looked in the arts there was a new vitality, a new confidence, a widening skill: Painters Eleven, Riopelle, Borduas, Pellan;
the Stratford Festival, which started in 1953; Glenn Gould, Oscar
Peterson, Mordecai Richler, Gilles Vigneault, Farley Mowat, Gabrielle
Roy, Hugh MacLennan, Kate Reid, Pauline Julien, Lorne Green, Lois
Marshall, Gratien Gélinas and his Théâtre du Nouveau Monde, Jon

Vickers, Melissa Hayden, Ernest Buckler, Leonard Cohen, Teresa Stratas, Christopher Plummer, Irving Layton, George London — the list goes on and on.

There was a darker side, of course. The literary and media cliques in Toronto fretted about the Canadian identity. Walter Gordon's 1958 royal commission report on Canada's economic prospects raised an alarm over foreign ownership of the economy. Ford of Canada, heeding its American head office, refused to ship Canadian trucks to China because it was "Red." And there also was a side where a self-indulgent intellectuality had distanced people. Jazz had turned cool, poets beat, and classical music atonal. But at the same time there was Elvis Presley telling the world to stay offa his blue suede shoes, appearing on "The Ed Sullivan Show" where the cameras were ordered not to shoot him below the waist, giving adults a psychic whiplash and yanking kids into a different century.

At the University of Toronto, says Frum, the way students stood out was with "extraordinary talent." The debaters of wit and humour, the ones who wrote skits or performed in them, actors, authors of student productions. Stars, she calls them. And the Junior Common Room at University College was where you could find them. "To get your oar in the JCR was tough. You were competing every lunch hour, struggling to join thirty-five other people listening to somebody being funny and talking and arguing and debating and discussing. . . . We certainly had stars."

Stephen was in that "upper level" of personalities, but "marked off in a different category". In his debating

> . . . he had a lemony wit. More biting. Fierceness. Passionate feeling. Whereas . . . most of us weren't politically engaged and politically affiliated. He was something of an unusual sort because of his political affiliation. . . . The general taste, . . . the people I recall drawing the biggest crowds, were the people who were funny. . . .
>
> What sticks in my mind is a kind of assurance and a kind of conviction of his own worth, his own contribution. He was so articulate. So verbal. But this skill was almost . . . a gift. It wasn't something that you could build up in yourself. It was just there. And it gave him a feeling, I think, of tremendous superiority.
>
> Now at the same time he was ravaged by doubt. He bit his nails and the result was unbearable to see. Half-nails. So you knew he was tormented by a requirement to excel and to succeed that I don't remember any of us feeling. . . .
>
> We all thought he was a winner because everyone saw all these great attributes in him [including] his own pain. . . . [We could see] there was equal, probably more possibility of failure than success in the course

he'd chosen for himself, so perhaps what we were responding to was the risk taker in him. The fact that he was staking it all on this one kind of thing, on success in transforming society.

But admired as he was, there was no herd of women chasing after him. He wasn't pursued. He wasn't perceived as a "catch," says Frum. Nevertheless, "He was very, very interesting to be with. I remember being alone with him once. It wasn't a date in any sense. It was all talk, but very interesting talk. I don't remember where we went or what we did or where it started or where it ended, but he was terribly interesting to be with."

Anxiety there may have been. Even extreme anxiety. But there also was a rollicking exuberance, a zest, a sense of humour that everyone who has known him remarks upon but finds difficult to provide examples of because it relies so much on intonation and the quickness of his responses and the way he reaches for words that are as rich as plum pudding. You laugh as much in the joy of the consummation of one of his verbal journeys as in what it is he's saying. His is not the humour of the one-liner or the pratfall. It looks pale on the printed page. But from the front benches of the Legislature, or from the speaker's podium, or given enough room on television news, it delights.

And there are the occasions when he relishes being slightly absurd. Gerry Caplan recalls going on a double date with Stephen one evening when Stephen had his father's car. "He stopped it right in the middle of the Yonge-Carlton intersection, about to do a left turn, and said to his date — a long-time flame and a nice person — 'I'm not going to move until you kiss me.' She refused on principle and there we sat for a long time with a lot of horns beeping," until finally she gave him a peck.

And there is the time when, as leader of the opposition, he rose in the Legislature to tell Tory Premier Bill Davis that much as it might embarrass him, he had to tell him that "I like you."

One of the things Frum noticed in her first encounters with Stephen was that "he offered you friendship as usually men would offer only to each other. So the kind of talk you could have with Stephen could be as human being to human being. He wasn't a bonding male."

It was one of the things that attracted Michele to him several years later when they met during an election campaign.

One of the reasons I married Stephen [she says] is that he was the first man I'd ever met who was spontaneously egalitarian. Of all the men I've loved or liked or thought of marrying, he was the first to whom it really came naturally — not feminism. That he had to learn over the years — but a sort of egalitarianism. There was no-deep down contempt of women in him.

This I loved about him. But even so, I was surprised at the extent of the partnership. It was not what any of my experiences led me to expect from men. Stephen has always phoned me at least twice a day, no matter where he was or what he was doing. . . . He's lonely without me. He wants to be in touch. . . .

Now when *I'm* away from home, I don't think about anyone. I just think about what I'm involved in. I'm working. I'm thinking about the work. If I'm with friends I forget about the family. I live for the moment. Not so with Stephen.

It's a characteristic that goes beyond any sense of equality that Stephen got from David, Michele says. David, in the tradition of the Bund, treated women entirely as colleagues while they were doing the work of socialism, and never would have considered them as lesser in any way. A belief in equality between men and women is part of the creed common to all socialist parties, including the CCF, but in David it was especially strong because it was rooted in the Bund and, says Michele, "the Bund was a far more intellectual and radical enterprise for its participants than the CCF or NDP ever were." Nevertheless, she adds, once David stepped outside the movement,

[he] was a most deeply dyed chauvinist and I think that, much as I loved and admired him. He was absolutely unable to acknowledge the claims of feminism. . . .

For example, any concern of Sophie's about furnishing the house or shopping for groceries or bringing up the children engendered in him this clenched-teeth impatience. He couldn't tolerate being bothered with such trivia.

And I remember once I deliberately enraged him because . . . I said something about pay for housewives. . . . It was outrageous because it would bankrupt the economy, he said. I wasn't willing to argue on that point because even I could see that. But that I dared to say that it was as important as anything that men did in the outside world, David was in a fury that I should say that — but [and she is openly delighted at the memory] Sophie gave a little contented smile.

You have to remember that most men of every generation base their ego strength on the fact that their work is more important than women's and that they are more important than women, and I think there was a large part of David like that. . . .

On the other hand, David would never have made the crude remarks about women that my father made. You know, women can't drive or washing dishes is women's work. All that kind of crap. . . . So Stephen wouldn't have been indoctrinated in any really basic misogyny. David's chauvinism came out when male hegemony was threatened or challenged in some way.

So Stephen was different from David in the depth of his egalitarian attitude, and if he didn't get this from David, where did he get it? Judith Golden recalls his already having it in high school. Stephen can offer no insights and neither can Michele. To her it is a wonderful mystery. Given Stephen's troubled relationship with Sophie, neither of them thinks that's where the extra dimension developed. Could it be that the treasured events of his childhood, long since passed from active memory, were the rare occasions when he could accompany his father somewhere? Most likely it would be to a party function; David and Sophie had no social life to speak of outside the party. It would be like other fathers taking their children to the office. There he would see equality in action and, having little to contradict it, would have every reason to think this was the way of the world outside the confines of the party business as well as within.

In any event, as Michele says, an egalitarian attitude is one thing but feminism is another.

I remember what a classic battle we had over taking turns with the dishes. Stephen was in the Legislature, I was working at the *Globe*, so we were both working weird hours. So I said, "Why should I both cook and serve and then wash the dishes?" Stephen agreed. That was fair. So we were going to take turns every other day. Only, Stephen would leave the dishes in the sink and I'd come home the next day and there'd be all these dirty dishes and I'd say, "Well, why didn't you wash them?" And he'd say, "I'm going to, but in my own sweet time," and we fought over that for a week because [and she is laughing because Stephen, who is sitting across the table, looks so dismayed], because he refused to accept that this was a way of sabotaging his end of the commitment and getting out of the work."

[Did I *really* say that, Stephen asks?]

It's a classic scenario. [Says Michele, still laughing.] It really is. I think a million other women had gone through the same thing, especially in the sixties when they were beginning to assert their rights and share the dishwashing. But when I finally made the argument cogently enough, Stephen accepted it and that was the end of the argument.

So now, says Stephen, "I have not only accepted feminism but have embraced it as a centrepiece of my socialism. . . . Now," and this time it is he who is laughing, "I'm a bore on the subject. I have all the fanaticism of the convert."

By the end of his first year at the U of T, Stephen had made his mark where he wanted it known, in debating and within the CCF club; so when his second year began and Lester Pearson, then minister of external affairs, came to Hart House to debate a resolution that "NATO has outlived its uselfulness," Stephen was chosen as one of the four debaters. He was the youngster among the four: two of the others were graduate students; the fourth was in second-year law.

Debates were held under parliamentary rules where two debaters spoke for the resolution, two against and the guest, in this case Pearson, spoke from the floor as the fifth speaker. Stephen was on the team supporting the motion and argued that NATO was ignoring the provision in its charter that called for economic and social collaboration, and therefore had doomed itself to be nothing more than a military alliance. "Great fun. Moments you cut your teeth on," he would say thirty years later. Pearson, of course, argued against the resolution and won the vote 203 to 65.[4] The debate, interestingly, was covered for The Varsity by Ed Broadbent, who reported occasionally for the paper.

This was the fall that Stephen and John Brewin changed campus politics. A mock parliament had been a yearly event but it had been only that: an event. Halfway through the fall of 1956 the two already seasoned campaigners had the CCF club romping before the footlights as no campus party had before. First there was an announcement that the club would hold a leadership convention; then leadership candidates announced themselves — Stephen and John Brewin among them — and policy resolutions were proposed; then the convention was held, policies were adopted — and Stephen was elected party leader and Brewin became deputy leader. Then another meeting was called to adopt more policy resolutions; then a pre-election rally was held at which Bert Gargrave, a Steelworker representative, and Andy Brewin, then national treasurer of the CCF, gave speeches. Finally there was the election. The university had never seen anything like it. Not a week went by without a front-page story in The Varsity about what the CCF club was doing. Even the name "mock parliament" was changed to "model parliament." On election day there was, according to The Varsity, "the largest vote ever recorded in a U of T election": 1,947 students turned out, 36 percent more than the previous year.

The Tories won forty of the seats, the CCF twenty-six, and the Liberals twenty-two; Varsity photographs of three nights of debate in the legislative chambers at Queen's Park show Stephen speaking from the same seat in the House that he was to occupy eighteen years later as a member of the Legislature and leader of the official opposition.[5]

Two weeks after the model parliament, Brewin was elected president of the CCF club and Stephen vice-president, and they immediately began a series of campus forums sponsored by the club and held in the various colleges and residences of the university. It was exactly the same kind of thing that David had organized through the Labour Club at Oxford when he was there as a student.

The summer of 1957 saw Stephen running Andy Brewin's campaign in the June federal election, working at Camp Ogama, and then, with Gerry Caplan and Owen Shime, heading south in David's car to Little Rock, Arkansas, where Governor Orval E. Faubus had called out the state militia to prevent black students from entering Little Rock High School, claiming that violence, bloodshed, and rioting might break out if blacks entered the school.

Heading to Arkansas was a spur-of-the moment decision. It was the beginning of September and university hadn't yet started, and since David was in Europe with the diesel firemen royal commission, his car, sitting in the driveway, was an open invitation. They got press passes from *The Varsity* and Stephen got authorization from CBC to say that he was preparing a freelance radio documentary, and they took off.

Their first encounter with Southern racism came in a little Mississippi town where they stopped at a snack bar. It happened that a black teenager in town had been shot by a storeowner for looking at his wife and the storeowner had just been acquitted by a jury. "I remember getting into a discussion with the snack bar owner," says Owen Shime, "and he looked at Stephen and Gerry and me and said, 'If you go out and kill a Nigra' — and that's how he pronounced it, Nigra — 'there won't be a white jury in all of Mississippi that'll ever convict you.'

"And he reached behind him and handed us a gun. I think that was probably the first time I had ever seen a gun. A real gun. And he was prepared to hand it right over to us. It was really very shocking."

Shime, two years older than Stephen, is chairman of the Ontario Grievance Settlement Board, a tall man of greying curly hair and languid energy, like a loose-limbed basketball player, whose words come in ordered sentences — monitored, examined in transit, and assessed on arrival. He speaks in facts, with few adjectives. The language of a man trained to daily precision. But it's precise without being clipped, factual without being dry. And tendrils of emotion now and then sneak around the corner of a word. Once in a while they balloon underneath so that the flat landscape of a sentence suddenly bulges. There must be a tune that he marches to, sombre sometimes, sometimes crisp, sometimes impassioned. Dark with undercurrents. But distant. It barely reaches the living room on the fringe of Rosedale where he is marshalling his memories, and when it does it lingers in the background with the dark oak. Tchaikovsky, is it? "The Capriccio Italien?"

With all the brashness of youth the three drove around Little Rock, once they arrived, talking to blacks — and were pulled over on a back road by state militia and questioned by a colonel. "I think if we had been from a Northern liberal newspaper we might have been in trouble," says Shime. "But we told him we were Canadians and . . . we were there as observers and we weren't there to cause trouble. . . . But they clearly indicated that we were being watched."

They even walked up to the front door of the governor's mansion and asked to speak to Faubus.

> We didn't get to see Faubus [but] we met with his two executive assistants. . . . Nothing much came of that. They were very uncertain. They were flapping about. They had no sense of what they would do. The national government was against them. My sense is that they were a very unsophisticated group. . . .
>
> My major recollection is of a master sergeant who had been with MacArthur either at Bataan or Corregidor, and he had a gun in his hand — a rifle or a Sten gun or whatever, I don't know the difference — and we were standing on the governor's back porch. He looked down to the very far end of the garden which was surrounded by a wall and he looked at me and he said, "If a Negro climbs over this fence, I could pick his ass off right from here." And I believed him.

They were invited to spend the night in one of the tents that the militia had set up on the governor's grounds. They accepted, and Stephen conducted a long interview with the colonel who had stopped them on the back road — "I remember he expressed the rawest racism I have ever confronted," he says — but they were kicked out in the small hours of the morning when a militiaman walked by their tent and overheard them talking about their impressions of what was happening.

They also sought out Daisy Bates, president of the Arkansas branch of the National Association for the Advancement of Colored People. Once again, they simply walked up to the front door and knocked. They stayed for an evening meeting held in a basement room where the decision was taken to try once more to send the students to school. The day before, nine black students had gone to the school but, according to The New York Times, "A mob of belligerent, shrieking and hysterical demonstrators forced [them] to withdraw."[6] On the outside eaves of the Bates house were scorch marks left by a burning cross that had been planted on the front lawn. There were nine or ten in the room, says Shime. Mrs. Bates and her husband, a neighbouring couple, a white mathematics professor "who also happened to be Jewish,

I think from the University of Arkansas," the three from Toronto, and possibly one other person. "I remember someone drawing the curtains," Shime says, "because they were afraid someone might shoot inside. It was dark and, as cars drove by, their lights flashed in the windows."

The decision was made to send the children to school. The following morning, federal troops of the 327th Airborne Battle Group of the 101st Airborne Division, ordered in by President Eisenhower, ringed the school, bayonets attached to rifles, and in the crowd outside the school the three met Harry Arthurs and Martin Friedland, the one later to become dean of Osgoode Hall law school; the other, dean of law at the University of Toronto. They were hitchhiking through the Southern states. The crowd was ugly, angry not only with the blacks but with Northern liberals and especially Jews.

> Being Jewish [says Shime], my inclination was to turn around and hit them. . . . I was really very angered. I looked at Stephen and Gerry and realized there was no point. If I hit them I was going to have to deal with three or four hundred others. . . .
> I remember a woman in front of me screaming and yelling at these young black children with such hatred . . . the spit was coming out of her mouth.
> The crowd started to press forward and the soldiers, holding their rifles in front of them, bayonets in place, started to march forward . . . pushing the crowd back. . . . Somehow, I think the people in the crowd realized that the soldiers meant business and when the kids got into the school they . . . dissipated and then we left.

On their way home they passed through Georgia, driving very carefully within the speed limit because they had heard about the "notorious" Georgia speed traps. Even so, they were stopped by a local policeman, told they were speeding, and advised that they could pay the $15 fine on the spot and be on their way.

"It was obviously some kind of payoff," Shime says, "and being young and idealistic, we said we would fight the speeding ticket." So they were escorted to a jail with a room where court was held in a place called Flowery Bluffs to wait for the judge, who also drove the school bus. He fined them $20, but since they had no money, they asked to pay in American Express traveller's cheques. The judge refused.

> Stephen was very eloquent [says Shime. People had come in from the street and were crowding around and] Stephen made a speech telling the local people how we, as Canadians, had been invited to come to

the United States by President Eisenhower and told to buy American Express traveller's cheques when we came.

Well, at that point they decided not to put us in jail, and called for the town treasurer, who said traveller's cheques would be fine. By this time there were about a hundred people standing around. . . . I gave them a traveller's cheque, but I didn't sign it . . . and as they were passing it around the crowd, we turned and walked to the car.

Stephen and Gerry were already in the car when the treasurer called me back, and I remember walking back through this ring of people, and he said, "Don't you have to countersign this?" I was scared out of my wits [but] I said, "I've already signed it. That's where you sign it." And I walked back through the crowd pretending I'd done nothing wrong. . . .

When we got to New York we reported the traveller's cheque stolen and they stopped payment. But months later, David Lewis was contacted by the Metro Toronto police — he was the lawyer for the police — who told him there was a warrant out that we had given a phony traveller's cheque to the police in Georgia. I remember David collecting $6 and change from Gerry and Stephen and me and sending it to Flowery Bluffs, Georgia.

Barely were they on the road again when they were pulled over once more and charged with speeding. Once again they were driven into a little town, this time accompanied by another accused, a black grandfather who had with him his daughter and her three pre-school children. The grandfather had been in an accident and was charged with being drunk while driving, but it was obvious, says Shime, that he was sober and it was the white driver of the other car who was drunk. On the way in, one of the children was crying. "I remember a police officer taking the gun out of his holster, holding it by the barrel, and threatening to hit the child with the butt if the woman didn't stop its crying. He was cursing. I was horrified. I'd never seen anyone treated that way."

The Toronto three paid their fine, the grandfather was jailed, and the woman and her children were driven out of town and left on the roadside. It was one in the morning. On the way out of town the three, followed by police, drove past her. When the police finally stopped tailing them, they doubled back and picked up the woman and her children and drove them to Atlanta. "The woman was shaking, the children were shaking; they were cold and upset. And because we were white, she was frightened. But I guess we were still the best alternative."

When they stopped at a roadside diner to get some milk for the children a crowd gathered, pointing and muttering, so they got out as quickly as they could. By the time they reached Atlanta they were sickened by the South. Later they stopped for dinner at a delicatessen and their revulsion was made all the worse when they discovered that their Jewish waitress was as racist as all the others they had met. "She poured out a stream of racist, anti-black invective that just traumatized us," says Caplan. "It was bad enough that everyone else that we'd seen was racist," But to be Jewish and racist "just blew us away again."

"By then our nerves were raw," says Shime. "We'd seen enough of Georgia. We'd seen enough of racism. I mean, I'd seen a police officer threatening an infant in his mother's arms with a gun. The waitress made a comment, the man behind the counter made a comment, and I lost my temper and I was over the counter to grab him by the throat. And Gerry and Stephen grabbed me."

Shaken, they took a room at the YMCA and, unable to sleep, they talked far into the night, and the longer they talked and the more unrelieved their outrage, the more their anger distilled into determination; and as the pre-dawn sky began to lighten they placed hand upon hand and swore a solemn pledge that they would never rest until they changed the world. "The whole situation made a tremendous impact on us," says Stephen. "Just being a witness to a social struggle. And then the subsequent travels and all we did out on the highways and byways and cotton fields and meeting people and making contacts.

"Yeah," he says, and you can sense him going back through time and feeling once again the emotions of that trip. "Yeah, it made a great impression."

It made a deep impression on Shime too. He found the discrimination so oppressive that, with one exception, he has refused ever since to return to the American South. The one exception was when his wife was ill, shortly before her death, and Florida was the only place he could take her for a winter holiday where there was convenient medical help.

Stephen arrived back in Toronto exhausted, gaunt, and half-sick. In addition to Little Rock and Atlanta, their trip had taken them to Jackson, Mississippi; New Orleans; Durham, North Carolina; Washington; and New York. "He looks frightful," Sophie wrote David, who was still in Europe. "He is terribly exhausted and says he lost seven pounds and has laryngitis and talks excitedly despite the raw throat and ears and croaking voice. . . . He set out tired and returned in what looks like the verge of collapse. I feel once this exhilaration passes, he's bound to feel let down."[7]

In Paris, David was worried about whether Stephen would be able to cope with repeating his second year at university.

I know that what I write next will annoy you [he wrote to Sophie]. Please don't be annoyed; I speak out of my anxiety. . . .

I wish I could persuade you to remove the resentment and ease the hurt in him for which we must be, in part at least, responsible. You always think I am appeasing him. That is wrong. I act the way I do for three reasons. First, because it's the only way to have any influence. There are people — you are one of them as well as he — who will react to love and understanding but who rear up on their hind legs whenever they are "told" or criticized. Second, because I firmly believe it to be my duty as a parent to subordinate my immediate inner reaction to the main purpose of considering the child's needs and position. Thirdly, because achievement of peace and understanding in a family is immeasurably more important than asserting parental sovereignty. I think — I am sure — I am right.

At all events, this is an absolutely crucial winter in Stephen's life. If we create an atmosphere of warmth and love and being wanted for him, and if he succeeds in disciplining himself and seeing things in a more mature perspective, he will be on the road to accomplishments and happiness which his great capacities and sensitiveness make possible. If we contribute to giving him another winter like the last couple, he may well be irreparably damaged. I do not claim infallibility, but I do not think I exaggerate.[8]

It was no easy undertaking that David was asking of Sophie. As Ray Stancer says, "Stephen and Sophie were both really high-strung and there were constant clashes." A week after David sent his letter, Sophie wrote to say that Stephen still looked "ghastly."

He still flies off the handle but I can see he's trying to control himself. We've had no tiff and each time I'm on the verge of answering back I see your face and stop. But *stop*. I think my silence is flooring him somewhat.

Michael keeps looking at me out of the corner of his eye as though to say, "Let him talk, mother, but don't say anything." I told Mike that I've caught his eye and felt his nudge a few times and I've paid attention to him.

Stephen still says, "Sophie," and uses his favourite expressions in speech. But I'm holding fast. He told me the letter from the dean of residence . . . told him "he probably could get into residence." "So," he said, "What do I do?"

"Do whatever you want," I told him. "I would want you to stay at home very much. Let's both try to get along from now on."

"That's what I want, mother. T'hell with the dean."

Let's hope it works out.[9]

It did work out. Stephen and Sophie managed a workable truce, even with the odd lapse, and Stephen passed second year and was a major figure on the university campus as he frolicked across the political footlights. He and John Brewin continued the program of CCF forums in the various university colleges which they had begun the previous spring[10] and the CCF club, according to *The Varsity*, "started off the year with a bang" by challenging the other campus parties to a debate.[11] The debate was held before a packed house and *The Varsity* declared Stephen the "strongest speaker": "Lewis . . . said the CCF was not in politics for power but to exert a moral influence."

"He outlined the basic beliefs of the CCF, that economics should be planned with 'ethics not expediency,' that the party would not yield to 'greed' in the face of 'need,' and that the concentration of wealth in the hands of so few stifles human initiative.'

"He said the CCF was fighting for 'the reformation of society.' "[12]

Once again a CCF campus convention was held; David was the keynote speaker and John Brewin was elected leader.[13] Once again there were a series of events that kept the club in the news and led up to a pre-election rally that this time featured Colin Cameron. Once again campus voting broke the record with 2,892 ballots cast. (The Conservatives won forty-nine seats, the Liberals twenty-two, and the CCF sixteen.[14])

And there were debates, debates, and more debates. Stephen toured U.S. universities as part of a U of T debating team;[15] he participated in an international debate at the U of T at which he and a U.S. debater were declared best speakers;[16] and, what has remained most in the memory of people who were at the university during those years, he participated in a debate with the junior senator from Massachusetts, John F. Kennedy. In 1956 Kennedy had been Adlai Stevenson's vice-presidential running mate and it was clear he was going for the presidential nomination in 1960. The debate at Hart House was in the same format as the Pearson debate: two for, two against, and Kennedy speaking from the floor as a guest. The resolution was "Has the United States failed in its responsibilities as a world leader?" Stephen was on the team arguing the affirmative; it lost by the narrow margin of five votes: 204–194. Kennedy stuck to his notes and gave a relatively flat speech.[17] But Stephen, accusing the United States of vacillating "in the face of pressure" and fumbling its role as "policeman, baby-sitter and bank of the world,"[18] transfixed the overflow crowd in Hart House.

"The speech that he made is still one of the best speeches I've ever heard," says John Brewin. "It was superb. . . . The place was jammed. Stephen had the whole room standing when he wanted to. Cheering and clapping. Or quiet. It was like conducting an orchestra. It was so powerful that I think it even shook Stephen, and I think that after that he felt he almost had to gear down in a speech.

"Kennedy's speech was nothing like as good."

Stephen's year at the University of British Columbia, where he obtained his third-year credits, was as different as night from day. For the first time he became a serious student. There was no involvement in student politics to speak of. He did take a seat in the university's model parliament and gave a speech that had all kinds of clubs and organizations after him to debate or to become a member, including the most exclusive fraternity. But he turned them all down. At the end of the year his professor of Canadian history told him that if he returned to UBC for his final year she was sure a post-graduate fellowship could be arranged for him at a major American university.[19]

However, he couldn't face another year so far away from home. His letters to his parents had been filled with a loneliness that often extended into depression. So it was back to Toronto — and to Kenneth McNaught at the U of T for his final year. In one of his letters home, he discussed the impending creation of the NDP with prophetic insight.

> I do not get the feeling that the New Party is going to have accrue to it the indispensable quality of "newness" requisite to success. Just a mere broadening of the base doesn't seem to be enough. . . .
>
> Even the argument of political education is somewhat specious since all that can really be accomplished in the short time remaining is stepped-up political propaganda — which, considering the party "machines" of our rivals, may prove of dubious effect. It would be a minor tragedy to put Tommy D. in the field in 1962 only to have him crucified. Or maybe we're now thinking even further ahead, and if that is so, what sustains us as a vocal political force in the interim?
>
> . . . I believe that one of the absolutely necessary aims is to jolt us out of our present directionless state. . . . Surely the inertia of modern 20th century socialism is at least partly attributable to the lack of "objectives" which tends to immobilize the movement within and without. Thus, I say, the old platforms have to be reinvigorated and the old philosophy reformulated or we shall pursue a frustrated course. . . .[20]

The highlight of Stephen's final year at the U of T was McNaught's seminar. But coming a close second was winning the election for the model parliament. The Varsity called it an "upset victory." The CCF won 754 votes, the Conservatives 601, and the Liberals 580 for a 39–31–30 standing.[21]

> The reason we won [says Gerry Caplan] was because Stephen intro-
> duced door-to-door canvassing at the university. . . . Actually, it was
> a precursor to Riverdale [four years later]. Ken Bryden in his end of
> Toronto [the Beaches] and Stephen and a couple of people in the west
> end in Davenport riding were playing with all these techniques. . . .
>
> We had canvassers knock on every single door of every residence.
> And we had tea and coffee parties. And it worked just like in the by-
> election [that elected Jim Renwick]. . . .
>
> A lot of people did the work but if it hadn't been for Stephen having
> the *chutzpah* and the creativity to say, "Why not?" it wouldn't have
> been done. But it was always Stephen.

Just reading some of the names in the CCF student cabinet conveys
a sense of the excitement that surrounded the victory. Gerry Caplan,
prime minister; Stephen Lewis, external affairs; Giles Endicott (later
a founder of the Waffle), arts and culture; Owen Shime, justice; Mac
Makarchuk (elected to the Legislature in 1975), defence production;
Margaret Brewin (Andy's daughter), agriculture; Hugh Peacock (elected
to the Legislature in 1967), trade and commerce; Larry Zolf, labour;
Harvey Levenstein, veteran's affairs, John Smart (later a leading
Waffler), postmaster-general; Marc Sommerville (nephew of Ted Jolliffe
and a lawyer in Galt who later ran provincially), northern affairs and
development; Ann Dale (who was to become Caplan's first wife),
immigration.

After university Stephen left for London, England, to work with
the Socialist International, and almost as quickly found himself in
Africa.

> I got this brochure about a World Assembly of Youth conference in
> Accra, and it was very appealing because it was clear that they were
> going to have a lot of people from around the world and Africa was
> an exhilarating continent at the time. Ghana had just become indepen-
> dent in 1957, the first African country to reach independence. . . .
>
> I wrote and said I would go and represent Canadian socialist youth
> and they said, sure. So I went and I was overwhelmed by the vibrancy
> and excitement of their society. [Kwame] Nkrumah was not yet mad,
> and everyone and everything was agog with the single-mindedness of
> independence. Everywhere you turned, the country was working as one
> to make of the independence something important, and I decided at
> the conference, the details of which I remember nothing, that I would
> look for a job in Ghana. And I did.

He got a job teaching extramural studies at the University of Ghana
at Legon, near Accra and, because the pay was low, a second job
teaching English and history at Accra High School. "Accra, to Africans,

was freedom," says Stephen. "This is where it all was happening. This was Africanism."

On the plane to the conference he sat with Joshua Nkomo, and the conference itself attracted "young, aggressive, radical African leaders who subsequently occupied senior positions in the republic." Shortly afterward he met Kenneth Kaunda, just released from a British prison and on his way to a Commonwealth conference in Lagos. As time went on, he met emerging leaders from all over black Africa. One of the people he met at the conference was Mukwugo Okoye, a Nigerian.

> I had been in Ghana for many months [Stephen says] and I suddenly got a letter from Muk saying "Come to the eastern region [of Nigeria], live with me in my village. There's a Peace Corps school, a high school that just opened, but the Peace Corps hasn't arrived. They need a principal. Please come and be principal."
>
> I was too excited to say no, so I went off to the eastern region and I lived with Muk in his village. I learned an enormous amount from him. He writes tracts and polemics: wild and stream-of-consciousness and incredibly rich with detail and quotation. He was determined never to enter politics himself. Just to be a gadfly of the left in that part of Nigerian society.
>
> He also had a great influence on me and I loved what I learned from him. The living was so intense and so intimate in the eastern region. My students were all vital and lively — thirteen- and fourteen- and fifteen- and sixteen-year-olds. It was the first year of high school, and I built the whole course and found texts and trained teachers. There had been nothing there. It was such an extraordinary experience to be part of that. And then to go back to the village and there was Muk expostulating on radical causes and pan-Africanism.

Obviously moved by the memory, Stephen looks away, across his UN ambassador's office, and for a moment the only sound is the ratchety hum of an old air-conditioner and the *thwak-thwak-thwak* of a helicopter passing somewhere out of sight along New York's East River. Then he resumes: "I genuinely had fallen in love with the continent and it preoccupied me in later years. Even while I was in the provincial legislature I would make speeches on Africa. I felt very deeply about the continent and what its future would hold."

It's only after you leave that you realize that what Stephen was talking about when he was describing almost two years in Africa was something that, for the first time in his life, was uniquely his own. This was not a CCF project. He was not organizing for the party. Managing a campaign. Debating. Being the brilliant son of a brilliant father. Carrying the flame. Here no one knew the name David Lewis.

No one had expectations or preconceptions. He was his own person, entirely and for the first time.

It was while Stephen was in Africa that the New Democratic Party was born. David, once again, was the central figure — both father and midwife.[22] The union of party and labour came twenty-five years almost to the day after his first formal attempt at bringing the two together in a resolution drafted by him and passed during the CCF's fourth convention at the beginning of August 1936. (See Appendix P.)

The party was quite frank about seeing the creation of the NDP as an effort to broaden its base — not just by incorporating labour but in attracting the community at large. What was particularly interesting about the six years of laying the groundwork for the NDP founding convention in July 1961 was how the party toned itself down in its formal declarations. It went from pledging support for public owner-ship, ending monopolistic control of the economy, and eliminating greed to innocuous statements about remaining loyal to principles of democratic socialism. During that time the CLC's formal declarations were consistently shying away from socialism, saying the NDP should be a home not just for socialists but for "liberally minded persons interested in basic social reform."[23]

Obviously the party was toning down to accommodate the CLC, and the climax came with the New Party Declaration passed at the found-ing convention which never once used the word "socialism." Nor did it refer to democratic socialism. And it referred to social democracy only once, and that was in a historical reference which said: ". . . this New Democratic party . . . adopts and will carry forward to new levels of achievement the best objectives of the farmer and labour, co-operative and social democratic movements for which so many progressive Canadians have striven in the past."[24]

In formal wording, this no longer was a socialist party, and indeed, the word "socialism" was banned from its official vocabulary for two years. The ban was so obvious that the editor of The Ottawa Journal published a ditty:

> Oh no! We never mention it;
> Its name is never heard.
> Our lips are now forbid to speak
> That once familiar word
> Socialism.[25]

It was only after the party's dismal showing in the 1963 federal election that the fearsome word was allowed back in. As historian Desmond Morton records, the party's August 1963 convention adopted a statement of Principles and Objectives in which "Little of the prose could have offended anyone to the left of the Chambers of Commerce but cautiously ensconced in the second sentence was the assurance that NDP principles were 'the principles of democratic socialism applied to our time and situation.'"[26]

The strongest rhetoric that the New Party Declaration could muster committed the party to putting "human rights and human dignity above the mere pursuit of wealth, and public welfare before corporate power" — a statement even the Liberal Party could live with. There were a couple of economic proposals that the Liberals would have balked at, such as the call for a federal Investment Board to regulate where companies could invest their funds and the proposal that all companies operating in Canada be required to have minimum Canadian ownership and representation on boards of directors. But aside from that, it was, indeed, a document aimed at the "liberally minded."

David worked very hard getting approval for the New Party, Ted Jolliffe says. "I'd say for at least three years. . . . I know he spent hours on the telephone and making trips here and there, all over the place. He was the key man. The key man in all those negotations. . . .

"He tried very hard to get Trudeau involved. . . . I remember a meeting in Montreal at the Mount Royal Hotel . . . shortly before the founding convention [and] Trudeau dropped in. He stood at the back of the hall beside me. He didn't say a word. He just listened. He was wearing his famous sandals. Very unconventionally attired."

The first step in creating the New Party Declaration was to get discussion groups across the country offering suggestions. According to Ken Bryden, who was provincial secretary for the Ontario wing of the party at the time,

> . . . we had two regional conferences [and] out of all this we got great masses of recommendations. Very fragmentary, as these things always are. The time for the founding convention was rapidly approaching and . . . David phoned up one day and said, "Look, we've got all this stuff on the program and nobody's doing a damned thing about it. So I want you down at my office on Sunday morning. . . ."
>
> It was late winter. A dreary, dreary day, as Toronto can be. So I go down and there's David, Mike Oliver who was brought in from Montreal — who [later] became president of the New Party — and Andy Brewin. The four of us. And we just divided it up. I took the economic

section. David took the international one, of course. Nobody would ever get that from him although Andy Brewin fancied it himself. As between Mike and Andy, I'm not sure who took which, but I think Andy had social programs and Mike had the institutions of government, the bill of rights, and that sort of thing. . . .

Anyway, we sorted out all this pile of junk we had and we wrote for the whole damned day. About four in the afternoon we had all our drafts completed, and we went over them and made some changes and then David turned the whole thing over to Bucky Buchanan, a journalist, to translate into readable English. And that, essentially, was the program of the New Democratic Party. . . .

You see, it was always David taking the initiative and getting things done. I must say I was getting worried.

Looking back on it from the 1980s, the document was exactly what Stephen, the young student at UBC, had warned his father against, saying that without revitalizing platforms and philosophy, "we shall pursue a frustrated course." David had realized the danger but saw little that could be done about it. He wrote Stephen six weeks after receiving Stephen's letter and described a New Party meeting in Oakville where he was "a little disturbed at the lack of an idealistic spark. The people are genuine enough in their interest and loyal enough. But it's too much 'bread and butter' and a little too much 'what the labour movement can get out of it,' and not enough selfless idealism, not enough of 'what can the labour movement give to it.' But I suppose that's merely a sign of our times; idealism, pure and simple, is not in fashion in a time of crass materialist expansion."[27]

Continuing a backward look, it's clear that somewhere along the way socialism in Canada gave up trying to change the system and settled instead for striving for a more humane and equitable distribution of wealth and power. Maybe July 1961 is as good a date as any to mark the switch.

There are arguments to be made that the change in direction may not be a bad thing. In his new book, Alan Borovoy warns against a belief that human nature will change if systems are changed. It's the redemptive fallacy, he says, adding that "The harbouring of unrealistic goals tends to erode the ranks of the social reformers." He suggests that "whatever we do in the area of public policy is likely to be bad. . . . We must guard against the temptation to escape into fantasy. Neither God nor socialism, neither the Ten Commandments nor the categorical imperative, can help us to transcend reality. If we are to solve our problems intelligently in the here and now, we must do so within the limits of unpalatable alternatives available. . . . The realistic *goal of looking beyond yesterday's solutions is not the good, it is the less bad.''*[28]

I.L. Peretz, telling his tale about Taming the Bear, quoted in the Introduction, travels the same territory.

Nevertheless, the irony was that at the very moment that the New Party Declaration was being prepared, C. B. [Brough] Macpherson, the brilliant professor of political science at the University of Toronto, was putting finishing touches to *The Political Theory of Possessive Individualism,* the book in which he was to burrow into the psyche of capitalism and lay bare its crucial flaw.

Macpherson maintained that deep within the id of liberal democracy lay a fundamental instinct that shaped its every action. It was the lust for personal property. That, he said, is what produced the excesses of capitalism.

Although he didn't say so explicitly because he was not employing Marxist terms, what he did was illustrate how historical materialism operated and, for the first time, he isolated the psychosis that it produced. It was a clinical demonstration of how values got twisted. Of how good and bad, right and wrong, came to be redefined in terms of the ownership of property. How the moral code of society came to be rewritten. He illustrated in chapter and verse how a market society (a system of production) shaped the values of liberal democracy (the attitude of a people) and raised an altar to property.

In its more extreme form, the possessive individualism in the title of his book is a doctrine of greed. It flourishes because, says Macpherson, at the root of traditional liberal democratic theory, at the starting point, is the concept that all people are equal because they have equal property in themselves. And since they own themselves, as it were, all the traditional freedoms follow. Other people, for instance, are barred from infringing on their property rights, meaning others cannot arbitrarily arrest, imprison, or try them or deny them freedom of speech, association, and religion. It's almost a parody of Descartes: *Habeo, ergo sum* — "I own, therefore I am."

The two corollaries of proprietorship of self are first, nobody owes anything to society. Ownership is a first principle and carries no obligation to the community at large. And second, what you own you can sell, so people, in actuality their labour, become commodities.

In a devastating analysis that runs through *The Political Theory of Possessive Individualism* and another of his books, *The Life and Times of Liberal Democracy* — and extends from Thomas Hobbes to John Stuart Mill — Macpherson argues that ownership of property was made the cornerstone of liberal democratic theory because philosophers,

beginning with Hobbes, saw it as the cornerstone of the private enterprise society that was evolving at the time, and they were trying to
incorporate reality into theory. As a result, liberal democracy was
fashioned to fit and to justify private enterprise. Consequently its function was to preserve class distinctions and give moral sanction to the
unequal acquisition of property. And that meant moral sanction for
acquiring as much as you possibly could with little responsibility for
those left behind.

There is a danger of over-enthusiasm in embracing Macpherson's
insights. He was not a behaviourist. He was not trying to analyze the
bewildering complexity of motivation that enters into human action.
There are always other desires and fears and ambitions and sympathies
that vie for pride of place in any decision. But in showing how ac-
quisitiveness came to be honoured and how it was reinforced with a
moral underpinning, he gave it an emphasis that can never be ignored.

Had David been aware of what Macpherson was up to, it would
have set him afire. He hated with a fury the twisted values, the distorted
priorities, that a hungry monopoly capitalism pressed on all below,
be they labourers, small business people, office workers, farmers, or
professionals.

Had he known, surely some of that fire would have found its way
into the New Party Declaration. The party was struggling to change
the false perception that it was obsessed with public ownership. Here
was Macpherson dealing with the greatest moral issue of all time. What
is good? What is bad? What is right? What is wrong? Surely this is
the stuff of socialism.

But David wasn't aware that the book was coming out.

And there was no fire in the declaration.

•CHAPTER TWENTY-ONE•

*I think I really am an ideologue. I think I have been driven
in a fashion often obsessive and sometimes unbalanced by
the need to better the world, to eradicate injustice, to
challenge the liberal premise.*

Stephen Lewis
May 1987

Two days after the NDP founding convention, Tommy Douglas dashed off a handwritten note to Sophie Lewis on the letterhead of the premier's office, Saskatchewan. Tommy had not sought the national leadership. In fact he determinedly had not wanted it. For one thing, he was on the verge of introducing medicare to Saskatchewan — the Legislature passed the medicare bill just a few days after he stepped down as premier on November 1.[1] But the leadership had been pressed upon him and the most relentless among those pressing had been David. Tommy had held out until June 28 — one month before the convention — and before he succumbed, he extracted from David the commitment that, if he agreed to go for the leadership, David would run in the next election.[2]

When David told Sophie, her heart sank with such force that she felt violated. Shoved aside and aborted of her most cherished hope. David was almost fifty-two years old, and even after he had resigned as national secretary of the party and they had moved to Toronto, he still kept her from the centre of his life. Made her stand in line. But finally that was going to change, she had told herself. So soon that she could feel the warmth of its nearness. And when it came, she would make it a rebirth. An intertwining they hadn't experienced since Oxford. But from the moment he mentioned his conversations with Tommy, she knew he was snatching that dream from her. Declaring that there would be no change. In fact, telling her that everything would be worse because daily politics, she knew, would force her still farther from the centre.

David had been consumed with other things — of necessity, she had told herself. He had to build a law practice. Provide for their security. But at last they were comfortable financially. And the frenzy of the past five years was almost over — the labour mergers, the declarations, the New Party, the incessant phone calls that came on her time, the evenings away, the weekend meetings, the preoccupation. So now, what was he doing? He was telling her he wanted to be a member of Parliament. Saying that all this had been only a prelude.

"Dear Sophie," Tommy began. "This is just a note I am dashing off before boarding a plane to Charlottetown, PEI."

If Tommy had had any idea of the memories that sentence would stir — of all those letters from David saying, this is just a note, my darling, written from God knew what place, waiting for God knew what train, going to God knew what town where he'd be for God knew how long — he never would have written it.

> I'm writing to urge you to persuade David to run in York South. . . . [W]e shall need him in the House of Commons. We can't do an effective job if one of the best debaters is sitting on the sidelines.
>
> However, my main consideration is for David himself. He belongs in the House of Commons and has always wanted to be there. If he doesn't fulfill his boyhood dreams he will he unhappy the rest of his life. Another election will be too late — if he is going to have a parliamentary career he has to run now!
>
> I recognize the necessity of having some financial arrangements with his law firm to guarantee an adequate income and I'm sure this can be done. However, it is equally important for a man to feel that he has kept his date with destiny — otherwise he becomes frustrated and develops a sense of futility.
>
> I'm sure Stephen would endorse what I'm saying. All of us who know David and love him realize that he can never have a full sense of fulfillment apart from the party he has laboured so hard to bring into being. Hope you'll help me in this my dearest wish.
>
> As ever,
> Tommy.[3]

One could say of the old master that he could be damned persuasive. One could also say he knew how to leave a woman with no alternative. How could Sophie say no? Tommy was right. If she stood her ground and held David to his commitment to her, he would be denying his "date with destiny." He would indeed become frustrated. He would indeed be "unhappy the rest of his life." And the finger would point straight at her. Tommy already was pointing it.

There was no way Sophie could win. Her only choice was how could she lose the least. Of course she agreed. At least this way there would be no resentment on David's part to distance them still further. But it wasn't without a struggle. Owen Shime was in the living room of the Lewis home when they were discussing Tommy's letter: "Sophie was very upset. There were tears [and] she was very vociferous. . . . Obviously she had erupted. And David in his sort of calm manner was saying, 'Now, now, Sophie dear.' . . . And I remember her pointing and saying, 'You know, this is the first time I've even had dishes for my dining room.'" For years they didn't even have a dining room table. "And the furniture was very battered."

On June 18, 1962, David became the member for York South in Toronto and his elation in entering the House was everything he ever expected it to be.

Stephen and Gerry Caplan were co-managers of his election campaign. Stephen had returned from Africa at Tommy's request after the party's founding convention. "He wrote me a letter," says Stephen, "which I simply could not possibly resist. I would have resisted any other invitation, but Tommy said, 'Come back and be director of organization for the New Party.' So I returned."

On his arrival he was sent immediately to Manitoba, where his first job was to find the party a provincial secretary, and he worked there until he came back to Ontario for David's York South campaign. The strategy for getting David elected was to break into the Jewish vote in Forest Hill, says Stephen, because the party didn't have enough votes from the working-class areas of the riding's west end.

There was too much of the riding which consisted of Forest Hill. If you couldn't break that, you were dead. It was my job to break it. . . .

What happened was that we went to key names in the Jewish community, to Leon Weinstein [then president of Power Super Markets Ltd. and later to become president of Loblaw Groceterias Co. Ltd.], to Mark Levy [chairman of Levy Industries Ltd.], to the big Jewish fundraiser, Stephen Berger, and we brought their friends together. We cracked the most notable personages of the Jewish community and they all signed a major letter in support of David.

They made it clear that they were not New Democrats . . . but that his election transcended party and, for the first time, they would vote NDP and, to an extent that nobody imagined possible, we cracked the Jewish vote in Forest Hill by appealing to them to [elect] a prominent voice, a social conscience — who happened also to be Jewish. But it was not mere ethnic solidarity. It went beyond that.

And to everybody's amazement, we won polls in Cedarvale and we got a share of Forest Hill which allowed us to take the riding.

Among the people Stephen recruited to work for David was Ray Stancer. "I took David through the apartment building I was living in at the time. Took him door to door. And I remember him sitting down — this was before medicare — and explaining why medicare was so important. He described in moving detail the death of his father and how the lingering nature of his illness had eaten up whatever resources the family had. And how he had vowed that if ever he had any control of it he would not allow that to happen to anyone. And I remember the people we were talking to who had been sort of hostile to him becoming really moved."

However, David held the riding for only ten months. In the April 1963 election he lost it to Marvin Gelber by a decisive 3,646 votes (21,042 to 17,396). Social Credit had jumped to thirty seats in the 1962 election, and Jewish voters turned out in droves in 1963 to vote Liberal and head off what they perceived as a party with a strong anti-Jewish strain. "We won the riding back in 1965 because the scare had gone," says Stephen. "David had performed magnificently, publicly, in the interim, and even in the eight months in the House of Commons, and the riding was increasingly Italian working-class and partial to the left so that we were able to win it back.

"But I remember so well as I went around . . . people would say, 'Your father has never done anything for the Jewish community. You're not United Jewish Appeal activists.' [He had] no particular identity [as a Jew within the Jewish community]. . . . It was not his natural community."

Yet David was proud of his heritage. And he was versed in it.[4] King Gordon tells of him reciting from memory Solomon's Song of Songs after dinner one night in the mid-forties at the Gordons' apartment in New York City — and reciting it with an emotional intensity and an obvious enjoyment. Kalmen Kaplansky remembers him humming old religious tunes at odd times. Certainly David knew Jewish history. And even in his oratory, Kaplansky says, there was the legacy of the Pale of Settlement. "David's way of speaking, his oratory, could only be understood if you had heard the itinerant [preachers] of the Jewish community. He had the same style, this mixture of pathos and [emphasis] on sinners and retribution."

But David's roots were in the Bund and the Bund had opposed the creation of Israel, as the Jewish community in Toronto and elsewhere knew, and knew also that his support for the state of Israel was tempered by political skepticism toward policies of the Israeli government.

Before the Second World War, David argued against establishing a Jewish homeland in Palestine. And he argued vigorously. One evening in Montreal, while he was still a student at McGill, King Gordon delivered a lecture at the Workmen's Circle — at David's invitation — and, as he was driving David home after the meeting,

> I said to him, half-laughing, that this was quite a weekend for me. "Here I am speaking at the Workmen's Circle tonight and to-morrow I've accepted an invitation to speak at a synagogue in Westmount."
> Well, David practically blew his top. "Those people there!" he said. "What do they know about suffering here in the East End? They aren't identified with us at all. They're Zionist!"
> I said quite innocently, "Well, what are Zionists?" And then he explained to me, "They've got this crazy view that the Jewish people have to eventually find their own destiny by returning to the Holy Land, which was their land." And David just brushed off Zionism as being a kind of elitist alternative to the kind of struggle of the Workmen's Circle.

Speaking in his memoirs fifty years later, David confirmed what Gordon recalled: that attention should not be diverted from the universal struggle against exploitation and discrimination. "I was also troubled," he wrote, "by the problems which the establishment of a Jewish state would create for Arabs then living in Palestine, and even more by the inevitable dependence of the new state on an imperialist power — at that time I had in mind Britain rather than the United States."[5]

It was not until the United Nations voted to partition Palestine in May 1948 that he came to support the state of Israel. "The dreadful tribulations of my people after Hitler came to power, and the heartless indifference of many men in power in the democracies, necessarily affected my ideas as well as my emotions," he wrote. "I did not become a Zionist but I ceased being critical of Zionism because the survivors of Nazism, at least, were entitled to find a home where they would feel secure and free as Jews."[6]

But dropping criticism of Zionism did not mean dropping criticism of the Israeli government. In a letter to Lorne Ingle, then national secretary of the CCF, he spoke of his concern about giving a speech in four days' time to a Histadrut conference in Montreal. Histadrut is the Israeli labour federation and its leadership was dominated by members of the Mapai Party. Gamal Abdel Nasser, president of Egypt, had nationalized the Suez Canal in July 1956, and on October 29, the day before David wrote the letter, Israel had invaded Sinai. The day after he wrote, Israel was to be supported by a French and British attack on Egyptian airfields.

I know that however much the Canadian Histadrut people might in their hearts be worried about the Israeli action [David said], they will expect me to show at least qualified sympathy with it, both as a Jew and as national chairman of the CCF — a sister party to the Mapai. I know this from experience and from my own Sophie's reaction.

I find it impossible to have any objective sympathy for the unprovoked adventure on which Israel has set out. . . .

It seems obvious to me that the Israeli authorities decided to take advantage of several facts in the international situation in order to achieve some purpose, the nature of which is not yet clear to me. The factors which they thought favoured their adventure were, obviously, the nearness of the American election, Egypt's preoccupation in the Suez, the likelihood of Britain and France taking advantage of the situation to reassert their position in the Suez, and the preoccupation of the Soviet Union in Hungary and eastern Europe generally. This kind of calculation may deserve some admiration for its alertness, but bespeaks a calculated and deliberate opportunism that ignores what should be a nation's international obligations.[7]

He suggested that he travel to Montreal and explain his position to Histadrut officials and asked for Ingle's advice.

It wasn't until early 1967 — before Egypt closed the Tiran Strait, the entrance to the Gulf of Aqaba and Israel's only access to the Red Sea, and the following Egypt-Israeli war — that David came to a more heartfelt support for Israel.

He went to Israel to visit Janet, who had been living on a kibbutz. After graduation from high school in June 1966 she had gone to Israel, much against her parents' wishes. "I had joined the Labour–Zionist movement . . . and they really felt that I had deviated from the family fold. Partly they were worried I'd stay and partly it was because it wasn't part of their tradition."

But Janet was searching for who she was and going to Israel was part of that search.

Religion not only was unimportant in our daily lives and unremarked in our daily lives; there was a real antipathy toward it. All I remember is that it was always a very significant part of my identity. And I fought with my parents all my life around it because I wanted to have some content to being a Jew and the only content growing up that I could see would be to celebrate the holidays or to go to the synagogue and my parents resented and resisted that. . . .

[When we'd go to a synagogue] because of some family function, you know, the bar mitzvah of a cousin or the marriage of a cousin, it was like who picked the short straw to sit beside my father and listen to him berate the rabbi. Not yelling at him, but loud enough that people around could hear. "Listen to that fool," he'd say. "There are impressionable minds here. Have you ever heard such nonsense?" He just hated it. Even though he could read it and sing it, he hated religion.

Despite David's knowledge and attachment to Jewish culture, he made no effort to pass it on — perhaps, says Janet, because it is so linked to the very religious observances that he hated. "My mother swears this is true: the only reason we had a menorah in the house for Hanukkah was because my father went to New York when I was about six years old, and when he asked me what he should bring back, I said, 'Do you think we can have a menorah like the other families do?' And that's why we had this silver menorah."

Religious holidays were never celebrated or discussed. And if the family went to Passover, it was at someone else's home. Janet resented that; Nina didn't. Janet found she was receiving "a very confusing and double message" because she was being told she was Jewish but saw nothing that was especially Jewish in their home life; Nina felt no such confusion because she felt that "Jewish culture, Jewish values, the Jewish sensibility, was always present and pervasive in our family" even though religious observance was absent.

Janet "always knew that being Jewish was a very important part of my father's identity and my father's socialism . . . but God knows, I didn't know how they were united." Nina "never found it at all difficult to understand the profound relationship and interrelationship between his socialism and his Judaism." Janet gravitated toward Labour Zionism; Nina toward the Bund.

Nina met her husband, Daniel Libeskind, in July 1966 while she was attending a Bund summer camp — called Hemshekh Camp — in northern New York State. "He is from Poland. Very much like my father: left Poland when he was eleven, went to Israel for two years and then came to America when he was thirteen. . . . His parents were in Russia during the war. His mother was in Siberia, his father in the Volga. His sister was born in Kirghizia and he was born in Lodz, Poland, one year after the war. . . . His father was one of the Bund in Poland; his mother was an anarchist. So between the Jewish anarchism and the Jewish Bund and my background, it's been an easy collaboration," she says with happy relish. She hasn't been to a synagogue in thrity years, she says, but "we bring up our children in an extremely Jewish household and we celebrate all the festivals and talk at great length all the time about Jewish things, about Jewish values, and that's why I don't find it difficult at all to understand the Judaism and the socialism. It's something that I feel we live."[8]

She and her husband are aetheists, as Sophie and David were and as are Janet, Michael, Stephen, and Michele.

As Nina was spending the summer after leaving high school at the Hemshekh Camp, Janet had begun a year-long stay at a kibbutz in Israel where David met her the following March, having taken advantage of an invitation from Histadrut to visit Israel.

It was quite an eye-opener for him [says Janet]. I'll never forget this memory. They gave him a lunch, a goodbye lunch, and all the bigwigs were there. Golda Meir was there. She wasn't prime minister as yet. She was minister of external affairs, I think. And the president of Israel was there. And Histadrut was there. And my father got up to thank them — they had taken him around for a couple of weeks — and he burst into tears and he couldn't carry on with his speech. The country had so moved him, filled him with such pride. The only other time I'd seen him burst into tears like this was when my grandmother, his mother, died.

It just took my breath away — maybe because Israel does that to Jews. I don't know. And certainly back then Israel's policies were a lot easier to take. A lot more palatable than they are today.

But I remember during elections [that] the Jewish community never forgave him his late acceptance of Israel. It never forgot.

Rose, David's mother, died just before the June 18 election in 1962 when David was elected. For ten years after Maishe's death she had lived with Doris and Andy Andras in Ottawa, and for the final two years with David and Sophie in Toronto. It happened suddenly in the living room. Rose said she wanted to sit down for a moment because she wasn't feeling too well, and thirteen-year-old Janet sat by her side holding her hand while David went upstairs to take off his jacket. When he came back only a few minutes later she was dead from a heart attack. She was buried beside Maishe in Montreal.

As soon as David was elected, Stephen and John Brewin were off to Saskatchewan to fight the doctors' strike, called in opposition to the introduction of medicare. "I remember Stephen going into these towns in Saskatchewan and getting groups of farmers to pony up $10,000 or $20,000 to support the creation of a local clinic," Brewin says. "The deal was that if the local committee would put together a doctor's office, the government would supply one of the British doctors it was bringing in to fight the strike."

At the end of July the strike fizzled out and an agreement was reached that saw the doctors return to work.

By now Stephen was reaching the end of what he calls his formative years, "the years when everything came together for me, intellectually, philosophically, ideologically. All of my convictions seemed to have practical applications — and it was quite a range in terms of impressions and opinions leaping into the mind and into the psyche."

He places that period as lasting from 1955 until 1963. If there was a formal end, it would be the date of his election to the Ontario Legislature: September 25, 1963. But before that happened, there was the April 1963 federal election that saw his father defeated — with Gerry Caplan working as his campaign manager and Stephen working as campaign manager for Val Scott in the North York riding of York Centre. It was Stephen's eighteenth election campaign, and at its end his record would stand at twelve won, six lost, and campaigns in five provinces. He was twenty-five years old.

Alan Borovoy was recruited by Stephen to work in the Scott campaign, and even though they failed to unseat the Liberal incumbent, he remembers how much he enjoyed the battle. "Stephen had the ability to make people enjoy working with him because he was so much fun.

"I'd walk into the committee room with him and he'd call out, 'Stop everything,' and then he and I would sing a chorus of something and everything would come to a halt. Telephones would come off the hooks and we wouldn't take calls. He just had charisma — and nerve. And the imagination to do things a little differently. And *chutzpah*. He always had that. And a sense of humour. . . . An imaginative sense of humour is a tremendous asset."

It was during this campaign that Stephen met Michele Landsberg, two years younger than he was and, in the words of Barbara Frum, "so dazzlingly pretty and tiny and lively and engaging [and] just as fervent and just as fluent and just as verbal and just as bubbling with ideas and theories and argument as he was."

Michele had gone to the University of Toronto but had never met Stephen there. In fact, she wasn't at all impressed by what she'd heard of him, and thought the whole business of campus politics was a little too precious. "I was just vehemently anti-establishment, anti-authority, anti-teachers, anti-principals, anti-kids-who-wore-saddle-shoes. I was just against it all. . . . So I didn't get involved in politics at university. I wasn't a joiner. Ironically, a friend of mine who was in my course had gone out with Stephen once or twice, and she would rave on about him endlessly and bore me to tears of wonderful Stephen Lewis, and I would sneer, 'Joe College.'"

She grew up poor and it was her mother, Leah, who kept the family together — and kept it fed. Her father, Jack, was a women's-wear salesman and not very good at it — a Willy Loman, Michele calls him. A handsome man with the build of a fullback but with little of the *joie de vivre* of her mother, and none of her determination. A nice enough person, but what Leah saw in him was something family friends never did understand. Unobtrusive, is how one of them delicately describes him. "She married him on the rebound and would never admit that she'd made a terrible mistake," Michele says. "So she put tremendous energy into our leading this very safe, secure, and proper little life." He died when Michele was in her mid-teens.

Michele was her mother's third child, born on July 12, 1939, when her mother was in her mid-forties. Her older brother, a doctor in Texas, is seventeen years older. The younger brother is only a year and a half older than she is and is in charge of systems programming for Revenue Canada.

Until she was about twelve, they lived in a little duplex on Burnaby Boulevard near Eglinton Avenue and Avenue Road in Toronto. "One side of the street was gentile and the other side all Jewish and never the twain did meet except to beat each other up," she says. "That was Toronto in the war years. A very rotten place."

In 1950 they were evicted. "They raised our rent and we couldn't afford to pay and my mother travelled the city by streetcar for weeks trying to find a place where we could afford to live. Finally she found a house way up in Willowdale [on Bogert Avenue at Sheppard Avenue and Yonge Street], which was the farthest reaches then, where a guy was going bankrupt . . . so we got this house for a bargain. My mother borrowed the money, scraped it together, and we moved into this un-finished house in Willowdale and I [ended up] one of the two or three Jews at Earl Haig Collegiate."

Leah became a real estate salesperson. "A very elegant lady," says John Pollock, a Toronto lawyer who used to refer clients to her, "slim, well groomed. Very trusted. Very well liked. Extremely honest." She was still working in her eighties when she died in 1982 in a tragic acci-dent. A plastic chair set too near her fireplace caught fire and she died from smoke inhalation.

It was a non-observant family. Leah rarely attended synagogue, even on holy days. The family wasn't then, and Michele isn't now, in the mainstream of the Jewish community, says Pollock. He marvels over Michele's intellectual curiosity. Where she got it, he doesn't know. It wasn't an intellectual family, he says.

> I grew up in St. Clements Public Library [says Michele].[9]
> Ours was a very conventional, lower-middle-class upbringing except I was wild and different from my family. I read. I was passionate about literature. . . . You could only take out three books at a time [at

libraries], so I would go on my bike to three or four . . . and in that way I could get nine books a week. I read existentialism when I was thirteen. I couldn't understand it, but I . . . plough[ed] through it.

I was reading Jean-Paul Sartre . . . and he made reference to Simone de Beauvoir in some essay. So . . . I went to St. Clements and in the card index was this book called *The Second Sex*. The librarian wouldn't let me have it because I had a child's card . . . and I fought with him for weeks. I would come in and try and find a young librarian who didn't know enough to keep it from me and I finally got it. Reading it was fantastic!

She discovered that she wasn't alone in objecting to the way women were marginalized. She had been writing essays privately for more than a year in which she argued that the use of the masculine to describe things — as in mankind — "excluded me from existence."

So I was mad about language and all that stuff long before the movement came along.

Around the time I was fourteen, somebody invited me to the Zionist Youth Movement and I joined, and that gave a focus to all my feelings of rebelliousness and left-wing sentiment. I was very involved until I was eighteen. The Zionist movement was frowned on by the Jewish establishment in Toronto. . . . We were all to assimilate, just like white people. . . .

The fifties were a horrible time. It wasn't just the McCarthy time. . . . The Canadian Jewish community was in shell shock over the Holocaust. You didn't talk about it. You didn't make noise. It was terrible. . . . [A]t Holy Blossom they delegated people to take me aside and convince me not to [join]. . . . It was a disgrace, and therefore I loved it. . . .

Initially it attracted me by being a group of youngsters . . . who didn't care about going to the sock hop or to the football games or all those stupid things that I despised. They wanted to debate and argue late into the night about the ideas of Theodor Herzl versus Chaim Weizmann versus Asher Ginsberg versus Aaron David Gordon.

It was ideology. It was passion. It was self-sacrifice. We pooled our pocket money. It was the sort of thing my soul was crying out for: passion, belonging, dedication, and rebelliousness. . . . I'd never had a group of Jewish friends. I'd always grown up in completely gentile surroundings. . . . It was a revelation. . . .

And then I went to Israel, right after high school, for a year. And then back to go to university. . . . I went right into English literature and here, at last, for the first time in my life, were other kids who liked to read. I had never found them before.

At Allenby Public School, if you liked to read — if you were a bit of an intellectual — you kept it quiet. I've since met people who were at Allenby . . . who were equally passionate readers [but] we never found each other. So university was wonderful.

It was at the University of Toronto that she first saw David in action. It was three months after the NDP's founding convention — December 5, 1961 — and he was debating against William F. Buckley, editor of *The National Review*, at that point author of three books and describing himself as "a radical conservative." The capacity crowd in Convocation Hall hung on every word, sometimes cheering, sometimes booing. There wasn't much new in the debate, said the *Toronto Star*; each claimed the other's system would produce nothing but ill. But their personal thrusts at each other "kept the crowd on seat edge" for two hours and forty-five minutes.[10] "The great line that just brought the house down," says Barbara Frum, "was David Lewis saying to Buckley — this was about the book *God and Man at Yale* that Buckley had written which was very critical of higher education — 'If I had gotten as poor an education at university as Mr. Buckley clearly got at Yale, I would have written that book too.' Something like that. But wittier. Anyway, it brought the house down."

Buckley, of course, had his own good lines. "Freedom is like baldness," the *Star* reported him as saying. "If a man loses hair after hair, you don't wait until the last one is gone before you say he is bald. Mr. Lewis doesn't want us to worry about our lost freedoms until he and his friends have taken away the last one."

At the beginning of the debate David was logical and tough, Michele recalls, but he wasn't knocking them dead. He was good but Buckley was equally as good.

Then Buckley started overdoing the sneering, the exaggerated mannerisms, the convoluted, sultry, fake elegant Yale number, and [made the mistake] of saying something sneering about working people.

Well, David stood up at the microphone and he was just flinging off the energy and the whole of Convocation Hall was rivetted, and he came up with one of those passionate, crowning images of speech. He pictured some poor working man who was locked out of his factory, on strike, hungry and cold and walking that picket line with nothing but his raincoat to wear. I don't know where he got it, but I can still see that man walking in the raincoat. It was one time David did come up with an image.

He said it with the whole dynamic force of his being and Convocation Hall just went ROAR! I think he won the debate a thousand to two. It was overwhelming. People were galvanized. . . .

I'm sure [the debate was the reason] why, when I decided to get active, I automatically went to the NDP.

She was working as a poll captain in Val Scott's campaign, and the first time she saw Stephen was when he spoke to a workers' meeting.

They had been canvassing all day and were tired and none too spirited after the endless repetition of trudging door to door, street after street, with the same message.

> The way he rallied us. The burning conviction, the humour of self-depreciation and mockery. The room was just roaring with laughter one minute, and at the next he made you feel that you'd get out there and give your life to get that very last vote for Val Scott.
>
> I was knocked over. I never thought of speaking to him personally or anything like that. I mean, he was the campaign manager. But I had the same admiration for him as I had for David.
>
> And after the meeting I was leaving and Stephen asked me would I stay for a planning meeting or something. I stayed but still I didn't think there was anything personal. And then he said, "What are you doing after the meeting?" and I said, "I'm going home." And so we went.

Six weeks later Stephen proposed — from a public platform as he delivered his acceptance speech after winning the nomination in Scarborough West for the upcoming provincial election.

> It was just the total, revolting bravado of a young man [he says now, laughing]. Just macho nonsense. I said to the riding association at the nominating convention that Reid Scott, who was the federal member of Parliament, had told me I had two serious liabilities. I didn't live in the riding and I should be married. So I announced that I was undertaking to move into the riding and that I wanted to announce my intended marriage to Michele Landsberg who was, even then, in the audience covering the meeting for *The Globe and Mail*.
>
> And Michele stood up, and she didn't know. I hadn't told her I was going to make this announcement. [He starts laughing again, adding], The spur of the moment wins it!

Later that evening they went over to Alan Borovoy's nomination meeting. He was running for the party in Downsview riding (where he lost to Vernon Singer, the Liberal candidate). Friends gathered around, overjoyed at the news. "Everyone was so happy for them," says Frum. "It wasn't at all clear how Stephen was going to come through the courtship wars. . . . He wasn't perceived as a catch at university. . . . That's why there was such joy about finding Michele. She was entrancing that night. She was just entrancing. So fresh and alive. And it just seemed absolutely perfect."

They were married seventeen days later, on May 30. Leah was shocked when Michele told her of the engagement. Michele already had a boy friend whom her mother liked very much.

Stephen just talked me into it. [Michele says]. It was a bravura performance. I was against marriage on principle. . . . [But] he phoned me night and day and I just laughed. I thought he was nuts. . . . I couldn't take him seriously at first. I said, "This is ridiculous. We don't even know each other." But he talked me into it. . . .

My mother burst into tears when I hit her with this incredible news. "But what does he do for a living?" she asked.

And I said, "You don't understand. He's going to be somebody. I'm sure of that. He's brilliant."

The truth is, Stephen didn't have a job and my mother knew nothing about politics. She barely knew the name of Lewis. So to her it was this risky, crazy thing. Here I was marrying this skinny guy. She just couldn't figure it out. She was sure I was making an awful mistake.

And even Michele was not altogether sure. "The night before I married I thought, 'Gee, what the hell am I doing. I don't even know this guy.' But I did it and I haven't been sorry very often. So that's not a bad record."

They were married in her mother's home and the only people present were parents, brothers, and sisters. The ceremony was brief and to the point. Michele disliked traditional weddings. "As I recall," she says, "the rabbi was standing in the hall eating a corned beef sandwich and he said, 'Is everybody ready?' And we went into the den and had this little wedding."

Then they were off to New York for the weekend, and the rest of their honeymoon they spent knocking on doors in Scarborough West. Even Leah, having concluded that there might be some good in Stephen after all, helped out. "People would say, 'What about this NDP?' and my mother would reply, 'I can't tell you too much about politics, but Stephen Lewis is my son-in-law and I can tell you he is a fine young man.' And they would go for it. Isn't that a scream!"

Stephen gave his maiden speech in the Legislature in mid-January 1964, arguing that the province should introduce medicare and, according to one observer, "stunned the Legislature with [his] eloquence and thoroughness."[11] Mind you, it was a partisan observer: Terry Morley, now married to Jane Brewin and a professor at the University of Victoria, but in a previous incarnation executive assistant to Donald MacDonald from 1969 to 1971. Even so, when Queen's Park journalists took to calling Stephen a boy wonder ten months later, it added some weight to the opinion.[12] And Don O'Hearn, the Queen's Park columnist for the Southam Newspapers, reported that

The Legislature may have seen in action the next NDP leader in Ontario.

It is years — perhaps as far back as the debut of Mitch Hepburn — since a new member has made his maiden speech in the Legislature with the impact that Stephen Lewis did.

Mr. Lewis . . . was as close to a sensation as you see in a parliamentary chamber. In a House where the standard of debate is very low he stood out like a beacon. . . .

He was so good even his colleagues on the NDP benches appeared startled.[13]

The speech was a warning of what was to come over the next thirteen years: the discomfitting questions in the House, the relentless digging into issues during debate, the resounding oratory that seemed to roll so effortlessly from him.

But what seemed so natural, so effortless was just the opposite. Behind the scenes, Stephen painstakingly prepared himself. "He spent much more time preparing than his father ever did," says Murray Weppler. "Stephen was much more meticulous. Much more careful . . . to the point of overkill."

And his memory was so good, says Weppler, that it was very close to being photographic. Weppler was a Queen's Park reporter for *The Citizen* of Ottawa for a year "when Stephen had just got the leadership." He went to work for David as his executive assistant in the spring of 1971 and "was promptly sent back to Toronto to help Stephen in his first campaign [as leader] in 1971." Stephen seemed to have read everything on the subjects he dealt with, Weppler says. He'd prepare something for him, and no matter how thorough Weppler had been, Stephen "would still find something that was left out and tell you where to find it and on what page almost."

During debates, if you watched closely, you could see Stephen's lips moving ever so slightly as he concentrated on what government speakers were saying. People speculated that he was committing to memory their statements because in debate he could quote what they'd said back at them, tearing it apart as he went. Actually, says Michele, it's something he doesn't realize he's doing and can't control. "All his life, when he's listening to someone speak, even on television sometimes, he listens so intently that without knowing it his lips are forming the words simultaneously." Stephen says he's not committing what he hears to memory. "I wish I had that facility. What I'm doing, I think, is anticipating what the person is about to say." Even so, to members speaking opposite in the Legislature, the sight of Stephen staring intently at them, lips moving, was as unnerving as watching some dreadful male gorgon licking its lips in anticipation of devouring them.

Before a major speech, he would disappear for a couple of hours. Hugh Mackenzie, research asssociate for the NDP caucus from 1973 until 1977, would discover him in the legislative library, hidden away in a corner, lost in total concentration over what he was going to say on the floor of the House. Oblivious to everyone.

> For the interest of the honourable members of this House [he began in his maiden speech], "a medical health insurance plan incorporating the principles outlined in [my] resolution . . . was enacted in Germany in 1883, in Denmark in 1892, in Norway in 1909, in the United Kingdom in 1911 and then elaborated on in 1948, in Japan in 1922, in France in 1928, in Spain — anti-democratic societies can apparently also have medical care for their people — in 1942, in Scandinavia in the post-war period. So that almost without exception every single country in western society has adopted a full and universal medicare plan. Only North America stands as the exception.[14]

The response of Premier John Robarts dwelt on the menace of the loss of individual rights: "We do not wish to take away from [the individual] every choice he has left and we do not wish to socialize him so that whatever he has is taken from him by the state and handed back by a bureaucrat, whether in fact he wants it or not. These things we do not believe in."[15]

Thus began what for Stephen were "the grinding years in the Legislature — from 1963 to 1967. . . . There were seven of us. And then eight when Jim Renwick came in in 1964. The Tories were so large that they slopped over onto our side of the House. . . . They were hard, hard years. We worked so bloody hard because we were the only real opposition to the government. And it was tough because I was being whipsawed in the Legislature over the involvement with Brown Camps and the attacks were personal and unpleasant. . . . It was one of those times when the world seemed to be crushing in a bit."

One by one, he took on responsibility for opposing the major government portfolios: education, health, welfare, corrections — and often they overlapped — but always it was the social-issue portfolios. Clare Westcott, Bill Davis's perennial executive assistant, remembers that what struck him most when Stephen entered the Legislature was that Stephen, like John Robarts, was remarkable most for his ambition, but "I've never seen anyone learn as fast as Stephen and he became one of the ornaments of the Legislature." For those who distinguish between the word "Tory," which has a tradition of humanism and dedication to the kind of values that George Grant espoused, and the phrase "Progressive Conservative," which oscillates to the expectations of the business elite, Clare Westcott was a Tory.

The whipsawing that Stephen received in the Legislature over John Brown was both deserved and undeserved. Deserved because Brown was using public money to run his group homes for distrubed children and everyone, including Stephen, suspected something fishy was going on; yet Stephen never pushed — or never pushed hard enough — to find out what was happening. Undeserved because Stephen fought passionately and unreservedly on behalf of the youngsters who so desperately needed Brown's help. There's no denying that Brown was a brilliant innovator who accomplished the seeming impossible, especially with youngsters whom people thought were hopeless cases. Had it not been for Stephen, many of those children might never have been rescued because Brown was under unceasing attack from all corners: by people who didn't want group homes in their neighbourhoods; by professionals upset by his various impertinences; by ordinary people scandalized by some of his methods, such as allowing a seventeen year old to suckle milk from a baby's bottle during a moment of regression; by Conservatives seeking to skewer the NDP.

Rarely, in the criticisms of Brown and Stephen, were efforts made to balance the good that was being performed against the bad that was suspected.

The focus of concern was that Brown's companies — first Brown Camps and then Browndale — overcharged the provincial government for taking care of the youngsters, even though they were charging more than 40 percent less than government-operated agencies. That suspicion was eventually confirmed when Brown pleaded guilty to frauds committed between April 1, 1971, and September 30, 1976, and was sentenced to three years in penitentiary by Mr. Justice R.E. Holland of the Supreme Court of Ontario. (See Appendix Q.)

In the early days of Brown's operations, before the period in which the frauds were committed, what Stephen did for Brown was "to bring Brown a legitimacy" — this in the words of Gerry Charney, who was the lawyer for Brown Camps as well as being a friend of Stephen.

For a time, Stephen was paid $12,000 to $15,000 a year to act as national director for Brown Camps, but he held no shares and was not on the board of directors.[16] His job was to try and extend Brown's system of group homes to other provinces and to help fight the political battles in Ontario, where Brown's treatment methods were seen by many as highly controversial and where homeowners objected to the establishment of group homes in their neighbourhoods. He and Michele were so committed to what Brown was trying to do that they had disturbed youngsters living with the family, "as so many of the Brown Camps people did . . . as part of a transition [for the youngsters]. These were really, really disturbed, acting-out kids," says Stephen. "It wasn't as though I was a staff member of the treatment centre. But we were so deeply involved."

Charney — the labour lawyer, the champion international bridge player, the former organizer for the International Ladies Garment Workers Union, the son, as coincidence would have it, of Faga Falk, the Montreal Bundist, the woman who helped take in Sofia Erlich when she escaped from Eastern Europe and arrived in Montreal in 1941 — puts both feet on the edge of the coffee table in his office and tilts his chair back, firing off thoughts so rapidly the words bump into each other on the way out. He is six feet and solid, with dancing brown eyes, and he conjures up merriment the way a theatre director does mist, behind which he sizes you up. Shrewdly. "It was like an armed camp," he says. "It's hard to describe. . . . There was a war going on. The Ontario government was determined to close Brown up, and it required a lot of time and effort to prevent that. . . . [It meant dealing with] various cabinet ministers and civil servants and lobbying and . . . explaining to the press and explaining to the public."

They had to fight to save the group homes, he says, because, as long as they survived, "never again would children be locked up in institutions. They would be treated with some kind of dignity and there would be attempts to rehabilitate them as opposed to keeping them drugged out and then intentionally shut away forever. I acted on some cases . . . and [before Brown's group homes] so many of the children had spent three or four or five years on medication. To keep them quiet. To calm them down. As far as I could make out, to keep them out of everyone's hair."

Everything about Brown was bigger than life — his compassion, his magnetism, his skill, his enthusiasms, and, unfortunately, his ambition. His staff worshipped him, child care officials were in awe of him, and emotionally disturbed youngsters responded to him almost instinctively.

He could perform miracles with children, Stephen says. "I have never seen anything like it and I don't ever expect to again. . . . I had the Warden Woods housing development in my riding and. . . . I can recall being called in one night for a terrible ruckus in a family with a little boy who was sitting banging his head against the wall as a tumultuous scene between his parents was taking place. The boy was terribly, terribly disturbed." In an effort to get help, Ellen Adams, who was secretary to Donald and me . . . phoned every single facility in Southern Ontario — psychiatric hospitals, general hospitals, treatment centres. Everybody. And everybody said no to her. Everybody said we can't look after this boy.

Finally it occurred to me to call John Brown. . . . John went in and in the midst of this chaos talked to the little boy in tones so soothing, so embracing, it was as though he had physically enveloped him as he walked through the door. The boy calmed down, John picked him up and carried him out. [He and his wife Debbie] drove back with him in their laps. They did an assessment evaluation. Put him in treatment. That little boy was the subsequent star of the movie *Warrendale*.

It was just incredible. They were so talented.

Even Mr. Justice Holland, delivering his sentence in November 1979, was impressed. He calculated that the amount defrauded came to $975,615 and then said:

John Brown is now fifty-seven years old and is an exceptional man. I have no doubt that he has contributed very much to the treatment and care of emotionally disturbed children, not only in Canada, but also in the United States and Europe. He is primarily responsible for developing what appears to be a unique programme for the care of such children. . . . [I]t appears to me that emotionally disturbed children in the plan received the best of care at a competitive cost. I am pleased to hear that the organization for which he and his wife are responsible continues to operate successfully in Ontario today. . . .

This is not the usual case of a fraud on the public motivated by greed with the proceeds going straight into the pockets of the accused for his personal use. Mr. Brown, in my opinion, was motivated more by a desire to protect the system of child care that he had developed and to extend the system to other provinces and to other parts of the world. There was no effort made to falsify the actual books of account or to hide [them] from the police or government inspectors or auditors.

At the end of June 1968 Stephen resigned as national director of Brown Camps[17] and by the summer of 1970 he had totally disengaged himself from Brown's operations. "John and I were in perpetual personal conflict," Stephen says. "Personal disagreement over everything. And, to be fair to John, he wanted me out as much as I wanted out. We just weren't getting along."

Brown had done the unpardonable in Stephen's eyes. Elected to the Legislature as the NDP member for Beaches–Woodbine in 1967, he behaved shabbily. He was distinguished more by his absence from the House than by anything he contributed to it, as one reporter recorded.[18] And he bad-mouthed the party, saying it was warped by the "glorious loser syndrome." As for the political system in Ontario, "It stinks," he said, later adding that he was disappointed and disillusioned not only with the Legislature but with the NDP membership, with his NDP colleagues in the House, and with Stephen.[19] He refused to run in the 1971 election.

One of the consequences of Stephen's disengagement was that he no longer could be accused in the Legislature of conflict of interest — the whipsawing he talked about which, though the accusation never prevailed, was emotionally draining.

Gerry Charney was to resign a short time later as lawyer for Brown Camps, so both were gone before the April 1, 1971, date at which Brown began overcharging the Ministry of Health. However, the group homes operated by Brown Camps remained the last hope for emotionally disturbed youngsters judged to be beyond the care of any other agencies and Stephen refused to relinquish his defence of them for several years after the April 1 date. And during that time he never pressed for a scrutiny of Brown's financial dealings. He would have, he says, if he had been aware of any evidence of wrongdoing. But he wasn't. All he had was an uneasiness — and the conviction that without the homes there could only be a reversion to what had gone on before, a horrible, heartless waste of lives. So he continued to face his critics in the Legislature. (See Appendix R.)

It was at Brown Camps that Janet met her husband, David Solberg, born in Norway; a lapsed Lutheran. Almost as soon as she was home from Israel in the late spring of 1967, she wanted to return but Sophie was adamant. Not back to a budding war zone, she said. Janet, eighteen years old, was furious and left home to live with Stephen and Michele and, at Stephen's suggestion, to get a job at Brown Camps.

Before the year was out, just after her nineteenth birthday, she and David moved in together — much to her parents' distress.

> This was the worst sort of thing I could have done to them. There were a lot of things they didn't approve of, but David could overcome those. He had a Grade Ten education, but then he went and got several master's degrees, so that was okay. But . . . he was ten years older and he wasn't Jewish.
>
> Not being a Jew, this was the thing that was brought up over and over again. I was very puzzled. My father would say, "You're the most Jewish of all our children. How could you do this to us?" And then I'd think, "How could you tell?". . .
>
> In fact, David and I came to an accommodation very early that I couldn't have a Christian household because I didn't know what that meant. And being Jewish was important to me, so, as much as I celebrated any holidays, they'd have to be Jewish holidays. And that was fine with him. And so we just carried on. We started having Passover

seders and lighting menorah during Hanukkah and sometimes going to synagogues during high holidays.

When my parents said, "Won't you convert?" I'll never forget. He turned to my mother and he said, "Sophie, am I over the age of six?"

And she said, "Yes."

"So who over the age of six can believe in God? Why are you asking me to do this?"

And that was the end of that.

But once we decided to get married [and they were married on November 13, 1970], we had to get married in their house. . . . I'd wanted a Jewish wedding . . . so we had it in my mother's living room. . . .

It was sort of brief, but it was Jewish. And it was in Hebrew. And this was very important to my parents. It was important to me, too, but it reassured them a great deal.

Nina's wedding was a year earlier, on May 26, 1969, and it was, in Janet's words, "one of the [family's] all-time great affairs. In fact, it was the last time that I saw some of my old relatives, my great uncles and aunts. There must have been sixty or seventy people and there was Hebrew dancing and singing. And they spoke Yiddish a lot and sang Yiddish songs and it was really lovely.

"Mine was much different because there were only eleven or twelve people there. David's family didn't come because he hadn't been in touch with them for many years. There was only my family and John and Debbie [Brown]." The disparity between the two weddings — because Nina's husband was Jewish and Janet's was not — left her feeling somewhat deprived.

Michael's wedding to Wendy Hughes was totally non-Jewish. It was performed by Stanley Knowles at a resort on Lake Ontario midway between Kingston and Toronto on August 16, 1975. It was a quiet ceremony with just the immediate families attending.[20]

John Brown affected Stephen and Michele in one other way. Stephen's championing of him in 1967 soured relations with the Brewin family. John Brewin had been planning to run in Beaches–Woodbine, which was considered a fairly safe seat because it incorporated much of Ken Bryden's old riding of Woodbine. (Beaches–Woodbine was created in a 1966 redistribution.) Stephen persuaded Brewin to move out and run in Scarborough North instead so that Brown could have the safe riding. Brewin did, and he lost in the October election by 1,527 votes to Conservative Tom Wells. Although he never complained, it rankled his family.

"They're all good friends now," says Peggy Brewin, John's mother. Interviewed in January 1987, she had just seen Stephen on televison giving a speech at the Empire Club in Toronto congratulating John's wife Gretchen, mayor of Victoria, on declaring the city a nuclear-free port. "So I rushed to the phone and Gretchen answered and I said, 'Gretchen, have you forgiven Stephen?' because Gretchen felt very strongly about Stephen having pushed John out, and she answered, 'Yes.' But there was a period when it was difficult. . . . It was one of Stephen's poorer judgments."

Today their friendship is as strong as it was during the heady days at the University of Toronto, and in the 1988 federal election Stephen was on the west coast and campaigned for a day in Brewin's successful bid to enter Parliament.

Stephen says he asked Brewin to shift ridings in 1967 because he thought there was a chance to win Scarborough North, which bordered on his own riding in an area where Stephen had a lot of support, but which could be won only by a party veteran such as Brewin who knew how to run a campaign. Brown, on the other hand, needed a much stronger riding to begin with because he'd never run before, wasn't identified with the party, and needed every bit of help he could get.

But then Stephen lapses into silence — and then says in a self-mocking way, "I like to think I've changed, that I've become a better person now. And I think that's largely due to Michele." And he laughs. But then his tone changes, becomes quieter, more introspective. "In those first few years it was possible that I was caught up in, not destructive things because you can't live in the party and be destructive, but maybe not entirely nice behaviour. If so, I look back on it remorsefully."

He turns silent again and then, speaking slowly and with a disquieting candour, adds, "I think I was narrow," and he pauses, "self-centred." He pauses again. "Egocentric." It's as if each additional word is a penitent's lash. "Driven . . . compulsive. Sometimes brutal. . . . With friends and with enemies."

He has been staring at the top of the table as he speaks. Now he looks up. "But I think those would have been character flaws [that] Michele ultimately assuaged, or at least . . . repaired. [It wouldn't be] a neglect of the party, or an insensitivity, because I don't think that was possible. The party I largely understood and respected and would not have wished to betray."

In the months that followed the 1967 election Stephen began to slip into a darkening mood. His humour began to border on black. He wore a button saying "Support mental health or I'll kill you." He grew increasingly restless and dissatisfied. The world around was struggling to break through its exoskeleton. To throw off the bindings, be they economic, philosophic, or political. But the Ontario Legislature seemed like a backwater, insulated by its heavy red sandstone walls, its own crustacean shell, to the point of suffocation. As Stephen would say in 1970, still chafing, "It's the unreality of the Legislature and the way we discuss vast quantities of trivia while the world is blowing up around us. You know, they're shooting people at Kent State [University] and we talk about amendments to the Warble Fly Act. I can't hack that; it drives me crazy."[21]

There were the violent assaults on the old order: the FLQ bombings in Quebec, the black riots in the United States, the student riots in Paris in May of 1968 that spread to nation-wide strikes paralyzing the country, the destruction of the computer centre at Sir George Williams University in Montreal — and there were the violent answers: Soviet tanks rumbling into Prague ending Czechoslovakia's brief flirtation with self-rule, the police beating demonstrators at the Democratic National Convention in Chicago, and, a little later, invocation of the War Measures Act in Canada.

There was "Burn, baby, burn," and the Black Panthers and the assassination of Martin Luther King in April 1968 and of Robert Kennedy two months later. But there also was the promise of peaceful change in the choosing of Pierre Trudeau as Liberal leader that same April and the June 25 election that followed, which people thought — naively as it turned out — would inaugurate a Just Society and participatory democracy.

There were the fiery figures of Ché Guevara, whose poster hung on the wall of every self-respecting radical, and Pierre Vallières, who was causing a sensation with *Negres blancs d'Amérique*, and even French President Charles de Gaulle who had grandiloquently sent *Vive le Québec libre* echoing coast to coast. But there also were platoons of young idealists, some misguided, some highly effective, wrestling with social issues almost everywhere you looked, thanks to the Company of Young Canadians. And there were people like Emmett Hall and Lloyd Dennis shaking up educational establishments with their report calling for the abolition of all grades, exams, and structured curricula and the substitution of a twelve-year "learning experience," and Mel Watkins rattling the nation's chain with his report on foreign ownership, and Jane Jacobs inspiring people to demand livable cities, and Kahn-Tineta Horn forcing people to look at Indian rights, and John Sewell and Wolf Erlichman driving around Toronto in a bright orange van called "teacup" organizing residents in Trefann Court to halt demolition and redevelopment,[22] and Paul Copeland and Clay Ruby publishing *Law Law Law*, otherwise known as the Hippies' Handbook, a civil-rights antidote to starchy, disgruntled — tight-assed — police.

There was Expo '67. There were communes and encounter groups and "Make love, not war." There was Stop Spadina, the anti-expressway coalition, and the Hassle Free Clinic for drug victims in Toronto's Yorkville. There was Rochdale, the eighteen-storey educational experiment in co-operatives that failed. There was Timothy Leary preaching "Turn on, tune in, drop out,"[23] and women's lib saying drop in, demand your place, be your own person. Private greed didn't go away, as Viola Macmillan and Windfall Oil and Mines proved, but public commitment produced the most influential building in Toronto's history, the new City Hall, which changed forever the city's attitude toward itself.

By 1965 half the population of Canada was under twenty-five years old and the Beatles had more fan club members here than anywhere else in the world — 50,000 paid-up Beatlemaniacs.[24] Flower children abounded. So, almost, did sit-ins. Unisex made macho pompous and silly. René Lévesque quit the Liberals in November 1967 and by October 1968 had formed the Parti Québécois.

Woodstock was on the horizon.

Possibilities were pinwheeling through the consciousness.

It was the Dawning of the Age of Aquarius, or so it seemed it just might possibly be — and Stephen wasn't sure he was on a commanding height to participate. Certainly the party was not. And the group within the party that did catch the spirit — and the excited attention of the media — began with a meeting on April 29, 1969, and died three years and a bit later of hyperkinetic confrontation. It was the Waffle.

The sense that the party was unresponsive to the spirit of the times is what persuaded Stephen to travel to Vancouver in March 1968 — just before Trudeau was elected Liberal leader — to ask Tommy Douglas to resign as leader of the federal party. There had been discussions within the Ontario caucus and, says Stephen, it was "the general caucus view," and that included the opinion of its chairman, Jim Renwick, that Tommy should be asked to step down.

> It was obviously potentially uncomfortable [says Stephen] because David Lewis would be . . . one of the likely successors. It was hard to dissociate from that. Although it was hard, it was primarily what was right for the party. I've always felt that in parties that are civilized and honest and straightforward, one can say these things as a friend and loyal colleague in confidence to leaders or to others. And I had, until then, a fairly good personal relationship with Tommy. . . .
>
> I can remember the hotel room. Tommy sitting in a corner chair, myself perched on the edge of the bed, putting to him a view that was shared by a majority of caucus members, and Tommy, as I recall,

saying he'd think about it but that it was not his instinct [to quit]. And I saying, "Fine. We'll be loyally with you." And that was that. . . .

I realized only in the aftermath that Tommy was clearly exercised about it. It didn't feel terribly difficult at the time. It felt like a fairly frank and open conversation. Obviously it felt like more than that to him.

Hundreds of New Democrats never forgave Stephen for taking that trip, says Gerry Caplan. "It came back to haunt us." Even though Stephen had conducted himself entirely openly and out of concern for the party. Even though the Ontario caucus was convinced there were problems in Ontario that should be communicated. Even though Stephen felt he could not avoid being the one to carry the message because he knew Tommy better than anyone else in the caucus.

Hans Brown, who became Tommy's executive assistant in the fall of 1968, says that in addition to never forgetting the hotel room discussion with Stephen, Tommy also never forgot that in 1944, six days after the CCF was elected in Saskatchewan, David wrote to suggest how Tommy should set up his government.[25] And then there was the business of Stephen and what he calls "the Toronto group" suggesting to Tommy that he change his image. "One had to be a little cooler," Brown recalls the message. "The little spectacles — those Leon Trotsky-type glasses, you know, the rimless ones — the hair style, the flaming oratory before mass audiences in Maple Leaf Gardens, the mass rallies, they were passé. One had to have a television manner. We were into *This Hour Has Seven Days* and people were very conscious of the impact of this new medium. And then there was the Kennedy debate [with Nixon]. . . .

"Well, he did change. The more windblown [hairstyle] as opposed to the wave that curled right up. Remember?"

All of this contributed to a slight tension that endured between Tommy and the Lewises, Brown says, and Tommy was always interested in knowing what Stephen and David were up to in the party, "and if they stubbed their toes, Tommy got a little chuckle out of it."

Stephen doesn't remember suggesting that Tommy change his image but acknowledges that the Ontario caucus "fooled around with this stuff about image." But it was far from its centre of concern. Certainly it was far from his. "Don't forget, David was in the federal House of Commons. He was very much there. I was in the provincial House. We were sharing things. He would not have allowed me to succumb disgracefully to this aesthetic dynamic that somehow, with the change of glasses and the suit, people would vote for you. David would have

. . . said it was all poppycock. If you don't have the policies, people won't vote for you. That's what he believed and I would have been enormously influenced by that."

The 1968 election came three months after Stephen's trip to Vancouver and Tommy lost his Burnaby–Seymour seat to the wave of Trudeaumania that was sweeping the country. He immediately announced to a post-mortem meeting of the party executive that he would retire at the 1969 convention — Tommy at that point was sixty-three years old — and attention instantly focused on whether David should become leader. But opinion was divided and among those opposed were some who harboured the memory of bruisings they had received from David. Robin Sears, knowing how to whet the appetite of a listener, begins his description of that period by saying, "This is a story I haven't told anybody about." Then he continues:

> At the first caucus following the election . . . my grandfather [Colin Cameron] was proposed to be chairman of the caucus [and] David was proposed to be parliamentary leader until such time as the question of the leadership was resolved.
>
> I am told that Colin said to David, "I will nominate you for parliamentary leader if you will nominate me for caucus chairman," which was seen as a very healing gesture. Tensions between left and right were beginning to bubble up into the Waffle and it would become a nightmare the following year. "But don't you ever use that position as a jumping-off post for the party leadership or I will ensure that it will be the end of your career."
>
> David accepted and acknowledged the understanding. Then Colin had a massive stroke and died a few weeks later. And that unlocked a series of events that makes it impossible to know what would have happened if he hadn't died precisely then. The seat was made available for Tommy. It was perfectly safe. [Colin] had just won one of the biggest landslides of his life and those who wanted Tommy to stay had a very good place to put him. . . .
>
> I don't know [how] David felt [about that]. Tommy's decision to retire at the 1969 convention was quietly and officially forgotten.

So, despite nearly tripling the seats in Ontario in the 1967 election — from eight to twenty — little seemed to be changing within the party at large. As Stephen says, looking back twenty years later, "The jump of seats in 1967 showed me the potential for the party rather than proving to me that somehow we were on the right track."

Politically, he was feeling more than a little cramped. On the margin of the currents sweeping society. And to top off everything, there were stories of genocide in the area of Nigeria where Stephen had started his school eight years before. At the end of May 1967 the Eastern Region in Nigeria, homeland of the Ibos, had declared itself independent and adopted the name Biafra. The summer of 1968 was the most active in the war that followed. Mukwugo Okoye's village, Ihiala, toward Biafra's western border with Nigeria, was only a few miles from Biafra's only functioning airstrip, a main target of Nigerian bombing.

Reports of starvation in Biafra were beginning to be labelled as genocide as the larger Nigerian army cut off supply routes. Pictures of starving Africans no longer are new. But then they were. And they shocked. Five years later Chinua Achebe, now an acclaimed novelist, would publish his poem "Christmas in Biafra (1969)," in which he wrote about a Biafran mother who visited a nativity scene set up by nuns at a local hospital and in his devastating understatement is reflected the horror of what was happening and the appalling indifference of the West, which was more interested in preserving Nigeria's old colonial boundaries and its capacity to deliver oil than it was concerned about the issues surrounding ethnic divisions and self-rule. In the poem the mother prays before the nativity scene, her son "like a flat dead lizard on her shoulder," and once finished, turns him around to look at the "pretty figures of God and angels and men and beasts,"

> But all he vouchsafed
> was one slow deadpan look of total
> unrecognition and he began again
> to swivel his enormous head away
> to mope as before at his empty distance.
> She shrugged her shoulders, crossed
> herself again and took him away.[26]

Stephen, by now father of three-year-old Ilana Naomi and a one year-old Avram David,[27] flew into Biafra to see for himself what was happening, landing at night at what was wryly called Uli airport — a strip of paved road about twenty-four kilometres from the front lines where landing lights were put on for only thirty seconds at a time and, beside the road, a small cemetery where twenty-five pilots and air crew who miscalculated were buried. The Nigerians were unable to force Uli to close because as fast as they bombed holes in the road, the Biafrans filled them in again.[28] British journalist John De St. Jorre in his book *The Nigerian Civil War* described what it was like to fly into Uli:

The last leg is flown at night and to avoid the Nigerian fighters and the flak a long devious route is followed. . . . There is no radar, no identification or landing equipment of any kind, only a primitive radio, and for what seems an eternity the flight continues in total darkness.

Then . . . [t]he pilot spirals down and down. . . . Now we are overhead and can see the lights and palm trees, though only intermittently through the gusts of rain and blotches of heavy tropical cloud. "Put your heads down and hold your knees," barks the guard. My hands are slippery with sweat. . . . The pilot circles, overshoots and then comes in with an awe-inspiring finality through the low-lying cloud and flying spume on to the road that is a runway. The plane lurches, lifts a little, then runs sweetly in. (Jesus Christ.)

"Christ," a veteran correspondent beside me, his voice muffled in his knees, says it. "I'm too old."[29]

There were some thirteen million people in Biafra when it seceded. By mid-January 1970, when the war ended, somewhere between 500,000 and a million people had died on both sides in the fighting. No records were kept. De St. Jorre estimates that deaths probably totalled in the vicinity of 600,000. But the deaths from starvation were something else again. On October 12, 1968 — while Stephen was in Biafra — the Dutch missionary doctor in charge of relief operations for the World Council of Churches cabled the UN secretary general:

ESTIMATED DEATH FROM STARVATION IN MONTH OF JULY 6,000 PER DAY, AUGUST 10,000 PER DAY, SEPTEMBER 12,000 PER DAY. PRESENT SITUATION HOLDS OR DECREASING SLIGHTLY WITH PRESENT LEVEL OF RELIEF FLIGHTS. HOWEVER UNLESS IMMEDIATE CEASE FIRE MONTH OF DECEMBER COULD SEE DEATH RATE UNITS OF 25,000 PER DAY. . . .[30]

The boy in Achebe's poem and one in every fourth child in the refugee camps[31] were suffering from kwashiorkor — extreme protein deficiency. Theirs has been the image most deeply graven on the history of this war.

Stephen flew into Biafra on two different occasions. "I felt very deeply about the continent and what its future would hold," he says, "and I felt especially deeply about Nigeria. . . . It was the Eastern Region that separated, and all my friends and students were there, and here they were involved in this terrible war and I didn't know whether they were dead or alive, but only that there was something terribly wrong with the whole business. With the whole war."

He filed freelance articles with the Toronto Star:

One of the factors which is lost sight of, but is driven home with enormous force on the scene [he wrote in October 1968], is the conviction of a whole generation of young Biafran militants that they are creating a revolutionary environment — a separate, autonomous nation-state, based on revolutionary principles and the eradication of social injustice. It is not Marxist or Maoist. . . .

Whether or not a military government can ever succeed in establishing a new kind of society is debatable. Just last week I spent an evening with Mr. Eke, Biafra's minister of information, and eight of his *young turk* radicals, all of them holding significant government positions. And it was for all the world like the best moments of those who fought on the Republican side in the Spanish Civil War or in the Cuban Revolution.[12]

But why should a Canadian get involved with the Spanish Civil War or the Cuban Revolution — or Biafra? The question is asked twenty years later in the ambassador's office at the United Nations. "Because it feels just," he says. "Because it's an important international cause. Because it speaks to the rights of a continent. Because it speaks to oppression, class struggle, all the things I felt politically and spiritually involved in. Because it was idealistic. . . .

"[Because] this was a cause that at that moment in time symbolized the struggle for freedom and against oppression in the world. What causes me some chagrin is I think it may have been the wrong struggle. I don't regret the experience, but I regret the lack of sophistication of the analysis."

He wrote bitterly of the starvation, of the *kwashiorkor*, of the malaria and tuberculosis that developed as complications, of one hospital where they were losing six children a day to tuberculosis alone, of the diarrhea that dehydrated and killed, of the "arbitrary, fitful slaughter" caused by bombing.

I realize that this will stand diplomatic hair on end [he wrote in the Star] and cause an apoplectic response from those who are given to rectitude and protocol in matters of foreign policy.

But the fact is — and one has only to spend some time in Biafra to realize it — that even one musket in the hand of every Biafran soldier would force an end to this war. I did not meet a single church relief worker, Protestant or Catholic, who didn't feel that guns were more important than food.

Though fraught with classic irony, it remains possible that the most humanitarian act we are capable of might be the provision of arms. It is not so easy an altruism as the giving of food, but it demands a commitment, an appreciation of the enormity of Biafra which mere relief does not insist upon. It would end the war, and one assumes that is the object to which all Canadians would be dedicated.[13]

As he looks back today, Stephen refuses to step back from that opinion. "I don't feel uncomfortable with that reaction at that point in time in my own evolution in thinking. I don't know what I'd do to-day. But I wouldn't feel uncomfortable if my children came to a similar conclusion in generally analogous situations. [But] times have chang-ed. Because the conventional arsenals that are available on battlefields now to any combatant are so terrifying that to talk about engaging in arms is to talk about horrible, horrible destruction. And in a fun-ny way, that still wasn't yet the case even in the sixties."

He returned to Canada from his first trip to Biafra three weeks before the Ontario leadership convention held November 15–17, 1968, at which Jim Renwick unsuccessfully challenged Donald MacDonald. Stephen supported Renwick and was nominally his chief adviser. But he arrived back from Biafra too late to be of any help in corralling delegates, and before leaving he had been distracted. John Brown, a strong Renwick supporter, was vicious in his criticism of Stephen during a 1971 interview, attributing his involvement in the Renwick campaign to nothing more than an unconscious attempt to undermine MacDonald and to set him up for Stephen's own leadership challenge two years later.[34] Acknowledging that it was not Stephen's intention, while at the same time saying it was his unrecognized motivation, has to stand as one of the more unsavoury gambits in the gallery of political smears. Impossible to prove wrong. Difficult to wash off. Stephen's own answer is:

> Obviously I didn't have my heart fully in it. How can I deny it? If I'd had my heart fully in it, I would have been there managing it morning, noon, and night. . . .
>
> Jim Renwick was a very strange and curious man, capable of streaks of brilliance and intuition and enormous capacity, and at times a little quirky and distant, but with great talent. . . . I think he could have led the party quite well . . . and I felt that he should be leader. But again, [looking back on it, I obviously] didn't feel it in a way that made me drive to make it happen.
>
> Was it so unconscious that it was a manipulative political act that I didn't realize I was engaging in? I don't know. . . .
>
> I think that I would certainly not have been wilfully destructive and I don't think unconsciously destructive, although I won't pretend that there wasn't ambition.

By the following summer, Stephen had decided to take his own run at the leadership. "Stephen called at midnight one night," says Gerry Caplan, "and we arranged to have supper at a restaurant on the Queensway that a friend of his now owns." At supper "he told me he'd be interested in taking a crack at the leadership and would I come in?"

Caplan said yes, even though at the time he was a member of the Waffle.

"It was somewhere in the summer of 1969. . . . When we came back from [the convention in] Winnipeg in October I called a meeting which was held at Mel Watkins' house for Mel, Jim [Laxer], Giles Endicott, and me and I told them about Stephen's intention. And I told them flatly that as for me I was moving out of the Waffle and into Stephen's leadership attempt, and I encouraged them to come. I argued that they could have far more influence with their ideas [if they worked with] the man I guessed would be the next Ontario leader, given Ontario's role in the country, than if they stayed as part of an internal protest group. [Only] Giles agreed.

On October 4, 1970, Stephen became leader of the Ontario New Democrats, beating out Walter Pitman by a vote of 1,188 to 642. Donald MacDonald had resigned at the end of June. His soundings had told him the party was fairly evenly split between supporting Stephen and him, and so he stepped down rather than put it through the trauma of what he thought would be a divisive battle. Pitman entered the race in early August.

MacDonald served loyally and enthusiastically under Stephen. But to this day he remains privately bitter that Stephen did not wait his turn. MacDonald had been leader since 1953, when the party held only two seats, and he had carried it through the lean years — three seats in 1955, five seats in 1959, seven seats in 1963 (eight with Jim Renwick in 1964) — and he had brought it to its breakthrough of twenty seats in 1967. He says in his recently published memoirs that, had he remained leader, he could have succeeded where Stephen failed in the 1971 election and could have forced the Tories into a minority government with the NDP as official opposition.[35]

His belief is one of those political "what ifs" that can never be answered completely. In coming to it, MacDonald assumed that what the public wanted was more of the same, and that assumption was dangerously weak. First of all, it ignored how he would have coped with the Waffle. Second, it was by no means certain that it was more of the same, and not significant change, that the public yearned for.

If MacDonald had coped badly with the Waffle, strife within the party could have been aggravated still further; and not only might the Ontario party have done worse in 1971; the federal party might have been hamstrung in the 1972 federal election. One thing is certain, his age, his manner, his mind set — in an interview he was strongly defensive of reaching out for "liberally minded people" — all would have made him more vulnerable than Stephen to dissatisfaction among those who believed the party needed a good shaking up. And Stephen was the person seen most likely to shake the party up — even the Waffle voted for him in the leadership contest with Walter Pitman.

John Brewin, who was a campaign manager for Pitman, puts it succinctly: "Don was a bit old hat and Don couldn't revitalize the party."

MacDonald's argument is that Stephen came across as too radical in the 1971 election and that lost votes. But the answer to that is not necessarily that a staid MacDonald leadership would have done better. It can be argued just as forcefully that the public was indeed in the mood for some thoroughgoing changes, but that Stephen was thoroughgoing on the wrong issues. If he had been talking about rent control instead of nationalization, as he was in 1975, who's to say the party might not have leapt ahead? And who's to say that, if MacDonald had been leader and preaching his policies for the "liberal-minded," the party might not have stalled at the polls?

Surprising support for the view that Stephen should have waited, however, comes from Gerry Caplan.

> I think it was a major mistake . . . to go after Donald for the leadership in 1970 [he says]. I think it was shallow ambition on both our parts that was responsible, and the lack of perspective that two guys just into their thirties had about how the world wasn't going to wait another three or four years for our time.
>
> But having said that, I believe there always was an overriding passion in Stephen . . . and if there was shallowness it was only because he was opportunistic about the issues, about forcing the party to confront a changing world. He was never going to sit in that Legislature the way all kinds of Liberals and Tories did for years, just getting involved when there was nothing else to do.

Caplan's opinion comes as a surprise to Stephen during a May 1987 interview. He hadn't realized that Caplan had changed his position, he says. Then he deals with the argument:

> I think there was undoubtedly an element of impatience. No question. I'm not sure, in retrospect that it was wrong. . . . The party was locked into a sort of repetitive way of doing things. Just enunciating old policies again and again in a way that captured the imagination hardly at all. . . .
>
> Looking at it historically, I think the maturing of the party and of myself between 1971 and 1975 was what took us to where we emerged in 1975 [as official opposition facing a minority government], and allowed us to make the contribution in the mid-seventies of which I feel quite proud — for the party and for Ontario.

He could have waited until 1975 before going for the leadership, Stephen says, in which case the maturing process would have taken until 1979. "The better test historically, for me, is whether it turned out that the change in leadership was premature for the party, and I don't think it was." In the early years of his leadership "a terribly important analysis" showed how important it was to understand the needs of the province at the grass roots level instead of trying to dictate policies and programs from on high.

> And that lesson [says Stephen] turned out to be enormously beneficial in the elections that were called immediately thereafter.
>
> In another odd way, we were probably a better leadership to face the Waffle [because], you see, the desire for change had obviously begun around 1968. So it wasn't a capricious move in 1970. I think, to be fair, one has to remember that. It obviously was a feeling over time. It wasn't the last minute.
>
> And it also was a feeling that clearly engaged the significant majority of the caucus because a very significant majority of the caucus was with us. In that sense, the leadership challenge mirrored a feeling that the time was ripe to make that change.

•CHAPTER TWENTY-TWO•

How to identify a Waffler: "You walk right up to him and whisper, 'Stephen Lewis.' If his eyes go all slitty, he's Waffle."

Mel Watkins
Maclean's *Magazine*[1]

In the end, the Waffle was just about everything anyone said it was. It was snotty and unruly and intemperate and abusive. It was a party within a party. It was riven with paranoia. It was irresponsible and insufferably holier than thou. It had more than its share of mouthy, fringe extremists. It had platoons of academics who had never been through a collective-bargaining session trying to tell unions how to run their affairs. It was Intolerant. Inconsistent. Undisciplined. Destructive.

It could even be — as Michele puts it with unabashed relish: "Entirely Oedipal. These were out-of-control bad boys who just wanted to screw Daddy and wreck the house. However sophisticated their political analysis, this was their emotional force."

At the same time, it was creative and idealistic and exuberant and full of ideas. It was democratic to the point of chaos. It was young. It was passionate and committed. Its outrage was fresh and uncompromised. It was undaunted by the big questions. It was articulate. Intellectually accomplished. Innovative. Droll.

It was bound to convulse the party. To uncork hostility, anger, frustration. Even bewilderment. There are all sorts of reasons for it. Everyone has a story, an anecdote. Every recounting of the history of the period has its perfectly logical rationale for the wild showdown that saw the party drive a stake through the heart of the Waffle.

Past a certain point, a vehement reaction was inevitable. But there had to be something that went beyond logic in the response to the Waffle. Something that could account for the savagery of the emo-

425

tions that were unleashed. Something subterranean. Something the Waffle triggered in the psychology of the party that made it call for no quarter. When you go looking for it, things slowly begin falling into place, and they point to feelings and experiences that at least to some degree must have tripped a reflex reaction learned during all those years of fighting Communists:

WINDSOR AND SUDBURY were among the largest centres of Waffle strength in Ontario — Windsor: home of the Autoworkers who had been led by George Burt in the days when the CCF was battling Communists in the unions; Sudbury: home of Mine Mill before it was driven out of INCO by Steel.[2]

AUTOWORKERS AND STEELWORKER DELEGATES from Stelco in Hamilton favoured Waffle leader Jim Laxer over David Lewis at the federal leadership convention in 1971.[3]

DAVID, in his memoirs, said that more than anything else the Waffle reminded him of the Socialist Fellowship in British Columbia in 1950 and 1951. The fellowship was a radical-left splinter group founded in opposition to the Winnipeg Declaration that, according to David, so bogged the party down in recrimination and intrigue it was at a standstill in the province for a year. It was dissolved midway through 1951.[4]

LYNN WILLIAMS, head of the Steelworkers, recalls that as the Waffle began to hit high stride, his reaction was "Here we go again!"[5]

JOHN BREWIN says his impression was that "David and my father and others tended to see the Waffle as the old-style type of Communist assault on the party. . . . It was yet another impulse of the left that needed to be put down."

STEPHEN says it wasn't just the attack on international unions that upset union leaders "because the labour movement knew in its soul that what eventually happened to the Canadian Autoworkers would happen. . . . They weren't as much frightened by the Waffle analysis as they were of an equivalent cell group [within their unions] which could make turmoil and trouble for a very long time."[6]

CLIFF SCOTTON, federal secretary from 1965 to 1975, says, "I think David saw the Waffle as another manifestation of the Trots, the Commies, or whatever, so he would go back to the old battle. David felt that you were either with us or against us."

CHARLES LYNCH, Ottawa columnist for Southam Newspapers, declared that the Waffle was acting in the interests of international communism.[7]

NORMAN PENNER in his book *Canadian Communism* notes that sprinkled through the Waffle were people who had quit the Communist Party in disgust, or whose parents had quit, after the Khrushchev revelations in 1956.[8]

OPPONENTS OF THE WAFFLE, when they speak of it today, time and again mention the "Trots" in the Waffle; it's like an eerie echo of the days when their counterparts used to talk of the "Commies" in Mine Mill — and in percentage terms there probably wasn't much difference.

THE 1948 EXPULSION OF BOB CARLIN from Mine Mill was on his mind, Stephen says when he declared war on the Waffle in his Oshawa speech in March 1972; he was worried about how to avoid a drought in party fortunes similar to what followed Carlin's ouster in the Sudbury basin for the next seventeen years.[9]

WHEN THE WAFFLE came into being, memories were still vivid of the bloody battles in the unions against Communists and those who were labelled fellow travellers. It was in:

1948 that the Communists were defeated in the UAW, that their control of the Vancouver Labour Council and the B.C. Federation of Labour was broken, and that they were driven out of the International Woodworkers of America;

1949 that Mine Mill was kicked out of the Canadian Congress of Labour and the notorious Hal Banks was brought into Canada to get rid of the "Communist" Canadian Seamen's Union;

1950 that the United Electrical Workers were expelled from the Canadian Congress of Labour;

1951 that the International Leather and Fur Workers Union was expelled from the Canadian Congress of Labour and Hal Banks' Seafarers' International Union (SIU) was brought into the CCL to replace the ousted CSU;

1959 that a slate sympathetic to the Steelworkers won control of the executive of Mine Mill's huge Sudbury local by the narrow margin of fifteen votes;

1962 that the Steelworkers finally won an organizing drive in Sudbury and kicked Mine Mill out of INCO;

1963 that the Norris Commission reported on the lawlessness of the SIU under Hal Banks;

1967 that Mine Mill merged with the Steelworkers and the battle with the Communists was formally over.

What the Waffle did was touch a nerve still raw with memories of thirty years of bruising struggle. Of insult and accusation. Of progress stalled. Of energies consumed. Of the frustration with endless meetings elbowing for advantages that often were stupidly tiny. Of being constantly impugned with charges of hypocrisy and betrayal and conspiracy and sucking up to the system.

Small wonder there was an oversized reaction. Small wonder especially when the Waffle began to spread its organization into union locals, raising for union leaders the spectre of a return to the kind of internal division and ideological turmoil they thought they had stamped out such a short time ago. The Waffle wasn't Communist — far from it — but that was no consolation. Because, if there were corners of the past, like the smear campaigns against Mine Mill, that they weren't particularly proud of, how much greater the reluctance to engage in a struggle that would evoke memories best forgotten?

It was in Ontario where most of the battles had been fought. It was in Ontario where the nerve was most tender. "It was a real shock to me," says Jim Laxer, "when I finally figured out that to some extent these guys [were] thinking that we were another version of the Communist menace. That was a shock to me. And pretty horrifying. . . .

"[It] made me bloody mad . . . the fact that they couldn't distinguish between what was obviously very much a youth political movement that was going on in the sixties [and the kind of thing the old CPers were up to]. . . . It really lowered my opinion of them very considerably."

Laxer, in his late forties, still has a boyish affability, and once he has you seated he takes a wooden armchair opposite, faces you squarely, leans forward, and grins. This is a man who loves his conversation. If he had feathers they would be ruffling in little shivers. He is leaner than in his Waffle days. To meet him for the first time is like jumping in the family album from photos of the pubescent teenager to the new college graduate. He has grown into his body and out of its softness. In the Waffle he had what you'd swear were the last vestiges of baby fat and a lot hair, watered down on top, bushy sideburns that went down to his jaw, and a moustache. Now he is clean-shaven — physically and doctrinally — although there still lingers about him that vulnerable openness of the peace generation. In 1969 he would describe himself as a "left nationalist" whose heroes were George Grant and Henri Bourassa. Now he thinks that in some ways he is turning into an anti-nationalist. "Look at what is happening in Europe. The idea of tearing down borders is pretty appealing to me. I don't like American nationalism much. And I certainly don't want to be dragged into the black hole of the United States as it goes down the drain. I think I'm turning into a globalist of some kind. But the burning thing that I cared about in the late sixties was U.S. control of Canada."

His father had been a full-time organizer for the Communist Party but quit in 1956 after Khrushchev disclosed the atrocities of Stalin. Laxer grew up hating the party because there was such opposition to it he felt like an outcast. "I didn't want to be associated with this goddam Soviet Union. I wanted to be part of the kids on the street," he says. He was delighted when his parents quit.

> So I suppose I'm a bit of an anti-Communist . . . [and] in that sense, I'm not terribly different from David Lewis.
>
> When I ran for the leadership in 1971, I used to travel with David Lewis and I used to spend a lot of time talking with him. . . . I saw him very much in a paternal kind of way. I always saw him as a great figure in Canadian social democracy because I was . . . a student of history. My degree is in history although I teach political science.
>
> To me he was a great hero in the way that twenty-seven-year-olds romanticize people. You know the Walter Young line about, "There wouldn't have been a Canadian social democracy without David Lewis"? I thoroughly believed that. I always wanted him to be leader of the party. . . .
>
> I remember one time we were sitting in the airport in Regina and he said. . . , "You know, Jim, I'm not angry with you. I know you're not running to be leader. You're running to put forward ideas. The people I'm really angry with are Harney and Broadbent." . . . And I always said, "Listen, you're going to be leader of the party and I'm going to support you."
>
> I saw myself as sort of a young rebel, but also as apprentice to somebody like that.

Of course there were some Trots in the Waffle, Laxer says. Not many, but some. And they were always "quite a small minority."

> There might have been meetings where they were 20 or 25 percent. But we always knew who they were and they never had their way in anything . . . and they detested us. They hated us. It's one of the things about the left that I don't like very much. . . . There's a tendency to develop the idea that your left-wing opponent is far more your enemy than any capitalist could be. . . .
>
> The Trots were anti-nationalist. They regarded us as some kind of petit bourgeois nationalists. In any serious revolution they would have regarded us with as much hatred as the Bolsheviks regarded the Bund, if you want to draw that analogy. . . . [T]he one thing I would not agree with is ever using the Trots as a way to talk about what the Waffle really stood for. . . .
>
> We used to play games [with them]. . . . [W]e used to say, "All right, let's have a standing vote on this," . . . and while the standing vote was being taken, somebody would take a picture . . . and you'd have a photograph and you'd be able to say, "You want to know who all

the Trots are? They're the fifteen people who are standing in this photograph." [He grins broadly.]

But I couldn't stand it now. My ability to sit in meetings has declined very significantly.

Laxer and Caplan and Mel Watkins and Giles Endicott were the forces behind the creation of the Waffle. Eleven, including Ed Broadbent, attended the first meeting on April 29, 1969.[10] Laxer's dominant concern was to get rid of a "Made in the USA" approach to social issues.

I thought the New Left was a totally Americanized phenomenon in Canada . . . which was [helping] to tear down Canadian institutions and to Americanize Canada. . . . What I was interested in was helping to move this stream of very powerful youth politics into Canadian social democracy. I was saying to people in the student movement, "There is a great Canadian institution which is quite different from anything the United States has and it's called the NDP." . . . So the furthest thing from my mind was the idea of destroying the NDP.

So when we drafted the Waffle Manifesto, I was full of virtue and belief that we were doing something that was good. . . . I didn't think that there was anything conflictual, or that David Lewis would hate this, or that trade union leaders would almost give themselves coronaries chasing twenty-six-year-olds from one side of a convention hall to another to stop us. . . .

And later to find out that people . . . thought of us as some sort of [threat equivalent to the] Red menace, that was really bizarre. But we started to get that feeling as early as the 1969 convention. And [even then] it was a kind of slow sense that "God, these guys, they're out of an old movie!"[11]

The Manifesto declared that "the major issue of our times is not national unity but national survival," and that it was American control of the Canadian economy, aided and abetted by a Canadian corporate elite, that had "opted for a junior partnership with . . . American corporate enterprises" that posed the major threat to survival. "By bringing men together primarily as buyers and sellers of each other, by enshrining profitability and material gain in place of humanity and spiritual growth, capitalism has always been inherently alienating," it said.

The leading features of its program included "extensive public control over investment and nationalization of the commanding heights of the economy, such as the key resources industries, finance and credit, and industries strategic to planning our economy."

The 1969 convention, held in Winnipeg during the last week of October, spurned the Manifesto by a vote of 499 to 268 in favour of what came to be known as the Marshmallow Resolution, drafted by David Lewis and Charles Taylor. Stephen wasn't there. He was back in Biafra.

The challenge of the seventies was "saving our country," the resolution proclaimed. Much more circumspect about nationalization, it said that the way to "strengthen and enrich Canada's independence" was through "Expansion of public investment and public ownership, government planning, investment controls, a just tax system, purposeful monetary policies freed from the restraints of a fixed exchange rate, and necessary laws to limit and regulate foreign investment and subsidiaries in Canada."

It also called for creation of a Canada Development Corporation, a "national commodity field throughout the world [to] reduce Canada's dependence on one unregulated market," and a "serious commitment in carefully chosen areas of science and technology."

It's a pity the Marshmallow Resolution had not been passed eight years earlier at the founding of the New Party. Then it might have given the sense of philosophic renewal to the party that it needed so badly. It was by far the most aggressive program for regaining control of the Canadian economy that the leadership had ever submitted. However, coming as a reaction to the Waffle Manifesto, the Marshmallow Resolution simply acknowledged that the initiative in developing policies had been seized by the Waffle, and by being much more restrained, it lacked the flair to attract what Laxer calls the powerful stream of youth politics. Its nickname stuck.

Laxer can't pinpoint when the Waffle reached the point of no return. The point at which compromise became impossible. The point after which it became inevitable that the NDP would decree that members could not belong to both organizations — would say, in practical terms, that anyone who insisted on remaining in the Waffle be expelled from the party. Nor can Watkins or Caplan or Lynn Williams.

But Stephen can. It was in late January 1972, three months after the Ontario election, when he and Michele had coffee and wine through one late afternoon and early evening with Laxer and his wife Krista Maeots. No one else knew of the meeting. Until recently asked about it, Mel Watkins was unaware of it. Stephen offered no specific proposals and neither did Laxer. "It was [just] the hand of friendship," says Stephen. "Jim was giving out signals everywhere that he wasn't comfortable" with how things had developed. "It was absolutely momentous" for Laxer and Maeots to agree to the meeting, says

Michele, and she and Stephen were in high hopes. "I remember our joking as we walked up to their house about an entente cordiale [and] Jim, who was sort of affable and charming and wanting to be friends and didn't seem to clue in to how much harm he was doing at all, was all ready . . . to work out a more benign way of behaving. [But] Krista all but hit the coffee table over his head and absolutely forbade any *entente*."

Stephen says that, even though nothing specific was mentioned, "we understood one another. We'd been fighting long enough." The party was "sufficiently flexible to accommodate the nationalist drives of the Waffle and some of what would be considered [its] radical prescriptions . . . if they could lay off the separate membership lists and the union bashing and that kind of stuff. We understood what the *quid pro quo* would mean." But, Stephen says, what Krista did was to say there were no grounds to talk, so, he says, "What the hell was left for the party?"

Laxer's memory differs. "I think what happened was that we got very close to agreeing," he says. "I thought we were going to get it together . . . a sort of *modus vivendi*. A kind of feeling of a pattern of behaviour that we weren't going to offend them as much as in the past. . . . And then at some [later] point they made a decision that they either didn't have enough or that they wanted to go all the way." In any event, the parting was friendly, Laxer says, with no sense of there being an unbridgeable gap. "Certainly not from my point of view. Maybe Stephen felt that. If Stephen felt that, then it matters."

For Michele, as with Stephen, there was no ambiguity. "We walked away depressed. And crushed. And furious," she says.

As for Krista's blocking any rapprochement, Laxer says, "Well, she was probably somewhat more hard-lined about this kind of thing . . . [but] I'm not sure there is any reality in all of that, except . . . if it made a difference in how [Stephen] would behave. Then that is important."

Regardless of which version is accepted, this was the point of no return if for no other reason than that's how Stephen perceived it. Equally certain is that Krista Maeots was a forceful personality. Some go as far as Murray Weppler, who worked with her at *The Citizen* in Ottawa and who says, "She was the brains behind the Waffle . . . a very single-minded person." What must be remembered, says Janusz Dukszta, without knowing of the Laxer–Lewis meeting, is that the three strongest people in the Waffle were all women: Krista Maeots, Kelly Crichton, and Jackie Larkin, and of the three Maeots was the strongest.

Dukszta was NDP member of the Legislature for Parkdale and a Waffle sympathizer at the time.

Even so, it was Laxer and Watkins who held the limelight, who were the stars of the Waffle — both of them charismatic, both fervid nationalists, with Watkins providing the piercing economic rationale for the Waffle's nationalism. Of the two, Watkins was the more unbending. "Gerry and I liked Jim," says Stephen, but not Mel. "Mel was much tougher, much more difficult, much more uncompromising. Jim was more malleable."

But although they were the spokesmen, the ones on whom the media focused, the ones who gave verve and inspiration to the Waffle, in Dukszta's view it was the three women who stood guard at the gates.

It's a view that Stephen shares. "They were the powerhouses," he says. During debates, "Laxer you could handle. Mel made you nervous. Mel's a very steady and intelligent debater. But when Jackie took the microphone, you wondered whether you'd carry the day." Maeots, he says, was "as bright as Mel . . . [and] the toughest and the most powerful Waffle member of them all. . . . Now, she did not manipulate Mel. He was a central force, no question. . . . [But] she and Jackie were on the [provincial] executive of the party," and the main battle with the Waffle wasn't fought in public meetings and press conferences. "It was fought in the heart and soul of the executive where [Waffle opposition] was implacable."

"The sadness of it [was that] the party could have come to terms with others . . . [people such as] Pauline Jewett, Jim Laxer himself, David Neuman, mayor of Brantford, [who] now sits in the Legislature for the Liberals. . . . We would have had trouble with Mel. We would have had trouble with the unions. Yet we might have orchestrated something. But it was that tremendously hard core at the centre, which was the women."

Speaking of Maeots is difficult because in 1978 she committed suicide. It had nothing to do with the Waffle, says Laxer. "By the time she died, psychologically she was very far away from the Waffle." In the intervening years she worked on CBC radio, becoming executive producer of *This Country in the Morning*. "She was extremely good," says Laxer. "She had a real genius for that . . . and was devoted to the idea of building local cultures across the country and finding people in the regions who were making a contribution . . . people in St. John's or in Saskatoon, and poets and writers, that sort of thing. I think she made a big contribution . . . so that now we get programs like *Morningside*."

Peter Gzowsky, current host of *Morningside*, worked with her on *This Country* and says of her in his latest book: "She left her mark on the radio forever, as well as on all of us who knew her . . . much of *This Country's* success was due to her dogged pursuit of the unsung." Despite her strong political views, "she was as fair-minded a producer as I have ever worked with."[12] In conversation he adds: "She had the most remarkable ability to separate her political commitment from her work in radio. She made more of a point of getting people on [the show] with views opposing hers than almost everyone I've ever known."

She was born in Sweden and when she was three years old, her parents immigrated to Calgary where she grew up. Her background was Estonian, says Laxer, "so she had a lot of that puritanism and work ethic . . . and she was never tremendously at ease with people. I think life to her was always tough, so what people would have seen as a stridency was really much more fighting her way through — you know, the girl from a small town who had those kinds of personality pressures. She was always making a tremendous effort to do the things she did." Her political views were not extreme, he says. "She came into politics only in her early twenties, so by the time we are talking about, she had evolved fairly quickly through a kind of romantic anarchism, which was a sort of New Leftism, to a more serious kind of socialism." Ideologically within the Waffle, she was smack in the middle, he says. Her death was the result of "the sort of life-long problem of dealing with the various ghosts and miseries that always afflicted her. She was a very strong person who managed to fight to keep herself going until she couldn't stand it any more."

After the Ontario election in October 1971 "things were really sliding downhill," says Stephen. "We fought the election with and against the Waffle rather than with and against the Tories. And the Steve Penners and others who were quite mischievous . . . helped to drive us down." Partly as a result of that, partly as a result of the Waffle moving in on the unions, meetings of the provincial executive became "awfully difficult. . . . You can't imagine those meetings. They were raw hatred. On both sides."

Elmer McVey was a member of that executive, having returned to the party after his suspension following the Bob Carlin affair, and by then was an anti-Waffler despite the fact that "support for the Waffle up here [in Sudbury] was out of this world." He remembers a classic meeting in Toronto.

We started debate at about nine o'clock, nine-thirty, in the morning and come lunch we were still on the same thing . . . because we were never able to get to a bloody vote. Now we had the majority and we could have voted, but Stephen believed in working by consensus. We wanted a goddammed vote to get the thing over with, but he wouldn't do it.

So we went out to lunch. There was Lynn Williams and a gang of us . . . and he said, "How the hell are we going to show this guy [Stephen] what these people are like?"

"Well, [someone said], "let's go back and agree to everything they want . . . and see what they do." It was a pisspot piddly thing anyway. . . . It was just a power struggle. I don't even remember the issue.

[So] we went back and the issue came on the floor and somebody said, . . . I believe we should accept the motion as it is without fighting it any longer. Goddammit! They turned right around and they wouldn't support it themselves. It was "There's something wrong here. What the hell's going on that these guys are suddenly supporting it?" They hadn't a clue . . . but they sure had the wind in their sails.

From the outset the Waffle had irritated union leaders by intimating, and sometimes saying explicitly, in fact sometimes saying tauntingly, that Canadian unions should be Canadian, not branches of American internationals.[13] Laxer says he and Watkins tried to restrain such provocations because "people would go absolutely around the bend. [So] we didn't do it very often. We resolutely tried to stop people . . . from raising the question of Canadian unions. We always talked about autonomy for unions and never talked about splits. We didn't call for anything as radical as Bob White ultimately did [with the Canadian Automobile Workers]. . . .

"What we didn't understand was that the whole logic of an independent Canada threatened . . . the trade union leadership. Because it raised the issue automatically . . . because after all, if General Motors should be Canadianized, why not the UAW?"

But even calling for autonomy was unwelcome. Union leaders like Dennis McDermott and Harold Thayer were not accustomed to having fellow party members thrash out union business in public, and they didn't like it one bit.[14] Nor did they like the Waffle's attempt to organize support within their locals. To hear Laxer explain the organizing, it sounds innocent enough:

One of the reasons that a caucus like the Waffle grows up is because people are tired of going to conventions where they find that all the decisions are being made in advance by various committees. . . . The Waffle organized to offset that kind of thing so you could have real debates. . . . [A]t the time I regarded that as democratic fairness . . . so that to get the reaction that we were highly structured, almost a political party, described in almost conspiratorial terms, was way out of line. It was extraordinarily paranoid. . . .

> The leadership of the party had a very direct line to people in every [union] local who worked with it. . . . It was very hard for us to get to [them] to . . . try to get support. They controlled the [membership] list and they wouldn't give it out . . . so you had this group who might have one-third of the delegates at a convention but who were very hard to get at. So we tried to organize to overcome that.

But any innocence that there may have been in the beginning was long gone by the time the election was over. By then there was only bitterness on both sides. A week after the vote the Waffle's newly created labour committee published a pamphlet called *A Socialist Program for Canadian Trade Unionists*, which declared that the "official trade union movement has become a major institution buttressing private corporate enterprise," and its "right-wing establishment believe[s] that corporate capitalism . . . is the best, most 'democratic' society for the workers. . . . [Moreover, it] accepts the multi-national corporations as the best form of economic activity in the world. . . . At bottom, they have no stomach for the struggle to free Canada from the American Empire. . . . In the long run Canadian workers must achieve full control of their unions which means completely sovereign and independent Canadian unions."[15]

As if that wasn't provocative enough, ten weeks later, on January 9, 1972, the Waffle and the Windsor and District Labour Council sponsored a symposium to protest against relaxation in safeguards in the Canada-U.S. Auto Pact, which news reports had said Ottawa was considering. The symposium was held in Windsor, site of the gruelling battles with Communists in the big UAW local, a local still rife with left-right divisions. If the Waffle had gone hunting for a symbolic location to highlight confrontation it couldn't have chosen better. As Laxer notes: "There was tremendous support for the Waffle in the big auto plants coming partly out of the radical tradition. . . . You got this incredible response. . . . The mayor of Windsor came. We had 500 Autoworkers there for two days." (News reports claimed 300 attended of whom fifty were UAW members.[16])

To people like UAW Canadian director Dennis McDermott, that radical tradition would translate straight back to 1948, to the bloody infighting with Communists and the legacy it left in the existing divisions within the local.

It was one thing to have to live with this radical division in the membership. It was quite another when the radicals were offered a political focus and the intellectual and organizing skills to mount effective ideological challenges — complete with the promise of endless efforts to turn the structure of the union upside down. Or, as the Waffle would say, right side up.

When the Waffle capped its criticism of the pact with a call for a one-day work stoppage and protest demonstration, that launched McDermott into a thundering rage. "The leaders of the Waffle are footloose academics with no affinity with and little understanding of labour," he fumed." Laxer, he said, was "an irresponsible academic, a headline hunter and an ego tripper par excellence." Waffle leaders ought to start the revolution in the universities where "they draw their fat salaries for lecturing a couple of hours a week and have all kinds of free time on their hands to meddle in other people's business. Meanwhile, why don't they . . . for want of a better expression . . . get lost? . . . This union has disassociated itself from the activities of the Waffle and in my view the NDP will have to do the same thing."[17]

Laxer was no less venomous. "I have no intention," he said, "of behaving like a compromised Canadian just because Mr. McDermott is more concerned about the heads of his union in Detroit than he is about the sellout of the auto pact safeguards. . . . For Mr. McDermott to regard a public conference on an issue of concern to all Canadians as an interference in the affairs of the UAW is simply fatuous."[18]

By now the two sides were rigidly entrenched in their opposition. It was time for Stephen to make his one last try at reconciliation.

When the Waffle was formed, Gerry Caplan had been delegated to ask Stephen to join. "There was no doubt that he was intrigued with the idea. . . . He had a regard for Laxer. And on the general analysis stressing the role of American imperialism [he thought] Laxer was right on. But from the beginning he said he didn't want any part of it. He just said leave me out. It's not an appropriate role for me to be a formal outsider.

"Looking back, I remember being pissed off with him for the first few months. But I came to have a great admiration for the intuitive shrewdness of that decision. It would have been nothing but trouble for him. . . . Stephen . . . can never be an outsider in that party."

And in any showdown there never was doubt where he would stand. It would be with the people who had supported the party through nearly forty years of gruelling struggle and with a conviction, reaching back to the Bund, that fusion of union and party were essential to political effectiveness.

Seven weeks after his meeting with Laxer — on Saturday, March 18, 1972 — Stephen took the podium in the UAW Centre in Oshawa and asked the provincial council to set in motion a process that would force the party to deal with the Waffle "once and for all." He asked the council to order preparation of a statement recommending what should be done. It was Stephen's declaration of war.

He warned of the polarization within the party that he had witnessed while crisscrossing the province, of acrimony and bitterness without precedent, of distrust and intolerance, of anger, of secret meetings of opposing factions, of hurtful and wounding statements. He defended the accusation that the Waffle had "virtually become" a party within a party. And he pointed to its attitude toward union leaders:

> [This attitude] arouses in me more feeling, and more incipient anger, than anything else I have to say today.
>
> There has developed in our party a sneering, contemptuous attitude toward official trade unionism and the labour leadership. The vocabulary used is mocking and scornful, replete with all the rhetoric about old-time, right-wing, reactionary, establishment, bureaucratic, power-hungry, porkchoppers — or brass, the terms are interchangeable. Every article and every pronouncement has to include this ritual and gratuitous abuse. . . .
>
> By what perverse assessment of reality does the New Democratic Party have to do Pierre Trudeau's dirty work for him? . . .
>
> These [so-called] patsies of the American Empire kept democratic socialism alive on this continent since 1933.

No one was prepared for the uncompromising finality of Stephen's speech. Not his supporters; not his opponents. Laxer was expecting an attack, he says, but "not the virulence." But in saying that, he says more about his own reaction than about the speech. Stephen was relentless, he was condemnatory, he was passionate. He was *not* virulent.[19]

Probably no one was more delighted than Lynn Williams, who says the speech

> was an absolute masterpiece. . . . Stephen sat up all night, or most of the night, and wrote it . . . by hand. It wasn't unusual for him to lose a lot of sleep. But it was unusual for him to speak from a handwritten speech because he speaks so magnificently extemporaneously anyway. . . .
>
> And I remember Mel Watkins, as we were leaving, just screaming at me, "What makes you think you're so much better than I am?" And I remember saying, "Mel, that's not the point at all. I don't think I'm any better than you are." I mean, I've dealt with many angry people [and] I've rarely seen anybody angrier than he was. I remember it, I guess, so clearly because I was really very taken aback at the depth of the feeling.

Watkins recalls the exchange but can't remember what was said. "But if Lynn remembers it so clearly, I probably did say something like that," he says. His outburst probably was rooted in a festering anger at continuing references to the Waffle as just a "bunch of intellectual troublemakers," he says. "They played this anti-intellectual game and I guess I felt that Lynn was leading the witch hunt — and for God's sake, he has his university degree in economics and I come from more of a working-class background than he does."

Williams now is head of the Steelworkers, the first Canadian to sit in the president's office in Pittsburgh with its commanding view over the headwaters of the Ohio River. Ushering the way to his office, an aide confides — reverently — "He's really fit, you know. Body and mind." And so he appears, although wiry would be more accurate — of body *and* mind. He is cautiously relaxed. And when questions come, he circles them warily, sniffing for hazards. Any found are neutralized in his answers. On a bookshelf, along with a row of books dealing with labour history, labour practice, labour law, sit three copies of David's memoirs.

There's a pride that underlines him. Pride in the Steelworkers. Pride in his party membership: "I joined the CCF when I was a kid, before I knew what a union was." Pride in the role of the Steelworkers in the party: "We were there when nobody else was. . . . Our own leaders, Larry Sefton, Charlie Millard, Eamon Park, Murray Cotterill, it's a litany of the people who built the CCF and the NDP."

When the final showdown came, this is the man who Stephen said stood like a stone wall against any backing off from a hard line with the Waffle. "Lynn Williams," Stephen said in a 1973 interview, "who was the bargainer for the trade union movement, was treating me like INCO and he just wasn't moving an inch." It reached a point where Stephen thought, "The party is going to absolutely disintegrate and there is nothing that can be done about it. . . ."[20]

Williams says he never threatened that the labour movement would withdraw financial support from the party if the Waffle was not expelled, as was alleged in newspaper reports at the time, nor did he suggest that it would leave the party as feared by Stephen who, in the same 1973 interview, said that was the "unstated ultimatum" of the unions.[21]

"My whole memory and my sense of myself was built around indignation that the Waffle was going to destroy my party," Williams says, "not that I was going to destroy my party. And my whole focus was that we had to win this argument." He felt a "personal sense of responsibility . . . [that] if this was all screwed up, it was during my

watch. Not somebody else's watch. . . . I can't imagine ever threatening that we were going to leave. Where would we go?"

However, he does acknowledge pointing out that if the Waffle remained in the party he would find it progressively more difficult to
muster support among union members. "I'm certain that I would have
made the argument that [the continued presence of the Waffle] would
jeopardize the union support the party enjoyed. That it [would] be
very difficult for members to support the party. . . . And I'm certain
that I would have argued that the trade union membership represented
much more of a cut of what Ontario citizens thought than did a meeting
of the council of the party."

It was the way the Waffle was behaving, he says, like a party within
a party, that convinced him it had to go. "I was really incensed by
that."[22]

Following Stephen's Oshawa speech in March, the provincial council
appointed a committee of Gerry Caplan, John Brewin (Ontario
treasurer), and Gordon Vichert (Ontario president) to hold hearings
across the province and submit a recommendation on what to do about
the Waffle. They recommended that it be dissolved and any member
who continued to be involved in it should be disciplined. In language
that rivalled the Waffle's for intemperate invective, the committee said
Waffle members had "a messianic fundamentalism, a bigotry and intolerance which echoed the American South . . . as dangerous to the
NDP as George Wallace's populism is to the Democratic Party in the
United States."

The recommendation was delivered on May 6 and adopted by the
provincial executive. On June 23 the council convened in Orillia and
passed an amended resolution having the same effect but softer wording.[23] The vote was 217-88.

For Stephen, the intervening weeks were anguishing. He was terribly worried that he had gone too far and unleashed forces that would
cripple the party — if not tear it apart. He was accused of arrogance,
of betraying the spirit of the party, and he agonized over whether that
might be true. "It was heartbreaking. Soul wrenching," he says. What's
more, he and David disagreed. David still wanted a compromise —
the first time in his life, Stephen said in a 1973 interview, that he had
ever seen his father at odds with trade union leaders.[24] In a June 8
letter to Lynn Williams, David urged him to relent: "A majority of
party members tend to recoil from the executive recommendation.
. . . I am forced to the conclusion that to try to bull through a step
which is clearly unpopular . . . is to take very great risks for the welfare
of the party. . . . But from what I heard Monday night [from you]

there is a danger that anything other than the executive recommendation may jeopardize the union support the party now enjoys."[25]

On the one side Stephen had Williams, undeterred by David, still brandishing his "unstated ultimatum," should Stephen back off from the committee's recommendation. "In the end," says Brewin, "a form of compromise was accepted which was no compromise at all. . . . There was enough of a change in wording which meant that my father and a whole bunch of people who fell in the centre could say that they accepted it. And yet the trade union caucus at the council could be persuaded that the compromise didn't water down the fundamental recommendation at all."

But once again, as with the old party stalwarts, so with Stephen, something doesn't sit quite right with a simple telling of the chronology. There's a sense of some kind of subterranean anger that goes unexplained.

It surfaces one afternoon while he is still ambassador to the United Nations in May 1987. He is sitting on a straight-backed chair on the other side of a coffee table, leaning forward, elbows loosely on knees, fingers interlaced, totally still. There is only the sound of his voice building up the familiar cadences until, without raising his voice, they almost throw the final phrases against the senses.

> Even as early as the convention when I was elected leader [in October 1970] I realized that they might be with me then, but that this was an undisciplined intellectual rabble. . . .
>
> I didn't trust them. I didn't sense in them a long-term commitment to democratic socialism, I didn't in the latter stages have real respect for their views because I'd sat with too many of them at provincial executive meetings of the leadership and had seen how destructive, perverse, angry, hostile they were.
>
> I had come to the conclusion that they wanted to wreck the party. Or turn it into a sectarian rump.
>
> I was frightened by the prospects of Orillia, but I truly felt that it had to be. . . .
>
> I hated the Waffle.

It's one thing to say the Waffle was wild, undisciplined, out of control and therefore destructive — and "destructive" is not a word that Laxer shies from. When it's put to him that the Waffle could be seen as radical, disruptive, destructive, just as the Communists had been, he says, "'Radical, disruptive, destructive' — in the late sixties those words didn't at all sound bad to me. Those were radical times. The word 'radical' sounded pretty good to me. 'Communist' didn't sound good."

It's quite a different thing to say the Waffle *wanted* to wreck the party. That it had a malicious desire to annihilate the party root and branch and to leave no part standing — as the Communists wanted to do with the CCF; as the Bolsheviks wanted to do with the Jewish Labour Bund. It stretches the imagination to accept that the Waffle wanted to do the same with the NDP.

When Stephen is confronted later with skepticism over his characterization of the Waffle, he holds fast. "My use of 'intent,' " he says, "is rooted in those recollections of the ferocity of the internal struggle [on the provincial executive] and the sense that no matter what one did, even when one capitulated to them, they were not prepared to make it possible for the party to continue to function." It might be irrational. It might be a reckless disregard for the party. It might be an ideological polarity too extreme to bridge. Whatever it was, the result was the same.

Indeed, the results could be the same — but the *motivations* would not be. Intentional acts are those that are punished most severely, those that disgust the most, and it's unusual for someone with Stephen's precision with language not to make distinctions. It seems that battle adrenalin still surges over reason at the memory — and that the memory is true to the actual struggle.

But why? He didn't have the raw nerve of a Lynn Williams or a Larry Sefton or a Dennis McDermott or all the others who had spent thirty years fighting with Communists. There was nothing in his direct experience to which he could compare it. In fact, David said as much in his memoirs when he said Stephen "had not before experienced the poisonous antagonisms of internal strife on an organized scale [and was] outraged by the fratricidal animosities which deformed relationships and crippled the will to constructive thought and work."[26]

What Stephen had instead was the long arm of family history. The stories bred into his bones of seventy years of struggle — his grandfather, his father, and now him — the Medems, the Abramovitches, the Henryk Erlichs; the Otto Bauers, the Stafford Crippses, the Jennie Lees; the Albert Carmans, the Irvines, the Woodsworths, the thousands in Canada he heard his parents, or the Coldwells, or the Brewins, or countless others talk about — who had given selflessly all their lives because they had a dream of a better way and a party that would find it. The memories handed down of dreams destroyed, of parties savaged by people like those David had described almost fifty years earlier as purists for whom dogma was more important than solidarity. And perhaps as important as anything else there was his own life, from the time of his earliest memories shaped to the contours of the party, confined to its ambitions, tuned to a sense of dedication.

For the Waffle to show disrespect for the party — and it did — was an affront; for it to lack loyalty was a sacrilege; but to persist in actions that seriously hurt the party as if all the history, all the sacrifice, all the struggles and advances, were worthless — could it be that that was so monstrous it beggared comprehension and could be seen only as malicious?

Looking back on the final confrontation, Stephen is satisfied with the outcome. The break was just as necessary for the NDP as was the rejection of Liverpool's Militant Tendency by the British Labour Party, he says. The difference is that the NDP's break was clean and the Labour Party's wasn't and — at the time he was speaking in 1987 — it continued to be plagued by strife.

He pauses over a suggestion that the Ontario party came of age in the process and then muses, "There's a lot of truth in that," but almost immediately disagrees.

"No," he says. "I came of age in the process. Yeah." He sits with the thought for a moment.

"Yeah."

For Mel Watkins, the party paid a price to dissolve the Waffle because "it turned off a generation of activists." The people he is speaking about are not the high-profile individuals whom newspapers liked to quote. They are people in towns and universities across the country, many of whom remained within the NDP but gave up working so hard. Or, if they were academics, turned elsewhere to express their ideas. He mentions eight or ten names, among them:

> Bruce Kidd, who's got an office two doors from me; Pat Smart, who just won a Governor General's award for nonfiction writing in French; Peter Usher, who does a lot of work in the North . . . there's a long list. . . .
>
> You know, in 1976, people created their own political economy group within the Learned Societies. There's now a journal that's been founded by this group, a very successful journal called *Studies in Political Economy*. Almost everybody involved in it has been to the left of the NDP, has not been in the NDP, and has been more Marxist than the NDP. So the NDP doesn't even relate to it. But I see that partly as a phenomenon that is a result of the complete break between the intellectual community and the NDP. And I think that is sad.

There are any number of people who agree with Watkins — some sitting in Parliament, some in the Legislatures today — who say the party has been intellectually stunted. If so, it would be history of a kind repeating itself. It took seventeen years for the party to recover from the expulsion of Bob Carlin. It's now seventeen years since the Waffle was told to disband.

> We weren't worth getting rid of [says Laxer].
>
> I think the NDP is a seriously intellectually underdeveloped party . . . maybe the most intellectually underdeveloped social democratic party in the Western world. . . .
>
> On the really interesting debates about the limitations of social democracy — what do you do with the welfare state; how do you do interesting things with your economy inside a context of globalization; how do you react to the pressures of the Reagan–Thatcher era — I think the NDP has been profoundly out to lunch. . . .
>
> Anybody who would defend traditional Keynesianism in the late 1980s as though it was a way to solve the problems of Canadians with their economy interlocked as it is with the United States, is perpetrating a cruel joke and everybody knows that. . . .
>
> [I've discovered] that the ideas that I've been painfully putting together in my backwoods way about Keynesianism in an open economy has been put together much more cogently and brilliantly by Europeans. . . . There's a real world out there . . . and I want to be part of it. And I think social democrats of Canada should also want to be part of it. And you know, I think Stephen thinks that too. Very strongly. And I think Gerry Caplan thinks that.

Watkins, gaunt back then, wispy-haired, the delight of cartoonists reaching for the stereotype of the cloistered professor, now bearded and barbered, not overweight but what beef farmers in the Georgian Bay area where he grew up would call well marbled, who talks pretty much as he writes in *This Magazine*, had been hunched over a ten-year-old Hyperion computer — Canadian designed and built but now a historical artifact, the company that made it long since pushed under by the giants of the business. He grins appreciatively when it's noticed. There's a network of Hyperion users who still stay in touch, he says. And grins.

Talk about symbolism!

He finally returned to the NDP because "I came to the view, particularly after Reagan was elected, that it was a luxury to imagine that you could be to the left of the NDP. You were involved in such a terrible struggle to have some kind of progressive politics left. As the spectrum of politics moved to the right, the NDP became much more something that you were prepared to go down fighting for and with . . . I felt too marginalized and too isolated."

No longer does he place such exclusive emphasis on nationalism. Like Laxer, he feels that

> There's a lot of water under the bridge since I worked for Walter Gordon in the late sixties. The economy is much, to use these awful terms, much more globalized. . . . I suspect that the question of [a corporation's] nationality is becoming less and less an interesting issue, harder and harder to establish what it is. . . .
>
> I remain convinced that who controls corporations matters to what they do . . . [but] the truth is, there are good branch plants and bad branch plants. There's no point in pretending that IBM is going to go away, and IBM Canada operates in a way that would be hard to characterize as some kind of deleterious branch-plant operation.
>
> The multi-nationals really do run the world now. The patterns of transnational trade and cross-border investments are so complex now that I can't see how you can unravel them. . . . I think now the question is: "How do we live with them?"

It's a question that troubled Stephen deeply as he watched the operations of multi-nationals, especially in connection with Africa, from his vantage point as ambassador to the United Nations. He was appalled "at the behaviour of international capitalism and what it's doing to many of these countries." And it "drove him crazy" that, as ambassador, he couldn't talk about it "honestly and publicly. . . . The creation of the great trading blocs — the European market, Canada and the U.S., Japan and the South Asia — is increasingly incestuous in the reinforcing of trade among the rich and increasingly awful in the exclusion of everybody else. It's yet another dimension of international capitalism which is excruciating in its consequences. What the hell is going to be done about it?"

In the end, all three of the main figures in the Waffle confrontation have come to a similar troubled view. None of the three will waver an inch from the positions taken over the Waffle. But they are finding themselves drawn together in their concern over international trends, over the burgeoning power of supra-national corporations. And since Stephen and they always had a mutual respect for political and intellectual abilities, they find themselves co-operating. And enjoying it.

"I use Jim's material for trading blocks and things because he's so goddam bright and interesting," says Stephen. "And Mel has me to his classes to lecture. Funny!"

The years seem to have stretched the way Laxer and Watkins look at socialism, made them more attentive to complexity. Those same years seem to have hardened Stephen's resolve. There is nothing wrong with an analysis of capitalism that's rooted in Marxism, he says, although Marxist solutions have been far too simplistic:

The analysis to this day remains sharp. Socialism rooted in the [Claude-Henri de Rouvroy, comte de] Saint-Simons and the [Paul] Faures of France and the early German socialists and the early British socialists and the utopians and Robert Owen, and all the others. All of that inheritance of the eighteenth and nineteenth centuries is a persistent philosophic underpinning. I never feel myself philosophically awash, rowing frantically. And as I grow older, I am more and more persuaded that a philosophic view is what is most important.

The problem with all the goddam small-l liberals in this world, who seem to be proliferating by the millions, is that they are infinitely adaptable on any issue because there is no consistent, philosophic underpinning. That's why I always got along so well with Tories and not at all with Liberals. Because even though I thought that what the Tories believed was horse shit, they did believe it. . . .

I think [he adds later] that the whole capacity of the party to distinguish degrees of dissent or radicalism or progressivism within the left was badly torn by the Waffle episode. Not that the Waffle set out to do that. But our perceptions begin to be distorted, as though the test of your radicalism now, in the eighties and nineties, is measured against rejection or embrace of the Waffle. . . .

I don't regard the Waffle as having been radical. In some ways it was reactionary in its prescriptions. So if one forgets that convulsion in the party and thinks of the party as more of a continuum, then I share my father's view — I always have — that the distinction between party and movement is silly. That the party is both a political machine seeking genuine political change and an ideal, logical force. . . .

Within the party movement, I am probably more radical in the critique of capitalism. That's why words like "socialism" and "class" will come freely from me. That's why I use "capitalism" in speeches all the time. Because in the analysis of capitalism I am pretty unrelenting. I see it, by and large, as an objectionable, abhorrent social and economic arrangement in society.

In my prescriptions to deal with capitalism, I am probably more in the mainstream, not because I feel less radical, but because I find the solutions very difficult. And that's why I feel the party at this moment in time needs a really serious rethinking of where it is going and what it is doing.

But I am not at all sure that radicalism is right. I'm not sure that it is possible. It's like the shift from an embrace of wholesale public enterprise to a mixed economy. You'd love to go back to nationalization and say, "Ah-hah! It really was a panacea and we made a mistake and now let's return to it." But that's not true at all. It raises more problems than solutions and it costs too much.

So the prescriptions to some extent elude me. But my view of capitalism is more unrelenting than many socialists would have. I am more impatient. I am angrier. I am perhaps a little fiercer in the analysis of capitalism and the way it behaves and what it does.

So in terms of the analysis or the critique, I would probably be on the radical wing of the party. In terms of prescriptions and solutions and approaches, probably in the mainstream because I crave, as I think others do, an effort to come to grips with what we should be doing. Because it is not all that clear any more.

Some of the issues, like the environment and economic arrangements and international trends, we just haven't addressed carefully enough. . . .

So, on balance, I would be a little bit to the left of the mainstream of the party, and on the critique very much so.

And I find myself increasingly so.

•CHAPTER TWENTY-THREE•

Stephen's never thought "What do I want out of life?"
It's always "What does life want out of me?"
                                    Michele Landsberg
                                    May 1987

For some people it comes early; for some late. But like an earth tremor it tilts the mirror on the wall, framing your image a different way. When that happens, do you quickly straighten the mirror? Or do you pause, for however short or long a time, to look?

For Stephen it happened when he was two and a half weeks from his thirty-fourth birthday — October 21, 1971 — the day when he fell seriously short of his own expectations. "I was dazed," he says, "but David was devastated. He desperately wanted me to succeed." It was the day of the Ontario election when the NDP was returned with nineteen seats, one fewer than it had won under Donald MacDonald in 1967. "Jesus, I remember the night," he says. "We gathered in mourning."

He had been through victories and losses with the party in the past, but always he had emerged as the figure of promise. The child of the party who one day would be its champion. Those days ended with his claiming the leadership, and what made this election different, he knew, was that it would be results, not promise, that would define him.

There were many encouraging signs. The NDP under Ed Schreyer had been elected in Manitoba in July 1969 and under Allan Blakeney in Saskatchewan in June 1970. Governments also had changed in Quebec, New Brunswick, and Nova Scotia. A desire for change seemed to be sweeping the land. Bill Davis, who won the Conservative leadership in Ontario four months after Stephen won his, was about as exciting as a tin of tomatoes, while Stephen had won the hearts of the press gallery with his self-depreciating humour and his performance in the House.[1] Also, the party had won the last by-election in Middlesex — in 1969 — by a comfortable margin.

Finally, the party was better organized for a provincial election than ever before, and for the first time was running a candidate in every riding. There was much talk, said *Globe and Mail* reporter Jonathan Manthorpe, of an NDP minority government.[2]

"He felt he had let the party down." says Michele. "He felt very guilty and traumatized because he had sailed into the leadership with confidence that he could improve the party's showing. It wasn't an egotistical thing. That's one thing that's always astonished me about Stephen. He doesn't take any of the political activity in the highly personal, egotistical way that you associate with politicians. His whole brief was for the party."

What puzzled Gerry Caplan was why Stephen, the veteran of so many campaigns, should react so strongly. After all, setbacks are part of politics, and although the party had experienced more than its share of those, it always had prevailed. "One of the things I didn't understand [before the vote] was that Stephen needed to be leader of the second party. It didn't matter to me whether we were second or third. It did matter that we should do better. But it mattered to Stephen that he was going back to be leader of the third party instead of leader of the official opposition, and I was shocked when I came to understand that. He really needed that public vote, that public sense that he had made it."

In retrospect it doesn't seem surprising that Stephen needed a sense of having proved himself, but it's only when his sister Nina talks of what it was like to be a child of a highly successful immigrant father that the depth of this need is sketched more clearly. The expectations Stephen placed upon himself were much higher than David himself laboured under, she says, so there was much more riding — emotionally — on success. Speaking generally and not of this election in particular, she tries to explain: "My father came to Canada as an immigrant, and therefore dealt with everything as a wonderment, including whatever success he had in his political life." When he had to, he could be satisfied with moral victories, never faltering in the the face of interminable setbacks because of that sense of wonderment.

When people live through that kind of life at the beginning, as Stephen did, then one's hopes and aspirations are higher [she says]. They're much more pragmatic. . . . We wanted to win. And that [pushes] people like Stephen into an entirely different realm of politics. Much tougher, requiring a very tough skin, and I don't think Stephen had that kind of skin. So in a sense, it was more of a problem for him. . . . When you have those kinds of aspirations, [defeats] are more difficult to take. . . .

My father's expectations were to build a political party and to have a functioning political opposition and to really try in Canada to present a better alternative. For Stephen and for me, and I'm sure for Janet and for Michael, the expectations were, okay, now we have this political alternative, now we want a different stage to evolve — and that brings with it a kind of notion of success which is very difficult to handle. Success no longer is how many members you have in the party and how effective the members of Parliament are; it is how many seats do you hold, what percentage of the popular vote did you get, and how well did you win your constituency?

Measuring success in terms of seats may be putting it a little too starkly in Stephen's case; his concerns never appeared to be dominated by seat counts. But that doesn't detract from the principle of what Nina is saying: that success meant going farther than David had gone.

Part of the difficulty in this election was that the eyes of the party were upon him — and Stephen knew it. Supporters of Donald MacDonald and Walter Pitman had united behind him but many still thought that electing him leader had been a mistake. So this was more than just an ordinary proving ground.

It was a difficult campaign. Although the view from the press gallery at Queen's Park was favourable to the party, the view in the hustings was different. Voters worried about the Waffle's influence within the NDP — and why shouldn't they? Only six months earlier, Jim Laxer had demonstrated its power by chasing David through five ballots in the federal leadership race before losing 1,046 to 612. Then there was the disenchantment with the NDP and the Liberals for supporting the highly unpopular proposal to extend aid to separate schools — which Davis opposed. And there was the problem of Stephen's image. Although he was effective in the Legislature, he came across on television, to use Manthorpe's description, like a cane cutter in Castro's Cuba.[3]

On top of everything else, the party's campaign plans kept unravelling. Murray Weppler, David's executive assistant who had been assigned to help Stephen with the election, says it was the worst campaign he's ever been in.

All the mistakes that one shouldn't make in a campaign were made in that one. . . . We were dealing with up to five issues a day — trying to deal with them. Stephen tended to be extremely long-winded, eclectic as hell on any subject. [And at the end of the day] when someone stuck a microphone in front of him and asked a question, he'd go off on another spiel and we might end up with six or seven issues.

There was no focus to the campaign at all. And because of Stephen's almost total recall — he's got a memory like a bear trap for numbers and details — he would turn a simple question into a new story. So we were dealing with too many issues. The campaign had no focus and the message was far too diffuse.

On top of that, Stephen was never a strong, healthy individual in terms of stamina. He lasted through the campaign, but he was strung out . . . and that reinforced the idea that he was . . . an aggressive, hawkish young guy.

What Weppler doesn't mention is that when someone stuck a microphone in front of Stephen and asked a question, nine times out of ten he'd be asked to respond to something the Waffle had said that differed from the party position. Day in, day out, it went on, all the way through the campaign. The press loved it; the Waffle loved it; it drove everyone else in the party crazy because it made it impossible to run a coherent campaign. And when the final results were in, showing that the party fell short by only one seat of beating the Liberals for the position of official opposition, anger and frustration with the Waffle were unbounded.[4]

"Strung out" as he was after the campaign, Stephen still had another eight months to go, battling every step of the way, before the Waffle was driven from the party. There were speculations in some corners of the press and the party during the winter of 1972 that he wanted to resign — but such was not the case. The wear and tear was showing, but there was no way that he would give a second's thought to leaving while the issue of the Waffle remained unresolved. The Waffle period, he was to say in 1989, "was the single most enervating period in my political life." But after it was over, he paused to examine his life and "in the year after the Waffle I was pretty buffeted by whether or not I wanted to continue to do this." He came close to quitting, but finally, in June 1973 at a provincial council meeting in Windsor, he put conjecture to rest and declared that he would lead the party through the next election.

The thing that Stephen has always disliked most about politics [says Michele] is rancour and enmity. . . . There's no personal hatred involved. Or personal venom. He'll fight on an issue he believes in, but he'll never go after anyone on personal grounds. And he hates it when other people do that.

The Waffle was a new thing in our experience. There was so much personal viciousness. . . . It left Stephen battered and depressed. He did what he felt it would be fair to do, though he didn't relish it. . . .

It took the zest out of politics for him. He hated seeing all the enmity in the party. He hated seeing the left tear itself apart — the old history of the left. . . . [After it was over] he felt that perhaps he was the wrong person to lead at that time. . . . And I remember that Gerry Caplan and I sat in our dining room in Scarborough and argued very passionately that he mustn't quit. . . .

I know that this sounds really odd, but when I look back on it, it was [because of] my feeling as a New Democrat and a socialist and not so much as a wife . . . that I persuaded him to go on. One of the reasons I loved Stephen and married him was because of his political views. This was inseparable to me from his whole character, and I was horrified at the thought that he should leave the leadership because as a party member I thought that he was the best leader. . . .

I was well able to bear the burdens of being a political leader's wife, thanks to the tolerance of our party for eccentricity and unconventional behaviour [and she pauses for a wicked chuckle], so I didn't have a personal stake in whether he stayed or went. . . . So I persuaded him to stay on. But it proved to be a mixed blessing because he did continue to be rather down in the dumps about politics. The heart seemed to have gone out of it for him, even though we became the official opposition after the next election [in 1975].

I can't say that it was all because of the Waffle. There may be other things that I am forgetting now, but it does seem that the Waffle was the main thing. . . .

One of the great deterrents to his going back into politics is that there seems to be so much personal viciousness and he's so repelled by that. . . . He reacts to it with horror. It offends his deepest sense of what politics should be.

Michele is speaking in late May 1989 — after Ed Broadbent has retired as federal leader and Stephen is steadfastly refusing to run for the leadership. If she is right in what she says, it means that Stephen came out of his struggle with the Waffle with the same kind of wounds that David carried with him from his election battle with Fred Rose in the Montreal riding of Cartier in 1943 — the difference being that David's wounds were allowed to heal. Stephen's were not.

What gives added weight to Michele's comments about Stephen's abhorrence of rancour is that when he became leader his first rule of conduct, laid down to the caucus, was that there would be no scandalmongering. In an interview in January 1987 while he was still ambassador, he recalls those days:

The one thing that my caucus mates used to yell and scream at me over, used to laugh at because it became a caucus joke, was that I would not permit them to get involved in any allegations. [It was] the only *sine qua non* I had. I wasn't sure what I believed in, but I was sure that what I didn't believe in was that we should be diverted from the basic issues by joining the Liberals on whether or not Bill Davis was receiving money on the side or somebody had signed a land deal. . . . It was such a distraction and it always served the government. . . .

Look at Ottawa now. We are as much interested in the scandal of Bissonette as we are in worker dislocation. . . . As a politician your job is to find out what you are going to do with 40,000 workers [who are going to be] dislocated[5] or what you are going to do with day care. It's funny how easily we get distracted. Look at the federal House. Jesus Christ, it is unbelievable.

Two years later, in another interview, he mentioned that it was David who "taught me it was wrong to attack individuals. It was really institutions [you should attack]. It was David who coined that lovely phrase about Tories not being evil. Just being wrong."

Next to David, Michele has had a more profound effect on Stephen's life than anyone else, widening the corridor of his resolve so that he has had room to move off centre, to flex other sensibilities. The narrowness of that corridor was something he was very much aware of:

A lot of things are very difficult for me to phrase in a way which either makes sense or isn't painful, but both David and I were a little unemotional about personal things. It's a weakness I share with him more than [Michael and the twins] do. [It's] almost an inability to register [emotion] at a personal level.

Curiously enough, emotions are more easily aroused in the service of the cause than on a personal level. I think it's a bit of an emotional vacuum, an emotional void. . . . [We have] this tendency to be — emotionally neutered isn't quite right, but close at times. Except for the grand scale. Except for fighting against injustice or fighting for change. Or building a great movement. Or exhorting a mob. Then emotion courses through body and soul.

Again, I owe to Michele a growing capacity over the years to be a fuller person and therefore to feel a little more of some of these things.

He says that to some extent he is like David in not thinking in images. "Michele does. I don't. I think more in images [than David did], but no, I'm not liberated either. I try a little. David wasn't willing even to try. [But] I never get away with it because it's not real."

Once the Waffle was gone, Stephen turned to repairing the party in Ontario. Never in his experience had it been so psychologically inert.

There was a drop-off [he says]. It was hard. It was painful. Exhaustion, pain and anguish, worry and recrimination, crises of faith and staying power, and all the things that were inevitable. But in the midst of that I remember how people persuaded me and Gerry and others to get out of Queen's Park. . . . To stop assuming that we at the party knew what was best for Ontario. . . .

I underwent the most extraordinary program of moving into the hinterland, day after day, week after week. On the road, meeting with little communities, bringing the issues back into the Legislature. We began to develop ties all over the province, . . . so the party became much more responsive to the realities of Ontario at the grass roots and much less imperious about imposing our prescriptions on the province. . . .

It was amazing. It began to take hold in the province, . . . so I feel that it was a turning point for the party. It was like returning to Donald MacDonald twenty years previously, in the 1950s, travelling the byways in a beat-up old car. That was a building process; this was an educative one. . . .

I realized far too late, I was just being obtuse and stupid, that Bill Davis [while he was minister of education] had spoken at every school in the province. He was grounded in the soil of Ontario and I wasn't at all.

The party still benefits "geographically and demographically" from Stephen's travels, Robin Sears says. For example, there's a dam just outside White Lake in Eastern Ontario that was built, Sears says, "quite unnecessarily, even provocatively," to supply surplus power to Arnprior. Stephen learned about its impending construction by travelling through the area, and fought to stop it because it would flood a lot of farmland. "He built a lot of support among farmers who, prior to that, would no more vote for the CCF or the NDP than they'd vote for communism."

At the same time, Stephen oversaw the expansion of the party into ethnic communities, especially the Italian community in Toronto, and that, says Sears, changed the party forever from being largely Anglo-Jewish.

In Toronto there were 600,000 Italians, a community so large it was under no particular pressure to adapt. That meant first-generation Italians, for the most part, didn't understand how the political system worked, and the party didn't understand the cultural dynamics of the Italian community. Too often the party made the false assumption that Italian workers would vote for it simply because they were workers.

In a way, says Oduardo di Santo, it was another kind of two solitudes. Di Santo is a diminutive man in his mid-fifties who looks fifteen years younger, black-haired with a robust Groucho Marx moustache and carrying himself with the straining erectness of a matador. Although he couldn't speak English when he arrived in Canada in 1967, he speaks it now with a precision that would shame many native-born Canadians. He was the NDP member for Downsview from 1975 until he was defeated in 1985. Now he is director of the Ministry of Labour's Office of the Worker Advisor, which assists injured workers with claims before the Workmen's Compensation Board.

In the late sixties, he says, members of the left-wing Italian Democratic Association made the decision that they should try to establish a significant presence within the party and seek to bridge the lack of understanding on both sides. Di Santo himself was elected to the national council in 1970 and was appointed as one of its delegates to the provincial executive. It didn't take them long to convince Stephen and his inner circle that an opportunity awaited, and early in 1973 *La Sezione* — which translates as "the affiliate" in English — was established. It was an organizing unit within the Italian community with offices on St. Clair Avenue West, two or three organizers paid by the party, a newsletter, and an arrangement that it would get a portion of every membership fee paid by a member of *La Sezione* to the party.

Its success was immediate. In 1975 four Italian candidates were elected: di Santo in Downsview, Tony Grande in Oakwood, Tony Lupusella in Dovercourt, and Ross McLellan, who learned to speak fluent Italian from his mother, the former Raphaelina Maria Costabile, in Bellwoods.

Immediately after Stephen became leader in October 1970, says di Santo, he grasped what the Italians on their own were trying to do, and "we started getting some concrete signs from the party that we should move . . . and [Stephen] took the lead."

In the Legislature Stephen dominated question period, drawing on his travels across the province and on the tireless work of a small band of NDP researchers. Peter Mosher covered Queen's Park for *The Globe and Mail* from the fall of 1973 until 1981, and his recollections of the run-up to the 1975 election remain vivid:

> There was a real difference [with Stephen]. Bob Nixon, the opposition leader . . . never bothered Davis and Davis . . . on occasion sniped at Nixon and some of his front benchers. But he never did it to Stephen Lewis because he was afraid of Stephen's tongue. . . .
>
> When Stephen got on to a good issue, he was able to hammer them in a manner that really frightened the Tories. Davis was usually able to get out of it, although in doing so he didn't look very good [because] he gave non-answers. . . . [But] there were some cabinet ministers who were scared to death of Stephen, such as Leo Bernier, who was minister of northern affairs and natural resources. All [Bernier and other cabinet

ministers] were able to do . . . was to try to get through question period without saying anything incredibly stupid. But that was all they could do. And as a result, Stephen . . . and his researchers . . . got all the media attention and the issues took off. . . .

Neither the Tories nor the Liberals planned in advance how to get a story out so that reporters could understand it, whereas Stephen did. He was very good at that. [For instance] agricultural land is disappearing. Well, divide the number of acres lost into the total number of acres in Ontario and it comes out to fifteen acres an hour. A great issue — even though there are many millions of acres in Ontario. . . .

The scrums in the hallway outside the Legislature were very important. . . . Stephen never stood out there without his researchers . . . and they always had sheets of material. . . . Nixon as often as not would lose stories to the NDP that he had raised in the Legislature [because with its] superior knowledge, [the NDP would] end up getting the lead of the story away from the Liberals.

To his credit, Stephen Lewis decided that research was where it was at, and he built a first-class team. And gave it credit. And that meant he kept very good people. They would have died for him.

By August 1973 Stephen had three full-time researchers working for the caucus. By the end of the year he had added a researcher to his own personal staff, and by June 1974 he had increased to five the researchers working for the caucus. Hugh Mackenzie, one of the five, hired in 1973, was then in his mid-twenties with a master's degree in economics.

It was was a very exciting time [he says]. It was an incredible amount of work, but we were all crazy. Working incredibly long hours. . . . We were all around the same age, and no one had kids to demand attention. And Stephen was so incredibly demanding that you sort of got whipped into a frenzy. . . . He was a very stimulating person. . . .

The payoff for doing all this work was in seeing it on the front page of *The Globe and Mail* or used in the House to belabour the government . . . and I've never encountered anybody who marshalls facts and information in an argument or a speech as effectively as he does. . . .

Mackenzie's first encounter with Stephen's ability to recall facts and figures left him shaken, he says. He had just started working for the caucus and was examining food prices and the profits of supermarkets, "and Stephen came wandering in. I'd left all my papers [in another room], but I've a pretty good memory for numbers, so I started talking to Stephen about what I'd been working on." After a while Stephen said he had to leave for a press conference and invited Mackenzie to join him.

Mackenzie, who had never been at a press conference, was delighted with the invitation. Stephen gave a statement to the press, and then someone asked a question "and out came all my numbers . . . how this company made so much this year and that much that year and that much more than ten years before and this percentage and that percentage . . . and I thought, wow, I'd better be careful. . . . And I sort of stored that away as an indication of how careful I must be. It's rather scary because you couldn't be sloppy."

At last the party was thundering along the way its people always dreamed it would. There hadn't been this kind of exuberance since the heady days running up to the 1945 elections. But unseen and un-suspected by everyone except his most intimate associates, in particular Gerry Caplan and his executive assistant Melodie Morrison, Stephen was becoming increasingly restive.

Partly it was because the battle with the Waffle had sliced with a terrible finality through the protective buffer that shielded a highly vulnerable inner person — the youth who was a sensitive musician, the man who collects children's books, the politician whose dedica-tion to helping disturbed children at times impaired his political judg-ment. He knew the nasty side of politics but was protected from it because his buffer was his belief in the good fight — the name that David gave to his memoirs — and in thirty years of training that in-cluded, as John Brewin recalled, learning how to subdue pain as a way of building leadership skills. The buffer was not destroyed. Far from it. But it was rent. And like so much in life, the tear had two sides: it allowed the darker side of politics to reach in where it could bruise, but it also allowed something else to get out, and although no one recognized it at the time, the issue would become what it was that had started to work its way out.

As success followed success in the Legislature, Stephen drove himself incessantly, and over time that began stretching his emotions tighter and tighter. He had always been an obsessive worker. Michele remembers that "when I first married him he would even forget to eat, for days on end if I didn't remind him. He'd completely forget. He is the only person I ever knew who was so little dictated to by his appetite that he would actually forget meals. He did without meals or sleep as the work demanded. Those other things, personal, sensual gratification or relaxation or rest, were absolutely secondary."

One of the consequences of this obsessiveness, and this was what Stephen identified as the cause of his restiveness, was an even more pronouced separation from his family. Even when he was home there were telephone calls and work to be done. It caused him endless agony because he had always sworn he would never, never impose the kind of isolation on his family that he had grown up with.

Nor was Michele one to let it be imposed — for Stephen's sake, for her own sake, or for the sake of the children. Ilana Naomi, the eldest, was then nine years old, Avram David was seven, and Jennie Leah was four. There is a perception within party circles that Michele by this time was pressing Stephen to get out of politics. It was even described by one intimate as a Chinese water torture that she imposed on Stephen. It's interesting to see the parallels — how the Lewis women, Sophie and Michele, were held to blame for upsetting the equilibrium of their husbands.

The truth is that Michele did want Stephen to spend more time with the family. His response, both to Michele and to his own burgeoning sense of guilt, was to say, increasingly, that the only way he could do this would be to quit politics. In fact, when he finally did leave politics, he worked just as obsessively as he had at politics and there was no perceivable change in his free time at home.

> I was quite inured by then to living on as a single mother [Michele says]. I'd brought up the kids alone with the help of *au pair* girls or whatever scrambling help I could organize on our limited budget. And I was used to it. And I was faring extremely well. And when Stephen could pry loose from his schedule, he was a wonderful father.
>
> So I felt that all was going fairly well. But there was an aura of strain and exhaustion about him and we both felt that if he could get more time to relax and be with the family, things would be much better. . . . I never wanted him to leave politics. I wanted him to be in politics. I thought he was the best leader the party could have. As a party member I wanted him to be leader. I didn't want to see him leave in 1977, except I could see that this was the end of the road. He just didn't want to do it any more. . . .
>
> I was heartbroken. I saw that he couldn't go on. He had to leave for his own sake. But . . . it was so sad for the party.

As the 1975 election approached, Stephen told Michele that it would be his last campaign. He would step down before the following election. However, he told no one else. Not even Gerry Caplan.

The election was called for September 18, 1975, but it was not until early spring that the party began developing its most potent issue: rent control. Hugh Mackenzie had been fiddling with research on the issue. There had been occasional stories in the newspapers about big rent hikes, and Mackenzie's overall figures were showing large increases. So he placed ads in the Toronto *Sun* and the *Star* asking people to telephone if their rents had shot up dramatically. He got enough responses that the caucus could begin to develop cases. Once the campaign started, the party was able to target specific buildings where rents had leaped upward, and it asked canvassers to find the people in them who were upset. "And then we were able to find the little old lady who'd had a 75 percent rent increase and she and her cat were going to have to leave." Two weeks before election day the issue caught on and the NDP's proposals for rent controls became the hottest item in the election.

There is a photograph that Stephen hung on the wall of his office at the United Nations showing David with his arm around Stephen's shoulders, the two of them standing with their backs to the camera. It's the photograph on the back of the dust jacket of this book. Stephen laughed when questioned about it. It was taken the night of the 1975 election. The party had just won thirty-eight seats compared to fifty-one for the Conservatives and nineteen for the Liberals. The NDP had become the official opposition in Ontario. In the photograph "I was just telling David, 'How am I going to tell Michele? I promised her I'd quit and now I can't,'" Stephen said.

He makes light of it now, but for Gerry Caplan it was unsettling to discover that Stephen seemed, indeed, ready to quit.

> One of our great, all-time moments was the morning after, when I went over to Stephen's house to start talking. We'd only both had an hour or two of sleep and it was the moment of great glory. . . . I went up to the bathroom and he was in his undershirt — he wore undershirts in those days — and he was shaving and he said, "I quit."
>
> I said, "I understand." I don't know what I understood, but I said, "I understand, but that would be really too bad for me. I really need a project. I am really feeling awful about my marriage" — my wife had left me two weeks earlier — "and I need something to do. It would help me a lot. You stay in, so I can work on it."
>
> We must have stayed up there for an hour with him saying he just didn't care any more and me saying, "Stephen, there are a lot of people who need it. Who want it."
>
> So finally he said, "Okay. Let's go and do it."

There is a disparity between the picture of a distraught Stephen that Caplan perceived through his own personal distress, and that of a wearied leader, with all defences down the morning after the end of a hard campaign, who was allowing himself a momentary diversion, which is how Stephen remembers it. Maybe it was just the effect of twelve years in the Legislature, Stephen says. Maybe, he laughs at himself, "I'm just haphazard and generally feckless." In any event, "It didn't take me very long to turn 1975 around; it took me about five minutes to look forward to leading the opposition."

The key to the disparity may lie in how Stephen uses language. When he speaks privately about a worry, it becomes a looming apocalypse. When things are not going well, it is to stare into the abyss of pending disaster. When dangers appear, they are catastrophic or cataclysmic. Even concerns can quickly become excruciating. Long-time associates all talk of what they call his streak of pessimism, his inclination to expect things to turn out far worse than they actually do and to see failure skulking in the shadows of success.

If you were to take such private expressions at face value, it would be like throwing your emotions into the Cuisinart and flipping the switch. But it's hard for people not to take them at face value because Stephen speaks with such assurance and authority on other occasions. And even for those who recognize the hyperbole it is no easy thing to deal with because it is put with such force and conviction.

Michele now calls this tendency of Stephen's "Sophiesque." Her way of looking at it is that:

"Stephen got his whole pattern of public speech from David, but of private speech from Sophie. And that negative, gloomy kind of construction he would put on things in personal terms was a kind of Sophiesque thing that didn't really reflect his [own reality]. I forget the formulation that some therapist came up with, but [it was to the effect that] your mother teaches you how to be in personal relationships and your father teaches you how you are to be with the world. . . . This apocalyptic language to [Stephen] is bantering. Or a mask because, you know, you don't say, "Gee, I feel inadequate." You say something more colourful and everybody around him, including me, takes it desperately seriously.

While he was still ambassador to the United Nations she was laughing one afternoon about how Stephen sometimes puts her through the wringer with this habit.

I've been struggling for the whole year I've been down here [in New York]. . . . I'm constantly shoring him up. Cheering him up. Pleading. Coaxing. Teasing him out of his moods to keep him going at it because I think he is accomplishing a lot. . . .

[I]t's one of the worst things I have to contend with in him. I don't want to be disloyal, but it's true that he has to exaggerate in his own mind futility or looming failure. He didn't use to be like that. It's gotten worse. When he got this appointment I couldn't move down until nine months later, and he wouldn't let me bring any of our books. He told me not to bring any of our personal things, which I didn't, . . . because, he said, it will only be for a few months anyway. "For sure I'll have to quit over some issue of principle." Oh [and she laughs in that deep-throated, infectious way of hers], he got me into so many fouled-up things because of this. . . .

I think Stephen is a driven man in lots of ways and doesn't allow himself the pleasure of accomplishment. He's got so many accomplishments that I admire and I'm allowed to admire them. But he won't admire them himself. He's always negating his own triumphs.

Looking back on that conversation in the summer of 1989, she adds: "When he talks that way . . . it afflicts me very much. I get worried and take it very seriously. And I'm a slow learner; it took me a long time to realize that he was not going to quit the next day. He just wants to be reassured by me. And so it comes out in this funny way."

Despite this idiosyncrasy — as Caplan would call it — that sometimes left a trail of frenzied associates in his wake, Stephen's actual performance remained largely unimpaired, and his accomplishments have passed into the folklore of the party. Robin Sears says he is still the Ontario leader that other leaders must measure themselves against, and he will remain that for a long time to come.

While he was opposition leader, the party forced the Conservatives to implement rent controls, to improve the legislation covering emotionally disturbed children, to provide greater protection for workers under the Occupational Health and Safety Act, especially those exposed to asbestos, to add controls for the preservation of agricultural land, and to place greater emphasis on providing affordable housing, and most important of all, he brought the party a level of acceptance and respectability that it had never had in Ontario. No longer would people fret over whether it would survive. It was here to stay.

He also brought the party to a heightened appreciation of the need for primacy of solid, continuous research and of how to humanize complex political issues. Also, says Robin Sears, "He taught many of the people here the importance of extra-parliamentary [approaches] in a world which can become enormously bound up in the ritual and minutiae of Queen's Park. He'd say, take a task force out to Sudbury and you're going to have more of an impact than a meeting in downtown Toronto. Organize a coalition of welfare mothers to come here and heckle from the gallery and you'll have more impact than if you ask the question without that kind of feeling. He had not only a sense of passion and theatre; he also had a brilliant organizational skill and an understanding of how to [pull all the pieces together] in a very clever way."

But his greatest achievement, as was David's, was the party itself. David built the party; Stephen embedded it in Ontario. He brought it to a level of acceptance and respectability that it had never had in

Ontario. He made sure it had become part of the culture, part of the psyche, of the province.

But as 1975 turned into 1976 and the year progressed, Stephen's restiveness began to take on more urgency, and at times it became almost fevered. Caplan recalls how every two or three months he'd get a call from Melodie Morrison saying, "You'd better find a day to get on the road with him. He's going off again," and, says Caplan, he'd send Stephen's chauffeur away and they'd spend the day "trying to cool him out for a month or two or three."

One of the problems was that Stephen had never escaped the exhaustion brought on by the Waffle period. Never blessed with great physical stamina, he had kept up a killing pace for six gruelling years. Gerry Charney says he and his wife would go out to dinner with Stephen and Michele "quite regularly" and "We had a standard sort of procedure. We'd order, Stephen would eat the first course, and then he'd fall asleep at the table. We'd sort of nudge him awake halfway through the meal and he'd eat the second course and go back to sleep. Going out to dinner with Stephen was sort of like the three of us just talking to ourselves."

An added problem was that the Conservatives had become more sophisticated in their own research and, says Peter Mosher, "The media didn't run with NDP issues the way it had before the 1975 election. There were several reasons for that. Reporters were getting much more cautious about figures. About what they could prove and what they couldn't prove. And the Tories were counterattacking more effectively. They were preparing their own research and . . . they were smart. They weren't going to get caught in the same old way without having figures available. So Davis would counter NDP assertions with the Tories' own assertions the next day, which would tend to confuse reporters. And with the resources of government, that was easy for them to do."

All this had an effect on the NDP researchers. Hugh Mackenzie found that, in the latter half of 1976, "It wasn't nearly as stimulating and nearly as much fun . . . working for Stephen as it was before . . . and [as a result] a lot of things just lost their cutting edge.

"I think he realized that they had and was dissatisfied with himself. But often that translated into being very hard on people around him. He felt sufficiently unhappy with the situation that he was unsure of himself. And the more unsure of himself he became, the more complete everything had to be, the more demanding he was about everything. And the more unhappy he was when things didn't meet his expectations. And that made life more difficult for everybody."

The wear and tear on Stephen was dramatic, and no one noticed it more than Michele.

> In those last two years, for the first time — and I was deeply, deeply appalled and troubled by this — Stephen would wake up in the morning and not get out of bed right away. He'd say, "I can't face it." I'd never seen him like that. . . .
>
> And so then I finally supported his leaving the leadership because I saw he was so oppressed in spirit that it was unendurable.
>
> I think people don't realize perhaps the burden of leadership when you don't have power. You've got a fractious caucus to deal with; you're trying to control a million uncontrollables; there's the constant glare of recognition and publicity. That's hard to deal with.
>
> We stopped going out to movies. He wouldn't even walk into the store with me. Any normal, little friendly things you do together as a husband and wife were curtailed because everybody recognized him and talked to him in a friendly way. . . . If we went to a dinner party, people who were not close friends would think, "Well, I'll invite a couple of Liberals and we'll make it very interesting," and we'd go to the dinner and instead of being people we'd have to be political all evening.

There was, she says, no surcease. "Never. Not for a second. You can't stand it night and day like that."

Finally, Peter Mosher of the *Globe* started picking up hints that everything might not be well, and in October asked to see Stephen. To Mosher's surprise, Stephen invited him up to his cottage. He was surprised because Stephen had been very protective of his time at the cottage. That was family time and reporters were never invited there. They talked shop and then, in Mosher's words, Stephen started musing about his future. Mosher returned to Toronto and wrote his story. It appeared as the dominant story on the front page under the headline, "Will Lewis Spoil Success?" At the time he was running well ahead of Bill Davis and Bob Nixon in popularity as party leader. It was an astonishing reversal from the 1971 situation. "Mr. Lewis yearns to do something else for a living before either his mind or the available opportunities narrow to the point where there is nothing else he wants to do or can do," Mosher wrote.

"That does not mean that he will resign after the next election, barring a disastrous showing that no party's polls show is likely. But he has confided to people close to him that if the party stays roughly where it is now, even if the Liberals again move ahead of the NDP in number of seats, he will not be around much longer than the time necessary for leadership potential to emerge among new caucus members."[6]

The story landed in the laps of party members like a bombshell. In retrospect, and from one point of view, it became a sort of self-fulfilling prophesy — although without any awareness or intention on Stephen's part. The party did do badly; the Liberals did move ahead of the NDP; and Stephen did quit immediately. If there is any validity in the thought that something was struggling to escape through the psychic tear left by the Waffle, it was apparent in the tumult of that struggle during the election campaign. In the last two weeks, says Caplan, "I had to bolster him on a stop-to-stop basis. He'd go into Orillia . . . and when he'd get back on the bus I'd say, 'Come on, we're going to Barrie next. We'll make it.'

"He'd say, 'I'm not going to go. I'm going back to Toronto.'"

"'Stephen, you're not going back to Toronto. We've got to go to Barrie. A lot of people. . . .'

"'I can't talk to another human being. I don't care. I don't want to.'

"So when we get to Barrie, [it'd be] 'Ahhhh. He's going to do it!'

"Stop by stop it happened. He just had lost it."

Where he finally lost it for all the world to see was in two television interviews, one shortly following the other, both by Fraser Kelly. The first occurred during the leaders' debate two weeks before the election on June 9, 1977. He was caught flatfooted when Kelly read a resolution passed at a party convention calling for nationalization of resource industries, and then asked him when it would happen and how much it would cost. The second came five days later when Kelly dug out a resolution passed at the party convention a year earlier calling for an increase in the minimum wage from $2.65 an hour to $4 an hour.

To the first, Stephen replied that he didn't have "the slightest intention of bringing any of the major sectors of the natural resource area under public ownership. It just doesn't make sense to me." Control, yes; ownership, no, he said.[7] It was a testy reply, handled without finesse and in direct contradiction to a speech he'd given a year earlier in which he said, "I'd happily nationalize Imperial Oil tomorrow if the New Democrats had the power to do so."[8]

When Kelly asked him about the minimum-wage increase, Stephen was vague and ill at ease. It might not be unreasonable, he said. However, in an interview with reporters later, he embraced it without reservation.[9] After the election he said he defended it because he had already backed off nationalization and "people generally would have had the right to say, 'What's real and what is not real in this program? What will the leader reinterpret next?'"[10]

Stephen performed wretchedly, Caplan says, and it "was all about just losing control. . . . And we got skewered on the $4 minimum wage because Stephen . . . [came across as if] he didn't give a rat's ass what happened to small business. It was a wonderful trap."

It was a mess but somehow, in the midst of it all, Stephen still maintained flashes of humour. Darcy McKeough, then provincial treasurer, calculated that NDP election promises would cost about $5.8 billion, which, under questioning by reporters, he admitted was exaggerated but, "give or take a billion dollars," was still right.

Stephen just laughed. Asking McKeough to practise restraint was like asking Evil Knievel to park your car, he said — and that was the end of that issue.

Then the Conservatives sent a television crew to British Columbia to gather man-in-the-street complaints about David Barrett's NDP government. They were used in Ontario ads against Stephen. "I thought we might go to Chile for ours," Stephen said when asked what he thought of them.[11]

When the votes were in, the NDP lost five seats and was knocked out as official opposition by one seat. The Tories won fifty-eight seats, the Liberals thirty-four, and the NDP thirty-three. The night of the election the party had planned its victory party at a tavern on Danforth Avenue in Stephen's riding, and had rented a trailer that was stationed in the parking lot for senior staff and Stephen and his family. Robin Sears was in the trailer watching the returns come in, and even though the party was dropping a few seats, "We were getting more and more happy about the fact that what we got in 1975 wasn't a glitch." The party was not slipping back to the nineteen or twenty seats of 1971. Nor was its percentage of the vote slipping back. It got 28.9 percent in 1975 and 28 percent in 1977.[12]

But Stephen was getting more and more depressed until, says Sears, "He and Gerry went into the bathroom and had a screaming match about what Stephen's prerogatives were at that point. I mean it was just totally crazy for him to be depressed about the outcome. It's like the guy who wins half a million dollars in the lottery and is furious because somebody else wins a million dollars. You forget that you won a goddammed lottery prize in the course of your unhappiness."

Four days later, Stephen announced that he was stepping down as leader because he "wanted to live a different kind of life with his family."[13]

Looking back on it today, his performance in the 1977 campaign sticks painfully in Stephen's memory.

> If I hadn't let the party down, we would still have been the official opposition. As it was, we dropped from thirty-eight to thirty-three seats.

It wasn't catastrophic but it was psychologically difficult. I would still have left because I intended to leave, but we might have been able to stay at a more pronounced level for a longer period of time. The fall from grace may not have been so precipitous in 1981. . . .

I think [my decision to leave] diminished my sharpness. I behaved very stupidly in [that] campaign. I don't know how else to describe it. I made a couple of horrible errors in judgment which were not characteristic of my behaviour. I walked into a leaders' debate knowing that the question of nationalization would undoubtedly be raised because they were looking for ways of not letting the NDP get away with everything it got away with in 1975. . . .

Had I my wits about me, had my mind not been somewhere else, had I done what a leader should do and that is anticipate the most obvious questions and think through how you handle them, I would simply have said with great ease that this was maybe a step down the road but like any left-wing party it will take us years to get there and parties change their policies and it's not on the horizon immediately. Instead, when the stark words were read to me I wasn't sure how to handle it.

And then the second thing was on the minimum wage. I hadn't read the program. I hadn't taken the trouble as leader to sit down and refresh my mind about all the nutty things that were in the NDP program, and there are always traps there. And that just wasn't characteristic of my behaviour.

Sure, you work hard and you're tired and you're depressed in a campaign. There are all kinds of excuses you can make. But you can't make excuses for things like that. There really aren't any. . . .

When it was all over and I said I was getting out, only one person nailed me to the cross and that was Clare Hoy [of the Toronto Sun]. He said, if you intended to leave, Lewis, why the hell didn't you say so? What right have you got to go running to the people of Ontario as a leader of a party, talking about running a government, and doing all the things you're talking about doing while you know that you're going to leave? And I remember thinking privately to myself that the sonuvabitch is right.

I didn't feel so badly about [not announcing I was leaving]. People are human, you know. You're not required by law to tell everybody of every intention. But you are required by moral and political imperative not to allow yourself to function less well — because the party's at stake — just because you know in your heart of hearts that you're going to be leaving. And I let my guard down.

As he talks, there is a distance that settles around him, stranding him on the landscape of his own judgment. His words become more drawn out, he becomes so introspective that you begin to feel he is having a conversation only with himself — and the mind flashes back to all the times he has talked about the need never to hurt the party. And to Robin Sears and the others who think Stephen did just that because he did not prepare it for an orderly transition — even though Stephen says he thought he had because Ian Deans was there to take over the leadership. "He was the deputy in the House, a superlative speaker, the House leader . . . the single best tactician in the party, bar none. . . . I genuinely felt that there would be no contest. That Ian would have it. . . . But his own arrogance and, alas, [his stand in favour of] the War Measures Act [did him in]." The party elected Michael Cassidy instead and suffered eclipse in Ontario for ten years. This is the political shadow under which Stephen still lives — although most of those who fault him still pressed for his return in 1989.

In a final conversation, Michele says she has been thinking about the repetitions in Stephen's life: his restiveness in 1968 when he returned to Biafra; his reaction to the 1971 election; his wrestling with whether to resign in 1973; a flicker of the desire to leave still apparent in the face of the 1975 victory; his inner turmoil in 1976 and 1977. She doesn't accept that it shows a pattern because, she says, the reasons in each case were different. Nevertheless,

> I wondered — in view of his resistance to going back into politics and running for the leadership [of the federal party], and how strangely happy and relaxed he is about not going back, and how he fought off the most sustained and unbelievable pressure over the past six months, even though he has all the talents and skills to do a very good job of being leader, and even though most people follow their talents and do whatever jobs they're really good at — I wondered if all his life Stephen was fulfilling a parental dictum. That he was just programmed from so early on to go into politics and work on behalf of the party, which he did with enormous skill and dedication. But was there another Stephen in there who was called back from Africa . . . where he wanted to stay forever? . . . And now in middle age he can be his own self and follow what he really loves?
>
> Thinking about this I remembered that when I met Stephen and we married, he was constantly talking about Africa — with passion and lyricism and joy. "Yes I've been elected, [he'd say] but we'll make our lives in Africa." And I was thinking "Oh my God, Africa!" I wasn't the least bit interested. I was so worried that he would actually follow this through. But gradually he got pulled into the life of politics and he gave up that thought.

Is this what had been struggling to get out all those years? Had Stephen been so encircled by expectations — his own and others — that he was never truly able to find out who Stephen Lewis really was? And was it only when the effort was made to conscript him back into the party that he finally came to terms with all those expectations? He himself doesn't know, and what the future will hold he is not sure;

but "I have this feeling," he says as his next-to-last words in a final conversation in late July 1989, "that maybe I've fought against politics all my life without realizing it."

Once again the mind flashes back, this time to the three-year-old child standing on a chair, so proudly giving his little speeches at Sophie's behest. And in one last leap it turns to something Michele said in New York that afternoon in May 1987. When Stephen was young, she said, the only person who ever accepted him totally and unconditionally, was Maishe. "He has very few memories of him, but, from the first time I knew Stephen, there was a tone of tenderness when he mentioned his grandfather. Even when he was denying that he had any memories of him, there was a tone that he had about no other person in his memory. I'm guessing that that was the one adult who said I love you unconditionally."

But there is one other person for whom Stephen uses that tone of voice. It is Mukwugo Okoye.

•CHAPTER TWENTY-FOUR•

Never say that this is the final journey;
the hour of fulfillment still will be ours.
                    Marching hymn of Jewish partisans
                    during the Second World War

                    Inscribed on the gravestone
                    of David Lewis

For David, 1971 to 1974 were the crowning years of his career, but they began in gloom and anger at what Gerry Caplan calls "one of the worst celebrations I've ever been at. It was like a wake . . . I've never been to a place at which the winner felt so much like a victim." It was in a conference room dressed up with a bar and little else at the Chateau Laurier in Ottawa on Saturday night, April 24, 1971, after David had won the NDP leadership.

At the convention, into the ballot box with all the Waffle votes for Jim Laxer, went all the grudges that people had nursed against David, sometimes for years. It took five ballots before David won 1,046 to 612. "David was our St. Paul," says Jean-Paul Harney, who was one of the leadership contenders. "Saul Alinsky describes it so well: 'Christ would have been just another guy hanging on the cross if it hadn't been for St. Paul.' He organized the church, you know, like David organized the party. He pushed, he fixed, he wrote some tough letters, he shoved, he cleaned up. When you do that, you are not going to be Pope." And when you do that in the party you become leader only after delegates get even. It was, says party historian Desmond Morton, shabby treatment for a man who deserved much better from his party.[1]

Not many people came to the celebration. Those who did stood around glumly, drinks in hand, trying, as Gerry Caplan says, "to pretend it was a great victory but knowing it was a humiliating moment for David. It was awful."

To go from there to winning the largest number of seats the NDP had ever held in the election a year and a half later was a stunning accomplishment — stunning because in the meantime so much time and energy and torment went into the struggle with the Waffle which ended only four months before the election, and into the struggle with the Quebec wing of the party over the issue of Quebec "self-determination" which was not shelved until a month before the election.[2] Moreover, through the winter and spring of 1972, unless the issue involved the Waffle or Quebec, the press was so uninterested that, says Lewis Seale, the party's press secretary in Ottawa, "If we got David to take off his clothes in Parliament I don't think we would have got front page." It didn't help that in Ontario the Conservatives were having a honeymoon following their great success in the provincial election.

"It was driving us around the bend," says Seale. "You couldn't turn on CBC radio without hearing about the Waffle, which had superb media access . . . In the meantime we couldn't get thirds (third-ranking stories) into the [Toronto] *Star* . . . But then, of course, August 1972 came along and the problems just vanished." They vanished because on August 3 in New Glasgow, Nova Scotia, David opened his Corporate Welfare Bums campaign.

It was, Paul Martin recalls in an interview, one of the greatest election campaigns of all time. Martin, having retired as minister of external affairs, was government leader in the Senate at the time of the election. The final result on October 30 gave the Liberals 109 seats, the Conservatives under Robert Stanfield 107, and the NDP, 31 — a 41 percent increase in seats and the balance of power in a minority government.[3]

It also is what springs first to mind so often when the name "David Lewis" is mentioned. Of course it was David who forced the Liberals into creating Petro-Canada, the national oil company; of course he was magnificent — as was Tommy Douglas — in the battle against imposition of the War Measures Act; of course his greatest accomplishment was the shape and strength of the party itself — and of course there are any number of other achievements that can be mentioned. But for firing the imagination, nothing can compare to that campaign. It was fact and it was fable: it was an attack on tax policies, grants, and incentives that pampered big business, and it was the prophet Isaiah crying "Woe unto them that decree unrighteous decrees" — one of the statements for which Woodsworth was charged with seditious libel when he repeated it in the Winnipeg General Strike; it was meticulous research on individual companies handed out day after day, each day on a different company, and it was the age-old struggle against privilege and favouritism; it was the leader of the small third party taking on the combined might of the government and big business, and it was the fifth labour of Hercules.[4] Without a doubt, it touched a chord that still reverberates, however faintly, to the Social Gospel, which sees greed as immoral and, in the words of Salem Bland, teaches that the purpose of Christianity is to persuade people to think socially and not for individual advantage. And for old socialists, however disguised in the language of tax policies and DIP, MACH, and TS incentive grants, it was a return to the heady theme of class struggle.[5]

"It took our research people at least three or four months to put [the material] together," says Murray Weppler, David's executive assistant at the time. "Over the summer [of 1972] they gathered [data on] about 250 corporations. . . . I think in the end we used only about fifty or sixty companies. But we did have a little portfolio on each of them. . . ."

Toward the end of the campaign "we were accused of having no solutions, but we did. The media never reported it. . . . We had a detailed industrial strategy. . . . Where the criticism is fair is that we were never able to turn it from the negative to the positive." Part of the reason, he says, was that the media loved the dramatic image of an underdog beating up bigger parties much more than a step by step outline of an industrial strategy, and "here was little David Lewis, who had been written off by most of them, running the best campaign. Dominating all the time."

According to Lewis Seale, "one of the really major developments was getting 'Bum Air'. That was the first time the party had a long-term charter [of an aircraft] for an election campaign. You actually had a captive audience [among the reporters on board . . . and] it was invaluable. Every day we had a new bum . . . and it made the news every night. . . . Maclean's [magazine] said [the NDP campaign] was informality bordering on art forms, but they didn't have it right. We were just going like hell."

And they never stopped going like hell right through to the next election a year and eight months later. From the beginning the question was: when will the NDP bring down the Liberal government? And then, when it didn't, it was accused of being in bed with Trudeau. It was a charge that rankled but which had a measure of truth because the party did co-operate in dealing with the business of the House, claiming that, as long as the Liberals governed responsibly, the NDP would not defeat them. Privately, however, the party couldn't take the initiative because the caucus was split into hawks and doves. "David was a hawk," says Weppler. "He would have been ready to dump the government as fast as possible. If he had been the only person to have a say, within four or five months of the election he would have forced another election. He just felt . . . it was a no-win situation and an election sooner rather than later would have been more beneficial — and in hindsight he was correct. . . . We couldn't control the parliamentary agenda and [we knew] it would take the Liberals only a short time to recover themselves — and they did recover themselves. . . . We got very little out of it, basically Petro-Canada and some changes in oil policy that had David's stamp on them." He also left his mark, Weppler adds later, on the election reform package and changes to tax policy.

About a third of the caucus were hawks, about a third doves, "and then there was a third that used to swing," says Weppler. "So every week in the caucus meeting you had this same discussion. Sometimes it was only half an hour or fifteen minutes; other times it would be two or three hours. It would go around the table with everybody having their speech. Sometimes it would start off because members had been to their constituencies and had been cornered by a group of people for supporting this terrible Trudeau. And then you have to remember that there were a lot of subjects during this session that were controversial in themselves."

Cliff Scotton was the federal secretary and his concern was that "I didn't get the sense that the party was itself ready to go. There was a great deal of fragility on the part of some of the MPs, particularly Western MPs who felt that their own seats weren't all that secure." He urged caution.

David thought that he would need about two-thirds of the caucus behind him before setting out to dump the Liberals, Weppler says. "At least twenty people." Don't forget, he adds, "that the NDP at that time wasn't as confident as it is now in raising money, so there was a lot of pressure from organizers and fund raisers saying no, we can't afford to. There was also the excuse that no one would want a winter campaign — which wouldn't wash nowadays, but then it still did. You needed Tommy on side and Tommy never got off the fence. You needed Stanley Knowles on side and Stanley was quite enjoying his time . . . It was a difficult period."

But David was never one to be retiring. If he had wanted to bring down the Liberals, why didn't he push that decision through the party? He'd done similar things in the past. Had he mellowed?

Not mellowed philosophically, says Weppler, but "by the time I was there he had learned to suffer fools." It was a rounding off of sharp edges that Weppler speculates happened during the time David worked as a lawyer. "You can't afford to offend clients. I suspect that's where he mastered it in his later years." While Weppler was executive assistant David was more interested in consensus than "trying to dominate the caucus." But ten years earlier, he again speculates, he probably would have pushed the caucus into throwing out the Liberals.

"I agree with Murray," says Scotton. "If he had been there five years earlier [he'd have had his way]. . . . There were occasions when he ran rough-shod over people. He had immense cachet within the party because of his long service, his intellect, his presence, because of his spirit. David did mellow, but it was not an amelioration of his passionate basic sense of bringing about democratic socialism."

To Lewis Seale, it simply seemed that David was at the end of his career and:

> [H]e was extremely deferential to everybody . . . I guess because — as he kept telling me — he felt he wasn't really a bastard despite what I might hear from other people. . . . He knew this was his last job, and that partly explains another type of deference he had, which was the deference to Stephen. He was transferring the mantle a bit. David thought Stephen was going to be prime minister or premier one day.
>
> I know he was very sensitive because we often talked about it . . . [especially] when we travelled. . . . David would be quite keyed up after a speech, so we'd go back to the hotel [and] if there was one of the big railway hotels in town that was always the one. . . . They were, to his mind, the classy hotels in town. I don't think he was aware of the niftier spots. So we'd always have a glass of Scotch — he was the first drinking leader the party ever had — and a sandwich and he'd talk. I used to get him to look back. I don't know why. I guess that's what interested me and I guess that's what brought him down from his speech. . . . That's when I got the feeling he was very sensitive. . . .
>
> He had become much more the conciliator and mediator.

Sensitive or not, even as leader David still got left with the dirty work, like slugging it out with Allan Blakeney in the spring of 1974 over the issue of oil prices. The West wanted no export tax and no price freeze, the East did, and, says Robin Sears, the two "went toe to toe in the Royal York [Hotel] at a [meeting of the national] council. . . . Nobody wanted to tackle that one. And nobody wanted to tackle Grant Notley. So David did."

But isn't it the leader's job to do that anyway? On a policy issue of that magnitude? "The hell it is," says Sears. "Not in private council. You don't use the leader in that circumstance. You keep him as far away from it as you can precisely because it is of that magnitude. It squanders his reputation and his capacity to govern. . . . The leader is the king who's kept in reserve, and that's why he has lots of captains and lieutenants to deal with these problems."

And there was the issue of special status for Quebec, Sears says. "David was the hard charger against special status in part because he believed in it and in part, . . . because others did not want any part of it, because it wasn't fashionable to be fiercely against the prospect of an independent Quebec." And, he says, turning to the year before David became leader,

> . . . there's the War Measures Act. . . . There were people in that [caucus] room who were very unhappy about the position the party took publicly, who subsequently have been very dishonest about what they argued in private. . . . A number of people said, and more thought, it's all right, I don't have to stick my head above the parapet because, after all, David will deal with it, David will go toe to toe with Trudeau, David will take the shit from the press about being too soft on the goddammed Frogs, et cetera.
>
> I don't know the more awful examples, but I have been told of them from the generation earlier when he was similarly used in a role inappropriate to his station because he was good at it. I mean, to justify it somewhat, if you needed shock troops and you needed heavy artillery, they didn't get any better for the role than David. But it doesn't entirely excuse it. . . . Tommy was as stern and as draconian in his private conviction as David, but he's rarely seen that way by some who were the victims of David's rhetoric. [Tommy] wouldn't be duplicitous and say, "Isn't that terrible what David did to you." But he certainly didn't discourage, and sometimes actively encouraged, a very fierce public attack on people or circumstances that he didn't personally want to be associated with."[6]

There were three or four major crises that could have provided the grounds for defeating the Liberals, says Weppler, but the one they both agreed was the best of all "both at the time and later in hindsight" was inflation. And the time to do it was August 7, 1973, the day *The Globe and Mail* published a front-page story on the jump in price over the weekend for a pound of bacon. A photograph with the story showed a package of bacon bought at a Dominion store carrying three price stickers — one on top of the other — for $1.26, $1.38, and $1.68.

"David lost the argument in caucus," says Weppler. "I think in hindsight that was the point at which the NDP probably could have salvaged a few more seats. Or at least could have run a campaign on its terms and not, as in the end, [on Liberal terms] . . . when the Liberals were ready to go."

Instead, the election was held on July 8, 1974, and, as Seale succinctly puts it, "The Grits threw us out, not the other way around." John Turner, then finance minister, produced a budget on May 7 that totally ignored NDP demands that it include government subsidies to assure mortgage rates of 6 percent, a big increase in corporate taxes, and a two-level pricing system for commodities such as gas, oil, and lumber, depending on whether the commodity was for domestic use or export. As the *Globe's* Ottawa columnist Geoffrey Stevens commented on budget night, "It left the NDP no way out."[7] The government fell — the first time in history that a government was defeated in a budget debate — and the final tally in July was Liberals, 141; Conservatives, 95; NDP,16; Social Credit, 11; and one independent from Moncton. The party dropped to a 15.1 percent share of the vote, the lowest since 1963, and David lost his seat in York South.

> One of the reasons why the 1974 campaign was so bad . . . is that everyone was exhausted [says Weppler]. In the minority government there never was any rest. There was crisis after crisis. Whether it was self-generated or from the other side, it didn't matter. That eighteen months was a very difficult, trying period . . . and at every caucus there was another rerun of whether we should dump the Liberals or keep them. . . .
> The 1972 campaign was run essentially by four or five people. Literally. And there were still only four or five people there in 1974 — with maybe one change in the senior staff. We just never stopped. . . . We had four or five months of preparation going into the 1972 campaign. We had nothing in 1974. Absolutely nothing.

The issue turned out to be Robert Stanfield's proposal for wage and price controls. "David made only three speeches on the subject attacking Stanfield," says Weppler, "two of them before the campaign started and one after. . . . We realized within the first week of the campaign that this was not an issue that we could win on and we stopped talking about it." But the press made it the issue of the campaign and the NDP got lost in the dust.

By then David knew he had leukemia, and, aside from Sophie, only Weppler, Scotton, and Seale were aware of it. Early in February there was a rumour going around because David had gone to the Ottawa Civic Hospital for Xrays and a technician leaked the news of his illness to a member of the press gallery with whom she was involved. "We managed to scotch it," says Weppler, "because David didn't show any indications." He appeared just as vigorous as ever. But on the campaign trail "my heart went out to him for the sheer will power that kept him going, mentally and physically. He never once failed to perform. And he never complained about our lack of preparation. Not once."

David was sixty-four years old and "he would do a sixteen-hour day and get up the next morning and do another sixteen-hour day, all with a fair bit of cheerfulness. . . . I have never worked for or with anyone with as much physical and mental stamina. . . . I think really it was his own desire. This is what he fought most of his life for, and no one was going to accuse him of failing to campaign properly . . . But the last three weeks of that campaign were unbelievably difficult to get through," Weppler says.

Sophie was with him through most of the campaign. "There's a great picture of Sophie and David sleeping on each other's shoulder in Frigid Air, the campaign airplane. We tried to call it Daisy Air [after Trudeau's taunts that David was like a person pulling the petals off a daisy trying to decide whether to vote against the government]. But the media insisted on Frigid Air." This is the same election for which Sophie was criticized so strongly for being troublesome and "impossible" — and no doubt she was. But weariness, a bad campaign, and the secret knowledge that her remaining time with David would be limited by his illness throws yet another light on her conduct.

On the night of David's defeat, when the returns had made it obvious that York South had been lost to the Liberals, and after David had delivered an extremely gracious speech to his campaign workers, saying that the strength of democracy rested in the right of voters to make their choice and that choice deserved respect, not grieving, Sophie stepped forward and in a voice that was firm but tremulous toward the edges, thanked them all and and added, "You may have lost a member of Parliament, but I have gained a husband." And she stepped back and slipped her hand gently into his. It was the end of almost forty years of active politics.

Sophie told no one, not even the children, of David's illness, and neither did he, until shortly before he died seven years later. It was a decision for which Stephen has found it difficult to forgive her because it deprived him of the opportunity to prepare for his father's death. "We became incredibly close during the last four years of his life," he says. These were the years immediately after Stephen left politics and established a labour arbitration practice, and part of the closeness came through the help he sought from David on labour issues. But mostly it was a kind of coming home for both of them.

I think it's fair to say we talked every day for four years and sometimes two and three times a day. I can't imagine a father and son closer than in those final years. . . . It was as though we were both frantically making up for lost time. I don't know how else to describe it. I cannot convey how complete was the love, loyalty, involvement, of those last few years of his life.

I think that's why there was the estrangement from my mother, and I am not passing judgment; I am just saying I never forgave her for my not knowing that he was dying . . . because inevitably there were things around the children in particular, and around his book, for which . . . a second volume [was never written] which I think was a great loss. . . . I think all of that would have been manageable, even if I had ended up writing [the second volume], or Janet had. . . . To this day I haven't really come to terms with that, I must admit.

However, in those last years I was running up to Ottawa once or twice a week. It was an intense, intense relationship as though at the end of his years and in my middle years we had somehow to compensate for all those early years when we were not together.

For David it must have been an especially rewarding time because not only had he missed so much of family life; he had lived with a growing sense of isolation from the Jewish community and, after retiring, from the party itself. In an obituary tribute, Ben Kayfetz noted that

Although [David] was a Jew in every fibre of his being and was helpful and co-operative when called upon, he was not at one with the trends in the Jewish community. Back in the late fifties he discussed this with [me]. . . . He had been for the proletarian all his life and the Jews were leaving the working class and moving into the middle class. He was not a religious believer and the centre of Jewish life was now being re-occupied by the synagogue. He had been a non-Zionist all his life and the focus of attention and zeal of the great majority of Jews was Israel. He had favoured Yiddish which did not seem to have a promising future. Where then was he to go in the Jewish community?

But he stayed, notwithstanding, and he helped where he could. . . . [At his funeral] I broke down and wept softly, something [I] had not done at funerals for persons who had been much closer . . . so strong was the impact of David Lewis, social democrat, Jew, and above all — mentsh!

After David retired, says Michael, "I think there was a loneliness and that might have been . . . [because of] a feeling of sort of not quite fitting in any more. That there was a new breed in the party, the young folks coming up. He never really talked about it, but I have that sense." And before his own death, King Gordon recalled an evening arranged by Andy Brewin to have some experts on international affairs, of whom he was one, discuss issues with "the top people in the NDP caucus," including Ed Broadbent, the new leader. "It was a very disappointing session. . . . David was sitting just over to the right of me, entering the argument from time to time, tending to come in on our side, but I think a bit embarrassed by the line that Broadbent was taking . . . which [came down to] saying that they were still determined to takepower and a lot of the stuff we were talking about was irrelevant. . . . To me it was very strange to find that [they] didn't really think that these [concerns] . . . that Olaf Palme [was expressing] and Willi Brandt was writing about . . . were priority items. David was worried about that."

He continued to attend meetings of the national council and sometimes of the executive and, says Robin Sears, "he was very good about not trespassing on Ed Broadbent's territory. It was a very admirable restraint on his part. . . . But then [Trudeau's plan to patriate] the constitution came along and he was just beside himself. . . . I guess it was probably the September 1980 federal council meeting where, after labouring all summer, we presented a document that was sort of our vision of what should be in the Charter [of Rights] and repatriation document and David was supportive and talked down some angry criticism from the West."

However, over the ensuing months the arguments became more and more bitter until it culminated in a meeting that, says Sears,

> . . . was the most personal, vituperative, unpleasant, unnerving, disillusioning, disheartening experience I have ever endured in my political life. And any of us who are veterans of that period in the party treat any disagreement today very gingerly as a consequence. . . . It was as serious as the Waffle. In a way it was more serious [because] the establishment itself was completely divided. At least in the Waffle period . . . there was unity among . . . the party's leadership about what should be done. . . .
>
> It was terrible. Absolutely terrible. And David had a keener sense of how terrible if could become because of his awareness of what dynamite was being played with. . . . The level of bitterness in the West was so profound and their institutional capacity to do basically what they wanted was so real that it could have gone into a dreadful, dreadful kind of denouement. And [Jim] Coutts and company [the key Liberal staff members] were doing their best to keep it that way. . . .
>
> At one point David actually burst into tears, which I had never seen in my life, before or after, and he said, "You're wrecking my life. You're destroying everything we have worked for. I can't let you do this." This was addressed to Allan Blakeney, in a sense, who was there, but really to all of us. It absolutely floored everyone because it was so uncharacteristic of David to intervene in that way or to behave in that way, and we all felt ashamed. Not embarrassed. We felt ashamed of ourselves that he would feel so frightened and troubled as to make himself that vulnerable.

In the end the party was able to patch up its differences. "I won't tell you all the details, but we did it. . . . We orchestrated a number of face-saving disengagements that came to fruition at the convention. That process paid off magnificently this year [1987] with how we handled Meech Lake. Whether one agrees or disagrees with the substance of the position, the respect and tolerance and restraint with which the differences were debated in caucus and handled in public was just another planet from 1980."

In 1978 David and Joe Ain, his lifelong friend, returned to Svisloch for one last look at their home town, but when they got there, according to David's notes, "There was not a sign of anything that we knew. There was not a Jew in the town or anywhere around it. The Nazis had razed the town to the ground. Part of a synagogue was left standing and it . . . is now a movie picture house. One other building which used to be a seminary remains standing. All the rest was destroyed." The town was rebuilt after the war, but "It was no more Svisloch than Ottawa."

They visited the grave of the 3,000 to 4,000 Jews — "every Jew in the area, man woman and child" — who were "all led out into the forest nearby and shot. . . . There is some kind of little memorial. But [It] does not state 'Jews Only.' It talks about the victims of Hitler. It's what they call, I think, a 'Brothers' Grave.' Thus there was not an inkling of our past anywhere. Not a person, not a building, not a thing."

At a reception in one of the schools David was asked to respond to a toast but "my voice broke and I did not carry on. I simply raised my glass and said 'To peace,' and sat down. I hadn't realized how much the visit had affected me. There is no way [to] describe the emptiness that one feels at seeing one's past deliberately and utterly moved out, obliterated by the Nazis, as if I had never been born there."[8]

When David died, the funeral service was held in the little synagogue on King Edward Avenue in Ottawa, just around the corner from where he and Sophie had their first apartment on Friel Street. All of official Ottawa was there, and Michael had loudspeakers set up outside for the crowd of people who couldn't get in, and Ed Broadbent, Frank Scott, Kalmen Kaplansky, and Dennis McDermott delivered the eulogies. And on the coffin was inscribed the Star of David.

The one honour that David wanted more than any other, he never got: an honourary degree from McGill University. When Stephen was offered one from McGill in 1987, he debated whether to accept it because the university's refusal to honour David "was the only thing I've ever known that hurt him . . . [because] he loved McGill. He felt it very deeply." When Carl Goldenberg suggested to university officials in 1979 that David be granted a degree, the response was: "Tell him to send in his CV and we'll see if we can consider him," Stephen says. He accepted his own degree because "Carl said, 'You give them another victory, Stephen, if you don't take it. You don't so much vindicate David as you allow them to keep the Lewis name dissociated from McGill forever. So take it and mention your father.' And I did. . . . "Still, the thing that I had wanted most of all, which was a posthumous honorary degree for my father, hasn't occurred. At least yet."

•CHAPTER TWENTY-FIVE•

The persistence of absolute poverty on this planet is ultimately inseparable from the issues of violence, instability, and environmental deterioration which affect us all and will affect us increasingly as we move toward the opening of a new millennium.

James P. Grant
Executive Director
UNICEF[1]

My involvement in the Africa Recovery Programme has been the single most intense and fascinating experience in my life. It even transcends politics, although I love and honour politics. I never learned so much as I have in the past year nor felt so useful.

Stephen Lewis
UN Ambassador
May 1987

A first response to Javier Pérez de Cuéllar, secretary general of the United Nations, is surprise that he's much taller than his photographs lead you to believe — about six foot two or three — but when he offers in greeting a hand that's so large your fingers can barely get around it, an awareness of his size, the thick, modular blocks of him, begins to seize hold. Even his sentences have that modular bulk, delivered in regular segments of strongly accented English, each stacked carefully on the one before. This is not a man who will run away with the imagination; this is a man who will be steadfast.

His office on the thirty-eighth floor of the UN building in New York is like a large den, all wood and burgundy leather and beige, and he has chosen not to return behind his desk but to settle into one of the burgundy armchairs in a corner of the room where he talks about other things as he sizes up a proposition that apparently is new to him — which is that the UN's Africa Recovery Programme is the most significant new undertaking of the United Nations since it intervened in the Suez Crisis of 1956, creating the United Nations Emergency Force and establishing a peacekeeping role it has maintained ever since. Would he agree with that assessment?

He takes a verbal excursion to Sudan and Mozambique and Ethiopia as he mulls it over and then, shifting in his chair to lean forward, he finally agrees: "I think so. I think so. I think it is right. Yes, I would agree."

It is an acknowledgment that needs a moment to digest. Put another way, the Africa program is the UN's most important initiative in thirty-three years and, if the Korean War is excluded, in the forty-one years since UN peacekeeping began in 1948. It's the biggest thing the United Nations has undertaken during the lifetime of Canadians now approaching middle age. What it has done to prevent war through its peacekeeping efforts, it is trying to do in sub-Saharan Africa to help drag the region back from the abyss of collapse, starvation, and human misery.

"And how important would you say Stephen Lewis has been to the recovery program?"

"He has been decisive." He repeats it: "Decisive."

Decisive not just because of his abilities but because he is trusted by Africans and because he has "the will and determination to serve." Even though he has left as Canada's ambassador to the United Nations, Stephen remains as special adviser to Pérez de Cuéllar. "He was an extremely dynamic ambassador," says Pérez de Cuéllar. "Courageous, which is not always the case, you know. Saying things that he had in mind even if he knew that would raise some eyebrows. But he was always, to me, a very honest, direct man, which I very much appreciated. . . . I think he was wonderful. And he was very helpful to the United Nations. . . . I think he was a man who dared to say things."

In all that he has done at the United Nations, Stephen says, his work on African recovery "is absolutely *the* most important thing. . . . I think building a constituency in support of the UN, fighting with the Heritage Foundation, making speeches against Afghanistan, dealing with the African famine — all those things are the the job of an ambassador. You do it. I [could] do it a little better than some because I have a political background and I had a little more liberty. . . . But that's a kind of repetitive job . . . and what the African involvement did was to give me a very considerable *raison d'être*, and so I plunged in and worked at it."

At five-thirty on a Sunday morning, June 1, 1986, after almost a year of discussing, pleading, and politicking — and more than five days of intense debate in a special session of the General Assembly — a tired and dishevelled, but exhilarated Stephen Lewis left a tiny room where he had resolved the last differences between African and European delegates and entered a large meeting room a floor below the General Assembly's great circular chamber. He walked up the few steps to the raised podium, paused for a moment as he looked out over the semi-circular rows of representatives from 158 other countries, then picked up the gavel, banged it, and announced: "Ladies and gentlemen, we have a document." Another pause, and then everyone burst into applause. As chairman of the session's ad hoc committee charged with reaching agreement on the Programme of Action for Africa's Economic Recovery and Action (1986–1990) he had steered the the way to what *The New York Times* would call a "landmark document" — and indeed it was.[2] He had won unanimous agreement of all countries, but most importantly of all industrialized nations and all forty-four sub-Saharan nations, plus the behind-the-scenes acceptance of the World Bank, to a 6,500-word program aimed at restoring self-sufficiency to Africa.

Eleven months earlier, the Organization of African Unity, acknowledging "some domestic policy shortcomings," had adopted a five-year program for economic recovery and had asked the UN for help. The fact that African nations had agreed to a unanimous, co-operative approach was an extremely important first step. The next step was politicking, negotiating, pleading, not only with representatives of other countries and with aid and lending agencies but with the Africans themselves, to get a document that could be placed before the United Nations with a reasonable expectation that it would be accepted. It was a task into which Stephen, the neophyte ambassador, threw himself with a consuming passion.

"You know," says Pérez de Cuéllar, "Africans sometimes are a little suspicious of people, but the great advantage of Stephen Lewis is that he was trusted by all Africans. Sometimes it is not enough to be in good faith or to intend well. If you don't generate confidence there's not much you can do. The Africans trust him very, very much. And that's an extremely important aspect that he has."

Even now that he has retired from the post of ambassador Stephen spends a quarter of his time on African affairs, all of it unpaid, travelling on behalf of the secretary general, attending meetings, advising, analyzing developments, raising money, and, says Pérez de Cuéllar, "galvanizing international public opinion . . . to the needs of Africa." Every year since the program was approved, Stephen has raised about $1.2 million (U.S.) — which has been matched by various UN agencies that provide staff and services — to maintain an administrative unit within the United Nations that oversees and helps implement the agreement. Up to now the UN has not had the money in its general budget to cover such expenses. It was only this year that the UN budget committee formally included the Africa Recovery Programme in its budget, allocating roughly $1 million (U.S.) for 1990 and 1991.

The program has the potential of becoming the Marshall Plan of Africa — if the industrialized nations maintain the will to make it so. For the first time there is unanimous North-South agreement on goals. For the first time, agreed priorities. For the first time there can be co-ordination among all sub-Saharan countries instead of a helter-skelter addressing of problems. For the first time the industrialized nations have a framework within which to synchronize their assistance. And perhaps most important of all, the program has created a forum in which progress can be monitored and discussed — and that turned out to be crucial in the spring of 1989.

The cost to 1990 — the agreement covers the period from 1986 to 1990 — was originally estimated to be $128.1 billion (U.S.) of which the African countries committed themselves to spending $82.5 billion, leaving a need for $45 billion — or $9 billion a year — in loans and grants from governments, banks, and agencies in the industrialized world. Of the total, $117.5 billion is for agriculture for improving everything from seeds and pesticides to credit programs, transportation, communication, and marketing. There are proposals for dealing with drought and expanding deserts, with education and better use of workers, with population growth and the role of women in development.

At the last moment — at 4 A.M. on that Sunday morning to be exact — agreement on the program almost collapsed. The Senegalese foreign minister said he couldn't give his approval unless the document said Africa's problems were "deeply rooted in its colonial past." What made his objection doubly distressing to thunderstruck delegates was that he spoke with the added authority that came from Senegal's chairmanship of the Organization of African Unity.

Predictably, the representatives of France and Britain bridled at the implication that their countries were principally responsible for Africa's dilemma, and it was immediately apparent that discussion before the full assembly would get nowhere. So Stephen adjourned to the small room next door and after an hour of hard bargaining with the foreign minister and British and French delegates — at which every skill he had learned at labour arbitrations came into play — he emerged with an agreed compromise and the program was passed unanimously. The compromise wording simply said: "The international community fully recognizes the pervasive and structural problems of the African continent. Some of these lie in the colonial past; some of these flow from the post-independence era; others are a combination of economic, political and endemic factors."

It soon became apparent, once the program was under way, that the World Bank's insistence on what it called "structural adjustment programs" was producing very mixed results, and they became the focus of a bruising fight between the bank and people working with the United Nations — especially Stephen, Adebayo Adedeji, the executive secretary of the UN's Economic Commission for Africa, and Richard Jolly, deputy director of UNICEF — as a result of which the bank received such a pummelling that it backed down. Never before had it found itself subjected to such an intense and such a public confrontation. It had become accustomed to more or less having its own way in setting the agenda for loans to Third World countries, and to be forced to eat humble pie with the major newspapers of the world looking on was, for it, disconcerting to say the least.

What the bank was doing was telling African countries that in order to qualify for full assistance from the bank they would have to organize their economies according to sound business principles — in other words, much more according to the free enterprise practices of the United States. The confrontation began to take public shape with a report by Pérez de Cuéllar to the General Assembly in August 1988, mid-way through the program.

> . . . the implementation of structural adjustment programmes has given rise to several concerns [the report said]. . . . Their human and social costs have often been seen as out of proportion with their real or intended benefits. The most vulnerable . . . groups, in particular women, youth, the disabled, the aged, have been severely and adversely affected . . . by such measures as the withdrawal of subsidies on staple food items, the imposition of wage increases at or below the inflation rate, the retrenchment of [low-paid] civil servants and private sector personnel . . . and the cutting of expenditures on social services, including health and education, and on basic infrastructure. [The result is] malnutrition has increased, particularly among children, infants and pregnant women. . . .
>
> Moreover, some of the main ingredients of the programmes, such as re-alignments of exchange rates and rises in producer prices, are not generating the full expected benefits. . . . Structural adjustment programmes need to be designed as an integral part of a long-term development strategy and the human dimension needs to be made a central concern.[3]

The report also dismissed as "a gross underestimation" calculations that African nations needed $14 billion a year, not $9 billion a year, in outside help. The figure that officials were trying to negotiate was $18 billion. Africa's total external debt, a subsequent report pointed out, rose from 52.6 percent of gross domestic product (GDP) in 1985 to 71 percent in 1987 and would be 81.1 percent for 1988.[4]

So the stage for confrontation was set: the World Bank stood accused of being short on social conscience; African debt was getting worse, not better; and more help was needed than was being given from the bank and other agencies in the industrialized world. The next step was a media tour of Ghana and Senegal in November and December "sponsored by the Recovery Programme's Steering Committee with funding from the Government of Japan." "Ghana now a World Bank showcase for free market policies," declared a headline in *The Times* of London. "In Ghana, The Leader At Full Sail," was *The New York Times* headline. "*Le Ghana, l'enfant chéri de la Banque mondiale, s'ajuste dans la douleur*," proclaimed a headline in *Le Soir* of Brussels. And so the headlines went, the stories saying, in effect, that judging from Ghana, the bank's structural adjustment policies were showing promise — even though Ghana was one of the least typical of the sub-Saharan countries.[5]

At that point the score stood even. The bank one, the UN one. Then, in March 1989, the bank issued a report called "Africa's Adjustment and Growth in the 1980s," which, according to the UN's Economic Commission for Africa under Adebayo Adedeji, falsely tried to prove "that in the wake of structural adjustment programmes, 'encouraging signs,' even 'signs of a turnaround,' can be detected in sub-Saharan Africa's economic standing." The UN agency said in so many words that the bank had cooked the statistics to make itself look good: ". . . the essence of the World Bank's conclusions . . . emanate from a compilation and presentation of basic statistics which differ from what is common practice . . . in other World Bank reports," it said.[6]

The showdown came in Paris, and Stephen prepared the way with the press. He was "very angry" about the World Bank report, he told *The Guardian*, the British newspaper. "It is a lousy document, prepared with a questionable data base, and is a gratuitous insertion into the debate on Africa's future. . . . [N]o hint was given to colleagues sitting on the Inter-Agency Task Force with them that the bank was preparing it." *The Guardian* called the upcoming confrontation with the bank "unprecedented." Seven UN agencies attended.[7] Two weeks after the meeting Stephen recalled the confrontation:

What happened, I think, is that the bank overplayed its hand in a very maladroit fashion. For the first time one of its major documents was being challenged on its analytic quality. That really rattled the bank. At the meeting I said, "I'm not going to worry about your document. It's flawed on every ground. You know that. I won't embarrass you by taking it apart. Others have done it.

"What I want to know is the motives. I want to know why this document came out when it did. Why, having worked together for two and a half years every step of the way, each of us knowing what the other was doing, the Economic Commission for Africa [ECA] having involved you every step of the way, why did none of us know about this publication? And why were 200 copies sent to a finance ministers' meeting in Malawi when they were debating an alternative to your structural adjustment programs? How can it be interpreted except as a way of pre-empting the ECA? Of denigrating what was coming out of Africa and securing your own version of structural adjustment?"

Then Adebayo Adedeji put himself on the line and set it out chapter and verse.

They were especially rattled because they had all of this stuff appearing in the international press. That just hadn't happened to them before. You had *The Economist* and *The Guardian* and the *Financial Times* of London — everybody writing about it, including David Crane in the *Toronto Star* — all of them talking about the terrible rupture between the two organizations.[8]

The following week the World Bank called a meeting at its Washington headquarters and invited the UN agencies, the Organization of African Unity and the African Development Bank — and the bank recanted. A joint statement issued after the meeting said: "[I]t has become clear that adjustment must be seen as part of a long-term development approach and that it must take full account of the human dimension. . . . Particular attention must be paid to protecting vulnerable groups during the adjustment process. . . . Increased donor assistance is . . . required to support the efforts of the African governments to expand their reform programs and promote sustained economic growth. . . . It was agreed that further steps should be taken to strengthen collaboration and the channels of communication. . . ."[8]

"It was an amazing shift for the bank," Stephen says. In many ways the bank's reputation is hanging on the success of the programs in Africa and, "They're not sure what's gone wrong. It's probably too early to tell if it has gone wrong. The results are mixed and disconcerting."

What the Africa program will test will be more than skill and determination and cooperative spirit and sheer staying power. It will be a test of civilization. How the most favoured will respond to the needs of the least favoured will tell, as it has through all ages, through all philosophies, through all religions, whether the light can indeed be divided from the darkness.

Stephen insists that it can.

• E P I L O G U E •

I am my brother's keeper.

David Lewis
federal leadership convention, 1975

Two years before Stephen resigned as ambassador, he warned that he would not be able to remain once Canada became a member of the Security Council. There would be issues where he would have to disagree with government policy — in particular on Nicaragua, on the Palestinian issue in Israel, and on South Africa. He could avoid taking a public stand while Canada was only a member of the General Assembly because the deputy ambassador could deal with those issues. But practice does not allow that in the Security Council.

He could have accepted any of a number of other postings. Instead, he resigned in the fall of 1988 — even though he would have become eligible for a government pension had he remained in service for another twelve months. The pension vests after five years of service and amounts to 30 percent of salary which, in Stephen's case, would have meant a pension of more than $30,000 a year. His answer to why he didn't stay long enough to qualify for a pension is that he didn't take the job for the money and he wouldn't stay for the money.

Where he will stay is at the side of Africa, doing everything he can to help it recover.

It is here, he will tell you, where North meets South, that the class struggle is most clearly defined. It is here that the struggle for human dignity is at its greatest. It is here, and he makes this apparent with every word he says, it is here that his heart is.

Nina and Daniel have just moved to Berlin where Daniel has won a competition for the design of the new Jewish Museum that will be an addition to the Berlin Museum.

Janet's husband David died of leukemia in 1986. In May 1988 Janet was elected president of the Ontario party after serving as chair of the election planning committee in 1986 and 1987. She is thinking of moving to Israel. What does it tell you, she asks, when the most famous immigrant from North America to Israel in the past twenty years is the ultra-right-wing rabbi Meir Kahane? She is fiercely opposed to the regime of Yitzak Shamir.

Michael was provincial secretary of the Ontario party from 1982 to 1985. He has worked in twenty-six election campaigns, federally and in every province, and is thought by many to be the best field organizer the NDP has ever produced. Now he is with the United Steelworkers of America as a staff representative responsible for political action and community outreach.

Doris Andras emigrated to Israel several years ago where she lives in Tel Aviv with her daughter Margot.

Jennie, the ebullient youngest daughter of Stephen and Michele, is entering her second year at York University where she is studying film and video arts. She has, she says, no interest whatever in politics. "I didn't grow up with it the way Avi and Ilana did." She was seven years old when Stephen quit the Legislature. She writes short stories for fun "like Mom did when she was young," and thinks she would like to work behind the cameras, maybe doing screenplays.

Avi graduated a year ago with an Honours BA in philosophy and English literature. He is the one with the penetrating logic that was David's. Quick to laugh, equally quick to cut to the centre of an issue, as yet he doesn't know what he wants. Perhaps journalism. Perhaps — and he says it with a chuckle that makes it seem that even he doesn't fully accept the thought — perhaps writing songs. He thoroughly enjoys working in political campaigns but he's not convinced that he wants to be a politician. "As far as making the arena of politics the main stage, I could do it," he says, "but I don't feel a compulsion to." What he does feel compulsive about is democratic socialism and it shows the moment he begins talking about the party. "As far as I'm concerned," he says, "winning has replaced change as the goal of the party and that's wrong." Public opinion polls are displacing socialist vision. "Once you use technology to try and determine what would be most effective as an argument, then you've totally switched the basis of argument. You've committed yourself to subjecting the means to the end. The argument in favour is, 'We know that we really represent working people more than the other parties, but they don't. So we have to find the most effective argument to convince them that we do.' But that's bullshit. The way to do that is not to find the pressure point where they're susceptible, the catch phrase or their particular fears or anxieties that need to be played on. That's manipulation. What you have to do is speak the truth. That will convince people eventually."

Ilana is entering Osgoode Hall Law School, "but I wouldn't be going if it weren't tied directly to politics. Certainly I have no interest in going to law school to be a lawyer." When she was ten years old "my grampa [David] sat me down and explained to me why I had to go to law school. He said you have to go because laws change society and society is politics." She delights in stretching language — as Stephen does — throwing in hypercharged words and laughing at what they do.

She's reluctant to say outright that she has her heart set on being a politician. "There's enough pressure through guilt by genetic association without going around saying sure, that's what you're going to do," and she grins infectiously. But five minutes later she is saying, "It's an inheritance like any other inheritance. If your daddy has a business it's hard to imagine doing anything else. Then you go to university and find out that there are lots of other things in life and either you move away . . . or you [don't]. Admittedly, when I think about my future in a serious way — and I've just turned twenty-four — I can't think of any other way to do all the things I believe in doing and enjoy. Politics fuses them all. So, in terms of effecting change in society, being a democratic socialist, being an ardent feminist, believing in making your life worthwhile by contributing and effecting some kind of change in the human condition, being happy, being motivated, being excited, being crazy, staying up all night, never sleeping — I like to do all those things — being overworked, obsessive, compulsive: that's politics. In every path that I turn . . . somehow it always comes back to some kind of political involvement."

•ACKNOWLEDGMENTS•

Had I never finished this book, it would have been reward enough that I came to know Emanuel Goldberg. He translated from the Yiddish for me; he guided me through the intricacies of Russian, European and Soviet histories; he shared his memories of Svisloch; but most of all he showed me — without realizing it, I am sure — what it means to be a good person. He has the knowledge, the gentleness, and the compassion to understand and the humility to remain true to his beliefs.

At a time when I was at an impasse because I could not reconcile past with present, David Rome, the former archivist of the National Archives of the Canadian Jewish Congress, took me by the hand into the world of nineteenth-century Eastern European shtetls and, in an afternoon and an evening, offered revelations so cogent and concise that they defined the path of this book.

Penny Gerrie helped me with some of the research on the CCF and the NDP and inevitably left me nonplussed at her speed and thoroughness.

Rabbi Gunther Plaut, generously allowing me to prevail on a long-cherished acquaintance, read the first sixteen chapters of the unfinished manuscript and offered advice that, as always, was penetrating in content and courtly in presentation.

Of all the people that I interviewed, Lewis Seale was the most diligent in his responses. The chief focus of our discussions was Quebec nationalism during the time David was leader of the federal party and Seale was his press secretary. He dug out copies of material for me and drafted extremely helpful memos. Although I didn't deal with the issue to any great extent in the book, his assistance was a significant help in shaping its final pages.

Betty Corson was my editor and there is but one word to describe her: superlative.

Finally, of the people I want to single out for particular thanks, I wish to mention Dorothy Jackson, my aunt, who was supportive at a time when I was especially needy.

One of the interesting things about my research is that I can't recall a single individual in all the many institutions I visited who wasn't helpful and good-humoured. I know that sounds excessive but it's true. Archivists and librarians must be a breed apart from the rest of us. Among those most deserving of praise are those at the Public Archives of Canada, the British Library, the Bodleian Library, the Bund Archives, the Robarts Library, the National Archives of the Canadian Jewish Congress, the Ontario Archives, the Jewish Public Library in Montreal, and the Metro Reference Library in Toronto.

With only one or two exceptions, people gave unstintingly of their time in interviews, even when they realized that I had views opposing theirs. For that I have not only to thank them but to point out that for the most part they also have given unstintingly toward making society a better place in which to live — regardless of whether they were in opposite camps — and that earns them a special place, at least in my affections.

Although I have expressed my appreciation privately, I also would like to extend it publicly to those who granted me major interviews, namely:

Fay Ain, Joe Ain, Doris (Lewis) Andras, Margot Andras; Tom Berger, A. Alan Borovoy, Andrew Boyle, John Brewin, Peggy Brewin, Hans Brown, Ken Bryden; Gerry Caplan, Gerald Charney, Bertram Collins, Murray Cotterill, John Cripps; Oduardo di Santo, Janusz Dukszta; Faga Falk, Israel Falk, Michael Foot, Eugene Forsey, Barbara Frum; Emanuel Goldberg, Judith Golden, H. Carl Goldenberg, King Gordon, Arnold Greenfield, Saul Gunner; Jean-Paul Harney, Jacob Hertz, T.E.B. Howarth; Lorne Ingle; E.B. (Ted) Jolliffe; Kalmen Kaplansky, Stanley Knowles; Michele Landsberg, Floyd Laughren, Jim Laxer, Margaret Lazarus, Morden Lazarus, Nina (Lewis) Libeskind, Avram Lewis, Jennie Lewis, Ilana Lewis, Michael Lewis, Sheldon Lewis, Sophie Lewis, Stephen Lewis, Yoel Litewka, Salim Lone; Donald C. MacDonald, Hugh Mackenzie, Josephine Malleck, Norman Massey (Noah Puterman), Kenneth McNaught, Elmer McVey, Allan Millard, Peter Mosher, Malcolm Muggeridge; Benjamin Nadel, Sir William Nield;

Javier Pérez de Cuéllar, Steve Perkal, John Pollock; Vyvian Rakoff, David Rome, Irving Rosenfeld; Cliff Scotton, Lewis Seale, Robin Sears, Thérèse Sevigny, Owen Shime, Gordon Shore, Bea Silcoff, Maurice Silcoff, Florence Silver, Janet (Lewis) Solberg, Mike Solski, Ray Stancer, Ray Stevenson; Charles Taylor, Jim Tester; Victor Willy; Mel Watkins, Murray Weppler, Herb Whittaker, Lynn Williams, Sir Geoffrey Wilson.

I am especially grateful to the Canada Council which assisted with a $10,000 grant midway through the preparation of this book when I realized I had taken on a much larger subject than I had anticipated.

Last of all, I hope someday this world will fashion a special tribute for long-suffering publishers. I came close, I fear, to sending mine into the world beyond. If I could, I would canonize Jim Williamson and Gordon Montador.

• P E R M I S S I O N S •

Excerpts from *Waiting for the Messiah* by Irving Layton, *A Red Carpet for the Sun* by Irving Layton and from *The Street* by Mordecai Richler all used by permission of the Canadian Publishers, McClelland and Stewart, Toronto.

Excerpts from *Angel Square* by Brian Doyle used by permission of Groundwood Books Ltd., Vancouver, Toronto.

The poem "The City of Slaughter", by Chain Bialik, translation by Joseph Leftwich, used by permission of Associated University Presses.

Excerpt from an obituary of David Lewis by Richard Gwyn is reprinted with permission of the Toronto Star Syndicate.

Excerpt from *Selected Stories* by I.L. Peretz, Edited by Irving Howe and Eliezer Greenberg, used by permission of Random House, New York.

Excerpt from *Like One that Dreamed: A Portrait of A.M. Klein* by Usher Caplan, used by permission of the author.

Appendix A. Chapter 2

The Decembrists: Although the Decembrists did little and achieved nothing concrete, they became a symbol of revolutionary daring and determination. They had their beginnings in a secret society formed in 1816 by six young noblemen, all officers in the Guards, called The Union of Salvation or the Society of the True and Faithful Sons of the Fatherland.

When Alexander I died a natural death in November 1825, there was a delay in the accession of Nicholas I because an effort was made to persuade his elder brother, the Grand Duke Constantine, to accept the throne, which he had earlier renounced. The efforts came to naught, but on December 13, 1825, before matters were resolved, leaders of the Northern Society of the union persuaded 3,000 soldiers to assemble and demonstrate for Constantine in St. Petersburg's Senate Square. Nicholas blasted them out of the square with cannons, hanged five of the ringleaders, and exiled hundreds to Siberia.

Nothing changed outwardly. Nevertheless, the spark of inspiration had been ignited and for that the Decembrists passed into revolutionary folklore. Alexander Herzen (1812–70), Russia's first great socialist, took a solemn vow to dedicate his life to continuing the Decembrist struggle for Russian freedom. He developed the pre-Marxist theory of peasant populism which stressed a unique Russian path to socialism.

Lenin, looking at his own revolutionary genealogy, commented that "The Decembrists awakened Herzen, and Herzen started the revolutionary agitation (and that) was taken up, widened and strengthened..."[1]

Appendix B. Chapter 2

The rate of industrialization: The 1890s are often regarded as the decade of Russian industrialization, but the previous thirty years set the pattern, as the following table indicates:

PRODUCTION IN SELECTED INDUSTRIES (in tons)*

Year	Coal	Oil	Iron	Pig Iron	Iron & Steel
1860	329,400			352,800	223,200
1870	763,200	32,400	825,750	372,600	261,000
1880	3,610,800	612,200	1,083,600	469,800	635,400
1890	5,049,600	4,348,000	1,913,400	993,600	871,200

*Walsh, *Russia and the Soviet Union*, p. 290.

The first railroad, which ran from Warsaw to Vienna, was built in 1851. Then came the St. Petersburg to Moscow (1851), the St. Petersburg to Warsaw (1859), the Riazin to Kozhlov to Moscow (1866). In the years 1870 to 1875 railway fever hit and 4,971 miles were constructed. For the next fifteen years there was a lag, but in 1891 the Trans-Siberian Railroad, the biggest project the world had ever seen, was begun, and in the period 1891 to 1895 a total of 4,148 miles were built. Over the next five years 10,036 miles were added, so that at 1901 the total mileage stood at 37,209.[2]

Appendix C. Chapter 2
Terrorism: In St. Petersburg, early in 1878, Trepov, the chief of police, ordered the flogging of a young revolutionary student who had refused to doff his cap when Trepov passed. In revenge a young woman, Vera Zasulich, shot Trepov. At her trial she didn't deny she had tried to kill him, but the jury acquitted her nonetheless. And when the police tried to re-arrest her, a jubilant crowd prevented it and she escaped.

Zasulich was a member of a secret society called Land and Freedom. It had turned to terrorism after its leaders had been thrown into the prison following a political demonstration in St. Petersburg. Having concluded that the masses were not about to rise and that political agitation only gave the Tsar's police a discernible target, they decided that the only alternative was to kill the most unpopular government leaders. That, they thought, would bring the entire regime tumbling down.

Through the spring of 1878 they tried unsuccessfully to kill other officials, often engaging in gun battles with police. But that summer they did assassinate the chief of the Third Section, the Tsar's secret police. The reaction was a massive crackdown. Fearing that there was an army of terrorists at work, although there probably were no more than a few handfuls operating in small groups, suspected terrorists were exiled, executed, expelled from the cities, and jailed. Reaction bred reaction and the terror increased, but the increase brought about a split in Land and Freedom.

One group, calling itself Black Partition, emphasizing reason and persuasion, concentrated on spreading propaganda in villages. By 1880 the police had smashed it and its leaders had fled abroad. The other, People's Will, Narodnaya Volya, became a small, highly disciplined group of professional revolutionaries with but a single thought: the assassination of Tsar Alexander II. Three times they tried to blow up the imperial train, each time unsuccessfully. They smuggled dynamite, stick by stick, into the Winter Palace, hoping to blow up the Tsar during a state dinner, but touched it off prematurely, killing eleven guardsmen, wounding fifty-six, and leaving Alexander unscathed.

In an atmosphere of mounting fear in St. Petersburg, Alexander appointed General Mikhail Loris-Melikov as head of a commission to break the terrorists. The immediate consequence was an attempt to kill the general. Within forty-eight hours the young would-be assassin was tracked down, arrested, and hanged. Then the general urged Alexander to institute reforms. Terror, he argued, was only the perverted manifestation of a deep public dissatisfaction. The Tsar should rekindle the reforming spirit of his early years. Alexander agreed. He abolished the Third Section (although its work and its members were simply transferred to the state police) and he agreed to allow broader participation in his State Council.

But while plans for the reforms were being drafted, new plans for his assassination were afoot and on March 1, 1881, he was killed. The assassination did not inspire people to revolt. Rather, it left them shocked and numb. Workers did not rise. All that students did was refuse to contribute to funeral wreaths. The greatest irony of all was that peasants thought noblemen anxious to restore serfdom had killed the Tsar.

The conspirators were caught and, a month later, were hanged before a crowd of 80,000 in Semeonovsky Square. The new Tsar, Alexander III, cancelled all reforms, saying, "The voice of God commands us to rule with faith in the power and the truth of the autocratic authority which we are called upon to confirm and to preserve." As Milton Meltzer has described it, the so-called Peasant Tsar, bent on repressing anything that had the slightest whiff of rebelliousness, "gave dictatorial power over the citizenry to his governors. It was a Magna Carta for police terror, renewed annually for the next 25 years."[3]

Nevertheless, terrorism continued. A year or so later, Narodnaya Volya assassinated the police chief of Odessa; two years later, the chief of Secret Police in St. Petersburg, Lieutenant Colonel G.P. Sudeikin, was clubbed to death in his own rooms. Meanwhile, at the universities, disturbances continued: in Kazan (1882), in Poland (1883), and in Moscow and Kiev (1884). Kiev University was closed completely in 1886 after demonstrations. The police were persistent, however, and by the mid-1880s they had succeeded in completely destroying Narodnaya Volya.

So when Alexander Ilyich Ulyanov and the other four conspirators who were hanged in 1887 shouted, "Long Live Narodnaya Volya," just before the trapdoors were sprung, they were proclaiming not the defiant spirit of an existing organization but the ongoing, if unfocused and poorly channeled, spirit of revolution. (In fact they were so poorly organized that they were discovered through a routine censorship check of letters, and the bombs that they intended to throw never would have exploded because of defective fuses.)

In his last words to the court that sentenced him to death, Ulyanov made it plain that they planned to kill the Tsar not because it was a rational thing to do but because they thought all other options were blocked.

Appendix D. Chapter 3

The Jewish advance into Russia; Robert Brym, in a 1978 study published while he was assistant professor of sociology at Memorial University in

Newfoundland, has traced the roots of anti-Jewish sentiment back 400 years to the fourteenth century when feudalism was just beginning to crystallize east of the Elbe River. To the west of the river, which runs diagonally northwest from Prague to Hamburg, feudalism had begun breaking up in the thirteenth century. In the feudalism of the West, Jews had been invaluable intermediaries.

As Brym puts it: "Serfdom implies decentralised extraction of tribute, not state-directed taxation; management of estates by agents of the landlord, not by [landlords] themselves; money-lending, not banking; [acquiring] scarce goods more through trade than [through purchase]."[4]

Jews excelled as estate managers, tax and toll collectors, money lenders, and traders. They were a necessary and integral part of the Western feudal system. So, when feudalism moved eastward, they moved with it, and by the middle of the fourteenth century 85 percent of the Jews in Poland were performing these functions.

In return for their services Casimir the Great granted them the right to their own political, judicial, administrative, and educational institutions. But, says Brym, "because the Jews were the immediate agents used by landowners to extract surplus from the peasantry, they were deeply despised in rural Poland. [Nevertheless] the chief opponents of the Jews were to be found in the cities. The monopolistic tendencies of medieval production encouraged the view among [local merchants] that Jews represented a great competetive threat. . . . It was here that the 'main source of anti-semitism in Poland originated.' Little wonder that opposition to the Jews increased as the Polish bourgeoisie grew."[5]

However, the bourgeoisie wasn't able to do too much about its anti-Jewish bent because in the sixteenth century the land-owning nobility developed at the expense of the bourgeoisie (and royalty) into the most powerful force in Polish society. Consequently, from 1500 to 1650, under the patronage of land-owning Polish nobility, there existed the "Golden Age of Polish Jewry." According to one account, the Jewish population increased from 12,000 in 1500 to 170,000 in 1650.[6] Another account has it increasing from about 30,000 in the fifteenth century to 500,000 in the seventeenth century.[7] As the aggressive nobility pushed eastward, it brought Jewish managers, merchants, and artisans with it.

Not all Jews migrated eastward with feudalism; some were among the 170,000 Jews forced to flee Spain in 1492 following the adoption of the fanatical policies of Torquemada, the first grand inquisitor; and some came from the East. Those coming from the East were Khazars, converts to Judaism. The kingdom of Khazaria flourished from the seventh to the tenth centuries as a major commercial empire in the area between the Black and Caspian seas, controlling and exacting tribute from tribes extending as far north as the Moscow area and as far west as Kiev. It was the Khazars who, in a hundred years of warfare, halted the advance of the Arab armies seeking an eastern entry into Europe that would match their advance into Spain in the west. Had they not blocked the Arab advance, the history of the West would have been radically different.[8]

However, after a steady decline through the eleventh and twelfth centuries, the Khazars were finally obliterated as a nation in the thirteenth century by the Mongol hordes of Genghis Khan. Some were absorbed into the Golden

Horde; some fled westward, following the paths of earlier migrants to areas
that later were incorporated into the Pale of Settlement; some didn't flee until the period of anarchy following disintegration of the Mongol empire, which
began in the fourteenth century. So as the Jews from the West were just beginning to move eastward, the Khazar refugees were moving westward, both
in the direction of Eastern Europe.

How large was the Khazar exodus is a matter of speculation. There are no
records, and when the Mongols threw the cloak of another Dark Age across
the eastern steppes, they smothered all knowledge of Khazar movements.[9]
There is evidence, however, of late medieval Khazar settlements in the Crimea
and in Ukraine, Hungary, Poland, and Lithuania.[10]

By 1569 Poland had pushed its borders to their farthest point eastward,
and there they remained until the partition of Poland 200 years later, despite
outward excursions that saw Poles capture Moscow and hold it for several
years in the early 1600s. So, in a large part of what is now Russia and Ukraine,
Jewish intermediaries grew roots under the sponsorship of the Polish nobility. At the same time, however, they attracted much the same resentment
among Russians and Ukrainians that they had attracted in the Polish
heartland.

Appendix E. Chapter 10

Hard times in the opening years of the 1920s; By 1921 the unemployment rate,
conservatively estimated, was 9.8 percent—192,000 people looking for work
in an industrial work force of 1,956,000. With the exception of the depression years, this was a higher unemployment rate than at any time until 1982.
And for the first five years of the decade (again with one exception, this time
in 1946) the proportion of time lost due to strikes and lockouts was higher
than at any point until 1966. See the following charts:

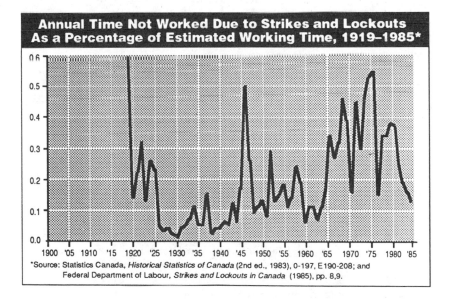

**Annual Time Not Worked Due to Strikes and Lockouts
As a Percentage of Estimated Working Time, 1919–1985***

*Source: Statistics Canada, *Historical Statistics of Canada* (2nd ed., 1983), 0-197, E 190-208; and
Federal Department of Labour, *Strikes and Lockouts in Canada* (1985), pp. 8,9.

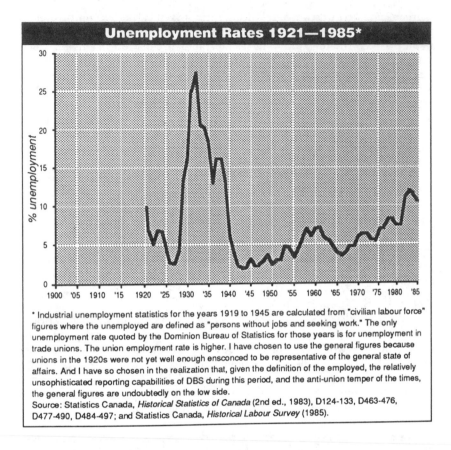

Unemployment Rates 1921—1985*

* Industrial unemployment statistics for the years 1919 to 1945 are calculated from "civilian labour force" figures where the unemployed are defined as "persons without jobs and seeking work." The only unemployment rate quoted by the Dominion Bureau of Statistics for those years is for unemployment in trade unions. The union employment rate is higher. I have chosen to use the general figures because unions in the 1920s were not yet well enough ensconced to be representative of the general state of affairs. And I have so chosen in the realization that, given the definition of the employed, the relatively unsophisticated reporting capabilities of DBS during this period, and the anti-union temper of the times, the general figures are undoubtedly on the low side.
Source: Statistics Canada, *Historical Statistics of Canada* (2nd ed., 1983), D124-133, D463-476, D477-490, D484-497; and Statistics Canada, *Historical Labour Survey* (1985).

Appendix F. Chapter 10

The Winnipeg General Strike: The city establishment, traumatized by the Red Scare that was sweeping all of North America,[11] formed a Citizens' Committee and started its own newspaper, a nasty enterprise that proclaimed the real threat was "alien scum."[12] Conspiracy theories abounded, the main one being that One Big Union (OBU) was planning to usurp the duly elected government.

One Big Union came into being in early June, right in the middle of the strike. By the following year it had 50,000 members.[13] Its chief spokesman, and the leading personality in the strike, was R.B. Russell, perceived as Canada's most notorious Bolshevist, a man who was not a Communist but who wanted to have One Big Union accepted into the Comintern. Membership was refused because the Comintern saw OBU as "secessionist" and this was a period when the Comintern wanted supporters to join mainstream unions.[14] After the strike Russell received the heaviest sentence of all that were handed down: two years in penitentiary for seditious conspiracy.

The OBU preached the overthrow of capitalism and direct control of the economy and politics through workers' councils and unions. Its revolutionary message never quite caught up with the strikers in Winnipeg. What was actually happening on Winnipeg streets, while the OBU was still trying to get organized, was far from revolutionary. Quite the contrary. Conspicuous efforts were being made to cool tempers, avoid violence, and prevent provocation. As Prof. Kenneth McNaught points out, A.E. Smith in his memoirs declared, "This was not a revolutionary struggle for power." Smith was a Communist and his autobiography stuck close to the party line. If any group had seen the strike as an attempt to overthrow local government, it would have been the Communists, says McNaught, so it's fair to take Smith's words at face value when he wrote that "The strike leaders in Winnipeg told the workers to stay home. They tried to keep the struggle strictly on an economic plane."[15]

Appendix G. Chapter 10

Trotsky's theory of permanent revolution (p. 000): Trotsky first expressed his theory in *Results and Prospects*, written in prison in 1906. It was an attempt to adapt Marxist theory to conditions where there were wide variations in development and in revolutionary fervour. In Russia his theory called for a bourgeois revolution, somewhat like that proposed by the Mensheviks, that would lead to a continuous state of revolution during which the proletariat would take power in urban centres. This seizure would inspire proletarian revolutions internationally which, in turn, would support the revolutionaries in Russia.

Stalin expounded his theory of socialism in one country shortly after Lenin's death. It was based on the belief that it was possible to build communism in the Soviet Union without the support of world-wide revolution and it was immediately popular with party middle managers whom Stalin was promoting to influential positions.

Stalin ousted Trotsky from the Politburo in October 1926 and by January 1929 had expelled him from the USSR. The move to Stalin's socialism-in-one-country policy was gradual, but by the time of the Comintern's 6th Congress in 1928, it was firmly in place. The 6th Congress also put formally in place what Norman Penner in *Canadian Communism* calls Stalin's ultra-left policy, first broached by him in 1924, of labelling democratic socialists the chief enemies of the working class. "Social fascists" is the phrase Stalin coined. It was a concept on which Stalin would flip-flop several times in the ensuing years.

Trotsky in exile was scathing about the Stalin regime, saying that it had betrayed the revolution, that it was a bureaucratic perversion, and that it was Bonapartist (meaning a personal dictatorship that had subverted the dictatorship of the proletariat). He maintained that as early as 1923 the revolution had begun to degenerate, isolated as it was by the failure of world revolution, the backwardness of Russia, and Stalin's static, inward-looking policies.

Appendix H. Chapter 15

Section 98 of the Criminal Code: Section 98 was infamous because:

1. An "unlawful association" was defined as having the "purpose . . . to bring about any governmental, industrial or economic change . . . by use of force, violence or physical injury to person or property." Consequently, it was not necessary for the association to actually commit a violent act. Or to plan one. Guilt would flow from intent alone, and this was contrary to the most basic principles of criminal law;

2. Individuals who attended meetings of an "unlawful association" or who distributed literature or spoke publicly in favour of it were assumed to be members and could be sentenced to twenty years in jail unless they could prove they weren't members. In other words, they were assumed guilty and had to prove their innocence;

3. Even if people weren't members, if they contributed money to an "unlawful association" or were "anywise associated" with it, or wore a badge or carried a banner "intended to suggest" they were members, they also could be convicted and jailed for twenty years. In other words, they could be found guilty regardless of what had been their intent, which also is contrary to basic principles of criminal law.[16]

Appendix I. Chapter 15

The attempted assassination of Tim Buck: Eight months after Buck was sent to Kingston Penitentiary a riot developed from a sit-down strike. Buck was convicted of inciting the riot, although he firmly denied it and testified that he had tried to prevent it;[17] and he was sentenced to an additional nine months in prison. According to Buck, during the disturbances a squad of guards outside his cell block marched to a point where they could see his cell through a corridor window, then they halted, wheeled, and fired eleven rifle shots into the cell, missing him only because he fell to the floor when he saw them wheel and then squeezed behind "about eight inches of wall that the cell gate was fastened into."[18]

The pockmarks left in the wall of his cell told the story, and as word of it spread across the land, outrage mounted and by November 1933, thirteen months later, 459,000 signatures had been collected to a petition demanding a full inquiry. When a delegation presented him with the petition, Bennett, in a fury, ordered the members out of his office. But there was no staying the public outrage. A year later — two years and nine months after he went to jail and with three years left to serve on his combined sentences — Buck was released, the last of the eight to get out. Deportation orders were dropped.[19]

Appendix J. Chapter 17

Make This YOUR Canada was more rigorously socialist than either the Regina Manifesto or *Social Planning for Canada*: Although the Regina Manifesto spoke of the need to replace the capitalist system and to end "the domination and exploitation of one class by another," it never once used the word "socialist" to describe its program. It referred to "class" only twice and never to the "class struggle." Revolution was never mentioned; neither was "proletariat" nor "the means of production." Nor did it exhibit any sense of historical materialism — the Marxist concept that it is the system of production that determines the shape of society and the attitudes of its people, not vice versa.

However, when it talked of public ownership, the Manifesto had a fat list. It called for nationalization of key undertakings such as utilities, transportation, communications, banking, insurance, hospitals, and medical and dental care, which would be followed by mining, pulp and paper, and the distribution of milk, bread, coal, and gasoline, to which it would add "other industries and services essential to social planning." Its final sentence had a radical ring, and it was to cause the party unending difficulty because it frightened people. "No CCF Government will rest content until it has eradicated capitalism and put into operation the full programme of socialized planning . . . ," it said. This was such a change from the rest of the language that it reads like something that was added as a token radical statement.

Social Planning for Canada, when it came out two years later, sounded much the same, and even though it didn't contain a radical statement, it did refer to itself as a socialist document. It prescribed an evolutionary, not a revolutionary, process. It did not talk of socializing the means of production. Its attitude can probably best be summed up in its approach to banks, which it recommended be nationalized, but "in general, the same executive staff would perform the same sort of jobs for the same sort of salaries."[20]

It was at pains to reconcile how it could recommend compensating capitalists for their industries with a socialist belief in economic equality. Its solution was to pay owners by issuing government bonds and then, as the bonds were paid off, to tax away the bulk of the profits. "Unless the bulk of the compensation is promptly taken back from the rich former owners by drastic income and inheritance taxes," it said, "the 'publicly owned' industries would still be run on capitalist principles . . . [and this] is not socialism but "state capitalism": the state operating industry on behalf of the capitalists."[21]

It proposed criteria for deciding what undertakings should be nationalized, and to the list of candidates suggested by the Manifesto, it added the iron and steel industry, flour and milling, and some parts of the construction industry. However, it cautioned that takeovers should proceed carefully step by step, so the government could learn from experience along the way. And it specifically affirmed that a place would remain for private enterprise although "At least a substantial part of productive activity must be socialized if planning is to have any fundamental and durable effects" (p. 242). It said "a number of individual industries [could] still remain in private hands" (p. 243), "for a considerable time to come" (p. 265), and called for measures to help "the small-scale business [so it] can be operated as efficiently as the big corporation" (p. 439).

Make This YOUR Canada might seem less radical since it was even more specific about retaining private enterprise and moved away from a general attack on capitalism in favour of attacking monopoly capitalism. On private enterprise, *Make This YOUR Canada* said: "The CCF economic programme will necessarily leave a considerable field for private enterprise since it will be undesirable and physically impossible to attempt the socialization of every industry. . . . Reasonable rates on profit in investment will be allowed. . . . The degree of private enterprise to be left is always a matter of debate, and circumstance — including the will of the electorate — will largely determine what policy should be followed."[22] As for monopoly capitalism, it was "irresponsible" and "It must and shall disappear."[23]

However, monopoly capitalism was not defined and *Make This YOUR Canada* had the same list of candidates for public ownership. But where it differed most markedly was that it had a much tougher approach to nationalization. It set down criteria for deciding which industries would not be nationalized. That approach assumed everything would be nationalized except those industries exempted. The approach adopted by *Social Planning for Canada* assumed the reverse, that nothing would be nationalized except those industries that fit the criteria for nationalization.

To escape nationalization, *Make This YOUR Canada* said companies had to (1) be in no position to exploit the public, (2) show no signs of becoming a socially dangerous vested interest, (3) be operated with reasonable efficiency under decent working conditions, and (4) be ready loyally to play their part in the fulfilment of the national plan. "Thus," it said, "small manufacturing and distributing concerns, businesses catering to local community needs, various forms of service and repair are examples of private enterprise which are likely to remain."[24]

In short, the approach of *Make This YOUR Canada* was much more aggressive because it shifted the onus of justification from those wishing to nationalize to those wishing to escape nationalization. Its language was also more confrontational. It declared that the basic nature of capitalism was to make profits (p. 9); that the choice was between planning by monopoly for monopoly or by people for people (p. 36); that the country's resources must be owned by the people (p. 37); that the primary cause for the breakdown of democracy, the raise of fascism, and the outbreak of war was the failure to recognize the logic of capitalist development (p. 38); that capitalism protected profit and investment, not human beings (p. 73); that robber barons, meaning oil companies, had to be prevented from gobbling up the Athabasca tar sands (p. 158).

The overall impression is that *Make This YOUR Canada* yearned more passionately for speedy and more extensive change. And it reinforced a declaration of aggressive intent by speaking in Marxist terms about the class struggle and taking over the means of production. However, in other ways, in groping toward a new definition of socialism limited to nationalizing monopolies and in being much more specific about leaving a "considerable field for private enterprise," it was more moderate. On balance, however, *Make This YOUR Canada* comes across as the more radical.

Appendix K. Chapter 17

Additional support for the view that David espoused a militant Parliamentary Marxism: David was still at Oxford when *Social Planning for Canada* came out, still talking in militant terms about the class struggle and the coming revolution and nationalizing the means of production. There, he laid his words on listeners like a lash, as in a May 1933 debate at the Oxford Union when he damned conventional morality for its ignorance, sham, and hypocrisy and, displaying his belief in historical materialism, condemned businessmen warped by the system. "Business men are people who pray on their knees on Sunday and on other people for the rest of the week. The very conditions under which we live force them to live in such an immoral way every hour of every day of their lives. . . .

"It is wrong, completely wrong, for a man who is starving to steal a loaf of bread, but the moment somebody swindles or steals £100,000 he becomes a financier and a saviour of the country. The whole body of our law is based on the conception of the protection of private property, without any consideration of the human element."[25]

He was still calling for precipitate action in August 1938, in what the press described as his maiden speech in Western Canada. Under a headline declaring "Young Ottawa Lawyer Holds Packed Audience Spell-Bound in First Speech Here," *The Vancouver Sun* reported David as saying: "Urgent times demand urgent measures. I have always marvelled at the patience and tolerance of the Canadian people. I hope it won't last too long. The whole future of civilization depends, not on centuries of slow progress, but on immediate and sweeping action by the workers and farmers of our nation. . . . We believe in giving the means of production to the people because we think it is the only way to give them back their happy and democratic way of life."[26]

And in October of the same year the *Sydney Post-Record* reported that, in a recent trip across Canada, David had found workers in "a state of hopelessness and helplessness" as a result of the concentration of wealth by capitalists. Private gain and private ownership of public property must be curtailed, he said. The report quoted David as saying that in fascist Germany and Italy people were living under "deplorable conditions. He compared this with Soviet Russia where the state pursues a policy of production for the masses instead of for the benefit of the wealthy few. He did not agree with the [Soviet] dictatorship and expressed the view that this form of government would eventually be replaced when the people could reach a more complete stage of cultural development."[27]

Three years later he was still lashing out against the capitalists. In March 1941 he gave a speech at Hobart College in Geneva, New York, condemning industrialists and privileged classes in France and Great Britain for selling out their countries by chasing profits instead of co-operating in the war effort.[28] And in June, in Vancouver, he declared that capitalist greed and monopoly interest were making the war effort ineffectual.[29]

Then came *Make This* YOUR *Canada* in 1943, his Dalhousie University speech in 1946, his interview in 1962 where he said the ultimate aim of the party should be public ownership of the means of production and distribution, and, in 1972, his Corporate Welfare Bums campaign.

This consistency, especially David's 1962 interview, contrasted with Frank Scott's views. By 1950 Scott was talking about a welfare state where "the profit motive, under proper control, is now and will be for a long time a most valuable stimulus to production."[30]

Appendix L. Chapter 18

Before 1945 David made exceptions in his opposition to Communists: David had returned from Europe in 1935 prepared to give some quarter to Communists if it was absolutely necessary for the overthrow of capitalism, or if it would significantly advance the CCF. He was haunted by the fact that warfare between the Communists and socialists had allowed Hitler to take power in Germany. Had they pooled their voting strength, they could have blocked his rise. It explains in part why, in the 1937 Ontario election campaign, David was prepared to have a CCF candidate withdraw from Toronto's St. Andrews riding and leave the field open to Joe Salsberg, a Communist running as a member of the Communist-dominated Labour Representation Association — and that earned him a resounding rebuke from J.S. Woodsworth.[31]

In part it explains why he was prepared to defend co-operating with other groups in popular-front organizations, providing it did not approach anything resembling fusion with the Communists — which was a policy approved by the CCF national convention in August 1936 in an effort to prevent splits within the CCF. David rationalized it on the basis that "the line of demarcation between non-political and political co-operation is fairly distinct."[32]

In part it explains why he and King Gordon tried, albeit without success, to promote "greater toleration of the Communists," at the August 1937 CCF convention.[33] And in part it also explains why, a week before the October 1937 election, David was urging CCFers to "participate with imagination, without fear, no matter who else may be participating," in various organizations — a stand that elated Communists.[34] Here, he was trying to keep the CCF in the centre of left-wing activity. The General Motors strike had occurred only six months before the election, and Communists already were organizing like mad in the industrial unions, while the CCF was disorganized and faltering.

After 1943 he was prepared to make exceptions in his opposition to Communists only where it would divide the party — some members made allowances for Communists because the Soviet Union was a wartime ally. For instance, in April 1944 he urged against attempts to push Pat Sullivan out as secretary-treasurer of the TLC because he was doing a good job, couldn't be replaced, and his ouster would backfire on the CCF in lack of support from unionists.[35] And in March 1944 he was prepared to give George Burt of the UAW the benefit of the doubt when Burt was accused of being a Communist lackey.[36]

After 1945 there would be no exceptions and no quarter. The party and the unions would be solidly behind him.

Appendix M. Chapter 18

David was at the centre of the drive to oust Communists from the trade unions: Ted Jolliffe, in an interview, commented that David "was constantly involved." His activities ranged from giving Charlie Millard very detailed notes on what to include in a speech and passing on to him articles published elsewhere for Millard to reproduce and distribute,[37] to setting the agenda for the National Trade Union Committee.[38] There were trade union committees at the provincial and local levels, too, and David was involved in their affairs as well. For instance, when James Russell of the Sudbury Trade Union Committee was in Ottawa, he made a point of meeting with Mosher and Conroy of the CCL and with David. The Ontario committee was established in July 1942 and was disbanded in December 1948. The committees at all levels were intended to be a liaison between the Ontario CCF and the trade union movement, and their goal was to organize support among trade unions "to neutralize the Communists' activities."[39]

David wrote pamphlets; he distributed a thirteen-page memo of unpalatable Communist quotations; he and Ted Jolliffe produced a memo outlining how the CCL union, the International Union of Electrical Radio and Machine Workers of America, could make better headway against the Communist United Electrical Workers; he sent a memo to all provincial secretaries advising them on how to confront attempts by Communists to infiltrate, and he corresponded with them on the subject; he kept up pressure on Walter

Reuther, for instance, as he reported in a 1950 memo following a meeting with him: "[Reuther's] assistant Jack Conway informed us that the Canadian District of the UAW had formally resolved at a recent meeting not to take sides in the IUE vs. UE struggle. Reuther agreed that this was not proper and that UAW should give every assistance to the struggle of the CCL and the affiliated unions concerned against the Communist-controlled unions."

And he spoke out whenever it was necessary, as at the Ontario CCF convention in October 1948 on the issue of expelling Bob Carlin from the CCF: "We are not attempting to interfere with any union; but we have a duty as a political party to state our policy: that we want to see every Communist out of any position of control of the trade unions, and they cannot use the clubs of the CCF to build Communist-controlled unions in Canada."

There are hundreds of other examples.[40]

Appendix N. Chapter 18

Big Bill Haywood and the Wobblies: The preamble to Mine Mill's constitution bore a striking resemblance to the preamble to the Wobblies' first constitution passed in 1905 and to the revised version passed a few years later.[41] A good description of Haywood, which he quoted with approval in his autobiography, was published in a conservative opposition newspaper in 1912. It reads as follows:

"Haywood does not want unions of weavers, unions of spinners, unions of loom fixers, unions of wool sorters, but he wants one comprehensive union of all textile workers, which in time will take over the textile factories, as the steel workers will take over the steel mills and the railway workers will take over the railways. Haywood interprets the class conflict literally as a war which is always on, which becomes daily more bitter and uncompromising, which can end only with the conquest of capitalist society by proletarians or wage workers, organized industry by industry.

"Haywood places no trust in trade [i.e., collective] agreements, which, according to his theory, lead merely to social peace and "put workers to sleep." Let the employer lock out his men when he pleases, and let the workmen strike when they please. He is opposed to arbitration, conciliation, compromise; to sliding scales, profit sharing, welfare work; to everything, in short, which may weaken the revolutionary force of the workers. He does not ask for the closed shop or the official recognition of the union, for he has no intention of recognizing the employer. What he desires is not a treaty of industrial peace between two high contracting parties, but merely the creation of a proletarian impulse which will eventually revolutionize society. Haywood is a man who believes in men, not as you and I believe in them, but fervently, uncompromisingly, with an obstinate faith in the universal goodwill and constancy of the workers worthy of a great religious leader. That is what makes him supremely dangerous."[42]

He was unalterably opposed to Gompers-type unions because he thought they sold out their brethren. For instance, he said, "The miners of Cripple Creek were scabs, many of them; the millmen of Colorado City were scabs, many of them. The railroads that connected them were manned by union men [belonging to a Gompers union] who were hauling scab ore to scab mills. That's craft unionism."[43]

Before long, America had enough of the Wobblies' pugnacity. Vigilante committees mushroomed against them. Their halls were attacked and destroyed. Sometimes there were gun battles killing men on both sides. In one case as late as Armistice Day, November 11, 1919, a Wobbly organizer was beaten, his genitals were ripped open, he was hanged, shot repeatedly, and dumped into a river.[44]

The downfall of the Wobblies was assured with American entry into the First World War. The IWW was the only labour organization to oppose U.S. involvement. A carnival of murder, Haywood called it. Over the next five years federal sedition acts and state acts against criminal syndicalism were used to hunt, arrest, and jail Wobblies, and the IWW became an underground organization. In 1921 Haywood skipped bail while an appeal to the U.S. Supreme Court was pending, and he left the United States for the Soviet Union. By the mid-twenties the IWW was dead — and in 1928, so was Big Bill Haywood. He died in Moscow, never having returned to the United States.

Appendix O. Chapter 18

The issue of Communist domination of Mine Mill, Local 598: The executive of the international board of Mine Mill in the United States and the executive of the national organization in Canada had a preponderance of Communists among their members. In the period between 1948 and 1959, about half of the international board was Communist, and from its inception on November 29, 1955, four of the six national board members were Communist.

However, Local 598 in Sudbury, because of its size, was the tail that wagged the dog; and even after the exodus from the CCF following Carlin's expulsion, Local 598 remained basically non-Communist. Former CCF members drifted to the Liberals or the Conservatives.

In the period 1949 to 1959, five out of thirty-seven men who served on Local 598's executive board were Communist and one was a member of an ethnic organization that was sympathetic. In 1949 there were no Communists on the board; in 1950, one; in 1951–52 there was one and one sympathizer; in 1952–53 and 1953–54 there were two and one sympathizer; in 1955–56 there was one and one sympathizer; in 1957–58 and until the board was ousted in March 1959, there were three. There were eleven board members in 1949. That increased to fourteen in 1952–53, and fifteen in 1954–55. None of the top four executive positions — president, vice-president, secretary-treasurer, and recording secretary — were held by Communists. A Communist sympathizer held one of those positions, a minor one, from 1951 through to 1956. A count of people prominent in the union from 1949 until the ouster of the Solski regime in 1959 — executive board members, committee chairmen, delegates to conferences, and members of negotiating teams who were mentioned in the local's minutes — shows that out of 113 people, twelve were Communist and four belonged to sympathetic organizations.

The issue that arises, then, is that if Communists were dominant on the international and national boards, why is it not legitimate to say that Local 598 was a Communist-dominated union? The answer is that they did not dominate Local 598.

Mine Mill, structured like the old Western Federation of Miners (WFM), was a federation of locals. The WFM began its existence in the days before telephones, before automobiles and airplanes, in many cases in areas remote from regular rail lines. Communication among locals and between locals and international headquarters was difficult at best and impossible more times than not. So WFM locals had a great deal of autonomy. They had to: it was the only way local problems could be confronted. If locals waited for word or assistance from international headquarters, nothing would ever get done.

Consequently, the WFM developed a horizontal structure instead of the hierarchical structure of most international unions. The same was true of Mine Mill. In Sudbury the local signed collective agreements, not the national or international. The local held the purse strings. Dues were paid to and held by it, and it doled out funds to the national and international offices, which is the reverse of the normal situation. Neither the national nor the international had power to override decisions by the local.

The consequence of this is seen in Local 598's first strike in 1958. The national executive was dead set against the strike, arguing that it would be disastrous — as it was. But it was unable to prevent the local from striking. Again, after the Solski executive was ousted in 1959, the national executive, still with four out of six members who were Communist, tried to exert control over the local's new executive, only to fail abysmally. The local rebuffed it and refused to forward money collected from dues. When the national tried to place the local under trusteeship, the local fought back and the courts ruled the trusteeship invalid.

Solski bristles when the question of Communist domination arises. "It's a lot of crap," he says. "I was the president of the biggest local in Canada — 18,000 members — and the certification was with the local, not the international. I could tell the international president to go to hell if I wanted to and if I could convince my members to back me up. For somebody to tell me that I was dominated by one political party or another was a whole lot of nonsense."

Ray Stevenson was the member of the national executive for Eastern Canada. He was then, and still is, a Communist. The only basic right the national and international executives had was the right to persuade. In the 1958 strike, "We couldn't stop them. . . . We were united pretty well on the national board. . . . I went to Solski myself and laid it on the line. I said [in an incredulous tone], 'What're you doin'?' . . . There was a massive buildup of nickel stockpiled in the States. It was the last time that we should be out [on strike]. . . . We had the right as the national executive to go over the heads of the 598 executive and go to the membership and say, 'Look, this is a mistake and you better reconsider the whole thing.' Why didn't we? Probably because we lacked the guts, to be frank about it."

If the national executive had gone to the membership, it would have risked a serious split in the union. That was what deterred the national board, he said.

The campaign in the press against Mine Mill was vitriolic. "Ontario Reds Recruit 7-Year Olds," blared a headline in *The Telegram* in December 1959. The story written by Frank Drea in breathless anxiety, quoting an anonymous source who "feared for the safety of his wife and himself," declared that

"Communism could destroy Canada. Communists gained control of an entire Ontario community and turned it to their captive city. They recruited children from the tender age of seven years [They] use anything — women, liquor, blackmail, hate and fear to get and keep members."[45]

The Ontario community was Sudbury, "the captive city that has become the nerve centre and lifeblood of the [Communist] party in North America." It was the lead story in a series that went on in the same sottish vein for six days. Drea later became public relations director for the Steelworkers and, later still, a Tory cabinet minister under Ontario premier Bill Davis.

In Timmins in March 1948 when the issue of the deportation of Communist organizers was being debated, a front-page editorial[46] referred to them as "lice infesting the labor movement," and then said, "Have you got a kid going to school? Well, when you go home tonight get his or her geography book and open it at the map of Canada. Take a good, long look at the map. You will see that if and when the next war occurs — and it is as certain as tomorrow's sunrise that it will — this section of Canada is the most strategically important piece of land on the North American continent. . . . Why do you think the concentration of Communists here is greater than anywhere else in the country?"

Other publications were less bombastic but equally adamant. None of the main-line press, with the exception of labour reporter Wilfred List writing in *The Globe and Mail* and perhaps one or two others, strove for objectivity.

The 1958 strike at INCO, the first since Mine Mill had organized the company, set the stage for defeat of the left-leaning Solski executive. The three-month strike was a total defeat for Mine Mill and resulted in a return to a forty-hour week and wage increases of only 1 percent in the first year, 2 percent in the second, and 3 percent in the third.

One of the theories behind the strike was that it would unify the workers. In fact, it had just the opposite effect. It was so unsuccessful it widened divisions instead of narrowing them. On top of that, the strike raised serious questions about the financial competence of the Solski board — not that members were using funds illicitly but that they had little expertise and confused priorities. And then there was bitterness, says Elmer McVey, because of apparent favouritism in distributing strike relief to board supporters.

It was fertile ground for Alexander Boudreau to run a union leadership training course at the University of Sudbury, a Jesuit university. He was hired in the fall of 1958 and began his course immediately with the support of the local clergy and Most Reverend Alexander Carter, bishop for the Archdiocese of Sault Ste Marie.[47] Boudreau dealt with industrial relations, the rules of parliamentary procedure, organizational techniques, economics, and the benefits of co-operative enterprise over monopoly capitalism. He also lectured on communism, but his lectures were simplistic in the extreme. He taught that:

"The philosophy of communism is based on hate. Hate and happiness are opposites, so you cannot hate and be happy.[48]

"Communism is an evil tree.[49]

"The Communist Party attempts to pass itself off as a bona-fide, political party like the Liberals and Conservatives. It is nothing of the sort. It is an active, militant, Soviet-dominated secret army of the hard trained troops of the Communist Conspiracy — open Party Members, undercover members, dupes and fellow travellers.[50]

"USSR *Illustrated News* and *Soviet Union Today* . . . are propaganda . . . largely financed through the collection of 'prepaid duty' on the food and clothing in the gift parcels sent by New Canadians to their unfortunate relations behind the Iron Curtain.[51]

"A complete denial of the very existence of God is the basic principle of Communism.[52]

"[Communists] have no moral scruples. Being atheists, they recognize no authority but the Party. In Communist 'NEWSPEAK' we learn that:

> Right is anything that is good for the Party
> Wrong is anything that is bad for the Party
> Truth is anything that helps the Party
> A lie is anything that hurts the Party."[53]

Boudreau made no bones about what his objectives were. In a fund-raising circular dated October 13, 1959, and addressed to "Dear Fellow Catholic Citizens," he wrote: "Educated Catholic Citizens have the reputation of being in the forefront in the defence of our religious principles and our democratic way of life. . . . It is an established fact that subversive elements are presently at work, and are endeavoring [sic] to gain control of an important sector of our economy and our social life. They are few in number, but well organized, WELL FINANCED and well known. It is imperative that we secure sufficient funds to counteract their iniquitous campaign."[54]

In a fund-raising letter to the Fatima Circle or the Daughters of Isabella in Capreol, Boudreau's assistant, Julien Pezet, wrote: "As you undoubtedly know, we are presently conducting an all-out war in Sudbury against Communist forces that are controlling the Union of Mine-Mill and Smelter Workers. . . . Ever since the campaign started, the University of Sudbury through its Extension Department and particularly through Doctor Alexander Boudreau, has been emphatically denouncing these Communist forces and attempting to educate the Sudbury population on the true nature of Communism."[55]

Boudreau obtained materials for union leadership training from the Steelworkers[56] and with the skills and outlook he taught, course members organized a campaign against the Solski executive and won the March 1959 election by the slim margin of fifteen votes.

A majority of the new Local 598 executive were Boudreau alumni. Eight months later, in November 1959, another election was held. Boudreau described it publicly as "a last ditch fight between Christianity and Communism,"[57] and again the Boudreau alumni were successful. A major factor in the election battle was the three-day Catholic Social Life Conference held in Sudbury one month before the election. Rev. Brian Hogan, in a 1985 academic paper defending the role of Boudreau and the Church, commented that "The Social Life conference was the largest gathering of Catholics ever witnessed in Sudbury. It drew bishops, priests, religious and hundreds of the most involved Catholic journalists and social activists across the country. For opening ceremonies in the Sudbury arena some 5,000 men and women gathered to welcome the 1,496 official delegates. . . . Inevitably, delegates and hosts reflected on the labour events of the past year and the forthcoming elections."[58]

Don Gillis, who had replaced Solski as president of Local 598, attended the next Social Life conference in Halifax two years later and, according to

The Sudbury Daily Star, ". . . not only paid tacit tribute to the support granted him by the previous conference held in Sudbury in 1959, but outlined the support he had received from the Roman Catholic Church. In his address he stated: 'As a result of a three-year course sponsored by the Roman Catholic Church in Sudbury, a group came in and ousted the Communist group from the Local.'"[59]

After the ouster Boudreau planned strategies with Canadian Labour Congress officials for keeping the new executive in power. "Mine Mill must be destroyed and disappear from the map of Canada," he wrote to CLC President Claude Jodoin. "This can be achieved only by depriving the Commies of their milch-cow, Local 598 of Sudbury."[60]

In his article, Brian Hogan denies vigorously that the university and the Church "deliberately introduced [Boudreau into Sudbury] to attack the incumbent leadership of the Mine Mill union." That may be so. But in that case, Reverend Hogan was asking the wrong question. The proper question was: Did the university and the Church know what Boudreau was doing and did they support him morally and materially? The answer to that can only be yes.

Appendix P. Chapter 20

Creation of the New Democratic Party: David's resolution, passed by the 1936 convention, called on CCF members "to associate themselves actively with the organization of their trade, industry or profession," and on unionists "to associate themselves in active membership of the CCF." He said, "I have become more and more convinced about the need for a Trade Union base for the party even though there are undoubtedly many disadvantages in a Trade Union political set up."[61]

Exactly who came up with the idea of creating a new party is a matter of gentlemanly disagreement. Some say David, some Stanley Knowles, some Eamon Park of the Steelworkers.[62] What's probably closer to the truth is that the new party idea evolved over time.

Murray Cotterill, who was publicity director of the Steelworkers, says that all through the mid-fifties the realization was growing in the labour movement — on the CCL side in particular but equally among the much smaller band of CCFers in the TLC — that there had to be a change in the party. It was obvious that the party was stalled.[63] As for David, certainly all his life he was convinced that labour should be persuaded to join the party — and that conviction went back to the Bund, which held that only if a party represented economic interests would it have the discipline for honing its policies and the finances for ensuring its survival.

What is clear is that the name "New Party" was hit upon at one of the Steelworkers' daily coffee klatches in the late fall of 1954. The question came up, what should the union of labour and CCF be called? "And the suggestion was made that from a PR point of view, what's better than 'New'? That's as simple as it was," Cotterill says. "Everybody sort of agreed." And who came up with the suggestion? "It was made by the public relations people. To wit, myself and one or two assistants." The name stuck until the founding convention changed it to "New Democratic Party."

It was then left to Eamon Park and Charlie Millard to take up the suggestion with other members of the party, Cotterill says.[64] The significance of promoting a name was that it underlined the determination of the leaders of some of the largest CCL unions to proceed toward formation of the new party.

The next event was a meeting held at Charlie Millard's home in Thistletown, just outside Toronto. David attended. So did Eamon Park, who in addition to being a Steelworker official was president of the Ontario wing of the party, Fred Young, Ken Bryden, provincial secretary of the Ontario wing, and several others whom Bryden can no longer remember. It was just before Christmas, 1954, and it was there, says Bryden, "where it really came to a head" and a strategy was developed to avoid alienating the TLC unions, which had resisted involvement with the CCF. The strategy required the CCF never to be seen to be pushing. Therefore, after the CCL and TLC were merged, the new congress would have to make all the advances. That meant (1) the issue of political affiliation would not be brought up at the CCL-TLC merger and (2) it would be left to the Canadian Labour Congress to invite the CCF to join in forming the new party.

In both steps of the strategy, David played a key role. According to Bryden, "The TLC was following the old Gompers policy . . . of political neutrality. Most of us in the CCF and indeed the leadership of the CCL did not want to ram the CCL policy down the throat of the merged congress," even though that's what about 40 percent of the secondary leadership wanted to do. "We had a lot of trouble getting those guys [to hold off] and David was fairly critical there. And also in getting the rest of the TLC to accept [political involvement]."

The following July, as the two labour organizations were gearing up for their merger, David reached an informal agreement with Claude Jodoin, who was to become the head of the new CLC, that it would be wise to steer clear of formal commitments at the CLC founding convention in April 1956, but within two years the CLC would move toward a political commitment "either through the CCF or through some broader political alignment." Thus, says Gad Horowitz in his book *Canadian Labour in Politics*, "The president-delegate of the new Congress had committed himself to a policy of positive political action by the CLC following the merger convention."[65]

Over the next six years everything fell into place — from setting up a joint committee to discuss the union to the founding convention in July 1961 — and throughout, the strategy was followed of having the CLC take the initial step and then invite the CCF to participate.

One of David's great victories was to persuade Frank Hall not to oppose the marriage. Hall was the best-known labour leader in Canada next to Claude Jodoin, and was Canadian head of the Brotherhood of Railway Clerks and a general vice-president of the CLC. He had been a strong Liberal and a strong supporter of TLC neutrality. Had he spoken out against the union at any stage — from the CCL-TLC merger to the NDP founding convention — he could have posed enormous problems. But he had come to trust David while David was working as a labour lawyer. "David [got] Frank Hall on side — who then got the other guys on side," says Ken Bryden. "And it was only because David had done such good work in negotiations with the railways. David was absolutely critical in getting this thing accepted without a great deal of contention at the founding convention."

David managed to persuade Hall to become a member of the joint committee that prepared the way for union, and even got Hall to sit on the platform at the founding convention — which was significant even though Hall said nothing.[66]

For all his efforts, once again David was hailed as "chief architect" of the party, this time by the historian Desmond Morton.[67]

Appendix Q. Chapter 21

The fraud of John Brown: Brown established two key non-profit companies: Brown Camps Residential and Day Schools, incorporated in 1967, and Browndale (Ontario), incorporated in 1972. Brown Camps had an Ontario division that ran treatment centres in Toronto and paid management fees to Browndale International Inc., a private company controlled by Brown. In December 1972 Browndale (Ontario) took over the Ontario operations of Brown Camps and continued paying management fees to Browndale International Inc.

The Ontario Ministry of Health paid Brown Camps and then Browndale to run treatment homes in Toronto. Brown pleaded guilty to fraudulently overcharging the Ministry of Health to cover so-called salaries and consulting fees paid to Brown's private company, Browndale International Inc.

Mr. Justice R.E. Holland of the Ontario Supreme Court calculated that the overcharging amounted to $564,574.[68] He also listed the amount of other fraudulent overcharges that inflated Browndale's bills paid by the ministry: $175,867 for a fictitious affiliation fee submitted directly to the ministry; $100,000 in excessive rent paid by Browndale to Brown Camps for Muskoka Lodge in 1974; and $135,174 in excessive payments for a property management fee.

Although it wasn't mentioned in Mr. Justice Holland's sentencing judgment, during the time Brown was overcharging the ministry he was still providing care for disturbed children at a much lower cost than that of government-operated institutions. Health Minister Frank Miller said the cost of caring for a child at the government centre in Thistletown was "over $100 a day" at a time when Browndale "is receiving $6.5-million from the Health Ministry to care for 300 children — a cost of $59.25 a child a day."[69]

Appendix R. Chapter 21

Stephen's relationship with John Brown and Brown Camps: Michele met Brown during the summer of 1964 while writing a feature article for *The Globe and Mail* about treatment for disturbed youngsters. Brown was executive director of the Warrendale treatment centre, and she was impressed with what he was doing. Stephen became interested and soon the two families became close — so close, in fact, that in June 1967 Stephen and Michele moved to Newmarket, directly across the street from the Browns. In August 1966 Brown resigned from Warrendale saying he was pressured into leaving because he intended to run for the NDP in the next provincial election. Most of the staff members resigned in sympathy and Brown — and they—left to establish Brown Camps.

Janet worked for six years as a staff counsellor at Brown Camps. At Stephen's suggestion, she applied and was hired during the summer of 1967 after she had returned from Israel. Brown's treatment methods were highly controversial and in an interview Janet described his approach:

"Once you get adolescents [who're disturbed], they're bigger, they're stronger, they're destructive. So John was desperate to get a mix of ages in both sexes [in group homes. And that was] one of the things that got him into a lot of trouble. [People thought that if you] put a teen-aged girl and boy together and they'll screw around rather than treat each other like brothers and sisters.

"In fact, they wouldn't think of going to bed with each other. They never did. In all the years I worked there . . . there wasn't a single pregnancy. Hundreds and hundreds of children.

"He also believed you should physically restrain kids so they don't hurt themselves, damage their surroundings, hit you. But they need to know that you care about them, and the way you do that is if you're physically close to them and you are controlling their aggression. Well, as soon as people saw an older man holding a fourteen- or fifteen-year-old girl, what next? They're going to screw in bed, right?

"Then there was the fact that if a kid at the age of thirteen or fourteen . . . felt like a bottle because he or she felt quite infantile, [he or she] got a bottle. Big kids. . . . Of course they didn't stay on the bottle very long. It was just a phase. It was a caring, growing kind of thing.

"I'm not sure John would do all those things again. You know, you learn. You've got to change and think about what you're doing. But at the time it was incredibly radical."

Stephen resigned as national director at the end of June 1968,[70] relations became strained by December 1969, and in May 1970 Stephen and Michele moved back to Scarborough. Stephen disengaged himself completely from Brown Camps a couple of months later.

"Stephen defended Brown politically," Gerry Charney says. "He worked for him in the field. He negotiated agreements in British Columbia and Saskatchewan. We tried to do a deal in Manitoba that never happened. We went down to the States."

In a separate interview Stephen adds, "I . . . persuaded Bramalea to sell houses to Brown Camps at lower values. My father got involved in negotiations with Muskoka Lodge for Brown Camps. I spoke to Greenwin and . . . Scarborough Homes Ltd., or whatever it is, and we managed to get, where it had never been done before in residential suburban areas, children into group homes doing exactly what, ten, fifteen years later became fashionable.

"[However,] there was always something unsettling. I never had anything to do with it. It wasn't part of my work. It just made me uneasy."

One of the main reasons there was such a hullabaloo about Brown Camps, says Charney, was that it was establishing group homes in residential neighbourhoods and homeowners didn't like it.

The uneasiness with Brown came to a head one evening when Brown tried to float an idea with Stephen and Charney. He was desperately anxious to buy more houses that he could turn into group homes, and was talking about a scheme whereby he would buy a house and enter into a lease with Brown Camps for an exorbitant rate. Since the high lease rate would increase the value of the house, he would then sell the house for an inflated price and

use the profit to buy more houses. He wouldn't have to worry about continuing to operate the group home in the house that was sold because he
could collect from the provincial government to cover the high lease payments.

"I remember vividly, to this day," says Stephen, "Gerry saying, 'John, if
you continue this way, you'll end up in jail.'"

Brown's answer was that he didn't need a lawyer to tell him he was going
to jail; he needed a lawyer to tell him how to stay out of jail.

Charney's reply was for Brown to get himself another lawyer.

Given this incident, why, in the years that followed, did Stephen continue
to support Brown's treatment programs? His answer is that Brown was so
volatile, neither he nor anyone else ever knew what Brown was doing financially and the treatment program was so essential that it couldn't be
abandoned.

"You never knew whether [what he was saying] was bluff, braggadocio,
or intention. I mean, the guy changed his mind from Wednesday to Thursday.
He had a constantly shifting universe of dreams, ambitions, hopes, expectations, concrete actions. You would never, never keep up at any given moment
in time with what he would do. And [the idea he floated past] Charney,
he might have abandoned the next day.

"[After that meeting] I had absolutely no contact and I had absolutely no
reason to believe he was going to get involved in actual wrongdoing for which
he could be prosecuted. I didn't think of it. . . .

"This is a man for whom life churned with such an intense volatility all
the time, twenty-four hours a day, that it was really impossible [for you to
keep up]. . . . One day there might be an educational foundation and the
next day there would be another treatment centre and the next day there'd
be a whole new vision of helping staff which would preoccupy it for one or
two months and then the next day, 'I'm getting rid of everything and I'm
going to teach school. No! I'm going to live in the South with my brother
and work at his treatment centre in Kentucky.'. . .

"One of the things I feel fairly good about in life is that I have always been
intensely scrupulous. . . . I think it is fair to say that if I had ever had evidence
of, or thought that it was more than a momentary craziness of a given assertion, I would have said something because I would have felt that I had an
obligation. But after I left [in 1970] I never had enough of a sense of what
was going on that I would have known. I was never privy to anything. Never
privy to any details. . . .

"Despite what is said, so much was checked by government. And one
forgets, but they were dealing with umpteen children's aid societies, all of
whom were in regularly and who satisfied themselves that the money was
being well spent and being well used. So I didn't feel as though I had an obligation to expose a potential bandit. . . . Everybody knew that something was
odd, but there was nothing demonstrable. And that's why I was better out
than in, because it was increasingly uncomfortable. . . .

"It was extremely hard to sort out what was an honest allegation and what
was motivated from some base purpose. . . . I was trying to defend the program because the program . . . if it were going to collapse, would be a tragedy.
These were the most disturbed kids in the province. [Brown Camps] was the
only place that would take them. These were kids who were destined

for adult wards in psychiatric hospitals if it weren't for Browndale or Brown Camps. It was that serious."

•NOTES TO APPENDICES•

1. Walsh, *Russia and the Soviet Union*, p. 187.
2. *Russia and the Soviet Union*, p. 289, and Moorehead, *Russian Revolution*, p. 15.
3. Meltzer, *World of Our Fathers*, p. 157.
4. Brym, *The Jewish Intelligentsia*, p. 9.
5. *The Jewish Intelligentsia*, p. 10.
6. Weinryb, *The Jews of Poland*, p. 115.
7. Vetulani, *The Jews in Medieval Poland*, p. 278. Vetulani specifies that his figure of 500,000 is for "the whole Polish–Lithuanian Commonwealth . . . which is about five per cent of the total population."
8. For a description and history of the Khazars, see Koestler, *The Thirteenth Tribe*.
9. The size of the exodus is a matter of some sensitivity because the Khazars were not descendants of the ancient Hebrews. They were of Turkish stock and the king, his court, and the ruling military class converted to Judaism around A.D. 740. If, as some historians claim, Khazars formed the bulk of the Jewish settlers in Eastern Europe several centuries later, it means that a majority of Jews in the world can trace some part of their ancestry to them. See *The Thirteenth Tribe*, p.16, which quotes A.N. Poliak of Tel Aviv University in *Khazaria — The History of a Jewish Kingdom in Europe* (in Hebrew).
10. *The Thirteenth Tribe*, pp. 15, 125.
11. Arthur Meighen, then acting federal justice minister and minister of the interior, was so frightened of "Bolshevism" that a month before the Winnipeg General Strike began, he and other cabinet ministers cabled Prime Minister Robert Borden in Versailles to say that "Bolshevism" and "socialism" were "rampant" in Vancouver, Calgary, and Winnipeg. The cable urged Borden to have the British station a cruiser off Vancouver to provide "a steadying influence." (Quoted in Penner, *Winnipeg 1919*, p. xvii.)

12. "Alien scum" is quoted in McNaught, *A Prophet in Politics*, p. 110.
13. The 50,000 members came mainly from Northern Ontario and the West, with a sprinkling of locals in Central and Eastern Canada and the United States. However, by 1923 OBU had been reduced to about 5,000 members through internal dissension and attacks from the Trades and Labour Congress, employers, and the federal government. It survived, mainly in Winnipeg, until 1957, when it merged with the Canadian Labour Congress.
14. Penner, *Canadian Communism*, p. 49.
15. McNaught, *A Prophet in Politics*, p. 104. However, since McNaught points to Smith's Communist beliefs as the reason for accepting his view, McNaught's reliance on that view may be suspect. Penner in *Canadian Communists* points out that the attitude of Communists to OBU was contradictory. Could it have been that it was against the interests of the Communists to describe the strike in terms that might have allocated a proper revolutionary zeal to OBU? A better reason for accepting Smith's version is that OBU was not in control of the strike. It had barely come into being and was not in a dominant position. Russell was the only OBU official on the fifteen-member Central Strike Committee and other strike leaders were not trying to overthrow capitalism. In fact, they did not have a cohesive philosophy. They ranged from "Liberals and Conservatives to single taxers, to radical and revolutionary socialists." (Penner, *Winnipeg 1919*, p. xv.) They were simply trying to win the right to collective bargaining.
16. See also Penner, *Canadian Communism*, p. 119.
17. Buck, *Yours in the Struggle*, pp. 214–41.
18. *Yours in the Struggle*, p. 221.
19. Avakumovic, *The Communist Party in Canada*, p. 90, and Betcherman, *The Little Band*, pp. 213–15.
20. LSR, *Social Planning for Canada*, p. 306.
21. *Social Planning for Canada*, pp. 175, 262.
22. Lewis and Scott, *Make This YOUR Canada*, pp. 162–63.
23. *Make This YOUR Canada*, pp. 154, 155. When *Social Planning for Canada* talked of nationalizing, it called for taking over "certain key functions and basic industries which are of strategic importance" (p. 243).
24. *Make This YOUR Canada*, p. 163.
25. *Oxford Mail*, May 25, 1933.
26. *The Vancouver Sun*, Aug. 8, 1938.
27. *Sydney Post-Record*, Oct. 17, 1938.
28. *The Geneva Daily Times*, March 17, 1941.
29. *The Vancouver Daily Province*, June 26, 1941.
30. Scott, *A New Endeavour*, p. 94. The remark was made in his speech as national chairman to the 1950 CCF convention in Vancouver.
31. "It strikes me," Woodsworth wrote to David, "that . . . you are going beyond what might be expected of the National Secretary of the CCF." PAC, MG 28, IV-I, Vol. 99, file: Lewis 1936–39, letter dated Sept. 27, 1937. David responded with a three-page letter that was uncompromising and unrepentant: "As I see it, the future of the CCF in Ontario depends on whether or not we shall succeed in winning the support and

goodwill of the trade unions. So far we have not won it. I am therefore convinced that any action of ours which is likely to hinder our progress in this direction is extremely harmful. It is my profound conviction that running [the CCF candidate] is a mistake from which the CCF in Ontario is likely to suffer from for some considerable time." (PAC, file: Lewis 1936–39, letter dated Sept. 29, 1937.)

Woodsworth retorted tartly that the Tory candidate also was pro-labour. Did this mean that the CCF should not oppose the Conservatives? (Letter dated Oct. 2, 1937, quoted in Young, *The Anatomy of a Party*, p. 168.)

Forty years later, in his *Memoirs* (p. 108), David would recant in a terse, two-line statement: "Later experience taught me that I was wrong in being taken in by a slick manoeuvre engineered by the Communists."

32. Avakumovic, *The Communist Party in Canada*, p. 105.
33. Young, *The Anatomy of a Party*, p. 79.
34. Avakumovic, *The Communist Party in Canada*, p. 106.
35. PAC, MG 28, IV–I, Vol. 59, file: Ontario Trade Union Relations, 1937–53, letter from D. Lewis to Eamon Park, chairman of the CCF Trade Union Committee, April 21, 1944.
36. Letter from D. Lewis to Ted Jolliffe dated March 9, 1944, quoted in Horowitz, *Canadian Labour in Politics*, p. 109, n. 83.
37. PAC, MG 28, IV–I, Vol. 102, file: C.H. Millard, letters from Lewis to Millard, Dec. 30, 1940, and April 15, 1940.
38. For instance, for the meeting of the CCF National Trade Union Committee on April 10, 11, 1948, David presented a detailed agenda for discussion, in York University Archives, Oliver Hodges Collection, Box 74, file: Minutes, Bulletins, Etc.
39. For the history of the Ontario TUC, see a memo by Larry Sefton prepared for a meeting on Sept. 13, 1947, in York University Archives, Oliver Hodges Collection, Box 74, file: Ontario CCF Labour Committee. For the demise of the Ontario committee, see letter from Hodges to Conroy, Dec. 10, 1948, in Oliver Hodges Collection, Box 75, file: To Be Entered and Filed in Letter Book. For liaison responsibilities, see letter from Hodges to H.G. Rhodes, Director of Organization, CCL, March 30, 1948, in Oliver Hodges Collection: Box 72. For its goal, see letter from Hodges to secretary of the British Labour Party, June 16, 1948, in Oliver Hodges Collection: Box 70. For James Russell, see his daily work sheet for April 5, 1948, where he noted, "Spent all day in Ottawa met with Conroy and Mosher also David Lewis," in Oliver Hodges Collection: Box 77.
40. For the pamphlet *Political Parties in Canada*, see Oliver Hodges Collection, Box 74, file: Minutes, Bulletins, Etc. For the memo of unpalatable quotations, see letter from Lewis to Hodges, April 6, 1948, in Oliver Hodges Collection, Box 73, file: Material for Use in Bulletins and Letters. For the IUE/UE memo, see Abella, *Nationalism, Communism, and Canadian Labour*, p. 161. For the memo to provincial secretaries, see memo dated Feb. 27, 1948, in PAC, MG 28, IV–I, Vol. 362, file: Communists 1938–51. For correspondence to provincial secretaries, see Zakuta, *A Protest Movement Becalmed*, pp. 78–79. For the memo on

Reuther, see memo dated May 12, 1950, in PAC, MG 28, I 268, Vol. 14, file: Jolliffe, Lewis & Osler. For remarks at convention, see Minutes of CCF (Ontario Section), 15th Annual Provincial Convention, Oct. 7–9, 1948, in Oliver Hodges Collection, Box 74, file: Minutes, Bulletins, Etc.

41. For the preamble to the Wobblies' first constitution, see Haywood, *The Autobiography of Big Bill Haywood*, p. 185; for the preamble to the revised version, see p. 245. The version quoted from the handbook notes that the constitution was "adopted by the 41st convention, Sept. 1944 and Referendum vote." See Oliver Hodges Collection, Box 74, file: Sudbury.

42. *The Autobiography of Big Bill Haywood*, p. 248.

43. *The Autobiography of Big Bill Haywood*, p. 154.

44. *The Autobiography of Big Bill Haywood*, pp. 355–356.

45. The series in *The Telegram* began as the flare headline, Dec. 21, 1959.

46. *The Porcupine Advance*, March 18, 1948. The editorial was signed by Don Delaplante, editor.

47. Hogan, "Hard Rock and Hard Decisions," pp. 22ff. In an interview with Hogan, Boudreau said that when he was trying to set up the training course he approached local pastors for assistance, but "they were not overly enthusiastic because they were afraid to come out openly. So I went to North Bay and talked to Bishop Carter — he knew everything about the situation, by the way — so I told him what I intended to do. He said he would help in any way he could. . . ."

48. From a student's notes, quoted in "Hard Rock and Hard Decisions," p. 23.

49. Ontario Archives, Mike Solski Collection, MU 8276, Series 17, Box 71, file: Workers' Education Association, Laurentian University Extension Department (University of Sudbury), file 1, Lesson 1.

50. Mike Solski Collection, file 1, Lesson 8.

51. Mike Solski Collection, file 1, Lesson 8.

52. Mike Solski Collection, file 1, Lesson 1.

53. Mike Solski Collection, file 1, Lesson 1.

54. Mike Solski Collection, file 1, letter from Boudreau to Fellow Catholic Citizens, Oct. 13, 1959.

55. Mike Solski Collection, file 1, letter from Pezet to Mrs. Stan Martin, Fatima Circle, Nov. 12, 1959.

56. Mike Solski Collection, file 2, letters between Boudreau and Gower Markle, Director of Education and Welfare, United Steelworkers of America, Toronto: letters from Markle, Jan. 20, Feb. 9, 1959; letters from Boudreau, Feb. 6, 18, 1959.

57. Lang, *A Lion in a Den of Daniels*, p. 255, quoting *The Sudbury Daily Star*, Oct. 23, 1959.

58. Hogan, "Hard Rock and Hard Decisions," p. 27.

59. Gillis is quoted by Hogan: "Hard Rock and Hard Decisions," p. 28.

60. Mike Solski Collection, file 2, letters from Boudreau to CLC President Claude Jodoin, April 15, June 5, 1959; letters to CLC Secretary-Treasurer Donald MacDonald, March 15, 1959, to June 5, 1959.

61. Young, *The Anatomy of a Party*, p. 77, 78.

62. See Azoulay, "The Politics of Pragmatism," p. 15. See also McLeod and McLeod, *Tommy Douglas*, p. 206, where Tom H. McLeod, a former deputy treasurer of Saskatchewan under Douglas, and his son say, "To a great extent the party is the work of David Lewis."

63. Cotterill dates his dissatisfaction by reference to the way things were going in the party in 1951 when he resigned as a director of the Political Action Committee (PAC) of the CCL. "That was the time that Pat Conroy also resigned [at the convention held Sept. 17–21, 1951]. I had frankly reached the parting of the ways with many of the party people who I felt were so insistent on a rather doctrinaire educate-the-masses approach that it was getting in the way of all the people in the unions who wanted to do things politically. And since I was a PAC director and I happened to agree with the union people, I finally ended up quitting."

64. Ken Bryden, who was CCF provincial secretary for Ontario at the time, says that it was Eamon Park who came up not only with the name but with the idea of the New Party at the coffee klatch. But Bryden wasn't there for that particular coffee klatch and Cotterill was. So Cotterill's recollection is probably the more reliable.

65. Horowitz, *Canadian Labour in Politics*, p. 168.

66. *Canadian Labour in Politics*, p. 249.

67. Morton, *The New Democrats*, p. 28.

68. Mr. Justice Holland's sentence was rendered Nov. 21, 1979. It is not reported in legal publications, but a transcript is available from B.R. Crockett, CSR, RPR, Supreme Court reporter at the office for the court reporters in Toronto. The judgment was reported by *The Globe and Mail* on Nov. 22, 1979.

69. *The Globe and Mail*, June 18, 1974.

70. *The Globe and Mail*, June 28, 1968.

• E N D N O T E S •

INTRODUCTION

1. Lenin, *Collected Works*, 24: 85, and 28: 108.

2. Peretz, *Collected Stories*, p. 34.

CHAPTER 1

1. Chamberlin, *The Russian Revolution*, II: 304ff. (hereafter cited as *Revolution*).

2. The forces were as follows: the British at Murmansk and Archangel in the Arctic and in the oil-rich Trans-Caucasus between the Black and Caspian seas; the French in the Crimea and neighbouring areas of Ukraine; the Czecho-Slovaks, conscripted by the Austrians and stranded in the Russian interior, who captured the Trans-Siberian Railroad all the way from Vladivostok on the Sea of Japan to about 1,000 kilometres east of Moscow, and the British, Americans, French, and Japanese who helped them guard the captured rail lines; and the Canadians at Archangel with the British and stationed in Vladivostok where they were never called into action. (Nicholson, *The Canadian Expeditionary Force*, pp. 510–23.)

3. Chamberlin, *Revolution*, II: 291.

4. *Revolution*, II: 291.

5. *Revolution*, II: 304.

6. Stalin is quoted in Davies, *White Eagle, Red Star*, p. 130.

7. Lewis, *The Good Fight*, p. 7 (hereafter cited as *Memoirs*).

8. Description of Svisloch from endpaper map in *Svisloch, Second Book*.

9. Recollection of the Bolsheviks singing the Internationale is from Kayleh Ain in "In Memory of the Jewish Community in Svisloch."

10. Chamberlin, *Revolution*, II: 309.

11. Account of Maishe's imprisonment and release is from Lewis, *Memoirs*, p. 10, and from Doris Lewis Andras.

12. Lenin is quoted in Watt, *Bitter Glory*, p. 134, and in Chamberlin, *Revolution*, II: 306.

13. Hiding of Maishe by Dr. Bittner recalled by Doris Andras.

CHAPTER 2

1. In the first ten years of the reign of Catherine the Great (1762–96) there had been forty major uprisings, including the greatest of them all led by the Cossack Emilian Pugachev who, in the years 1772–74 rallied 25,000 peasants to his banner and was finally defeated only because Catherine recalled Suvorov, Russia's greatest general then or since, from a war with Turkey. Suvorov captured Pugachev and he was executed in 1775.
   During the short reign of Catherine's son Paul (1796–1801), there were 278 peasant disturbances. Under Nicholas I (1826–55) uprisings steadily increased. In the period 1826–34 there were 148; in the period 1835–44 there were 216; and from 1845–55 there were 348.

2. There were 326 strikes from 1870–79 and 446 from 1880–85. The first trade union, called the South Russian Workers' Union, was formed in Odessa in 1875 and the second, the Northern Union of Russian Workers, was founded in St. Petersburg in 1878. Despite continuing repression, the number of strikes kept increasing through the last half of the 1880s and the 1890s. (Salisbury, *Black Night, White Snow*, p. 7, and Walsh, *Russia and the Soviet Union*, p. 301.)

3. The Tsars had a council of ministers, and through the 1800s some of those ministers were very accomplished. But all ministers reported to the Tsar personally and the power of decision was his alone.

4. Wolfe, *Three Who Made a Revolution*, p. 33.

5. Shmarya Levin's Svisloch was located between Minsk and Bobruysk. "On one side ran the Berezina [River] and on the other, parallel with it, the Svislo," says Levin at the outset of his memoirs, *Forward from Exile*. The English translation of the town's name is also given as Svislovitch and Swislotsch. (Cohen, *Shtetl Finder Gazeteer*, p. 100.) The additional English spellings given for Maishe's Svisloch are Svislotch, Sislevitch, Svislovitz, and Swislocz.

6. Levin, *Forward from Exile*, p. 11.

7. Ain, "Swislocz," pp. 86ff.

8. "In the 1830s a conflagration destroyed the stores. . . . In the course of the 19th century the town burned to the ground twice. In 1910 half the town was destroyed by fire again" ("Swislocz", p. 87).

9. "Swislocz," pp. 101ff.

CHAPTER 3

1. Descriptions of ceremonies are from Zborowski and Herzog, *Life Is with People*, pp. 315ff.; Rabbi Donin, *To Be a Jew*, pp. 271ff.; Trepp, *The Complete Book of Jewish Observance*, pp. 214ff.; Gottlieb, *A Jewish Child Is Born*, p. 41ff.; Ain, "Svisloch", p. 99; and from discussions with Doris Andras and Emanuel Goldberg, who was born and raised in Svisloch, escaped to the Soviet Union when the Nazis invaded, returned to Svisloch in 1946, and immediately immigrated to Toronto.

2. The word "pale" is derived from the Latin *palus*, meaning "stake," and, according to the *Encyclopaedia Britannica*, refers to a district separated from its environs by definite boundaries or distinguished by a different legal and administrative system. In addition to the Pale of Settlement in Russia, pales also existed in Ireland and France where they were established by the English. "The Pale" in Ireland was named in the late fourteenth century, but was established at the time of Henry II's expedition in 1171–72 and comprised the territories conquered by England which were most secure. It lasted until all of Ireland was subjugated under Elizabeth I (1558–1603). In northern France, the Calais pale lasted from 1347 to 1558 and extended from Gravelines to Wissant on the coast and inland for six to nine miles.

3. Zborowski and Herzog, *Life Is with People*, pp. 61–62.

4. Ain, "Swislocz," p. 96.

5. "Swislocz," p. 101.

6. Levin, *Forward from Exile*, p. 242.

7. *Encyclopaedia Judaica*: s.v. Pale of Settlement.

8. The term "White Russian" derives from the dissolution of the ancient Russian empire called the Kievan Rus that stretched from about 300 kilometres north of present-day Leningrad southward to Dnepropetrovsk, which is about 400 kilometres along the Dnieper River south of Kiev. The destruction of Kiev by Genghis Khan in 1240 marked the end of the Kievan Rus. With a population of about 100,000, Kiev had been one of the largest cities in medieval Europe. The Kievan Rus had a population of about 7.5 million, but after its dissolution it eventually divided into Ukrainians, who came under Polish control; White Russians, in an area that lay between Poland and halfway to Moscow, who came under the control of the Lithuanians; and Great Russians, who were under the control of the Mongols.

9. Meltzer, *World of Our Fathers*, p.17.

10. Brym, *The Jewish Intelligentsia and Russian Marxism*, p. 53 (hereafter cited as *The Jewish Intelligentsia*).

11. Recollections of Emanuel Goldberg. See also Levin, *Forward from Exile*, p.116.

12. *Forward from Exile*, p. 45.

13. Zborowski and Herzog, *Life Is with People*, p. 90.

14. Descriptions based on *Life Is with People*, pp. 88ff., and recollections of Emanuel Goldberg.

15. Levin, *Forward from Exile*, p. 53.

16. Zborowski and Herzog, *Life Is with People*, p. 92.

17. *Life Is with People*, p. 95.

18. *Life Is with People*, p. 96.

19. Levin, *Forward from Exile*, p. 149.

20. *Forward from Exile*, p. 54.

CHAPTER 4

1. Peretz is quoted in Meltzer, *World of Our Fathers*, p. 142.

2. David Lewis says his father "showed himself to be a brilliant student in Yeshiva, the Jewish religious seminary and [Ezekial] had looked forward to seeing him become a leader in Judaism. But the bug of socialism and agnosticism had infested the Yeshiva and influenced my father to drop out of school and to become an ordinary worker in the leather factory. When he would not even join his father's business, my grandfather was heartbroken" (*Memoirs*, p. 3).

   Doris has similar recollections. However, there was no yeshiva in Svisloch, and no one knows where Maishe went for his training. According to Emanuel Goldberg, Volkovysk was the closest town that had a yeshiva of any substance. Consequently, I have taken the liberty of placing Maishe in Volkovysk for his yeshiva training, acting on the assumption that Ezekial would have sent him to the closest town with a yeshiva substantial enough to prepare him for becoming "a leader in Judaism." Closeness is a factor because it probably meant Ezekial had contacts there, possibly developed through his business as a grain dealer, which would make it easier to arrange *tegh* (eating days) for Maishe. Descriptions of yeshiva life have come from Zborowski and Herzog, *Life Is with People*; Howe, *The World of Our Fathers*; Meltzer, *World of Our Fathers*; Ain, "Svisloch"; Brym, *The Jewish Intelligentsia*; Levin, *Forward from Exile*; and recollections of Emanuel Goldberg and David Rome, historian and former archivist of the National Archives of the Canadian Jewish Congress.

3. Howe, quoting from a memorial book on Volkovysk published by emigrants, in *The World of Our Fathers*, p. 190.

4. Lewis, *Memoirs*, p. 4.

5. Zborowski and Herzog, *Life Is with People*, pp. 97–99.

6. In his novel *The Brothers Ashkenazi*, I.J. Singer described the fever of discovery experienced by a thirteen-year-old student: "He read day and night . . . without system. . . . Mendelssohn's modernist commentary on the Bible, Maimonides's Guide to the Perplexed, German translations which he only half understood, articles in the modernish Hebrew periodical Ha-Shahar, stories and poems and treatises by Smolenskin, Mapu and Gordon, rationalist essays by Krochmal and Adam Ha-Cohen, fantastic travel books, Hebrew treatises on astronomy and higher mathematics, of which he understood nothing but which attracted and fascinated him because they represented that great, brilliant, forbidden world which was opposed to everything held sacred by his father. From Mendelssohn he passed on to Solomon Maimon, and from him to Spinoza and Schopenhauer. He mumbled the German words to himself, caught part of their meaning, tried to guess the rest, lived in a fever of intellectual effort and wild hopes. And with all this he still managed to learn [his] weekly lesson." (Quoted in Meltzer, *World of Our Fathers*, p. 127.)

7. Ain, "Swislocz," p. 109.

8. Jones, *A History of Western Philosophy*, p. 808.

9. Ain, "Swislocz," p. 96.

10. Howe, *The World of Our Fathers*, p. 20.

11. *The World of Our Fathers*, p. 11.

12. Pushkin is quoted in Walsh, *Russia and the Soviet Union*, p. 203.

13. Herzen is quoted in Meltzer, *World of Our Fathers*, p. 48, and Howe, *The World of Our Fathers*, pp. 6–7.

14. Meltzer, *World of Our Fathers*, p. 49.

15. Brym: *The Jewish Intelligentsia*, p. 28, quoting Dubnow, *History of the Jews in Russia and Poland*, III: 222–23; Mahler, *A History of Modern Jewry*, pp. 377ff., 406ff.; Rubinow, "Economic Condition of the Jews in Russia," p. 556; Von Laue, *Sergei Witte and the Industrialization of Russia*, pp. 102–04.

16. Alexander II liberalized education, allowing much larger quotas of Jews into secondary schools and, of special interest to Jews, into universities; Alexander III and Nicholas II tightened the quotas, cutting the number of Jews in universities by half. Alexander II cut back on censorship; Alexander III and Nicholas II intensified it. Alexander II allowed Jews to move freely within the Pale and small numbers of Jewish artisans, merchants, distillers, and artisans' apprentices to go beyond; Alexander III cut off Jewish excursions beyond the Pale and forced many Jews to return, especially Jews who had settled in Moscow, forbade free movement within the Pale, banned settlement outside of cities and small towns, and prohibited Jews from having anything to do with land, even going so far as to disallow extension of existing leases. Nicholas II maintained the strictures.

17. Brym, *The Jewish Intelligentsia*, pp. 28–29, and Levin, *Forward from Exile*, p. 241.

18. Report is quoted in Meltzer, *World of Our Fathers*, pp. 158–159.

19. *World of Our Fathers*, p. 158.

20. *World of Our Fathers*, pp. 160–61.

21. Brym, *The Jewish Intelligentsia*, p. 30.

22. Levin, *Forward from Exile*, p. 175.

23. Lewis, *Louder Voices*, p. 118.

24. Levin, *Forward from Exile*, pp. 188–89.

25. Count Nikolai P. Ignatiev (1832–1908) was minister of the interior under Alexander III for little more than a year (1881–82), during which time he carried responsibility for the laws of 1882 under which Jews were forbidden to buy or rent land or to live outside cities and towns within the Pale. The terrible pogroms that ran unchecked following the assassination of Alexander II also fell within his period of office.

    George Ignatieff, his grandson, who became a prominent Canadian diplomat and subsequently chancellor of the University of Toronto, says in his memoirs, "I find it hard to believe that he could have been the instigator of an anti-Semitic policy, particularly since it is a matter of record that he was dismissed because of his supposed democratic tendencies" (*The Making of a Peacemonger*, p. 13). However, the fact is that aside from the Tsar, the primary responsibility for dealing with the pogroms rested with him — and he turned a blind eye.

26. According to the Book of Esther in the Old Testament (7:1–10), Haman, vizier to the Persian King Ahasuerus (Xerxes I), was hanged at the behest of Esther to prevent Haman from fulfilling his plan to kill all the Jews in the realm. The Jewish feast of Purim is held to commemorate the rescue of the Jews.

    Nebuchadnezzar (630–562 B.C.) was the greatest king of the Chaldean (Neo-Babylonian) Empire. In 586 he destroyed Jerusalem and led much of its captive population to Babylonia. Levin's reference to Nebuchadnezzar's eating the grass of the field for seven years relates to the Book of Daniel (4:33), which describes the madness God visited upon Nebuchadnezzar. Outside of the Bible, there is no independent support for the assertion of Nebuchadnezzar's madness.

27. Sipyagin was assassinated by Stefan Balmashev. (Tobias, *The Jewish Bund in Russia*, p. 151.)

28. Meltzer, *World of Our Fathers*, pp. 186, 187.

29. *World of Our Fathers*, p. 188, and Abramovitch, "The Jewish Socialist Movement in Russia and Poland," p. 374.

30. Salisbury, *Black Night, White Snow*, p. 643, n. 10.

31. Meltzer, *World of Our Fathers*, pp. 185–86.

32. Poem quoted in *World of Our Fathers*, pp. 188ff.

CHAPTER 5

1. See the recollections of Hillel Katz-Blum in Tobias, *The Jewish Bund in Russia*, pp. 20–21, 43.

2. Recollection of Doris Andras.

3. Ain, "Swislocz," p. 102; map showing locations of factories published in *Svisloch: The Second Book.*

4. Howe, *The World of Our Fathers*, p. 21.

5. *The World of Our Fathers*, pp. xix, 26, 120.

6. The Second Temple in Jerusalem, the most important religious institution of the Jews, was destroyed by Roman legions in A.D. 70, and when an effort was made to rebuild it sixty-two years later, the Romans razed it, and Jerusalem, to the ground. From A.D. 135 onward, says historian Cecil Roth, "the Jews were a minority in the land of their fathers" (*A History of the Jews*, pp. 98–115).

7. Tobias says, "The Bundists took advantage of every opportunity to gain exposure. They posted leaflets on synagogue walls on Friday nights, for example, where they were bound to remain through the Sabbath unless a Christian could be found to remove them" (*The Jewish Bund in Russia*, p. 97).

8. *The Jewish Bund in Russia*, p. 229.

9. Both Litvak quotations are in *The Jewish Bund in Russia*, p. 245.

10. Phylacteries: two small, cube-shaped, black leather cases, each containing an excerpt from Holy Writ inscribed on parchment. Attached to each cube is a long leather strap. During morning services, observant Jewish men fasten one cube on the left arm next to the heart and the other to the centre of the brow to remind them of their duties to God and His commandments.

11. The Bund hymn is quoted in Tobias, *The Jewish Bund in Russia*, p. xiii.

12. *The Jewish Bund in Russia*, p. 140.

13. The Fifth Congress is quoted in Tobias, *The Jewish Bund in Russia*, p. 226.

14. *The Jewish Bund in Russia*, p. 229.

15. Der Fraind is quoted in *The Jewish Bund in Russia*, p. 227.

16. *The Jewish Bund in Russia*, p. 238.

17. Keep, *The Rise of Social Democracy in Russia*, p. 288 (including n. 2); Abramovitch, "The Jewish Socialist Movement," p. 389; and Tobias, *The Jewish Bund in Russia*, p. 239.

18. Brym, *The Jewish Intelligentsia*, p. 78; Schwarzbart, "General Zionism," p. 29; and Abramovitch, "The Jewish Socialist Movement," pp. 380, 389.

19. "The Jewish Socialist Movement," p. 369.

20. Samuel Gozhansky, one of the original members of the Vilna Group, ia quoted in Tobias, *The Jewish Bund In Russia*, p. 24.

21. Kosovsky, "V. Medem," p. 133.

22. Brym, *The Jewish Intelligentsia*, p. 96.

23. *The Jewish Intelligentsia*, p. 96

24. Lenin is quoted in Salisbury, *Black Night, White Snow*, p.44.

25. Sukhanov is quoted in Moorehead, *The Russian Revolution*, p. 38.

26. Zasulich is quoted in Salisbury, *Black Night, White Snow*, p. 143.

27. Medem is quoted in Brym, *The Jewish Intelligentsia*, p. 86.

28. Lenin is quoted in *The Jewish Intelligentsia*, p. 86.

29. Medem is quoted in Tobias, *The Jewish Bund in Russia*, p. 217.

30. Lenin is quoted in *The Jewish Bund in Russia*, p. 272.

31. *The Jewish Bund in Russia*, p. 276.

32. Levin, *Forward from Exile*, pp. 298–99.

33. Brym, *The Jewish Intelligentsia*, p. 1.

34. *The Jewish Intelligentsia*, p. 85.

35. Der Bund is quoted in Tobias, *The Jewish Bund in Russia*, p. 253.

36. *The Jewish Bund in Russia*, p. 175.

37. *The Jewish Bund in Russia*, p.129.

38. *The Jewish Bund in Russia*, p. 317.

39. *The Jewish Bund in Russia*, p. 309.

40. Litvak is quoted in *The Jewish Bund in Russia*, p. 309.

CHAPTER 6

1. Valery Bryusov's poem "The Pale Horse," written two years before the 1905 Revolution, became the most popular poem in Russia. Harrison Salisbury quotes it, without putting it in verse form:
"The street was like a storm. The crowds passed by as if pursued by inevitable fate. Cars, cabs, busses roared amid the furious endless stream of people. Signs whirled. . . . Wheels hummed proudly, newsboys screamed, whips cracked. Suddenly amid the storm — a hellish whisper. There sounds a strange dissonant footfall, a deadening shriek, a tremendous crash. And the flaming Horseman appears. The horse flies headlong. The air still trembles and the echo rolls. Time quivers and the Look is Terror. In letters of fire the Horseman's scroll spells Death. The crowd tramples madly. Terror stays no one. . . . It lasts a moment. Then on the streets there is fresh movement. All is ordinary in the bright sunshine and no one notices in the noisy rush whether an apparition has passed by or simply a dream — only a woman from a whorehouse

and an escaped madman still stretch their hands toward the vanished vision" (*Black Night, White Snow*, p. 193).

2. Ain, "Swislocz," p. 98.

3. Tobias, *The Jewish Bund in Russia*, p. 44.

4. Gorky is quoted in Salisbury, *Black Night, White Snow*, p. 127.

5. The Central Committee is quoted in Abramovitch, "The Jewish Socialist Movement," p. 376.

6. Tobias, *The Jewish Bund in Russia*, p. 301.

7. Moorehead, *The Russian Revolution*, p. 55.

8. The Black Hundreds leaflet is quoted in Tobias, *The Jewish Bund in Russia*, p. 312. See also p. 313.

9. *The Jewish Bund in Russia*, pp. 315, 316.

10. Dubnow is quoted in Meltzer, *World of Our Fathers*, p. 194.

11. Tobias, *The Jewish Bund in Russia*, p. 306.

12. Where the Bund was strongest, the strikes were heaviest. Official strike reports show that from January through September 1905, the worker turnout was: Lodz, 95.1%; Latvia, 97%; Kovno, 82.1%; Vilna, 81.4%; Grodno, 79.9%; Minsk, 66.2%; Vitebsk, 54.3%; Mogilev, 47.5%; and Warsaw, 40.7%.

13. The chairman of the St. Petersburg Soviet was G.S. Nosar, who used the pseudonym Nostaliev Khrustaliev. (Keep, *The Rise of Social Democracy in Russia*, pp. 235ff.) Trotsky, however, "was undoubtedly the stronger personality and exerted a great deal of influence on Nosar." Some, such as Harrison Salisbury, incorrectly identify Trotsky as chairman of the 1905 Soviet (*Black Night, White Snow*, p. 457). He was chairman of the 1917 St. Petersburg Soviet.

14. *Black Night, White Snow*, p. 653, n. 16.

15. Levin, *Forward from Exile*, pp. 415ff.

16. Shulgin is quoted in Salisbury, *Black Night, White Snow*, p. 133.

17. Ain, "Swislocz," p. 89.

18. Meltzer, *World of Our Fathers*, p. 199.

19. Ain, "Swislocz," pp. 110ff.

20. Minutes of a general meeting of the Bund in Svisloch, 1907, Bund Archives, file MG 2-359. The minutes (called protocols in the document) note that L. Maishka was chairman of the praesidium (the board of directors) of the Bund. In 1907 the Bund was still an illegal organization and real names were rarely used in documents. Putting two facts together makes it a very near certainty that L. Maishka was Maishe Losz. Those two facts are: (1) Many people have described Maishe as "the leader"

or "the head" of the Bund in Svisloch (although I have not been able to find anyone who could say at what specific date he became leader), and (2) L. Maishka can be read as the transposition of Maishe Losz's first and last names and Maishka is, of course, the diminutive (the affectionate use) of Maishe.

Jacob Hertz, editor of *Unser Tsait* (the Bundist newspaper) in New York, and Dr. Benjamin Nadel, director of the Bund Archives, both confirm that there is an extremely high probability that L. Maishka was Maishe Losz. Both men were Bundists in the Old Country. Mr. Hertz, who was born in 1893 and grew up in Warsaw, is emphatic in saying that it was not at all unusual for a nineteen-year-old to be chairman of a local Bund organization in a small town such as Svisloch. A great many prominent Bundists were very young.

The minutes note that L. Maishka, as chairman, and two others were on the praesidium of the Svisloch Bund and that the meeting had been called to elect delegates to attend a regional conference of the Russian Social Democratic Workers' Party. Four were elected, including L. Maishka, who got the second highest number of votes.

Finding the minutes was, for me, one of the more exciting moments of research in the preparation of this book. They are written in Yiddish on a scrap of paper roughly four inches square.

That tiny piece of paper had a remarkable journey. The Bund archives were established in 1899 in Geneva, Switzerland. This site was chosen because the archives would have been too vulnerable in Russia; in the previous year the Tsarist government had made an all-out effort to destroy the Bund.

After the First World War the archives were transferred to Berlin, which was "the main centre of the great Social-Democratic movement of the German working class." However, after Hitler assumed power in 1933, Nazi Storm Troopers occupied the building housing the German Social Democrats and confiscated all their property. Fearing that the Bund archives would suffer a similar fate, the Bund nominally sold them to the French ambassador in Berlin who had them transferred to Paris.

When the German army occupied Paris in 1940, the archives were crated and given to a Frenchman who was paid for hiding them. However, when the Germans evacuated Paris four years later, they seized the archives and took them with them. Obviously they had known of the hiding place all along.

After the end of the war the archives couldn't be found. Months passed and then Bundists heard that the Nazis, unable to carry with them all that they had seized, had simply thrown things away in a field outside Paris. Members of the Bund found the field and there, "strewn about, [were] libraries, art objects . . . other treasures" — and the archives.

Since one-half of world Jewry now lived in North America, it was decided to move the archives to New York City.

So eighty years after this protocol was secretly written at an underground meeting in the tiny shtetl of Svisloch, I arrived in New York to actually hold it in my hand and wonder at the hazardous journeys that had brought it there and to admire yet again the determination of the people who insisted their history would live. (See *A Great Collection, The Archives of the Jewish Labour Movement.*)

21. Keep, *The Rise of Social Democracy in Russia*, p. 288.

22. Ain, "Swislocz," p. 111.

23. "Swislocz," pp. 112-13.

24. In 1905 there had been 13,995 strikes and employers had won only 29.4%. In 1906 there were 6,114 strikes and in 1907 only 3,573 and of them employers won 57.6%. (Keep, *The Rise of Social Democracy in Russia*, p. 283.)

25. In 1912 there were 2,032 strikes involving 725,491 workers. In 1913 the number of strikes reached 2,404 involving 887,096 workers. (Salisbury, *Black Night, White Snow*, pp. 197, 252.)

26. *Black Night, White Snow*, p. 197.

CHAPTER 7

1. Kayleh Ain, as told to Doris Andras' daughter Margot.

2. The five books are Solomon's Song of Songs, Ruth, Lamentations, Ecclesiastes, and Esther.

3. Lewis, *Memoirs*, p. 3.

4. Recollections of Doris Andras and Emanuel Goldberg; and Zborowski and Herzog, *Life Is With People*, pp. 281ff., and Ain, "Swislocz," p. 98.

5. "Swislocz," p. 113.

6. Medem, *The Life and Soul of a Legendary Jewish Socialist*, p. 440 (hereafter cited as *Life and Soul*).

7. *Life and Soul*, pp. 446, 447.

8. Litvak is quoted in Abramovitch, "The Jewish Socialist Movement," p. 390.

9. Poalei Zion is quoted in "The Jewish Socialist Movement," p. 390.

10. Gutman is quoted in "The Jewish Socialist Movement," p. 390.

11. Krupskaya is quoted in Salisbury, *Black Night, White Snow*, p. 220.

12. Lenin is quoted in *Black Night, White Snow*, p. 224.

13. Ain, "Swislocz," p. 96.

14. "Swislocz," p. 97.

15. This anecdote is recalled by Norman Neslen, who joined Maishe's branch of the Workmen's Circle in Montreal in the late twenties and who now lives in Toronto.

16. Tobias, *The Jewish Bund in Russia*, pp. 325, 305.

17. Medem, *Life and Soul*, p. 396.

18. Tobias, *The Jewish Bund in Russia*, p. 334.

19. Medem, *Life and Soul*, p. 476.

20. Abramovitch, "The Jewish Socialist Movement," p. 386n.

21. Actually, late October is a guess. David's daughter Janet does not recall the exact date. She remembers only her parents saying David was born "right after the first snows" in 1909.

22. Ain, "Swislocz," p. 87.

23. Descriptions are taken from "Swislocz," p. 100; and Zborowski and Herzog, *Life Is with People*, pp. 376ff.

24. Ain, "Swislocz," p. 93.

25. Zborowski and Herzog, *Life Is with People*, p. 377.

26. This assessment of Maishe is based on recollections people had of him in Montreal. I could find no one who remembered his specific activities in Svisloch in these matters, but there were many who recalled others in the 1930s and 1940s saying that he had been the leader of the Bund in Svisloch. So I have assumed that if he showed these characteristics in Montreal, he would have exhibited them in Svisloch too.

27. Abramovitch, "The Jewish Socialist Movement," p. 391.

28. Ain, "Swislocz," p. 113.

29. Abramovitch, "The Jewish Socialist Movement," p. 392.

30. Salisbury, *Black Night, White Snow*, p. 232.

31. Abramovitch, "The Jewish Socialist Movement," p. 392; and Roth, *A History of the Jews*, p. 353.

32. Abramovitch, "The Jewish Socialist Movement," p. 392.

33. "The Jewish Socialist Movement," p. 393.

CHAPTER 8

1. Reed, *Ten Days That Shook the World*, p. 171. Reed does not name the person making the statement. Instead, he says: "Again the representative of the Bund," and then he proceeds to relate what the representative said. Since his previous reference to a Bund speaker had been to Erlich (see p. 131), I have assumed it was Erlich who was speaking. The full context of the passage bears this out.

2. Lewis, *Memoirs*, p. 7.

3. Conversations with Joseph Ain in Montreal and Emanuel Goldberg in Toronto; and Ain, "Swislocz," p. 96.

4. "Swislocz," p. 90.

5. Levin, *Forward from Exile*, p. 287.

6. *Forward from Exile*, p. 365.

7. Recollections of Emanuel Goldberg.

8. A modicum of conjecture is present here. David implies that the Germans closed schools when they entered Svisloch (*Memoirs*, p. 8). Yet Abraham Ain wrote that the Yiddish school was opened "under German occupation." Emanuel Goldberg recalls that his father taught in a German school in Svisloch, and so did Kayleh Ain. The Hebrew school must have been closed, Mr. Goldberg reports, because his father spoke perfect Hebrew and would have taught in the Hebrew school if it were still operating.

9. Ain, "Swislocz," p. 113.

10. Lewis, *Memoirs*, p. 8.

11. Brusilov is quoted in Salisbury, *Black Night, White Snow*, p. 268. Even though production had increased rapidly — rifle production rose from a rate of 525,000 a year to 1.6 million by Jan. 1917 and artillery from 2,106 guns in 1915 to 5,135 in 1916 — the increase in demand far outstripped production gains (p. 667, n. 7).

12. *Black Night, White Snow*, pp. 280, 322.

13. Report is quoted in *Black Night, White Snow*, p. 321.

14. Chelnokov is quoted in *Black Night, White Snow*, p. 321.

15. First of all, a Provisional Executive Committee of the Petrograd (St. Petersburg) Soviet was formed on Monday, March 12. It called for a meeting of the new Soviet that evening and immediately set about organizing food supplies and creating the embryo of a military organization. The leaders in organizing the St. Petersburg Soviet were Henryk Erlich, the prominent Bundist, two members of the Workers Section of the Military–Industrial Committee, a Menshevik, a right-wing Menshevik, and a Social Democrat. Significantly, there were no Bolsheviks involved in the original organizing.

   Lenin, who was in Switzerland immersed in arguing with other émigrés, didn't even know that the revolution had occurred. He left Zurich by train on April 9 in a party of thirty-two made up of nineteen Bolsheviks, six Bundists, three Mensheviks, and four others, one of whom was a fourteen-year-old boy. Lenin arrived at Finland Station in St. Petersburg on April 16, ten years after he had last set foot in Russia. (Salisbury, *Black Night, White Snow*, pp. 329, 363, and Alan Moorehead, *The Russian Revolution*, p. 182.)

16. Ascher, *The Mensheviks in the Russian Revolution*, p. 27 (hereafter cited as *The Mensheviks*).

17. After rejoining the Russian Social Democratic Workers' Party in 1906, the Bund had allied itself with the Mensheviks, and when the Bolsheviks and Mensheviks split for good in 1912, the Bund stayed within the Menshevik Social Democratic Party, and the Mensheviks changed their position to support the Bund's concept of national cultural autonomy.

So there was a strong bond between the two groups. (*The Mensheviks*, p. 12.)

18. *The Mensheviks*, p. 31.

19. Abramovitch, "The Jewish Socialist Movement," p. 394.

20. "The Jewish Socialist Movement", p. 395.

21. Henryk Erlich and Victor Alter, would be executed by Stalin in 1941. After 1918 both moved to Warsaw and became members of the city council and the most prominent leaders of the Polish Bund. Alter became president of the Council of Jewish Trade Unions in independent Poland. (Scherer, "The Bund," pp. 143, 146, and Salisbury, *Black Night, White Snow*, p. 363.)

22. Description of the hall taken from Reed, *Ten Days*, p. 121.

23. *Ten Days*, p, 131. Reed identified the speaker as Raphael Abramovich, but an editor's note says: "Reed is mistaken as to the speaker. He took the name from the Petrograd press, which made the same mistake. The speaker he is describing was Henryk Ehrlich of the Bundist Right, an ardent defensist. Abramovich was of the Bund Left and a Menshevik-Internationalist. In 1917 he did not wear glasses, thick or otherwise."

24. Salisbury, *Black Night, White Snow*, p. 528.

25. Trotsky, *Lenin*, p.127.

26. "Cheka" is how the Russian letters Ch and K are pronounced; they stood for "Extraordinary Commission." It was the forerunner of the GPU, the OGPU, the NKVD, the MVD, and now the KGB. Its full title was the All-Russian Extraordinary Commission for Struggle Against Counter-Revolutionary Sabotage. Lenin created it Dec. 20, 1917. (Salisbury, *Black Night, White Snow*, p. 545, and Chamberlin, *Revolution*, II: 79.)

27. *Revolution*, II: 75.

28. *Revolution*, II: 352.

29. Wolfe, *Three Who Made a Revolution*, p. 253.

30. *Encyclopaedia Judaica*: s.v. The Bund: The 1917 Revolutions and Their Aftermath.

31. Ascher, *The Mensheviks*, p. 37.

32. Abramovitch, "The Jewish Socialist Movement," p. 396.

CHAPTER 9

1. Calculation of the timing of events in Svisloch is based on the assertion of Doris Andras that Maishe hid at Dr. Bittner's for ten days. The Soviet retreat from Warsaw brought their army to Bialystok on Aug. 23, 1917, which means that by the 25th it would have been safe for Maishe to come

out of hiding. That means he would have gone into hiding on the evening of the 14th.

2. D'Abernon is quoted in Kirkien, *Russia, Poland and the Curzon Line*, p. 38.

3. Recollections of Doris Andras and Emanuel Goldberg from stories told to them.

4. A preliminary peace treaty between Russia and Poland was signed at Riga on Oct. 18, 1920, and it set the armistice line that on an average was only about eighty kilometres short of what had been the historic borders of Poland in 1772 before the first of the partitions. The final treaty, confirming those borders, was signed on March 18, 1921. Svisloch is roughly 200 kilometres directly west of present-day Timkovichi, which was at the new Polish–Russian border. (See English text of preliminary treaty in *Soviet Treaty Series*, p. 67, and Watt, *Bitter Glory*, p. 151.)

5. By the end of 1921 the Bund "held the overwhelming majority" in the national council of Jewish Trade Unions, which had seven unions with 205 branches and 46,000 members. By 1939, with the Bund still in the majority, there were fourteen unions with 498 branches and about 99,000 members. Also by 1939 the Polish Bund had a youth organization (Zukunft) with 15,000 members, a chidren's organization (SKIF), a women's organization (YAF) and a sports organization (Morgnshtern). (*Encyclopaedia Judaica*: s.v. The Bund: The Polish Bund.)

6. Lewis, *Memoirs*, p. 12.

7. *Memoirs*, p.13.

8. Sack, *Canadian Jews*, p. 2; and Kage, *With Faith and Thanksgiving*, pp. 14–24. The following table shows the growth of Jewish communities in Canada.

Jewish Population*

Year	Montreal	Quebec	Ontario	Manitoba	Canada
1851		348	103		451
1861	403	572	614		1,195
1871	N.A.	549	636		1,333
1881	811	989	1,245	31	2,456
1891	2,473	2,703	2,540	791	6,566
1901	6,941	7,607	5,337	1,514	16,717
1911	28,807	30,648	27,015	10,741	75,838
1921	45,802	47,977	47,798	16,669	126,201
1931	58,032	60,087	62,383	19,341	156,725
1941	63,937	66,277	69,875	18,879	170,241
1951	80,829	82,701	85,467	19,282	204,836
1961	102,420	104,727	109,344	19,981	254,368
1971	109,480	110,880	125,310	18,770	276,025
1981	101,365	102,355	148,255	15,670	296,425

* Compiled from Kage, *With Faith and Thanksgiving*, p. 261; Rosenberg, "Changes in the Jewish Population...in Montreal," p. 3; Rosenberg, "Jewish Population of Canada"; and Statistics Canada.

9. On the contrary, there are people who say Maishe was less impressive than others of his contemporaries. One such person is Arnold Greenfield, born in 1903 and since 1932 a member of the same branch of the Workmen's Circle that was renamed in Maishe's honour. For seventeen years he was its recording secretary and for another five its financial secretary, and he remembers Maishe as being less prominent than others: "We had more active people than him," he says, "people who were active in the unions. People who were active in other ways. . . . That's the only way I can talk about him. I mean I couldn't tell you that he was a giant. He wasn't. We didn't have anybody like that. You see, everybody did as much of what he could for the organization."

10. Interview with Emanuel Goldberg.

11. Peretz, *Selected Stories*, p. 38.

12. *Selected Stories*, p. 13.

CHAPTER 10

1. Program: Workmen's Circle Choir performing "Legend of Toil" (Goichberg), arranged by Lazar Weiner, at the Monument National Theatre, Sunday evening, May 9, 1943. Guest conductor Lazar Weiner with soloists, chorus, and string orchestra. Program also included Alexander Brott, violin; Doris Silverman, piano; and a wide selection of other music including Beethoven, Bloch, De Falla, Heifetz, Eisenstatt, and other composers. Maishe Lewis was in charge of publicity (Jewish) and also was on the four-member Arrangements Committee. (Canadian Jewish Congress Archives, ZB/Workmen's Circle, hereafter cited as CSCA.)

2. Richler, *The Street*, p. 53.

3. Rosenberg, "Changes in the Jewish Population . . . in Montreal," p. 2.

4. "Changes in the Jewish Population . . . in Montreal," p. 1.

5. Richler, *The Street*, p. 58.

6. Layton, "Piety," in *Engagements*, p. 285.

7. Sack, "Canadian Jews Early in This Century," p. 41.

8. Goldman, "Seven Years of the League," in *In Honour of the Dedication of the Workmen's Circle Centre*, p. 7. In CJCA.

9. Afros, "A Place for Youth," in *In Honour of the Dedication of the Workmen's Circle*, p. 8. In CJCA.

10. PAC, MG 28, V 75, Vol. 2, file 5: Jewish Labour Committee of Canada — Minutes, banquets, and conventions.

11. Lewis, *Memoirs*, p. 15.

12. *Memoirs*, p. 17.

13. Young, *The Anatomy of a Party*, p. 81.

14. Howe, *The World of Our Fathers*, pp. 292ff. Howe was writing of Bundists who immigrated to New York after the 1905 Revolution, but his remarks apply equally to Maishe immigrating to Montreal in 1921.

15. Short biography of Maishe Lewis in *The Workmen's Circle*.

16. Recollection of Faga Falk in an interview.

17. Recollection of Israel Falk in an interview.

18. Lewis, *Memoirs*, p. 18. David did not mention that Raphael Abramovitch was also a Bundist. Abramovitch served as the Bund's representative in the St. Petersburg Soviet in 1905. He was arrested and exiled in 1910–11, but fled from exile to Western Europe. He returned to Russia in 1917 as a leader of the internationalist wing of the Bund and as a Menshevik.

19. Green, *Children of the Sun*, p. 206.

20. McNaught, *A Prophet in Politics*, p. 134.

21. Penner, *Winnipeg 1919*, p. viii.

22. The Second Comintern Congress in 1920 approved a list of twenty-one points proposed by Lenin which organizations seeking to affiliate would have to adopt. They were called the Conditions of Affiliation to the Communist International and stated in part: "Parties desiring to affiliate to the Communist International must recognize the necessity of a complete and absolute rupture with reformism and the policy of the 'Centre," and they must carry on propaganda in favour of this rupture among the broadest circle of party members." (Lenin is quoted in Penner, *The Canadian Left*, p. 143.) Lenin's statement that reformists were the principal social bulwark of the bourgeoisie was made at the 1920 congress. (*The Canadian Left*, p. 144.)

23. MacDonald is quoted in *The Canadian Left*, p. 148.

24. Hurwitz, *The Workmen's Circle*, p 57.

25. The Communist Party of Canada was born in "deep secrecy" at night in a small barn on Fred Farley's farm near Guelph. Guards were posted and "strict security" prevailed although, unknown to the twenty-two delegates representing Communist groups from Manitoba, Ontario, and Montreal, one delegate was an undercover RCMP agent. Delegates adopted a constitution declaring the new party to be highly centralized and they decided it would be "an underground, illegal organization." They felt that the experience of the Winnipeg General Strike made it obvious that if the new party stated its objectives clearly, it would be prosecuted.

The convention agreed that "the Communist Party of Canada [would] systematically and persistently propagate to the working class the idea of the inevitability of and the necessity for violent revolution, and [would] prepare the working class for the destruction of the bourgeois state and the establishment of the proletarian dictatorship based upon Soviet power." (Rodney, *Soldiers of the International*, pp. 37–40; Avakumovic,

The Communist Party in Canada, pp. 21, 28; and Hurwitz, *The Workmen's Circle*, p. 58.)

26. Epstein, *The Jew and Communism*, p. 144; and Shapiro, *The Friendly Society*, p. 80.

27. Epstein, *The Jew and Communism*, p. 145; and Hurwitz, *The Workmen's Circle*, p. 63.

28. *The Workmen's Circle*, p. 65.

29. *The Workmen's Circle*, p. 70.

30. Interview with Norman Massey; and Paris, *Jews . . . in Canada*, p. 135; and Hurwitz, *The Workmen's Circle*, p. 72.

31. "Ethnish" is an obsolete word that's worth bringing back — at least in this context. It means "heathenish." (See *Shorter Oxford English Dictionary*.)

CHAPTER 11

1. Lewis and Scott, *Make This YOUR Canada*, p. 190.

2. Layton, *Waiting for the Messiah*, p. 143.

3. Roth, *A History of the Jews*, p. 386.

4. Rubinstein, "Ten Years of Strife, Rescue and Aid," p. 6.

5. According to a report of the Jewish Labour Committee of Canada to the 1975 Biennial National Convention of the Jewish Labour Committee, held at the Hotel Roosevelt, New York City, Oct. 24-26, 1975, Maishe was the Canadian committee's first secretary. According to Kaplansky, "History of the Jewish Labour Committee in Canada," p. 6, Maishe was its third secretary after, "Ch. Papiernick of the 'left' Poale Zion and Moishe Trossman of the Workmen's Circle." Doris Andras recalls that it was "about three years" after Maishe started with his concession booth in late 1932 that he became secretary. Mr. Kaplansky in his history says it was "several years" after "the organization" was founded. Since the organization was created in New York in 1933 and the Montreal branch was started in 1936, both are probably correct on that point. The 1975 report announced establishment of the Moishe Lewis Foundation: "The aim of the foundation is to actively educate the public with respect to human rights and, in doing so, assist in ending discrimination based on race, colour, creed, nationality or ethnic origin."

6. In "History of the Jewish Labour Committee in Canada," Kaplansky says Maishe was paid $8 a week. However, Doris Andras says it is her distinct memory that her father was paid $10 a week, not $8. Perhaps Maishe received $2 a week for expenses. If not, I can't explain the difference.

7. *Jewish Labor Committee*, p. 1.

8. Scherer, *The Bund*, p. 150. In the area of the old Pale of Settlement prior to the war (Hungary, Romania, Bulgaria, Czechoslovakia [the

Protectorate of Bohemia and Moravia], Slovakia, Poland, Lithuania, Latvia, Estonia, and parts of White Russia and Ukraine), there were 6,922,000 Jews. At the end there were 1,625,000. A total of 5,297,000 were killed. A further 975,000 lived beyond the Pale in Russia. Of them, 868,000 survived. (Dawidowicz, *The War Against the Jews*, p. 403.)

9. *The Role in Relief and Rescue During the Holocaust*, pp. 3, 5, 8. For Canada's tight quota, see Abella, *None Is Too Many*.

10. Paraphrased from "The Campaign" by Joseph Addison (1672–1719):
    And pleas'd th' Almighty's orders to perform,
    Rides in the whirl-wind, and directs the storm.
    (Smith, *The Oxford Book of Eighteenth Century Verse*, p. 33.)

11. Lewis, *Memoirs*, p. 21.

12. *Memoirs*, p. 20.

13. Layton, *Waiting for the Messiah*, p. 135.

14. Quoted in U. Caplan, *Like One That Dreamed*, p. 99.

15. Layton, *Waiting for the Messiah*, p. 137.

16. Lewis, *Memoirs*, p. 21.

17. *Memoirs*, p. 21.

18. U. Caplan, *Like One That Dreamed*, p. 36.

19. *Like One That Dreamed*, p. 39.

20. "Identity," p.6.

21. At the time of writing, Sophie was unable to be interviewed. After two years of extreme medical hardship — several heart attacks, a stroke, an operation to install a pacemaker, and severe infection resulting from the operation — she was admitted to a nursing home, her concentration and ability to remember severely impaired.

22. Lewis, *Memoirs*, p. 22.

23. Sophie told this story at a preliminary meeting to arrange time for interviews, just days before her first heart attack. She never was well enough after that attack to give an interview.

24. Interview with Joe Ain; and Lewis, *Memoirs*, pp. 29, 30.

25. *Memoirs*, p. 29.

26. Layton, *Waiting for the Messiah*, p. 146. In 1935, however, "the Toronto CCF established a special Welfare Committee to co-ordinate party relief and eviction protest activity throughout the city" (G. Caplan, *The Dilemma of Canadian Socialism*, p. 72).

27. Layton, *Waiting for the Messiah*, p. 124.

28. Lewis, *Memoirs*, p. 29.

29. *Memoirs*, p. 31.

30. U. Caplan, *Like One That Dreamed*, p. 55.

31. Layton, *Waiting for the Messiah*, p. 135.

32. Lenin, *Collected Works*, 28: 108.

33. Lewis, *Memoirs*, p. 27.

34. *Memoirs*, p. 34.

CHAPTER 12

1. Layton, *A Red Carpet for the Sun*. The poem is located on the title page.

2. Ted Jolliffe recalls, "quite distinctly," Sir Carlton Allen making this remark at a luncheon arranged for him at the University of Toronto, "I believe in 1935."

3. Lord Lothian (Philip Henry Kerr, 11th Marquess of Lothian) was quoted in an editorial published in *The Ottawa Journal*, Jan. 27, 1950. In addition to being secretary of the Rhodes Trust and ambassador to Washington, he had been editor of the Round Table (1910–16), secretary to the prime minister (1916–21), and parliamentary under-secretary of the India Office (1931–32).

    The McGill Daily also published a story under the headline "Lewis Discusses Students' Relations to Government" (Dec. 13, 1933), which begins: "'There is a boy speaking regularly in the [Oxford] Union just now who will be famous before very long, although being a Canadian, we may not hear so much about him over here. His name is David Lewis, and he is a Socialist. For sheer brilliance as a speaker he has no equal in Oxford, except for the President of the Union, Mr. Michael Foot, about whom I have written before.'

    "This was said of the speaker at the meeting of the McGill Labour Club last night in McGill Union in 'Oxford and Cambridge' for November 1933, of David Lewis by Sir Anthony Jenkinson in an article entitled 'Oxford Comments.'"

4. In describing the influences on him, Foot said: "I became a socialist, I joined the Labour Party, when I just left Oxford in 1934. David had some part in all that, you know. It was a mixture of arguments with David Lewis and John Cripps and Tony Greenwood and other people that I met there and the reading I was doing. But David Lewis certainly . . . played a part in converting me to socialism." *The Isis* announced Mr. Foot's conversion in its issue of Feb. 27, 1935, p. 6, describing him as "the most brilliant post-war figure in Oxford politics, who was the youngest President the Union ever had."

5. This view is confirmed by Michael Foot, Sir William Nield,, John Cripps, and Ted Jolliffe, all of whom were at Oxford with David and all of whom were members of the Oxford Labour Club.

6. Boyle, *The Fourth Man*, p. 74.

7. At the end of 1932 membership was 484 (Ashley and Saunders, *Red Oxford*, p. 45). In Nov. 1934 it was 700, as mentioned in the profile on David after he won the presidency of the Oxford Union, (*The Isis*, Nov. 28, 1934, p. 7); in Jan. 1935 it was 650 (*The Isis*, Jan. 23, 1935, p. 6.)

8. Brooke, *The Collected Poems*, p. 245.

9. Muggeridge is quoted in Boyle, *The Fourth Man*, p. 48.

10. Betjeman, *Mount Zion*, p. 22.

11. Cornford, *Understand the Weapon, Understand the Wound*, p. 32. See pp. 11–17 for appreciation of Cornford.

12. Connolly is quoted in Green, *Children of the Sun*, p. 157.

13. Background information on the Children of the Sun comes primarily from *Children of the Sun*; and Pryce-Jones, *Cyril Connolly: Journal and Memoir*.

14. Rebecca West, discussing Burgess, Maclean, and other traitors in *The New Meaning of Treason* (1964), said that many English people "would have felt more at ease with many of the traitors in this book" than with a British hero who died in the Korean war whose "heroism has something dowdy about it, while treason has a certain style, a sort of elegance." Graham Greene wrote an introduction to Philby's *My Silent War* (1968) in which he said, "Who has not committed treason to something or someone more important than a country?" He then compared Philby to an English Catholic living under Elizabeth I, refusing to conform, and becoming by necessity a traitor. Evelyn Waugh, introducing the 1955 autobiography of William Weston, who was the kind of recusant that Greene was talking about, said that England under Elizabeth I needed political betrayal and military defeat by Philip of Spain "for the full development of our national genius." (The works of West, Greene, and Waugh are quoted in Green, *Children of the Sun*, pp. 467, 468; and Brown, "C," *The Secret Life of Sir Stewart Menzies*, pp. 729, 747.)

15. Green, *Children of the Sun*, p. 246.

16. *The Lincoln Imp* VII, no. 8 (Hilary Term, 1934), 7.

17. MacNeice is quoted in Penrose and Freeman, *Conspiracy of Silence*, p. 53.

18. **UNEMPLOYMENT IN ENGLAND, 1929–37:**
    Number of unemployed (in millions)*

Month	1929	1930	1931	1932	1933	1934	1935	1936	1937
Jan.	1.43	1.53	2.67	2.79	2.98	2.46	2.39	2.23	1.77
July	1.19	2.07	2.78	2.89	2.51	2.19	2.05	1.72	1.45

* Total number of persons (insured and uninsured) registered as unemployed in the United Kingdom (Great Britain and Northern Ireland). *British Labour Statistics*, Table 162.

19. In more technical terms, the revolutionary insight that Keynes had was that, contrary to what had been believed, the level of investment was

not set by the amount people saved from consumption, but consumption itself set incomes at a level that was necessary to cover investment.

20. See Ashley and Saunders, *Red Oxford*, p. 16, for a discussion of Cole's efforts to maintain the socialist tradition at Oxford up to the time of the depression.

21. Howarth, *Cambridge Between Two Wars*, p. 213.

22. Penrose and Freeman, *Conspiracy of Silence*, p. 45 (description of Runciman), p. 108 (quotation).

23. Roy Harrod, Keynes's biographer is quoted in Penrose and Freeman, *Conspiracy of Silence*, p. 110. See also Howarth's comment in *Cambridge Between Two Wars*, p. 217.

24. Layton, *Waiting for the Messiah*, p. 125.

25. Lewis, *Memoirs*, pp. 38, 39.

26. Notes for memoirs in PAC, MG 32, C 23, Vol. 105, file: David Lewis Random Notes.

27. PAC (see n. 26).

28. Lewis, *Memoirs*, p. 41, and PAC (see n. 26).

29. Lewis, *Memoirs*, p. 42.

30. *Memoirs*, p. 45.

31. *Memoirs*, p. 45.

32. Strachey, *The Coming Struggle for Power*, p. 396.

33. Green, *Children of the Sun*, p. 319.

34. Lewis, *Memoirs*, p. 298.

35. Bell is quoted in Howarth, *Cambridge Between Two Wars*, p. 156.

36. *Cambridge Between Two Wars*, p. 156.

37. "Identity," p. 8.

38. PAC (See n. 26).

39. Unless otherwise noted, all references to Union debates are from the minute books of the Oxford Union Society found in the Oxford Union Society Library.

40. *The Isis*, Feb. 15, 1933, p. 7.

41. *The Times*, Feb. 13, 1933.

42. *The Isis*, Feb. 15, 1933, p. 1.

43. Lewis, "Nursery for Statesmen," *This Month*, May 1946, p. 50.

44. Freeman in *Young Oxford at War*, p. 87.

45. *The Isis*, Oct. 25, 1933, p. 12; Nov. 15, 1933, p. 8; Jan. 24, 1934, p. 9; Jan. 31, 1934, p. 6; June 6, 1934, pp. 2 and 5; Nov. 28, 1934, p. 8.

46. Lewis, *Memoirs*, p. 53.

47. *The Isis*, Nov. 28, 1934, p. 7. The minutes of the Oxford Union Society recording David's election as president are dated Nov. 29, 1934. Presumably the election was held on Nov. 27 or earlier and recorded at the next meeting of the union which fell on the 29th.

48. Foot, *Anuerin Bevan*, p. 158.

49. Up to the time of the 1917 Revolution, this certainly was the position of the Bund. However, beginning in late 1918 and carrying through 1919 — in other words, during the civil war — there were terrible pogroms against Jews in Ukraine, and this tended to further radicalize members of the Bund. At the same time, the Communists prevented pogroms in the areas they controlled, calling them counter-revolutionary. As a result, the Bund in Russia came to support the theory of a dictatorship of the proletariat as a means of preventing the violence of reactionary groups. Nevertheless, it was support for a dictatorship of the proletariat only in extreme cases and then only for as short a time as possible.

   Maishe belonged to the Russian Bund. But after the war most members were no longer in Russia, and those who were fled or became passive or were exiled or shot or joined the Kombund (a section of the Bund in Ukraine that broke away and joined the Bolsheviks under the name "The Communist Bund"). The centre of the Bund transferred to Poland because that's where most of the Jews were. However, the Polish Bund had declared itself an independent party when the Germans invaded in 1916, and at its congress in Dec. 1917 it had accepted the theory of dictatorship of the proletariat — although it said it would restrict its application to such situations as a prolonged civil war when it might curtail the civil rights of "social groups that do not belong to the democracy of socially productive work." However, the curtailment would be minimal and aimed at drawing unproductive classes into workers' associations. Nevertheless, by 1924 the Polish Bund was opposing the Comintern on the grounds that the Central Committee of the Soviet Communist Party was imposing a dictatorship over workers. (Hertz, *History of the Bund*, Vols. I–II.) According to Kaplansky, Maishe never accepted the theory of dictatorship of the proletariat. He belonged, says Kaplansky, to the more moderate wing of the Bund.

50. Ascher, *The Mensheviks*, p. 22.

51. Penner, *Canadian Communism*, p. 8.

52. See Trotsky's account of the meeting between Wells and Lenin in Trotsky, *Lenin*, pp. 180–182.

53. *The Isis*, Feb. 7, 1934, p. 9.

54. *The Isis*, Feb. 7, 1934, p. 9.

55. Lewis, *Memoirs*, p. 67.

56. Recollection of Ted Jolliffe.

57. Lewis in *The Oxford Forward*, pp. 10, 14.

58. "The Red Flag" is sung to the tune of "Tannenbaum." It was written by Jim Connell, an Irish journalist, for the London dock strike of 1889, and is still sung at Labour Party conventions and in Parliament to celebrate Labour victories.

59. PAC, Reel M–3619, A.M. Klein Papers: letter to Abe Klein, pp. 000006–000017.

60. Lewis, *Memoirs*, p. 72.

61. *The Isis*, Nov. 8, 1933, p.1.

62. *The Isis*, Feb. 14, 1934, pp. 3, 11.

63. The October Club was formed in Dec. 1931. Two months earlier, similar clubs had been formed at the London School of Economics and at London's University College. In April 1932 the first Communist cell at Cambridge was formed. By early 1932 Oxford's October Club had about 150 members and, by the end of the year, about 300. (Ashley and Saunders, *Red Oxford*, p. 45.)

64. *The Isis*. May 29, 1935, p. 4.

65. *The Isis*, June 5, 1935, p. 13.

66. *The Isis*, Dec. 4, 1935, p. 3.

67. The figure of more than 1,000 comes from Hilton, *Oxford Left in the Thirties*, p. 13. Approaching 1,200 was the recollection of Sir William Nield, chairman of the Labour Club in 1935, and that recollection was confirmed by John Cripps, who was chairman in 1934, and by Sir Geoffrey Wilson, who was chairman in 1933. Student population figures for 1938–39 are from the Oxford University Registrar's office.

68. Green, *Children of the Sun*, p. 325.

69. Lewis, *Memoirs*, p. 75.

70. PAC (see n. 26): letter from Woodsworth, June 19, 1935.

71. PAC (see n. 59): letter to Bessie Klein, pp. 000026–000037.

CHAPTER 13

1. David's favourite song, "A Dudu": *Riboinoi shel oilem, / ich vel dir a dudu zingen! / ayei emtzoecho? / vu ken ich dich yo gefinen? / v' ayei loi emtzoecho? /un vu ken ich den nisht gefinen? /az' vu ich gei, iz nor du, / un' vu ich shtei iz doch vider du, / rak' du, / ach' du, / nor' du, / du, du, du, du, du. . . .*

You are to be found everywhere. / Wherever I go — Du, / Wherever I stand — Du, / When I am well — Du, / When misery befalls me / It is certainly Du; / In the East — Du, / In the West — Du, / In the North — Du, / In the South — Du; / In Heaven — Du, / On earth — Du; / Everywhere — only Du, Du, Du.

2. For example, a Simpsons newspaper ad invited readers to compare "our copies" which were selling $4 to $11 cheaper than the New York originals. (*Montreal Star*, Nov. 28, 1951.)

3. *The Gazette*, Nov. 9, 1942.

4. The reviews of *Death of a Salesman* appeared on Monday, Jan. 26, 1953. The reviewer for The Gazette was Harold Whitehead (Whittaker by then having left to work for *The Globe and Mail*). Reviewing for *The Montreal Herald* was Pat Pearce.

5. *Kanada Adler* (Montreal), Aug. 31, 1941.

6. Interview with Faga and Israel Falk; and Kaplansky, "History of the Jewish Labour Committee," p. 8.

7. "History of the Jewish Labour Committee," p. 8.

8. *Kanada Adler* reported the arrests (Dec. 18, 1941). Erlich and Alter had been arrested previously in Oct. 1939, following the Hitler-Stalin Pact and had been sentenced to death "For active subversive work against the Soviet Union and assistance to Polish Intelligence organs in armed activities." They were released in Sept. 1941 under an amnesty for all Polish prisoners negotiated by the Polish government in exile. Their death sentence in 1942 was ordered, the Soviets said, because they were engaged in hostile activities, and the example given was that they had been urging Soviet troops "to stop the bloodshed and immediately conclude a peace with Germany." The charges were baseless. In fact, Erlich and Alter topped the Gestapo list of dangerous enemies who were to be liquidated when caught.

9. PAC, MG 28, IV I, Vol. 363, file: Erlich and Alter, letter D. Lewis to Frank J. McKenzie, May 28, 1943.

10. Typed copy of resolution with list of council members (including the executive) and how they voted attached. The vote was 14-9 in favour of the resolution. (PAC [see n. 9]. See also Young, *The Anatomy of a Party*, p. 271.)

11. PAC (see n. 9): letter Hillary Brown to D. Lewis, May 1, 1943.

12. PAC (see n. 9): letter D. Lewis to Frank J. McKenzie, May 28, 1943. In his recounting of the actions undertaken, David overlooked a resolution of protest and a "Special Manifesto of Protest," published by the Quebec section of the CCF. (See also Young, *The Anatomy of a Party*, p. 272.)

13. PAC, MG 28, V 75, Vol. 7, file 10: letter from the Foreign Exchange Control Board to Michael Rubinstein, chairman of the Jewish Labour Committee, citing David Lewis's intervention, April 23, 1942.

14. See numerous letters in PAC (see n. 13): Vol. 16, file 7.

15. *The Role of Relief and Rescue*, p. 8.

16. *The Role of Relief and Rescue*, p. 11.

17. The Tree of Life is referred to in Genesis 2:9: "And out of the ground made the Lord God to grow every tree that is pleasant to the sight, and good for food; the tree of life also in the midst of the garden, and the tree of knowledge of good and evil." (See also Genesis 3:22 and Proverbs 3:18.)

CHAPTER 14

1. *The Canadian Methodist Quarterly*, July 1891, p. 297.

2. For weather conditions, from the Atmospheric Environment Service, Environment Canada. For state of the parliamentary grounds, from photographs at the Parliamentary Library.

3. Heaps, *The Rebel in the House*, p. 118. See also pp. 14, 4, 131.

4. McHenry, *The Third Force in Canada*, p. 24.

5. *The First Ten Tears, 1932–1942*. Grace MacInnis says she is "pretty sure" that Scott and Underhill were there. But the historian Michiel Horn says that he talked with both men in 1966–67 and neither recalled being there.

6. Floor plan, sixth floor, Centre Block, House of Commons, by A.W. Reynolds, Nov. 1940. The office numbering was changed by Prime Minister John Diefenbaker in 1958, as shown in floor plan by O. Huggard, Sept. 25, 1958. Both plans are filed in Ottawa, Public Works Canada, Records Division, "A" Wing, Room 033.

7. The minutes of the meeting at which the CCF was conceived are quoted in McNaught, *A Prophet in Politics*, p. 259.

8. Interview with Stanley Knowles.

9. Psalm 137:1,4: "By the rivers of Babylon, there we sat down, yea, we wept, when we remembered Zion. . . . How shall we sing the Lord's song in a strange land?"

   "Jerusalem" was the preface to Blake's book *Milton*, published in 1808. It was put to music by Charles Hubert Hastings Parry and was first sung in 1916 in Albert Hall, where it was an immediate success. For the remainder of the First World War, and for a time afterward, it was almost a second national anthem. It found its way into the English public school hymn book, and no doubt every public school graduate at Oxford during David's time there knew it intimately. See Osborne, *If Such Holy Song*, Item 157. According to Osborne, Blake was not referring in the poem to righting social wrongs in the sense perceived by the Social Gospel, even though that is how the poem came to be read in the twentieth century. "The 'dark satanic mills' [in the poem] have nothing to do with factories and sweated labour," he says. "[T]hey represent 'the chopping block of logic and science' to which Blake was unalterably opposed, and which he found in the philosophies of men like Locke and Bacon. . . . Thus for him, Jerusalem stood for an ideal life of liberty, of divine freedom. For us today, it is the City of God."

10. George is quoted in Cook, *The Regenerators*, p. 120.

11. *The Regenerators*, p. 107.

12. *The Regenerators*, p. 173.

13. McNaught, *A Prophet in Politics*, p. 26. At about the same time A.E. Smith was saying, "[Jesus] was not so much concerned about the salvation of the souls of men as he was about the salvation of their social relations" (quoted in Cook, *The Regenerators*, p. 225). And in a speech to the Social Service Congress in March 1914 Charles Stelzle said: "[Jesus] thought not so much of individual salvation . . . [He] thought supremely of social salvation" (quoted in Allen, *The Social Passion*, p. 29).

14. Chown is quoted in Cook, *The Regenerators*, p. 230.

15. Thompson is quoted in *The Regenerators*, p. 171.

16. Carman is quoted in *The Regenerators*, p. 192.

17. Silcox is quoted in Allen, *The Social Passion*, p. 7.

18. Cook, *The Regenerators*, p. 179.

19. Allen, *The Social Passion*. For Jesus as the first labour leader, see p. 14; for Bland, see p. 264; and for Ivens, see p. 51.

20. *The Social Passion*. For conscription of wealth, see p. 42; and for corporate structures accepting social guilt, see p. 45.

21. *The Social Passion*, p. 64.

22. *The Social Passion*, p. 74.

23. *Social Welfare* is quoted in *The Social Passion*, p. 66.

24. *The Social Passion*, p. 84.

25. *The Social Passion*, p. 85.

26. McNaught, *A Prophet in Politics*, p. 137.

27. Allen, *The Social Passion*, p. 116.

28. Cook, *The Regenerators*, p. 226.

29. Allen, *The Social Passion*, p. 97.

30. *The Social Passion*, p. 121.

31. Thomas is quoted in *The Social Passion*, p. 157.

32. *The Social Passion*, p. 152.

33. *The Social Passion*, p. 155.

34. *The Social Passion*, p. 216.

35. Levin, *Forward from Exile*, p. 389, where Levin was referring to his move to Vilna in late 1903 or 1904 and the help he received there from businessmen: "It was a generation of businessmen which has by now died out in the Jewish world — individuals who regarded business only as a means that would enable them to serve the community." Levin left

Russia in 1906, never to return. His comment was made in the 1930s when he was writing his memoirs. He died in 1935 with his memoirs finished only up to his fortieth year. Vilna, of course, is where the Bund was founded.

36. Cook, *The Regenerators*, p.169.

37. PAC, MG 32, C 23, Vol. 105, file: David Lewis Random Notes, letter D. Lewis to Ray Hayes, secretary-treasurer, B.C. Federation of Labour, Dec. 16, 1971.

CHAPTER 15

1. PAC, MG 28, IV I, Vol. 102, file: MacInnis, letter Grace MacInnes to D. Lewis, May 15, 1944.

2. York University Archives, Oliver Hodges Collection, Ontario CCF Labour Committee. See correspondence throughout this area of the collection.

3. PAC (see n. 1): Vol. 59, file: Ontario Trade Union Relations 1937–1953, letter D. Lewis to Bert Leavens, Sept. 25, 1942.

4. Lewis, *Memoirs*, p. 151. Ted Jolliffe, in an Oct. 1986 interview, confirmed that David's goal was to "get the Communists out of there [out of the unions] and build a new party of which labour would be a constituent part. Hence the New Democratic Party. . . . In his philosophy, in his political theory, I suppose it's part of the materialist interpretation of history, he thought that most parties are dependent on economic interests for their survival."

5. York University Archives, Oliver Hodges Collection, Box 70, file: Windsor, letter from E. Park to O. Hodges, March 6, 1946. The committee was created in July 1942 and would go out of existence in Dec. 1948 (see memo by Larry Sefton re the Ontario CCF Labour Committee, Sept. 13, 1947, Oliver Hodges Collection, Box 74, file: Ont. CCF Labour Committee; see also letter Oliver Hodges to Pat Conroy, Dec. 10, 1948, Box 75, file: To Be Entered and Filed in Letter Book.)

6. LSR, *Social Planning for Canada*, pp. 115, 116.

7. For unemployment figures, see Table D124–133: Labour Force and Main Components . . . 1921 to 1960, *Historical Statistics of Canada*.
   In Feb. 1935 there were 1,054,821 on direct relief. A year earlier there had been 1,154,822. These figures included the families of the unemployed but did not include men in work camps, in farm placements, those doing relief work for wages, those in relief settlement schemes, or those on relief in dried out areas. If they were all added, the figure for 1935 would rise to 1,342,000 and that for 1934 to 1,490,000. (LSR, Social Planning for Canada, p. 13.)

8. Drystek, "The Simplest and Cheapest Mode of Dealing with Them," p. 427.

9. Penner, *Canadian Communism*, p. 110.

10. Thompson and Seager, *Canada 1922–1939*, p. 269.

11. For a description of the riot see, *Canada 1922–1939*, pp. 271–72; and Avakumovic, *The Communist Party in Canada*, pp. 78–81.

12. By L.A.M(acKay), quoted in Betcherman, *The Little Band*, p. 105.

13. *The Little Band*, p. 44.

14. *The Globe and Mail*, Aug. 1, 1929.

15. *The Mail and Empire*, Dec. 8, 1932.

16. *The Globe and Mail*, Nov. 15, 1937.

17. Dafoe Papers, University of Manitoba, quoted in McNaught, *A Prophet in Politics*, p. 269.

18. In 1934 a pastoral letter from Archbishop Gauthier, read from pulpits throughout his archdiocese, condemned the CCF as godless, Communist, and materialistic. And four years later, in Nov. 1938, Cardinal Villeneuve, head of the Church in Quebec, levelled the same charges in a widely reported speech to the Montreal Junior Board of Trade. What was especially irksome, said David in his memoirs, "was the fact that CCF doctrine and practice owed more to the Social Gospel and the search for a Christian Social Order than to any other source. It was difficult to understand how learned church leaders could fail to perceive this obvious aspect of the CCF" (*Memoirs*, p. 459). Villeneuve also joined Spanish bishops and came out in support for soon-to-be dictator General Francisco Franco during the Spanish Civil War, declaring that Franco was waging a holy war against Bolshevik atheism.

19. Hutchison, *Mr. Prime Minister*, p. 243. Hutchison says Bennett "worked steadily for fifteen or sixteen hours [a day], with a brief interruption for lunch and a leisurely dinner in his suite."

20. Penner, *Canadian Communism*, p. 23, citing Harvey Klehr, *The Heyday of American Communism*.

21. Horn, *The League for Social Reconstruction*, p. 127.

22. Under the Immigration Act any immigrant who was not yet a citizen could be deported if he or she had ever been a public charge or was convicted of a crime, even something as minor as vagrancy, loitering, or obstructing a footpath. In the ten years before the Second World War, about 30,000 were deported and about 28,000 of those were during Bennett's period as prime minister, 1930–35. Most were deported for being a public charge (Drystek, "The Simplest and Cheapest Method of Dealing with Them," pp. 427, 439).

   When the number of deportations peaked in 1932–33, the causes were listed (p. 430) as: public charge, 8,758; medical, 1,493; criminal, 876; other, 538. Total: 11,665.

In addition, section 41 of the Immigration Act was amended at the time of the Winnipeg General Strike to give the federal government power to deport anyone who advocated or taught the unlawful destruction of property or who was "a member of or affiliated with any organization entertaining or teaching disbelief in or opposition to organized government." As Drystek says (p. 422), consequently "every radical not born in Canada was liable to deportation." He says (p. 440) that "about 100 individuals who were considered by the government to be radical agitators were deported prior to WW II."

23. LSR, *Social Planning for Canada*, p. 116.

24. Avakumovic, *The Communist Party in Canada*, p. 74. The LSR attributed 21,253 members in affiliated unions to the WUL in what, judging from the text, appears to be the year 1933. (See *Social Planning for Canada*, p. 116.)

25. *Historical Statistics of Canada*, Table E190–197; Avakumovic, *The Communist Party in Canada*, p. 70; and Penner, *Canadian Communism*, p. 106, quoting Tim Buck, *Thirty Years 1922–1952*.

26. Avakumovic, *The Communist Party in Canada*, p. 77.

27. Betcherman, *The Little Band*, p. 161.

28. *The Communist Party in Canada*, p. 78; and *The Little Band*, p. 151.

29. Eleven weeks after arrest, they were convicted. The sentence included a recommendation that Buck and the seven others sentenced to Kingston Penitentiary be deported after their release. Thirteen weeks after that, on Feb. 20, 1932, their appeal was thrown out. (*The Little Band*, pp. 171–211, and *The Communist Party in Canada*, pp. 87, 88.)

30. Penner, *Canadian Communism*, p. 121.

31. Avakumovic, *The Communist Party in Canada*, p. 89.

32. Penner, *Canadian Communism*, p. 137.

33. Penner, *Canadian Communism*, p. 142; and Abella, *Nationalism, Communism, and Canadian Labour*, p. 4.

34. *Nationalism, Communism, and Canadian Labour*, p. 5.

35. PAC (see n.1): Vol. 99, file: Lewis 1936–39; letter G. Spry to D. Lewis, written from Toronto, Dec. 9, 1936,

36. Letter G. Spry to D. Lewis, April 30, 1937, quoted in Horn, *The League for Social Reconstruction*, p. 142; and Abella, *Nationalism, Communism, and Canadian Labour*, p. 24.

37. Letter D. Lewis to Sophie, June 28, 1937. This letter, used with permission, is from the Lewis family's private collection of letters between David and Sophie, hereafter referred to as "the family collection."

38. Avakumovic, *The Communist Party in Canada*, pp. 115 n., 117. However, as Avakumovic points out, even though membership was high, so was the turnover.

39. Penner, *Canadian Communism*, pp. 143,144.

CHAPTER 16

1. When David quit as national secretary in 1950, he was earning $3,900 a year.

2. G. Caplan, *The Dilemma of Canadian Socialism*, p. 56. Woodsworth's action was "swiftly endorsed by the National Council" (Morley, *Secular Socialists*, p. 201). See also McNaught, *A Prophet in Politics*, p. 266.

3. ### CCF ELECTION RESULTS IN ONTARIO*

Year	Type	Votes	%	Seats Won
June 1934	Provincial	108,961	7	1
Oct. 1935	Federal	129,457	8	0
Oct. 1937	Provincial	77,744	5	0
Mar. 1940	Federal	61,166	3.8	0
Aug. 1943	Provincial	418,520	31.9	34
June 1945	Provincial	390,910	22.5	8
	Federal	260,502	14.4	0
June 1948	Provincial	465,834	26.5	21
June 1949	Federal	306,617	15.2	1

* McHenry, *The Third Force in Canada*, p. 164.

4. Recollection of Kalmen Kaplansky.

5. Lewis, *Memoirs*, p. 375.

6. See, for example, *Memoirs*, p. 118.

7. Letter D. Lewis to R.I.C. Picard, The Graduates' Society of McGill University, Aug. 26, 1976.

8. Unless otherwise noted, the letters quoted here are in the family collection and are used with permission.

9. Maclean's Magazine, April 1971, p. 21.

10. PAC, MG 32, C 23, Vol. 116: letter D. Lewis to S. Lewis, Sept. 12, 1957.

CHAPTER 17

1. Lewis, *Louder Voices*, p.61.

2. In David's words, the Manifesto "applied the Fabian approach" (*Memoirs*, p. 85). The six surviving signatories were Eugene Forsey, King Gordon, Leonard Marsh, Frank Scott, Graham Spry, and J.F. Parkinson. There were seven signatories to the first edition — Frank Underhill, who died in 1971, was the seventh — and there were a number of additional contributors. Some were thanked in the preface; some requested anonymity. Michiel Horn names them all (*The League for Social Reconstruction*, p. 68).

For the comment that the program was reformist, see LSR, *Social Planning for Canada*, p. xviii.

3. Lewis, *Memoirs*, p. 198.

4. Horn, *The League for Social Reconstruction*, p. 69.

5. References, in the order of the paragraphs quoted, are Lewis and Scott, *Make This YOUR Canada*, pp. 88, 103–04, 189, 197. The third and fourth of these quotations come from the last chapter in *Make This YOUR Canada* which was drafted "mainly" by Frank Scott. It had David's enthusiastic approval, however, and he participated in the editing of the chapter (Lewis, "F.R. Scott's Contribution to the CCF," pp. 81, 82).

6. David is quoted in Young, *The Anatomy of a Party*, p. 61, from an interview by Prof. Paul Fox.

7. *The Anatomy of a Party*, p. 166.

8. Speech at Dalhousie University delivered Oct. 30, 1946, PAC, MG 28, IV I, Vol. 100, file: Miscellaneous.

9. *Toronto Star*, May 27, 1981.

10. Lewis and Scott, *Make This YOUR Canada*, p. 55.

11. *The Globe and Mail*, Sept. 29, 1988.

12. Quoted without source in LSR, *Social Planning for Canada*, p. 199.

13. PAC (see n.8): Vol. 363: letter Bill Temple to M.J. Coldwell, May 28, 1936.

14. Report of the Executive to the Ontario Provincial Convention, 1936, quoted in Zakuta, *A Protest Movement Becalmed*, p. 37.

15. Scott, *A New Endeavour*, p. 38.

16. See David's letters to Sophie (Chapter 16) and also Young, *The Anatomy of a Party*, p. 79.

17. *The Gazette*, Feb. 6, 1936.

18. For this and other examples, see Young, *The Anatomy of a Party*, p. 88.

19. See pamphlets in PAC (see n.8): Vol. 126, file: Elections Literature, and Vol. 406, file: Federal Election 1945 — in English.

20. The proper name of the report was *Social Insurance and Allied Services*. Its author, Sir William Beveridge, was created 1st Baron Beveridge of Tuggal in 1946.

21. In his speech David said: "Socialism says to you that in the same manner in which you went from the mere umpire function of the state to the social service function, so that instead of the state sitting back and watching the citizens going at each other, merely making sure the rules were observed, it became the duty of the state to see to it that sick people were not wanting for doctors, homeless people, old people, et cetera, were looked after. You now have to go from that to the third step [to a

democratic socialist system] just as logically and just as relentlessly in the development of your society." PAC (see n.8): Miscellaneous, pp. 3, 1, 2.

22. *The Gazette* is quoted in Lewis, *Memoirs*, p. 250.

23. In tape-recorded notes for his book, David had this to say: "The Dec. 14 issue of *The New Commonwealth* . . . does not contain . . . any reference to the argument on the floor of the convention with respect to the section of the election manifesto headed Social Ownership. My memory is that it was a very severe debate with respect to the second paragraph providing that private business, if it was not exploitative, will be given every opportunity to function and to provide a fair rate of return. There was a great deal of argument about this." The tapes are in the possession of the Lewis family and are referred to hereafter as "family tapes."

24. Lewis, *Memoirs*, p. 251.

25. The resolution said that "Where private business shows no sign of becoming a monopoly, operates efficiently under decent working conditions, and does not operate to the detriment of the Canadian people, it will be given every opportunity to function, to provide a fair rate of return and to make its contribution to the nation's wealth." Instead of the word "monopolies," *Make This YOUR Canada* had used the phrase "socially dangerous vested interests"; and instead of "operate to the detriment of the Canadian people" it had used "exploit the public."

26. The letter, dated Oct. 1, 1940, is quoted in Young, *The Anatomy of a Party*, pp. 115–16.

27. PAC (see n.8): Vol. 59, file: Ontario Trade Union Relations 1937–1953; letter D. Lewis to Dr. C.A. King, Oct. 18, 1944.

28. For another account of David's encounter with the lady at the bookstall, see Shackleton, *Tommy Douglas*, p. 225.

29. McLeod & McLeod, *Tommy Douglas*, p. 281.

30. Lewis, *Memoirs*, p. 326.

31. *The Canadian Forum*, April, 1952.

32. Underhill is quoted in Francis, *Frank H. Underhill*, p.153.

33. Lewis, *Memoirs*, pp. 422, 423.

34. *The Canadian Forum*, May, 1952, p. 34. In the same issue Underhill responded to Brewin's letter, saying: "Anybody can easily make a test for himself of the real interest in education that prevails in CCF Toronto headquarters. Take a look at the files of the Ontario CCF *News* over the past few years and see if they give you the impression of a management solicitous to building up a CCF membership who shall be intellectually alert and well informed about the issues that have caused storms in world socialism over the past two decades, or of a management that

encourages discussion. They give me the impression of a management that regards the CCF members as sheep."

35. Lewis, *Memoirs*, p. 423.

36. Francis, *Frank H. Underhill*, p. 178.

37. Matthew 3:30.

CHAPTER 18

1. Hellman, *Scoundrel Time*, p. 75.

2. Cf. Lewis, *Memoirs*, p. 261, where David says, "We did not realize it at the time but, in retrospect, it seems clear to me that 1945 was the year which decided the fate of the CCF." I think the statement is equally applicable to the battle between the CCF and the Communists. Ted Jolliffe in an Oct. 1986 interview said, "I would say the battle [to oust the Communists from the labour movement] really began in 1945."

3. *Memoirs*, p. 269.

4. Scott is quoted in Young, *The Anatomy of a Party*, p. 119.

5. There are any number of references to support this description of David. Walter Young points out that after 1937, when illness reduced Woodsworth to being only the titular head of the CCF, David became the undisputed administrative and ideological leader. (See *The Anatomy of a Party*, p. 162.) Young adds at p. 164: "He was not a particularly charismatic leader; he was a manager, if not a boss. . . . [His] domination [was] complete."

   Terry Morley says that David couldn't dominate the Ontario CCF as he could the national party because among the provincial oligarchy there were people of competing talent. Nevertheless, he was consulted about all major decisions and he gave "constant advice" and "People of such stature, with one or two exceptions in Saskatchewan and English-speaking Montreal, were not available to the party elsewhere in the country" (*Secular Socialists*, p. 170).

6. Lewis, *Memoirs*, p. 261.

7. The results were: Fred Rose (Labour-Progressive) 5,767
   Paul Massé (Bloc-Populaire) 5,506
   Lazarus Phillips (Liberal) 4,120
   David Lewis (CCF) 3,267

8. Avakumovic, *The Communist Party in Canada*, p. 162.

9. Lewis, *Memoirs*, p. 231.

10. See *The Gazette* for the three weeks before the election.

11. The novel was called *Come the Revolution*, and the passage is quoted in the transcript of a radio documentary called *Cold War in Canada*, prepared by Gary Marcuse and broadcast on CBC's "Ideas" program, March 6–27, 1984. (Transcript, p. 9.)

12. Attendance figures for the Lewis and Bloc Populaire rallies: *The Gazette*, Friday, Aug. 6, 1943; for the LPP rally: *The Gazette*, Monday, Aug. 9, 1943.

13. Penner, *Canadian Communism*, p. 205. A CCF candidate would have split the left-wing vote and Samuel Schwisberg, the Liberal candidate who came second, would have won.

14. *Canadian Communism*, p. 206, quoting a letter to A. Shurem, March 11, 1944.

15. Lewis, *Memoirs*, p. 232.

16. *Memoirs*, p. 232.

17. Joe Zuken, the Communist candidate, was a Jewish Winnipeg lawyer who was a board of education trustee at the time. Stewart polled 13,011 votes; Zuken, 9,116; the Liberal candidate, 8,839; and the Conservative, 2,584. After winning York South in 1962, David lost it twice, first in 1963 (winning it back in 1965) and again in 1974. In Winnipeg North he might never have been defeated, even in the 1958 Diefenbaker landslide, when a Conservative won the seat by 215 votes.

    As for his 1945 candidacy in Hamilton West — the riding of Ellen Fairclough and Lincoln Alexander and never, in its eighty-four-year history, held by anyone but a Liberal or a Conservative — he gives the skimpiest of coverage in his memoirs: two and a half sentences in all, claiming, unconvincingly, that he thought there was a chance of victory. (*Memoirs*, pp. 261, 266.)

18. In the Ontario election, the Communists ran thirty-seven candidates, twenty-seven of them against sitting CCFers and only five against sitting Tories. Going into the election the CCF had thirty-two seats; it ended up with eight — and the Tories went from thirty-eight seats and a minority government to a majority with sixty-six out of the ninety seats. Estimates are that the CCF would have won five more seats in the Ontario election (and would have remained as official opposition) and ten more across Canada in the federal election if LPP candidates had not deliberately split the vote. (Young, *The Anatomy of a Party*, pp. 276, 277; Lewis, *Memoirs*, p. 268; and G. Caplan, *The Dilemma of Canadian Socialism*, p. 158.)

    A Sept. 1943 Gallup poll ranked the CCF highest in voter support with 29% across the nation compared with 28% for Liberals, 28% for Conservatives, 9% for Bloc Populaire, and 6% for others.

19. Op-ed feature article by John Weir in *Canadian Tribune*, Dec. 16, 1944, p. 7.

20. *The Winnipeg Tribune*, May 29, 1944. David responded to McLean's endorsement of co-operation by pointing out that "The only objective of the [LPP] . . . is to try to prevent the CCF from winning power." (*The Winnipeg Tribune*, May 30, 1944.)

21. Pickersgill, *The Mackenzie King Record*, I:467.

22. Pickersgill and Forster, *The Mackenzie King Record*, II:316.

23. Lewis, *Memoirs*, p. 291. If it was not a formal alliance, it was close to it. Sam Carr, testifying in his trial on a charge of conspiring to utter a forged passport for a Soviet agent, said that he had been to Ottawa quite a number of times to confer with Liberal leaders on "election negotiations." He had met Allan McNeill of the Liberal Federation (obviously Carr, or the reporter, meant Allan G. McLean) and Health Minister Paul Martin, who had a lot of Labour-Progressive supporters in his riding. (*The Globe and Mail*, April 8, 1949.)

24. Mackenzie King's diary for Feb. 18, 1944, records that TLC president Percy Bengough "did not want to see the CCF make any headway," although in a 1962 interview Bengough denied that's what he told King. (Horowitz, *Canadian Labour in Politics*, p. 104.) Whatever was the truth, Bengough *was* worried about growing CCF strength. He thought the labour movement should be non-partisan, which was the exact opposite of what the CCF wanted. The congress's 1945 action was the only time the TLC endorsed a party and, as Gad Horowitz describes it, the step it took was "small and cautious, almost terrified . . . and it was never repeated." (*Canadian Labour in Politics*, p. 106.) At best the support was marginally effective, but it further divided the left and enraged the CCF.

25. Buck, *Yours in the Struggle*, p. 328.

26. Sullivan was a solid trade unionist; nevertheless, his election as secretary-treasurer owed much to the liaison between Bengough and Buck. (Penner, *Canadian Communism*, p. 190, and Buck, *Yours in the Struggle*, p. 328.)

27. Gallup poll results are from McHenry, *The Third Force in Canada*, p. 136.

28. The 1944 edition of *Who's Who in Canada* lists Victor Drury as holding the posts of president and chairman of Canadian Car & Foundry Co. Ltd.; president and director of Canadian Car Munitions, Limited; Canadian General Transit Co. Limited, Hydro-Electric Securities Corporation, Limited, and International Holdings, Limited, vice-president and director of The Foundation Co. of Canada Ltd., and director of Calgary & Edmonton Corporation Limited, Canadian Vickers Limited, Carter White Lead Company of Canada, Limited, Construction Equipment Company, Eddy Match Co. Limited, Gatineau Power Company, Gunite Waterproofing Co., Limited, The Hull Electric Company, Montreal Dry Docks, Limited, Montreal Trust Company, The Sherwin-Williams Co. of Canada Ltd., and The Guardian Insurance Co. of Canada.

    Bud Drury served as president of the Treasury Board from 1968 to 1974. He also served as minister of public works and minister of state for science and technology from 1974 to 1976.

29. *Montreal Standard*, Sept. 1, 1945. At the time, Canadian Car & Foundry was laying off employees because it had stopped production of fighter aircraft and trainers. Meanwhile it was paying employees an average of less than $28 a week in take-home pay, and its net profits after taxes and

depreciation for the previous year were $1,130,000. At the same time, C.D. Howe was saying that two jobs were available for every applicant and a million additional jobs "definitely are in sight." (*Toronto Star*, Sept. 17, 1945.)

30. Regarding the Ford strike, see Abella, *Nationalism, Commmunism, and Canadian Labour*, p. 143.

    Regarding strikes in 1946, see *Historical Statistics of Canada*, Series E 190–197, Numbers of strikes and lockouts, employers and workers involved and time loss, Canada, 1901 to 1975. Although there were years between 1946 and the mid-seventies during which there were more people on strike and more time lost, the average number of days lost per worker in 1946, calculated on the basis of the total number of workers in Canada, was more than double that in the other intervening years. The value of this particular statistic is that it takes into allowance a smaller work force when demonstrating the impact of the strikes.

31. In Canada the Cold War began in earnest on Sept. 7, 1945, five days after the surrender of Japan, when Igor Gouzenko fled the Soviet Embassy in Ottawa with news of a Communist spy ring operating in Canada. Throughout 1946 and right up to the end of 1948, front pages across the country focused on the trials of people implicated by Gouzenko and by a royal commission into his allegations. Churchill's famous speech in Fulton, Missouri, coining the phrase "iron curtain," was delivered in March 1946, just one week before Fred Rose, MP for Cartier, was arrested as one of the people incriminated through Gouzenko's disclosures. Rose and sixteen others were charged. Rose, Sam Carr, and six others were convicted and sent to prison. The last appeal was heard on Dec. 1, 1948.

32. Gardiner is quoted in G. Caplan, *The Dilemma of Canadian Socialism*, p. 128, and taken from *The Telegram*, Toronto, Nov. 30, 1943.

33. The statement was made in a Liberal Party advertisement in *The Globe and Mail*, July 28, 1943, and is quoted in G. Caplan, *The Dilemma of Canadian Socialism*, p. 100.

34. The Kirkconnell speech was made to the Canadian Club in Toronto. (*The Telegram*, Toronto, February 16, 1948, p. 31.)

35. PAC, MG 28, IV I, Vol. 362, file: 1945 Election, letter Coldwell to C.W. Price, New Brunswick section of the CCF, March 8, 1945.

36. The CCL expelled the UE for non-payment of its per capita tax. The union had been late in its payment because of an administrative oversight but CCF officials expelled it even though it tried to pay the tax as soon as it knew of the oversight. (Abella, *Nationalism, Communism, and Canadian Labour*, pp. 156–60.) The TLC expelled the CSU in 1949 and by early 1950 the union no longer existed. In 1951 it allowed the SIU to replace the CSU in the congress. (Kaplan, *Everything That Floats*, pp. 61, 63, 66, 68, 84.)

37. *Everything That Floats*, p. 71.

38. PAC (see n.35): Vol. 59, file: Ontario Trade Union Relations 1937–53, letter D. Lewis to O. Hodges, 29 Oct. 1948.

39. Mine Mill was organizing the local at INCO and the raid apparently was aimed at getting the records of who had signed union cards. Mike Solski described the raid: "On Feb. 22, 1942, a dozen goons ransacked the office in broad daylight, beating union workers Forrest Emerson and Jack Whelahan so badly they had to be hospitalized. A former union officer said of Jack Whelahan, 'His face was like an old piece of liver.'

"In response, Mine Mill secretly distributed 10,000 handbills protesting this outrageous act of terrorism by the company and revealing the names of some of the attackers, several of whom were INCO shift bosses apparently at work at the time of the attack." Sudbury police didn't arrest the attackers, says Solski. "Rather, police apprehended two Mine Mill representatives for distributing the handbill, and at the police station warned them they were breaking a city bylaw prohibiting littering" (Solski and Smaller, *Mine Mill*, p. 103). See also Abella, *Nationalism, Communism, and Canadian Labour*, p. 90.

40. The Taft-Hartley Act said that unless union officials signed an affidavit declaring that they were not Communists, their union would be refused the services of the U.S. Labor Relations Board. Millard was supporting a statement by U.S. Senator Robert Taft, who had said the exodus was "swamping mining unions in Canada" (*New York Times*, Feb. 12, 1948). For Millard's comments, see *The Globe and Mail* and *The Evening Telegram*, Feb. 12, 1948. Taft was referring primarily to Reid Robinson, Mine Mill's international vice-president, and a couple of other Mine Mill organizers who had come to Canada to assist in organizing the gold fields in Northern Ontario. Two days after Taft's statement, Prime Minister Mackenzie King announced that Taft's claim was being studied, and within two months Reid Robinson and two other organizers were deported. For both McVey's and Solski's comments, see *The Globe and Mail*, Feb. 23, 1948.

41. "The Ballad of Joe Hill" is quoted in Solski and Smaller, *Mine Mill*, p. 14.

42. I grew up in Sudbury and remember neighbours telling how they had to pay shift bosses with liquor. Mike Solski recalls many instances, too, and adds that as a boy he remembers his father's shift boss at the Coniston smelter coming to their home to pick up bottles from his father. Nick Stempien, a miner, claimed that at least one miner a week was killed (Solski and Smaller, *Mine Mill*, p. 102). Jim Tester recalls the practice of clipping dismissal notices to time cards. I recall old-time miners telling me how hot it was underground, much hotter because of poorer ventilation than when I was working in mines such as Creighton and Garson during the 1950s. I also worked in the Copper Cliff sintering plant in the mid-fifties and my nose would bleed spontaneously, the sulphur fumes were so sharp. Other workers told me the same happened to them and that things weren't as bad as they used to be before Mine Mill. Hugh Kennedy, a long-retired miner, Mike Solski, and Jim Tester are sources

for the recollection of the Frood shift boss boasting of the men he fired. Carl Warder, who worked at Frood Mine in 1936 and 1937, recalled in a tape-recorded interview (Ontario Archives, Sound and Moving Images Section, Jim Tester Collection: Collection 219, Reel 27) that miners figured 10 to 15% of workers were company informers, that shift bosses used to order grizzlies removed, that crowds of 400–500 unemployed men would gather at the mine gates, that working in the gold mines was a cinch compared to the nickel mines because company efficiency experts kept insisting on greater production, that Frood fired about forty men a month and that he, finally, was one of those fired with no reason given.

43. Lang, *A Lion in a Den of Daniels*, p. 161. See also Solski and Smaller, *Mine Mill*, p. 14.

44. The trial began in May 1907 and lasted six weeks, at the end of which Clarence Darrow, defending Haywood, delivered one of the finest summations of his career. It lasted eleven hours, following which the jury acquitted Haywood. For extracts of Darrow's summation see Haywood, *The Autobiography of Big Bill Haywood*, pp. 214–216.

45. *The Autobiography of Big Bill Haywood*, p. 181.

46. *The Autobiography of Big Bill Haywood*, p. 230.

47. *The Autobiography of Big Bill Haywood*, p. 172.

48. *The Autobiography of Big Bill Haywood*, p. 243.

49. Laurel Sefton MacDowell describes National Selective Service provisions thus: "No employer could advertise for employees except by arrangement with an NSS officer. No employer could interview or hire a person who did not possess a NSS permit to seek and accept empoloyment. Seven days' 'notice of separation' was required before an employer could fire an employee or an employee could quit. After October 1942, 'labour exit permits' were required before workers could seek or accept employment in the United States. The explicit ban on 'poaching' of employees indicates the fierce competition for workers existing at the time" ("*Remember Kirkland Lake*," p. 17).

Ray Stevenson, who worked as an organizer for Mine Mill — and as a member of the Labour Progressive Party — at this time, says that because of the NSS provisions (and because of the tight labour market), "Thousands and thousands of people flooded into the unions because they knew they couldn't be fired."

50. The charter for Local 598 was taken out in April 1942.

51. *The Case for Sudbury*, p. 4.

52. I am not going to name the people who were Communist, nor am I going to name the people who went over lists I made of the names of Mine Mill members, pointing out who were party members or members of sympathetic Finnish or Ukrainian organizations. I compiled the lists from executive board minutes of Local 598 contained in the Mike Solski Collection at the Ontario Archives (MU 8251, Series 3, Box 9). I spoke

with five people, two who were Communist then and still are, two who were CCF then and are NDP now, and one who was CCF then and is a Liberal now. All were members of Local 598. There were variations in the people identified as Communist, and where there were, I used the higher number in calculating Communist membership. Moreover, some were Communist Party members for relatively brief periods and, in their cases, I continued to count them among the Communists on the rationale that they would retain some sympathy for the party. So, if anything, the figures are on the high side.

53. A report by Oliver Hodges, full-time organizer for the Ontario CCF Trade Union Commitee, following a trip to Sudbury on Feb. 8, 1948, confirmed that Communists did not control Mine Mill. In his opinion, however, they did maintain a "barrage of Communist propaganda." His report said: ". . . not one of the Mine Mill Locals is actually dominated by the Communist Party, although the membership is continually subjected to the influence of Party appointees. One of the latest efforts is the appointment of the Negotiating Committee 'Co-Ordinator' for the Sudbury and Port Colborne Locals. This individual is a known Communist and was foisted upon the Negotiating Committee without said Committee having any say in the matter.

"If it is possible to register an opinion here, it is most unfortunate that Canadian workers should be continually subjected to a barrage of Communist propaganda and to the influence of Communist organizers imported from the United States" (York University Archives, Oliver Hodges Collection, Box 74, file: Sudbury).

54. The CCF provincial constitution required "all CCF candidates to be endorsed or otherwise by the Provincial Council." See Procedures for the Nomination of CCF Candidates, PAC (see n. 35): Vol. 51, file: Ontario Council and Executive Minutes.

55. For David's appointment, see minutes of the Provincial Executive Council, 27 April 1948. For Grube's appointment, see minutes of the Provincial Executive Council, May 1, 1948. Both in PAC (see n. 54).

56. For David's arrival time, see telegrams April 30, 1948, PAC (see n. 35): Vol. 59, file: Ontario/Sudbury. The argument is based on a tape-recorded interview of Einer Johnson in the hospital just before he died. (Ontario Archives, Sound and Moving Images Section, Jim Tester Collection: Collection 219, Reel 22.) Johnson described the elements of the argument; I have tried to reconstruct the words because Johnson did not recount anything of what David said.

In the recording Johnson said: "Him and I had a big chewing match that morning when I met him at the train. And I said that this whole thing's wrong. I said you got no business coming from Toronto telling us who we're going to run for a candidate here. And I said if you'd have left it alone, maybe nine times out of ten Carlin would never have got nominated. Because there was a lot of dissatisfaction with him. You know. At the time. Because he drank too much, eh. But that's like old Margaret Ruth said, 'Toronto, they were the brains.' "

57. *The Case for Sudbury*, p. 15. Tape-recording of interview with Eric Johannson, Ontario Archives, Sound and Moving Images Section, Jim Tester Collection: Collection 219, Reels 20–22.

58. On July 3, 1948, the provincial council established a tribunal composed of C.C. (Doc) Ames, Donald MacDonald, and Morden Lazarus to hear evidence concerning the six and to report back to the council, which subsequently suspended them. Provincial Council minutes for June 29 and July 3, 1948, PAC (see n. 35) Vol. 51; and *The Case for Sudbury*, p. 19.

59.   **SUDBURY BASIN CCF PARTY MEMBERSHIP***

Year	Sudbury Riding	Nickel Belt Riding (created provincially in 1955 and federally in 1957)
1948	419	
1949	243	
1950	67	
1956	14	19
1957	59	39
1958	95	24
1959	167	216
1962	148	105
1963	157	212
1964	131	195
1966	441	403

* Figures are taken from membership lists broken down by federal ridings. PAC (see n. 35): Vol. 51, file: Ontario Council and Executive Minutes for 1948–49 and 1950–51; Vol. 452, file: Ontario Membership 1956–60; Vol. 57, file: Ontario Membership 1958; Vol. 453, file: Ontario Membership 1961 67. Membership lists for some years were missing.

60. In the federal riding of Nipissing, which at that time included Sudbury, Communists ran in 1945, won 1,525 votes out of 45,644 cast, and came second last. Also in 1945 they ran in the provincial riding of Sudbury and came last with 1,692 votes out of 28,791 cast. This was Carlin's riding, which he won for the second time with 13,627 votes. In the federal riding of Nickel Belt they ran in 1953 and came last with 687 votes out of 15,062 cast.

61. Bill Mahoney and Larry Sefton announced the start of the Sudbury campaign on Sept. 15, 1961, and, at the same time, announced that Bob Carlin had defected to Steel. The Port Colborne campaign began with the defection to Steel of the local's president on Oct. 5, 1961.

62. "Facts on File," *World News Digest*, March 21–27, 1956.

63. See the first paragraph of Chapter 15 for Solski's condemnation. The Port Colborne vote was 1,033 to 763 in favour of Steel. The votes in Port Colborne and Sudbury were only three months apart — Port Colborne on Dec. 4–6, 1961, and Sudbury from Feb. 27 to March 2, 1962.

64. Ray Stevenson, in an interview, accused David of having been ruthless: "Let me draw one small picture of David Lewis in action. It was soon after he became full time as an attorney for the Steelworkers. We were involved in a struggle with Upper Canada Mines in Kirkland Lake in the early fifties . . . [and] there was a little fellow who had signed up a lot of our cards by the name of Paul Bergeron, . . . French Canadian, broken English. So on. The question was whether Paul had falsely sign-ed some of these cards. David gets him on the stand, and he'd done his homework. . . . He had discovered that Paul Bergeron was really Napoleon Bergeron . . . and he went after poor Paul on this issue. . . . 'I will prove,' says David, 'that if Mr. Bergeron is capable of misstating and lying about his name, he is also capable of misstating and lying about these cards.' This is a poor worker, understand? . . . What was he doing to the guy? That's what I mean by ruthless."

65. Lang, "A Lion in a Den of Daniels," pp. 194, 195.

66. David argued that the trespass law was invalid, the province had no jurisdiction to pass it, and the court had no jurisdiction to hear the case because the law was an attempt to legislate criminal law, which was a preserve of the federal government.

67. The vote was held Aug. 4–5, 1959.

68. Lang "A Lion in a Den of Daniels," p. 310. Under a petition in the name of "Robert F. Kennedy, Attorney General of the United States, Peti-tioner," the U.S. Subversive Activities Control Board reopened pro-ceedings that were begun on July 28, 1955. See the board's recommenda-tion dated Dec. 26, 1961, in PAC, MG 28, I 268, Vol. 57, file: Com-munist Party.

69. *The Globe and Mail*, Sept. 23, 1961.

70. *The Globe and Mail*, Oct. 14, 1961.

71. *The Sudbury Daily Star*, Oct. 7, 1961. The *Star* also carried a large front-page photo showing Goldberg meeting with Claude Jodoin and Donald MacDonald, president and secretary-treasurer of the Canadian Labour Congress, accompanied by Labour Minister Michael Starr.

72. Lang, "A Lion in a Den of Daniels," p. 311.

73. Board recommendation dated Dec. 26, 1961, in PAC (see n. 68). Also *The Globe and Mail*, Dec. 29, 1961. The board's order dated May 4, 1962, in PAC (see n. 68): Vol. 31, file: Mine Mill.

74. In early Jan. 1962 Prime Minister John Diefenbaker appointed Don Gillis, president of Local 598 and a proclaimed Steel supporter, as labour represen-tative in a Canadian delegation to a NATO conference in Paris to be held later that month. (Lang, "A Lion in a Den of Daniels," p. 312, quoting *The Sudbury Daily Star*, Jan. 6, 1962.) In early February, a month before the Sudbury vote, the Ontario government appointed Gillis as a labour representative to the Ontario Economic Council. ("A Lion in a Den of Daniels," p. 312, quoting *The Sudbury Daily Star*, Feb. 2, 1962.)

CHAPTER 19

1. Moses Maimonides (1135–1204) was a philosopher, jurist, and physician, and the greatest intellectual of medieval Judaism. The quotation is from *Eight Chapters*, Chapter IV, "Concerning the Cure of the Diseases of the Soul," quoted in *A Maimonides Reader*, p. 374.

2. According to a *Toronto Star* "Insight" story, the Heritage Foundation is, "one of the most powerful and influential right-wing lobby groups in the [United States and] is part of the U.S. power elite. Foundation policy papers are handed out at cabinet meetings in the White House along with government briefing documents. Each week 8,000 political decision makers across the country are bombarded with the foundation's . . . 'background' papers on issues of concern to conservatives." (*Toronto Star*, May 10, 1985.)

   In his speech to the General Assembly assailing the Soviet Union for its invasion of Afghanistan, Stephen said it had ". . . reverted to the excrescences of Stalinism. . . . If we are back here next year [still debating a pullout of Soviet forces] it will be solely because the Soviet Union continues to believe that nihilism is preferable to negotiation; that butchery is preferable to bargaining. . . .

   "My distinguished Soviet colleague talks about 'objective facts.' He mangles the use of language. The phrase 'unselfish revolutionary assistance' actually means the premeditated military decimation of a nation. If I may be allowed to paraphrase from Shakespeare's *Macbeth*, 'All the perfumes of Araby will not wash the blood from those hands' (*The Globe and Mail* — news story and editorial — Nov. 14, 1985.) After the speech Stephen's office was flooded with invitations from across the United States asking him to speak at local functions.

3. "Identity," p. 15.

4. Interview with Sophie Lewis, May 15, 1985.

5. "Identity," p. 16.

6. "Identity," pp. 14–15.

7. "Identity," p. 15.

8. Letter Sophie to David, Aug. 17, 1939, family collection.

9. For creating a new room, see Lewis, *Memoirs*, p. 369; for no rug, interviews with Kalmen Kaplansky and Bea Silcoff; for dresser drawers as cribs, interview with Florence Silver, to whom Sophie told of it. In 1938 David's salary was $1,800 a year; in 1946 it was $3,200 a year. (*Memoirs*, pp. 127, 370.)

10. Letter Sophie to David, Nov. 24, 1942, family collection.

11. Doyle, *Angel Square*, pp. 9, 15, 16.

12. *Toronto Star*, Oct. 25, 1975.

13. Lewis, *Memoirs*, p. 243.

14. *Memoirs*, p. 228.

15. Newspaper clippings in the possession of Sophie Lewis for the years 1946, 1947, and 1950. Also an undated written assessment of Stephen's playing by Sidney Harrison at the Ottawa Music Festival giving Stephen marks of 85 for both technique and interpretation.

16. Dyck, *Running to Beat Hell*, p. 135.

17. Lewis, *Memoirs*, p. 190.

18. *Maclean's*, April 1971. Prof. Kenneth McNaught, the teacher Stephen most admired at the University of Toronto and a good friend of Sophie and David, agrees that Stephen has more the temperament of Sophie than David.

19. Recollection of Irving Rosenfeld of Toronto.

20. The province-wide public-speaking contest Michael entered was organized by the Ontario Educational Association. Stephen debated Kennedy on Nov. 14, 1958. The public-speaking award he won at Harbord was sponsored by the Lions Club. Stephen's speech was a plea for more aid to "the two thirds of the world that go to bed hungry every night. . . . We need a vast program of aid," he said, "one far exceeding that given by the Marshall and Colombo Plans. If we ignore it, we ignore humanity. . . . What we desire for ourselves we should wish for all." (*Toronto Star*, April 27, 1955.) The trip to New York was sponsored by Massey-Harris-Ferguson, Ltd., and the Toronto branch of the United Nations Association.

21. Interview with Stephen Lewis: "He would have been embarrassed by what he was making. He was embarrassed."

22. "*Freiheit*" ("*Freedom*") was written in 1936 by volunteers in the German contingent of the International Brigade. La Quince Brigada, the 15th Brigade, *was* the International Brigade, and although most in it couldn't speak Spanish well, many were able to get by. "*Viva la Quince Brigada*" was based on an old Spanish folk song.

23. See Morley, *Secular Socialists*, p. 83.

24. *Secular Socialists*, p. 65.

25. Young, *The Anatomy of a Party*, p. 216.

26. According to Leo Zakuta, the 1950s brought a decline in factionalism (*A Protest Movement Becalmed*, p. 100); Walter Young says that, by the mid-fifties, "The nature of the CCF had changed. More time and attention were devoted to organization and winning votes than to discussion of the many aspects of socialism and the development of more telling social criticism" (*The Anatomy of a Party*, p. 122).
    The CCF at this time was not unique in turning from ideology to the mechanics of winning votes. The same shift away from the argumentative and toward the practical was happening all over the place, in all kinds of organizations, private and public. David Rome saw it in the Jewish

community in Canada and elaborated in a July 1985 interview: "The world of ideologies ceased; it was cut like a knife around 1955. There was a reason for that . . . [and] it probably was true for everybody [although] I haven't studied it. Canada became rich . . . and poverty virtually ceased in this country. So you have the process of the whole country becoming bourgeois. Now in this bourgeois society, ideology and discourse and argumentation . . . ceased in Canada for everybody. Everybody became polite. . . . Controversy ceased. And we all became homogenized. We feel that, in order to live decently, we have to discard argument."

27. Crosland, *The Future of Socialism*, p.2.

28. *The Future of Socialism*, pp. 65, 148.

29. *The Future of Socialism*, p. 76.

30. *The Future of Socialism*, p. 361. Crosland notes that the quotation is from Keynes' *Essay in Persuasion*, pp. 371–72.

31. Bryan Gould in *The Guardian*, Dec. 11, 1987.

32. Morley, *Secular Socialists*, p. 87. Looking back in 1963, M.J. Coldwell described as "a millstone around the party's neck" the final sentence of the Regina Manifesto which declared: "No CCF government will rest content until it has eradicated capitalism and put into operation the full programme of socialized planning which will lead to the establishment in Canada of the Co-operative Commonwealth." (Young, *The Anatomy of a Party*, p. 44, n.16.)

33. Cross, *The Decline and Fall of a Good Idea*, p. 13.

34. Young, *The Anatomy of a Party*, p. 127.

35. Zakuta, *A Protest Movement Becalmed*, p. 96.

36. For the position that it marked a shift from public control, see Horowitz, *Canadian Labour in Politics*, p. 173; that the CCF ceased to be a movement, see Lewis, *Memoirs*, p. 445; that it substituted social planning for ending capitalism, see Young, *The Anatomy of a Party*, p. 137; that more property for more people, see *The Anatomy of a Party*, p. 137; that it helped turn the CCF into a liberal, reform party, see Zakuta, *A Protest Movement Becalmed*, p. 103.

37. Interview with Stephen Lewis.

38. Lewis, *Memoirs*, p. 432.

CHAPTER 20

1. David Lewis speaking to a New Party seminar in Montreal in Dec. 1960, quoted in Knowles, *The New Party*, p. 110.

2. Interviews with Kalmen Kaplansky and Ted Jolliffe.

3. This information was received on condition of anonymity.

4. *The Varsity*, Oct. 11, 1956.

5. *The Varsity*, Jan.14, 16–18, 1957.

6. *The New York Times*, Sept. 24, 1957.

7. Letter Sophie to David, Sept. 20, 1957, family collection.

8. Letter David to Sophie, Sept. 15, 1957, family collection.

9. Letter Sophie to David, Sept. 23, 1957, family collection.

10. *The Varsity*, Sept. 17, 1957.

11. *The Varsity*, Sept. 27, 1957.

12. *The Varsity*, Oct. 24, 1957.

13. *The Varsity*, Nov. 15, 1957.

14. *The Varsity*, Jan. 13, 1958.

15. *The Varsity*, Oct. 31, 1957.

16. *The Varsity*, Feb. 3, 1958.

17. *The Varsity*, Nov. 15, 1957; *The Globe and Mail*, November 15, 1957; and recollections of John Brewin and Gerald Caplan.

18. *The Varsity*, Nov. 15, 1957.

19. Letter Stephen to Sophie and David, March 15, 1959, family collection.

20. Letter Stephen to Sophie and David, Jan. 29, 1959, family collection.

21. *The Varsity*, Jan. 11, 1960.

22. Think of this as a gender-free mixed metaphor!

23. The CLC passed a resolution at its convention in April 1958 instructing its executive council to open discussions and declaring: "There is a need for a broadly based people's political movement, which embraces the CCF, the Labour movement, farm organizations, professional people and other liberally minded persons interested in basic social reform and reconstruction through our parliamentary system of government."

   The CCF, at its convention three months later, welcomed the CLC move and agreed to enter into discussions. For its part, it declared that: ". . . the CCF reaffirms its belief . . . [in] a broadly based people's movement. As democratic socialists, we believe that such a movement must continue to be dedicated to the principles of democratic social planning and to the widest forms of social security and individual liberty. It must remain steadfast in its determination to introduce, where appropriate, public control and public ownership in place of the present monopolistic domination of our economy. . . . [And it] must dedicate itself to the task of democratically rebuilding society so that co-operation will replace greed, constructive development will replace exploitation of man by man."

   Two years later, at its April 1960 convention, the CLC gave the go-ahead to prepare for a founding convention, reaffirming that the New

Party "shall be organized . . . [to] be fully representative of farmers, members of the CCF and other liberally minded groups and individuals as well as of labour."

The CCF gave its go-ahead at its convention the following August and said only that the New Party was necessary "so that we may unitedly carry forward still further the philosophy and principles of democratic socialism to which the CCF has been dedicated since its foundation." (For the full text of the resolutions, see Knowles, *The New Party*, pp. 127–33.)

24. For the full text of the New Party Declaration, see Cross, *The Decline and Fall of a Good Idea*. Manifestos and declarations are published in chronological order.

25. *The Ottawa Journal*, Feb. 4, 1960, quoted in Horowitz, *Canadian Labour in Politics*, p. 207.

26. Morton, *The New Democrats*, pp. 44, 45.

27. PAC, MG 32, C 23, Vol. 105, file: David Lewis Random Notes, abstract of letter David to Stephen, April 18, 1959.

28. Borovoy, *When Freedoms Collide*, pp. 13, 11.

CHAPTER 21

1. See McLeod & McLeod, *Tommy Douglas*, pp. 218–220. And see pp. 196-202 on the introduction of medicare.

2. Interview with Owen Shime, who was present for the discussion between Sophie and David and recalls David speaking of the agreement with Tommy Douglas.

3. PAC, MG 32, C 23, Vol. 105, file: David Lewis, letter Tommy Douglas to Sophie, Aug. 6, 1961.

4. Lewis, *Memoirs*, p. 226.

5. *Memoirs*, p. 226.

6. *Memoirs*, pp. 31, 227.

7. PAC, MG 28, IV I, Vol. 99, file: Lewis 1950–58, letter D. Lewis to Lorne Ingle, Oct. 30, 1956.

8. Nina's children are Lev Jacob, born Oct. 31, 1977; Noam Isaac, born Dec. 14, 1979; and Rachel Dora, born March 7, 1989.

9. The library has been closed. It used to be at St. Clements Avenue and Yonge Street in Toronto.

10. *Toronto Star*, Dec. 6, 1961.

11. Morley, *Secular Socialists*, p. 81.

12. *The Telegram*, feature article, Nov. 14, 1964.

13. Quotes about Stephen in PAC, MG 28, IV I, Vol. 447, file: Lewis (Southam News).

14. For Stephen Lewis's maiden speech, see *Hansard* (Ontario), 1963–64, I:117.

15. *Hansard* (Ontario), 1963–64, I:126.

16. *The Globe and Mail*, June 28, 1968.

17. *The Globe and Mail*, June 28, 1968.

18. Michael Enright in *The Globe Magazine*, Sept. 26, 1970. See also Ross Munro in *The Globe and Mail*, Aug. 4, 1971.

19. *The Globe and Mail*, Aug. 4, 1971.

20. Michael's and Wendy's children are Ben, born April 6, 1981, and Sarah, born December 4, 1984.

21. *The Globe Magazine*, Sept. 26, 1970.

22. Teacup was spelled TCUP, which stood for Toronto Community Union Project.

23. Leary is quoted in Kostash, *Long Way From Home*, p. 131.

24. Edmonds, *The Years of Protest*, pp. 18, 31.

25. See Young, *The Anatomy of a Party*, p. 148, n.37, where Young says David wrote on June 21, 1944, to "advise [Tommy] as to who should be hired or fired in the establishment of the first CCF government in [Saskatchewan]."

26. Achebe, *Christmas in Biafra*, p. 26.

27. Stephen and Michele's first child, Ilana Naomi, was born on July 26, 1965; their second, Avram (Avi) David, on May 15, 1967; and their third, Jennie Leah, on July 8, 1970.

28. For landing lights, see De St. Jorre, *The Nigerian Civil War*, p. 317; for the cemetery, see p. 329; for repairs to the Uli runway, see p. 317.

29. *The Nigerian Civil War*, pp. 24–25.

30. Jacobs, *The Brutality of Nations*, p. 3.

31. *The Brutality of Nations*, p. 11.

32. *Toronto Star*, Oct. 18, 1968.

33. *Toronto Star*, Oct. 18, 1968.

34. *The Globe and Mail*, Aug. 4, 1971.

35. MacDonald, *The Happy Warrior*, p. 175.

CHAPTER 22

1. *Maclean's*, April 1971, p. 22.

2. Other centres of the Waffle were Ottawa, Toronto, London — which drew the core of their members more from universities and the civil service than from blue-collar workers — and Hamilton, St. Catharines, and

St. Thomas, where members were basically blue-collar. These designa-
tions came from Jim Laxer in an interview.

3.   Watkins, "Learning to Move Left," p. 88.

4.   Lewis, *Memoirs*, pp. 385–87. See also McLeod & McLeod, *Tommy
     Douglas*, p. 277.

5.   Interview with Lynn Williams at Steelworkers headquarters in Pittsburgh,
     Pennsylvania.

6.   Interview with Stephen Lewis.

7.   Charles Lynch is quoted in Bullen, *The Ontario Waffle*, p. 195.

8.   Penner, *Canadian Communism*, p. 260.

9.   Interview with Stephen Lewis.

10. Bullen, *The Ontario Waffle*, p. 193.

11. With a sense of humour characteristic of its early days, the Waffle took
     its name from the derisory headline of a *Globe and Mail* editorial com-
     menting on the Manifesto. During the course of drafting the Manifesto,
     someone said — memories are vague as to who it was; Desmond Morton
     claims in *The New Democrats* (p. 92) that it was Ed Broadbent — that
     if they had to choose between waffling to the left and waffling to the
     right, they should waffle to the left.

     The editorial was written by Jean Howarth, the Globe's chief editorial
     writer, and as it was being set into type, Hugh Winsor mentioned the
     waffling comment to her. Winsor, then a Globe editorial writer and now
     national political editor for the paper, participated in the drafting of the
     Manifesto and was a signatory. Howarth quickly changed the headline
     to read, "Waffle Manifesto" and added three short references to it in
     the body of the editorial.

     When Laxer and others saw the headline, they adopted the name.
     "We might not have had it [the name] without the editorial," Laxer
     says. "We knew it would be a problem to have a left-wing group that
     was seen as too serious, so to have a name that was humorous was just
     great. We knew right away that it was a great name." For the editorial,
     see *The Globe and Mail*, Sept. 6, 1969.

12. Gzowski, *The Private Voice*, pp. 214, 216.

13. See Bullen, *The Ontario Waffle*, pp. 198–200, 206–07.

14. *The Ontario Waffle*, p. 198.

15. *A Socialist Program for Canadian Trade Unionists*, pp. 6, 7, 9.

16. Wilf List in *The Globe and Mail*, Jan. 17, 1969.

17. *The Globe and Mail*, Jan. 17, 1972.

18. *The Globe and Mail*, January 18, 1972.

19. For the transcript of Stephen's speech, Mar. 18, 1972, see PAC, MG
     32, C 23, Vol. 51, file: Stephen Lewis 1964–72.

20. Morley, *Secular Socialists*, p. 217.

21. See Bullen, *The Ontario Waffle*, p. 209, 210.

22. Laxer is reluctant to acknowledge that the Waffle acted as a party within a party, pointing out that all politicians have mailing lists, all politicians raise money, all politicians have organizers helping them. Watkins, on the other hand, admits the strength of the accusation: "I have to grant that we were a very highly organized caucus. We had our regular meetings; we had our own executive; we had our own membership lists; we imposed a tithe on people to raise money for the organization; we had our own press conferences."

23. Ed Broadbent submitted the amendment through the Riverdale riding association two days before the Orillia meeting. It said that "The present structure and behaviour of the Waffle cannot continue," but that members could opt to remain in the party if they ceased public activity as part of an unauthorized group.

24. Stephen is quoted in Morley, *Secular Socialists*, p. 217.

25. PAC (see n. 19): Vol. 78, file: 22–33 Waffle, letter D. Lewis to Lynn Williams, June 8, 1972.

26. Lewis, *Memoirs*, p. 387.

CHAPTER 23

1. The image of Davis as a tin of tomatoes is graphic in another sense. The Conservatives mounted a massive advertising campaign during the election which prompted a Tory researcher to comment that they were selling Davis like a can of tomatoes. (Manthorpe, *The Power and the Tories*, p. 189.)

2. *The Power and the Tories*, p. 180.

3. *The Power and the Tories*, p. 181. There were other causes, of course. For instance, the Conservatives used sophisticated polling techniques and about $1 million in advertising. The NDP relied on intuition and TV clips produced at no charge to the party by filmmaker Allan King. (*The Power and the Tories*, pp. 199, 197, and Morton, The New Democrats, p. 114–16.)

4. The results were Conservatives, 78; Liberals, 19; NDP, 19; Liberal–Labour, 1.

5. George Peapples, president of General Motors of Canada Ltd. had just announced that up to 40,000 Canadian jobs would be in jeopardy by the early 1990s because of overexpansion in the auto industry. (*The Globe and Mail*, Jan. 20, 1987.)

6. *The Globe and Mail*, Oct. 9, 1976.

7. *The Globe and Mail*, May 25, 1977.

8. *The Globe and Mail*, May 26, 1977.

9. *The Globe and Mail*, May 30, 1977.

10. *The Globe and Mail*, June 18, 1977.

11. Both quips were reported in *The Globe and Mail*, May 28, 1977.

12. The results of the three elections during which Stephen was leader were:

Year	Party	Seats	Percent*
1971	Conservatives	78	44.5
	Liberals	20	27.8
	NDP	19	27.1
1975	Conservatives	51	36.1
	Liberals	36	34.3
	NDP	38	28.9
1977	Conservatives	58	39.7
	Liberals	34	31.5
	NDP	33	28.0

* Office of the Chief Election Officer of Ontario: Electoral History of Ontario, Candidates and Results 1867–1982, pp. J11, J12.

13. *The Globe and Mail*, June 14, 1977.

CHAPTER 24

1. Morton, *The New Democrats*, p. 128.

2. In 1965 the NDP's national council accepted the principle of "special status" for Quebec. In Feb. 1971 the Quebec wing (NDP-Q), led by Raymond Laliberté, called for self-determination for Quebec (*La Presse*, Feb. 15, 1971), and for the next eight months pressed for a program that would commit it to "the right of divergence" from federal policies and to "political self-determination for the Quebec community as a whole; economic self-determination for the workers as a whole; [and] social self-determination for the citizens [of Quebec] as a whole." (For draft program, see "Document sur l'orientation du NPD–Québec," PAC, MG 32, C 23, Vol. 76, file: 22-17 NDP Québec 1971.) David engineered a truce at the Oct. 1971 convention of NDP-Q by getting agreement on a "New Canada" policy that called for holding a constitutional convention of "elected representatives of Canada's eleven Parliaments . . . and of the native peoples of Canada" to propose a new constitution. (PAC, see above.)

The truce became under increasing strain during the spring of 1972 and by June had evaporated. Laliberté issued a new program that once again stressed Quebec's right to self-determination, declaring that "Under real federalism, the central government has no other powers than those that are delegated by the different parts that make up the country." David immediately repudiated the program and said no one subscribing to the program could be an NDP candidate in the election. "My party and I are determined to resist every attempt to break up the country," he said. (See press statement, June 19, 1972.)

According to Lewis Seale, a Quebec native who accompanied David in meetings with Laliberté and NDP-Q, David involved himself deeply in dealings with NDP-Q and "made it clear from the start that constitutional policy would have to be oriented toward unity." Moreover, much of the drafting of key documents was done by David, he says. Charles Taylor was the principal adviser and "led the federal side in arguments about details and phrasing," Seale adds. In an aside, John Harney notes that "David was a dualist very much in the tradition of Trudeau [who] is a linguistic dualist . . . and he was profoundly anti-nationalist [as far as Quebec was concerned]."

Charles Taylor observes that "David really understood the mind-set of the people in Quebec — what they were worried about, what they were afraid of, what they wanted — and he was sensitive to the kind of unconscious slights being given in English about multiculturalism . . . and that was very rare." Claude Ryan thought that "of all four federal leaders, Lewis is the one who accepts most clearly Quebec's position in the constitutional discussions. . . . He is not concerned with who signs the cheques. He is concerned with ensuring national standards of social welfare." (*Le Devoir*, June 28, 1971)

3. In 1968 the Liberals won 155 seats; the Conservatives, 72; and the NDP, 22.

4. Hercules was given twelve seemingly impossible labours to perform. The fifth was to clean the Augean stables belonging to King Augeas of Elis. The stables housed a herd of 3,000 oxen whose stalls had not been cleaned in thirty years. Hercules diverted the rivers Alpheus and Peneus through the stables, thereby cleaning them in one day.

5. DIP-Defence Industry Productivity Program; MACH-Machinery Program; TS-Transport Subsidies. A couple of dozen other programs, each with its own acronym, were discussed.

6. Hans Brown was executive assistant to Tommy Douglas, and the morning after the War Measures Act was invoked, says Brown, "All the MPs showed up in caucus and I remember the people who had the most to say were Andrew Brewin and David. . . . Tommy was quite categorical about it: we were opposed to it. . . . David and Andrew talked about the ins and outs . . . until finally Tommy said, 'Well, carry on, but I'd better go and finish off my notes for my speech,' and away he went. Bang, he walked into the House and gave one hell of a speech . . . one of the finest speeches that he made."

For Robin Sears, Brown's anecdote is illustrative of the relationship between David and Tommy: "Tommy could leave the caucus meeting when the question was far from resolved, secure in the knowledge that it was left in the hands of someone who would make sure that it was resolved in the way he wanted without having to say that *and* resolved in terms of how everybody had to comport themselves publicly. . . . There was an understanding that when it came to doing the real heavy-duty stuff, David was there."

7. *The Globe and Mail*, May 8, 1974.

8. PAC (see n. 2): Vol. 127, file: Swislocz Reference, transcript, "Lewis Trip to Soviet Union & Poland — May 1978."

CHAPTER 25

1. Preface to *The State of the World's Children*, 1989, published by Oxford University Press for the United Nation's Children's Fund (UNICEF).

2. *The New York Times*, June 5, 1986. See also "United Nations Programme of Action," pp. 7–24.

3. *Critical Economic Situation in Africa*, items 111–12, pp. 29, 30.

4. *Economic Report on Africa 1989*, Table XI, p.28.

5. Package of press clippings available from the Africa Recovery press office at the UN. *The Times* (London), Jan. 5, 1989; *The New York Times*, Dec. 11, 1989; *Le Soir*, Jan. 11, 1989; and others.

6. ECA *Preliminary Observations*, "Summary."

7. *The Guardian*, May 4, 1989. The UN agencies attending were: Economic Commission for Africa (ECA), United Nations Development Programme (UNDP), International Labour Organization (ILO), World Food Program (WFP), United Nations Childrens's Fund (UNICEF), United Nations Fund for Population Activities (UNFPA), and International Fund for Agricultural Development (IFAD).

8. Among the publications reporting the rupture in the spring of 1989 were: *The Guardian*, May 4; *The Economist*, April 29; *Financial Times of London*, April 25, May 3; *The Christian Science Monitor*, May 8; *The Wall Street Journal*, May 10; *The Independent* of London, May 4; *The New York Times*, April 25; *South Magazine*, May 1989; *Financial Post* (Canada), April 25; *Jeune Afrique*, April 26; *International Herald Tribune*, April 19; *Toronto Star*, April 25.

9. Text of a "Joint Statement on Africa's Long-Term Development," UN Information Office, New York, May 10, 1989.

• B I B L I O G R A P H Y •

BOOKS AND PERIODICALS

Abella, Irving. *Nationalism, Communism, and Canadian Labour.* Toronto: University of Toronto Press, 1973.

———, ed. *On Strike: Six Key Labour Struggles in Canada, 1919–1949.* Toronto: James Lorimer & Co., 1975.

Abella, Irving, and Harold Troper. *None Is Too Many: Canada and the Jews of Europe 1933–1948.* Toronto: Lester & Orpen Dennys, 1982.

Abramovitch, Raphael R. "The Jewish Socialist Movement in Russia and Poland (1897–1919)." In *The Jewish People Past and Present,* II: 369–98. New York: Jewish Encyclopedic Handbooks Inc., Central Yiddish Culture Organization (CYCO), 1948.

Achebe, Chinua. *Christmas in Biafra and Other Poems.* New York: Doubleday, 1973.

Aharoni, Yohanon, and Avi-Yonah, Michael. *The Macmillan Bible Atlas.* Toronto: Collier-Macmillan Canada, 1968.

Ain, Abraham. "Swislocz: Portrait of a Jewish Community in Eastern Europe." YIVO *Annual of Jewish Social Sciences* IV, 1949: 86–114.

Ain, Kayleh. "In Memory of the Jewish Community in Svisloch." In *The Community of Svisloch in the Province of Grodno.* In Yiddish. Tel Aviv: Association of People from Svisloch in Israel, the Jewish year 5721.

Allen, Richard. *The Social Passion: Religion and Social Reform in Canada 1914–1928.* Toronto: University of Toronto Press, 1973.

Arnopoulos, Sheila McLeod. *Voices from French Ontario: A Vivid Portrait of the French-Speaking Community of Nouvel-Ontario.* Kingston and Montreal: McGill–Queen's University Press, 1982.

Ascher, Abraham, ed. *The Mensheviks in the Russian Revolution: Documents of Revolution*. London: Thames and Hudson, 1976.

Ashley, M.P., and C.T. Saunders. *Red Oxford: A History of the Growth of Socialism in the University of Oxford*. 2nd ed. Oxford: The Oxford University Labour Club, 1933.

Avakumovic, Ivan. *The Communist Party in Canada: A History*. Toronto: McClelland and Stewart, 1975.

Azoulay, Dan. "The Politics of Pragmatism: The Founding of the Ontario New Democratic Party, 1958–1961." Master's thesis. York University, 1984.

Betcherman, Lita-Rose. *The Little Band: The Clashes Between the Communists and the Political and Legal Establishment in Canada, 1928–1932*. Ottawa: Deneau Publishers, 1983.

Betjeman, John. *Mount Zion, or In Touch with the Infinite*. London: St. James Press, 1931; reprint ed. for the British Library, London, 1975.

Borovoy, A. Alan. *When Freedoms Collide*. Toronto: Lester & Orpen Dennys, 1988.

Bothwell, Robert, and William Kilbourn. *C.D. Howe: A Biography*. Toronto: McClelland and Stewart, 1979.

Boyle, Andrew. *The Fourth Man: The Definitive Account of Kim Philby, Guy Burgess, and Donald Maclean and Who Recruited Them to Spy for Russia*. New York: The Dial Press/James Wade, 1979.

British Labour Statistics: Historical Abstract 1886–1968. London: Department of Employment and Productivity, 1971.

Brooke, Rupert. *The Collected Poems, With a Memoir by Edward Marsh*. 3rd ed. London: Sidgwick & Jackson, 1983.

Brown, Anthony Cave. *"C": The Secret Life of Sir Stewart Menzies, Spymaster to Winston Churchill*. New York: Macmillan Publishing Co., 1987.

Brym, Robert J. *The Jewish Intelligentsia and Russian Marxism*. New York: Shocken Books, 1978.

Buck, Tim. *Yours in the Struggle, Reminiscences of Tim Buck*. Edited by William Beeching and Phyllis Clarke. Toronto: NC Press Ltd, 1977.

Bullen, John. "The Ontario Waffle and the Struggle for an Independent Socialist Canada: Conflict Within the NDP." *Canadian Historical Review* LXIV, no. 2, June 1983: 188–215.

Cameron, Duncan. "I Went to an Election and Politics Broke Out." *This Magazine* 22, no. 7, February 1989: 16–18.

Caplan, Gerald. *The Dilemma of Canadian Socialism: The CCF in Ontario*. Toronto: McClelland and Stewart, 1973.

Caplan, Usher. *Like One That Dreamed: A Portrait of A.M. Klein*. Toronto: McGraw-Hill Ryerson, 1982.

The Case for Sudbury. Booklet. Published by the "Elect Carlin Committee" of Sudbury Riding. The Mike Solski Collection, Ontario Archives, MU 8270, Series 9, Box 23, file: 32.

Chamberlin, William Henry. *The Russian Revolution.* Vols. 1–2. New York: Grosset and Dunlap, 1977.

Cohen, Chester G. *Shtetl Finder Gazeteer.* Los Angeles: Periday Co., 1980.

Cold War in Canada. Transcript of CBC "Ideas" broadcast, March 6–27, 1984.

Cook, Ramsay. *The Regenerators: Social Criticism in Late Victorian English Canada.* Toronto: University of Toronto Press, 1985.

Cornford, John. *Understand the Weapon, Understand the Wound: Selected Writings.* Edited by Jonathan Galassi. Manchester: Carcanet New Press, 1976.

Critical Economic Situation in Africa: United Nations Programme of Action for African Economic Recovery and Development 1986–1990." Report of the Secretary-General. Mid-term review of the implementation . . . UN General Assembly, UN Information Office, A/43/500, August 10, 1988.

Crosland, C.A.R. *The Future of Socialism.* Revised. New York: Shocken Books, 1963.

Cross, Michael. *The Decline and Fall of a Good Idea:* CCF-NDP *Manifestoes 1932–1969.* Toronto: New Hogtown Press, 1974.

Davies, Norman. *White Eagle, Red Star: The Polish–Soviet War 1919–1920.* London: Macdonald & Co. (Publishers), 1972.

Dawidowicz, Lucy. *The War Against the Jews: 1933–1945.* New York: Holt, Rinehart and Winston, 1975.

De St. Jorre, John. *The Nigerian Civil War.* London: Hodder and Stoughton, 1972.

Deacon, Richard. *A History of the British Secret Service.* London: Panther Books, Granada Publishing, 1980.

Djwa, Sandra. *A Life of F.R. Scott: The Politics of the Imagination.* Toronto: McClelland and Stewart, 1987.

Djwa, Sandra, and Ronald St. J. MacDonald, eds. *On Frank Scott.* Kingston and Montreal: McGill–Queen's University Press, 1981.

Donin, Hayim Halevy. *To Be a Jew: A Guide to Jewish Observance in Contemporary Life.* New York: Basic Books, 1972.

Douglas, T.C. *The Making of a Socialist: The Recollections of T.C. Douglas.* Edited by Lewis H. Thomas. Edmonton: University of Alberta Press, 1982.

Doyle, Brian. *Angel Square.* Vancouver and Toronto: Douglas & McIntyre, 1984.

Drystek, Henry F. "'The Simplest and Cheapest Mode of Dealing with Them': Deportation from Canada before WWII." *Histoire sociale/Social History* 15, no. 30, Nov. 1982: 420–40.

Dubnow, S.M. *History of the Jews in Russia and Poland: From the Earliest Times Until the Present Day*. Translated by I. Friedlaender. Vols. 1–3. Philadelphia: The Jewish Publication Society of America, 1920.

Dyck, Betty L. *Running to Beat Hell, A Biography of A.M. (Sandy) Nicholson*. Refina: Canadian Plains Research Centre, University of Regina, 1988.

ECA *Preliminary Observations on the World Bank Report: "Africa's Adjustment and Growth in the 1980s."* Booklet. United Nations Economic Commission for Africa: Statistics and Policies, April 24, 1989: pp. 1–25.

Eckman, Lester Samuel. *The History of the Musar Movement (1840–1945)*. New York: Shengold Publishers, 1975.

Economic Report on Africa, 1989. Booklet. Addis Ababa: United Nations Economic Commission for Africa, April 1989.

Edmonds, Alan. *The Years of Protest, 1960/1970*. Canada's Illustrated Heritage Series. Toronto: N.S.L. Natural Science of Canada Ltd., Jack McClelland, Publisher, 1979.

Epstein, Melech. *The Jew and Communism: The Story of Early Communist Victories and Ultimate Defeats in the Jewish Community, U.S.A.* New York: Trade Union Sponsoring Committee, 1959.

Ferns, H.S. *Reading from Left to Right: One Man's Political History*. Toronto: University of Toronto Press, 1983.

The First Ten Tears, 1932–1942: Commemorating the Tenth Anniversary of the Co-operative Commonwealth Federation. Booklet. Ottawa: CCF, 1942. Thomas Fisher Rare Books Library, University of Toronto.

Foot, Michael. *Aneurin Bevan*. Vols. 1–2. London: Granada Publishing, 1982.

For an Independent Socialist Canada. Pamphlet. Public Archives of Canada, MG 28, I268, Vol. 14, file: Waffle.

Francis, R. Douglas. *Frank H. Underhill, Intellectual Provocateur*. Toronto: University of Toronto Press, 1986.

Gilbert, Martin. *The Jews of Russia: Their History in Maps and Photographs*. 3rd ed. Israel: Steimatzky and The Jerusalem Post, 1979.

Gottlieb, Nathan. *A Jewish Child Is Born*. New York: Block Publishing, 1960.

Grade, Chaim. "My Quarrel with Hersh Rasseyner." In *A Treasury of Yiddish Stories*. Edited by Irving Howe and Eliezer Greenberg. New York: Viking Press, 1954.

A Great Collection, The Archives of the Jewish Labour Movement. Booklet. New York: Committee for The Archives, 1965.

Green, Martin. *Children of the Sun: A Narrative of Decadence in England After 1918*. London: Constable, 1977.

Gzowski, Peter. *The Private Voice: A Journal of Reflections*. Toronto: McClelland and Stewart, 1988.

Hansard. Toronto: Official Reports of Debates, Legislative Assembly of Ontario.

Haywood, William D. *The Autobiography of Big Bill Haywood: William D. Haywood's Own Story of the Industrial Workers of the World (IWW).* New York: International Publishers Co., 1969.

Heaps, Leo. *The Rebel in the House: The Life and Times of A.A. Heaps,* M.P. London: Niccolo Publishing Co., 1970.

Hellman, Lillian. *Scoundrel Time.* New York: Bantam Books, 1976.

Hertz, I. Sh., ed. *The History of the Bund.* In Yiddish. Vols 1–3. New York: Farlag Unser Tsait, 1960.

Hilton, Rodney. *Oxford Left in the Thirties.* Oxford: Oxford University Labour Club, 1953.

Historical Labour Survey. Ottawa: Statistics Canada, 1985.

Historical Statistics of Canada. Edited by F.H. Leacy. 2nd ed. Ottawa: Statistics Canada, 1983.

Hogan, Brian F. "Hard Rock and Hard Decisions: Catholics, Communists and the IUSW — Sudbury Confrontations." 47 pp. Paper presented to the Canadian Historical Association, May 30, 1985, and noted in *Historical Papers: A Selection from the papers presented at the Annual Meeting Held in Montreal,* 1985, p. 236.

Horn, Michiel. *The League for Social Reconstruction: Intellectual Origins of the Democratic Left in Canada 1930–1942.* Toronto: University of Toronto Press, 1980.

———. "Lost Causes: The League for Social Reconstruction and the Co-operative Commonwealth Federation in Quebec in the 1930s and 1940s." *Journal of Canadian Studies* 19, no. 2, Summer 1984: 132–56.

Horowitz, Gad. *Canadian Labour in Politics.* Toronto: University of Toronto Press, 1968.

House of Commons Debates. Ottawa: Parliament, House of Commons, Offical Reports.

Howarth, T.E.B. *Cambridge Between Two Wars.* London: Collins, 1978.

Howe, Irving. *The World of Our Fathers: The Journey of the East European Jews to America and the Life They Found There.* New York: Simon and Schuster, 1976.

Hurwitz, Maximilian. *The Workmen's Circle: Its History, Organization and Institutions.* New York: The Workmen's Circle, 1936.

Hutchison, Bruce. *Mr. Prime Minister, 1867–1964.* Don Mills: Longmans Canada, 1964.

"Identity." Transcript of CBC broadcast, January 19, 1976, Public Archives of Canada, MG 32 C 23, Vol. 128, file: Identity CBC broadcast.

Ignatieff, George. *The Making of a Peacemonger*. Toronto: University of Toronto Press, 1985.

In Honour of the Dedication of the Workmen's Circle Centre. A Souvenir Book. Montreal: National Archives, Canadian Jewish Congress, file ZB/Workmen's Circle.

In Memoriam: Victor Alter, Henryk Erlich. Booklet. New York: Erlich–Alter Memorial Conference, 1943.

Jacobs, Dan. *The Brutality of Nations*. New York. Alfred Knopf, 1987.

Jewish Labor Bund 1897–1957. Booklet. New York: The International Jewish Labor Bund, 1958.

The Jewish Labor Bund: A Pictorial History 1897–1957. Compiled by J.S. Hertz. New York: Farlag Unser Tsait, 1958.

Jewish Labor Committee. New York: Pamphlet published by the Jewish Labor Committee, n.d.

Jones, W.T. *A History of Western Philosophy*. New York: Harcourt, Brace and Co., 1952.

Kage, Joseph. *With Faith and Thanksgiving: The Story of 200 Years of Jewish Immigration and Immigrant Aid Effort in Canada 1760–1960*. Montreal: The Eagle Publishing Co., 1962.

Kaplan, William. *Everything That Floats: Pat Sullivan, Hal Banks, and the Seamen's Unions of Canada*. Toronto: University of Toronto Press, 1987.

Kaplansky, Kalmen. "History of the Jewish Labour Committee in Canada." 1986. Typescript. Ottawa: Public Archives of Canada, MG 30, A 53, Vol. 20, file 2.

Keep, J.L.H. *The Rise of Social Democracy in Russia*. Oxford: Clarendon Press, 1963.

Kinder, Hermann, and Werner Hilgemann. *The Penguin Atlas of World History*. Vols. 1–2. Revised ed. Hammondsworth, England: Penguin Books, 1984.

Kirkien, L. *Russia, Poland and the Curzon Line*. Edinburgh: Caldra House (Publishers), 1945.

Klein, Lawrence R. *The Keynesian Revolution*. 2nd ed. New York: The Macmillan Press, 1966.

Knowles, Stanley. *The New Party*. Toronto: McClelland and Stewart, 1961.

Koestler, Arthur. *The Thirteenth Tribe*. London: Pan Books, 1977.

Kosovsky, Vladimir. "V. Medem and the Nationality Question." In Yiddish. In *Vladimir Medem on the Twentieth Anniversary of His Death*. New York: American Representation of the General Jewish Workers' Union of Poland, 1943, p. 133.

Kostash, Myrna. *Long Way from Home. The Story of the Sixties Generation in Canada*. Toronto: James Lorimer & Co., 1980.

Landsberg, Michele. *Women and Children First: A Provocative Look at Modern Canadian Women at Work and at Home*. Markham: Penguin Books Canada, 1982.

Lang, John B. "A Lion in a Den of Daniels: A History of the International Union of Mine Mill and Smelter Workers in Sudbury, Ontario, 1942–1962." Master's thesis, University of Guelph, 1970.

Laxer, James. "Taking Stock, an Excerpt from James Laxer's Report to the NDP Federal Caucus on NDP Economic Policy." *Canadian Forum* LXII, no. 736, Feb. 1984: 8–16.

Layton, Irving. *Engagements: The Prose of Irving Layton*. Edited by Seymour Mayne. Toronto: McClelland and Stewart, 1972.

———. *A Red Carpet for the Sun*. Toronto: McClelland and Stewart, 1960.

———. *Waiting for the Messiah*. Don Mills: Totem Press, 1986.

Lenin, V.I. *Collected Works*. Vols. 1–45. Moscow: Progress Publishers, dates vary according to volume.

Levin, Shmarya. *Forward from Exile: The Autobiography of Shmarya Levin*. Translated and edited by Maurice Samuel. Philadelphia: The Jewish Publication Society of America, 1967.

Lewis, David. F.R. Scott's Contribution to the CCF." In *On Frank Scott*. Edited by Sandra Djwa and R. St J. Macdonald. Kingston and Montreal: McGill–Queen's University Press, 1963.

———. *The Good Fight: Political Memoirs 1909–1958*. Toronto: Macmillan of Canada, 1981.

———. *Louder Voices: The Corporate Welfare Bums*. Toronto: James, Lewis and Samuel, 1972.

———. "A Tale of Two Cities." *The Oxford Forward* I, no. I, Nov. 1934: 9.

Lewis, David, and Frank Scott. *Make This YOUR Canada: A Review of CCF History and Policy*. Toronto: Central Canada Publishing Co., 1943.

Lewis, Stephen. *Art Out of Agony: The Holocaust Theme in Literature, Sculpture and Film*. Toronto: CBC Enterprises, 1984.

LSR (The Research Committee of the League for Social Reconstruction). *Social Planning for Canada*. Introduction by F.R. Scott, Leonard March, Graham Spry, J. King Gordon, Eugene Forsey and J.S. Parkinson. Reprint. Toronto: University of Toronto Press, 1975.

Lyashchenko, Peter I. *History of the National Economy of Russia to the 1917 Revolution*. New York: The Macmillan Co., 1949.

MacDonald, Donald C. *The Happy Warrior: Political Memoirs*. Markham: Fitzhenry & Whiteside, 1998.

MacDowell, Laura Sefton. *"Remember Kirkland Lake": The History and Effects of the Kirkland Lake Gold Miners' Strike, 1941–42*. Toronto: University of Toronto Press, 1983.

Macmillan, Harold. *The Past Masters: Politics and Politicians 1906–1939.* London: Macmillan London, 1975.

Macpherson, C.B. *The Life and Times of Liberal Democracy.* Oxford: Oxford University Press, 1977.

———. *The Political Theory of Possessive Individualism: Hobbes to Locke.* Oxford: Oxford University Press, 1962.

Mahler, R. *A History of Modern Jewry, 1789–1815.* Translated by Y. Haggai. London: Valentine Mitchell, 1971.

Manthorpe, Jonathan. *The Power and the Tories: Ontario Politics 1943 to the Present.* Toronto: Macmillan of Canada, 1974.

Masters, D.C. *The Winnipeg General Strike.* Toronto: University of Toronto Press, 1973.

McHenry, Dean E. *The Third Force in Canada: The Co-operative Commonwealth Federation 1932–1948.* Berkeley: University of California Press, 1950.

McLeod, Thomas H., & Ian McLeod. *Tommy Douglas: The Road to Jerusalem.* Edmonton: Hurtig Publishers, 1987.

McNaught, Kenneth. *A Prophet in Politics: A Biography of J.S. Woodsworth.* Toronto: University of Toronto Press, 1963.

Medem, Vladimir. *The Life and Soul of a Legendary Jewish Socialist.* Translated by Samuel A. Portnoy from *From My Life,* published 1923. New York: Ktav Publishing House, 1979.

Meltzer, Milton. *World of Our Fathers: The Jews of Eastern Europe.* New York: Farrar, Straus and Giroux, 1974.

Moorehead, Alan. *The Russian Revolution.* New York: Harper and Row, 1958.

Morley, J.T. *Secular Socialists: The CCF/NDP in Ontario, A Biography.* Kingston and Montreal: McGill–Queen's University Press, 1984.

Morton, Desmond. *The New Democrats 1961–1986: The Politics of Change.* Toronto: Copp Clark Pitman, 1986.

Nettl, J.P. *Rosa Luxemburg.* Abridged ed. Oxford: Oxford University Press, 1969.

Nicholson, G.W.L., C.D. *The Canadian Expeditionary Force 1914–1919: The Official History of the Canadian Army in the First World War.* Ottawa: Army Historical Section, Queen's Printer, 1962.

Osborne, Stanley L. *If Such Holy Song: The Story of the Hymns in the Hymn Book 1971.* Whitby: The Institute of Church History, 1976.

Oxford Union Society. *Minute Books.* Vols. Nov. 1932–June 1935. Oxford: Oxford Union Society Library.

Oxford University Labour Club. *Minute Books.* Vols. 1921–1931. Oxford: Bodleian Library, Oxford University, Mss. Top. Oxon. d. 296–8.

Paris, Erna. *Jews: An Account of Their Experience in Canada*. Toronto: Macmillan of Canada, 1980.

Penner, Norman. *Canadian Communism: The Stalin Years and Beyond*. Toronto: Methuen Publications, 1988.

―――. *The Canadian Left: A Critical Analysis*. Scarborough: Prentice-Hall of Canada, 1977.

―――, ed. *Winnipeg 1919: The Strikers' Own History of the Winnipeg General Strike*. 2nd ed. Toronto: James Lorimer & Co., 1975.

Peretz, I.L. *Selected Stories*. Edited by Irving Howe and Eliezer Greenberg. New York: Shocken Books, 1974.

Pickersgill, J.W. *The Mackenzie King Record, 1939–1944*. Vol. 1. Toronto: University of Toronto Press, 1960.

"Preliminary Treaty of Peace with Armistice Conditions." No. 58, Poland–R.S.F.S.R. and Uk.S.S.R. Signed Riga, Oct. 12, 1920; ratified Libau, Nov. 2, 1920. *Soviet Treaty Series*. London: Royal Institute for International Affairs.

Pryce-Jones, David. *Cyril Connolly: Journal and Memoir*. New York: Ticknor & Fields, 1984.

Raisin, Jacob S. *The Haskala Movement in Russia*. Philadelphia: The Jewish Publication Society of America, 1913.

Ravel, Aviva. *Faithful Unto Death: The Story of Arthur Zygielbaum*. Montreal: Arthur Zygielbaum Branch, Workmen's Circle, 1980.

Reed, John. *Ten Days That Shook the World*. Introduction by Bertram D. Wolfe and Foreword by V.I. Lenin. New York: Random House, Vintage Books, 1960.

Richler, Mordecai. *The Street*. Toronto: McClelland and Stewart, 1969.

Robertson, David, and Chuck Rachlis. "Replying to Laxer." *Canadian Forum* LXIV, no. 740, June/July 1984: 10–14.

Rodney, William. *Soldiers of the International: A History of the Communist Party of Canada, 1919–1929*. Toronto: University of Toronto Press, 1968.

The Role of Relief and Rescue During the Holocaust by the Jewish Labor Committee. Pamphlet, Appendix 4-2. New York: The Jewish Labor Committee, 1987.

Rome, David. *On Our Forerunners — At Work*. New Series no. 9. Montreal: National Archives, Canadian Jewish Congress, 1978.

―――. *On Our Forerunners — At Work: Epilogue, Notes on the Twentieth Century*. New Series no. 10. Montreal: National Archives, Canadian Jewish Congress, 1978.

Rosenberg, Louis. "Changes in the Jewish Population in the Old Area of Jewish Settlement in Montreal Within a Radius of One Mile from Corner of Jeanne Mance St. & Villeneuve Ave., in the Period from 1951 to 1957." *Research Papers, Bureau of Social and Economic Research, Canadian Jewish Congress* no. 3, April 24, 1958.

————. "Jewish Population of Canada: A Statistical Summary 1851–1941." *Canadian Jewish Populations Studies* no. 2, Bureau of Social and Economic Research, Canadian Jewish Congress, 1948.

Roth, Cecil. *A History of the Jews from the Earliest Times Through the Six Day War*. New York: Shocken Books, 1970.

Rubinow, I. "Economic Condition of the Jews in Russia." *Bulletin of the Bureau of Labor* 72, 1907: 487–583.

Rubinstein, Michael. "Ten Years of Strife, Rescue and Aid." *The Jewish Labour Committee in Canada*. Tenth anniversary commemorative booklet. Montreal: Jewish Labour Committee, 1946. Bund Archives, New York, JLC 50, pp. 6–9.

Sack, B.G. *History of the Jews in Canada*. Montreal: Harvest House, 1965.

————, with Benjamin Gutl Sack. *Canadian Jews — Early in This Century*. New Series no. 4. Montreal: National Archives, Canadian Jewish Congress, 1975.

Salisbury, Harrison. *Black Night, White Snow: Russia's Revolutions 1905–1917*. Garden City: Doubleday & Co., 1978.

————. *Russia in Revolution, 1900–1930*. London: Andre Deutsch, 1978.

Scherer, Emanuel. "The Bund." In *Struggle for Tomorrow: Modern Political Ideologies of the Jewish People*. Edited by Basil J. Vlavianos and Feliks Gross. New York: Arts Incorporated, 1954.

Schwarzbart, Isaak Ignacy. "General Zionism." In *Struggle for Tomorrow: Modern Political Ideologies of the Jewish People*. Edited by Basil J. Vlavianos and Feliks Gross. New York: Arts Incorporated, 1954.

Scott, F.R. *The Collected Poems of F.R. Scott*. Toronto: McClelland and Stewart, 1981.

————. *A New Endeavour: Selected Political Essays, Letters, and Addresses*. Edited and with an Introduction by Michiel Horn. Toronto: University of Toronto Press, 1986.

————, and A.J.M. Smith, eds. *The Blasted Pine: An Anthology of Satire, Invective and Disrespectful Verse — Chiefly by Canadian Writers*. Toronto: Macmillan of Canada, 1967.

Shackleton, Doris French. *Tommy Douglas*. Toronto: McClelland and Stewart, 1975.

Shapiro, Judah H. *The Friendly Society: A History of the Workmen's Circle*. New York: Media Judaica, 1970.

Shewchuk, Serge Michiel. "The Russo–Polish War of 1920." Ph.D. thesis, University of Maryland. Copy in Imperial War Museum, London, 82/2767.

Smith, David Nicol. *The Oxford Book of Eighteenth Century Verse*. Oxford: Oxford University Press, 1926.

A Socialist Program for Canadian Trade Unionists. Pamphlet. Movement for an Independent Socialist Canada. Public Archives of Canada, MG 28, I 268, Vol. 14, file: Waffle.

Solski, Mike, and John Smaller. *Mine Mill: The History of the International Union of Mine, Mill and Smelter Workers in Canada, Since 1895.* Ottawa: Steel Rail Publishing, 1985.

The State of the World's Children, 1989. Booklet. United Nation's Children's Fund. Oxford: Published by Oxford University Press for UNICEF, 1989.

Steed, Judy. *Ed Broadbent: The Pursuit of Power.* Markham: Penguin Books Canada, 1988.

Strachey, John. *The Coming Struggle for Power.* London: Victor Gollancz, 1936.

Strikes and Lockouts in Canada. Ottawa: Federal Department of Labour, 1985.

Svisloch, The Second Book. Edited by Yerakhmiel Lifshitz. Netanya: Association of People from Svisloch in Israel, 1984.

Teeple, Gary. *Capitalism and the National Question in Canada.* Toronto: University of Toronto Press, 1972.

Thompson, John Herd, and Allen Seager. *Canada 1922-1939, Decades of Discord.* Toronto: McClelland and Stewart, 1985.

Thwaite, Ann, ed. *My Oxford.* Essays by Martin Amis, John Betjeman, Antonia Fraser, and Others. London: Robson Books, 1977.

Tobias, Henry J. *The Jewish Bund in Russia from Its Origins to 1905.* Stanford: Stanford University Press, 1972.

Trepp, Leo. *The Complete Book of Jewish Observance.* New York: Behrman House/Summit Books, 1980.

Trotsky, Leon. *Lenin.* New York: Minton, Balch & Company, 1925.

Tulchinsky, Gerald. "The Third Solitude: A.M. Klein's Jewish Montreal, 1910-1950." *Journal of Canadian Studies* 19, no. 2, Summer 1984.

Twersky, Isadore. *A Maimonides Reader.* New York: Library of Jewish Studies, Behrman House, 1972.

"United Nations Programme of Action for African Economic Recovery and Development 1986-1990." Annex to Report of the Ad Hoc Committee of the Whole of the Thirteenth Special Session, UN General Assembly. UN Information Office, A/S–13/15, June 4, 1986.

Ury, Zalman F. *The Musar Movement: A Quest for Excellence in Character Education.* Studies in Torah Judaism. New York: Yeshiva University Press, 1969.

"V. Medem and the Nationality Question." In Yiddish. New York: *Vladimir Medem on the Twentieth Anniversary of his Death,* The American Representation of the General Jewish Workers' Union of Poland, p. 133.

Vetulani, Adam. "The Jews in Medieval Poland." Translated from Polish by Marek Wajsblum. *The Jewish Journal of Sociology* 4, 1962: 274-94.

Von Laue, T. *Sergei Witte and the Industrialization of Russia*. New York: Columbia University Press, 1963.

Walsh, Warren Bartlett. *Russia and the Soviet Union*. Ann Arbor: University of Michigan Press, 1958.

Watkins, Mel. "Learning to Move Left." *This Magazine Is About Schools* 6, no. 1, Spring 1972: 68–92.

———. "Once Upon a Time: The Waffle Story." *This Magazine* 22, no. 8, March–April 1989: 28–30.

Watt, Richard M. *Bitter Glory: Poland and its Fate, 1918–1939*. New York: Simon & Schuster, 1979.

Weinryb, Bernard D. *The Jews of Poland: A Social and Economic History of the Jewish Community in Poland from 1100 to 1800*. Philadelphia: The Jewish Publication Society of America, 1972.

Whitehorn, Alan. "An Analysis of the "Historiography of the CCF-NDP: The Protest Movement Becalmed Tradition." In *Building the Co-operative Commonwealth: Essays in the Democratic Socialist Tradition in Canada*. Regina: Canadian Plains Research Centre, University of Regina, 1983.

———. "The CCF–NDP: Fifty Years After." In *Party Politics in Canada*. Edited by Hugh Thorburn. 5th ed. Douglas-Coldwell Foundation. Forthcoming.

———. "The New Democratic Party in Convention." In *Party Democracy in Canada*. Edited by George Perlin. Toronto: Prentice-Hall, 1985.

Wolfe, Bertram D. *Three Who Made a Revolution, A Biographical History*. 4th revised ed. New York: Dell Publishing Co., 1964.

Woodcock, George. *The Rejection of Politics and Other Essays on Canada, Canadians, Anarchism and the World*. Toronto: New Press, 1972.

———, ed. *The Anarchist Reader*. Glasgow: Fontana/Collins, 1977.

The Workmen's Circle: Builders and Activists. A Compendium of Members. New York: Minston Press, 1962.

Wright, Peter. *Spy Catcher: The Candid Autobiography of a Senior Intelligence Officer*. Toronto: Stoddart Publishing Co., 1987.

Young Oxford and War. Essays by Michael Foot, R.G. Freeman, Frank Hardie and Keith Steel-Maitland. Preface by H.J. Laski. London: Selwyn & Blount, 1934.

Young, Walter. *The Anatomy of a Party: The National CCF 1932–1961*. Toronto: University of Toronto Press, 1969.

Zakuta, Leo. *A Protest Movement Becalmed: A Study of Change in the CCF*. Toronto: University of Toronto Press, 1964.

Zborowski, Mark, and Elisabeth Herzog. *Life is with People: The Culture of the Shtetl*. New York: Shocken Books, 1952.

NEWSPAPERS AND MAGAZINES

The Canadian Forum: A Monthly Journal of Opinion and the Arts. Toronto.

Canadian Tribune. Toronto.

The Citizen. Ottawa.

The Evening Telegram. Toronto.

The Gazette. Montreal.

The Geneva Daily Times. Geneva, New York.

The Globe. Toronto.

The Globe and Mail. Toronto.

The Guardian. Manchester, England.

The Isis. Oxford University.

Kanada Adler. In Yiddish. Montreal.

The Lincoln Imp. Lincoln College, Oxford University.

Maclean's Magazine. Toronto.

The Mail and Empire. Toronto.

Montreal Standard. Montreal.

Montreal Star. Montreal.

The National Review. New York.

The New Commonwealth. Toronto.

The New York Times. New York.

The Ottawa Journal. Ottawa.

Oxford Mail. Oxford, England.

The Porcupine Advance. Timmins, Ontario.

The Sudbury Daily Star. Sudbury, Ontario.

Sydney Post-Record. Sydney, Nova Scotia.

The Telegram. Toronto.

The Times. London, England.

Toronto Star. Toronto.

The Vancouver Daily Province. Vancouver.

The Vancouver Sun. Vancouver.

The Varsity. University of Toronto.

Winnipeg Free Press. Winnipeg.

The Winnipeg Tribune. Winnipeg.

ARCHIVES

Bodleian Library. Oxford University.

British Library. London.

Bund Archives of the Jewish Labour Movement. Astran Centre for Jewish Culture, New York.

Fisher Rare Book Library. University of Toronto.

Imperial War Museum. London.

Jewish Labor Committee. New York.

Jewish Public Library. Montreal.

Library of Parliament. House of Commons. Ottawa.

National Archives, Canadian Jewish Congress. Montreal.

Ontario Archives. Toronto.

Oxford Union Library. Oxford University.

Public Archives of Canada. Ottawa.

Reference Library of Metropolitan Toronto.

Robarts Library. University of Toronto.

Royal Institute for International Affairs. London.

Workmen's Circle. Montreal.

Workmen's Circle. New York.

YIVO Scientific Institute for Jewish Research. New York.

York University Archives. Toronto.

• I N D E X •